Praise for *Marketing: Based on First Principles*

"Palmatier and Crecelius brilliantly simplify complex concepts
Derived from decades of teaching experience and hundreds of re
is a must-read for every student in marketing. Each chapter is a bite-sized portion of insight, perfect for effortless comprehension and application. In my mind, this is more than a book—it is a comprehensive, simple, and exciting knowledge support system for instructors."

Shrihari Sridhar, ***Professor of Marketing, Texas A&M University, USA***

"Palmatier and Crecelius offer a refreshingly clear and practical approach to modern marketing. By organizing the discipline around four fundamental truths, the authors provide a framework that is both intuitive and powerful. The book seamlessly integrates cutting-edge digital strategies with timeless marketing wisdom, making it invaluable for students and practitioners alike. Its emphasis on data-driven decision-making, coupled with engaging case studies and ethical discussions, ensures readers are well-equipped to navigate today's complex marketing landscape. This text doesn't just teach marketing; it reshapes how we think about the entire discipline."

Anthony Patterson, ***Professor of Marketing, Lancaster University, UK***

"Marketing: Based on First Principles offers a modernized framework for understanding marketing concepts, blending foundational theories with real-world case studies. An essential resource for students aiming to master contemporary marketing strategies and tackle global challenges, this textbook sets a new standard for marketing education."

Fine Leung, ***Associate Professor of Marketing, Hong Kong Polytechnic University***

"Palmatier and Crecelius's textbook balances profound theoretical insights with engaging real-world anecdotes. Using a First Principles framework, the book brings strategy, global perspectives, and a strong application focus to the forefront. By seamlessly integrating consumer and B2B perspectives, it offers a comprehensive and enriched view of marketing. Truly, a must-read for anyone serious about mastering the field."

Eugene Sivadas, ***Dean, Lam Family College of Business, San Francisco State University, USA***

"This truly groundbreaking textbook sets a new standard for marketing education by organizing content around the four First Principles. This outcome-based framework equips students to effectively approach real-world marketing challenges. The coverage of omnichannel strategies, service-based approaches, and business-to-everyone (B2E) models reflects the complexities of today's global marketplaces. The text's emphasis on ethics and sustainability aligns with the evolving demands of contemporary marketing practice, and the integration of global case studies offers valuable insights that inform marketing strategy. This is an indispensable tool for anyone aspiring to excel in the field of marketing."

Scott Weaven, ***Professor of Marketing, Griffith University, Australia***

"This informative, well-structured, and pleasant-to-read textbook offers a unique blend of the theory and practice of marketing, with emphasis on decision making, the complex reality of the business world, and up-to-date examples and cases from around the world. It stands out from the crowd and is certain to be one of the classic textbooks in marketing."

Constantine S. Katsikeas, ***Professor of Marketing and International Management, University of Leeds, UK***

"This excellent marketing textbook compellingly integrates Palmatier's powerful First Principles of marketing with essential marketing mix decisions, offering students a comprehensive framework and an accessible toolbox to structure and navigate the complexities of modern marketing. The diverse examples, exercises, and cases featured throughout the book are highly effective in stimulating critical thinking and enriching class discussions."

Lena Steinhoff, ***Professor and Chair of Marketing and Digital Transformation, Paderborn University, Germany***

"This book offers a fresh, practical approach to marketing, organized around the four First Principles. With global examples, relevant cases, and a strong focus on application, it prepares students to tackle modern marketing with confidence. Instructors will benefit from seamless resources that enhance teaching and engagement. A must-read for every student of marketing."

Frank Germann, ***Associate Professor of Marketing, University of Notre Dame, USA***

"Most marketing textbooks are just minor variations of the 'Kotlerian' view on marketing, hence little new is offered. This book, however, offers something completely fresh and different. The First Principles provides a uniquely strategic and analytical approach to marketing. This, combined with the excellent support material, makes this the book that all universities should base their marketing courses on."

Eirik Haus, ***Lecturer, BI Norwegian Business School, Norway***

"I organize all my classes around the First Principles developed by Palmatier. My undergraduate students appreciate the logical flow of one principle to the next, which makes it easy for them to gain confidence in understanding and analyzing marketing problems, from the product/brand level to the customer level. My MBA students love the universality of the First Principles approach because they can apply the frameworks and analytical tools to their businesses. I'm excited to introduce this book to students as a great learning and reference resource."

Conor M. Henderson, ***Associate Professor of Marketing, University of Oregon, USA***

"The First Principles offer an insightful and realistic framework for understanding today's fast-changing marketing environment. Palmatier and Crecelius expertly cover critical areas such as digital marketing, data analytics, B2B buying behavior, sales force management, and the challenges of cross-cultural and global markets. This book is an indispensable resource for students eager to learn the complexities of modern marketing and the competencies needed for success in today's dynamic business environment."

Danny P. Claro, ***Professor of Marketing, Insper, São Paulo, Brazil***

"*Marketing: Based on First Principles* offers thought-provoking examples, cases, and point-counterpoint discussions. The ways in which these compelling features support the Four Principles of marketing create a highly effective student learning experience."

Kelly D. Martin, ***Professor of Marketing, Colorado State University, USA***

MARKETING

BASED ON FIRST PRINCIPLES

ROBERT W. PALMATIER
ANDREW T. CRECELIUS

BLOOMSBURY ACADEMIC
LONDON • NEW YORK • OXFORD • NEW DELHI • SYDNEY

BLOOMSBURY ACADEMIC
Bloomsbury Publishing Plc
50 Bedford Square, London, WC1B 3DP, UK
1385 Broadway, New York, NY 10018, USA
29 Earlsfort Terrace, Dublin 2, Ireland

BLOOMSBURY, BLOOMSBURY ACADEMIC and the Diana logo are trademarks of Bloomsbury Publishing Plc

First published in Great Britain 2025

Cover design: Jess Stevens and Eleanor Rose
Cover image © Yagi Studio / DigitalVision / Getty Images

A catalogue record for this book is available from the British Library.

Library of Congress Cataloging-in-Publication Data
Names: Palmatier, Robert W., author. | Crecelius, Andrew T., 1987- author.
Title: Marketing : based on first principles / Robert Palmatier, Andrew Crecelius.
Description: London ; New York : Bloomsbury Academic, 2025. | Includes bibliographical references and index.
Identifiers: LCCN 2024031777 (print) | LCCN 2024031778 (ebook) | ISBN 9781350327900 (hardback) | ISBN 9781350327894 (paperback) | ISBN 9781350327917 (epub) | ISBN 9781350327924 (pdf)
Subjects: LCSH: Marketing.
Classification: LCC HF5415 .P2337 2025 (print) | LCC HF5415 (ebook) | DDC 658.8–dc23/eng/20240823
LC record available at https://lccn.loc.gov/2024031777
LC ebook record available at https://lccn.loc.gov/2024031778

ISBN: HB: 978-1-3503-2790-0
PB: 978-1-3503-2789-4
ePDF: 978-1-3503-2792-4
eBook: 978-1-3503-2791-7

Typeset by Integra Software Services Pvt. Ltd.
Printed and bound in Great Britain by Bell and Bain Ltd, Glasgow

To find out more about our authors and books visit www.bloomsbury.com and sign up for our newsletters.

BRIEF CONTENTS

LONG CONTENTS

LIST OF FIGURES

LIST OF TABLES

LIST OF CHAPTER CASE STUDIES

LIST OF ABBREVIATIONS

3E	experimentation, execution, evolution
4P	product, price, place, promotion
5C	customers, company, collaborators, competitors, context
7P	4P + people, processes, physical evidence
AER	acquisition-expansion-retention
B2B	business-to-business
B2C	business-to-consumer
B2G	business-to-government
BOR	brands, offerings, relationships
BRIC	Brazil, Russia, India, China
CEO	chief executive officer
CIO	chief information officer
CLV	customer lifetime value
CRISP-DM	cross-industry process for data mining
CRM	customer relationship management
EU	European Union
GDPR	General Data Protection Regulation
GIGO	garbage in, garbage out
GRP	gross rating points
IMC	integrated marketing communications
Inc	incorporated (US corporate affix)
MENA	Middle East and North Africa
MP	marketing principle
NFT	non-fungible token
PC	personal computer
PLC	public limited company (UK corporate affix)
PR	public relations
R&D	research and development
RFP	request for proposals
RM	relationship marketing
ROI	return on investment
SCA	sustainable competitive advantage
SE	societas Europaea (EU corporate affix)
SEM	search engine marketing
SEO	search engine optimization
STP	segmentation, targeting, positioning
UGC	user-generated content
UK	United Kingdom
USA	United States
VRIO	valuable, rare, inimitable, organized
WOM	word of mouth

AUTHOR BIOGRAPHIES

Robert W. Palmatier is Professor of Marketing and John C. Narver Chair of Business Administration at the Foster School at the University of Washington where he founded and serves as the research director of the Sales and Marketing Strategy Institute (SAMSI). He earned his bachelor's and master's degrees in electrical engineering from Georgia Institute of Technology, as well as an MBA from Georgia State University and a doctoral degree from the University of Missouri, followed by postdoctoral research at Northwestern University's Kellogg School of Management. Prior to entering academia, Professor Palmatier held various industry positions, including president and COO of C&K Components and European general manager at Tyco-Raychem Corporation. He also served as a US Navy lieutenant on board nuclear submarines.

Robert's research interests focus on marketing strategy, relationship marketing, data analytics, branding and trademark, misleading advertising, and marketing channel theory and practice with an emphasis on customer relationships, loyalty, and privacy in the business-to-business, online, technology, service, healthcare, and retail markets. His research has appeared in *Harvard Business Review*, *Journal of Marketing*, *Journal of Marketing Research*, *Marketing Science*, *Journal of Academy of Marketing Science*, *Journal of Retailing*, and *Journal of Consumer Psychology*. He has also published over ten books including *Marketing Channel Strategy* (2014, with Eugene Sivadas, Louis W. Stern, and Adel I. El-Ansary), *Marketing Strategy: Based on First Principles and Data Analytics* (2017, with Shrihari Sridhar), *The Intelligent Marketer's Guide to Data Privacy* (2019, with Kelly D. Martin), and *Marketing Analytics: Based on First Principles* (2022, with J. Andrews Peterson and Frank Germann). His research has been highlighted in *Nature*, *The New York Times Magazine*, *The Economist*, and *Los Angeles Times*, as well as on NPR and MSNBC.

Robert was ranked as the sixth most productive scholar based on publications in premier marketing journals (2013–2022) and ranked in the top 0.10 percent of most-cited scientists in Stanford's study that calculated the total number of citations ascribed to 9,071,122 researchers who have published at least five academic papers between 1960 and 2020.

Among the numerous industry and governmental committees on which Robert has served, he chaired proposal selection committees for the National Research Council (NRC), National Academy of Sciences (NAS), and the Wright

Centers of Innovation, which awarded grants of $20 million for the development of a new Wright Center of Innovation based on joint academic–industry proposals. He has served on NASA's Computing, Information, and Communications Advisory Group, with the AMES Research Center. This advisory group assessed the current state of technology development within academia, governmental agencies, and industry related to NASA's information technology activities and space exploration requirements.

He also consults and serves as an expert witness for companies including Foley, Kirkland & Ellis, Knobbe Martens, the US Treasury, Bates White, BraunHagey & Borden, Sidley Austin, Microsoft, Telstra, Amazon, Starbucks, Emerson, Fifth Third Bank, Wells Fargo, Genie, Health Stories Projects, Cincom, World Vision, Belkin, Tableau, Everett Clinic, Expedia, Concur, New Innovations, and Wells Fargo.

He has served as Editor-in-Chief of the *Journal of Academy of Marketing Science* and co-editor for *Journal of Marketing*. His publications have received multiple awards, including the Maynard, Sheth, Davidson, Buzzell, and Stern awards. He also has received the Mahajan Award for Lifetime Contributions to Marketing Strategy and the Interorganizational Research Award for Lifetime Contributions. He has received multiple awards as a teacher of marketing strategy in the doctoral, EMBA, and MBA programs at the University of Washington.

Andrew T. Crecelius is Associate Professor of Marketing at the Ivy College of Business at Iowa State University. He earned his bachelor's degree in finance from the University of Notre Dame, and his MBA and doctoral degrees in marketing from the University of Missouri.

He conducts empirical and conceptual research across a variety of topics in marketing strategy and business-to-business marketing, with a focus on managing customer relationships via multiple interpersonal and digital channels. His research leverages collaborative arrangements with firms in industries such as financial services and industrial distribution, along with rigorous quantitative analyses, to highlight practical and actionable solutions to pervasive marketing problems. More recently, he has begun studying disruptive forces in the digital realm, including issues related to marketing analytics, e-commerce, and live streaming. His work can be found in outlets such as *Journal of Marketing Research*, *Journal of Marketing*, *MIS Quarter*ly, and *Journal of the Academy of Marketing Science.*

His past and ongoing work has been recognized with multiple awards and grants. These include multiple grant awards from the Marketing Science Institute, the AMA Sales SIG Excellence in Research Award, AMA Conference Best in Sales Track award, finalist recognition for the Shelby D. Hunt/Harold H. Maynard

Award, and the Ivy College of Business Early Career Achievement in Research Award. He also serves on the editorial review boards of the *Journal of the Academy of Marketing Science*, *Journal of Retailing*, and *Journal of Business Research*.

Andrew has extensive experience in instruction and course development. He has taught ten different classes in his career across the areas of marketing, finance, professional selling, operations management, channels of distribution, and research methods. He has developed online coursework and taught a variety of classes in both traditional and distance formats for diverse populations of traditional and nontraditional students at multiple institutions. At the University of Alabama at Birmingham, he taught multiple courses in the Industrial Distribution program, providing students with job-relevant skills and knowledge for positions with major industrial, electrical, and medical distributors. At Iowa State, he developed a unique and innovative course in Sales Enablement Tools, Technology, and Analytics. Inspired by the ongoing digital transformation of the business world, the course teaches future salespeople and sales managers the fundamentals of analytical intuition, data structure, and visual insights while laying a practical foundation of skills in Salesforce and CRM Analytics. Most recently, he developed a doctoral-level empirical modeling seminar, in which he taught econometric methods and the software tools necessary for modern quantitative research. His teaching has been recognized with the Ivy College of Business Assistant Professor Achievement in Teaching award.

He lives with his wife and four children in Ankeny, Iowa.

ACKNOWLEDGEMENTS

Robert Palmatier thanks his colleagues and doctoral students whose ongoing insights into marketing strategy and data analytics have helped inform this book in multiple ways: Todd Arnold, Carlos Bauer, Joshua T. Beck, Alexander Bleier, Abhishek Borah, Natalie Chisam, Fred C. Ciao, Daniel Claro, Andrew Crecelius, Beibei Dong, Kenneth R. Evans, Eric Fang, Shankar Ganesan, Frank Germann, Gabriel Gonzalez, Srinath Gopalakrishna, Dhruv Grewal, Rajdeep Grewal, Flora F. Gu, Wenjun Guo, Bita Hajihashemi, Colleen Harmeling, Conor Henderson, Mark B. Houston, John Hulland, Brett Josephson, Vamsi Kanuri, Frank R. Kardes, Jisu Kim, Irina V. Kozlenkova, V. Kumar, Justin Lawrence, Jongkuk Lee, Ju-Yeon Lee, Fine Leung, Xiaoling Li, Gary L. Lilien, Kelly Martin, Martin Mende, Fred Miao, Jordan Moffett, Mehdi Nezami, Sara Quach, Carla Ramos, Stephen Samaha, Lisa K. Scheer, Maura Scott, Arun Sharma, Jan-Benedict E.M. Steenkamp, Lena Steinhoff, Park Thaichon, George Watson, Scott Weaven, Stefan Worm, Diandian Xiang (Vincent), Jonathan Zhang, and Zelin Zhang. Robert would especially like to thank his co-author, Shrihari Sridhar, from the initial book based on the First Principles Approach, *Marketing Strategy: Based on First Principles and Data Analytics* as many aspects of this book borrow from this previous book. His debt to numerous past MBA, EMBA, and PhD students is unbounded; they were instrumental in shaping many of the insights in this book. He is also very grateful to Charles and Gwen Lillis for their generous support of the Foster Business School and his research, which helped make this book possible. Finally, Robert would like to acknowledge with gratitude the support and love of his daughter, Alexandra, which made this effort worthwhile.

Andrew Crecelius thanks his mentors, colleagues, and doctoral students who shaped and continue to shape his perspective about the theory and practice of modern marketing. These individuals include Divya Anand, Bitty Balducci, Peter Bloch, Michael Brady, Nawar Chaker, Thomas DeCarlo, Andrea Dixon, Srinath Gopalakrishna, Dwayne Gremler, Mohammad Hakimi, Colleen Harmeling, Vamsi Kanuri, Youngtak Kim, Subodha Kumar, Son Lam, Justin Lawrence, Ju-Yeon Lee, Chengzhe Liu, Shijie Lu, Detelina Marinova, Colleen McClure, Hans Nguyen, Jessica Ogilvie, Robert Palmatier, Alec Pappas, Ashutosh Patil, Harrison Pugh, Sekar Raju, Adam Rapp, Marina Scatolin Murarolli, Lisa Scheer, Mike Wittmann, Amir Zahedi, and Jonathan Zhang. Andrew is also very thankful to the many students that have been through his undergraduate and graduate classes over the years, especially those whom he taught in Principles of Marketing at Iowa State. These students directly informed his overall approach, perspective, and voice in writing this textbook. Finally, and most importantly, Andrew is eternally grateful to his family—his wife Elysia, and his children Marcus, Haydn, Kyllian, and Lysette—for providing meaning to this endeavor and for their unconditional love and understanding.

PREFACE

GOAL AND OVERALL APPROACH

This book serves as a guide to a student's first course in marketing. The text is designed to introduce key concepts and real-world applications to help students understand the challenges that twenty-first-century marketers face. Naturally, the chapters survey the key decision areas that marketers handle, including digital marketing, global marketing, marketing research, product design, pricing, advertising, marketing planning, and many others. But the text also breaks with the tradition of "principles of marketing" courses in several ways:

- *Organizing the material around four, central First Principles of Marketing.* These marketing principles provide structure to the topics and connect the concepts to core challenges that marketers must solve.
- *Taking a global perspective.* In line with today's interconnected world, examples and cases are sourced with a balanced approach, representing firms and consumers from North America, Europe, Asia, and numerous other markets. These diverse examples highlight both the universal challenges that marketers face (encapsulated by the First Principles) and the unique headwinds in different geographies and cultures.
- *Diving head-first into marketing controversies.* Today's world is polarized and filled with ambiguity and shades of gray. This book captures that reality by presenting multiple sides of thorny issues, and by emphasizing that marketers sometimes fail to navigate the stormy seas of today's economic and sociopolitical environment.
- *Adopting an application-first stance.* A large share of each chapter's text is devoted to cases, mini-cases, and other features that bring the material to life and ask students how they would solve real marketing challenges. In other words, the emphasis of this text is not on rote memorization of terms and process steps, but on building understanding through application, reflection, and discussion. The industry coverage of these applications is designed to emphasize industries that are relevant and engaging to today's students, such as film, fashion, gaming, and social media.
- *Minimizing friction for instructors***.** The book is accompanied by a full suite of instructional resources, including online course-ready lecture videos. These resources are meant to minimize tedium for novice and experienced instructors alike, redirecting effort toward high-impact student engagement.

WHY TAKE A FIRST PRINCIPLES APPROACH?

This is the first marketing principles textbook grounded in the "First Principles" of marketing, specifically: (1) All customers differ, (2) All customers change, (3) All competitors react, and (4) All resources are limited. Why does this matter? The First Principles approach provides four critical advantages for learners and instructors:

1. **The First Principles serve as a streamlined organizing framework for marketing concepts.** Challenges such as understanding differences in consumer behavior, allocating advertising budgets, and building channel partnerships do not exist in isolation, but rather they reflect specific facets of the First Principles. Tying each chapter and module back to elements of a core framework enables a more coherent and cohesive course delivery without sacrificing academic rigor or the importance of each topic. By framing each concept and tool as a potential solution to the marketing problems represented by the First Principles, the text will also satisfy modern students' preference for efficient, outcome-based learning. The First Principles have proven potential as an organizing framework for instructors. For example, as Conor Henderson (University of Oregon) explains, "I have used a First Principles-based approach in my class for the past three years. Students come to recognize that they should not begin to address any marketing-related issue without considering how all of the First Principles come to bear on it. There is a lot of wisdom in starting with First Principles."
2. **The First Principles integrate idiosyncratic business contexts.** Whether offline or online, B2C or B2B or B2G, products or services, domestic or international, the same First Principles apply. This allows more diverse illustrations and applications to be embedded in each chapter. For example, consumer and B2B buyer decision processes are embedded in the same chapter, rather than the traditional format of separate B2C and B2B chapters; the challenges of global and cross-cultural marketing are examined as a special case of FP#1 (All customers differ); product strategy and services strategy are likewise incorporated into a single chapter focused on developing sustainable competitive advantage (FP#3: All competitors react). This approach better prepares students for today's omnichannel, service-dominant, business-to-everyone, and globally competitive world.
3. **Each principle builds on the last.** For example, the unique needs of customer segments at a point in time (FP#1: All customers differ) is a foundation for the firm's view of customer dynamics (FP#2: All customers change). As a result, learners will be able to articulate how successful firms assemble, piece by piece, a marketing mix that seizes and defends a position of superiority over competitors. This approach also makes the links between modules more apparent. For example, the marketing research chapter focuses on its connection to understanding and managing customer differences and dynamics, unlike in traditional texts where marketing research is often siloed.

4. **The approach brings ethical considerations to the fore.** Recognizing that ethics, sustainability, and conscious marketing are a critical component of marketing principles curricula, these topics pervade the text. They are a major focus in the first chapter and recur frequently in later chapters and sidebars. For example, when FP#4 (All resources are limited) is introduced, the ethical challenges of managing resource trade-offs among stakeholders are a central concern. Compared to the traditional approach of an isolated "ethics chapter," which in our view diminishes and tokenizes this content, this approach bolsters the case for ethical considerations to permeate marketing decision-making processes.

STRUCTURE OF THE TEXT

The textbook is divided into five units, first introducing the First Principles framework, then organizing marketing concepts around each of the four principles:

Part 1—Introduction: An Overview of Modern Marketing

- **Chapter 1: The Modern Marketing Concept**
- **Chapter 2: The First Principles of Marketing**
- **Chapter 3: First Principles in Action—Navigating the World of Digital Marketing**

Part 2—Marketing Principle #1: All Customers Differ

- **Chapter 4: Managing Customer Differences**
- **Chapter 5: Understanding Consumer and Organizational Buyer Behavior**
- **Chapter 6: Marketing for Global and Cross-Cultural Differences**

Part 3—Marketing Principle #2: All Customers Change

- **Chapter 7: Managing Customer Dynamics**
- **Chapter 8: The Changing World of Retail and Omnichannel Marketing**
- **Chapter 9: Marketing Research & Analytics for Managing Customer Dynamics & Customer Differences**

Part 4—Marketing Principle #3: All Competitors React

- **Chapter 10: Managing Sustainable Competitive Advantage**
- **Chapter 11: Brand-based Advantages and Advertising**
- **Chapter 12: Offering-based Advantages, Innovation, and Product-Service Strategy**
- **Chapter 13: Relationship-based Advantages, CRM, and Channel Management**

Part 5—Marketing Principle #4: All Resources Are Limited

- **Chapter 14: Managing Resource Trade-offs and Pricing Strategy**
- **Chapter 15: Managing Resource Trade-offs in Integrated Marketing Communications and Personal Selling**

As the above outline illustrates, the traditional marketing principles topics (e.g., advertising, consumer buyer behavior, etc.) are here presented not in siloed modules, but instead as key decision areas that embody fundamental challenges that marketers must face. This framework gives greater weight to the *why* of marketing decisions—that is, why do these decisions matter so much and what happens if marketers fail? This is in contrast to the traditional approach of a first textbook in marketing, which stops at *what* (key terms and concepts) and *how* (mechanistic marketing process steps).

Each chapter proceeds in a systematic way:

- It opens with an overview, specific learning objectives, and a preview of the chapter's outline and its various cases and features.
- The chapter proceeds in a structured format, introducing the topic, explaining its importance, and comparing different marketing tools and approaches.
- Cases and features are woven throughout the text and are intended to be read in tandem with the text so that students understand the real-world importance, as well as uncertainty and controversy, surrounding the chapter concepts.
- The chapter concludes with a summary, end-of-chapter case, and discussion questions.

TAKEAWAYS FOR INSTRUCTORS AND STUDENTS

We thank you for considering using this textbook. We believe that it provides a novel and valuable approach to teaching a principles of marketing class. This approach should be more interesting for students, more relevant to modern marketing practice, and simple for instructors to adopt. The key benefits of the text are:

- Strong coverage of marketing principles content for the modern era.
- A First Principles approach to provide structure and meaning to the content.
- An extensive set of instructional resources, including ready-made online lectures.
- A uniquely global focus, without a bias toward the United States or any other country.
- Fresh examples from industries that matter to today's students, such as gaming and fashion.
- An application-first emphasis with thought-provoking, timely, and engaging cases.
- A firm grounding in both classic marketing theories and the latest research.

TOUR OF THE BOOK

Chapter Overview and Learning Objectives

Each chapter begins with a preview of what the chapter is about and what you are expected to learn, helping you to plan your study.

CHAPTER OVERVIEW

Chapter 6 looks at the problem of Marketing Principle #1 (all customers differ → managing customer differences) through a global lens. It explains how globalization has historically created more differences for marketers to manage and will continue to do so. It then outlines the distinct strategies that marketers can use to enter global markets. Finally, it introduces a cultural framework for managing customer differences across different country markets. The chapter will proceed by answering the following questions:

- Backlash against skin products designed to make skin less dark (Marketing Fail).
- E-commerce giant Alibaba's dramatic entry into the US market (Chapter Case).
- Ethical and moral dilemmas in managing global customer differences, such as dubious sustainability claims by fashion brands such as H&M (Shades of Gray) and the globalization of cultures (Opposing Views).

LEARNING OBJECTIVES

- Identify the factors that have contributed to a globalized world.
- Recognize key terms and concepts in global marketing.
- Evaluate moral and ethical considerations in global marketing, with attention to their historical and cultural context.
- Compare various marketing strategies for managing global and cultural differences.

Glossary

Definitions of essential marketing terms appear alongside where they are first mentioned in the text.

functional risk The risk that the purchase will not fulfill *functional needs* (see above)

emotional risk The risk that the purchase will not fulfill *emotional needs* (see above)

Imagine

These engaging thought exercises, found at the start of every chapter, put you in the shoes of marketers, encouraging you to think deeply about a variety of today's marketing challenges.

IMAGINE Expanding your Business Abroad

Imagine that you own a small business in Australia selling women's hair accessories (jeweled barrettes, fashion clips, graphic headbands, vintage ribbons, etc.) via an online shop. In addition to your own website, you have an online storefront on Gumtree Australia, an ecommerce platform that is especially popular for handmade and niche apparel. You noticed over the last year that, despite continuing to introduce new styles, your business's growth has stalled. You are beginning to wonder if you are saturating the Australian market for your admittedly niche product.

Therefore, you decide that you will try to start selling products outside of Australia. You are already selling online and shipping products out—

- Second, you realize that a large percentage of women in Indonesia and Malaysia wear head coverings such as hijabs when in public. Who will buy your hair accessories? Is there any way you can still sell your products in these countries?

As much as you hate the idea of completely ignoring these two large, alternative markets, you do not see an easy path forward.

Critical thinking

1. Can you think of any way to tap into the Indonesian and Malaysian markets in this scenario? Feel free to get creative in devising a solution.

In Other Words

Crucial learning points are highlighted throughout the text.

IN OTHER WORDS ...

Firms begin in their home market, and often later enter new country markets. Over time, they can then expand into additional new country markets, build up their presence in existing country markets, or reduce their investment in existing country markets.

Marketing Fail

Flipping the usual success stories on their head, this feature invites you to diagnose the problems with the failed marketing tactics of well-known businesses.

MARKETING FAIL Backlash against "Fairness Creams" in India

The colonial history of early globalization has echoes today, and nowhere is this clearer than in the case of "fairness creams" (products that make the skin lighter). Although these products are popular in many countries, they have received a great deal of attention recently in India. As of 2013, the country consumed 233 tons of skin-lightening cosmetics annually.[31] The demand for these products serves a cultural norm that views lighter skin as more attractive and darker skin as less desirable. Social scientists and popular narratives attribute this norm directly to the nation's colonial heritage, harkening back to a time when having lighter skin was associated with wealth and status.[32,33] Sales of skin-lightening products in India have surged in the last fifty years and are believed to account for more than one-third of profits in the country's cosmetics industry.[34] Although domestic brands have had some success, a large share of skin-lightening products in India are sold by US-based and European cosmetics brands: Fair & Lovely by Unilever, White Light by Estée Lauder,

India

Opposing Views

See the issues from both sides in these accounts of contemporary marketing dilemmas.

OPPOSING VIEWS Cultural Globalization in Consumption

Although globalization has doubtless accelerated peaceful trade relationships and contributed to worldwide growth, it has also received criticism from various quarters for its unintended consequences. One of the more troubling criticisms is that globalization, while forging connections between diverse peoples, has actually diminished global diversity by homogenizing products, services, and even cultures around the world. This phenomenon is known as "cultural globalization." It can be observed in several spheres, but is perhaps most observable in the entertainment industry, where Hollywood claims a vastly disproportionate slice of global film culture.

The critique most famously came from German-American economist Theodore Levitt, who claimed that "The world's needs and desires have been

markets begin to develop preferences increasingly similar to those in the corporation's home market. The process repeats in a new country, until everyone wants the same products and the multinational corporation has become global. Or so Levitt argues. Nonetheless, the free movement of ideas and goods across borders will likely continue to lead to blending and blurring of cultural lines.

Global

See the issue from two sides:

1. Craft an argument in favor of Levitt's side: that in every sector, customers will increasingly consume essentially the same goods, and the world will shift toward a single global culture. In your argument, be sure to acknowledge the

Shades of Gray

Examples of moral and ethical dilemmas from throughout the business world, allowing you to think critically about marketing practice.

SHADES OF GRAY "Sustainable" Claims in the Apparel Industry

Consumers increasingly care about the sustainability of the brands they purchase. Although definitions vary, **sustainable business practices** are widely viewed as broader than environmental concerns and may also include holistic strategies that consider impacts on communities, treatment of employees, product safety, and diversity.[51] Consumers are concerned not only with the business practices of brands themselves but also about sustainability all the way up the brands' supply chains, often to nations in the Global South supplying raw materials. Thus, **sustainable sourcing**—choosing suppliers with sustainable business practices—is increasingly emphasized, especially at large firms.[52]

Sweden Spain

Theory Spotlight

Important theoretical insights are offered here in digestible form.

THEORY SPOTLIGHT Hofstede's Cultural Dimensions

Shalom Schwartz was not the only social scientist to develop a theory of cultural dimensions. The leading alternative framework belongs to Dutch psychologist Geert Hofstede. Hofstede characterizes cultures along six dimensions: power distance (tolerance of societal inequality), individualism (extent of independence from family), masculinity/femininity (extent to which typically masculine or feminine traits are considered desirable), long-term orientation (degree of reliance on adaptation/pragmatism versus tradition), and indulgence (whether it is acceptable to focus on having fun). Hofstede's dimensions are useful, and share several themes with Schwartz's model. The Schwartz framework is better suited to understanding global customer differences, though, because (i) the values explicitly exist at the individual level (consistent with MP#1), with cultural values representing an average of individual values in a group, and (ii) Schwartz's dimensions do a better job predicting consumer behavior and international trade.

Chapter Case Study

An extended case study exploring how real-life businesses, including AstraZeneca, Uniqlo, and Primark, dealt with the key issues discussed in the chapter.

CHAPTER CASE STUDY

ALIBABA OPENS DOORS FOR US-BASED SELLERS

When Chinese entrepreneur Jack Ma visited the United States in 1995, he saw which way the wind was blowing. Globalization 3.0 was underway, and Silicon Valley's internet companies were at the heart of it. Ma decided to start his own e-commerce platform. After two failed attempts and a pivotal $20 million investment from Softbank, he founded Alibaba.com, an online, business-to-business (B2B) marketplace that enabled organizational buyers from

Chapter Summary and Application Questions

A useful summary of the key points of each chapter along with a list of questions to help you put what you have learnt into practice.

56 MARKETING PRINCIPLE # 1: ALL CUSTOMERS DIFFER

CHAPTER SUMMARY

In pursuit of growth, firms large and small increasingly enact their marketing mix across national and cultural borders. Globalized competition heightens the challenges of managing customer differences, as offerings must be brought to market in a way that is sensitive to differences in norms between regional cultures while also recognizing the unique forms of customer differences within each market. To provide a framework for understanding within- and between-culture customer differences, this chapter presents an overview of key terms, concepts, and strategies employed by today's global marketers. The chapter begins with a detailed history of the four eras of increasing globalization, to provide context for understanding many of the thorny ethical and cultural challenges that marketers face today. Criteria for deciding to enter a new country market, as well as various modes of entry such as international joint ventures and direct investment, are reviewed. Finally, approaches for managing cultural differences in new country markets are examined in the context of Schwarz's cultural dimensions, with particular attention to the simultaneous importance of within-culture and between-culture customer differences.

APPLICATION QUESTIONS

1. Think of a time when you, or someone you know, ordered a product from another country. What technologies facilitated this purchase? How would this person have placed the order without these technologies?
2. Think of at least one specific criticism of globalization that you have heard (if you cannot think of any, you can use the cultural globalization issue from this chapter).

TOUR OF THE WEBSITE

This book is accompanied by a freely available website that provides an array of resources designed to support teaching and learning. These resources have been designed with flexibility in mind. At one end of the spectrum, an instructor (for example, a novice graduate student-teacher) could adopt the entire suite of resources to enable a ready-to-use online course. At the other end of the spectrum, an instructor can pick and choose specific resources to suit the class's needs.

Visit **https://bloomsbury.pub/palmatier-marketing** to find:

- Fully produced ***PowerPoint lecture videos*** for all chapters (along with the original slide decks) that can be plugged into online courses, or used as makeup lectures for in-person classes.
- An extensive ***testbank*** for building quizzes and examinations.
- A set of ready-made ***sample syllabi*** for principles of marketing courses of various term lengths and formats.
- **A *library of external video resources*** to supplement class lectures and further illustrate concepts from the chapters.
- ***Interactive flashcards***, based on the glossary terms from the book, to aid students.
- A set of ***bonus videos*** of author Rob Palmatier's lectures on the First Principles of Marketing.

You can also visit **https://samsinstitute.com/resources** for additional learning and teaching tools.

Part 1

INTRODUCTION: AN OVERVIEW OF MODERN MARKETING

Part Overview

Welcome to *Marketing: Based on First Principles.* This book will give you a clear picture of the challenges that marketers face today and some of their tools for solving these challenges. To begin with, though, we must answer two questions. First, what is marketing—that is, what is the definition of marketing, and what does it mean to "do" marketing? Chapter 1 focuses on this question. Second, what are First Principles, and how do we take a First Principles approach to marketing? Chapter 2 lays out four First Principles that apply to virtually all marketing decisions and that form a roadmap for the rest of the topics in this book. Finally, Chapter 3 illustrates how to apply the First Principles approach to one of the world's most challenging and rapidly evolving marketing environments: digital marketing.

Chapter 1

THE MODERN MARKETING CONCEPT

CHAPTER OVERVIEW

Chapter 1 introduces the world of today's marketer. It emphasizes that marketing is so much more than advertising and explains how most of the high-profile business decisions we hear about are, in fact, marketing. It then lays out a process that companies use to develop marketing strategies and explains the "marketing mix" that is involved in executing these strategies. The chapter will proceed by answering the following questions:

- What is modern marketing?
- How do businesses develop a marketing strategy?
- What is the marketing mix?

In the chapter's cases and features, you will get a more detailed look at how companies have managed the marketing concept well (or poorly). These include:

- Quibi's doomed entry into the streaming wars (Marketing Fail).
- Ethical and moral dilemmas in marketing, such as companies relying on customers for product ideas (Shades of Gray) and the potential pitfalls when marketers try to align with company shareholders (Opposing Views).

LEARNING OBJECTIVES

- Identify the three facets of the marketing concept.
- Recognize basic terms such as customer centricity, sustainable competitive advantage, and marketing mix.
- Explain the steps in the marketing planning process and how they lead to the development of a marketing strategy.
- Identify the four components of the 4P marketing mix—and the additional three components of the 7P marketing mix—and their role in marketing strategy.
- Evaluate potential ethical consequences of marketing, such as effects on stakeholders.

IMAGINE What Marketing Is

It will be useful to begin with a simple thought exercise. Do the following:

- Get a blank sheet of paper and write the word "marketing" in the center.
- In a circle surrounding this word, write the first four words that come to mind when you think of marketing.
- Finally, in an outer circle, write the next six words that come to mind when you think of marketing.

After doing this, begin a session with your favorite AI chat tool (ChatGPT, Copilot, Gemini, etc.). First, ask it "What is marketing?" Then, ask it "Who does marketing?" Compare these answers to the words that you associated with the marketing concept.

Critical thinking:

1. Did anything surprise you about the "What is marketing" answer? What kinds of aspects came up in this answer that were not covered by the words that you wrote?
2. Consider the "Who does marketing" answer. Which of these roles sounds the most appealing to you? Which is the least appealing? Why?

WHAT IS MODERN MARKETING?

What does **marketing** mean today? It is helpful to think of examples of marketing from everyday life:

marketing Decisions and actions that seek sustainable competitive advantages to achieve objectives of stakeholders

- A television advertisement is marketing.
- The design of your favorite website or app is marketing.
- The way that a customer service representative on the phone talks to you is marketing.
- The prices at your supermarket are marketing.
- The product selection that Amazon shows you on its front page is marketing.
- The location, architecture, and music of your favorite clothing store are marketing.
- The features and specifications of an iPhone are marketing.
- It is also common to talk about "marketing yourself" when looking for a new job or other opportunities, as you tailor a resume or CV and attend networking events.

So many choices and actions by businesses are part of marketing, it may be harder to think of ones that are not marketing!

Thus, the challenge of defining marketing is drawing borders around a broad and ever-evolving concept. Many definitions of marketing exist, and each of these serves a purpose in understanding marketing (see Theory Spotlight). Given the focus of this book on action and application, we define marketing not in terms of what it *is* from a theoretical perspective, but what it *does* from a practical perspective—that is, what it aims to achieve.

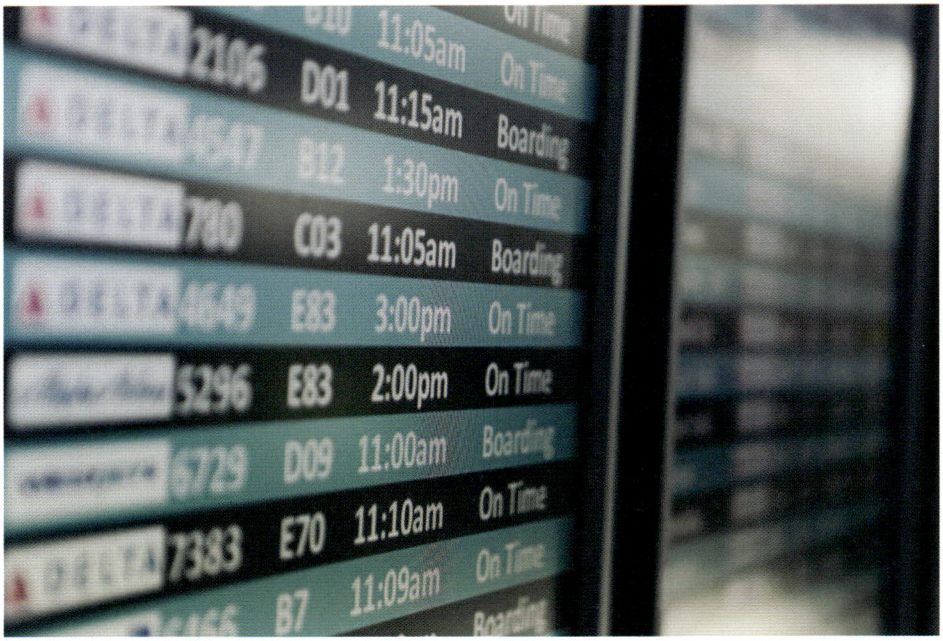

Source: Matthew Smith/Unsplash

An airline's choice of which routes to offer between cities, and how often, is a marketing action that affects its advantage relative to competitors.

We define **marketing** as follows: *decisions and actions that seek sustainable competitive advantages to achieve objectives of stakeholders.*[1] This definition is useful because it is concise and has a meaning on the surface. For example, if German airline Lufthansa adds a new set of daily flights (a decision or action) on routes where its competitors cannot profitably operate (seeking sustainable competitive advantage) in the hopes of growing market share and profit (to achieve objectives of stakeholders), this clearly fits the definition of marketing. Nonetheless, each of the definition's three parts has terms that are worth a deeper explanation.

THEORY SPOTLIGHT Other Definitions of Marketing

Several other definitions exist. Generally, these definitions serve a different purpose because they have less focus on actions and objectives. We provide a few notable examples of alternative definitions and highlight some strengths of these definitions below.

Dictionary definitions are a good way to see how a word is popularly understood. In the *Oxford English Dictionary* marketing is "the action, business, or process of promoting and selling a product, etc., including market research, advertising, and distribution."[2] Also, in *Merriam-Webster Dictionary* it is defined as "the process or technique of promoting, selling, and distributing a product or service."[3] These are simple definitions that fit most everyday uses of the word. However, they have two main limitations. First, they are too specific. "Promoting and selling" are indeed part of marketing, but so are designing products, setting prices, and myriad other actions. Second, they lack a goal orientation. By these definitions, selling seems to be an end unto itself. What does all this marketing activity accomplish?

We next turn to a more rigorous definition, developed by a committee of marketing scholars. The American Marketing Association (AMA), one of the marketing profession's premier professional associations, defines marketing as "the activity, set of institutions, and processes for creating, communicating, delivering, and exchanging offerings that have value for customers, clients, partners, and society at large."[4] This definition focuses on the important concept of **value**—the financial, emotional, or social benefit that a person or company receives. Value is folded into the "sustainable competitive advantage" portion of our definition, since creating value is necessary for an advantage.

The AMA definition has a focus on covering the theoretical breadth of the marketing concept, and certainly does not leave anything out. However, this strength can also be a weakness. By incorporating a "set of institutions," and employing the general "offerings that have value for ... partners" the definition loses some of its action-focus and its specificity. For example, Nokia's accounting department (an institution) produces income statements. These documents have value for potential suppliers (i.e., partners) that want to evaluate the financial stability of Nokia before working with them. Are Nokia's corporate accountants now marketers? It seems absurd on the surface, but the expansiveness of this definition leaves the question open. This shows the trade-off between usefulness and breadth when defining marketing.

Marketing Consists of Decisions and Actions

In this book, we view marketing with an action focus; we emphasize what marketing does, and what it aims to achieve. Hence, the first component of our definition is **decisions and actions**—choices, activities, expenditures, and initiatives made by individuals, teams, and firms. Figure 1.1 illustrates several examples of marketing decisions and actions, and how they fit neatly into our overall definition of marketing. For example:

value The financial, emotional, or social benefit that a person or company receives from a product or service

decisions and actions Choices, activities, expenditures, and initiatives made by individuals, teams, and firms

- In 2020 Indian e-commerce giant FlipKart launched a complex rewards program called SuperCoin Pay. Under this program, customers earned points by buying products on FlipKart, and then could spend these points at brick-and-mortar retailers (e.g., coffee shops and clothing stores) that partnered with FlipKart.[5]
- Also in 2020, French hypermarket chain Carrefour spent €60 million ($73 million) to acquire a Parisian chain of organic supermarkets called Bio c' Bon; this single action significantly expanded Carrefour's presence both in the Paris geographic market and in the organic food segment.[6]

Planning and executing the elements of the "marketing mix" described later in this chapter also involve multifaceted decisions and actions. Thus, marketing decisions and actions are many. But surely marketing cannot include *all* decisions and actions. A sales team's choice of what to order for lunch on Tuesday is a decision, but it is obviously not marketing. The second part of our definition specifies which decisions and actions fall under the umbrella of marketing.

Marketing consists of:

DECISIONS AND ACTIONS...	... THAT SEEK SUSTAINABLE COMPETITIVE ADVANTAGE...	... TO ACHIEVE OBJECTIVES OF STAKEHOLDERS
FlipKart *(Indian online retailer)* Launched SuperCoin Pay reward program, where customers earn points they can spend at partner stores...	... to create extra benefits from buying products at FlipKart, rather than other online retailers...	... to improve market share and strengthen partnerships with brick-and-mortar retailers.
Carrefour S.A. *(French super/hypermarket chain)* Spent €60m (~ US $73m) to buy organic, Paris-focused supermarket chain Bio c' Bon...	... to gain access to unique and valuable store locations in the growing organic foods segment...	... to earn new customers and advance its ACT FOR FOOD initiative to support food quality and nutrition.
Walt Disney Co. *(US entertainment conglomerate)* Launched a streaming service called Disney+, featuring hundreds of movies and television series...	... to bring its unique catalog of intellectual properties to the rapidly-growing streaming market...	... to create a stable subscription-based revenue stream and enable new ways to engage with customers.
Nokia Corp. *(Finnish telecoms conglomerate)* Partnered with Polish firm Polkomtel to build out 5G cellular networks in Poland's major cities...	... to capture a sought-after opportunity to build a nation's next generation of cellular infrastructure...	... to grow sales in its 5G technology division and strengthen international corporate/government partnerships.
Epic Games, Inc. *(US entertainment software firm)* Paid game publishers large sums to offer their games for free to users on the Epic Games Store platform...	... to rapidly build a userbase to compete with existing digital game storefronts that dominate the market...	... to grow future game/add-on revenue on its platform and help promote Epic's own games such as Fortnite.
Baidu, Inc. *(Chinese search/internet giant)* Used its advanced AI technology to launch driverless taxi service Apollo Go in Beijing and other large cities...	... to gain a foothold in a cutting-edge, disruptive market that relatively few firms have the technology to enter...	... to set the stage for more widespread autonomous vehicle sales and build Baidu's profile among tech giants.

Figure 1.1 Examples of Marketing.

Marketing decisions and actions can take many forms and be executed by different groups, but they share a goal orientation: achieving sustainable competitive advantage to achieve stakeholder objectives.

Marketing Decisions and Actions Seek Sustainable Competitive Advantages

Marketing actions are intended to protect or advance the firm's position in the marketplace. Apple's famous advertising campaigns create and maintain its unique and recognizable brand image. UAE-based airline Air Emirate's sought-after first-class seats protect the firm's reputation among high-spending, luxury-focused customers. International bakery chain Le Pain Quotidien seeks out highly visible locations on busy streets in major cities, preventing competitors from obtaining these choice locations.

Thus, a defining characteristic of marketing decisions and actions is the marketer's intention to achieve or protect a **sustainable competitive advantage**, defined as an edge in the marketplace that a competing organization cannot easily imitate or overcome. There are several factors required for a sustainable competitive advantage:

sustainable competitive advantage An edge in the marketplace that a competing organization cannot easily imitate or overcome

- To get an edge in the marketplace, the firm must create more value (see Theory Spotlight).
- **Customer centricity**—viewing decisions from the customer's point of view—is a critical element of this value.[7] This means that *customers* must perceive more value, not merely that the firm believes it offers more value. For example, if Chinese smartphone manufacturer OnePlus designs a new phone with double the screen size of its existing flagship device, the firm might well believe it is offering more value. But consumers will not necessarily see it this way if the device does not fit in their hands!

customer centricity Viewing decisions from the customer's point of view

- "Sustainable" refers to whether the advantage can be readily imitated or overcome; if a competitor can immediately take the same action and be equally successful, the advantage will not last. When an electronics store cuts prices on living room televisions, for example, it aims to gain market share, and hopes that competing stores will not be able to profitably match its prices.
- Decisions and actions can also be *reactive* in nature, aiming to protect an existing advantage or prevent a competitor from acquiring an advantage. In the price cut example, a competing store that can match the reduced price and still turn a profit might do so to maintain the competitive status quo.

Figure 1.1 lays out several cases of firms making marketing decisions to protect or advance sustainable competitive advantages. Finnish telecommunications company Nokia, for example, partnered with Polkomtel to build 5G cellular towers and related infrastructure in Polish cities, under the oversight of the Polish government. This created an edge for Nokia that was strongly protected from competitors, since the deal effectively locked these other telecoms firms out of using their 5G radio equipment in Polish cities.[8] US-based videogame developer and platform provider Epic Games also made a play for a competitive edge when it paid videogame publishers millions of dollars to offer their games for free on the Epic Games Store platform. While costly, this move enabled the platform to quickly build a userbase and erode the competitive edge of the market-leading Steam platform.[9]

IN OTHER WORDS ...

Marketing decisions and actions help a firm create more value than competitors, create value in a unique way, or prevent a competitor from creating more value. This allows the firm to sustain its competitive advantage and ultimately protect and advance its position in the marketplace.

Sustainable Competitive Advantages Achieve Objectives for Stakeholders

While a sustainable competitive advantage is an important and immediate goal of marketing decisions and actions, it is not the reason these decisions and actions exist. Rather, their ultimate objectives are guided by the objectives of the firm.

shareholder view The perspective that when the firm makes decisions, all that matters is whether it does the best thing for its owners (in the case of a publicly traded firm, its shareholders)

benefit The value that the product's features provide

stakeholder view The perspective that when the firm makes decisions, it should holistically evaluate those decisions, considering everyone who is affected by those actions—typically shareholders, employees, customers, suppliers, local communities, the environment, and society

There are two perspectives on the firm's objectives. The older perspective is the **shareholder view**. Under this view, all that matters is whether the firm does the best thing for its owners (in the case of a publicly traded firm, its shareholders).[10] So, marketing decisions and actions should increase long-term shareholder value by enhancing present and future profits.

Marketing scholars and the general populace are increasingly aware, though, that a firm's choices affect far more people and businesses than its shareholders—sometimes in drastic ways. For example, in 2008 UK-based oil and gas firm BP began operating an offshore oil rig in the Gulf of Mexico called Deepwater Horizon. The goal of this action was to increase BP's oil throughput and **benefit** shareholders. But in April of 2010, Deepwater Horizon exploded, killing eleven workers as well as spilling 4 million barrels of oil into the Gulf, resulting in immense damage to wildlife and the Gulf Coast economy. In the end, even BP's shareholders suffered as the firm's reputation was tarnished and it was forced to pay billions of dollars in civil and criminal penalties arising from charges of negligence.[11]

Incidents such as the Deepwater Horizon disaster have given greater popularity to the **stakeholder view** of the firm. Under this perspective, marketers (and managers in general) should holistically evaluate their decisions and actions, considering *everyone* who is affected by those actions—typically shareholders, employees, customers, suppliers, local communities, the environment, and society.[12] It is possible, for example, that a more robust stakeholder view could have resulted in BP assigning greater importance to costly preventative measures such as safety inspections, personnel training, and preemptive maintenance aboard the rig. This chapter's Opposing Views features additional examples and discussion of this issue.

Source: USEPA Environmental-Protection-Agency/Flickr

Controlled burns of spilled oil following the Deepwater Horizon disaster; this event was one of many that prompted businesses to seriously consider a stakeholder perspective.

OPPOSING VIEWS Shareholders versus Stakeholders

Many corporate scandals have arisen over the past several decades. For example:

- In 2013, German automaker Volkswagen was caught using special software in its diesel cars to cheat on emissions tests. These "clean diesel" vehicles seemed to pass these tests, but in real-world conditions they exceeded allowable emissions by more than ten times.[13]
- In 2016, US-based financial services firm Wells Fargo's executives put excessive financial pressure on the firm's branch employees to get customers to open more accounts. Eventually, these employees began to open accounts in customers' names without their permission! In addition to causing notoriety (and a half-billion-dollar legal settlement) for Wells Fargo, this event was costly for the employees and customers involved.[14]

These and other scandals involved marketers and other managers pursuing profits for shareholders without regard for how their decisions could adversely impact other parties, such as customers, employees, and the environment. Thus, the stakeholder view grew in popularity. However, there has also been a pushback against this view. Based on the legal structure of a corporation, the board of directors has a fiduciary duty to maintain and increase the value of the firm, which many have interpreted as an exclusive legal obligation to grow shareholder value.[15] This view was famously summarized by economist Milton Friedman as: "the social responsibility of business is to increase its profits."[16]

Global

An important and often forgotten portion of Friedman's argument, though, is that doing the right thing for stakeholders (not taking advantage of customers, not poisoning the environment, etc.) in fact tends to increase profit in the long run. This argument seems to align with the examples above, as well as the Deepwater Horizon disaster: the wrongdoing was caught, and the firm suffered financially for not considering impacts on other stakeholders. With increasing public access to information, rapid sharing of business scandals on social media, and a seemingly increasing tendency for negative stories to leak via whistleblowers, it may be difficult to avoid financial blowback from taking a narrow, shareholder perspective. Major companies still have not reached a consensus on this issue.

See the issue from two sides:

1. Craft an argument in favor of the shareholder view. How might this view indirectly protect the interests of other stakeholders?
2. Craft an argument in favor of the stakeholder view. In what ways might the shareholder view be insufficient to protect the interests of other stakeholders?

Thus, marketing decisions and actions create sustainable competitive advantages to *achieve stakeholder objectives*. Under this view, broader moral and ethical considerations, rather than only a profit motive, should influence marketing decision-making. Despite the prevalence of a stakeholder view, the stakeholders prioritized by most marketing decisions and actions are ultimately the owners of the firm, as Figure 1.1 illustrates. For example:

- In 2019, US-based entertainment firm Disney entered the streaming wars with its Disney+ service, featuring hundreds of movies and TV shows. Ultimately, this service aimed to advance shareholder objectives by creating a stable, subscription-based revenue stream and creating more touchpoints to engage with (and profit from) customers.[17]

- Similarly, in 2020, one of China's largest technology companies, Baidu, launched its Apollo Go autonomous taxi service in several major Chinese cities, hoping to create a new revenue stream. However, Baidu's objectives differed from Disney's in two ways: (1) Apollo Go was likely unprofitable at launch, aiming instead for longer-term shareholder value by enhancing the popularity of autonomous vehicles, and (2) Given the relative scarcity of firms with effective autonomous driving technology, Apollo Go was also a prestige project, raising the profile of Baidu's employees and other lines of business.[18]

As these and the preceding examples show, this action-oriented definition of marketing—*decisions and actions that seek sustainable competitive advantages to achieve objectives of stakeholders*—makes it easier to view marketing activities through a lens of intended competitive outcomes and organizational objectives.

Types of Marketing

A definition of marketing is not complete without considering the various "flavors" of marketing. Marketing is often described in terms of the setting where it occurs. It is important to recognize these descriptive terms and what they mean, since they are used often in this book and in the business world. One of the most common distinctions is based on whom marketing actions target: business-to-consumer (B2C), business-to-business (B2B), and business-to-government (B2G):

business-to-consumer (B2C) marketing Marketing decisions and actions targeted toward individual people

- **Business-to-consumer (B2C) marketing** is familiar to almost everyone and consists of marketing decisions and actions targeted toward individual people. For example, UK-based telecoms provider Vodafone offers several phone plans for individuals and families, such as its pay-per-gigabyte Red plans.

business-to-business (B2B) marketing Marketing decisions and actions targeted toward businesses

- **Business-to-business (B2B) marketing** is equally important but less commonly encountered in everyday life. It is made up of marketing decisions and actions targeted toward businesses. Vodafone also offers plans for businesses, such as its Business Freedom unlimited plan that easily scales with the size of a business, whether it has one employee or hundreds.

business-to-government (B2G) marketing Marketing decisions and actions targeted toward entities in the public sector, such as city and national governments, law enforcement organizations, the military, and government agencies

- Finally, **business-to-government (B2G) marketing** is targeted toward entities in the public sector, such as city and national governments, law enforcement organizations, the military, and government agencies. Vodafone also serves these organizations—including around two-thirds of fire, police, and EMS services in the United Kingdom—with special features such as network monitoring to ensure maximum uptime.[19]

DEVELOPING A MARKETING STRATEGY

Marketing Strategy versus Marketing Actions

No individual marketing decision or action, on its own, is responsible for creating a firm's competitive advantages or achieving all stakeholder objectives; it is the combination of numerous decisions and actions over time. This combination is achieved through a **marketing strategy**. A marketing strategy is a plan that answers three questions:

1. What does the firm aim to accomplish?
2. Which competitive advantages will advance the firm's objectives?
3. What decisions and actions will achieve those competitive advantages?[20]

marketing strategy A plan with three parts: (1) it spells out the firm's objectives, (2) it specifies the competitive advantages that will achieve those objectives, and (3) it lays out the decisions and actions that will achieve those competitive advantages

For example, UK-based grocery chain Sainsbury's strategy could be described as follows: (1) it aims to continue to grow its share in the mid-range grocery market while helping communities "live well for less," (2) by offering more convenient locations and high-quality, high-value brands than competitors, (3) through continued openings of full-service and convenience store locations and promotional support for in-house brands.[21]

It should be apparent that the definition of marketing strategy feels like the definition of marketing actions, but in reverse. This is no accident. Marketing decisions and actions work toward a firm's strategy. If marketing actions are jigsaw puzzle pieces, marketing strategy is the artwork that those puzzle pieces form.

marketing planning process A series of steps to formulate a marketing strategy—(1) stakeholders objectives, (2) analysis of the marketing environment, and (3) designing the marketing mix

mission statement A document that spells out high-level goals with respect to various stakeholders

The Marketing Planning Process

If marketing strategy is a jigsaw puzzle, this poses a challenge for marketers: puzzles are difficult and require time, trial, and error to complete. In business, time is money as competitors will seize on any delay to gain an edge. Therefore, instead of coming up with a strategy through trial and error—experimenting with different tactics at random—strategy should be developed through a **marketing planning process**, or a series of steps to formulate a marketing strategy. Continuing our metaphor, this is a bit like completing a puzzle using an instruction booklet. It might be less fun, but it is quicker and more effective. Figure 1.2 shows the steps in the marketing planning process, culminating in a fully developed marketing strategy. These steps are:

1. defining stakeholder objectives;
2. analysis of the marketing environment; and
3. designing the marketing mix.

Step 1: Defining stakeholder objectives. The first step in the marketing planning process maps onto element (1) of marketing strategy, spelling out the firm's objectives. This step is typically highly formalized into two components. First, the firm has a **mission statement** that lays out high-level goals with respect to various stakeholders. For example, a sustainable apparel brand's mission statement might feature the following: "to create durable and appealing clothes made in the domestic market." The mission statement serves

Source: Wonderlane/Unsplash

Marketing strategy can be thought of as a complex jigsaw puzzle, with the pieces representing various marketing decisions and actions.

Figure 1.2 The Marketing Planning Process.

The three steps in the marketing planning process answer the three questions addressed by a marketing strategy. The process is cyclical as objectives, advantages, and performance are continuously reevaluated.

firm-wide objectives Specific and measurable goals for the firm's activity and performance

as an inspiration for **firm-wide objectives**, or specific and measurable goals for the firm's activity and performance, such as "achieve 10 percent year-over-year sales growth."

Step 2: Analysis of the marketing environment. The second step maps onto element (2) of marketing strategy, answering the question: which competitive advantages will advance the firm's objectives? There are many ways to answer this question, but generally there are two steps marketers must accomplish before answering it. First, they must identify **external opportunities**, meaning circumstances outside the firm that facilitate the achievement of organizational objectives. For example:

external opportunities Circumstances outside the firm that facilitate the achievement of organizational objectives

- Recall Nokia (Figure 1.1). Nokia's executives wanted to forge closer international partnerships with firms and foreign governments. The desires of countries such as Poland to build 5G cellular infrastructure have been golden opportunities for Nokia to advance this objective.
- Or consider the earlier example of Carrefour. One of Carrefour's corporate objectives was to advance its ACT FOR FOOD initiative to support food quality and nutrition. Therefore, the chance to grow its presence in the organic food market—for example, by acquiring Bio c' Bon—was a valuable opportunity.

segment A group of customers with similar preferences

More generally, identifying opportunities often involves finding a **segment**, or group of customers with similar preferences, that is not as well-served as it could be by the products and services on the market. French fashion house Louis

Vuitton, for example, exclusively pursues consumers who desire unique and glamorous luxury apparel and accessories.

Second, marketers must recognize **internal capabilities**, meaning the ability to create value from hard-to-duplicate combinations of firm assets and expertise.[22] Consider:

internal capabilities The ability to create value from hard-to-replicate combinations of firm assets and expertise

- Nokia, for example, has extensive technology and innovation capabilities, arising from its rich history of innovation, its expansive patent portfolio, and the large number of engineers and scientists in its employ.
- Disney has a wide array of intellectual properties under brands such as Pixar and Marvel, enabling the creation of valuable new films and TV series.
- Or, returning to the Sainsbury's example, the grocery chain benefits from a strong geographical footprint and well-liked brand name, enabling it to gain consumer acceptance for its own store-brand products as well as other food and beverage brands.

In each of these examples, the firm's internal capabilities pointed to natural opportunities to pursue. Nokia could use its technology capabilities to close in on cutting-edge markets such as 5G infrastructure; Disney can use its many franchises to serve consumers hungry for family-friendly content, cinematic universes, and nostalgia; and Sainsbury's can use its geographical footprint and brand name to sell higher-priced groceries to quality-focused shoppers. Hence, the heart of the marketing planning process is *aligning internal capabilities with external resources* to advance stakeholder objectives.

Of course, if aligning internal capabilities with the right external opportunities was easy, marketers would rarely fail. As this book will show in the "Marketing Fail" feature of every chapter, marketers do fail! Understanding the marketing environment is growing more difficult as this environment grows more complex. Chapter 3, on digital marketing, addresses this challenge in greater detail. Increasingly, marketers also rely on **marketing analytics**—using data to solve marketing problems—in identifying external opportunities and matching those opportunities with current or potential internal capabilities. Various analytics techniques are noted throughout this textbook, especially in Chapter 9 (marketing research).

marketing analytics Using data to solve marketing problems

Step 3: Designing the marketing mix. The final step in the marketing planning process maps onto element (3) of marketing strategy, answering the question: what decisions and actions will achieve the firm's competitive advantages? This involves planning the tactics, the individual actions, that will be used to execute the strategy. These actions are often collectively referred to as the **marketing mix**. Returning to the example of FlipKart (Figure 1.1), its SuperCoin Pay program was an individual promotion in the firm's marketing mix, designed to bolster the unique benefits of buying from FlipKart rather than other online retailers.

marketing mix All of the various decisions and actions that implement the firm's strategy

The marketing mix is a broad and growing concept that means something slightly different for every firm and defies a neat and quick summary. The next section provides details on each of the various types of elements in the marketing mix, and how they can serve a firm's strategy.

EXECUTING MARKETING STRATEGIES THROUGH THE "4P" AND "7P" MARKETING MIX

"7P" marketing mix A framework that separates marketing decisions and actions into categories of product, price, place, promotion (4P) in addition to people, processes, and physical evidence

There are many individual marketing decisions and actions that comprise marketing strategy. It is useful, then, for managers to be able to categorize these actions into different spheres (i.e., groups). These categories can then serve as a sort of "checklist" so managers can be sure that they have considered the implications of their strategy for each sphere. For example, if a discount store wants to start carrying high-end jewelry, they must surely think about what this action means for their prices and the design of their stores.

"4P" marketing mix A framework that separates marketing decisions and actions into categories of product, price, place, and promotion

Beginning in the 1960s, the most common way to categorize marketing choices and actions was the **"4P" marketing mix**.[23] Separating decisions into those pertaining to **p**roduct, **p**rice, **p**lace, and **p**romotion—each explained in the sections that follow—this framework is still valuable and widely used because it concisely describes most of what marketers do. When asked by a person on the street, "What sorts of things do marketers spend their time on?", the 4P categories are a perfect place to start.

The 4P Marketing Mix

marketing mix element #1: product The physical items and/or intangible services offered by the firm

offering Another term for the physical items and/or intangible services offered by the firm

Marketing mix element #1: Product. The first and core element is the **product**, which in the context of the marketing mix is a catch-all term referring to the physical items and/or intangible services offered by the firm. Another term for the product element of the marketing mix, used frequently in this book, is the firm's **offering**.

Products take many forms. Volkswagen's product includes not only its cars, but the after-the-sale service it offers through its add-on service plans and its authorized dealerships. Amazon's product includes the various products that the company stocks in its warehouses, the Marketplace service that connects other sellers with Amazon customers, the growing in-house Amazon Logistics shipping service, the Prime Video streaming service, and various services connected to the firm's other business units (e.g., Amazon Web Services website hosting). Café Coffee Day's (India's biggest coffee chain) offering includes specialty coffees and teas, food items such as chicken burgers, the service experience within its stores, and home delivery service.

features What the product is and what it does

benefits The value and usefulness that a product's features provide to its end user

A product can be described in terms of **features** and **benefits**. Features describe what the product is and what it does—for example, the horsepower of a car or the storage space of a smartphone. Benefits characterize the value those features provide—for example, the car's feeling of excitement and adventure or the phone's ability to carry many apps and photographs. The product's features and benefits should advance the firm's competitive advantage. This means that the product should provide value for customers in some situations or use cases to a greater extent than other options on the market. For example, the core product of Google's YouTube—a platform for sharing and watching videos—generates unmatched value for video content creators, as YouTube's massive userbase provides an audience that these content creators cannot find elsewhere. Chapter 12 elaborates more on gaining competitive advantages through products.

MARKETING FAIL Quibi Goes Small and Goes Home

Source: Hugh Han/Unsplash

US-based streaming service Quibi featured short-form shows designed exclusively for smartphones, not for TVs. In theory, people would watch during short breaks; for example, they might watch a ten-minute episode during a train ride. The service folded within a year of launching.

Netflix, Prime Video, Disney+, HBO Max: these are all familiar names in the world of streaming television and movies, bringing to mind evenings curled up on the sofa binge-watching the latest series, comforted by the cool glow of a high-definition TV. And then there was Quibi. What was Quibi? Launched to great fanfare after raising $1.75 billion in venture capital, this streaming service went small where others went big. It launched in the United States and Canada (and later Australia and New Zealand) with around 5,000 "quick bite" videos (under ten minutes) and no long-form programming. Additionally, at launch it was *only* possible to watch Quibi on handheld smart devices, with limited smart TV functionality added months later.[24] The ad-free version of the service cost $8/month, which was more expensive than Disney+ in 2020.

A bold strategy, but it did not pay off for Quibi or its investors. A mere eight months after its launch, the service shut down as it failed to attract enough subscribers. Its entire library of original content was later sold for less than $100 million—around 5 percent of what investors originally put into the company.[25] This streaming service was an embarrassing failure.

USA

Why did Quibi fail? Among other reasons (e.g., a high price and low consumer awareness of the service's existence), it was a classic case of a product looking for a purpose. Given the short-form, mobile focus, one might be forgiven for assuming that Quibi was looking to compete with apps such as YouTube and TikTok for users' eyeballs and attention on commutes, breaks from work, and similar "in-between" situations. Not so, according to CEO Meg Whitman: "YouTube has done a fantastic job, but what we want to do is to do what HBO did when they launched. It will be that much of a step up in quality and storytelling."[26]

But Quibi could not compete with HBO; few consumers wanted to watch *Game of Thrones*-style prestige dramas in ten-minute bites, and even fewer wanted to watch them alone on their phones. And Quibi also failed to recognize that apps such as YouTube were *already* producing high-quality content, with thousands of dedicated creators pouring their time and livelihoods into their videos, with many YouTube channels securing millions of subscribers. One media commentator succinctly summarized the issue: "Quibi didn't work because no one at Quibi knew what it should be, what people wanted, or how people use their phones."[27]

Diagnose the problem:

1. Without changing Quibi's core offering—short-form, high-production-value series—can you think of a way to bring this streaming service to the market more successfully? Are there particular types of consumers, or situations, or even parts of the world where Quibi's offering might have found a home?
2. The streaming service space, once dominated by Netflix, saw many new competitors in the latter half of the 2010s. Given how crowded the market is, do you think there is room for more streaming services? Is there something you would like to see a streaming service do, that none of them currently offer?

marketing mix element #2: price What the firm demands in exchange for its offering

Marketing mix element #2: Price. The second element of the marketing mix is **price**, or what the firm demands in exchange for its offering. A firm's menu of prices, negotiation tactics, and various discounts and sales are all part of this element. It is worth noting, though, that this definition does not mention money, because price is not always monetary. Consider Twitter's social media platform. Twitter has two sets of customers. Advertisers pay a monetary price to place promoted posts at highly visible positions within users' search results and feeds. Twitter users are also customers, but they do not pay a monetary price. Instead, they pay with *data* about their own usage of Twitter. If a user consents to combine this data with information from third-party services such as Google Ads—most users consent, whether they realize it or not—then this data tells a powerful story about the user's online life and becomes even more valuable to advertisers.

Like the product, the price should serve a competitive advantage. German supermarket chain Aldi is well-known for offering the lowest prices available for food and drinks in many cities. Competitors cannot match these prices because of the other elements of Aldi's marketing mix (limited staff, small stores, narrow selection, etc.) that keep costs extremely low.[28] This is a common theme with price. To use *low* prices as a competitive advantage, other parts of the firm's strategy must keep costs below competitors' costs. Otherwise, competitors will react with an even lower price, potentially starting a harmful price war. High prices can also support a competitive advantage, for example by acting as a signal of high quality or exclusivity. Epic Games' popular multiplayer videogame Fortnite sells premium "skins"—digital add-ons that change the cosmetic appearance of the player's character—for as much as $20, with these skins providing a sense of status to the game's players.[29] Pricing strategies such as these are discussed in greater detail in Chapter 14.

marketing mix element #3: place How the firm ultimately gets its offering to its customers

Marketing mix element #3: Place. The third element of the marketing mix, **place**, is about how the offering ultimately gets to the customers. There are numerous types of place decisions, answering questions such as: In which countries, cities, or regions should our product be sold? Should we sell through a distributor or wholesaler, or direct to a retailer? In which types of shops should our product appear? Should we have our own retail stores? Where should our stores be located? How should our products be laid out or organized within a store?

The nature of these questions varies by firm. For example:

- For South Korean electronics firm LG's television division, essentially all the questions above are applicable. LG has decided to directly sell its TVs to more than sixty different brick-and-mortar and online retail store chains in over forty countries.[30] It does not operate its own stores but uses partnerships with retailers to secure prominent wall displays in "big box" electronics stores and to be shown in "featured" search results in online stores.
- On the other hand, consider a local plumber. She only carries parts commonly used in her repairs, so she does not have any products to sell in a store. Most of her services cannot be performed from a single location, instead requiring her to travel and visit customers. Most of LG's questions

become irrelevant in this case. The plumber's main place-related questions might be: What is my business address, so I can be convenient to customers looking for local service? How far away should I be willing to travel to service customers?

- Or, for sellers of digital products such as smartphone apps, there are still other "place" questions: In what countries will the app be available? On which app stores should the app be sold? Should users also be able to access the app through a web browser?

Whatever the nature of the firm's place-related decisions, they are a part of its competitive advantage. Unlike price, place decisions can sometimes create significant advantages on their own. This is especially the case for the location of a retail store or service center because *locations are inherently non-substitutable.* If a restaurant opens in the single-story building at the corner of Main Street and 1st Avenue, it is physically impossible for a competing restaurant to copy this location! A similar, equally attractive location may or may not exist or be available, depending on the circumstances. Additional nuances related to place decisions are explored in Chapters 6 (country market entry decisions), 8 (retail location decisions), and 13 (marketing channel management).

Marketing mix element #4: Promotion. If place defines how and where customers can get their hands on the product, then the fourth element, **promotion**, encourages customers to go there. That is, marketing promotions persuade or encourage customers to try, or continue purchasing, the product. Promotion comes in many flavors:

marketing mix element #4: promotion Actions that persuade or encourage customers to try, or continue purchasing, the product; includes advertising, public relations, the sales force, and sales promotions

- **Advertising**—messages paid for by the firm and aimed at current and potential customers—is the classic form of promotion, often taking the form of television, billboard, or print advertisements targeting wide audiences. Increasingly, firms are using highly targeted forms of advertising such as promoted Twitter posts, mentioned earlier in this chapter, that appear to specific users based on their browsing patterns.

advertising Messages paid for by the firm and aimed at current and potential customers

- **Public relations (PR)** are another common form of promotion, in which the firm weaves a narrative about its activities using formal statements to the press, interviews, and social media posts. PR can be proactive, but it is often *reactive*, a way to mitigate harm from negative events. The infamous European horsemeat scandal in 2013, for example—in which "ground beef" on store shelves turned out to contain as much as 29 percent horsemeat—prompted a flurry of public statements, announcements of investigations, and apologies from affected retailers such as Tesco.[31]

public relations The firm's use of public communications such as formal statements to the press, interviews, and social media posts to weave a narrative about the firm's activities

- The **sales force** comprises personnel, such as salespeople and in-store sales associates, who directly interact with current or potential customers to inform and persuade about the firm's offering. It is also critical to promotions in many firms. French pharmaceutical company Sanofi, for example, has one of the world's largest professional sales organizations, featuring approximately *10,000 salespeople.*[32]

sales force Personnel who directly interact with current or potential customers to inform and persuade about the firm's offering

- Lastly, **sales promotions** describe any other tactics to encourage purchase, such as sweepstakes entries, free gifts, and shipping deals.

sales promotions Miscellaneous other activities to encourage purchase, such as sweepstakes entries, free gifts, and shipping deals

Promotions tend to work synergistically with product, price, and place to forge a competitive advantage. By communicating with customers, persuading them, and encouraging them to buy, promotions magnify the ability of the first three Ps to generate an advantage. A firm with a great product will be better off if customers can be convinced that the product is great; a firm with low prices benefits when consumers learn about those low prices; and a firm with convenient locations wants its customers to see how convenient those locations are. Due to the breadth of promotions, additional details about them are spread throughout this book, including in Chapters 3 (social media marketing), 11 (advertising strategy), 13 (relationship marketing actions), and 15 (integrated marketing communications).

IN OTHER WORDS ...

The four categories of marketing promotions are advertising, public relations, the sales force, and sales promotions. Marketing actions in these categories usually do not achieve advantages on their own, but instead use information and persuasion to magnify the advantage obtained from the other marketing mix elements.

The Value of a "7P" Marketing Mix in Service Settings

Thus, the 4P framework is extremely useful and has long been descriptive of most marketing activity. But as time went on, and particularly as services (banking, subscription programs, restaurants, health care, etc.) have grown as a share of major economies since the 1980s, marketing scholars and other observers realized that the 4P approach was being stretched to its limit. While still functional, it did not fit naturally with some important parts of service businesses.

For example, the customer service counter at a retail store has employees that must handle returns in a certain way, following the store's return policies (e.g., how many days have passed) and sometimes even following a "script" mandating what phrases they should say. The firm makes choices about which employees work at this counter, and how to train them on these policies and scripts. Are these choices about place because they relate to the store? Are they about promotion because they involve communications with customers? Are they about products because product returns are involved? Are they about price because they determine whether a refund is given?

These, and similar limitations of the 4P marketing mix, are addressed by expanding the framework to accommodate important aspects of marketing strategy more comfortably. One of the most popular expanded frameworks is the **"7P" marketing mix**, which takes the initial four categories and adds three: **p**eople, **p**rocesses, and **p**hysical evidence.[33] People, processes, and physical evidence play primarily supporting roles in the marketing mix but are nonetheless crucial to a successful marketing strategy. These additional elements, as well as the original four, are described in Table 1.1.

Table 1.1 Marketing Mix Examples and Coverage in this Book.

A firm must make marketing decisions and actions in up to seven interrelated spheres. The first four are the classic 4P elements.

"P" Element	Definition	Examples	Coverage in this book
#1: Product	The physical items and/or intangible services offered by the firm	Volkswagen's cars and after-sale service; Café Coffee Day's food, drinks, and home delivery	Chapter 12 (offering-based advantage and innovation of the offering)
#2: Price	What the firm demands in exchange for its offering; can be monetary or non-monetary (e.g., personal data)	Aldi's low food prices; Fortnite's costly videogame character "skins"	Chapter 14 (pricing strategy)
#3: Place	How the firm ultimately gets its offering to its customers, whether it is a physical product, a digital product, or a service	LG's partnerships with dozens of authorized retailers; Google Maps' availability on the Apple App Store	Chapter 6 (country market entry decisions) Chapter 8 (retail location decisions) Chapter 13 (marketing channel management)
#4: Promotion	Actions that persuade or encourage customers to try, or continue purchasing, the product; advertising, public relations, the sales force, and sales promotions	Promoted Twitter posts; Tesco's public relations response to 2013 horsemeat scandal; Sanofi's 10,000-strong army of salespeople	Chapter 3 (social media marketing) Chapter 11 (advertising strategy) Chapter 13 (relationship marketing actions) Chapter 15 (integrated marketing communications)
#5: People	The personnel that execute the firm's marketing strategy, especially on the front lines	The 10 million retail store workers in the United States; Amazon's team of 150 PhD economists	Chapter 8 (omnichannel marketing mix) Chapter 15 (personal selling)
#6: Processes	Standardized procedures for solving problems that arise in implementing and evaluating the marketing strategy	Territory design process for salespeople (e.g., using Javelin software); Segmentation, targeting, and positioning process; Price adjustment/optimization process (e.g., using PROS software)	Chapter 4 (segmentation, targeting, positioning) Chapter 9 (marketing research) Chapter 11 (advertising planning) Chapter 13 (relationship marketing process)
#7: Physical evidence	Evidence (not always physical!) that the firm will serve customers well into the future, including stores and brands	Target's physical stores and branded packaging for online orders; IKEA's e-commerce website	Chapter 8 (retail store management) Chapter 11 (branding)

Marketing mix element #5: People. The firm's marketing mix cannot be executed without the fifth element, the **people** who implement marketing decisions and actions both within and outside the firm. Within the firm, personnel support and execute marketing actions in countless ways, such as by translating firm-wide objectives into team and individual performance goals, designing (or contracting out) materials for advertising campaigns, training and guiding customer service employees, and performing various analytics functions. Amazon, for example, employs around 150 PhD economists that specialize in tasks such as creating

marketing mix element #5: people The personnel who implement marketing decisions and actions both within and outside the firm

demand forecasts for specific product categories and quantifying the effects of price increases.[34]

frontline workers Personnel, such as salespeople, who interface directly with customers

Many other individuals support the firm's marketing strategy by taking outward-facing actions and communicating with external stakeholders such as customers. The most important of these are **frontline workers**, those who interface directly with customers. Phone-based customer service representatives and retail store sales associates dominate this category. In the United States alone, nearly 10 million people (*almost 5 percent of adults*) work in retail sales.[35] Professional salespeople, such as Sanofi's 10,000-strong force mentioned earlier in this chapter, are also a key part of the firm's frontline personnel.

The careful reader will note that salespeople seem to fall under both the promotion and people elements of the marketing mix. While it is true that the persuasive and informative communications of salespeople are central to the firm's promotions, the "people" element acknowledges that salespeople are fundamentally different from promotional tools such as advertising and giveaways. This is because salespeople are *human* resources, and like all parts of the fifth marketing mix element, require a complex web of resources such as training, financial compensation, motivation, mentoring, and support for physical and mental health. In general, people will be more effective in executing marketing decisions and actions when these supporting resources are properly configured and funded. For example, in 2009 Swiss food and beverage giant Nestlé built a massive wellness center for employees at its Vevey headquarters, with an extensive cafeteria of healthy dining options, dozens of fitness clubs, and a bike-sharing program.[36] The "people" element receives additional attention in Chapters 8 (omnichannel marketing mix) and 15 (personal selling).

marketing mix element #6: processes The firm's standardized procedures for solving problems that arise in implementing and evaluating the marketing strategy

Marketing mix element #6: Processes. The sixth element of the marketing mix, **processes**, includes the firm's standardized procedures for solving problems that arise in implementing and evaluating the marketing strategy. Like people, processes are a supporting element of the marketing mix that enable the other elements to enhance competitive advantage. Processes can take many forms depending on the firm and the situation, but they increasingly rely on data and marketing analytics. For example:

- A formal process for deciding the shapes and sizes of salespeople's sales territories—using tools such as ZS Associates' Javelin software to incorporate data about customers and their buying potential—supports effective marketing actions using people and promotions.
- The segmentation, targeting, and positioning process covered in Chapter 4 complements the rest of the marketing mix by helping the firm decide which customers to sell to and how to appeal to them.
- Pricing can also be formalized into a process, where prices are reviewed and adjusted at regular intervals using data and pricing optimization software—such as the artificial intelligence-based platform offered by PROS.

Like promotions, processes are a diverse subject, and hence receive coverage throughout the book. Key topics include Chapters 4 (segmentation, targeting, and positioning), 9 (marketing research), 11 (advertising planning), and 13

SHADES OF GRAY Co-Creation or Appropriation?

Global

Individual customers are increasingly participating in and supporting the firm's marketing mix, thus it can be viewed as part of the "people" element. They participate most often through the process of **value co-creation**. Through co-creation, customers contribute to the value created by the firm, such as by providing product ideas. Co-creation was likely happening long before marketers gave it a name. Good salespeople, especially in business-to-business settings, have long been able to learn about what a specific customer wants and customize that customer's experience and, to an extent, the product or service the customer receives.

However, co-creation took on an expanded meaning with the increasing focus on **lead users** in the last several decades.[37] These are consumers with a lot of knowledge and enthusiasm about a given product category, who tend to know exactly what they want and have proven to be a valuable source of product ideas. For example, in 2012 Dutch beer conglomerate AB-InBev hosted competitions between thousands of small breweries, where consumers would taste and rate new beers. The winning beer inspired AB-InBev's "Black Crown" lager.[38]

The premise of co-creation is that consumers and firms both benefit from co-creation; the firm gets pre-vetted, successful product ideas, while consumers get the products they really want. But when do firms cross the line from co-creation to appropriation—simply stealing ideas from their own customers? In the case of AB-InBev, the firm never publicly announced any royalties or significant compensation for the competition winner. Similarly, US-based tool manufacturer DeWalt developed an online, interactive "insight community" where users could submit and judge product ideas, saving DeWalt approximately $1 million in research and development costs per year without compensating users.[39]

On the other hand, some firms go out of their way to compensate users for their co-creation efforts, a practice that seems to be becoming more popular. Danish toy brand LEGO is among the most salient examples. Its Fan Designer program gives select users formal recognition on product packaging and sometimes a percentage of sales.[40] This program has remained popular and led to many popular "Lego Ideas" playsets.

Identify the ethical dilemmas:

1. Who is harmed if a firm sells products based on a user's idea without compensating that user? How so?
2. Suppose that a user agrees to Terms of Service that do not specify any compensation, and voluntarily submit ideas to the firm. How should the firm handle recognition and compensation of this user if her ideas are used? Is there any downside to withholding recognition or compensation from users, even if the firm is not legally required to grant them anything?

(relationship marketing process). In each of these cases, formal processes play a key role in enabling the effectiveness of other marketing mix elements.

Marketing mix element #7: Physical evidence. The seventh and final element of the marketing mix is **physical evidence**. Although the word "physical" gives this element its "P" initial, this name is somewhat misleading because the evidence is not always physical! Rather, this element consists of evidence that the firm will continue to serve customers well into the future. Like promotion, physical evidence encourages customers to try or continue purchasing a product or service; it inspires confidence in the legitimacy and longevity of the firm and its offering.

value co-creation The process by which individual consumers contribute to the value created by the firm, such as by providing product ideas

lead users Consumers with a lot of knowledge and enthusiasm about a given product category

marketing mix element #7: physical evidence Evidence (not always physical!) that the firm will serve customers well into the future, such as physical stores and recognizable brands

Source: Claudio Schwarz/Unsplash

The storefront of a retail store is one form of physical evidence, but not the only one; the existence of physical products or a prominent website can also be considered physical evidence.

Physical evidence can be tangible or intangible. The most common tangible evidence is a physical store or service center. US-based retailer Target's large and instantly recognizable stores, with their consistent internal layouts, create a sense of permanence and continuity in the minds of consumers, assuring them that a positive experience at Target can be repeated in the future. Target also provides tangible evidence for online orders, as they come shipped in a Target-marked box with a printed receipt inside. This once again reinforces the consumer's sense that she is dealing with a legitimate and reasonably permanent organization and can hope to buy from them again.

Intangible physical evidence—despite not being, strictly speaking, physical—is equally important and common. A website provides evidence in almost exactly the same way that a brick-and-mortar store does, encouraging confidence and the sense of a consistent experience that can be repeated in the future. Swedish furniture company IKEA, for example, offers a full-featured web-based store, with extensive product details and typical features such as virtual wish lists and shopping carts. Brands are perhaps an even more important form of evidence and enhance the effectiveness of other forms such as stores and websites. Brands are tied to not only the name of the firm but typically to signifiers such as logos, colors, and slogans. When stores, packaging, and websites feature these signifiers—such as the massive "bullseye" brand logo on Target's storefronts—the consumer's sense of familiarity and confidence in buying from the firm is reinforced.

Thus, physical evidence rounds out the "7P" marketing mix by supporting and reinforcing advantages gained from other elements of the mix, in a similar manner to the complementary effects of people and processes.

CHAPTER SUMMARY

The marketing concept has three key facets: (1) decisions and actions, (2) leading to sustainable competitive advantages, (3) that advance objectives of stakeholders. Stakeholders include not only proprietors or shareholders but also customers, society at large, and other parties affected by marketing decisions. Market-leading firms increasingly embrace a holistic set of ethical considerations when making marketing decisions, rather than only profit. Marketing can be B2C, B2B, or B2G.

Marketing planning is used to develop a marketing strategy. There are three planning steps: (1) defining stakeholder objectives, (2) analyzing the marketing environment, and (3) designing the marketing mix. The marketing mix consists of decisions and actions that can be grouped into several distinct categories. Traditional marketing management defined the 4P approach to the marketing mix: Product, Price, Place, and Promotion. However, as marketing increasingly pivots toward a greater emphasis on services, there is growing recognition that the 4P approach does not always emphasize all relevant categories of marketing decisions. Many marketers therefore now consider a 7P view of the marketing mix: the original four (Product, Price, Place, Promotion) in addition to People, Processes, and Physical Evidence. Together, these seven elements are the core execution dimensions in a marketing planning process. This chapter details the types of choices that surround each of the marketing mix elements, and how they advance the firm's marketing strategy.

APPLICATION QUESTIONS

1. Think of two recent marketing actions by companies that you saw in the news or in advertisements.
   a. Which of the seven marketing mix elements was each action? Explain your answers.
   b. Explain how each of these actions advanced a company's competitive advantage.
2. Think of a recent time that you made a small purchase, such as food or household supplies. Which marketing mix elements had the greatest influence on what you decided to buy? Why?
3. Think of a recent time that you made a *large* purchase, such as a computer or car (or a similar purchase by a family member or friend). Which marketing mix elements had the greatest influence on what you (or this other person) decided to buy? Why?
4. Pick one of the companies mentioned in this chapter that you know at least a little bit about and look up its mission statement (sometimes only a "vision" statement can be found; this also works). Do you feel that this company is enacting this mission? What is this company doing that helps its mission, and what is it doing that is not helpful?
5. Think of your favorite company. To what extent do you think this company makes decisions from a stakeholder (vs a shareholder) point of view? Which stakeholders do they care about, and how do you know they care?

Visit the companion website, **https://bloomsbury.pub/palmatier-marketing**, or **www.samsinstitute.com**, for additional learning and teaching tools, including professional videos outlining the Four Principles, PowerPoint tutorials with voice-over commentary, sample syllabi for marketing courses, testbank and more.

Chapter 2

THE FIRST PRINCIPLES OF MARKETING

CHAPTER OVERVIEW

Chapter 2 introduces the First Principles perspective, which is the guiding framework for this book. It explains the "what" and "why" of this approach, with examples of how these principles are underlying truths that marketers must handle. It links each of the principles to the marketing mix decisions from Chapter 1 and explains how marketers integrate all four principles as they develop and implement marketing plans. The chapter will proceed by answering the following questions:

- What are the First Principles of marketing?
- Why should we use a First Principles approach?
- What are the four Marketing Principles and how do they affect the marketing mix?
- How do the four Marketing Principles work together to influence marketing decisions?

In the chapter's cases and features, you will see examples of marketing decisions that either incorporate or fail to account for the four Marketing Principles. These include:

- Motorola's attempt to launch a modular smartphone (Marketing Fail).
- The growth and challenges of plant-based meat (Chapter Case).
- Marketing controversies such as the role of mathematical analysis versus intuition (Opposing Views).
- Moral dilemmas such as Amazon's treatment of Marketplace sellers (Shades of Gray).

LEARNING OBJECTIVES

- Identify the four First Principles of marketing.
- Recognize the marketing challenges associated with each First Principle.
- Associate each First Principle with various marketing mix decisions.

IMAGINE Opening a Coffeehouse

Imagine opening a coffeehouse in your hometown. To start your business, there are a lot of steps you need to complete, such as writing a business plan, securing financing (e.g., from a bank), leasing or buying a store location, designing a menu of drinks and food, making deals with suppliers, and hiring employees. You also must contend with your town's current preferred coffee destination—let's assume that it's Costa Coffee, a UK-based Coca-Cola subsidiary with thousands of locations worldwide.

Your challenge is convincing enough consumers in your town to come to your shop instead of Costa Coffee so that you can turn a profit. You must do this using the initial funding that you secured from the bank and ongoing funds from operating the shop (undoubtedly far less than an international chain such as Costa Coffee has at its disposal). In summary, you face a David versus Goliath scenario. Where can you go to find customers, and what can you do differently than Costa Coffee to win them over? Perhaps you might find some consumers who are not well-served by Costa's menu, such as those who want various alcohol-spiked coffee drinks. Or you might identify a way that Costa has failed to keep up with the times, for example, by not having an area for children to read or play while their parents enjoy a coffee. Implementing marketing mix elements (e.g., Product and Physical evidence) to fill these needs represents an opportunity to satisfy certain customers that a larger, slower-moving chain might ignore.

Critical thinking:

1. Aside from the examples noted above, can you think of at least *two* other types of customers that might not be well-served by Costa Coffee? You may find it helpful to look up Costa's menu and services. Why does Costa not meet these needs?
2. Which marketing mix elements from Chapter 1 would you deploy to meet these customers' needs, and how?
3. How do you think the Costa Coffee in your town will respond to you opening a coffeehouse with the unique features that you have described?

WHAT ARE THE FIRST PRINCIPLES OF MARKETING?

As the marketing field evolves, managers are overwhelmed with more and more concepts, analysis tools, and research techniques (e.g., geotargeting, big data, artificial intelligence) for specific marketing tasks (e.g., segmenting, branding). Although these new approaches offer value, a marketer is left with unanswered questions. For example, when is each approach appropriate and worthwhile to use? How does each concept or technique improve the firm's performance? And are some tools best left inside the toolbox?

Marketing textbooks are typically organized around separate chapters that deal with each element of the 4P marketing mix (product, price, place, promotion), suggesting ways for dealing with competitors or performing marketing functions such as advertising. This functional or task-based perspective provides a lot of concepts and frameworks distributed across different areas. But it offers little overall guidance on when to use the various frameworks, how they work, which ones are most valuable, or how they all fit together.

This book takes a different approach. We attempt to simplify managers' marketing decisions by arguing that these decisions should focus on solving four underlying "problems" or "complexities" that all marketers face. These four

First Principles of marketing (or "Marketing Principles") Four fundamental complexities that guide all marketing decisions; (1) all customers differ, (2) all customers change, (3) all competitors react, and (4) all resources are limited

problems represent the most critical hurdles to marketing success; they also define the organization for this book. We refer to them as the **First Principles of marketing (or "Marketing Principles")** because they reflect the foundational assumptions on which marketing decisions are based.[1] They are:

1. All customers differ.
2. All customers change.
3. All competitors react.
4. All resources are limited.

This First Principles approach is different because its goal is to align the concepts, processes, and data-driven tools that guide modern marketing practice, together with existing frameworks and insights on the marketing mix (4P or 7P), competitors, and marketing tasks from traditional textbooks.[2] Organizing the varied discussions around four fundamental principles means that every decision appears within its meaningful context, which includes its impact on other decisions. This view establishes a guiding purpose for marketing efforts.

For example, segmentation and customer centricity are both tactics that deal with a First Principle: all customers differ. By taking the First Principles approach, we offer a toolbox for dealing with a broad range of marketing challenges, rather than learning unique techniques for each specific marketing event. That is, the guiding framework can solve a wide range of marketing problems. Conceptually, the application is similar to using Newton's laws of motion (i.e., First Principles of basic physics) to solve diverse physics problems, rather than learning different process steps for each type of problem.

Source: Sunder Muthukumaran/Unsplash

The ever-popular Newton's cradle sustains its motion thanks to Newton's laws of physics; likewise, the First Principles of marketing affect and guide the outcome of all marketing actions.

This chapter therefore begins with the rationale behind the First Principles approach. With an overview of each of the four principles, we prepare readers to dive deeper into the concepts, tools, and decisions addressed in the rest of this book. Finally, this chapter integrates the four Marketing Principles to show how they allow a better understanding of marketing decisions and how they map onto the contents of this book.

WHY SHOULD WE USE A FIRST PRINCIPLES APPROACH?

In Chapter 1, we defined marketing as decisions and actions that seek sustainable competitive advantages to achieve objectives of stakeholders. One might wonder whether there is an easier way to make these decisions. For example, couldn't a manager simply look at past marketing mix deployments, identify those that generated the highest performance, and implement those same tactics, again and again? Some firms can follow this approach to generate success in the short run. But as customers, competitors, and conditions continue to evolve, approaches that created success in the past may become inappropriate. In some cases, past successes using a particular approach even can hinder a firm's ability to develop necessary capabilities to address new conditions. Copying the successful strategies of a competitor also might fail to yield the same results, because each firm has different capabilities and conditions. No marketing mix is ever going to be consistently effective in all conditions or for all firms; the effectiveness of a particular mix depends on a multitude of underlying customer, competitor, and contextual factors.

A key requirement for making good marketing decisions, then, is to identify these underlying factors. Without such information, a firm might copy the successful marketing actions of a competitor, only to find that those actions work only for certain segments of customers, only at particular points in the customer's life cycle, only in response to specific competitive actions, or only in certain conditions. Identifying the underlying factors or complexities that determine the efficacy of marketing decisions also requires digging deeper than reading about the most recent marketing fad in the business press. By definition, these fads tend to apply only for a short period of time or in certain situations.

For example, Microsoft saw that Apple was successful in creating a complete software ecosystem for its customers, offering seamless compatibility across Apple's desktop (macOS) and mobile (iOS) operating systems. Microsoft attempted to replicate this success by getting its massive Windows desktop userbase to adopt the Windows Phone mobile operating system. Unfortunately, Microsoft failed to account for an unfortunate truth: *tempus fugit* (time flies). In the mere three years since the launch of iOS, the mobile operating system market had matured and solidified; whereas in 2007 consumers' preferences were fluid and emerging, by 2010 iOS and Android enjoyed dominant positions and highly loyal users. Microsoft was never able to obtain a foothold and eventually retreated from the market.

Thus, effective marketing decisions require accounting for four underlying complexities that are inherent, at least to some degree, to all business' interactions:

(1) All customers differ; (2) All customers change; (3) All competitors react; and (4) All resources are limited. Of course, you will recognize these four facts as the First Principles of marketing noted at the beginning of the chapter. This approach involves grouping or aligning key marketing decisions with these four assumptions, in such a way that managers can understand and account for their interdependencies and sequencing when making decisions. Each Marketing Principle is closely associated with a category of marketing decisions. For example, all customers differ, so firms must manage customer differences when deploying the marketing mix (e.g., customer segmentation).

marketing effectiveness The strength of the link between resources deployed to the marketing mix and stakeholder outcomes

The end goal of the First Principles approach is to improve **marketing effectiveness**—that is, to strengthen the link between resources deployed to the marketing mix and stakeholder outcomes. It does not imply removing or preventing underlying complexities; it recognizes that in most cases, the First Principles are given, so firms need to understand and effectively manage each of them. The units of this book focus on each Marketing Principle in detail. In the remainder of this chapter, we offer short overviews to help readers understand just what we mean by the four MPs and available tactics for making decisions relevant to that MP.

IN OTHER WORDS ...

The First Principles approach is designed to maximize the "return on investment" of the marketing mix. It does this by (1) grouping the key obstacles and complexities that often hinder marketing effectiveness into four categories, and (2) connecting marketing concepts and tools that account for these complexities to these four categories.

MARKETING PRINCIPLE #1: ALL CUSTOMERS DIFFER

All Customers Differ

Marketing Principle #1: all customers differ The idea that customers vary widely in their needs and preferences

managing customer differences Tailoring products and services to meet the unique needs of one or more segments or individual customers

The first and most basic issue affecting marketing mix decisions is **Marketing Principle #1: all customers differ.** Customers vary widely in their needs and preferences, even for basic commodity products such as bottled water (mineral water, spring water, flavored water, etc.) and milk (skim, 2%, organic, etc.). Large grocery stores and online retailers offer thousands of different products in their efforts to match each individual customer's preference. Hence, MP#1 leads to a key challenge in designing the marketing mix: **managing customer differences**.

Various factors lead customers to differ in their preferences, including:

1. unique functional needs for the product;
2. previous marketing activities focused on changing their preferences;
3. basic, personal differences;
4. varying life experiences; and
5. distinct aspirational self-identities.

These sources all work together to drive variation in customers' preferences, as Chapter 4 explains in detail.

If a firm ignores this principle and offers a weak selection, they may gain sales in the short term, particularly if competition is limited or the product is scarce. Netflix provides an informative example. When its online streaming service launched in 2007, it faced relatively few mainstream competitors and earned a large subscriber base with a catalog of mostly older scripted shows and movies. As time went on, though, streamers such as Hulu and Amazon Video offered a wider selection of new content across diverse genres, including reality shows and documentaries. To maintain its market dominance, Netflix poured billions of dollars into acquiring or producing "Netflix Originals" that could appeal to each demographic across various genres. For example, in 2021 Netflix paid $450 million for the rights to two sequels to the 2019 mystery film *Knives Out*.[3]

As demand for any new offering grows, competitors recognize opportunity and begin supplying differentiated products that match the preferences expressed by specific segments of the overall market. If a firm fails to respond with refined offerings, customers move. The firm thus loses sales revenue. In addition, because competitors are likely to go after the fastest growing or most profitable segments, the firm is left with customers in slow growing and less profitable segments. Failing to manage customer differences has been the death knell for many firms.

Managing Customer Differences in the Marketing Mix

The different sources of individual variation work together in multifaceted ways. Although customer differences are a fundamental challenge that all firms need to address when developing an effective marketing mix (MP#1), the ways to do so are not always clear. That is, how should each firm deploy its marketing mix to manage customer differences?

- First, it could ignore these differences and provide an offering (i.e., *Product*) that matches the average customers' needs. Many customers will be dissatisfied, but in a large enough market, "average" customers could be numerous enough to keep the firm profitable—at least temporarily. If the market keeps growing though, a competitor likely will appeal to some group of customers who are interested in a better fitting solution. The original firm then is left with an oversized infrastructure and associated costs. Combined with lost sales and profits, this situation greatly erodes its financial performance.
- Second, a firm could offer a range of products and services to satisfy many different customer segments. This strategy can be highly effective; it also can be very costly and difficult (see this chapter's Marketing Fail feature on Motorola's attempt at this). A single firm rarely satisfies all these different customers simultaneously. Imagine, for example, trying to appeal to high-end markets, as with BMW cars and Yves Saint Lauren clothing, while also catering to lower-end markets, as with Volkswagen and H&M. From a marketing mix perspective, such efforts can seem virtually impossible; communications (*Promotion*) and store aesthetics (*Place* and *Physical evidence*) could become confused and conflicting.

Source: Valeria Odnovol/Unsplash

Selling luxury apparel and accessories is about more than an appealing product; it is supported by the entire marketing mix, including high-end boutique retail stores. It would be difficult for the same retailer to appeal to both luxury and discount apparel consumers.

- Third, firms might embrace the notion that customers will sacrifice desired product attributes if the price is low enough. With a classic low-cost strategy, firms attempt to identify core, must-have attributes that will satisfy consumers' functional needs, then focus all their efforts on reaching the lowest cost for an offering that meets those needs (i.e., a low *Price*). Here again, the strategy can be viable, depending on the size of the low-cost segment and the firm's ability to gain differential cost advantages over its competitors.
- Fourth, to deal with customer differences, a firm might select a specific segment of customers and target them by positioning its offering as the best solution, compared with those available from any competitors, for that particular segment (i.e., segmentation, targeting, and positioning, or an STP approach; see Chapter 4). This approach requires strong support from skilled analysts (*People*) and an effective segmentation scheme (*Processes*). The result is often a strong brand that customers in the segment know and respect. This strategy often incorporates a customer-centric approach to promote further growth in the targeted segment. For example, Apple knew that its core, loyal customer base wanted high-end, stylish, and reliable smartphones, and continued to meet these needs over successive generations of iPhones. But by focusing on the needs of these customers more broadly, rather than viewing them merely as a segment in the smartphone market, Apple has been able to provide new products such as the Apple Watch and AirTags to meet these customers' needs and to complement other Apple products.

Thus, "all customers change" is a constant principle that managers must account for when designing the marketing mix. This Marketing Principle is the focus of Chapters 4 (managing customer differences and STP), 5 (understanding differences in consumer and industrial buyer behavior), and 6 (marketing for global and cross-cultural differences).

MARKETING PRINCIPLE #2: ALL CUSTOMERS CHANGE

All Customers Change

Marketing Principle #2: all customers change The idea that customers' needs change over time

managing customer dynamics The key marketing mix challenge associated with MP#2

In addition to considering differences across customers (MP#1), managers need to account for **Marketing Principle #2: all customers change.** They must deploy a marketing mix that accounts for variation as a customer's needs change over time. In other words, the marketing mix challenge arising from MP#2 is **managing customer dynamics**. These changes might happen at the individual customer level, reflecting specific customer, product market, and contextual factors. At any point in time, customers might be grouped and targeted based on their needs and desires. Soon thereafter though, customers' needs start to evolve. Even within a well-defined segment, members' individual needs often evolve at different rates or directions. At some point in the future, two customers who once were part of the same segment might exhibit widely divergent needs and desires. For example, two senior college students might buy a lot of the same products; but after they graduate, one might continue in graduate school while the other begins in a career in sales, resulting in very different spending and consumption habits.

The changes also can be market-level evolutions in customer preferences that come from new technologies. In these cases, nearly all customers eventually change, albeit at different rates, so the firms that fall behind suffer a risk of extinction. For example, as electric and hybrid automobiles become more popular and cost-effective, they are growing more acceptable to a larger swathe of consumers. Many automakers have picked up on this trend and started emphasizing various fully electric models (e.g., Tesla, Nissan, Ford, Volkswagen), but others lag behind and risk losing brand-loyal consumers.

Thus, the different sources and drivers of customer dynamics combine to make change inevitable. Most of these drivers can be grouped into five categories:

1. seminal events in a person's life (e.g., birth of a child);
2. distinct stages in a person's life (e.g., middle age);
3. changes in product knowledge (e.g., familiarity with the features of a voice-activated smart assistant);
4. changes in maturity of the product category (e.g., preferences change more rapidly for new types of products); and
5. influence from marketers.

Chapter 7 addresses each of these drivers in detail. Because all customers change over time, a failure to understand and address customer dynamics ultimately will undermine marketing effectiveness.

Managing Customer Dynamics in the Marketing Mix

The marketing mix often takes a significant amount of time to implement and begin producing results. Therefore, waiting for sales data to show that customers have begun their inevitable change before responding is not an effective plan. So how should a firm manage customer dynamics?

There are three main approaches firms can use to manage changing customers:

1. It is sometimes possible to strategically ignore changing preferences and continue to provide an identical offering (*Product*) and even replay the same commercials (*Promotion*). For example, for iconic consumer brands such as Coca-Cola and M&M, the notion that these products have endured for decades with minimal changes is part of the appeal. This leads these brands to maximize continuity in the product's flavor and packaging and use "classic" advertisements over and over (e.g., M&M's famous Santa ad). However, this approach only works for a select few firms, and even

then, only for a portion of their offering. After all, both Coca-Cola and M&M continue to introduce different flavors, variants, and commercials alongside the classic ones.

2. A firm can gain insight into customer dynamics by applying life cycle perspectives to customers, products, or industries. A life cycle perspective specifies the stages that a customer, product, or industry experiences over time. For example, a customer life cycle refers to the average change among customers as their relationship with the firm ages. A car insurance company might notice that early on, customers want a lot of personal contact with a representative (*People*) to answer questions about their policy and a professional-looking mobile app and website (*Physical evidence*). But after several years, they care much more about a smooth policy renewal process with transparency on price changes (*Processes*). Likewise, a product or industry life cycle approach captures typical user experiences and industry developmental effects that can be observed as the product category matures. These life cycle approaches are simple and easy to use, which probably explains why they remain predominant in many marketing courses and textbooks. While they account for changing preferences over time (MP#2), they ignore how these changes might differ between customers (MP#1).
3. By applying insights from MP#1 to the customer dynamics problem, firms can segment their existing customers according to how they expect the customers' preferences or behaviors to change over time. One formal way to do this is using the dynamic customer segmentation approach, which we explain in detail in Chapter 7. Briefly, grouping existing customers into three stages—those recently acquired, longer-term customers, and those lost or at risk of being lost—can offer insights into how customer segments change their relationships with the firm over time. Returning to the car insurance example, the life cycle approach likely oversimplifies matters. Consider two segments: the "high-relational" and "low-cost" consumers. The high-relational group wants high-touch personal contact not only early in the relationship but also years later. Personalized emails and letters (*Promotion*) can further cement this relationship. The low-cost group, on the other hand, might be increasingly susceptible over time to discounted offers from competitors. Maintaining the lowest profitable premium for this group (*Price*) and reminding them of the discounts that they already receive could become especially important to retaining this group.

In summary, managing customer dynamics across the marketing mix is critical to marketing effectiveness. We explore this idea further in Chapters 7 (managing customer dynamics and dynamic customer segmentation), 8 (evolution of retail and omnichannel marketing), and 9 (using marketing research to manage customer dynamics).

MARKETING FAIL Motorola Tries to "Mod"-ify Its Destiny

Motorola Mobility (formerly Motorola, Inc.) has a storied history, with Neil Armstrong's declaration "one small step for a man, one giant leap for mankind" being spoken into a Motorola radio.[4] It once owned many of the patents commonly used for cellular antennae and other components and was the number two cell phone brand in the mid-2000s. However, the advent of the smartphone era was not kind to Motorola. Two acquisitions later (first by Google in 2012, then by Lenovo in 2014), it had become a niche player in the phone market.[5]

Looking to stage a comeback, in 2016 the Lenovo-owned Motorola launched the Moto Z. Motorola recognized that people used their phones in different ways. Some were on the go constantly and needed a lot of battery life; others used their phone as a music speaker; still others enjoyed photography or gaming. Whereas other smartphone makers approached these customer differences with a varied product line, Motorola took a new approach with the Z: modularity. The Moto Z was ultra-thin but came with a unique connector on the back. Motorola hoped to start an ecosystem of "Moto Mods," produced by Motorola itself as well as partner firms, that would attach to the Z's connector. Mods available over the years included a battery expansion, an advanced camera with a zoom lens, a gamepad, a speaker with kickstand, a video projector, and a handful of others. To support this mod ecosystem, Motorola committed to the same phone shape and connector on each of the Z's successors, including the Z2, Z3, Z4, and several variants.

USA

Unfortunately, Moto Mods and the Moto Z line did not take off, with Motorola's market share peaking at 8 percent in 2019 in the United States and even lower in other markets.[6] The mods themselves were not all available at launch, were pricey to collect, and could be cumbersome to carry around. Even setting these problems aside, Motorola faced another challenge: the mod ecosystem required retaining the same phone design for several years while consumer preferences rapidly changed. For example, by 2019 most consumers liked taller screens and bigger built-in batteries, making the Z4 unappealing.[7] Motorola's market share never recovered following the failure of this product line.

Diagnose the problem:

1. Explain what went wrong with the Moto Z line of phones, including the role of both MP#1 and MP#2.
2. Was the Moto Mods idea doomed to fail from the start? If so, why is it impossible to make this idea work? If not, what could a smartphone maker (not necessarily Motorola) do differently to make this idea successful?

MARKETING PRINCIPLE #3: ALL COMPETITORS REACT

All Competitors React

The first two marketing principles are focused on potential and existing customers because understanding and managing customer differences and dynamics allows a firm to match its targeted customers' needs and manage these needs as the firm engages with those customers over time. The selection of target markets and positioning strategies is based on the firm's relative strengths compared with existing competitors', but the firm's long-term success and financial performance also depend on how competitors react now and in the future. No matter how well a firm addresses MP#1 and MP#2, competitors will constantly try to imitate its success or develop business processes and offerings to match customers' needs and desires better. The persistent effort by other firms to copy and innovate implies **Marketing Principle #3:**

Marketing Principle #3: all competitors react The idea that other firms will persistently try to innovate, copy, and respond to marketing mix actions

managing sustainable competitive advantage The key marketing mix challenge associated with MP#3

all competitors react. Marketers must address MP#3 by building and maintaining barriers to competitive attacks. This leads to a challenge in **managing sustainable competitive advantage** (SCA) when designing the marketing mix.

History shows that no firm can withstand the competitive onslaught forever. In 1896, industrialist Charles Dow created the Dow Jones Industrial Index, a market index that comprised twelve giants of American industry at that time (e.g., US Rubber, American Sugar, Chicago Gas). With the exit of General Electric from the Index in 2019 due to its declining share price, *none* of the original members remained.[8]

Competitors have many avenues for undermining a firm's position:

1. Technical innovations can render a firm's existing product or services obsolete. For example, horse-drawn carriages once crowded the streets of the world's cities. In late-1800s London, for example, it is believed that purchases of one popular design—the sporty, single-horse "Hansom cab"—numbered in the thousands.[9] By the 1920s, automobiles had almost completely displaced these carriages on the city's streets.
2. Customers' desires may change when cultural, environmental, or other unpredictable factors cause the firm's brand to appear no longer relevant or even harm the firm's performance. For example, the coronavirus pandemic temporarily made many restaurant brands seemingly irrelevant, forcing them to temporarily find alternative ways to serve customers, such as expanded delivery or grocery offerings.
3. The entrepreneurship and creativeness of diverse actors are constantly being leveraged to find different, better, alternative solutions to problems and offer new products and services (e.g., Airbnb cutting into hotels' revenues).

Source: RL Sirius via The National Archives UK/Flickr

The sporty Hansom cab once dominated the streets of London, but technological innovation led to the decline of horse-drawn carriage makers as automobile manufacturers generated a new type of competition.

4. Competitors can copy the firm's offering but also be better at executing its strategy. This is arguably the case for Impossible, whose plant-based ground beef poses a serious threat to Beyond Meat's product, which launched several years earlier (see Chapter Case Study).

Thus, technology, customers, and business environments keep changing, and among these changes, a firm's competitors are constantly trying to create new ways to satisfy customers' needs and desires. Those efforts have great potential to disrupt the firm's market position. The more successful a firm is, the more effort its competitors will expend to attack its position.

Managing Sustainable Competitive Advantage in the Marketing Mix

Because competitors are always attacking the firm's position, marketers cannot solely focus on customers' unique needs now (MP#1) and manage the changes in these needs over time (MP#2) but also must anticipate future competitors' reactions, then build barriers to withstand the never-ending competitive assault (MP#3). These barriers arise when a firm builds sustainable competitive advantages. A firm should develop SCAs that are relevant for a specific target segment; if those customer needs change then the firm has to adapt its competitive advantage to protect that segment or consider moving to a different customer segment. Accordingly, firms often spend much of their marketing budget to shore up their SCA, relying on the three, key **marketing-based sources of sustainable competitive advantages:** brands, offerings, and relationships.

marketing-based sources of competitive advantage Brands, offerings, and relationships, which individually and collectively form barriers against competitors

- **Brands** are memorable names that are attached to products or services. As noted in Chapter 1, brands themselves can be viewed as "*Physical evidence*" of the firm's reliability and continuity. As sources of sustainable competitive advantage, they often are most effective in large consumer markets (e.g., soft drinks, beer, fashion, automobiles). Firms invest heavily in advertising, public relations, and celebrity sponsorships (*Promotion*) to build brand awareness and brand images in customers' minds and match the firms' own positioning strategy. Brands create SCA in multiple ways, but in the simplest form, strong awareness can cause customers to buy based on recognition and habit. When brands have a strong, unique meaning, customers might purchase them out of a desire for status, to enhance their self-identity, or because of their strong positive attachment to the brand. If the firm's brand aligns better with customers' desires than other, competitive brands, it provides an advantage. Brands are also difficult to copy because of trademark laws and other legal restrictions.

brand The memorable name attached to a product or service; one of the marketing-based sources of sustainable competitive advantage

- Offerings (by definition, *Product* in the marketing mix; see Chapter 1), such as innovative products or services, can be effective sources of SCA in many markets. Firms allocate large budgets to research and development departments, which develop prototypes and perform tests (*Processes*) to achieve and patent the most innovative product, add supplementary services, or reduce their costs to undercut competitors (*Price*). The firm can also innovate in terms of delivering the offering in new places or channels (*Place*), such as restaurants selling frozen dishes in grocery stores. Offerings create SCA if they meet customers' needs better or provide more value than existing offerings. This route also requires that customers care about the new feature, innovation, or value proposition established by the offering (consistent with the customer centricity concept from Chapter 1). Offerings can be hard to imitate because of patent laws, trade secrets, and a firm's general knowledge and experience providing the offering.

relationship A connection between a buyer and a seller, typically including personal interaction; one of the marketing-based sources of sustainable competitive advantage

- Finally, **relationships** are especially effective sources of sustainable competitive advantage in business-to-business (B2B), service, or complex business settings. Building strong relationships between customers and the firm's salespeople or other boundary-spanning employees (*People*) can prompt enduring customer loyalty and ensure superior financial performance. Most B2B transactions are fairly complex, require two-way communication, and span long periods, so strong interpersonal relationships between buyers and sellers can help establish the necessary cooperation and flexibility for these exchanges. Relationships thus lead to SCA through factors such as trust, commitment, and interpersonal reciprocal bonds. Relationships are not easy to copy, since the fabric of the relationship is unique to the individuals involved.

Thus, when a firm focuses on building strong brands, developing new innovative offerings, and devotes resources to build enduring customer relationships, the results should be strong and difficult-to-replicate barriers against competitive attacks. This textbook explains how several marketing mix elements can be deployed to achieve these barriers and manage MP#3: branding and advertising techniques (Chapter 11), innovation and product/service strategy (Chapter 12), and CRM and channel management (Chapter 13).

MARKETING PRINCIPLE #4: ALL RESOURCES ARE LIMITED

All Resources Are Limited

Marketing Principle #4: all resources are limited The idea that firms have finite pools of resources but many different priorities to address

managing resource trade-offs The key marketing mix challenge associated with MP#4

The final issue is constant for managers: **Marketing Principle #4: all resources are limited.** Firms have finite pools of resources but many different priorities to address. Thus, in deploying limited resources to the marketing mix, firms are constantly **managing resource trade-offs**. When marketers allocate spending to brand advertising, or innovating new products, or expanding the sales organization to build stronger relationships, they often rely on the same fixed resource pool. With finite resources, important trade-offs are unavoidable. For example, allocating thousands of square feet of retail shelf space to products that serve an unprofitable consumer segment could lead to substantial losses; these resources should be shifted to alternative products. Managing resources judiciously also is critical because, to implement what the firm has learned from MP#1 to MP#3, the firm needs resources on hand to fund the appropriate marketing mix elements.

Multiple factors impact these complex resource trade-offs, though four are perhaps the most critical:

1. changes in the needs of different customer segments (MP#1 and MP#2), which affect how the firm prioritizes different segments;

? SHADES OF GRAY Does Amazon Abuse the Competition?

Amazon has many advantages: universal brand recognition; a dizzying selection of products across almost every retail category along with its own Alexa-powered devices and complementary services; and sticky relationships with consumers and businesses, thanks to the Prime membership program and its assorted benefits. Amazon's dominance partly arises from its Marketplace program, where third-party sellers—be they individuals, small businesses, or sophisticated international operations—can set up a storefront that is fully integrated into Amazon's e-commerce site. By all accounts, the program is extremely successful, accounting for the majority of merchandise sold on Amazon in 2019.[10] Sellers pay a monthly subscription and a "referral fee" up to 15 percent on each item.[11] But perhaps even more important than these fees is the hidden cost of Marketplace participation: an agreement to share detailed sales data with Amazon.

Consider an example to highlight how Amazon could exploit this agreement. An interior designer—let's call him Marco—notices a growing trend in the design world, in which large stencils are used to spray-paint bold, artistic designs on the walls. Feeling entrepreneurial, Marco designs a collection of stencils, engages a Ukrainian contract manufacturer to produce them in large quantities, and creates an Amazon Marketplace storefront. In a short while, Marco grows a successful side business, and happily continues designing and selling new stencils. Yet after a few months, he notices that sales have slowed. He searches Amazon to see if he has a new competitor, and indeed he does. And worse, it's one of Amazon's own brands and the stencils are being sold for less than Marco's production cost! Due to Amazon's size, it was able to negotiate a better deal with a manufacturer.

USA

Marco's case illustrates what some accuse Amazon of doing: using Marketplace sellers' own sales data to identify successful products and launch competing brands. This would not be a problem if sellers could just move to a competing marketplace. However, critics argue that Amazon's dominant position in most markets—controlling as much as half of the e-commerce market in the United States, for example—gives it virtual monopoly power over its sellers and elevates its tactics to the level of abuse.[12]

Identify the ethical dilemmas:

1. Who is harmed by Amazon's use of Marketplace data? How are they harmed?
2. How does Amazon's behavior illustrate an aggressive application of MP#3?
3. In your opinion, is Amazon's behavior abusive? If so, is it sufficiently abusive that regulators and/or legislators should intervene? Why or why not?

2. the entry or exit of competitors (MP#3), as the most competitive segments become potentially less attractive resource targets;
3. the firm's available slack resources such as cash on hand; and
4. changes in the environment, such as new or aging product categories and/or shifting effectiveness of specific media (e.g., mobile advertising) affecting the profitability of resource allocations.

These different sources work together to create the need for complex trade-offs when firms execute their marketing mix. Chapter 14 expands on these four sources.

Firms that neglect the complexity of resource allocations may succeed in the short term, particularly if they have a very large cash pile and can afford expensive and inefficient investments (e.g., modern technology companies such as Google continuously launching and shuttering new services and applications). But it rarely works in the longer run. Trading off among marketing mix elements is inevitable in a dynamic business environment where multiple factors simultaneously influence firm performance. If firms do not develop effective methods to manage these complex trade-offs, they risk losing whole customer segments or significant market share to competitors that have become more effective at allocating their resources.

Managing Resource Trade-offs in the Marketing Mix

A firm's resource trade-off strategies define how much it allocates to each target market segment and marketing mix activity. If these or any other factors (e.g., changes in the composition of a firm's customer segments or product portfolio, changes in the effectiveness of marketing activities) induce additional resource trade-offs, the firm also must adapt its marketing mix to acclimate to these changes. A firm's resource allocation decisions can be informed by two broad approaches:

1. Firms use simple rules to make resource trade-offs when they lack hard data about the attractiveness of each resource option. Managers solve the resource trade-off problem by using basic rules of thumb, driven by intuition and judgment. Such easy-to-use heuristics might suggest allocating a percentage of sales to advertising (*Promotion*) or adopting the same markup rate for all products (*Price*); these approaches can be adapted quickly and seem appealing in complex situations. However, heuristics are often incorrect. They lack any forward-looking, scientific basis for the decisions, relying instead on past successes or managers' gut feelings about what the right resource allocations are. For example, hiring the same amount of salespeople each year as the business grows (*People*) violates MP#3, as competitive reactions in each year might require a lesser or greater number of salespeople to support further growth.
2. A more successful option is the use of attribution-based approaches, especially as modern managers capitalize on their improved computing power, database management, and analytics techniques (*Processes*). Firms are in a better position to review their historical data and measure the impacts of various marketing resource allocations on outcomes such as sales and profits. Historical data contain insightful information about whether and how much marketing resources truly increase economic outcomes. With a well-executed attribution approach, marketing managers can answer critical resource allocation questions, such as, "How much would our sales change if we increased advertising expenditures by 1 percent?" For example, a restaurateur could use attribution approaches to estimate the impact of investing in expanded delivery services (*Product*) or opening additional restaurant locations (*Place/Physical evidence*). If marketing managers use more than one marketing resource, or resources in multiple markets or categories (as is almost always the case), they can discern the relative impact of each resource. In the preceding example, the restaurateur may find that expanded delivery services have a proportionately greater sales impact in urban (compared to rural) markets, suggesting that more delivery resources should be allocated to such markets.

In summary, all resources are limited, and a firm's marketing mix must effectively allocate resources to maximize marketing effectiveness. Chapter 14 expands on MP#4, particularly in the context of pricing, while Chapter 15 explores resources trade-offs in integrated marketing communications and personal selling.

OPPOSING VIEWS When Intuition and Analysis Disagree

Source: Luke Chesser/Unsplash

Packaging marketing analytics in dashboards and other types of data visualizations not only make it faster and more convenient for managers to access these analytics but also makes them easier to interpret and use.

At a macro level, the evidence is clear: when firms organize and integrate their databases, view decision-making as a data-driven enterprise, and employ sophisticated analytic approaches, they tend to perform better. In one study, firms with above-average use of marketing analytics achieved 8 percent higher returns on their assets than firms with moderate usage of marketing analytics; this advantage was even more pronounced in highly competitive industries and when consumer preferences were rapidly changing.[13] The continued growth of business intelligence platforms such as Tableau and PowerBI, as well as customer relationship management systems such as Salesforce and HubSpot, demonstrate the consensus view: the collection and analysis of customer data to support marketing decisions is a vital capability for any firm.

But at a micro level—that is, for certain individual decisions—this consensus seems to crumble.[14] In some cases, marketers are simply overwhelmed with data and can suffer from "analysis paralysis," leading them to fall back on what worked in the past. This can often be resolved with better presentation and "packaging" of marketing analytics, for example with intuitive data visualizations and dashboards.

Global

In other cases, marketers are presented with analyses that are too simple or rough-grained, such that the implications for an individual customer are unclear. For example, a B2B seller of enterprise software might find from past transactions that offering a customer a 10 percent price discount per software license leads to a 20 percent increase in the number of licenses sold to the customer, on average. But how can a salesperson apply this insight when dealing with a customer that might behave differently from those in the past, such as a customer in a new foreign market or an especially large customer? And still in other cases, even with fine-grained and easily interpretable analytics, a marketing decision-maker might simply disagree with the implications of the analysis. This is particularly a problem with some veteran managers who argue that their intuition is also driven by data, in the form of their extensive observations and experiences.

See the issue from two sides:

1. Craft an argument in favor of the universal (i.e., in all situations) use of formal analytics to support marketing decisions. How would you convince an experienced manager that their intuition is often flawed?
2. Craft an argument in favor of the situational appropriateness of intuition to support certain marketing decisions. How would you convince a skilled analyst that their output is sometimes unreliable or incomplete?

INTEGRATING THE FIRST PRINCIPLES INTO MARKETING DECISION-MAKING

The four Marketing Principles guide marketing decisions in two ways. First, they have a holistic and combined impact on the decision-making process. Addressing one principle requires knowledge of the other principles. Imagine a firm faced with developing a sustainable competitive advantage by devising a marketing mix that will appeal to its customers and sustain attacks from competitors (MP#3). It would be impossible to build this marketing mix unless the firm knows what customer segments it wants to pursue and how it can uniquely fulfill their needs and benefits (relative to other offerings). That is, it would need to understand MP#1 to even begin building an SCA. Moreover, it needs to account for how customers might change over time and understand when customers might start or stop buying from it or competitors (MP#2). The same challenges apply to managing MP#4, because making resource trade-offs requires a clear understanding of the first three Marketing Principles.

Second, while all four Principles are universally applicable to marketing decision-making, each one is particularly evocative of a specific set of decisions or marketing mix elements and should be given special focus when dealing with these elements. The structure of this textbook, as well as Figure 2.1, draws out these connections. Part 2 (Chapters 4, 5, and 6) focuses on MP#1, which has heightened

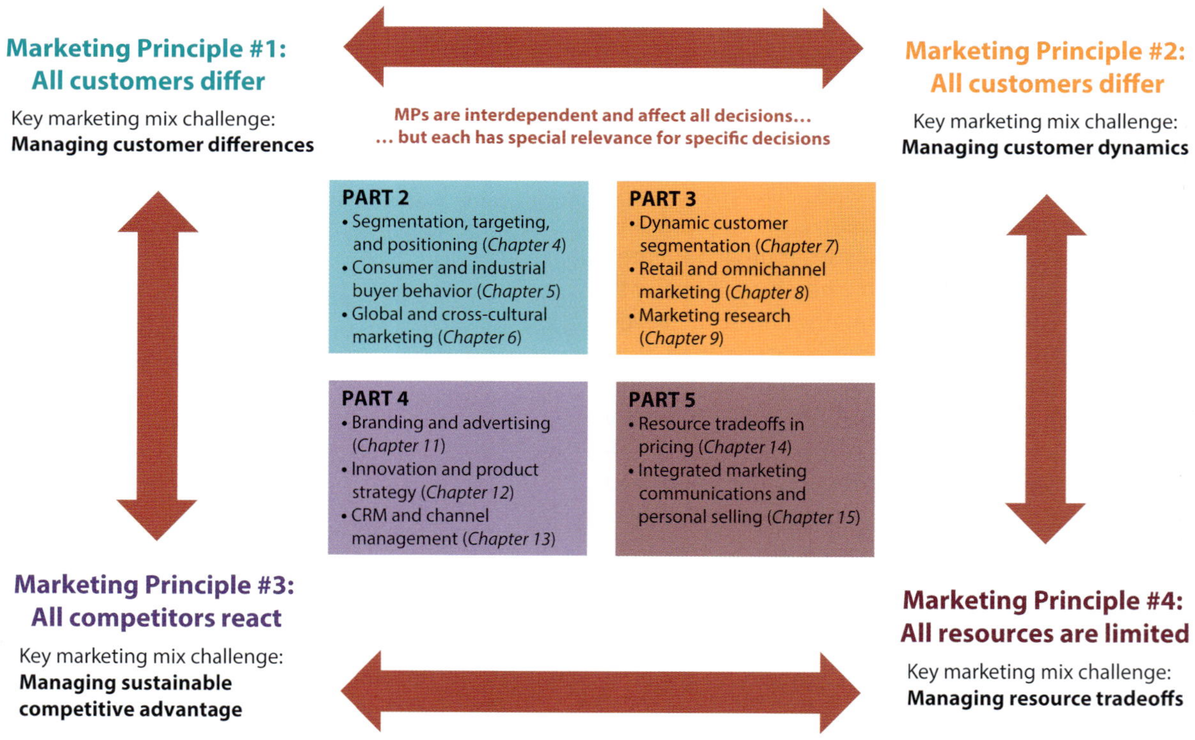

Figure 2.1 First Principles Guide Marketing Decisions.

All four Marketing Principles influence the outcomes of all marketing decisions, but each principle is particularly relevant to a specific subset of decisions. The structure of this book follows these links.

THEORY SPOTLIGHT Resource-Based Theory

The four Marketing Principles aim to integrate marketing decisions into an overarching framework. It is important to acknowledge that other established frameworks can complement our understanding of marketing and strategy. One important framework can be broadly described as **resource-based theory**, the view that a firm's resources and capabilities explain its advantages over competitors and its performance.[15] Under this theory, the firm is a collection of resources. Resources can include strong brands, patented products, facilities and other capital investments, loyal employees, and unique business processes, as well as more intangible benefits such as supplier relationships and innovation capabilities.

The firm derives an advantage over competitors from its resources, depending on four factors: the financial *value* of the resources themselves, the *rarity* of those resources among competitors, the degree to which the resources are difficult to imitate, namely, *inimitable*, and the level of synergy or complementarity in the firm's *organization* of resources. These four factors are known as the **VRIO framework** and lie at the core of resource-based theory. For example, one of Real Madrid's most important resources is the club's name itself; it is extremely valuable (as evidenced by lucrative licensing agreements), impossible to perfectly imitate (due to trademark laws), and rare in that very few sports organizations' names carry such weight. Thus, this resource greatly contributes to Real Madrid's strong competitive position. A firm's level of advantage over competitors, in turn, determines its profitability.

Thus, resource-based theory is useful for understanding how marketing decisions drive performance, insofar as these decisions affect the firm's pool of resources. With its focus on competitive advantage, it can supplement our understanding of Marketing Principle #3 (all competitors react) by helping to explain why strong brands, offerings, and relationships drive sustainable competitive advantage. Chapter 10 explores these ideas in more detail.

relevance for understanding buyer behavior and cross-cultural marketing. Part 3 (Chapters 7, 8, and 9) highlights MP#2 and its importance to marketing analytics and the world of omnichannel marketing. Part 4 (Chapters 10, 11, 12, and 13) emphasizes MP#3 and demonstrates the elevated significance of this principle for brand management, product strategy, and customer relationship management. Finally, Part 5 (Chapters 14 and 15) covers MP#4 and its special relevance for pricing and integrated marketing communications.

resource-based theory The view that a firm's resources and capabilities explain its advantages over competitors and its performance

VRIO framework The core of resource-based theory—the idea that a firm's resources provide competitive advantage to the extent that they are *valuable, rare, inimitable,* and *organized* in a complementary way

CHAPTER CASE STUDY

USA

THE "MEATLESS MEAT" MARKET HEATS UP

In 2009, Ethan Brown started Beyond Meat with the stated goal of replacing livestock-based meat products with appealing but sustainable alternatives. Brown recognized that the traditional market for meat alternatives—vegans and vegetarians—was being supplemented with a growing segment of consumers that were concerned with the environmental impact of livestock. Cattle ranching was of particular concern to these individuals, due to the large amount of land and resources consumed and methane emissions from cattle. After successfully selling "chicken-free chicken strips" in Whole Foods supermarkets, the company launched its signature ground beef alternative in 2014. This product differentiated itself from other options on the market (e.g., tofu burgers) through a unique recipe that derived proteins and iron from peas and other vegetables to closely mimic the texture, flavor, and appearance of beef. By 2020, Beyond products were available at grocers or restaurants in dozens of international markets.[16]

Success breeds competition. The success of Beyond showed consumers that vegan "meatless meat" could taste a lot like the real thing but with over 80 percent less environmental impact.[17] In one poll, for example, the percentage of adults willing to eat plant-based meat products grew from 8 percent to 15 percent in a one-year span; this growth was even greater for high-income consumers.[18] As the market grew and mainstream restaurants adopted "meatless meat" offerings, several competitors arose to challenge Beyond. Most notably, the start-up Impossible—founded by a Stanford University chemistry professor—launched their

Source: Izzy Park/Unsplash

Creating ground beef that faithfully reproduces the entire experience of grilling and eating a hamburger—right down to the "bleeding" of the meat—has been a major flashpoint for competition between Beyond Meat and Impossible.

Impossible Burger in 2016. This product was unique in that it featured heme, a soy-derived iron source that imparts a flavor similar to animal blood. The Impossible Burger gained rapid adoption in restaurants, in particular, such as Burger King in the United States. Although both firms experienced growth and success, by 2019, Impossible had exceeded Beyond's market share in some regions.[19]

Pandemic throws a wrench in the works. In 2020, both Beyond and Impossible faced a new challenge: a global slump in the restaurant industry caused by the coronavirus pandemic. This generated tough questions for both firms. Should they reduce their investments in restaurant partnerships and increase their distribution to grocers? How would such a change impact their supply chains? Would consumers—many of whom had lost their jobs—still be willing to pay a premium for plant-based meat? How long would the pandemic last, and would the firms be able to quickly retool their supply chains when restaurants reopened and consumers' finances improved? Beyond had one advantage relative to Impossible: thanks to a successful initial public offering (IPO) in 2019, it was sitting on a large stockpile of funds. Nonetheless, it was forced to incur significant costs. For example, it had to pay $6 million in the second quarter of 2020 to repackage meat that was originally destined for restaurants and send it to grocers instead. As Ethan Brown explained, "We had 50% of our infrastructure set up for a sector that essentially disappeared."[20] Although the pandemic faded, both Beyond and Impossible still face complex challenges as they handle nuanced and evolving consumer preferences and the likelihood of additional new competitors.

CASE QUESTIONS

1. Explain the role of Marketing Principle #1 in the meatless meat market, focusing on the different types of customers that exist in the market.
2. Explain the role of Marketing Principle #2 in the meatless meat market, focusing on how preferences have evolved over time, how they are likely to evolve in the future, and how this has guided competitors' strategies.
3. Explain the role of Marketing Principle #3 in the meatless meat market, focusing on how the actions of Beyond and/or Impossible can be viewed as responses to one another.
4. Explain the role of Marketing Principle #4 in the meatless meat market, focusing on how and why priorities for resource allocations have shifted over time.

CHAPTER SUMMARY

Modern marketers have access to a wealth of frameworks, tools, and concepts. But there is little overall guidance on when to use the various frameworks, how they work, which ones are most valuable, or how they all fit together. This chapter provides an overview of a very different approach grounded in the First Principles of marketing. Rather than adding complexity, this approach simplifies it by arguing that marketing decisions should focus on solving four underlying complexities that all organizations face when designing their marketing mix. These four problems represent the most critical hurdles to marketing effectiveness; they also define the organization for the remainder of this book. They are called First Principles because they reflect the foundational assumptions on which marketing decisions are based. In short, marketers' most critical decisions must address the following First Principles of marketing: (1) all customers differ, (2) all customers change, (3) all competitors react, and (4) all resources are limited. Organizing the varied decisions around four fundamental principles means that each decision appears within its meaningful context, which includes its impact on other decisions. This view and context establishes a guiding purpose for marketing mix decisions.

APPLICATION QUESTIONS

1. Choose your favorite company or brand—let's call it Company A. In your view, does Company A effectively account for MP#1 and MP#2? Why or why not?
2. Continuing from #1, think of a major competitor to Company A. Let's call the competitor Company B. What is it about Company A that prevents Company B from simply copying Company A's marketing mix? Be sure to reference brands, offerings, and/or relationships.
3. Continuing from question 1, can you think of any segments that Company A ignores, or marketing activities that Company A does not emphasize? Why do you think Company A seems to favor investing resources in other segments/activities?
4. Make a case that MP#1 is the most important Marketing Principle. Find an example of a company's marketing mix element (e.g., an advertisement or a new product) that failed to account for MP#1.
5. Build an argument for MP#2 as the most important Marketing Principle. Find an example of a company's marketing mix element that did not account for MP#2.
6. Craft an argument for MP#3 being the most important Marketing Principle. Provide an example of a company's marketing mix element that failed to account for MP#3.
7. Make the case that MP#4 is the most important Marketing Principle. Find an example of a company's marketing mix element that did not sufficiently account for MP#4.

Visit the companion website, **https://bloomsbury.pub/palmatier-marketing**, or **www.samsinstitute.com**, for additional learning and teaching tools, including professional videos outlining the Four Principles, PowerPoint tutorials with voice-over commentary, sample syllabi for marketing courses, testbank and more.

Chapter 3

FIRST PRINCIPLES IN ACTION—NAVIGATING THE WORLD OF DIGITAL MARKETING

CHAPTER OVERVIEW

Chapter 3 illustrates how to apply the First Principles approach to one of the most important challenges for modern marketers: digital marketing. The chapter introduces the concept of digital transformation and how it has given rise to digital marketing. It then lays out the digital tools that marketers use. Finally, it explains how the First Principles framework both guides and simplifies marketers' decisions about how to use their digital marketing tools. The chapter will proceed by answering the following questions:

- What is digital transformation?
- What tools can modern digital marketers use?
- How does a First Principles approach help marketers manage their digital toolboxes?

In the chapter's cases and features, you will run into companies that have struggled, and sometimes excelled, at managing resource trade-offs while sustaining profitability. These include:

- Walker's botched snack food Twitter campaign (Marketing Fail).
- The digital collaboration between fashion brand Amaro and the Animal Crossing videogame (Chapter Case).
- Ethical and practical dilemmas in digital marketing, such as Facebook's past data scandals (Shades of Gray) and the persuasive power of influencers (Opposing Views).

LEARNING OBJECTIVES

- Recognize key concepts and terms in web, mobile, and social media marketing.
- Evaluate moral and ethical concerns in the current practice of digital marketing.
- Apply the First Principles framework to various digital marketing decisions.
- Compare approaches to implementing the digital marketing mix.

IMAGINE Promoting a New Product in 1990

Imagine that you have developed a business idea: you want to craft and sell knit socks with designs based on characters from popular movies and television shows. But there's one catch—the year is 1990. Although a growing number of households have computers, no one is online. The World Wide Web is not yet accessible to the public and cell phones are the size of small bricks. As for social media, Mark Zuckerberg is rather preoccupied with his schooling at the tender age of six.

This is a problem for your fledgling side business, since you live in a small town. You've sold socks to your friends and family, but you are running out of acquaintances. You are also not exactly a big enough operation to buy primetime television advertisements. You consider other options for finding new customers in your town and beyond. Is it worth buying an advert in the local newspaper? Are there any local businesses that might help you? You ponder these and other possibilities as you weigh the future of your enterprise.

Critical thinking:

1. What strategies might you use to identify and reach new customers for your socks in 1990? How would you grow your business? Think like an entrepreneur and be as creative as you like.
2. Now, fast-forward to 2024. How would your approach change? What role would social media and other modern technologies play in reaching your customers?

THE RAPID PACE OF DIGITAL TRANSFORMATION

digital transformation The ongoing overhaul of customer expectations, market environments, and business processes in response to evolving digital technologies

digital marketing The use of web, social media, and mobile tactics to support the marketing mix

three eras of digital transformation Three distinct stages of changes in the role of digital technology, marked respectively by the growth of e-commerce and internet advertising; the rise of social media; and the ubiquity of smartphones

user-generated content (UGC) Consumer contributions to interactive online platforms, such as reviews and social media posts

The decades from 1990 onward have been marked by **digital transformation**: the ongoing overhaul of customer expectations, market environments, and business processes in response to evolving digital technologies.[1] The pace of this transformation has been remarkable, as the "Imagine" exercise illustrates; 1990 and 2024 are worlds apart in terms of how businesses and customers understand and interact with the world and each other. **Digital marketing**—the use of web, social media, and mobile tactics to support the marketing mix—has come to the fore.

This change did not occur overnight but proceeded over **three eras of digital transformation.**[2]

- The *ecommerce era*, from approximately 1993 (the birth of user-friendly web browsers) to approximately 2002, was characterized by the nascent web growing into a booming online marketplace and advertising platform, facilitating transactions and marketing communications.
- The *social network era*, from approximately 2003 (the launch of the first widely successful social networking platforms such as Myspace) to roughly 2010, saw the growing importance of consumer-to-consumer interactions online. Social networks and **user-generated content (UGC)**—consumer contributions to interactive online platforms, such as reviews and social media posts—took center stage.
- The *always-on era*, from roughly 2011 (when smartphones began to saturate developed markets) onward, is defined by the "always-on" connectivity that is familiar to today's consumers and businesses. In this era, individuals carry the web, various social media platforms, and numerous other connected services with them in their pocket, literally, virtually every minute of each day.

This rapid and dramatic change has not been without challenges. New laws and regulations have been passed to protect privacy and intellectual property, as well as limit digital marketing of illegal products and services. Individuals young and old have also been required to retool their skillsets as digital savvy becomes more central to both personal and professional lives.[3] And marketers themselves have sometimes struggled to understand how and when to use the dizzying array of digital marketing tools available. This chapter outlines what these tools are and then applies the First Principles framework to organize and guide the use of these tools.

UNDERSTANDING THE DIGITAL MARKETING TOOLBOX

Digital marketing is best understood as a set of tools that, when properly employed, will comprise a valuable part of the marketing mix and advance stakeholder objectives. When used haphazardly or without an understanding of their purpose though, these tools can be a waste or even a hindrance—much like how using the wrong screwdriver can strip a screw's head, making it impossible to remove. This section highlights numerous digital marketing tools (Figure 3.1) and explains their roles in the marketer's toolbox.

5Cs framework A perspective that highlights the interplay of five factors in the digital marketing ecosystem (or the marketing environment more broadly): customers, company, collaborators, competitors, and context

THEORY SPOTLIGHT 5Cs of the Digital Marketing Environment

Although this chapter focuses on applying the First Principles approach to the digital marketing toolkit, other frameworks are useful for understanding the unique role of digital marketing. The **5Cs framework** is one such example. This perspective highlights the interplay of five factors in the marketing environment: customers, company, collaborators, competitors, context.[4] Applying this framework to the digital marketing ecosystem yields useful insights:

- *Customers* use social media, review platforms, and shopping apps to access products and information in rich, diverse ways.
- The *company* must design its marketing mix, including digital elements, to account for this complexity.
- It can leverage *collaborators*, such as social media platform operators or influencers, to enact elements of the marketing mix.
- However, *competitors* have access to these same resources; moreover, the digital space generally reduces barriers to entry, enabling new competitors.
- Throughout, the *context* of digital marketing, including social media platforms and search engines, serves as a battleground that both customers and the company must navigate.

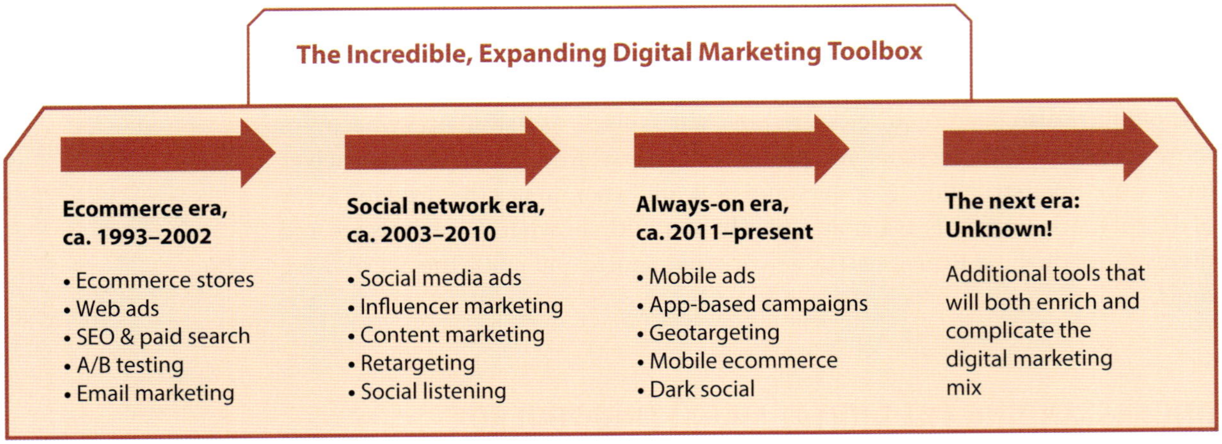

Figure 3.1 The Digital Marketing Toolbox.

Digital marketers have an ever-growing array of tools in their toolbox, distributed across web, social media, and mobile marketing categories. The biggest challenge is knowing what tool to use, and when.

Web Marketing: The Original Digital Marketing

web marketing Marketing mix elements that rely on basic internet functionality such as web browsing and email

e-commerce Buying and/or selling products via an online storefront

The World Wide Web predates social media and smart devices. Thus, **web marketing** tools—marketing mix elements that rely on basic internet functionality such as web browsing and email—are the oldest and most established component of digital marketing. Website design is perhaps the first such tool. Savvy marketers figured out early on that a website was an analogue for a store. Therefore, its design should be treated with the same care and attention to detail in evoking customers' thoughts and feelings.[5] Web design is especially important for firms with **e-commerce** operations, such as Indian retailer Flipkart, as few consumers want to buy or sell products on an unappealing website. Even B2B sellers, such as wholesalers selling hardware and tools to contractors, are discovering the importance of appealing and effectively designed e-commerce functionality.[6]

search engine optimization (SEO) A firm's selective use of relevant keywords on its website, to improve its standing in search results

click-through rates The percentage of time that an advertisement or email is clicked on when it appears

content marketing Drawing in customers with substantial, thoughtful content such as blog posts

Search engines and email are also old standbys of marketers. Firms use **search engine optimization (SEO)**, or selective use of relevant keywords on their websites, to improve their standing in search results and to be found more easily by customers.[7] Email marketing follows a similar tack; after receiving a potential customer's email address (due to the customer signing up with the firm or with a partner firm), the firm deploys tailored messages featuring key words and phrases to avoid spam filters and attract the reader's attention. Likewise, web adverts, such as those plastered across every corner of each Forbes article, and paid search results ("sponsored" links at the top of search results) use key phrases or imagery to grab attention. Web marketing campaigns, such as email marketing, web adverts, and paid search results, can all measure their success with **click-through rates**, or the percentage of time that the advert or email is clicked on when it appears. Lastly, **content marketing**—drawing in customers with substantial, thoughtful content, such as blog posts or "think pieces" about product trends—is an increasingly important digital marketing tool.[8] For example, Luxury watch brand Rolex launched a transaction-less website https://

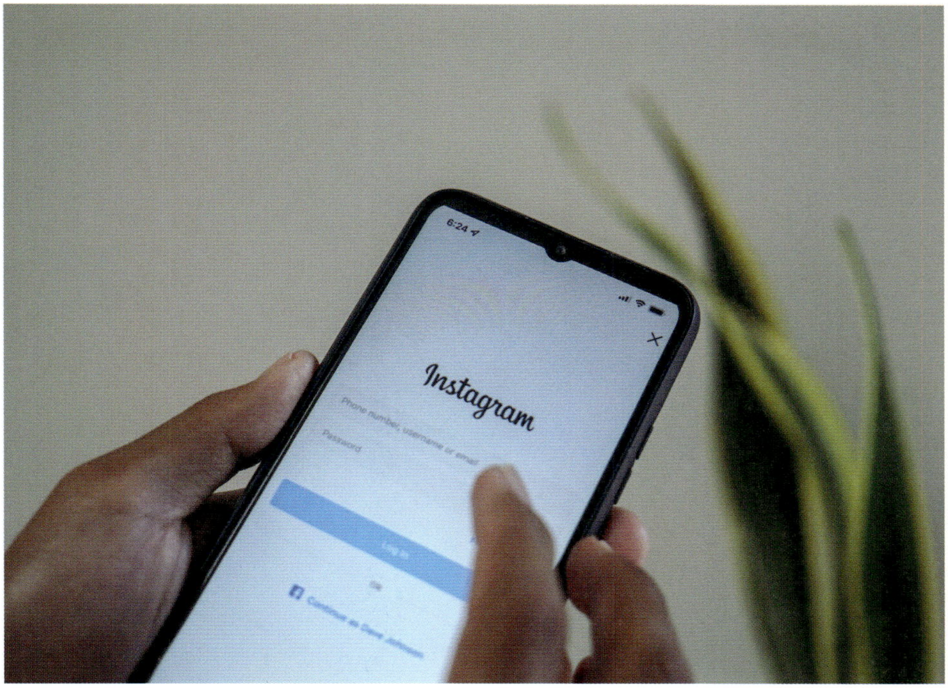

Source: Mourizal Zativa/Unsplash

Website design is a core feature of web marketing. Prompting users to log in is a ubiquitous feature on e-commerce, news, and other sites, and provides an easy mechanism for the site's content and/or layout to be customized based on the user's preferences.

www.rolex.org in 2018. Instead of being greeted with products or promotions as on rolex.com, visitors to the website were presented with expansive and slickly produced content, such as a documentary about the brand's founder Hans Wilsdorf.[9]

Social Media: Marketing Gets Networked

Like web marketing, social media tools are now considered among the core of digital marketing. **Social media** platforms are interactive websites or applications that allow users to create or share messages, images, or related content with other users of the platform. At the heart of social media lies the premise that the many connections between individuals (LinkedIn connections, Facebook friendships, Twitter follows, etc.) collectively comprise a **social network.**

social media Interactive websites or applications that allow users to create or share messages, images, or related content with other users of the platform

social network A collection of links (such as friendship or social media connections) between individuals

Social networks are powerful in their ability to amplify and disseminate information across many individuals. As a post is shared and reshared, an audience of a handful of friends can grow to thousands of strangers—much like a contagious disease spreads through tight living quarters, hence the idiom *going viral*. As long as the post can keep finding links to new clusters of the network, it can grow indefinitely.[10] It was this viral spread that allowed 2012 K-pop hit "Gangnam Style" to become the first YouTube video with one billion views in a mere five months.[11]

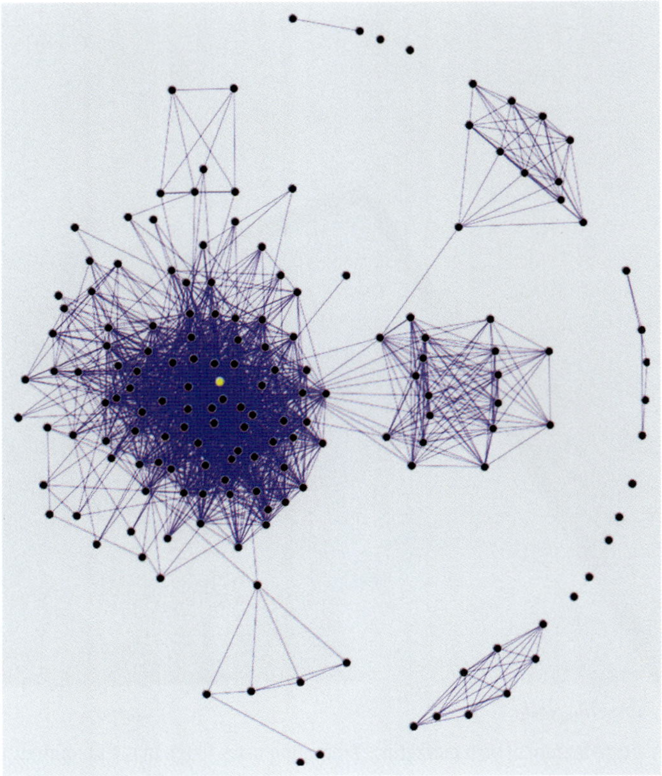

Source: Screenshot of GUESS by DarwinPeacock/Wikimedia Commons

In this diagram of social media "friendships," a densely connected core is linked to several smaller clusters by "bridge" friendships. These bridges are critical to the spread of marketers' messages through social networks.

Marketers today try to achieve this kind of viral buzz with their own posts, with varying results. Often, a perceived lack of authenticity in content produced by marketers—after all, it is ultimately produced to sell something—leads posts to wither away in irrelevance or, worse, go viral for the wrong reasons (see this chapter's Marketing Fail). For example, Pepsi's 2017 advertisement, in which Kendall Jenner diffuses a heated political protest by handing out a Pepsi, was widely shared and ridiculed across social media, prompting intense backlash.[12] Researchers suggest that consumers are more likely to engage positively with social media posts when they are informative, timely, and targeted to the right individuals within the network.[13] For example, if Louboutin exclusively announces a brand-new shoe line to followers of the brand's Twitter account, this message is likely to receive positive engagement, likes, and shares. Similar to clickthrough rates for web adverts, **engagement rates** for social media posts measure the percentage of times that the post is engaged with (e.g., liked or shared) when it is seen.[14]

engagement rates The percentage of times that a social media post is engaged with (e.g., liked or shared) when it is seen

Alternatively, the firm can try to avoid perceptions of inauthenticity through **influencer marketing**. This strategy relies on sponsorship deals with established social media personalities such as YouTubers and has seen rapid growth; as of 2024, it was a $24 billion market.[15] For example, popular YouTuber Doug Walker

influencer marketing Using sponsorship deals with established social media personalities to promote the firm's messages

SHADES OF GRAY Cambridge Analytica Exploits the Network

UK USA

The broad strokes of Facebook's Cambridge Analytica scandal might be familiar to you. Using a Facebook app, British consultants Cambridge Analytica delivered surveys to users and collected additional data about users and their Facebook friends, to generate insights for political campaigns.[16] When these practices came to light in 2018, outrage ensued. Cambridge Analytica was forced into bankruptcy, while Facebook had to pay a $5 billion fine to the US Federal Trade Commission plus a nominal fine to the UK Information Commissioner's Office for failing to protect users' privacy rights.[17]

But what exactly did Facebook and Cambridge Analytica do? The core of Cambridge Analytica's surveys delivered via a Facebook app was run-of-the-mill, asking questions about users' personalities. But these surveys also downloaded information from participants' Facebook profiles, including information about their friends who had *not* agreed to participate in any study. By marrying the personality data from the surveys with the survey-takers' rich Facebook data, Cambridge Analytica was able to accurately predict the personalities of those who did *not* take the survey, using their Facebook data.[18] In total, tens of millions of US Facebook users had their Facebook data collected and their personalities analyzed without their knowledge. For its part, Facebook has committed to a "privacy-focused future," but it remains to be seen how exactly that will manifest.[19]

Identify the ethical dilemmas:

1. Who was harmed by Cambridge Analytica's and Facebook's actions, and how? How much of the blame does Facebook carry?
2. To what extent do social media platforms such as Facebook have a duty to protect users' privacy? What policies, if any, should Facebook adopt to avoid a repetition of this type of scandal?

(the "Nostalgia Critic") reviews old films for his one million-plus subscribers. In these reviews, he includes lengthy and elaborate skits promoting services such as ExpressVPN and Stamps.com. Despite its greater perceived authenticity, though, influencer marketing is not without its pitfalls (see Shades of Gray feature in Chapter 4) and its effectiveness varies (see Opposing Views in this chapter).

Finally, marketers can also use social media for more passive strategies, rather than actively sending messages through the network. This is most commonly accomplished through **social listening**, or monitoring social media for mentions of a firm's products, competitors, or other relevant topics.[20] For example, cosmetics brand L'Oréal uses social listening to spot trends regarding which products are being featured more in users' posts and images, and even identify users that have similar profiles to those that currently favor the brand. As Adrienne Rostaing, Market Insights Manager for L'Oréal summarizes: "Social allows us to refocus our actions on the present moment, tracking and adapting in real time to continuously improve the link with our consumers."[21]

social listening Monitoring social media for mentions of a firm's products, competitors, or other relevant topics

OPPOSING VIEWS Are Influencers Losing Their Influence?

Global

Almost 90 percent of marketers believe that influencer marketing is at least as effective as other types of marketing communications, and most consumers admit to being influenced at least somewhat by these personalities.[22] And yet at the same time, recent data shows that engagement rates for influencers' posts are declining to levels as low as 2 percent. Experts suggest that a surfeit of influencers is crowding users' feeds with sponsored content on Instagram and other platforms, reducing attention to the posts and even prompting frustration.[23] Popular perceptions of influencers have also been uneven, with news articles commonly reporting that businesses are tired of providing influencers with free products (a typical part of the arrangement) when their actual influence is hard to observe and quantify.[24]

Still, others suggest that properly executed influencer marketing has not lost its punch. One suggested solution is to identify the right type of influencer for the firm's offering. Five recognized categories exist:

1. micro-influencers, who have several thousand social media followers but typically greater engagement;
2. social media influencers, who have larger audiences but lower engagement rates;
3. blog influencers, who have established blogs and loyal readers;
4. opinion leaders, who are recognized experts with specialized knowledge in a field; and
5. celebrity influencers, bona fide celebrities who happen to use social media.[25]

Selecting which categories will most benefit a brand, however, remains a challenge.

See the issue from two sides:

1. Craft an argument in favor of reducing investments in influencer marketing. What is the biggest obstacle to influencer marketing effectiveness? Why should consumers and firms be skeptical of influencers?
2. Craft an argument in favor of increasing investments in influencer marketing. How would you enhance influencer marketing effectiveness? Which category of influencers do you believe has the most actual influence on consumers, and why?

Mobile: Marketing Is Everywhere

mobile marketing Deploying the marketing mix via mobile devices and applications

Mobile marketing, or deploying the marketing mix via mobile devices and applications, is distinct from web and social media marketing. Rather than being characterized by a defining functionality (e.g., e-commerce or social networks), mobile marketing is important due to the prevalence and ubiquity of smartphones in the lives of consumers and B2B buyers. A staggering 80 percent of the world's population owned smartphones in 2020, up from 50 percent in 2016, with most of this growth coming from smartphones finally approaching saturation in lower-income countries.[26] Smartphones by nature accompany individuals throughout their days, providing a unique opportunity for marketing mix elements to reach current and potential customers anywhere, anytime.

Implementing mobile elements in the marketing mix depends on an understanding of how customers use smart devices. The planned mobile strategy

Source: Mika Baumeister/Unsplash

Nearly 80 percent of the world's population has a smartphone—an eye-popping statistic that drives home the importance of smartphones in both the Global North and the Global South.

must align with one of the ways that the target segment uses their devices. For example, Peloton knew that its customers used their smartphones to search for fitness information and watch training videos on the go; therefore, it launched a digital membership that included access to a full-featured mobile application.[27] Generally speaking, there are **seven reasons that people use their mobile devices.** These include, from most to least common:

seven reasons that people use their mobile devices The use cases of smart devices, which guide mobile marketing strategy; they include "me time," socializing, shopping, accomplishing, preparation, discovery, and self-expression

1. "me time" such as watching funny videos or reading comics;
2. socializing and chatting with others;
3. shopping on websites and apps;
4. accomplishing tasks with productivity and email apps;
5. preparation for trips or other plans, such as looking up tickets;
6. discovery of new information via news outlets and other sources such as Wikipedia; and
7. self-expression via recording videos and other hobbies.[28]

Each of these use cases provides opportunities for engaging with customers, typically using tactics from web marketing (e.g., offering apps with e-commerce functionality) or social media marketing (e.g., incorporating sharing and "friends"

geotargeting Delivering marketing mix elements when a specific consumer enters a specific physical area, typically using mobile phone location data

features into mobile apps and social games). In other cases, marketers can deploy tools that are exclusive to the mobile environment. For example, **geotargeting**, or delivering marketing mix elements when a specific consumer enters a specific physical area,[29] provides unique communications approaches; Starbucks used this technique when it made a deal with UK telecoms provider O2 to send text messages to customers based on their phones' location data.[30]

IN OTHER WORDS . . .

Mobile marketing's uniqueness comes from smartphones themselves and how they are used. Mobile marketing should begin with an examination of how targeted customers use their devices, and design tactics to meet customers where they are in their digital lives.

APPLYING A FIRST PRINCIPLES APPROACH TO ORGANIZE AND USE THE DIGITAL MARKETING TOOLBOX

If the various techniques and concepts of digital marketing comprise a toolbox, it seems often to be a disorganized and misunderstood toolbox. The confusion around digital marketing is evident in marketers' haziness around the very meanings of these tools. For example, popular business blogs and consulting white papers are rife with conflicting definitions about the definition and boundaries of content marketing, with some placing virtually all of digital marketing under the content marketing umbrella.[31] Beyond definitions, it is unclear how to apply these tools. Should you use both SEO and email marketing? When is influencer marketing appropriate, and which of the five types of influencers should be deployed? Will your customers view geotargeted messages as informative or invasive?

This section uses the First Principles approach to aid decisions about which tools are appropriate for the firm's purposes and to organize the digital marketing toolbox. Specifically, the four Marketing Principles can be incorporated into digital marketing decision-making by asking a series of four fundamental questions.

Four Questions for Digital Marketing Effectiveness

four questions for digital marketing effectiveness Four questions that probe whether a digital marketing strategy accounts for the First Principles: (1) Does your strategy reach the customers that you want to target? (2) Can your strategy keep up with customers that are "moving targets"? (3) Will your strategy stand out favorably among current and potential competitors? (4) Do you understand your strategy's resource commitments?

As with the marketing mix more broadly, digital marketing effectiveness is maximized when the four Marketing Principles are fully accounted for in the decision-making process. To achieve this, firms should probe each proposed digital marketing strategy with a series of **four questions for digital marketing effectiveness**. These questions and their associated Marketing Principles, as detailed in the following subsections, are:

1. Does your strategy reach the customers that you want to target (MP#1)?
2. Can your strategy keep up with customers that are "moving targets" (MP#2)?
3. Will your strategy stand out favorably among current and potential competitors (MP#3)?
4. Do you understand your strategy's resource commitments (MP#4)?

MP#1: Does Your Strategy Reach the Customers That You Want to Target?

As illustrated in the preceding discussion of the seven reasons that people use mobile devices, digital marketing tools should meet customers where they are. Based on this insight, a retailer might note that most of its customers use Facebook and place extensive advertising on that platform. But such an approach fails to align with MP#1: *all customers differ*. While the firm's average customer might use Facebook, specific subgroups might favor Twitter or Instagram, while other customers avoid social media altogether. Customer segmentation schemes (see Chapter 4), then, should categorize buyers in part based on where they spend their digital lives, so that the right digital tools can be deployed to the right segments.

Therefore, marketers must ask the following: "*Does your digital marketing strategy reach the customers that you want to target?*" This test can be difficult to pass due to the fluid transmission of information over social networks. Often, messages originally reaching the right customers in the right digital channels can "leak" via shares and retweets to unintended audiences. For example, when UK restaurant chain Gourmet Burger Kitchen launched a tongue-in-cheek campaign promoting its burgers with slogans such as "Vegetarians, resistance is futile," the advertisements were widely shared on Twitter and other platforms with unintended recipients: vegetarians and vegans, who found the messages insulting and belittling. The backlash hurt the brand across all segments.[32] Thus, marketers must also account for the porousness of barriers between segments in the digital space.

MP#2: Can Your Strategy Keep Up with Customers That Are "Moving Targets"?

The first question acknowledges that marketers should categorize customers based on where they spend their digital lives. But MP#2 implies further complexity that must be accounted for: *all customers change*. Customers have multiple "digital homes" that they might occupy depending on the time of day, day of the week, their mood, and countless other factors. For example, the same consumer might search for job opportunities on LinkedIn in the morning, read friends' Facebook posts during lunch, and browse Reddit before going to bed. In addition, as emphasized in the beginning of this chapter, the digital marketing toolkit and customers' digital behaviors are rapidly evolving.

Thus, marketers should ask: "*Can your strategy keep up with customers that are 'moving targets'?*" For example, a marketer in 2012 looking to target 16–24 year olds on social media might focus resources on Facebook; by 2015, those in this age bracket prefer Instagram and see Facebook as a platform for their parents. Three years later, in 2018, TikTok is the latest craze for this age group. And now, new trends are taking hold, such as **dark social**: communications via groups in private messaging apps such as Telegram and WhatsApp, which are growing in popularity but remain inherently difficult for marketers to penetrate.[33] Marketers without their ears to the ground, failing to follow their segments as they change and migrate to different platforms, are likely to find that their digital marketing efforts veer off-target.

dark social Communications via groups in private messaging apps such as Telegram and WhatsApp

MP#3: Will Your Strategy Stand Out Favorably among Current and Potential Competitors?

Of course, digital marketing tools are not deployed in a vacuum. Even if the right mix of techniques and platforms is employed to account for MP#1 and MP#2, *all competitors react* (MP#3). It is not enough that a post, for example, gains some threshold level of likes or shares. One of the strengths of digital marketing, particularly social media, is its comparative transparency; marketing strategies and their responses (e.g., a sponsored tweet and its retweets) are instantly and publicly observable in a way that most marketing mix elements are not. This feature enables social listening, in fact. But the flipside is that a firm's competitors also engage in social listening and often learn about customer responses to digital initiatives at the same time that the firm does. These competitors can launch rival campaigns that copy or even mock the firm's social media posts, for example. Social media and other digital marketing mix elements must anticipate and withstand such reactions.

Hence, marketers must question: "*Will your strategy stand out favorably among current and potential competitors?*" This is especially difficult when numerous, well-known competing brands are likely to react via social media. For example, in 2018 the breakfast restaurant chain IHOP (International House of Pancakes) temporarily changed its name to IHOb—inverting P to "b" to mark the addition of burgers to the menu. Although the menu change itself was necessary and moderately successful, IHOP's communication of this change via social media likely limited this success.[34] The renaming gimmick immediately attracted scorn and withering jokes from other restaurants' social media accounts. Burger chain Wendy's was particularly aggressive, launching salvos such as "Not really afraid of the burgers from a place that decided pancakes were too hard," and "Remember when you were like 7 and thought changing your name to Thunder BearSword would be super cool? [This is] like that, but our cheeseburgers are still better."[35] In this case, IHOP failed to anticipate that other brands would steal the show on social media.

Source: Karsten Winegeart/Unsplash

It takes more than a few likes for a social strategy to stand out. Firms are often looking to make a post that goes "viral," generating thousands of shares across different platforms.

MP#4: Do You Understand Your Strategy's Resource Commitments?

Digital marketing is well-known for carrying a lower cost than traditional marketing mix elements. Discussion forums on a firm's website can allow consumers to replace part of the job of customer service personnel, answering technical questions from other users. Posting non-sponsored messages on social media costs only the time of the personnel handling the messaging. And other elements, such as hosting a blog (i.e., content marketing), investing in SEO, and marketing via influencers come at a much lower cost than, for example, buying primetime television advertisements.[36]

This sometimes leads to a perception that digital marketing is costless, which is simply untrue. Every digital marketing tool consumes at least some resources, in the form of employees' time and/or fees paid to third parties (e.g., social media platforms). Because *all resources are limited*, firms must account for their resource deployments and possible trade-offs among them (MP#4). In other words, marketers must ask themselves: "*Do you understand your strategy's resource commitments?*" Failure to consider the costs of digital marketing tools can lead to suboptimal resource allocations. For example, assuming away the cost of paying someone to write content for a company blog will overestimate the return on investment from this tool. Worse still, ignoring such costs at the outset may lead the firm to neglect these investments entirely, leaving the firm's digital strategy with glaring vulnerabilities. The case of Walkers Crisps (Marketing Fail) provides one such example.

Putting It All Together: Constructing the Digital Marketing Mix

Accounting for the four First Principles helps ensure that marketers select the most appropriate digital marketing tools and heightens digital marketing effectiveness. But in practical terms, after building out a digital marketing mix that passes the "four questions" test, how can marketers roll out and revise this mix over time (e.g., as customers change and competitors react)? They can use the **3E digital marketing process** (Figure 3.2) consisting of three steps: *Experimentation, Execution, Evolution*.

3E digital marketing process A sequence of steps for enhancing digital marketing effectives; the three steps are *experimentation, execution,* and *evolution*

1. The first step, *experimentation*, involves testing each proposed digital marketing tool to ensure that it has the expected impact, and to uncover any gaps or oversights in accounting for the Marketing Principles. For example, the firm might believe that its older customers will engage more heavily with a Facebook post while its younger customers will react more positively to an Instagram post, but it might wish to confirm this intuition before launching an entire campaign around this assumption. Thankfully, experimentation is uniquely suited to the digital arena. The design of website elements, for example, can be randomly altered based on the user's IP address. Subsequent behavior on the website can then be analyzed, perhaps finding that a more muted color palette is associated with a greater likelihood of making a purchase online. This **A/B testing** (so called because it compares outcomes from two versions of the content, A and B) is prevalent not only in web design but also in social media marketing and content marketing. Because markets rapidly evolve—all customers change, after all—the most important, most visible, and most costly elements of the digital marketing mix should be prioritized for testing, rather than spending months testing each detail of a message or advertisement before launching a campaign.
2. Once experimentation has yielded a digital marketing mix that handles the First Principles as intended, the next step is *execution*. In this phase, implementing resource deployments and the planned timing of elements is key. For example, if a social media campaign is central to the firm's strategy, then sufficient personnel must be in place with time available to devote to managing the firm's various social media accounts and engaging with users across platforms. Or if the strategy requires specific timing of messages,

A/B testing An experiment comparing outcomes from two versions of content (e.g., clickthrough rate for two different versions of an advertisement)

internet trolls Users who intentionally seek to upset others and provoke heated responses, and who can undermine social media marketing efforts

MARKETING FAIL Twitter Crumbles Walkers Crisps

Source: Yulia Khlebnikova/Unsplash

Walkers Crisps—known elsewhere as Lays Potato Chips—were supposed to be the highlight of the "Walkers Wave" campaign. Instead, the firm's Twitter feed accidentally featured infamous criminals and historical dictators.

Walkers Crisps—better known in many countries as Lays Potato Chips—is an iconic and ubiquitous British brand, controlling about half of the market in the United Kingdom.[37] For such a brand, its 2017 partnership with renowned former Leicester City and Tottenham player Gary Lineker seemed like a no-brainer. In the "Walkers Wave" campaign, Twitter users could respond to the Walkers Twitter account with any selfie for a chance to win tickets to the UEFA Champions League final. The brand would then *automatically* tweet a short, altered video featuring Mr. Lineker appearing to hold a large printout of the selfie, in front of a stadium of fans performing a Mexican wave.[38]

UK

Predictably, **internet trolls**—users who intentionally seek to upset others and provoke heated responses—caught on to the apparent lack of oversight for this campaign. They began sending in photographs of less-than-savory characters such as Josef Stalin, rather than selfies. In one particularly egregious example, a user submitted a photograph of Harold Shipman, a British serial killer infamous for using poison injections on his victims. Walkers' automatic post featuring Shipman's portrait and the tagline "Great shot!" was not well-received.[39] Following this and other incidents in which photographs of murderers and dictators slipped through undetected, Walkers was forced to apologize and discontinue the campaign.

Diagnose the problem:

1. Explain how such photographs could slip through and be featured in videos posted by a major brand. What resource investments could Walkers have made to avoid this problem?
2. More generally, internet trolls pose a threat to digital marketing campaigns. Do marketers have a duty to proactively invest resources to limit the impact of trolls? Or should marketers be held blameless for the actions of trolls, such as those in the Walkers example? Why or why not?

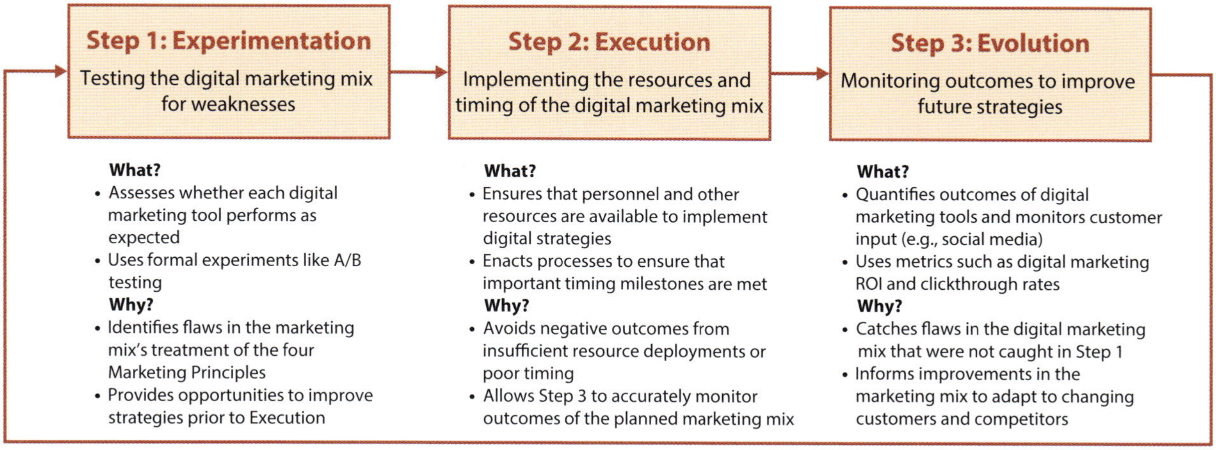

Figure 3.2 Deploying the Digital Marketing Mix.

The 3E digital marketing process contains three steps: experimentation, execution, and evolution. After designing a digital marketing mix that accounts for the four Marketing Principles, the 3E process can be deployed to implement these strategies and refine them over time.

processes must be in place to coordinate this timing (e.g., across steps in the campaign or across time zones). For example, Japanese apparel brand Uniqlo uses **retargeting**—serving adverts on other websites based on a customer's browsing of specific products on Uniqlo's website—to encourage consumers to complete purchases that they previously contemplated. If retargeting occurs too soon, the consumer may become annoyed; if it is too late, the consumer may no longer care about the product. Likewise, Amaro's collaboration with Animal Crossing (see Chapter Case) required precise execution. These approaches and others require strict timing in their execution.

retargeting Serving advertisements on other websites based on a customer's browsing of specific products on a firm's website, to encourage the customer to come back and complete a purchase

3. Finally, and arguably most critically, deploying the digital marketing mix requires *evolution* over time. The performance of a digital marketing campaign should be observed and quantified. Typically, this is accomplished through metrics such as clickthrough rates and engagement rates, as well as some sort of **digital marketing ROI** (return on investment).[40] Marketers also measure whether resource investments exceeded expectations, leading to potentially greater costs; for example, delays in the creation of posts and videos for content marketing may lead the firm to incur additional expenses to "catch up" on content.[41] Closely watching these metrics and other outcomes of digital marketing tools has two advantages for marketers. First, it can spot any flaws in the digital marketing mix, essentially catching after the fact what experimentation hoped to catch prior to execution. Second, it helps marketers stay attuned to changes in customers or the environment, such as fundamental shifts driven by the Marketing Principles (i.e., all customers change, and all competitors react). For example, in 2009 Southwest Airlines overhauled its blog to include more interactive and engaging content such as videos. In doing so, it encouraged users to comment on important topics such as assigned seating

digital marketing ROI Any metric used by marketers to quantify the rate of return on resource investments in the digital marketing mix

and snack selections. With this approach, monitoring users' engagement on the blog could inform Southwest's future marketing mix deployments.[42] This example highlights that evolution is not the end of the 3E process, but rather the end of one *iteration* of the process; marketers continuously cycle through experimentation, execution, and evolution to refine and update their digital marketing strategies (similar to the marketing planning process from Chapter 1).

By planning a digital marketing mix that affirmatively answers the four questions for digital marketing effectiveness, and implementing and refining this marketing mix using the 3E digital marketing process (experimentation, execution, evolution), marketers can deploy digital marketing strategies that account for the four Marketing Principles and achieve positive outcomes for stakeholders.

CHAPTER CASE STUDY

AMARO BRINGS REAL-WORLD FASHION TO ANIMAL CROSSING

Brazil

Amaro was founded in 2012 in São Paolo, Brazil with a mission to provide women with trendy and functional products across the apparel, beauty, and wellness categories through its online stores. Amaro gained popularity within Brazil particularly through its unique fashion line. Over time, Amaro expanded its offering by selling select items from over 100 partner brands. Eventually, the digital-native retailer also established a brick-and-mortar presence, opening fifteen boutique "guide shops" staffed by customer service personnel that the company calls "influencers"—not to be confused with the social media influencers employed in influencer marketing.[43]

A unique social media opportunity presents itself. In 2020, brands in apparel and other categories each took their own spin on a social media tie-in unlike any other. The focal platform was not Facebook or Twitter—its primary function was not even as a platform at all. It was *Animal Crossing*, a game launched in March of 2020 for the Nintendo Switch. The cartoonish, low-key town-life simulator allowed personalized in-game objects and avatars, enabled friends to chat and visit each other's towns, and allowed various objects to be sold via an in-game marketplace. Perhaps owing to the game's inherent appeal, the growing videogame market in general, then-common coronavirus lockdowns, or some combination of the three, the game become a nexus for social activity in 2020, selling over *30 million* copies by the end of the year to a female-skewed audience.[44]

Brands took note of the game's status as a de facto social media platform and jumped in on the action. Apparel brands Highsnobiety and 100 Thieves recreated their own clothing within the game, sharing it with players. Similarly, the Getty Museum in Los Angeles provided in-game versions of the museum's artwork, which could be used to decorate players' houses. Social strategist Moshe Isaacian explains the appeal: "It's a space where people are trying to live out their ideal lives and create a space that's just their own. If a brand can organically contribute to people's peaceful simulations, whether that's with clothes or doing something silly on their own, then they have the most to gain."[45]

Amaro jumps on the opportunity. Amaro saw the popularity of *Animal Crossing* and recognized a perfect match. Amaro exclusively focuses on women, the majority of Brazilian gamers are women, and *Animal Crossing* became extremely popular in the country. But the firm took a different approach in leveraging this opportunity. Rather than using the game as a new platform to push and promote existing products to consumers, Amaro decided to use it as a platform for developing new products.

The brand created an in-game character named Mara—a "virtual model and trendhunter"—to visit players' towns and allow them to present *their own* in-game fashion creations.[46] Players were promised future discounts if their creations were chosen for adoption into Amaro's product line. As designs were chosen, the brand even created Instagram videos to show how the in-game artwork would be transformed into real-world clothing. The end result was a set of fifteen to eighteen items called the Amaro Cross Collection. The unique campaign and resulting apparel collection generated a great deal of positive press coverage and brand awareness for Amaro, but it is unclear whether it can replicate this success in the future.

CASE QUESTIONS

1. Which elements of the digital marketer's toolkit were used in Amaro's *Animal Crossing* campaign? What was unconventional about how these tools were used?
2. Pose the "four questions for digital marketing effectiveness" with respect to Amaro's strategy. For each question, explain how this approach aligns (or does not align) with the corresponding Marketing Principle.
3. Tie-ins to social videogames represent a new and growing frontier for social media marketing, and one that is not usually included in typologies of digital marketing. Do you believe that this trend is a passing fad, or a strategy that is here to stay? Justify your response.
4. Choose your favorite brand. Devise a creative approach that this brand could use to incorporate a social videogame, such as *Animal Crossing*, into its marketing mix.

CHAPTER SUMMARY

Twitter, Instagram, SEO, SEM: modern marketing is dominated by terms unheard of thirty years ago. Yet the same four Marketing Principles guide effective marketing decisions in the digital arena. This chapter provides an overview of customer engagement strategies for online, mobile, and social media marketing, while providing a first illustration of how the First Principles framework is applied. Each principle informs the development and implementation of digital marketing strategies. Customers differ in not only which aspects of online, mobile, and social media they use—based, for example, on their nationality and whether they are a business or an individual—but also in how they engage with various platforms (MP#1). These differences between customers can dissipate or further diverge over time, as both customers and marketers gain experience with digital media (MP#2). Digital marketing is unique in its enablement of near-instantaneous competitive reactions, exacerbating the need for advantages that are not easily replicated (MP#3). And despite being known for a relatively low cost of deployment compared to non-digital media, digital marketing is subject to numerous resource constraints, such as the cost of search engine marketing and limited customer attention (MP#4).

APPLICATION QUESTIONS

1. Digital marketing continues to grow and evolve. Describe one important change in digital marketing (e.g., social media or the web) that you have witnessed in your lifetime.
2. Think of a time that you found a company's or brand's digital marketing tactic to be deceptive or misleading. What about the tactic was problematic for you, and how should the company have behaved differently?
3. Think of your favorite brand. Name three elements of the digital marketing toolkit (Figure 3.1) that this brand uses. Provide an example of each.
4. Do you personally engage with social media influencers? Why or why not?
5. Considering the seven reasons that people use their mobile devices, which is the most typical activity for you? Which is the least typical? How could a firm use this knowledge to better reach you with digital marketing tools?
6. Think of a recent digital marketing campaign (or at least part of a campaign) that you witnessed, such as a brand's social media posts or sponsored search results. Analyze how well this campaign accounted for the Marketing Principles by using the four questions for digital marketing effectiveness.
7. Consider a streaming service that wants to use celebrity influencers on Twitter to promote the service's new lineup of original series and movies. Apply the 3E digital marketing process to explain how you would roll out and revise this strategy over time.

Visit the companion website, **https://bloomsbury.pub/palmatier-marketing**, or **https://samsinstitute.com**, for additional learning and teaching tools, including professional videos outlining the Four Principles, PowerPoint tutorials with voice-over commentary, sample syllabi for marketing courses, testbank and more.

Part 2

MARKETING PRINCIPLE #1: ALL CUSTOMERS DIFFER

Part Overview

Welcome to Part 2. The three chapters in this unit explain how unavoidable differences between customers create challenges for marketers. The chapters also introduce tools and concepts for addressing these challenges. Chapter 4 highlights historic and ongoing trends that make customer differences more important, illustrates five ways that customer differences arise, and lays out a segmentation, targeting, and positioning (STP) process for managing customer differences. Chapter 5 expands the concept of customer differences by elucidating some of the varied ways in which consumers and businesses make buying decisions. Finally, Chapter 6 spotlights the marketing challenges of globalization and of managing multinational firms while accounting for cross-cultural and within-cultural customer differences.

Chapter 4

MANAGING CUSTOMER DIFFERENCES

CHAPTER OVERVIEW

Chapter 4 introduces Marketing Principle #1: all customers differ. It introduces the concept of customer differences and highlights the importance of these differences. The chapter then outlines the five diverse reasons that customer preferences vary. Finally, it describes the steps in the segmentation, targeting, and positioning (STP) process and explains how marketers can use this process to manage customer differences. The chapter will proceed by answering the following questions:

- What is Marketing Principle #1 and its accompanying managerial challenge?
- What makes customer differences so important?
- What are the five sources of customer differences?
- How can segmentation, targeting, and positioning (STP) help manage customer differences?

In the chapter's cases and features, you will see examples of some firms that excel in managing customer differences, and some that fall short of this challenge. These include:

- Google's poorly conceived videogame streaming service (Marketing Fail).
- Tata's expansion in the luxury segment through its Jaguar acquisition (Chapter Case).
- Ethical and moral dilemmas in managing customer differences, such as the danger of influencer fraud (Shades of Gray) and BuildDirect's behavior-based segmentation (Opposing Views).

LEARNING OBJECTIVES

- Define Marketing Principle #1 and its associated key marketing challenge.
- Compare the importance of managing customer differences across three historical marketing eras.
- Recognize the five primary sources of customer differences.
- Identify the steps involved in the segmentation, targeting, and positioning process.
- Evaluate moral and ethical concerns in managing customer differences.

IMAGINE Buying a Car

Imagine that you are preparing to buy your first car. You have long dreamt of this moment, and you are excited to explore your options. Unfortunately (as often happens), your dreams are tempered by reality: your budget is modest, and your automotive expertise is limited. You make a sensible choice and resolve to purchase a well-known, affordable, and reliable brand. You scour internet listings such as autotrader.com and dealer websites before eventually settling on a pre-owned Hyundai Elantra. You enter the local used car dealership—an uncomfortable experience—pay the advertised price, sign the paperwork, and drive off in your new vehicle.

Now, imagine a quite different scenario. Your aunt Ava, a successful real estate investor, is shopping for a new car—her fifth time doing so. For Ava, money is a secondary concern; she loves the performance and styling of BMW vehicles. As always, she visits her local BMW dealer and chats with her favorite salesperson Arvind. After talking things over, Arvind affirms Ava's interest in a brand new 7 Series sedan. She buys the car and makes sure to sign up for a maintenance plan, as she is fond of the dealer's service department.

Critical thinking:

1. What are the key differences between your priorities and Ava's priorities? Be sure to consider not only the vehicle itself, but the entire purchase process.
2. For each of these key differences, speculate about why Ava's priorities are so different from yours.
3. Consider the perspective of a local car dealership selling new and used vehicles. Is it possible for this dealership to appeal to both you and Ava? If so, how? If not, why?

INTRODUCTION TO MARKETING PRINCIPLE #1

The stark contrast between the two scenarios in the opening example—in terms of priorities for price and vehicle performance, the shopping and dealership experience, and behavior after the sale—evokes a central truth (i.e., a First Principle) of marketing. According to **Marketing Principle #1,** ***all customers differ***; customers tend to exhibit diverse preferences for goods and services.[1] As the chapters in this unit will show, these customer differences explain why it is so important to "know your customer."

Marketing Principle #1 *All customers differ;* customers tend to exhibit diverse preferences for goods and services

Managing Customer Differences

"*All customers differ*" is first among the Marketing Principles because it implies a marketing challenge that has troubled businesses for generations: **managing customer differences**.[2] The most successful firms do not worry about this challenge, but embrace differences by tailoring products and services to meet the unique needs of one or more segments or even individual customers. The Coca-Cola Company takes this premise to the extreme and offers over 3,000 different beverages—including drinks under the Sprite, Fanta, MOJO Kombucha, Powerade, vitaminwater, Ayataka, and Topo Chico brands, to name a few—to meet virtually every conceivable customer need that exists in the beverage category.[3] More typical is the approach of craft entrepreneurs and artists on Folksy, a UK-based e-commerce marketplace similar to US-based Etsy.

managing customer differences Tailoring products and services to meet the unique needs of one or more segments or individual customers

Source: istock.com/BongkarnThanyakij

Craft marketplaces such as Etsy and Folksy offer small merchants a way to satisfy diverse customer needs.

These entrepreneurs make products by hand in extremely specific categories—think handmade monogrammed belts and papercraft animals—and sell them to small, niche groups of customers via their Folksy storefronts.

Both Coca-Cola executives and Folksy entrepreneurs in these examples succeed by answering the **three questions for managing customer differences**:

three questions for managing customer differences (1) What types of customer preferences exist? (2) Which types of customers should the firm pursue? (3) By what means will the firm satisfy the chosen customers' needs?

1. ***What types of customer preferences exist?***
   These are the segments and individual customers that a firm and its competitors can try to satisfy. Coca-Cola might identify one segment interested in sweet, fizzy, non-caffeinated sodas, one segment that prefers low-calorie caffeinated drinks, another looking for hydration to supplement athletic activities, and still another shopping for nutritious children's beverages.
2. ***Which types of customers should the firm pursue?***
   Here, Coca-Cola might answer "all of them" while a Folksy entrepreneur may reply "connoisseurs of reproduction vintage farm signs."
3. ***By what means will the firm satisfy the chosen customers' needs?***
   Coca-Cola creates numerous products with unique flavor, mouthfeel, nutrition, and packaging features to meet diverse target customers' needs, while the Folksy farm sign shop might focus on made-to-order, custom commissioned works for customers.

Now imagine if Coca-Cola were unable to identify what types of customer preferences exist. They might still produce a broad product line to satisfy diverse hypothetical needs, but the design of individual products would be stabs in the dark, not tailored to any specific existing needs. Or consider what would happen if the Folksy entrepreneur only produced one, standardized vintage farm sign—would this meet the needs of "connoisseurs" who collect products in this niche category? Thus, failing to tackle these three questions for managing customer differences can be one of the reasons that marketers fail.

IN OTHER WORDS ...

The three questions for managing customer differences can also be understood through a military analogy. First, what types of customer preferences exist? These varied preferences are the "battlefield" where your company and others compete to satisfy needs, and it is critical that you know the geography. Second, which types of customers should you choose to pursue? This is the specific "terrain," within the battlefield, which you aim to wrest from competitors and to occupy. Third, by what means will you satisfy the chosen customers' needs? These are the "stratagems" you will deploy to capture that terrain.

WHY ARE CUSTOMER DIFFERENCES SO IMPORTANT?

As a First Principle, the idea that "all customers differ" has always held true, but the recognition of this truth has progressed through three distinct eras: (1) the mass-marketing era, (2) the niche marketing era, and (3) the one-to-one marketing era:

1. There existed a time, beginning over a century ago, when firms largely ignored or overlooked customer differences and focused on mass-producing standardized products. This **mass-marketing era** saw the growth of many of today's most recognizable brands. German lighting manufacturer OSRAM focused the bulk of its efforts from the 1910s to the 1930s on a single product: the tungsten lamp. This standardized lightbulb, featuring an innovative durable metal filament, was widely used in both residential and commercial applications for decades.[4] Similarly, US automaker Ford spent most of these years manufacturing only one passenger vehicle: the famous Model T, explicitly designed as a car for everyone.[5] Firms such as OSRAM and Ford succeeded in this era because competitors had not yet significantly eroded their positions with more specialized offerings.

mass-marketing era An era in the first half of the 1900s characterized by firms mass-producing standardized products

2. But two simultaneous and interdependent trends would eventually disrupt the success stories of the mass-marketing era (see Figure 4.1). First, *marketers in the latter half of the twentieth century began to view their trade as a science*, and increasingly used data—for example, sales patterns and marketing research studies—to systematically inform decisions.[6] Naturally, these enhanced capabilities led to more sophisticated **segmentation** schemes and the identification and targeting of more specific customer preferences. Second, owing to marketers' enhanced targeting capabilities, *these years saw an explosion of product variety*. As noted earlier in this chapter, the Coca-Cola Company now offers over 3,000 different beverages worldwide, but this was not always the case. The company focused exclusively on its core red-label soft drink in the mass-marketing era.

segmentation The process of dividing the overall market into groups, such that potential customers *within* each group have highly similar needs and preferences for a particular product or service category, but the groups are highly different from one another

niche marketing era An era in the latter half of the 1900s characterized by a greater use of data-driven decision-making and growing product variety, allowing firms to serve small segments

one-to-one marketing era An era in the twenty-first century characterized by the use of dynamic, individual-level information to effectively target a segment of one customer

personalization The firm tailors marketing mix elements such as communications and other promotions to the individual customer

customization The firm enables the customer to *choose* their own elements of the marketing mix

It was only in 1955 that the firm introduced Fanta, and Sprite did not hit the scene until 1961.[7] Additional brands such as Mello Yello, Minute Maid, and Mr PiBB were launched in the remaining years of the **niche marketing era.** In the niche marketing era, ignoring customer differences would bear a high cost. Throughout this era, increasingly sophisticated segmentation fueled growing product variety to meet the diverse needs of smaller groups of customers. Meanwhile, heightened competition—due to firms introducing so many new products to capture various corners of the market—created an incentive for further advances in marketers' collection of data and understanding of smaller and smaller segments.

3. These ongoing trends have culminated in the **one-to-one marketing era** of the twenty-first century, in which marketers can use dynamic, individual-level information, such as data recorded by smartphone applications and e-commerce websites, to effectively target a segment of one customer. Chinese e-commerce giant AliExpress aims to achieve one-to-one marketing by presenting unique product recommendations based on a customer's purchasing and browsing history with AliExpress. Under a one-to-one marketing approach, services such as AliExpress focus not on share of the overall market but on the firm's share of each individual customer's wallet.[8] The key features of successful one-to-one marketing are **personalization** and **customization**. Personalization means that, as in the AliExpress example, the firm tailors marketing mix elements such as communications and other promotions to the individual customer. Customization goes a step further and enables the customer to *choose* their own elements of the marketing mix.[9] The ubiquitous streaming platform Netflix offers extensive customization of the core service itself; users can create multiple profiles with unique taste preferences, and change which shows and films are recommended by proactively rating programs

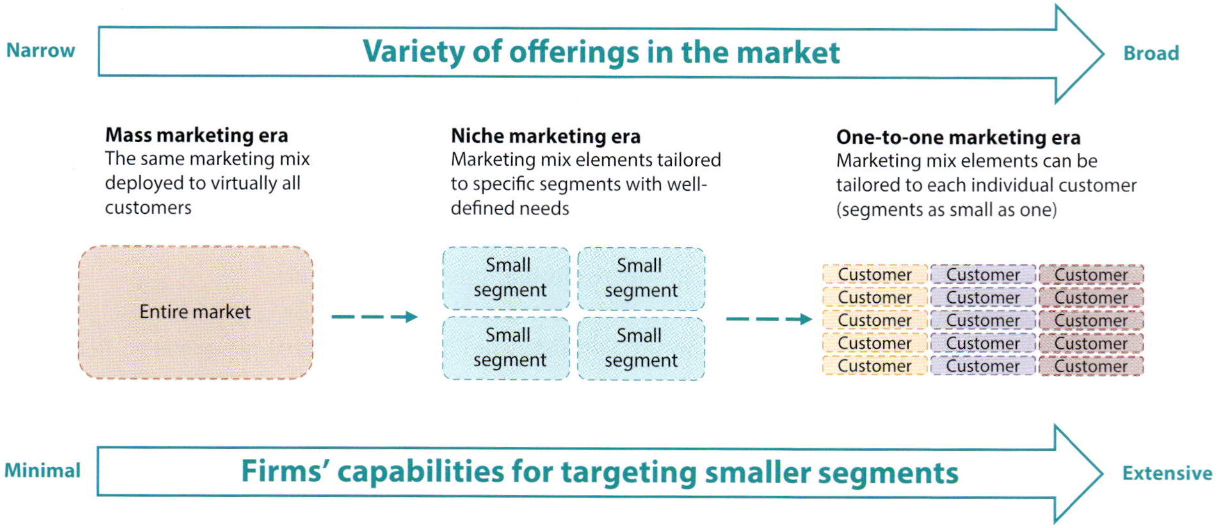

Figure 4.1 Growing Importance of Managing Customer Differences.

The importance of managing customer differences continues to grow over time.

with "thumbs up" or "thumbs down."[10] Entrepreneurs on the Etsy craft marketplace, on the other hand, offer a variety of product customization options, from color choices, to engraving, to commissioned works. As a growing number of firms leverage the power of personalization and customization to tailor customer experiences and marketing mix elements to individual customers, the cost of failing to manage customer differences will only increase.

MARKETING FAIL Google Stadia's Launch

Source: Florian Olivo/Unsplash

Was Google's Stadia service equipped to attract the enthusiast segment of video gamers?

Its name has become a verb; it owns the online search industry and dominates the global smartphone operating system market; and a year with under $100 billion in revenue would be cause for concern.[11] Yet US-based Google LLC (a subsidiary of Alphabet Inc.) is also known for experimenting with its products and is no stranger to failure.

Consider Stadia, Google's foray into video games, a service heralded as the future of interactive entertainment. Stadia was supposed to be different: gamers did not need an expensive, clunky box next to the television, or any special hardware at all, to play the latest big-budget games. With a gamepad, a stable internet connection, and a smartphone or laptop, modern video games could be streamed from the cloud and played anywhere, anytime.[12] All customers had to do was buy the games (for the full retail price) and start playing.[13]

But Stadia's launch in November 2019 did not go well. Complaints of technical problems abounded; the bandwidth demands of streaming games proved too much for customers with unreliable internet access, such as those in rural areas.[14] While technical hurdles could be overcome with time, the reports of fading interest and declining active users were more troubling.[15] It quickly became apparent that Google had positioned itself into a corner. The casual segment of gamers—for example, people who play free mobile phone games—were most likely to find Stadia's lack of expensive physical hardware appealing; but these same individuals were also the least likely to pay full retail price (typically $60 in 2019) for video games. Conversely, the enthusiast segment of gamers, who would happily pay $60 for a game, typically already owned a traditional hardware-based gaming system such as Sony's PlayStation 4.[16] Google aimed to please both segments but captured neither, causing Stadia's launch to perform far below expectations and the service to later be discontinued.

USA

Diagnose the problem:

1. Recall the three questions for managing customer differences. On which of these questions did Google stumble with Stadia, and how?
2. Why would Google attempt to target Stadia to both the casual and enthusiast segments of video game players? In particular, how might the novelty and innovativeness of Stadia have made this strategy appealing to Google?
3. What would you have done differently with the design and launch of the Stadia service to target only the casual gamer segment? What would you have done differently to target only the enthusiast gamer segment?

FIVE REASONS WHY CUSTOMERS DIFFER

Customers differ in more ways than can be counted, but their differences fall into five identifiable categories detailed in this section: functional needs, influence from marketers, individual differences, life experiences, and self-concept. These **five sources of customer differences** are critical to enacting the segmentation, targeting, and positioning strategies described later in this chapter (Table 4.1). The five sources are:

five sources of customer differences The five reasons why all customers differ: functional needs, influence from marketers, individual differences, life experiences, and self-concept

1. functional needs;
2. influence from marketers;
3. individual differences;
4. life experiences; and
5. self-concept.

Source #1: Functional Needs

functional needs How important each of a product or service's functional attributes is based on personal circumstances

The most straightforward source of different preferences among customers is an individual's **functional needs** for a specific offering. A product's or service's

Table 4.1 Five Sources of Customer Differences.

Individuals diverge in their needs and preferences for many reasons, which can generally be grouped into five categories.

Source	Definition	Examples
Functional needs	How important each of a product's or service's functional attributes is based on personal circumstances	Customers differ in their budgets for a given purchase (based on income and frugality), their need for overall performance (based on product category experience and enthusiasm), and a desire for specific features (e.g., a larger screen on a smartphone)
Influence from marketers	The impact of advertising, branding, and other marketing activities on customers' preferences	Lexus signed an agreement with Marvel Studios to promote its LC500 in its films, most prominently in a major chase scene in *Black Panther*. Lexus hoped that this tie-in could make its brand more approachable to younger consumers
Individual differences	Psychological traits that characterize each person's stable and consistent way of responding to the environment	The "Big 5" personality traits (openness, conscientiousness, extraversion, agreeableness, neuroticism)
Life experiences	Events and experiences that are unique to her or his life and that have lasting impact on the value the person places on products and services, affecting preferences independently of the individual differences	A person who comes of age during an epidemic or pandemic, such as SARS or COVID-19, maybe develop different attitudes toward hygiene and wearing protective equipment such as masks
Self-concept	An individual's view of himself or herself from a social, physical, and moral point of view	Fans of K-pop (Korean pop music) may aspire to and identify with a particular star's image, and alter their own hairstyle or wardrobe to align with this image

THEORY SPOTLIGHT Salesperson Customer Orientation

Salespeople are charged with matching customers' functional needs to the company's products and services. For example, when a customer walks into one of French telecommunications provider Bouygues' retail stores, sales associates must learn how much cellular data a customer will need, what kind of phone they might want to purchase with the plan, and whether they want to bundle television and home internet services. The sales associate might try to sell every customer the most comprehensive and expensive service; this would reflect a **selling orientation**, or a focus on "winning" the exchange by extracting as much money as possible from the customer in that single transaction. Marketing theorists, however, suggest (and find) that salespeople are better served by adopting a **customer orientation**, which is focused on learning about the customer's functional needs (e.g., by asking probing questions) and ultimately meeting those needs.[17] This keeps customers satisfied and coming back for more.

functional attributes are based on a customer's personal circumstances: What price can they afford to pay (income)? How long does the product need to last (quality, warranty)? When will they use the product or service (battery powered, portability)? Are there any special usage features that they need (waterproof)? Higher quality, more features, and additional capabilities are almost always desired, but they come with a higher price or other physical trade-offs in size or weight. These trade-offs prevent firms from making any single, "ideal" product that could meet every customer's needs at an attractive price. Thus, understanding how customers perceive the relative importance of, or prioritize, a product or service's attributes is paramount in understanding how customers differ depending on their different functional needs.

selling orientation A focus on "winning" the exchange by extracting as much money as possible from the customer in that single transaction

customer orientation A focus on learning about the customer's functional needs and ultimately meeting those needs

Source #2: Influence from Marketers

A second and particularly intriguing source of customer differences arises due to **influence from marketers.** Over time, firms use marketing activities to persuade customers that certain functional attributes are more or less important (e.g., recent years have seen the removal of the headphone jack from smartphones) and to build linkages between their brands and core identities or meanings. By building a strong association between their product and a specific identity, marketers increase the likelihood that a consumer will purchase an offering that matches their aspirational self-image. For example, the luxury car brand Lexus signed a two-year agreement with superhero filmmaker Marvel Studios to promote the upmarket LC500 car. This deal culminated in the vehicle's starring role in a pivotal car chase in the 2018 film *Black Panther*.[18] Lexus' strategy was predicated on the belief that the characters in the Marvel Cinematic Universe, such as Black Panther, would be aspirational to potential target customers (e.g., men aged under fifty years). Notably, applying this strategy with social media influencers (instead of films and celebrities) can fail to shift preferences if those influencers deceptively overstate the product to their followers (see Shades of Gray in this chapter).

influence from marketers The impact of advertising, branding, and other marketing activities on customers' preferences

In a simpler approach, launching and aggressively marketing a new product can change customers' needs. The wide availability of cold brew coffee at major coffee chains such as Starbucks, for example, has granted this beverage greater exposure and fueled growing preferences for it over the last several years.[19]

IN OTHER WORDS ...

Earlier in this chapter, customer differences were described as a "battlefield" or landscape. Consider the implications for this analogy of influence from marketers. This influence means that the landscape is not constant; the marketer's toolkit can alter the terrain. Marketers can not only *use* customer differences but also proactively *create* them.

Source #3: Individual Differences

individual differences Psychological traits that characterize each person's stable and consistent way of responding to the environment

Other sources of customer differences have deeper roots in individuals' minds. First and most basic among these are **individual differences**: psychological traits that describe the stable and consistent characteristics of a person's response to the environment. There are innumerable ways in which people differ psychologically. The most popular typology organizes these differences into the "Big 5" personality traits: openness, conscientiousness, extraversion, agreeableness, and neuroticism.

1. *Openness to experience* captures an individual's curiosity and breadth of interests.
2. *Conscientiousness* involves self-discipline and striving for achievement.
3. *Extraversion* indicates gregariousness and a tendency to draw energy from social situations.
4. *Agreeableness* refers to a warm and compliant nature.
5. *Neuroticism* denotes a lack of emotional stability.[20]

These traits drive striking differences in customer behavior, such as an interest in artistic products (openness) and a willingness to spend money on highly social experiences such as cruises (extraversion). Other less central traits, such as favorite colors, also fall into this category and underscore the importance of product customization (e.g., being able to choose a smartphone color). Similarly, people vary in their favorite flavors, textures, sounds, and smells. Many individual difference-based preferences are ingrained at birth, due to random or genetic variation, or else develop in very early childhood. As a result, this source of customer differences can generate a diversity of customer needs in virtually any product category.

Source #4: Life Experiences

life experiences Events and experiences that are unique to her or his life and that have lasting impact on the value the person places on products and services, affecting preferences independently of the individual differences

A person's **life experiences** are made up of events and experiences that are unique to her or his life and that have lasting impact on the value the person places on products and services, affecting preferences independently of the individual differences. Some geographic, temporal, and cultural factors have systematic impacts on an individual's worldview, propensity to take risks, or desire to consume specific product categories; for example, an individual who came of age in the 1960s in the United Kingdom or United States may be more likely to prefer music from the Beatles and other popular groups from that period. Other factors, such as controversial geopolitical events (e.g., pivotal elections and wars), have an impact but the nature of that impact is unclear. Furthermore, some individual difference-based psychological factors likely interact with characteristics of an individual's environment to cause varying reactions. Thus, life experiences are a source of customer differences, but their actual linkages to preferences are often difficult to predict.

Source #5: Self-concept

Consumers often purchase a specific product or service to support their actual or aspirational **self-concept**, defined as "the concept the individual has of himself as a physical, social, and spiritual or moral being."[21] While individual differences and life experiences influence purchase behavior at a subconscious or unintentional level, consumers' desires to buy products and services that match their self-concepts entails a more proactive, conscious decision process. Consumers seek out products that they believe reflect their unique self-concepts. The wide variety of consumer choices in aesthetically focused categories such as fashion and home décor speaks to the diversity of self-concepts that drive purchases of these products. A product's image can also come from a link to an iconic figure or celebrity or what is popular in a peer or aspirational social group. Style-focused YouTube influencers, for example, are often aspirational figures to their followers. When these influencers praise specific products or trends, they align these

self-concept An individual's view of himself or herself from a social, physical, and moral point of view

Source: istock.com/Rawpixel

The desire for a unique self-concept is an important source of customer differences.

products with their followers' aspirational self-concepts. Some people, on the other hand, have a self-concept focused on uniqueness and actively avoid popular products. The practice of dyeing hair unusual colors, and unusual combinations of colors, often reflects this desire for uniqueness.

MANAGING CUSTOMER DIFFERENCES THROUGH SEGMENTATION, TARGETING, AND POSITIONING (STP)

targeting Deciding which segment or segments to pursue

Segmentation, **targeting,** and positioning (STP) has been the primary tool for answering the three questions for managing customer differences throughout the niche marketing era and one-to-one marketing era. In STP, marketers characterize customer groups based on their needs, then document the observable demographics and behaviors of these groups (segmentation). With this information, marketers then select the most favorable and profitable segment or segments to pursue (targeting) and devise a marketing mix (see Chapter 1) to appeal to each targeted segment's needs (positioning).

Step 1: Segmentation

Segmentation is the process of dividing the overall market into groups, such that potential customers *within* each group have highly similar needs and preferences for a particular product or service category (e.g., high preference for quality and service warranties, low need for large assortments), but the groups are highly different from one another. The specific customer needs that delineate these differences between segments are the **basis of segmentation.** Segmentation is a critical tool for answering the first of the three questions: what types of customer preferences exist?

basis of segmentation The specific customer needs that delineate the differences between segments

Segmentation's importance is rarely questioned, but the underlying process is poorly understood. The use of demographic characteristics to describe customer segments in marketing parlance and in the popular press (e.g., "that TV show captures the desirable 21- to 45-year-old viewer") makes it easy to assume, mistakenly, that demographic groups such as males and twenty-one to forty-five year olds are segments. These demographics are instead **segment descriptors**—observable characteristics that are useful in finding and targeting members of the segment.

segment descriptors Observable characteristics that are useful in finding and targeting members of the segment

Confusing segment descriptors with the basis of segmentation overlooks the core purpose of segmentation: to identify groups of customers with similar needs. Occasionally, needs are directly determined or at least heavily influenced by demographics. The need for specific primary school textbooks is driven heavily by age. But for most products, any single demographic characteristic fails to clarify who does or does not have a need or desire for that product. Customers in a specific age group might share some preferences for clothing, but the differences in their preferences—driven by personal tastes, experiences, functional goals, and so on—so far outweigh the shared preferences that age alone is of little use as a basis for segmentation. In the same way, business customers (i.e., firms) in the same industry share some common preferences, due to industry standards and similar end-customer expectations. But one business customer's unique strategy and context might cause it to emphasize cost control over all other attributes, whereas a second firm might make choices based on customer service, and a third focuses on the depth of its supplier relationship. The focus of segmentation therefore should be differentiating consumers according to their unique needs and desires (basis of segmentation), not demographic characteristics (segment descriptors). The most precise evaluation of customer needs is obtained from marketing research studies (see Chapter 9), although it is increasingly common for marketers to segment customers based on search and purchasing behaviors tracked in digital channels (e.g., mobile application and e-commerce platforms), as this chapter's Opposing Views feature highlights.

OPPOSING VIEWS Behavior-Based Segmentation

Segmenting customers based on their behaviors, and then proceeding with targeting and positioning using this behavioral segmentation, is not a new practice. Shopping and purchasing behaviors are widely viewed as a more valid way to infer customer needs than simple demographics or other segment descriptors and are thus a useful tool in applying segmentation schemes.[22]

New technologies have enhanced the power of behavior-based segmentation to precisely define the needs of smaller and smaller segments. For example, Canadian home improvement retailer BuildDirect.com tracks customer behavior online using DoubleClick, a Google service that logs users' visits to various webpages—such as BuildDirect.com's product listings.[23] This data is then used to infer underlying customer needs; if an individual frequently browses products across a wide range of product categories, BuildDirect might infer that this individual belongs to the "handyperson" segment.

But as technology has advanced, these increasingly sophisticated tools for tracking customer behavior have come under fire. Advocacy groups such as the Electronic Frontier Foundation have expressed concern over companies tracking children on the web, for example,[24] leading to regulations in some countries that restrict data collection on minors.[25] Even with such regulations, critics say that the sheer volume of data collected from online tracking can paint a rather detailed picture of any individual's life and interests.[26] This alone can be construed an invasion of privacy to some. When this data is combined with geolocation tracking (e.g., from Google Maps on Android phones) and the ambiguous data collected through "always on" listening devices such as smartphones and home automation hardware (e.g., Amazon's Alexa-enabled devices), critics' concerns are amplified.[27] This controversy has only grown in recent years as firms collect more data about user behaviors.

Canada

See the issue from two sides:

1. Craft an argument in favor of continuing to use more advanced, potentially intrusive technology in behavior-based segmentation. Why do the advantages outweigh the disadvantages? How would you minimize harm to consumers with this approach?
2. Craft an argument in favor of more stringent industry standards and/or regulation to restrict the use of more advanced, potentially intrusive technology in behavior-based segmentation. Why do the disadvantages win out? How would you minimize costs to firms (e.g., regulatory burden, opportunity cost of less refined segmentation) with this approach?

Step 2: Targeting

After segmenting potential customers into groups based on their preferences for a specific product or service category, marketers must select which segments to target. **Targeting,** the second step in STP, answers the second of the three questions: which types of customers should the firm pursue? If segmentation is like cutting the market into slices of pie, then targeting is deciding which slice (or slices) you want to eat. The GE Matrix developed by McKinsey is a long-standing and useful decision aid for targeting (Figure 4.2). In this framework, each market segment is rated on two dimensions: market attractiveness and competitive strength:

market attractiveness External market characteristics that make a given segment strategically and financially valuable to serve

competitive strength The relative strength of a firm, versus competitors, at securing and maintaining market share in a given segment

- **Market attractiveness** captures external market characteristics that make a given segment strategically and financially valuable, such as size, growth rate, and price sensitivity. Generally, an attractive segment is equally appealing to all firms competing in that market.
- **Competitive strength** captures the relative strength of a firm, versus competitors, at securing and maintaining market share in a given segment. Thus, this dimension is specific to each firm's competitive situation and core competencies.

By evaluating the market attractiveness and competitive strength of each segment of potential customers, a marketer can weigh their desirability against the firm's ability to win them, then select the segment or segments to target. Performing this evaluation is essential for the firm to craft a strong positioning for the targeted segments. For example, in this chapter's Marketing Fail feature, Google seemingly had no notion of which video game player segments it was targeting, leading to a weak positioning.

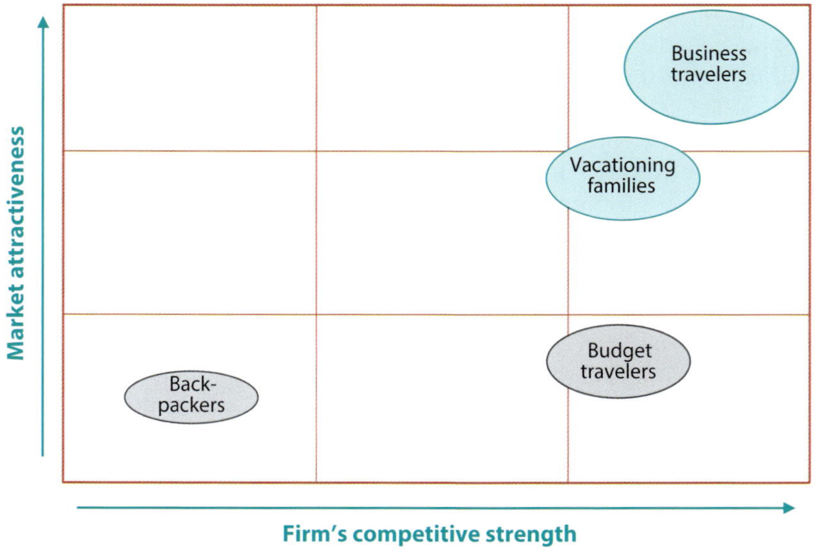

Figure 4.2 GE Matrix.

Example of a GE Matrix, which maps the attractiveness of segments according to the attractiveness of each market and the firm's ability to effectively compete in each market. This example is for Intercontinental Hotels Group (IHG), a British firm that operates well-known chains' brands across the price spectrum, such as Holiday Inn and Intercontinental. One of the most appealing segments for IHG (as for most hotel groups) is business travelers.

Firms often target multiple segments simultaneously with different offerings to match different customer preferences and gain access to a larger market. In some cases, a firm can use similar or related brands with different offerings and price points. For example, Japanese automaker Honda Motor Company is well-known

SHADES OF GRAY "She Has 1 Million Followers!"

Source: istock.com/Xavier Lorenzo

The influencer market has gone from a hobby to big business, and it has not always been smooth sailing.

If you spend much time on social media such as Instagram, YouTube, and TikTok, you have likely encountered more than one influencer, a social media personality who has many followers and who can affect those followers' purchases and other behavior. When influencers discuss products—often in categories such as apparel, cosmetics, movies and television, video games, and health and wellness—people listen; the majority of consumers trust what influencers say about a brand more than that brand's advertising.[28] A typical influencer has a captive audience with a well-defined set of interests. For example, a YouTuber who reviews action movies will draw followers who love action movies. Followers' interests, in turn, sometimes align with a firm's target segment; a film studio might be interested in the action movie YouTuber's followers. Thus, delivering messaging through influencers is a potentially powerful targeting tool.

Brands have taken notice and spend more than $8 billion annually on sponsored messages and endorsements from influencers to their followers. Influencing has therefore become a potentially lucrative profession. An influencer with 75,000 followers could expect several thousand dollars for every sponsored post; an influencer with over 1 million followers can exceed $100,000 per post.[29]

Global

The vast sums of cash being tossed about in the influencer market, often by marketers with limited understanding of how influencers work, has led to a growing trend of fraud and abuse. On the one hand, when influencers make sponsored posts, they sometimes—without or perhaps with the knowledge of their partner brands—neglect to mention that they are being paid for said posts (a practice known as *influencer payola*). Department store Lord & Taylor infamously colluded with fifty influencers in this practice.[30] On the other hand, 15 percent of marketers' influencing spending is wasted on *fake influencers*.[31] These are social media accounts that use bots and other fraudulent means to accumulate a large number of followers, likes, and shares, but lack a significant authentic following or actual influence. Thus, influencer marketing is plagued by deceptive practices, and these practices affect both consumers and marketers.

Ethical dilemmas:

1. Who is harmed when an influencer is paid to promote a product, but does not disclose that they are paid? How exactly are these individuals/organizations harmed?
2. How can marketers use influencers to reach their target segments while reducing the occurrence of influencer payola?
3. Who is harmed by fake influencers? How exactly are these individuals/organizations harmed?

for its Honda passenger vehicles, which target multiple segments at moderate price points. However, Honda Motor also markets the Acura brand, with a similar overall aesthetic to Honda vehicles (and even a similar logo design) but a greater focus on luxury segments and an upmarket price point. Similarly, Tata Motors Group acquired the premium brand Jaguar to gain a stronger foothold when targeting luxury car consumers (see Chapter Case).

Step 3: Positioning

positioning Deploying the marketing mix to establish and communicate that a firm's offering meets the needs of targeted customers better than competitors do

The last step in the STP process is **positioning**, which entails deploying the marketing mix to establish and communicate that a firm's offering meets the needs of targeted customers better than competitors do. Positioning answers the final of the three questions: by what means will the firm satisfy the chosen customers' needs? Positioning entails changing both the actual offering (innovating products or reducing manufacturing costs) and the perceived offering (building a new brand image). Nearly every marketing mix decision that managers make, including all decisions pertaining to the 7 Ps discussed in Chapter 1, affects the positioning of the firm's offering in customers' minds.

repositioning The process by which a firm shifts its target market for a product or service

Product design and performance represent perhaps the most straightforward way to change an offering's position. In 2020, television network HBO, a division of WarnerMedia, expanded its content library to include a wide array of WarnerMedia films and television series, to ultimately position itself as a new streaming service competing for the same target market as Netflix: HBO Max.[32] Marketing communications drive positioning as well, as US automaker Buick attempted with its "That's not a Buick" advertising campaign to refresh its image and appeal to a younger target market.[33] This campaign was also a prime example of **repositioning**, or the process by which a firm shifts its target market. Distribution strategy and pricing are also key tools to achieve a desired positioning; consider premium jeweler Tiffany & Co., which sells its products almost exclusively through its own stores and almost never discounts its products to support a positioning focused on luxury and exclusivity.

positioning statement A strategy document that captures key marketing decisions, ideally in the form "For [target segment] the [product/concept] provides [benefit], which [compelling reasons for buying versus competition]."

Firms often find it helpful to write a **positioning statement** to capture the key marketing decisions that appeal to customers in the firm's target segment. An effective positioning statement can be expressed in the form, "For [target segment] the [product/concept] provides [benefit], which [compelling reasons for buying versus competition]." This statement then becomes the roadmap for implementation decisions involved in marketing a product or service, both inside and outside the company. In larger firms, different groups of employees (e.g., from sales or design departments) design, implement, or affect customer perceptions, so a clear positioning statement is critical to aligning everyone's decisions and actions. Inconsistency across sales organizations, advertising materials, channel members, and product management has the potential to undermine the effectiveness of an otherwise well-designed positioning.

As a powerful external and internal communication tool, the positioning statement provides clear guidance and minimizes the potential that any employee or outside vendor will make decisions incongruent with the firm's positioning strategy. For example, an aspirational positioning statement for McDonald's might read: For budget- and time-conscious diners, McDonald's provides friendly service and operational excellence across thousands of worldwide locations, which delivers a more consistent and enjoyable customer experience than other quick service restaurants.

Thus, positioning helps a firm manage customer differences because it can use the marketing mix elements to position or reposition both tangible and intangible elements of its offering to align with target segments' preferences. To visualize and develop effective positioning strategies, many marketers use **perceptual maps**, which depict customer segments, competitors, and a firm's own perceived position on a two-dimensional grid characterized by key customer needs (e.g., durability and visual appeal).

perceptual map A marketing tool that depicts customer segments, competitors, and a firm's own perceived position on a two-dimensional grid characterized by key customer needs

Figure 4.3 is an example of Buick's perceptual map, before and after its "That's not a Buick" repositioning effort; it tried to retain its image as a slightly upmarket brand, while offering a more modern and youthful appeal. Perceptual maps are useful not only for positioning, but also for providing a high-level overview of the entire output of the STP process. The various segments on the map illustrate what types of customer preferences exist, and the perceptions of the firm's offerings reflect which segments are being pursued and how effectively the firm's offerings are meeting the needs of the chosen segments. Thus, segmentation, targeting, and positioning—when properly executed and based on an understanding of the sources of differences in customer needs—are effective tools to address the three questions for managing customer differences.

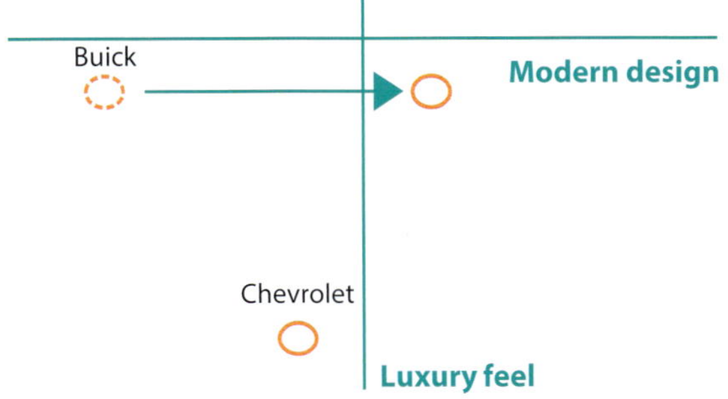

Figure 4.3 Perceptual Map Example.

Example of a perceptual map showing the goal of Buick's "That's not a Buick" repositioning campaign, and other GMC car brands. GMC tried to create a more modern and youthful image for Buick while retaining its somewhat upmarket reputation.

CHAPTER CASE STUDY

India

TATA MOTORS ENTERS THE PREMIUM CAR SEGMENT

"Life. It's not about figures. It's about feelings. The moments that feed your soul. The occasions that take your breath away. The instances that leave you speechless. These are the moments we live for."[34] These words convey a brand ethos that premium automobile manufacturer Jaguar has maintained since 1935 and communicate the core needs of Jaguar's target segment: superior performance and refined design aesthetics.[35] As it happens, these words also spoke to the aspiration of Indian automaker Tata Motors to enter the premium car segment.

Enter Tata Motors. Founded in 1945 in Mumbai, India as a steam engine manufacturer, Tata Locomotive and Engineering Company (now known as Tata Motors Group) gradually expanded into commercial vehicles and, in 1991, began manufacturing passenger cars.[36] By 2008, its annual sales had climbed to over 330 billion Indian rupees ($7 billion) on the backs of two key categories: subcompacts and sports utility vehicles (SUVs).[37] Its subcompacts, including the Indica, Indigo, and Nano, were targeted and positioned for the economy segment, whose primary needs were a low purchase price and a low cost of ownership. The Nano, in particular, was targeted at "bottom-of-the-pyramid" buyers who otherwise would have been priced out of the automobile market altogether.[38] Tata's SUVs, the Safari and Sumo, were targeted to multiple utility-focused segments, such as middle-class families needing greater seating capacity than a compact and rural buyers seeking better performance on unpaved roads.

Yet Tata continued to eye an unmet set of needs in its product line: the needs of the lucrative premium car segment. Like other automakers, Tata Motors projected rapid growth in this

Source: istock.com/Boris25

Luxury and premium automobiles were not Tata Motors' forte prior to the Jaguar acquisition.

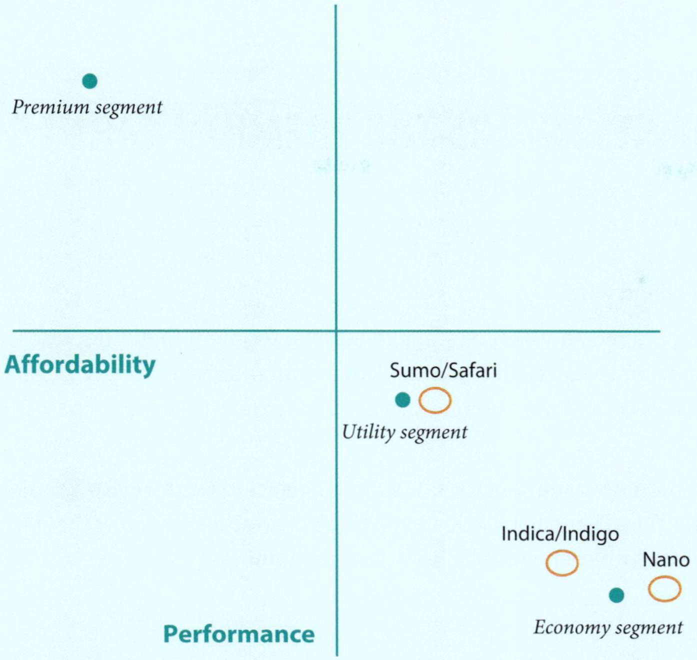

Figure 4.4 Tata Perceptual Map.

Stylized perceptual map of Tata Motor's offerings and target segments' needs at the beginning of 2008. At the time, Tata lacked a well-defined offering for the premium segment.

segment due to the ever-increasing number of affluent buyers in emerging markets such as the Middle East and India—indeed, this market's size would double in the ten years following 2008.[39] Although the premium car segment was appealing, Tata had nothing in its product line that was suitable for the aforementioned needs of these buyers: superior performance and refined design aesthetics (Figure 4.4). The company had to find another route to meeting this segment's needs

The acquisition of Jaguar. In March of 2008, Tata Motors Group announced that it would purchase both of the Ford Motor company's premium British car brands, Jaguar and Land Rover, for $2.3 billion.[40] At the time, the optics of the acquisition grabbed headlines; an Indian firm purchasing British brands from a US company was uncommon, and evoked a sense of "reverse imperialism"—but this was not Tata's concern.[41] Rather, the Jaguar brand's strong awareness, as well as its associations in the minds of consumers around the world (as captured in the opening quote of this case), gave Tata Motors exactly the opening it needed to target and enter the premium car market.

Tata's gambit paid off. Following years of stagnation, the automaker's revenue expanded by 64 percent in the year following the acquisition, owing almost entirely to global sales of the newly acquired brands.[42] This trend continued in the years to come; by 2019, Tata Motors reached annual sales of over 3 trillion Indian rupees ($40 billion), with 74 percent of this total—and the majority of revenue growth since 2008—arising from the premium car segment.[43] By understanding and leveraging customer differences, Tata successfully targeted and positioned a new offering to a lucrative untapped segment, and turned a $2.3 billion acquisition into over $30 billion of revenue growth.

CASE QUESTIONS

1. Compare the needs of the premium car segment to the needs of the economy segment. Considering the five sources of customer differences from this chapter, why do you think these buyers have such different needs?
2. Imagine you are the CEO of Tata Motors Group at the beginning of 2008 (prior to the acquisition). Use the two dimensions of the GE Matrix from this chapter to evaluate the premium car segment. Which dimension was favorable, and which dimension was unfavorable—and why?
3. Tata Motors acquired another company to target a segment that otherwise would have been very difficult to target. Can you think of any alternative routes, besides acquisition, that Tata Motors could have taken to successfully target the premium passenger car segment?
4. Devise a positioning statement for Tata's Jaguar vehicles. Next, devise a positioning statement for Tata's Nano vehicle. Can you think of another company that has products and/or services with such radically divergent positionings?

CHAPTER SUMMARY

The foundational assumption that customers vary widely in their needs and preferences is encapsulated in Marketing Principle #1. This principle implies a key marketing challenge: managing customer differences. Managing customer differences requires answering three questions. First, what types of customer preferences exist? Second, which types of customers should the firm pursue? And third, by what means will the firm satisfy the chosen customers' needs? Some firms assume away customer differences by offering a single product to the entire target market. This approach may work in special circumstances, particularly if competition is weak or scarce (as in the mass-marketing era), but it rarely works in the long run. As a category grows, competitors recognize untapped opportunity, identify niches of customers whose needs are insufficiently met by existing offerings, and then target those customers with a tailored offering that is better aligned with those unique preferences. This process resulted in the evolution of the niche marketing era and, later, the one-to-one marketing era. Customers' unique preferences may arise due to (1) functional needs, (2) influence from marketers, (3) individual differences, (4) life experiences, and (5) self-concept. If a company fails to map new or refined offerings to the different segments characterized by these sources of customer differences, then customers have a compelling reason to purchase a competitor's product. STP (segmentation, targeting, and positioning) is highlighted in this chapter as a critical tool to answer the aforementioned three questions and successfully manage customer differences.

APPLICATION QUESTIONS

1. Can you think of any firm that seems to ignore Marketing Principle #1? How does this firm get away with it?
2. Think about a product or service that you love. Now think about one that you hate. Why do you feel this way about these products? How do your reasons align with the five sources of customer differences?
3. In your experience, and what you have observed from family and friends, which of the five sources of customer differences is most important? Why do you think some sources are less important?
4. Think of a time when you experienced a salesperson (for example, a retail sales associate) attempting to enact a customer orientation. What kinds of things did this salesperson do to learn about your needs? Did you feel that the salesperson was effective in understanding your needs? Why or why not?
5. Pretend that you are opening a shop in your favorite neighborhood—it might be a café, a bar, or a clothing store, for example. Design a segmentation, targeting, and positioning plan for this shop in your neighborhood by answering "the three questions."
6. Choose two important needs that consumers consider when purchasing an airline ticket. Pick three airlines. Draw a perceptual map, and plot how well you think each of these airlines meets these two needs. Which airline is closest to your "ideal" point?

7. Imagine that you are a senior leader in Twitter's analytics division. Your department devises a variety of tracking procedures and metrics pertaining to individual users, and these tools are critical to advertisers who want to target a "segment of one" on Twitter with personalized advertisements. One of your analysts comes to you with a promising idea to harvest consumers' interests and sentiments about brands from a new source: their DMs (private, direct messages between Twitter users). How could you gain additional insights about differences in customer preferences from this data? What kinds of privacy concerns or other moral issues does this data harvesting pose? Can you see any way to overcome these concerns?

Visit the companion website, **https://bloomsbury.pub/palmatier-marketing**, or **https://samsinstitute.com**, for additional learning and teaching tools, including professional videos outlining the Four Principles, PowerPoint tutorials with voice-over commentary, sample syllabi for marketing courses, testbank and more.

Chapter 5

UNDERSTANDING CONSUMER AND ORGANIZATIONAL BUYER BEHAVIOR

CHAPTER OVERVIEW

Chapter 5 elaborates on Marketing Principle #1 (all customers differ) by exploring the diverse decision journeys that lead different customers to purchase. The chapter first explains how buying decisions can be divided into consumer and organizational buying. It then lays out the consumer decision journey. Finally, it outlines the steps in the organizational buying decision journey and highlights where these steps differ from the consumer journey. The chapter will proceed by answering the following questions:

- What are the two main types of buyer decision journeys?
- How do the different steps in the consumer decision journey unfold?
- What is the organizational buying decision journey and how does it differ from the consumer journey?

In the chapter's cases and features, you will encounter companies struggling, and often succeeding, in efforts to influence customers at various stages of the decision journey. These include:

- A divisive Vera Bradley social media campaign (Marketing Fail).
- Zoom's rapid adoption by corporations and educators (Chapter Case).
- Ethical and practical issues in managing customer decision journeys, such as the dangers of YouTube Kids (Shades of Gray) and the ongoing convergence of consumer and organizational buying habits (Opposing Views).

LEARNING OBJECTIVES

- Compare consumers and organizational buyers.
- Identify the steps in the customer decision journey.
- Describe the ways in which consumer behavior shapes consumer decision journeys.
- Associate differences between consumers and organizational buyers with key features of the organizational buyer decision journey.

IMAGINE Buying Products for a Business

Source: Calugar Ana Maria/Unsplash

Retailers must decide which coffee machines to purchase, based on what they think their customers will buy.

Imagine that you have just been hired as an assistant manager at a store in a major supermarket chain. This position promises the possibility for advancement within the company, so you are eager to make a strong impression. Due to a company-wide push to stock more cookware, appliances, and dishes along with groceries, your manager wants to start selling coffee machines in the store. For one of your first major assignments, she has tasked you with proposing an assortment of coffee machines to sell.

Your manager did not give you very specific instructions for this task. She said an assortment of three different machines, each suitable for different types of customers, would be ideal. But she also noted that stocking larger models could mean a smaller assortment—two or fewer types—due to shelf space limitations. She made it clear that, although you will propose an assortment, the final decision is subject to her approval. You are aware of several major coffee machine brands, such as Breville, Nespresso, De'Longhi, and Keurig, each with various models available, but you are certain there must be more worth considering. You begin to do some research to determine which coffee machines the store should buy.

Critical thinking:

1. It is often useful to break a complicated decision into a series of smaller steps. List the steps you would go through before deciding on an assortment of coffee machines to present to your manager.
2. Imagine that, instead of buying coffee machines to sell in the store, you are buying coffee machines to install in the store's employee breakroom. In what ways would your decision-making steps differ?
3. Now imagine that you are buying a coffee machine for your own home. List the steps you would go through before buying a machine. How do these steps differ from your answers to #1 and #2?

THE TWO FACES OF CUSTOMER BEHAVIOR

Chapter 4 established various reasons that customers differ. This chapter delves deeper and explores how customer differences influence the series of events that lead a customer to buy. **Customer decision journeys** characterize the steps on the path toward an initial purchase, as well as toward potential repeat purchases, of a product or service.[1] Figure 5.1 illustrates a typical customer decision journey; the individual steps are discussed later in this chapter. Two different customers may follow divergent journeys prior to buying a given product. Understanding

customer decision journey The steps on the path toward an initial purchase, as well as toward potential repeat purchases, of a product or service

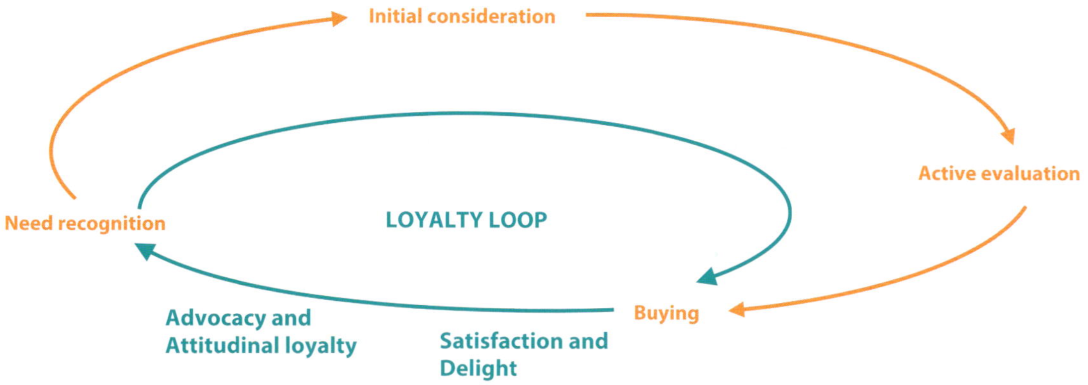

Figure 5.1 Customer Decision Journeys.

Consumers and organizational buyers proceed through a series of steps leading to initial and repeat purchases.

these differences—and in turn, understanding *why* different customers behave differently before, during, and after the purchase—enables more fine-grained tailoring of marketing efforts. Ultimately, marketers aim to apply Marketing Principle #1 to guide customers in their target segment(s) down pathways to purchasing and loyalty.

Historically, decision journeys have been segregated according to one critical distinction, that is, whether the customer is a consumer or an organizational buyer:

consumers Individuals who buy a product or service for personal use, including items bought for one's own consumption as well as gifts

- **Consumers** are individuals who buy a product or service for personal use; this includes items bought for one's own consumption as well as gifts. People making purchases from shopping malls, hair salons, and restaurants are all consumers. Major retailers, such as Best Buy and MediaMarkt, sell most of their products to consumers.

organizational buyers Individuals who buy a product or service on behalf of a business, institution, or government organization

- **Organizational buyers** are individuals who buy a product or service on behalf of a larger entity; these entities include businesses such as supermarkets, institutions such as schools and hospitals, and government organizations such as police departments. It is important to remember that a *customer* can be either a consumer or an organization; therefore, consumer and customer are not always synonyms. As the opening example implies, organizational buyers must approach a purchase somewhat differently than consumers.

This chapter first discusses the consumer decision journey, before considering how decision journeys play out for organizational buyers.

IN OTHER WORDS ...

Customers can be consumers or organizations. Consumers buy for themselves, and organizational buyers buy for their company or organization. Organizational buyers have different things to worry about when making purchase decisions, so they have different decision journeys from consumers.

CONSUMER BEHAVIOR

Purchases by individual consumers make up a sizable portion of the economy and are the main source of revenue for many of the world's most iconic brands. Globally, considering e-commerce purchases of products alone, consumers bought approximately $3.5 trillion of goods in 2019.[2] Thus, firms have long been highly motivated to understand both *what* consumers buy and *why* they buy it, and consumer behavior has attracted a great deal of attention from market research firms and academic researchers. This attention has resulted in a deep collective understanding of the consumer decision journey, as well as various factors that shape this journey.

Mapping the Consumer Decision Journey

The consumer decision journey involves five steps, although the customer does not always proceed through these in a linear fashion:

1. need recognition;
2. initial consideration;
3. active evaluation;
4. buying; and
5. post-purchase and the loyalty loop.[3]

Step 1: Journey's Beginning—Need Recognition

need recognition The first step in the decision journey, involving the identification of a specific necessity or desire that is not currently satisfied

personal needs Needs motivated by a consumer's desire to create utility (happiness or comfort) for themselves or, in the case of a group/gift purchase, for others

functional need A type of personal need related to the utilitarian, performance-related criteria that a product or service fulfills

emotional need A type of personal need characterized by a desire to feel a specific way

social need A type of personal need driven by an individual's sense of identity in relation to others

The refrigerator breaks. A teenager hears about a new video game being released. A young couple decide to plan a tropical getaway. Each of these events leads to a consumer's **need recognition,** or the identification of a specific necessity or desire that is not currently satisfied. Consumers are focused on **personal needs;** they are motivated by a desire to create utility (happiness or comfort) for themselves or, in the case of a group/gift purchase, for others. Repairing the refrigerator, buying a new video game, and going on a tropical vacation would all satisfy personal needs.

Since all customers differ (MP#1), consumers' personal needs are diverse. They can be broken down into three needs:[4]

1. **Functional needs** relate to the utilitarian, performance-related criteria that a product or service fulfills. If a consumer searches for a new computer because her old computer does not have enough storage space, this reflects a functional need.
2. **Emotional needs** are characterized by a desire to feel a specific way; when a child wants to watch a cartoon that will make him laugh, he is experiencing an emotional need. Or, for example, an adult's desire to feel fulfilled and self-actualized can be viewed as an emotional need.
3. **Social needs** are driven by an individual's sense of identity in relation to others; in other words, fulfillment of this need is achieved only if other people respond in a particular way. This type of need can include a desire for higher status or a desire for a sense of belonging and relatedness.

> A woman who thinks about buying a new dress to impress former peers at a school reunion, and a father who wants to get himself tennis equipment so he can bond with his daughter over her love of the sport, are both guided by social needs. Or, in the case of altruism (e.g., donating to charity), the individual can be driven by a desire for a positive moral self-image.

Multiple types of needs can apply simultaneously. Consider a man visiting a hair salon. He might be driven by a functional need to shorten his hair, so it stays out of his eyes and is easier to comb. At the same time, he could also feel an emotional need to feel relaxed and pampered during the salon experience. Additionally, a social need could apply, as he hopes others will compliment him on his new haircut.

These three types of needs individually and jointly influence the remaining steps in the consumer decision journey. Marketers must be attentive to the types of needs that consumers value across diverse segments. As this chapter's Marketing Fail illustrates, in the case of Vera Bradley's hashtag campaign, misjudging these needs can backfire on the firm.

Step 2: Initial Consideration

Recognizing a need immediately prompts the next step. In **initial consideration,** consumers formulate in their minds the set of products or services that could meet their recognized needs: the **consideration set.** For example, a thirsty patron walking into a bar might immediately consider several brands of beer such as Guinness, Paulaner, and Pilsner Urquell. The consideration set is informed by numerous factors, such as an individual's own goals and priorities, memories of past consumption experiences or conversations about the brands, and awareness of brands based on advertising and other outside influences.[5] A more complicated set of needs—for example, both an emotional need to enjoy the drink and a social need to appear to have sophisticated tastes—naturally constrains the number of viable options in the consideration set. In some cases, hype or news coverage can dramatically influence this stage as outsized attention on one option forces it into the consideration set—consider, for example, the growth of Zoom during 2020 (see Chapter Case).

initial consideration The second step in the decision journey, in which customers formulate in their minds the set of products or services that could meet their recognized needs

consideration set The set of products or services that could meet recognized needs

Step 3: Active Evaluation

After forming an initial consideration set, a consumer enters **active evaluation,** a stage marked by the search for relevant information and the assessment of alternatives. A consumer can search for information in many ways, such as by reading product descriptions and specifications, visiting stores to physically examine items, scanning reviews written by other consumers, seeking out expert reviews, and asking friends for their opinions. As noted in Chapter 4, influencers on YouTube and other social media platforms are an increasingly trusted source of information about products and services.

active evaluation The third step in the decision journey, marked by the search for relevant information and the assessment of alternatives

This search process can not only reveal information about brands already under consideration but also pare down or even expand the consideration set. Imagine a consumer looking to replace an aging mid-range Android phone.

She initially considers Google Pixel, based on her current phone, as well as Samsung and Xiaomi, based on phones she has seen her friends use. But after doing some research online, she rules out Samsung based on its price while adding Motorola and Sony to her list.

After gathering relevant information, a consumer next assesses the alternatives, weighing the pros and cons of each option in the consideration set. This assessment involves the **attributes,** or important characteristics, of each alternative (performance, price, convenience, etc.). Consumers can consider these attributes in different ways.

attributes Important characteristics of a product or service

- One seemingly rational way to compare the attributes of various alternatives is **compensatory assessment.** Compensatory assessment may be compared to the scoring for Olympic events such as figure skating and floor gymnastics, where competitors receive an "Artistic score" and a "Technical score." A high artistic score can make up for (i.e., *compensate* for) a low technical score, and vice versa. Similarly, applying compensatory assessment to the Android phone example, the consumer could judge that the Motorola phone's strong battery life makes up for its weak camera performance. Table 5.2 illustrates the logic of compensatory assessment (although that table focuses on the business-to-business context, consumers can also make judgments in this way).
- In reality, though, consumers often make decisions based on **non-compensatory assessment.**[6] As the name implies, under this approach, a strong attribute does not necessarily compensate for a weak attribute. In practice, this leads to a much simpler assessment. Continuing the same example, imagine the consumer *only* cared about battery life; if this were the case, the phone with the longest life would prevail and the other attributes could be ignored. For budget-minded consumers, price is often the driving attribute in non-compensatory assessment.

compensatory assessment Evaluating alternatives such that a strong attribute can make up for a weak attribute

non-compensatory assessment Evaluating alternatives such that a strong attribute cannot make up for a weak attribute; a single attribute can drive the evaluation

Not all purchases warrant extensive search and assessment. The extent of effort exerted in the active evaluation step depends on the costs and benefits of evaluation. The **costs of evaluation** consist of the time, effort, and money expended to search for information and compare alternatives. For some purchases, these costs are not justified. Low-importance or routine purchases, such as salt or printer paper, may proceed without any evaluation at all; the consumer simply buys the first item they see. Similarly, for impulse purchases (e.g., buying a candy bar at the supermarket checkout), the rushed circumstances surrounding the purchase make extensive evaluation prohibitively inconvenient. This phenomenon—choosing something that is "good enough" because it is not worth looking for something better—is known as **satisficing** and applies to a wide range of consumer decisions.[7]

costs of evaluation The time, effort, and money expended to search for information and compare alternatives

satisficing Choosing something that is "good enough" because it is not worth looking for something better

But in other cases, such as the Android phone example, the **benefits of evaluation** outweigh the costs. These benefits entail the reduction of risk surrounding the potential purchase. The nature of these risks mirrors the needs that drive decision journeys:

benefits of evaluation What is gained by incurring the costs of evaluation, namely, a reduction of the risk surrounding the potential purchase

- **Functional risk** is associated with the potential failure to fulfill functional needs.
- **Emotional risk** involves the potential failure to fulfill emotional needs.
- **Social risk** entails the potential failure to fulfill social needs.

functional risk The risk that the purchase will not fulfill *functional needs* (see above)

emotional risk The risk that the purchase will not fulfill *emotional needs* (see above)

social risk The risk that the purchase will not fulfill *social needs* (see above)

A recent college graduate buying professional attire for his first job might invest heavily in researching and evaluating alternatives (trying on clothes at different stores, etc.) to mitigate all three types of risk: the functional risk of having an ill-fitting, uncomfortable suit; the emotional risk of having clothes that fail to instill a sense of confidence and self-worth; and the social risk of sporting a drab or dated look that leaves a poor impression on coworkers. This example also highlights that each type of risk necessarily has a financial dimension; despite spending a sizable chunk of his first paycheck on new clothes, this recent graduate might still be left with the same unmet needs. Thus, highly risky purchases enhance the benefits of evaluation, such that extensive information search and a more formal assessment of alternatives—for example, with compensatory decision rules—are more likely.

Step 4: Buying—Journey's End?

After evaluating alternatives, the natural next step is purchasing the chosen brand and the focus shifts from *what* to buy to *how* to buy. Which retailers stock the product? How trustworthy and convenient are they? Is it more convenient to buy in the store or online? Should the purchase be made in cash, or with financing? These are all questions the consumer must answer at this stage, each implying miniature decision journeys—there are journeys within journeys! Sometimes these questions result in insurmountable obstacles to buying. For example, if financing is unavailable for a major furniture purchase, the consumer may give up or move back to the evaluation step to identify cheaper alternatives. But if the consumer does complete the purchase, this is *not* the end of the journey.

Step 5: Post-Purchase and the Loyalty Loop

Marketers hope that a single purchase results in a loyal customer over time. While **attitudinal loyalty**—feelings of attachment to the brand—are desirable, the ultimate goal is **behavioral loyalty,** meaning a pattern of repeat purchasing. In the decision journey, behavioral loyalty is represented in the **loyalty loop:** an abbreviated repeat journey leading directly back to buying (see Figure 5.1).[8]

attitudinal loyalty Feelings of attachment to the brand

behavioral loyalty A pattern of repeat purchasing

loyalty loop The final piece of the decision journey, consisting of an abbreviated repeat journey leading directly back to buying (bypassing initial consideration and active evaluation)

Consumers enter the loyalty loop by being satisfied with the product or service. This satisfaction can stem from the initial need fulfillment at the time of purchase, as well as service provided after the sale—for example, prompt and responsive warranty service on a new laptop. Marketers can maximize satisfaction by aiming to generate **customer delight**—going beyond expectations by providing a product or service that does more than what it promises to do.[9] In turn, delighted consumers advocate for the

customer delight Going beyond expectations by providing a product or service that does more than what it promises to do

SHADES OF GRAY Advertising on YouTube Kids

Source: istock.com/Jelena Stanojkovic

YouTube Kids provides a unique outlet for children's entertainment and creative expression, but it has been plagued by content control and privacy concerns.

YouTube is one of the world's most dominant social media platforms, allowing creators a wide-open avenue for self-expression in short- or long-form videos and providing viewers a near-infinite stream of ad-supported entertaining and informative content. YouTube is the second-most visited site worldwide, claiming almost 40 percent of internet traffic from mobile devices, and boasts over 30 million channels with roughly *1 billion* hours of videos watched each day.[10]

But with this wealth of content came a challenge: How can a platform whose key selling point is boundless creativity nurture a more controlled environment for younger viewers? The solution was YouTube Kids, a separate platform containing walled-off content suitable for children under thirteen years of age. This platform took a major stride in 2018 when it introduced the option to restrict viewing to human-curated videos; this change overcame the limitations of automated, algorithmic identification of mature content.[11] Children could watch channels such as Bounce Patrol, which provides upbeat renditions of nursery rhymes, and also access a unique outlet for their own creativity. In turn, advertisers gained unique access to children's decision journeys, introducing new brands into their consideration sets and influencing their evaluation of toys and other products.

USA

Unfortunately, the platform was dealt a major blow just one year later: It lost a $170 million lawsuit. What went wrong? YouTube Kids ran afoul of an important US law known as the Children's Online Privacy Protection Act (COPPA). This law requires that websites obtain consent from parents before collecting personal information from children.[12] As it turned out, the platform had been installing tracking cookies—text files that can be read by other sites to target advertisements—on children's devices without such consent. In effect, YouTube Kids was permitting its advertising partners to access information about children's profiles and viewing habits on the platform.[13] Thus, in pursuing its core business model of helping advertisers influence consumer decision journeys, YouTube found itself on the wrong side of the law. It has since had to maintain strict controls on the platform to avoid further legal troubles.

Identify the ethical dilemmas:

1. Who was harmed when YouTube Kids shared children's viewing habits with advertisers without parental consent? Why do you think the platform did not attempt to obtain parental consent?
2. Setting aside the issue of collecting personal information, do you believe it is appropriate to advertise directly to children, without a parent or guardian present? Explain why or why not.

THEORY SPOTLIGHT Decision Journey vs Purchase Funnel

The customer decision journey differs from the classic concept of the **purchase funnel,** wherein the consumer follows a linear sequence of steps each featuring a decreasing number of brands.[14] The consumer begins with *awareness* of a large number of brands, has *familiarity* with a smaller number, entertains *consideration* of still fewer, and completes the *purchase* of one (Figure 5.2). While a useful tool, the purchase funnel does not envision the set of brands potentially growing from one step to the next, as can happen in a decision journey—funnels are narrower at the bottom! Nor does the funnel explicitly allow frustration or backward progression, such as the reversion to active evaluation after a failure to purchase. Moreover, the funnel is primarily intended to explain an initial purchase and is ambiguous about how repeat purchases and loyalty work. Thus, the decision journey is a useful evolution and expansion of the purchase funnel concept.

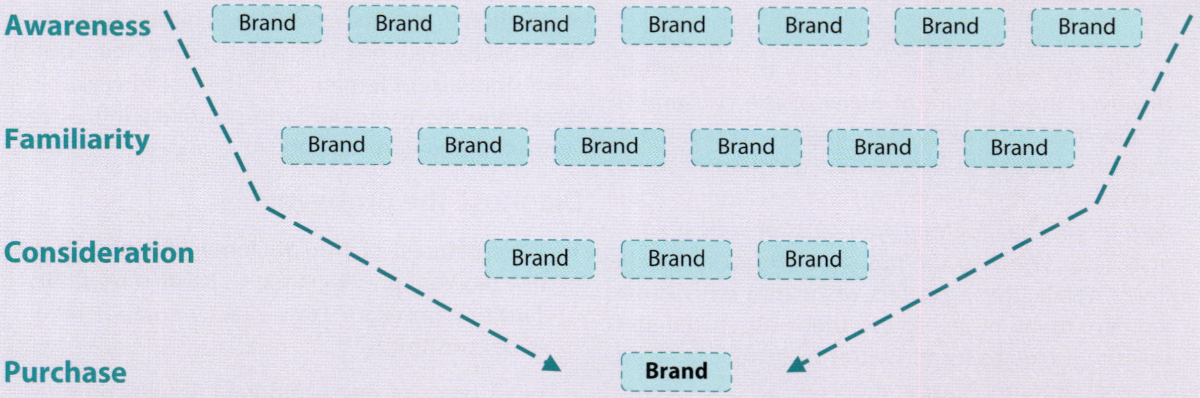

Figure 5.2 Traditional Purchase Funnel.

Traditionally, purchasing decisions were viewed as a funnel: a linear series of steps featuring a decreasing number of brands under consideration. This approach is useful but incomplete.

brand when interacting with others, leading to positive word of mouth, and experience a deeper bond with the brand themselves, generating attitudinal loyalty.

These attitudes trigger the continuation of the loyalty loop; the consumer short-circuits the longer journey that passes through initial consideration and active evaluation, and instead proceeds directly to purchasing once again. The loyalty loop repeats itself, reinforcing attitudinal and behavioral loyalty with each cycle. Consider, for example, a college student trying Starbucks coffee for the first time. Although this student is initially skeptical of the coffee's high price, he finds himself pleasantly surprised by the breadth of available flavors, the personalized service, and the pleasant store atmosphere. His view of the Starbucks brand

purchase funnel A traditional way of viewing purchasing, wherein a customer follows a linear sequence of steps each featuring a decreasing number of alternatives

MARKETING FAIL Vera Bradley and #itsgoodtobeagirl

USA

In 2016, handbag, luggage, and accessory retailer Vera Bradley hoped to revitalize its image for millennial professionals. The brand aimed to use viral content on social media to inject their message into channels popular among these consumers, thereby altering their decision journeys and creating new customers. The most visible component of Vera Bradley's efforts was a Twitter campaign entitled #itsgoodtobeagirl. The campaign's starting point was innocent enough: a single tweet reading *"There are so many reasons why #itsgoodtobeagirl. What's yours? Share it with us: verabradley.com/girl."*[15]

The reasons the brand chose to emphasize, however, drew the ire of many of the consumers it had hoped to woo. The brand tweeted motivational posters that communicated such sentiments as *"Using Chinese food and ice cream to cope with a breakup," "Getting your glass of wine poured first,"* and *"Wielding the power of lipstick and high heels."* While these posters resonated with some women, many others found them superficial and belittling. True to form, Twitter users reacted with a mix of outrage, exasperation, and sarcasm. Some responses highlighted that the brand's target market consisted of women, not "girls" as the hashtag implied. Others sarcastically invoked the brand's hashtag while noting inequities such as the gender wage gap that persists in most countries. And still others noted the irony that Vera Bradley's handbags are only needed because women's clothing notoriously lacks functional pockets.

In response to the viral backlash, Vera Bradley quietly changed course. The brand retained the more successful elements of the campaign, such as YouTube videos featuring in-depth discussions with female professionals. Meanwhile, the brand's motivational posters on Twitter pivoted to focus on explicitly feminist messages, rather than outward signifiers of femininity.[16] The brand was able to salvage the campaign and positively influence consumer decision-making.

Diagnose the problem:

1. Which step(s) of the consumer decision journey did Vera Bradley hope to influence with its Twitter campaign? How exactly could it influence consumers?
2. What types of needs did Vera Bradley emphasize with its Twitter campaign? Why did these needs resonate with some consumers but not others?

improves, he is more likely to recommend Starbucks coffee to others, and he plans a return visit.

ORGANIZATIONAL BUYER BEHAVIOR

Airgas. SAP. Maersk Group. Companies that sell primarily to organizational buyers are typically not household names and do not often make headlines outside of business and financial outlets. But as important as it is to understand consumer behavior, businesses and other organizations worldwide actually purchase nearly *twice as much* as consumers.[17] The US government alone—the world's largest buyer—made roughly $600 billion in purchases in 2019, exceeding the gross domestic product (GDP) of Switzerland.[18] It is unsurprising, then, that marketers and scholars have also sought to understand the organizational buyer decision journey.

Major Differences between Consumers and Organizational Buyers

Organizational buyers differ from consumers along three key dimensions, which each inform divergent aspects of the organizational buyer decision journey (see Table 5.1). These differences relate to the motivation for purchasing, scale of purchasing, and complexity of purchasing.

Difference 1: Motivation for Purchasing

The first and most fundamental of these is the **motivation for purchasing.** As noted earlier, consumers buy to fulfill personal needs, meaning that they aim to create utility (happiness or comfort) for themselves or others. Buying a new television for the living room, ordering a gift for a friend, and providing beverages for a house party all fulfill personal needs.

motivation for purchasing The fundamental reason behind the initiation of a decision journey: a personal need (for consumers) or an organizational need (for organizational buyers)

Organizational buyers, on the other hand, buy based on **organizational needs,** such that the purchase should help accomplish the objectives of their organization's stakeholders. Creating economic value (for example, by increasing profit), reducing environmental impact, and improving employee welfare are all among the various stakeholder aims that a purchase might advance. The opening example of this chapter illustrated buying to fulfill an organizational need. Similarly, when a local restaurant owner decides which disposable plates and cups to purchase, this decision is based on an organizational need. And when a fire department aims to purchase a helicopter, organizational needs are the driving force. Although the traditional view holds that exclusively organizational needs motivate organizational buyers, mounting evidence suggests that personal needs can also subtly influence these buying decisions, as discussed later in this chapter.

organizational needs Needs that relate to accomplishing objectives of the organization's stakeholders

Table 5.1 Differences between Consumers and Organizational Buyers.

The distinction between consumers and organizational buyers is the most significant dividing line affecting customer decision journeys. This distinction can be defined along three key dimensions.

Dimension	Consumers	Organizational buyers
Motivation for purchasing	Personal needs, aiming to create utility for self and/or other individuals. Examples include buying a new television for the living room, ordering a gift for a friend, and providing beverages for a house party.	Organizational needs, advancing the objectives of the organization's stakeholders. Examples include buying coffee machines to sell in a retail store, switching to a more environmentally friendly paper in a corporate office, and ordering raw materials for an assembly line.
Scale of purchasing	Typically small, with everyday purchases such as groceries having little broader economic impact.	Can be small, moderate, or large. A small-scale organizational purchase would be a local coffee shop buying a new French press. A large-scale purchase would be an airline buying a dozen new long-haul planes.
Complexity of purchasing	Minor to moderate; increasing with the number of available options as well as the breadth of different functional, emotional, and social needs to consider.	Minor to extensive. Buying products for resale tends to increase complexity exponentially, as different products can serve both distinct and overlapping needs with many other products in the assortment.

Difference 2: Scale of Purchasing

scale of purchasing The monetary size of purchases

The second major difference between consumers and organizational buyers is the **scale of purchasing,** meaning the monetary size of purchases. The typical consumer has limited buying power. Even a purchase that is quite significant from an individual's perspective is typically small-scale in its economic impact and the resources spent during the decision journey. Consider, for example, a family buying a $1,500 Samsung television. The effort devoted to this choice might include several hours of a family member researching televisions online and in stores, as well as a few minutes of a sales associate's time in a store.

Some organizational purchases are small-scale as well. For example, the choice of eight $200 benches to install in a local gym's locker rooms might be finalized in an hour or less; if the benches are later found to have defects (cracks, paint chipping, etc.), this $1,600 decision can be changed later for a significant but manageable cost. However, organizational buyers differ from consumers in that the *potential* scale of their purchases is enormous. Consider the choice of benches not in a local gym's locker room, but in the locker rooms of PureGym, a chain with over 500 company-operated gyms across the United Kingdom, Denmark, Switzerland, and six other countries. The chain aims to provide a consistent and reliable customer experience across PureGym-branded locations, and part of that experience comes from the chain's use of nearly identical equipment, décor, and fixtures across locations. Renovating locker rooms across the entire chain would, as in the local gym example, require choosing a locker room bench. But in this case, *thousands* of these benches must be purchased, for a total cost in the realm of $1,000,000. The impact of a poor choice, and the cost of rectifying it, are much greater. Because the stakes are raised, more resources—the input of multiple personnel and discussions with potential suppliers, for example—will be brought to bear on the decision.

Difference 3: Complexity of Purchasing

complexity of purchasing The number of factors that are relevant to the purchase decision

Third, consumers and organizational buyers differ in their **complexity of purchasing,** meaning the number of factors that are relevant to the decision. Although some business purchases are straightforward (e.g., the local gym example), the complexity ceiling for organizational buyers is virtually unlimited. As an extreme example, consider Amazon. The e-commerce giant stocks *tens of millions* of different products across *hundreds of thousands* of brands, with countless more offered by other sellers via the Amazon Marketplace.[19] When deciding which products to purchase and keep in its warehouses, Amazon must not only decide what its customers might like to buy, but also how stocking a given product could affect other products. For example, carrying a new brand of toothpaste could actually reduce sales of other toothpaste brands on the site, while potentially boosting sales of complementary dental hygiene products such as floss. Given the sheer number of different products sold on Amazon, the complexity of these organizational purchasing decisions can be daunting. Although consumers sometimes feel overwhelmed by their breadth of options—and this challenge is doubtless exacerbated by the breadth of offerings from retailers such as Amazon—the number of decision factors is inarguably more manageable at an individual consumer level than at an organizational level.[20]

Key Differences in the Organizational Buyer Decision Journey

The customer decision journey is a generalizable concept, and the same five steps from the consumer decision journey apply to the organizational buyer decision journey. However, the content of each step can differ dramatically.

Step 1: Recognizing an Unmet Need

Rather than personal needs, organizational buyers are motivated primarily by organizational needs. Organizational needs can be further categorized into derived needs and operational needs. **Derived needs,** uniquely possessed by retailers, wholesalers, and distributors, are based on reselling products; they are *derived* from the needs of the organization's customers.[21] For a retailer, the personal needs of the individual consumers who shop in the store become the needs of the retailer; it is in the retailer's best interests to buy and stock products that consumers will ultimately want to purchase. This is the premise of the chapter's opening example about buying coffee machines to sell at a supermarket. The functional, emotional, and social needs that drive consumers to buy coffee machines are all relevant when the retailer decides which machines to buy from its suppliers.

derived needs A type of organizational need based on reselling products and derived from the needs of the organization's customers

Similarly, for a wholesaler (and other distributors), the needs of the organizations that buy from them become the needs of the wholesaler, which in turn is motivated

Source: TheStandingDesk/Unsplash

Distributors of groceries and other consumer packaged goods, whose primary business is selling such products to retailers, are concerned with recognizing derived needs.

to purchase and stock products that meet those needs. Consider W.W. Grainger, a multibillion-dollar US-based wholesaler. Among numerous other products, Grainger sells janitorial supplies for use in factories and office buildings. When buying cleaning products from its own suppliers, Grainger must keep abreast of which attributes various types of businesses prefer (cost, potency, toxicity, environmental impact, applicable surfaces, etc.) to stock an assortment that will meet its customers' needs. As these examples imply, derived needs contribute greatly to the complexity of organizational purchasing, due to the many, varied, and potential overlapping needs for various products that a reseller might stock.

operational needs A type of organizational need involving the consumption of products or services to support the organization's continuing operations

In contrast to derived needs, all organizations possess **operational needs,** which drive the consumption of products or services to support the organization's continuing operations. Manufacturers such as Intel have the most prominent operational needs, as they consume raw material and components to create a finished product. Non-manufacturers also have operational needs, though. As India's largest provider of wired internet service, Bharat Sanchar Nigam Limited (BSNL), is engaged in neither reselling nor manufacturing products. Instead, BSNL continuously consumes resources to support service provision to its customers. Products and services purchased in support of BSNL's operational needs are many and varied, including everything from supplies used in the maintenance of internet lines, to vehicles for service technicians, to Styrofoam coffee cups for breakrooms in the firm's headquarters, to relocation and moving services for newly hired executives.

IN OTHER WORDS ...

If an organization purchases a product or service to use in manufacturing a different product or to help provide a service, that purchase is in service of an operational need. If an organization buys a product to resell that very same product to the organization's customers, the purchase fulfills a derived need.

Step 2: Initial Consideration

The fundamentals of this step mirror its cousin in the consumer decision journey, in that organizational buyers enter the decision journey with a preliminary consideration set. A key distinction, though, is *who* is involved from this point onward. Small organizations such as local businesses might begin with an individual organizational buyer's (e.g., the owner's) consideration set. But for most nontrivial purchases by larger organizations, the decision journey involves a **buying system:** "patterned, repeated interactions among social actors ... who participate in one or more of the purchasing-related flows."[22] In other words, multiple voices in the organization contribute to the consideration set and subsequent steps.

buying system The multiple voices in the organization that contribute to the consideration set and subsequent steps of the organizational buyer decision journey

For example, consider a hospital looking to buy a magnetic resonance imaging (MRI) machine. These large medical devices, typically used to assess tumors and other abnormalities, cost at least $150,000 and typically much more than that.[23] Numerous hospital personnel could inform the decision journey:

- The hospital's managing director might have the final say on the purchase.
- Radiologists and radiology technologists, who work closely with this equipment, will undoubtedly have opinions on which specific machines would make them more effective in their jobs.
- Meanwhile, the hospital's medical physicist is likely already aware of which machines on the market meet the hospital's radiation safety guidelines.

Thus, many individuals in the organization can influence the consideration set and subsequent steps. Additionally, the job titles of people involved in the purchase, and their roles in the purchase, can vary across different potential buyers for the same product. For example, at a different hospital, the organization's board of directors might directly make the final decision on the purchase. As a result, it is not only customer needs but also the nature of the purchase decision that varies across customers and segments.

Step 3: Active Evaluation

Information search and assessment of alternatives vary dramatically across organizational buying situations but tend to be quite a bit more involved than the corresponding activities in the consumer decision journey. Highly sophisticated buyers such as Amazon automate this step, conducting information searches using the firm's endless trove of data to learn which products sell well, and assessing alternatives with finely tuned algorithms before deciding which items to buy and keep in stock.[24] More typical buying systems involve one or more individuals manually researching alternative products/services and suppliers. Although organizational buyers traditionally relied on a supplier's salesperson as a major source of information, they increasingly turn to many of the same sources that consumers do, including online reviews, word of mouth, and social media.[25]

Assessment of alternatives is usually more formalized in organizational buying decisions. Compensatory assessments are prevalent and often quantified in the form of scorecards or other **multi-attribute models.** These models assign a numerical weight to each attribute based on how important that attribute is, then assign numerical ratings to score each alternative product or service on each attribute. Table 5.2 illustrates how a multi-attribute model can be used to assess alternatives—in this case, for a commercial property company choosing between potential cleaning service providers for a cluster of office buildings. As the table shows, the importance weights and rating scores are multiplied and summed to generate an overall score for each option.

multi-attribute model A model used to assess alternatives; with this model, an organizational buyer assigns a numerical weight to each attribute of the product/service based on how important that attribute is, and then assigns numerical ratings to score each alternative product/service on each attribute

In some organizations—especially institutions (e.g., hospitals and schools) and government agencies—the active evaluation step is even more rigid and formalized. In these settings, regardless of the organization's initial consideration set, a **request for proposals (RFP)** is issued. An RFP is a document, posted where all potential suppliers can see it (e.g., a public online database), detailing the exact nature of the organization's need, the minimum acceptable levels of various product or service attributes, and often the process by which a proposal will be chosen. For example, a government statistical agency could post an RFP seeking a new supplier of workstations for its headquarters. The RFP would, at a minimum, include such

request for proposals (RFP) A document, posted where all potential suppliers can see it (e.g., a public online database), detailing the exact nature of the organization's need, the minimum acceptable levels of various product or service attributes, and often the process by which a proposal will be chosen

Table 5.2 Multi-attribute Model for Buying B2B Services.

A multi-attribute model is a useful way to formalize and quantify an assessment of alternatives. This example pertains to a commercial property company's choice of cleaning service providers for office buildings.

Attribute	Importance	Option A: Quik Clean	Option B: MopRite	Option C: Spit Shiners
Price	**0.30**	9	2	6
Reputation	**0.30**	3	9	7
Experience level of staff	**0.15**	3	8	4
Quality of cleaning equipment	**0.15**	5	10	4
Scheduling flexibility	**0.10**	5	7	2
OVERALL SCORE (sum of option's [importance × rating] for each attribute)		5.3	**6.7**	5.3

details as the purpose of the workstations (conducting computationally intensive statistical analyses) and minimum specifications (processor speed and memory requirements for the workstations, as well as maintenance and replacement schedules). The agency's current supplier and competing suppliers could all submit proposals. The agency would then choose the lowest-priced proposal that meets or exceeds the required specifications. Each supplier is not meant to know who else is bidding or at what price; indeed, suppliers are expected to have minimal contact with buyers in RFP purchases.[26] Thus, an RFP acts as a "reverse auction," where suppliers silently aim to place the lowest bid without sacrificing profits while buyers hope to see each supplier's best price.

Step 4: Buying

As in the consumer decision journey, organizational buyers can be stymied at this step and forced to go back to the drawing board without finalizing a purchase. Perhaps a multi-attribute assessment of alternatives reveals that none of the options on the table score acceptably well, prompting a need to expand the consideration set. But the most straightforward way an organizational purchase can fail to materialize is through the RFP process. The RFP could receive no responses because the minimum specifications are unrealistic or prohibitively costly to deliver. Alternatively, the responses received could all be priced too high for the organization's budget. Nonetheless, a productive organizational buyer decision journey culminates in a purchase, triggering the all-important post-purchase step of the journey.

Step 5: Post-Purchase and the Loyalty Loop

Organizational buyers, like consumers, can proceed through the loyalty loop and experience accelerated repeat purchases. The steps in this loop, however, play out differently. Little evidence supports the existence of customer delight in organizational buying, suggesting that satisfaction alone, based on the product or service meeting organizational needs, kickstarts the loyalty loop.[27] Advocacy and word of mouth do occur, though, both within the organization (i.e., talking to other individuals in the buying system) and outside the organization.[28]

Attitudinal loyalty is also critical to fostering behavioral loyalty in the organizational buyer decision journey. Interpersonal relationships with supplier salespeople, as well as preferences for specific brands, influence attitudinal loyalty by enhancing **affective commitment**—that is, an emotional desire to continue purchasing from a given supplier.[29] Further, the increasing interconnectedness of buyers and suppliers over time, based on personal connections and sharing information, heightens attitudinal loyalty via **calculative commitment.**[30] This type of commitment reflects a desire to continue purchasing from a given supplier based on a cost-benefit analysis, including the potential costs of having to develop an equally deep relationship with a different supplier. Given the importance of close partnerships between firms in organizational buying, calculative commitment is a powerful driver of attitudinal loyalty that reinforces the loyalty loop.

affective commitment
An emotional desire to continue purchasing from a given supplier

calculative commitment
A desire to continue purchasing from a given supplier based on a cost-benefit analysis, including the potential costs of having to develop an equally deep relationship with a different supplier

OPPOSING VIEWS The Convergence of Organizational and Consumer Buying

Organizational buyers have traditionally been viewed as rational economic agents, maximizing value for stakeholders while remaining unclouded by personal biases or emotions. In recent years, this view has been challenged in light of the apparently converging behaviors of consumers and organizational buyers. Younger organizational buyers, in particular, perceive less of a wall between their personal and professional lives, and exhibit similar preferences in both spheres.[31] Buyers are increasingly recognized as having personal agendas and being driven, in part, by personal (including social and emotional) needs.[32] For example, buyers can approach the decision journey with the goal of improving their own reputation within the organization. Consideration sets in organizational purchases are also affected by individual brand preferences.[33] In smaller buying systems, these personal biases at the front-end of the journey can substantially affect purchasing outcomes. And later in the process, organizational buyers increasingly rely on the same sources they consult in their personal lives, such as social media and friends' opinions.[34]

Global

Do these personal influences contribute to a refreshing modernization of organizational buying? Do they interfere with accomplishing stakeholder objectives? Or perhaps a mixture of both? Imagine you are the manager of an outlet of a large electronics retail chain, selling products in categories such as smartphones, televisions, video games, audio equipment, and smart home technology. You have some authority over what products to carry in your store.

See the issue from two sides:

1. Craft an argument in favor of allowing your personal brand preferences, and sources such as social media and friends, to influence which products you buy and stock in the store.
2. Craft an argument in favor of relying *exclusively* on sales and marketing research data from your own store and corporate headquarters (e.g., sales trends, market forecasts) in forming the assortment of products your store carries.

CHAPTER CASE STUDY

US

ZOOMING IN THE TIME OF CORONAVIRUS

Zooming was ubiquitous by 2020, but the video conferencing service is surprisingly younger than many other high-technology brands. Founded in 2011, Zoom Video Communications, Inc. traces its ancestry to 1997 when Eric Yuan developed video conferencing service WebEx. Yuan stayed on after Cisco Systems acquired WebEx in 2007 for $3.2 billion but grew frustrated with Cisco's seeming inflexibility and lack of attention paid to the service. Yuan and numerous colleagues left Cisco in 2011 and founded Zoom.[35] The new firm aimed to create a simpler but more robust service, with capabilities and pricing that could scale to suit enterprises of all sizes. This approach particularly resonated with smaller tech-oriented organizations and, in the years that followed, Zoom experienced explosive growth—for example, 300 percent revenue expansion in 2017.[36] Although anyone can use Zoom, the firm collects virtually all of its revenue from organizations that purchase subscription plans to enable larger and longer meetings.

However, Zoom still struggled to gain traction with slower-moving organizations, such as large multinational corporations and governments. As of 2018, 64 percent of organizations with at least 500 employees used Skype for Business instead of Zoom.[37] Through inertia, history, and force of habit, these firms had established a loyalty loop with Skype. How could Zoom break this loop?

The pandemic begins. In 2020, the world turned upside down. The SARS-CoV-2 virus spread like wildfire in China's Hubei province beginning in December 2019, causing a potentially deadly

Source: Government of Japan/Wikimedia Commons

Zoom has exploded beyond its niche in the tech industry to become the de facto standard for businesses, virtual social gatherings, and even many government functions.

respiratory illness named COVID-19. Outbreaks in Italy, Spain, France, and the rest of the world soon followed. The virus not only had a tragic human cost but also plunged the world into a sudden and deep recession; major economies such as the United Kingdom shrank by 20 percent as businesses closed and individuals stayed home to slow the disease's spread.[38]

Tough times demanded resilience and flexibility from individuals and organizations. Entire organizations moved to remote operations, as WFH (work from home) became the new normal in many professions. This trend is expected to persist beyond the time of coronavirus, as approximately half of corporate employees expect to engage in at least partial WFH after the pandemic (versus 30 percent before).[39] This trend accelerated an ongoing trajectory in some sectors, such as high technology firms. But in others, such as primary and secondary education, it required a complete rethinking of how organizational objectives could be accomplished.[40] Schools' operational needs previously focused on creating an effective learning environment in physical classrooms on school property. The pandemic shifted these needs toward enabling a distributed and decentralized learning environment to foster academic progress in hundreds of students' homes—no small feat, given limited school budgets and inequality among students. Slow-moving government entities likewise faced a radical disruption in their operational needs. Nowhere was this truer than in parliamentary bodies, where physical presence and arcane procedural norms are based on long-standing historical precedents.[41] Even individual consumers, driven by social and emotional needs, sought new ways to connect, with virtual versions of parties and other social events rapidly evolving from a joke into a regular occurrence.[42]

Zoom's growth. Organizations' changing operational needs created a unique opportunity for video conferencing services. Zoom was especially well-suited to meet this opportunity. Its ease of use facilitated adoption by heavily disrupted sectors such as primary and secondary education, which were unaccustomed to virtual meetings, as well as by individual consumers looking for a convenient social tool. Meanwhile, its cost-effective scalability created an opening for Zoom to make inroads with larger organizations that faced a sudden need to drastically ramp up WFH operations. Organizations aiming to fulfill these altered operational needs adopted Zoom en masse. In a single month, March 2020, first-time installations of Zoom's mobile app increased *over 700 percent*.[43]

Despite the unparalleled success of Zoom during the pandemic, the service experienced notable growing pains. Eric Yuan himself conceded in March that such pains arose because he lacked "the foresight that, in a matter of weeks, every person in the world would suddenly be working, studying, and socializing from home."[44] The spring of 2020 was marked by numerous reports of security holes, such as a lack of encryption, meetings' video feeds being replaced with offensive content, and unknown individuals "Zoom-bombing" conferences. Zoom moved to address these issues, but not before facing a significant public relations backlash.[45] Still other problems persisted, such as operator error from an inexperienced userbase. UK Prime Minister Boris Johnson, for example, infamously live-tweeted a screenshot from an ongoing Zoom cabinet meeting, including sensitive details about the meeting and its participants.[46] And due to the bandwidth requirements of video conferencing, infrastructure limitations continue to impede Zoom's adoption in remote and rural areas. In the United States, at least 18 million individuals—many of these being small business operators or employees of larger organizations—lacked access to broadband internet service in 2020, creating challenges for both the WFH paradigm and Zoom's solution.[47] Although Zoom undoubtedly benefited from the unfortunate events of 2020, its path forward remains unclear. This ambiguity has gained force as more firms—including Zoom itself—require firms to return to the office, leading to an inevitable decline in the amount of video conferencing services that companies need.[48]

CASE QUESTIONS

1. Describe at least three needs that might initiate a decision journey ending with a consumer or organizational buyer choosing Zoom. Based on your knowledge of other communications platforms, how would the consideration sets diverge according to these three different needs?
2. A lack of user knowledge and infrastructure limitations remain stumbling blocks in the decision journey for many potential customers. In what step of the decision journey would these stumbling blocks become apparent to these consumers and organizational buyers? What strategies could Zoom enact to remove or mitigate these obstacles?
3. As the case illustrates, a radical external event realigned customer decision journeys with Zoom's existing strategy, leading to rapid growth in novel markets. Had the pandemic not occurred, what could Zoom have done to accelerate its growth in untapped segments? For example, in the absence of pandemic-induced remote learning, what could have led primary and secondary schools to adopt or increase their use of Zoom?

CHAPTER SUMMARY

Customers follow complex decision journeys to arrive at purchases, and these journeys differ greatly across customers. The most important distinction with respect to these journeys is between consumers and organizational buyers. Although both groups proceed through the same basic journey steps—need recognition, initial consideration, active evaluation, buying, and the loyalty loop—these steps can play out quite differently. This is because consumers and organizational buyers differ fundamentally in terms of their motivation for purchasing, their scale of purchasing, and their complexity of purchasing. As a result, consumer behavior and organizational buyer behavior are distinct domains that each merit attention. Consumer behavior is driven by personal needs, including functional, emotional, and social needs. Organizational buyer behavior, on the other hand, is driven by organizational needs, including derived and operational needs. Several other key distinctions separate the consumer and organizational buyer decision journeys, such as the importance of consumers' individual attachments to brands and the involvement of multiple individuals—the buying system—and formalized processes in significant organizational purchases. Marketers attempt to understand heterogeneity within consumer and organizational buyer decision journeys to craft more finely tailored strategies.

APPLICATION QUESTIONS

1. Think of a purchase you made in the last year that satisfied at least two of the following: a functional need, an emotional need, and a social need. How did the desire to satisfy multiple types of needs affect your decision journey?
2. Recall a purchase from the last year for which you did not spend much time considering alternatives but instead was just satisfactory. Why did you do so?
3. Think of a purchase you made in the last year when you evaluated alternatives using either a compensatory or a non-compensatory assessment. Explain why you took this approach.
4. Think of your favorite retailer. Name both a derived need and an operational need that the retailer has.
5. Do you believe that you are in the loyalty loop with respect to any repeat purchases you have been making? Looking back, how/why do you think you entered this loyalty loop?
6. Imagine that you are a salesperson selling major soft drink brands to a regional supermarket chain. Estimate how many individuals might influence the supermarket chain's choice of which soft drinks to buy and stock across its locations. How does the involvement of a buying system of this size affect your job as a salesperson?
7. Can you think of a time that you expanded your consideration set after searching for information? Did you end up buying one of the options that was added to your set? Why or why not?

Visit the companion website, **https://bloomsbury.pub/palmatier-marketing**, or **https://samsinstitute.com**, for additional learning and teaching tools, including professional videos outlining the Four Principles, PowerPoint tutorials with voice-over commentary, sample syllabi for marketing courses, testbank and more.

Chapter 6

MARKETING FOR GLOBAL AND CROSS-CULTURAL DIFFERENCES

CHAPTER OVERVIEW

Chapter 6 looks at the problem of Marketing Principle #1 (all customers differ → managing customer differences) through a global lens. It explains how globalization has historically created more differences for marketers to manage and will continue to do so. It then outlines the distinct strategies that marketers can use to enter global markets. Finally, it introduces a cultural framework for managing customer differences across different country markets. The chapter will proceed by answering the following questions:

- Why is globalization important and how has it influenced customer differences across history?
- What are the different strategies companies can use to enter global markets?
- How can companies successfully navigate different cultures and preferences when entering new country markets?

In the chapter's cases and features, you will hear about products and services that have successfully, or unsuccessfully, managed Marketing Principle #1 while expanding their cultural reach. These include:

- Backlash against skin products designed to make skin less dark (Marketing Fail).
- E-commerce giant Alibaba's dramatic entry into the US market (Chapter Case).
- Ethical and moral dilemmas in managing global customer differences, such as dubious sustainability claims by fashion brands such as H&M (Shades of Gray) and the globalization of cultures (Opposing Views).

LEARNING OBJECTIVES

- Identify the factors that have contributed to a globalized world.
- Recognize key terms and concepts in global marketing.
- Evaluate moral and ethical considerations in global marketing, with attention to their historical and cultural context.
- Compare various marketing strategies for managing global and cultural differences.

IMAGINE Expanding Your Business Abroad

Imagine that you own a small business in Australia selling women's hair accessories (jeweled barrettes, fashion clips, graphic headbands, vintage ribbons, etc.) via an online shop. In addition to your own website, you have an online storefront on Gumtree Australia, an e-commerce platform that is especially popular for handmade and niche apparel. You noticed over the last year that, despite continuing to introduce new styles, your business' growth has stalled. You are beginning to wonder if you are saturating the Australian market for your admittedly niche product.

Therefore, you decide that you will try to start selling products outside of Australia. You are already selling online and shipping products out—how hard can international expansion be? You settle on Malaysia, Indonesia, and the Philippines as potential expansion targets, due to their size and relative proximity to Australia:

- The Philippines seems promising, and the Gumtree platform operates there, which should make your expansion easier. But as you begin to explore the other two possibilities, you run into some issues.
- First, Gumtree does not have a dedicated platform for Indonesia or Malaysia. Unless you want to create yet another storefront on another platform, you would have to count on getting shoppers from these countries to visit the Australian Gumtree site.
- Second, you realize that a large percentage of women in Indonesia and Malaysia wear head coverings such as hijabs when in public. Who will buy your hair accessories? Is there any way you can still sell your products in these countries?

As much as you hate the idea of completely ignoring these two large, alternative markets, you do not see an easy path forward.

Critical thinking:

1. Can you think of any way to tap into the Indonesian and Malaysian markets in this scenario? Feel free to get creative in devising a solution.
2. Assume that you identify a significant number of consumers in Indonesia and Malaysia who might buy your products. How would you overcome the practical challenge of entering these markets, considering that the Gumtree platform does not operate there? Specifically: (1) How would you make it possible for these consumers to order your products? (2) How would you ensure that these consumers were aware of your products?
3. Although expanding into the Philippines seems promising on the surface, international expansion is seldom easy. Think of at least one challenge you might encounter entering this market and explain how you would address it.

GLOBALIZATION AND ITS IMPORTANCE FOR MARKETERS

As you are reading this, you might be sitting on a chair made in Mexico or a desk from Malaysia. Perhaps you are also looking at a laptop with an LCD display made in Vietnam and assembled in Singapore. Or you could be taking notes on paper from Canada. And when you opened your favorite news app this morning, perhaps you saw top stories from Russia, India, the United States, and France.

These everyday experiences illustrate the irreversible interconnectedness of a world that has undergone intense globalization. **Globalization,** defined as "the process by which the whole world becomes a single market," has complex implications for everything from finance to politics, to religion, to culture.[1] Marketing is no exception. Swiss conglomerate Nestlé S.A., the world's largest food and beverage company, provides a dramatic example of the complexity of

globalization The world's movement over time toward a single global market

marketing efforts in multinational firms. Nestlé sells over 2,000 brands across 187 countries, managed across three divisions: the Americas; Asia, Oceania, and sub-Saharan Africa; and Europe, the Middle East, and North Africa.[2]

home market A firm's native base of operations

existing country markets Nations where a firm already operates

new country market A nation where a firm does not yet operate but potentially could

This structure is typical for a large multinational corporation. Nestlé's Europe, Middle East, and North Africa division includes its **home market,** its native base of operations in Switzerland. This home market is one of Nestlé's many **existing country markets**—nations where it already operates—such as France, Brazil, and Japan. As Nestlé's worldwide expansion shows, it routinely considers **new country markets,** or nations where the firm does not yet operate but potentially could. Nestlé's marketers must strategically manage the company's portfolio of brands across home and other country markets, deciding which brands will be profitable to sell in each country. Although the company frequently introduces its brands to new country markets, it also occasionally exits existing country markets; in 2019, the firm sold products in *fewer* countries than it did in 2014.[3] At other times, Nestlé expands its presence in existing country markets, investing in additional factories or selling its products in additional cities; for example, in 2020, the company announced a $700 million investment to upgrade its existing manufacturing plants in Mexico.[4]

Although Nestlé is a classic example of the challenges of global marketing, the conglomerate's extreme scale and complicated multinational structure belie an important implication of globalization: even small firms can be global. It is common for small businesses that sell through e-commerce platforms such as eBay, the Amazon Marketplace, or Alibaba to accept orders from all over the world; this is the premise of the chapter's opening example featuring Gumtree.

Source: Austin Distel/Unsplash

Lunya uses an aggressive digital advertising campaign to gain online customers in both its home market (the United States) and new country markets. Campaigns like these can reach consumers across multiple devices and applications.

Even without the aid of these platforms, an international presence is possible thanks to digital advertising, trusted payment processing services such as PayPal, and lower cost international shipping. Consider, for example, boutique sleepwear brand Lunya. Founded in 2014 in Santa Monica, California by entrepreneur Ashley Merrill, the company sells products almost exclusively via its website.[5] Lunya leveraged an aggressive advertising campaign, featuring the tagline "sleepwear for the modern woman" along with quotes from glowing customer reviews, across a broad range of websites and social media to promote its brand first in its home market and then abroad.[6] As a result, the brand expanded sales to Canada, the United Kingdom, the Netherlands, Italy, France, Germany, Spain, and Ireland in a relatively short period of time. Yet the company later faced financial difficulties, suggesting that managing this rapid growth across diverse markets was a challenge.

IN OTHER WORDS ...

Firms begin in their home market and often later enter new country markets. Over time, they can then expand into additional new country markets, build up their presence in existing country markets, or reduce their investment in existing country markets.

The Evolution of Globalization

Lunya's story is typical of fast-growing brands in today's globalized world. Now, it is common for "born global," international new ventures to launch initially into multiple country markets simultaneously. As a result, modern marketers must often wrestle with cross-country differences from a company's inception.[7]

To understand how this world came to be, it is worth stepping back into history to see how nations' economies became increasingly intertwined. Understanding this history is also critical to approaching global marketing with tact and sensitivity (see Marketing Fail in this chapter). The evolution of globalization can be divided into the four periods discussed in this section: pre-globalization (1st century BCE—*c.* 1800 CE), Globalization 1.0 (*c.* 1800–1945), Globalization 2.0 (1945–95), and Globalization 3.0 (1995–present).[8] As will be shown, these periods saw globalization emerge and then grow as a result of two interdependent trends (Figure 6.1):[9]

- The **expansion of international markets** refers to the growing scale of trade between countries—for example, the United States buying more semiconductors from Taiwan.
- The **integration of international markets,** on the other hand, is the removal of barriers to trade. Integration means that trade between nations becomes more like trade *within* nations, as unified trading rules and low-cost transportation make selling products in other countries easier—for example, a new trade agreement between the United States and Malaysia could reduce taxes on imports and exports between the two countries.

expansion of international markets The growing scale of trade between countries

integration of international markets The removal of barriers to trade between countries

Figure 6.1 Evolution of Globalization.

The history of the world's movement toward a global market can be roughly divided into four eras, each with greater expansion and integration of international markets than the preceding era.

Pre-globalization: 1st century BCE*–c. 1800* CE

The pre-globalized era can be divided into two broad phases:

early trade The sporadic, segmented formalized trade from the ancient world through circa 1400 CE

- **Early trade** describes the segmented, sporadic existence of formalized trade from the ancient world through roughly 1400 CE. International trade was not uncommon even for ancient empires such as those of Rome and China. The most well-known example of early trade is the Silk Road. This is the modern name for a loosely connected network of ancient trade routes from Xi'an in China, all the way to the Mediterranean and to the Black Sea.[10,11] Parts of the route were even protected by Han dynasty soldiers, a clear indication that the value of trade was recognized.[12] It is vital to understand, though, that the presence of international trade did not mean the world was globalized. Integration was practically nonexistent. Trade barriers made the average merchant wary of selling their goods abroad. These barriers included steep **tariffs** (taxes on imports), difficulty communicating with potential buyers in foreign markets, and treacherous trade routes over both land and sea.

tariffs Taxes imposed by a nation on imports

Age of Exploration A period from roughly 1400 to 1800 characterized by naval innovation, aggressive imperialism, and expanded trade

- The **Age of Exploration,** from roughly 1400 to 1800, saw the growth of European empires such as Spain and Britain, and witnessed rapid scientific advancements that improved navigation and shipbuilding.[13] These innovations enabled European empires to aggressively expand into new lands. The hallmark of this era of globalization was a robust international trade system built on the exploitation of the people and natural resources of indigenous societies, mostly in the Americas, Africa, and Southeast Asia.[14] Thus, although improved naval technologies reduced barriers to trade, integration was limited. For example, when Spaniards colonized Mexico in the 1500s, this market and its resources were forcibly integrated into the Spanish empire's market. There was no trade deal, but rather an exploitative arrangement benefiting the colonial power. European empires each formed separate, integrated markets, while extensive barriers to trade between empires (e.g., high tariffs) persisted.[15]

Source: The Chinese town, West Point, Hong Kong. Photograph by W.P. Floyd, c. 1873. Wellcome Collection. Public Domain.

This photograph of a port in Hong Kong was taken in 1873. Although the Industrial Revolution was well underway, industrialization was uneven and slow to reach most of the world.

Globalization 1.0: c. 1800–1945

The first true driving force toward a single global market was spurred by the **Industrial Revolution:** the age of steamships and railroads, telegraph and textile mills, and the most dramatic transformation of manufacturing technology in human history. The United Kingdom was a major driver of manufacturing and international trade for much of this era; from 1809 to 1849, British exports grew almost 400 percent.[16] Soon, the innovations of the Industrial Revolution spread throughout much of the world, drastically increasing businesses' capacity to harvest raw materials and manufacture products while improving transportation and communication.

Industrial Revolution A period of unprecedented global innovation beginning roughly in 1800, best known for the popularization of railroads and factories

The exploitative, colonial trade of the Age of Exploration persisted and even grew throughout Globalization 1.0. France acquired most of its North African colonies in these years, and the British Empire reached its apex.[17] The fact that the Industrial Revolution occurred during a period of such imbalance between colonial powers and the rest of the world had far-reaching consequences that reverberate to this day.

Industrialization was uneven; areas of the world with smaller populations of westerners experienced a comparatively smaller infusion of industrial infrastructure such as factories and railroads.[18] As a result, this era greatly contributed to the partition between the **Global North**—nations that benefited from early industrialization, also known as the developed world—and the

Global North Nations that benefited from early industrialization, also known as the developed world

Global South Nations that did not benefit from early industrialization, also known as the developing world

Global South—nations without this benefit, also known as the developing world. The terms Global South and Global North do not strictly refer to latitude (Australia, for example, is considered part of the Global North), but most nations in the Global South happen to have territory in the southern hemisphere.[19]

Globalization 1.0 The shift toward more integrated markets from 1800 to 1945, characterized by a growing number of significant trade agreements

Despite this imbalance, industrialization contributed to what can be called **Globalization 1.0,** an early shift toward the unification of markets. The massive upscaling of production meant that a lot more goods were entering the global economy, leading to an expansion of international trade. This expansion, in turn, created a strong incentive for nations to forge trade agreements; the value to be gained from easing tariffs and other barriers soared. For example, the Treaty of Wanghia in 1845 formalized trade relations and reduced tariffs between the United States and the Qing dynasty's Chinese Empire.[20] Meanwhile, in the scattered German states of central Europe, the 1833 Zollverein treaties created the first customs union. This completely removed barriers to trade between the member states and effectively formed a single market.[21] Thus, the integration of international trade, and movement in the direction of a unified global market, had begun.

Globalization 2.0: 1945–95

The world wars of the first half of the twentieth century slowed and reversed the progress of imperial expansion, while leaving in their wake a strong desire for peace, prosperity, and trade. Against this backdrop, members of the newly formed United Nations sought a comprehensive trade pact that would establish consistent, lower tariffs for trade between all countries in the pact.[22] Eventually, in 1948, twenty-three nations—including the United States, the United Kingdom, China, India, and Brazil—agreed on a set of rules called GATT: the General Agreement on Tariffs and Trade. So began **Globalization 2.0,** a period from 1945 to 1995 featuring the first true single market covering a significant portion of the globe. The GATT pact, with 45,000 specific provisions, reduced tariffs from an average of 40 percent to 22 percent on $10 billion of international trade (roughly $100 billion adjusted for inflation).[23] Dozens of additional countries joined the agreement in the ensuing decades, eventually accounting for over 75 percent of global trade.[24]

Globalization 2.0 The period of world trade from 1945 to 1995 governed by the rules of the General Agreement on Tariffs and Trade (GATT)

GATT was a dramatic step forward for the expansion and integration of markets. The decades following its signing saw 8 percent average annual growth for its member nations' economies, and average tariffs declined to just 5 percent by 1995.[25] However, several factors hampered its success:

- First, much of the Global South suffered from its colonial legacy, with a lack of industrial infrastructure in these nations inhibiting growth and expansion of trade. India, for example, had experienced *deindustrialization* in some sectors under British rule.[26]
- Second, poor diplomatic relations between the Soviet Union and much of the rest of the world naturally limited the integration of trade between these nations.
- Finally, the GATT was not as comprehensive as it could have been; agriculture and textiles were excluded entirely, and many nations in the Global South were permitted to join on a partial basis—leaving higher tariffs in place for many of these countries' goods.[27]

Globalization 3.0: 1995–Present

Globalization 3.0, today's interconnected world economy, arose from three major events in the closing years of the twentieth century:

Globalization 3.0 The period of world trade from 1995 onward governed by the rules of the World Trade Organization (WTO)

- First, the World Trade Organization (WTO), a successor to the GATT with more comprehensive rules lowering tariffs for 123 nations, was born, further integrating world markets in both the Global South and North.[28]
- Second, the Soviet Union fell and its successor countries (e.g., Russia) adopted capitalist systems, while China significantly opened its economy to foreign businesses, expanding international trade.
- Third, the internet, invented decades earlier, saw its popularity accelerate with rising personal computer ownership and web browsers such as NetScape; by 1995, 10 percent of the world's population used the internet.[29] The internet made it easier than ever before for companies to sell products in foreign markets, as well as for customers to find products from outside their home countries. Today, consumers can easily browse an e-commerce site such as Amazon or AliExpress and order products from countries around the world in minutes. This factor has particularly enabled "born global" companies, discussed earlier, to quickly launch operations in multiple country markets.

These events have created new dynamics in the world economy. The **BRIC** countries (Brazil, Russia, India, and China) as well as nations in the Middle East and North Africa (**MENA**) experienced rapid economic growth in this period, attracting the attention of investors and multinational companies. Starbucks, for example, opened its first stores in Brazil and Egypt in 2006.[30] It is worth noting that countries beyond BRIC and MENA, such as Indonesia and Mexico, have similarly benefited from this shifting dynamic and continue to attract foreign businesses. More than any prior era, Globalization 3.0 has created extremely compelling incentives for companies to seek out new country markets. Thus, the challenge of addressing customer differences now takes on a global dimension.

BRIC Brazil, Russia, India, and China

MENA The Middle East and North Africa

MARKETING FAIL Backlash against "Fairness Creams" in India

The colonial history of early globalization has echoes today, and nowhere is this clearer than in the case of "fairness creams" (products that make the skin lighter). Although these products are popular in many countries, they have received a great deal of attention recently in India. As of 2013, the country consumed 233 tons of skin-lightening cosmetics annually.[31] The demand for these products serves a cultural norm that views lighter skin as more attractive and darker skin as less desirable. Social scientists and popular narratives attribute this norm directly to the nation's colonial heritage, harkening back to a time when having lighter skin was associated with wealth and status.[32,33] Sales of skin-lightening products in India have surged in the last fifty years and are believed to account for more than one-third of profits in the country's cosmetics industry.[34] Although domestic brands have had some success, a large share of skin-lightening products in India are sold by US-based and European cosmetics brands: Fair & Lovely by Unilever, White Light by Estée Lauder,

India

Source: Collection of the Smithsonian National Museum of African American History and Culture, c. 1930.

A print advertisement from the 1930s advertises cream for "lighter looking skin." These creams have enjoyed popularity among some consumers in Southeast Asia, creating complex problems and, more recently, backlash for global skincare brands.

Active White Line by Clinique, Blanc Cristal by Lancôme, and White Perfect by L'Oréal.[35]

The world is more interconnected, brands are more visible, and information spreads more rapidly via social media. As a result, the popularity of skin lightening cosmetics—specifically, the involvement of Western companies and individuals in helping to perpetuate their popularity—has come under fire. British actress Emma Watson, for example, was heavily criticized for being the face of Lancôme's Blanc Expert advertisements in Southeast Asia from 2011 to 2013.[36] Matters came to a head in 2020, when global protests drew even greater scrutiny to global brands' handling of race-related issues, and a storm of negative social media comments descended on the brands involved in this market. Unilever, for example, was called out for consistently portraying light-skinned women as confident, but darker-skinned women as insecure, in its advertisements. In response, it changed the name of Fair & Lovely to Glow & Lovely to de-emphasize whiteness (although the product itself remained unchanged). Neutrogena, on the other hand, discontinued its skin-lightening products in India entirely.[37] Yet some consumers argued that these actions did not undo the damage that had already been done, such as perpetuating unfair beauty standards and indirectly motivating consumers to try alternative skin-lightening products—some of which contain mercury.[38] Clearly, global cosmetics brands face a complex path forward in India, and this issue still does not have a clear resolution.

Diagnose the problem:

1. Explain precisely why the involvement of Western brands in promoting skin-lightening products in India began to provoke pushback from consumers. Be sure to reference the relevant historical context surrounding this backlash.
2. Unilever's response, simply changing the name of Fair & Lovely, did little to appease upset consumers. Aside from simply pulling the product line from the market, as Neutrogena did, what other options did Unilever have? In your opinion, what was the morally right thing for Unilever to do?

ENTERING NEW COUNTRY MARKETS

Rapid globalization has firms large and small scrambling to evaluate potential new country markets. Developing a marketing strategy for new country markets can be broken down into three distinct issues: deciding *whether* to enter a market, deciding *how* to enter a market, and creating value *after* entering the market.

Whether to Enter New Country Markets

No single company operates in every country in the world. This is, of course, in part because it is virtually impossible to do so. Sanctions against North Korea, for example, make doing business there illegal for a large portion of the world's largest firms.[39] But many large firms simply choose not to expand, or to limit their expansion. Of the *Fortune* 500 largest US firms, over 30 percent have *zero* locations outside the United States, and a further 25 percent have twenty-five or fewer international locations.[40] Perhaps some of these firms are laggards and should accelerate their global expansion. But nonetheless, there are valid reasons for staying put. Entering a new country market requires that the company can answer "yes" to the **three questions for entering new country markets:**

three questions for entering new country markets (1) Can you supply it? (2) Can they buy it? (3) Can we make a profit?

1. Can you supply it?
2. Can they buy it?
3. Can we make a profit?

Question 1: Structural Factors—Can You Supply It?

The first question pertains to whether a company can feasibly provide its goods and/or services in the country—both at the time when the company first enters the market and on a reliable, consistent basis thereafter. The answer to this question is typically driven by high-level structural factors. The nation's government as well as international law, such as the sanctions against North Korea, can obviously create a barrier to supplying products. Political instability and civil unrest are also a threat to providing a reliable supply; if the current regime is toppled, for example, the next leader could ban imports of certain products or from certain nations.

Additionally, the market's distribution infrastructure can pose hurdles. Physical infrastructure, such as highways, railroads, telephone lines, and internet access are necessary to cost-effectively transport goods and communicate with customers. Channel infrastructure—the presence of wholesalers or distributors with existing customer relationships—is also critical.[41] Consider, for example, a kitchen appliance manufacturer wanting to expand to a country without a significant national distributor, or even a big box retailer, for such appliances. Expansion would then require establishing and maintaining relationships with countless local shops that carry limited inventory, which could make it too expensive to keep products on store shelves.

Question 2: Financial Factors—Can They Buy It?

Even if products make it onto the shelves, other factors can create barriers to customers actually buying. The second question, therefore, pertains to whether potential customers in the country possess both the money and freedom to buy. As with the first question, a company should consider both the current situation and the country's trajectory.

Numerous economic indicators have been linked to potential customers' ability to buy. The size of the market (e.g., gross domestic product), national income levels and standards of living, the availability of loans and credit lines from banks, and the economy's growth rate all contribute to purchasing power.[42] Notably, customers' ability to buy is also influenced by structural and legal factors to some extent. This is because economic freedom varies across nations; rampant corruption, the threat of inflation due to economic mismanagement, and poorly protected property rights all diminish economic freedom and reduce spending by households and businesses.[43]

Question 3: Cultural and Competitive Factors—Can We Make a Profit?

It goes without saying that "My customers are able to buy my products" is not a sufficient condition for a business to succeed, at home or abroad. Entering a country market often thrusts the new entrant into a fierce rivalry with other domestic and international competitors. As an **insurgent** competitor, meaning one that is new to the market, the firm has a natural disadvantage to **incumbents**—the existing competitors. This chapter's case illustrates this challenge in the context of China's Alibaba opening its business-to-business marketplace to US-based sellers and challenging the incumbent Amazon Business platform.

insurgent The quality of being a new, unestablished competitor in a market

incumbent The quality of being an established competitor with existing market share

The level of competitive intensity in the market will determine how much resistance the company can expect to encounter when trying to acquire customers from incumbents.[44] The famous Porter's **Five Forces** model explains how this competitive intensity reduces the potential profit a firm can achieve, as prices fall and customers are more costly to win over. Other relevant forces that could lead to lower profit include the potential for new entrants (since this will increase competition), powerful suppliers and powerful customers (as both could bully the firm in price negotiations, cutting into margins), and the threat of substitute products (since these could reduce overall demand).[45]

Five Forces The forces of competitive rivalry, potential for new entrants, powerful suppliers, powerful customers, and the threat of substitute products, which each threaten a market's profits

The new country market's culture also affects potential profits to be earned. If certain dimensions of the culture make the firm's product less appealing, the firm can clearly expect to earn less sales and profit unless it forms a strategy that accounts for this shortcoming. The dimensions of culture, and the steps the firm can take to enhance profit while managing cultural differences, are discussed in detail in the section "Creating Value in the Face of Global Customer Differences."

IN OTHER WORDS ...

The first two questions for entering new country markets, "Can you supply it?" and "Can they buy it?" address whether the expansion is feasible at all. If the answer to either question is no, the expansion should not even be considered. The third question, "Can we make a profit?" involves a deeper analysis of the competitive and cultural environment, and the answer depends in part on the firm's own choices and strategy in the new market.

How to Enter New Country Markets

After deciding to enter a market, the next question is *how* to enter. A new entrant firm must make two choices: where will operations (e.g., manufacturing or distribution centers) be located, and who will own them?[46] Operations can be located in the new country or an existing country market. Setting up operations in the new country market is costlier and riskier but provides more control over how the products are distributed in that market.

Ownership can take on three flavors: owned by the new entrant firm, owned jointly with a domestic firm, or owned by a domestic firm that enters a contract with the new entrant firm. As with location, ownership involves a trade-off of risk and control; the new entrant solely owning operations allows total control but can be extremely risky. If, for example, the business does not take off in the new market, or the business is seized by the government during political turmoil, the loss is borne entirely by the new entrant firm.

There are four common modes of entry into a new country market, each representing a different combination of location and ownership of operations: (1) exporting, (2) licensing, (3) international joint venture, and (4) direct investment (Table 6.1).[47] The simplest and least risky is **exporting.** This involves operations in an existing country market and ownership by the new entrant firm; it is simply using existing operations to ship products to a new country. In the chapter's opening example, the hair accessory business was considering export-based market entry.

exporting Using existing operations to ship products to a new country

Table 6.1 Entering New Country Markets.

There are four primary ways to enter a new country market, reflecting combinations of where operations are located and who owns the operations.

Market entry	Definition	Where are operations located?	Who owns the operation?
Exporting	Using existing operations to ship products to a new country	Home market	New entrant firm
Licensing	An arrangement in which a domestic partner owns the facilities in the new country market and operates them through a contract with the new entrant firm	New country market	Domestic market (i.e., new market) firm that has a contract with the new entrant firm
International joint venture	An arrangement in which the new entrant and a domestic partner both invest capital in setting up operations in the new country market	New country market	Shared between new entrant and domestic market firm
Direct investment	The new market entrant paying the entire cost and fully owning operations in the new country market; can be greenfield (built from scratch) or acquired	New country market	New entrant firm

licensing An arrangement in which a domestic partner owns the facilities in the new country market, and operates them through a contract with the new entrant firm

international joint venture An arrangement in which the new entrant and a domestic partner both invest capital in setting up operations in the new country market

direct investment The new market entrant paying the entire cost and fully owning operations in the new country market

greenfield investment A type of direct investment; the new market entrant builds the business in the new market from scratch, rather than buying an existing operation

Other modes of entry involve operations in the new country market:

- **Licensing** entails facilities that are owned by a domestic partner (i.e., a partner from the new country market) and operated through a formal contract where the new entrant firm collects a portion of earnings. Franchising is the most well-known version of this arrangement. For example, in 2009 US-based fast-food chain KFC entered the Nigerian market through franchised stores owned and operated by Devyani International Nigeria Ltd.[48]
- An entrant wanting more control than licensing allows, and willing to take on more risk, can instead consider an **international joint venture:** a commercial arrangement in which the new entrant and a domestic partner both invest capital in setting up operations in the new country market. This approach has historically been extremely popular with large firms setting up operations in China. BMW, for example, partnered with Brilliance China Automotive Holdings in 2003 to create a joint venture called BMW Brilliance Automotive for the purpose of selling BMW cars in the Chinese market.[49]
- The last and riskiest method of market entry is **direct investment.** This involves the new market entrant footing the entire bill and fully owning operations in the new country market. This ownership can occur through a simple acquisition of existing operations—for example, buying manufacturing facilities from a competitor in the new market. It can also occur through **greenfield investment,** meaning the business is built up from scratch in the new market; this gives the new entrant significantly more control in shaping how the business is run, but comes with a greater start-up cost.

The choice of entry strategy is directly tied to the three questions for entering new markets. The more the answers to the three questions imply a risk of losing money, the greater caution the firm should exercise in considering direct investment or other costly entry modes. It should be noted that a firm need not pick just one entry strategy. It can hedge its bets with a hybrid entry approach, choosing a different level of risk for different portions of the business.[50] For example, Apple can directly invest in a new country market by opening a company-owned and company-operated retail store there, but it has no need to build local manufacturing facilities; it can retain an exporting model for production of phones for the new market.

CREATING VALUE WHEN CUSTOMER DIFFERENCES ARE GLOBAL

After entering a new market, the firm must try to profitably create value for its target segment(s) following the principles established in Chapter 4. But doing so in a global context raises an additional challenge: cross-cultural differences. When assessing the impact of culture in country market opportunities, it is tempting to simplify and generalize. "Filipinos tend to be highly self-conscious, so they will not buy garish clothing," one might claim. But global consumers are people, with all the complexity that entails. Each person in the Philippines is an individual, with her own personality and set of preferences that are not determined merely

? SHADES OF GRAY "Sustainable" Claims in the Apparel Industry

Consumers increasingly care about the sustainability of the brands they purchase. Although definitions vary, **sustainable business practices** are widely viewed as broader than environmental concerns and may also include holistic strategies that consider impacts on communities, treatment of employees, product safety, and diversity.[51] Consumers are concerned not only with the business practices of brands themselves but also about sustainability all the way up the brands' supply chains, often to nations in the Global South supplying raw materials. Thus, **sustainable sourcing**—choosing suppliers with sustainable business practices—is increasingly emphasized, especially at large firms.[52]

Brands in the apparel industry have gone to great lengths to tout their sustainable business practices and sustainable sourcing:

- H&M launched its "Conscious Collection" in 2010, claiming it was made with "sustainable materials."
- Meanwhile, Zara proclaimed that its clothing lines would focus on using "more sustainable" materials.

But neither brand actually clarified how exactly the cotton and polyester used in these clothing lines were any more sustainable than before.[53] Brands such as H&M and Zara are not unique; the apparel industry has a history of taking advantage of the fact that most consumers do not agree on what exactly it means to be an ethical or sustainable product. Under the cover of this ambiguity, it is hard to say that sustainability claims are outright lies. Still, these fast-fashion brands are increasingly accused of failing to engage in sustainable sourcing—relying on laborers in the Global South earning less than a living wage—while "greenwashing" their sustainability records to boost their images.[54] As consumers become increasingly knowledgeable about brands' global supply chains, this behavior could backfire. Therefore, companies will need to be increasingly mindful of whether their sustainability claims are credible—and the extent to which their customers care about this.

Sweden

Spain

Identify the ethical dilemmas:

1. Who is harmed by apparel brands' "greenwashing" (artificial or exaggerated sustainability claims)? How are they harmed?
2. Given the low-price business model of fast-fashion brands such as H&M, how should they balance sustainability concerns with maintaining low costs in the supply chain? Put another way, how can fast-fashion and sustainable sourcing be reconciled?

by her nationality. Like all consumers, she has preferences that are influenced by the five sources of customer differences from Chapter 4: her individual traits, life experiences, self-concept, functional needs, and influences from marketers. The preferences of some consumers in this country, in fact, might mirror those of a group of consumers in another country with a starkly different culture. This leads to the idea of **strategically equivalent segments**: customers in different parts of the world that nonetheless respond similarly to specific product features and other marketing mix elements.[55]

Individuals, though, grow up in societies with well-established norms. Societies have evolved these norms to produce specific end-states (a peaceful life, economic growth, safety and security, etc.). These norms typically take the form of values: "desirable goals, varying in importance, that serve as guiding principles

sustainable business practices A business's holistic strategies that consider impacts on the environment, communities, treatment of employees, product safety, and diversity

sustainable sourcing The business practice of choosing suppliers that practice sustainable business practices

strategically equivalent segments Customers in different parts of the world that nonetheless respond similarly to marketing mix elements

in people's lives."[56] These values are important to understand because they can affect sources of customer differences, such as life experiences and self-concept. For example, if a girl grows up in a culture that values upholding family unity, she might have more life experiences with extended family members such as cousins and grandparents, potentially affecting her preferences as an adult.

There are several theories to describe differences in values between cultures. One of the most relevant theories is **Schwartz's cultural framework**. This theory argues that each individual has his or her own values, and cultural values are defined as the overall (or average) values of a group.[57] This focus on individuals allows Schwartz's framework to adapt to the modern era; as an increasing number of consumers identify with two or more cultures, the framework allows these multicultural influences to shape the overall culture of a nation without ignoring the underlying diversity.[58] By building the theory on individual-level differences, Schwartz also aligns with Marketing Principle #1 and supports the notion that all customers differ—both across and within cultures.

The theory relies on three underlying cultural dimensions, depicted in Figure 6.2:

1. embeddedness–autonomy;
2. hierarchy–egalitarianism; and
3. mastery–harmony.

embeddedness–autonomy One of Schwartz's cultural dimensions; an individual on the embeddedness end of the spectrum values reliance on tradition and the established social order; someone at the autonomy end believes that satisfying curiosity and seeking excitement in life are more worthwhile

Dimension 1: Embeddedness–Autonomy

Schwartz's framework defines three dimensions of values, each representing opposite ends of a spectrum.[59] The first is **embeddedness–autonomy.** An individual on the embeddedness end of the spectrum values reliance on tradition

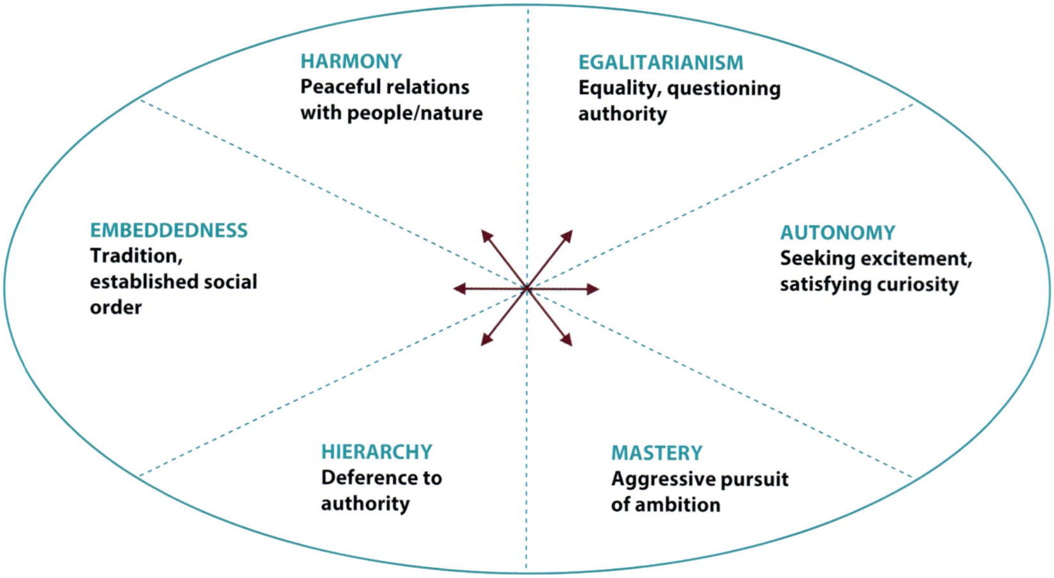

Figure 6.2 Schwartz's Cultural Framework.

Schwarz's cultural framework proposes three dimensions, each with two poles.

and the established social order; they view themselves as embedded within these norms. Conversely, someone at the autonomy end of the spectrum believes that satisfying curiosity and seeking excitement in life, even if they defy tradition, are worthwhile. Consider a family with two daughters. The elder daughter, Sofia, feels an obligation to go to law school because her father's law practice has been in the family for three generations. The younger daughter, Anastasia, has no interest in the family's traditions and intends to pursue her dream of being an artist—much to the chagrin of her father, who wonders how she will make money. In this example, Sofia clearly values embeddedness, while Anastasia values autonomy.

The values of a nation's individuals collectively define its national culture. For example, Oman, a country on the Arabian Peninsula, has a relatively high cultural emphasis on embeddedness, rather than autonomy.[60] Although individuals vary greatly, *on average*, people in Oman care a great deal about the established social order and its traditions. In Oman, this social order is closely tied to the country's Muslim faith and socially conservative traditions, such as limiting consumption of alcohol. Imagine how the owner of a major hotel chain might view the Omani market through a cultural lens. Perhaps the chain should re-evaluate the minibar offering in the rooms and examine whether the on-site restaurant's menu should be altered. Even the hotel's décor and regional web advertisements might be altered to better suit more conservative local tastes. These are all examples of **adaptation**—altering elements of the marketing mix to satisfy customer needs and create value in a new country market. Alternatively, the hotel owner might note that, cultural differences notwithstanding, Oman has many business travelers and tourists with very similar preferences to the chain's guests in other countries. In other words, the hotel could identify a strategically equivalent segment in Oman instead of adapting the marketing mix.

adaptation Altering elements of the marketing mix to satisfy customer needs and create value in a new country market

Dimension 2: Hierarchy–Egalitarianism

The second dimension is **hierarchy–egalitarianism.** Hierarchy indicates a great deal of importance placed on deferring to authority and remaining humble toward perceived social betters. Egalitarianism is the opposite end, and reflects a belief in equality, social justice, and openly questioning authority figures. Imagine, for example, college roommates Marco and Jacob who attend some of the same classes. Jacob makes a point of calling professors "Sir," "Ma'am," or their full titles; Marco makes up nicknames for them. When Jacob performs poorly on a test, he is apologetic toward the professor and asks for strategies to do better; Marco insists the test was poorly designed and mocks the professor behind her back. Jacob clearly values hierarchy, while Marco has a more egalitarian outlook (and is also possibly a bad student).

hierarchy–egalitarianism One of Schwartz's cultural dimensions; hierarchy indicates a high importance placed on deferring to authority and remaining humble toward perceived social betters; egalitarianism is the opposite, and reflects a belief in equality, social justice, and questioning authority

Nations with individuals who, on average, value hierarchy (or egalitarianism) can be said to have a hierarchical (or egalitarian) culture. Bulgaria scores highly on the hierarchy cultural dimension.[61] If individuals, on average, tend to value deference to authority, then it stands to reason that products or services with anti-authority messaging could be at a disadvantage in Bulgaria. Consider, for example, an event promoter looking to schedule a concert in Bulgaria. Booking

Source: JoshBerglund19/Flickr

Japan scores higher than most countries on the hierarchy cultural value dimension. This means that, on average, people in Japan place more importance on showing deference to authority figures. This value is instilled from a young age, as these schoolchildren bowing show.

acts from punk rock groups might not be ideal. The event could be adapted to meet the market's needs by avoiding this genre. Or, if there are enough punk rock fans in Bulgaria (despite the overall cultural tendency to the contrary), perhaps these acts can be booked after all. Once again, pursuing a strategically equivalent segment is an alternative to adapting the service.

Dimension 3: Mastery–Harmony

mastery–harmony One of Schwartz's cultural dimensions; an individual who values mastery is ambitious and is willing to take from others to serve his ambition; one who favors harmony values peaceful relations with other people and with nature above his own ambition

Mastery–harmony is the third and final dimension. An individual who values mastery is ambitious and is willing to take from others and from the environment to serve his ambition. Conversely, an individual at the harmony end of the spectrum values peaceful relations with other people and with nature above his own ambition. Imagine two colleagues, Shelley and Raj, have just submitted a project to their boss. They each contributed equal work to the project. Shelley overhears Raj talking to her boss afterwards, and notices that he is taking most of the credit. If Shelley confronts Raj about this in front of her boss, knowing that Raj will be diminished in the process, this is consistent with mastery-focused values. If Shelley lets it slide because she does not want to cause trouble, she is exhibiting the importance she places on harmony.

THEORY SPOTLIGHT Hofstede's Cultural Dimensions

Shalom Schwartz was not the only social scientist to develop a theory of cultural dimensions. The leading alternative framework belongs to Dutch psychologist Geert Hofstede. Hofstede characterizes cultures along six dimensions: power distance (tolerance of societal inequality), individualism (extent of independence from family), masculinity/femininity (extent to which typically masculine or feminine traits are considered desirable), long-term orientation (degree of reliance on adaptation/pragmatism versus tradition), and indulgence (whether it is acceptable to focus on having fun). Hofstede's dimensions are useful, and share several themes with Schwartz's model. The Schwartz framework is better suited to understanding global customer differences, though, because (i) the values explicitly exist at the individual level (consistent with MP#1), with cultural values representing an average of individual values in a group, and (ii) Schwartz's dimensions do a better job predicting consumer behavior and international trade.[62, 63]

To understand the implications of this value dimension for culture at the national level, and for Marketing Principle #1, an example is instructive. Finland scores highly on the harmony cultural dimension.[64] This means that, despite potentially dramatic differences within the country, the *average* individual leans toward a desire for harmony. This desire has implications for customer preferences in Finland. Because harmony with nature is a key part of this value, it should directly affect preferences for functional attributes of products—specifically, those attributes related to sustainability or eco-friendliness.

Marketers can use this insight in several ways. A manufacturer of recycled shoes might view Finland as a more appealing market to enter. A typical shoe brand such as Adidas, on the other hand, might see less potential in the Finnish market. Or perhaps the brand's advertising messages, or the product itself, can be adapted for the Finnish market. Yet another possibility exists: despite the average individual in Finland having a desire for harmony, a manufacturer with questionable "green" bona fides might simply take advantage of Marketing Principle #1 by identifying individual consumers within Finland who place less importance on sustainability: a strategically equivalent segment. This target segment might be smaller than in other nations, but it surely exists.

Importance of Schwartz's Dimensions

Thus, Schwartz's three cultural dimensions have significant implications for successful ventures in new country markets and should be considered in concert with the five sources of customer differences identified in Chapter 4. Cultural differences are intertwined with customer differences. It should be noted though, that despite these implications, each example in this section highlights that within-culture differences are just as important as between-culture differences. This is the very reason that identifying strategically equivalent segments can be a viable alternative to adaptation in some markets. Firms that treat foreign nations as cultural monoliths, therefore, do so at their own peril.

OPPOSING VIEWS Cultural Globalization in Consumption

Although globalization has doubtless accelerated peaceful trade relationships and contributed to worldwide growth, it has also received criticism from various quarters for its unintended consequences. One of the more troubling criticisms is that globalization, while forging connections between diverse peoples, has actually diminished global diversity by homogenizing products, services, and even cultures around the world. This phenomenon is known as "cultural globalization."[65] It can be observed in several spheres, but it is perhaps most observable in the entertainment industry, where Hollywood claims a vastly disproportionate slice of global film culture.[66]

The critique most famously came from German American economist Theodore Levitt, who claimed that "The world's needs and desires have been irrevocably homogenized. This makes the multinational corporation obsolete and the global corporation absolute."[67] Essentially, Levitt argues that powerful multinational firms enter new country markets, forcing out less well-financed local competition. These corporations flood the market with the same goods they produce in their home markets. Because marketing actions contribute to customer preferences, customers in the new markets begin to develop preferences increasingly similar to those in the corporation's home market. The process repeats in a new country, until everyone wants the same products and the multinational corporation has become global. Or so Levitt argues. Nonetheless, the free movement of ideas and goods across borders will likely continue to lead to blending and blurring of cultural lines.

Global

See the issue from two sides:

1. Craft an argument in favor of Levitt's side, that is, in every sector, customers will increasingly consume essentially the same goods, and the world will shift toward a single global culture. In your argument, be sure to acknowledge the fact that firms can adapt products and services to new markets.
2. Craft an argument against Levitt's side, that is, there exist barriers to cultural globalization that will sustain different preferences and cultures in different countries. Be sure to specify what these barriers are, and how your argument relates to the Hollywood example provided above.

CHAPTER CASE STUDY

ALIBABA OPENS DOORS FOR US-BASED SELLERS

China

When Chinese entrepreneur Jack Ma visited the United States in 1995, he saw which way the wind was blowing. Globalization 3.0 was underway, and Silicon Valley's internet companies were at the heart of it. Ma decided to start his own e-commerce platform. After two failed attempts and a pivotal $20 million investment from Softbank, he founded Alibaba.com, an online, business-to-business (B2B) marketplace that enabled organizational buyers from around the world to easily buy large quantities of products listed on the platform by China-based exporters.[68] Alibaba opened new doors for these sellers, who gained customers abroad, as well as for buyers, who gained low-cost suppliers that would have been difficult to find without the platform. This self-service platform was viewed as vastly more efficient than relying on export agents, who traditionally had personally brokered deals between importers and exporters for a hefty commission. As a result, the company grew rapidly and started a number of other platforms and services: Alipay (a payment processing service like PayPal), Taobao (a direct eBay competitor), and Aliexpress (a wholesale platform specializing in small buyers). By 2014, when the firm's initial public offering on the New York Stock Exchange raised $25 billion, it represented 80 percent of all online transactions in China.[69] The original B2B platform, Alibaba.com, was still an important part of the firm's business.

Opening to US sellers. By 2019, the global B2B e-commerce market had grown to $23.9 trillion—ten times the value of the consumer market—enabled largely by Alibaba.com and the US-based Amazon Business platform. The market was continuing to grow rapidly, as B2B sellers had previously lagged behind their consumer-focused counterparts in taking their businesses online. In July of that year, Alibaba.com made a major move to capitalize on this growth and expand its global footprint: for the first time, it opened the platform to sellers based in the United States.[70] Alibaba's primary target was small- to medium-sized wholesalers, distributors, and manufacturers—similar to its core sellers in China—that were looking to grow their business both within the United States and abroad.

Source: Alf van Beem/Wikimedia Commons

A Chinese cargo plane lands at Schiphol in the Netherlands. Before Alibaba, Western firms seeking Chinese suppliers often had to rely on costly export agents to broker deals.

Targeting these sellers, of course, put Alibaba.com on a collision course with Amazon Business. In 2019, roughly 10 percent of all B2B sales in the United States occurred over Amazon's platform. For example, most major universities as well as most of the *Fortune* 100 largest companies in the country counted themselves among the customers of Amazon Business. The platform enticed new sellers to the platform with its ease of use and the ability to set up a storefront for free, charging a percentage commission on each transaction. The breadth of sellers attracted buyers to the marketplace, more buyers made the platform more appealing to sellers, and so on, leading to a dominant market position.[71]

A path to growth. Alibaba had an uphill battle to compete with Amazon in the United States. The company aimed to win sellers to its platform with three main points of differentiation from Amazon Business. First, Alibaba.com charged sellers an annual subscription to set up and maintain their storefront, whereas Amazon Business collected commissions on every sale. Second, Alibaba insisted that it would limit its own access to sellers' data about their buyers.[72] Third, compared to Amazon, Alibaba had a larger base of buyers based outside the United States. These differences were meant to enhance sellers' ability to profitably grow their businesses on the platform and address distrust about Amazon's use of marketplace sellers' data (for example, to decide which of Amazon's own products to stock).[73]

Alibaba has made clear that it views this market entry as a testing ground for future expansion. The director of the firm's North American Supply Chain division, Jamin Dick, succinctly explains the company's vision: "We see this as an anywhere-to-anywhere type business."[74] The stakes for Alibaba's US market success, then, are quite high. Early results are positive but inconclusive. In its first year, the US platform recorded a 100 percent year-over-year growth in transactions and 76 percent growth in the number of buyers, but these percentage gains might be relative to small starting values; the company has not released exact numbers of buyers or transactions in the United States.[75] Alibaba continues to explore new ways to provide value to US B2B sellers, such as offering useful case studies, technical reports, and webinars on the platform, but it remains unclear whether these efforts will move the needle for businesses that have become accustomed to Amazon's platform.[76] Alibaba will need to continue to mind the unique needs of US businesses to compete in that market.

CASE QUESTIONS

1. Answer this chapter's "three questions for entering new country markets" for the case of Alibaba entering the market for US-based sellers. In answering the three questions, pay close attention to: (1) What exactly is the Alibaba platform selling, and to whom? (2) What are the implications of a product or service being entirely software- or cloud-based for these three questions?
2. Legal and government issues feature prominently in market entry decisions. Obviously, China and the United States had a fraught trade relationship at the time of Alibaba's entry (2019), and this posed a significant risk. Why do you think Alibaba decided to move forward anyhow?
3. What sorts of cultural challenges might Alibaba run into when dealing with US-based, rather than China-based, sellers? What should Alibaba do to account for these cultural differences?

CHAPTER SUMMARY

In pursuit of growth, firms large and small increasingly enact their marketing mix across national and cultural borders. Globalized competition heightens the challenges of managing customer differences, as offerings must be brought to market in a way that is sensitive to differences in norms between regional cultures while also recognizing the unique forms of customer differences within each market. To provide a framework for understanding within- and between-culture customer differences, this chapter presents an overview of key terms, concepts, and strategies employed by today's global marketers. The chapter begins with a detailed history of the four eras of increasing globalization, to provide context for understanding many of the thorny ethical and cultural challenges that marketers face today. Criteria for deciding to enter a new country market, as well as various modes of entry such as international joint ventures and direct investment, are reviewed. Finally, approaches for managing cultural differences in new country markets are examined in the context of Schwarz's cultural dimensions, with particular attention to the simultaneous importance of within-culture and between-culture customer differences.

APPLICATION QUESTIONS

1. Think of a time when you, or someone you know, ordered a product from another country. What technologies facilitated this purchase? How would this person have placed the order without these technologies?
2. Think of at least one specific criticism of globalization that you have heard (if you cannot think of any, you can use the cultural globalization issue from this chapter). Do you think this criticism has merit? Why or why not?
3. Provide at least two specific reasons why an incumbent competitor would have a natural advantage over an insurgent competitor in a market.
4. Assume you have addressed the three questions for entering a new country market, and you determine that the venture is feasible but there is a significant risk of losing money. Assuming you are set on moving forward, which mode of entry would you prefer, and why?
5. Assume you have addressed the three questions for entering a new country market, and you determine instead entering the new market is almost certain to be highly profitable. Which mode of entry would you prefer, and why?
6. Pick one of Schwartz's value dimensions. Describe a person you know who falls on one end of the spectrum, and another person you know who falls on the opposite end.
7. Pick any of Schwartz's value dimensions. How would you characterize your own country's culture on this dimension? How, if at all, has this element of your country's culture influenced your own preferences for products/services? Be sure to consider effects on the five sources of customer differences from Chapter 4.

Visit the companion website, **https://bloomsbury.pub/palmatier-marketing**, or **https://samsinstitute.com**, for additional learning and teaching tools, including professional videos outlining the Four Principles, PowerPoint tutorials with voice-over commentary, sample syllabi for marketing courses, testbank and more.

Part 3

MARKETING PRINCIPLE #2: ALL CUSTOMERS CHANGE

Part Overview

Welcome to Part 3. The three chapters in this unit build on Marketing Principle #1 (all customers differ) by exploring what happens as customer needs and preferences continue to diverge or converge over time. Chapter 7 introduces this core idea in the form of Marketing Principle #2 (all customers change). This chapter also depicts several strategies for handling the accompanying challenge of managing customer dynamics, such as the acquisition, expansion, retention (AER) framework. Chapter 8 examines customer dynamics in one of the most rapidly changing sectors—retail and omnichannel marketing—while introducing key terms and concepts in retail marketing strategy. Finally, Chapter 9 focuses on marketing research and analytics, and highlights the processes and tools that modern marketers use to understand and manage customer differences and customer dynamics.

Together, these chapters highlight that “change is the only constant” for marketers looking to maintain a competitive advantage.

Chapter 7

MANAGING CUSTOMER DYNAMICS

CHAPTER OVERVIEW

Chapter 7 introduces Marketing Principle #2: all customers change. It explains the nature of changing customer preferences and why managing customer dynamics is vital to the firm's survival in a shifting market landscape. It then outlines the five reasons why customer preferences change. Finally, the second half of the chapter introduces various practical tools and approaches for managing customer dynamics, including traditional approaches such as life cycle models and more current tools such as acquisition, expansion, retention (AER) models. The chapter will proceed by answering the following questions:

- What is Marketing Principle #2 and its accompanying managerial challenge?
- What factors make managing customer dynamics especially important?
- Why do customer preferences change over time?
- What tools do marketers have to manage customer dynamics?

In the chapter's cases and features, you will run into companies that have struggled, and sometimes excelled, at managing resource trade-offs while sustaining profitability. These include:

- Pizza Hut's efforts to adapt to more modern pizza preferences (Marketing Fail).
- AstraZeneca's work to adapt to a changing world during the pandemic (Chapter Case).
- Ethical and moral dilemmas in managing customer dynamics, such as the nebulous value of firms adopting blockchain-based technologies (Shades of Gray) and brands' attempts to weather politically oriented boycotts (Opposing Views).

LEARNING OBJECTIVES

- Define Marketing Principle #2 and its associated key marketing challenge.
- Recognize the importance of managing customer dynamics.
- Identify the five primary sources of customer dynamics.
- Compare strategies for managing dynamics, such as AER and life cycle approaches.
- Evaluate moral and ethical concerns in managing customer dynamics.

IMAGINE Planning a Software Lineup

Imagine that you are an executive for Japanese video game company Nintendo, and the company is planning its investments in major game releases for the next five years. Nintendo is known for family-friendly software such as the Super Mario series, which has always helped it attract younger gamers. However, these younger gamers inevitably grow older. Some stop gaming entirely; some others may be enticed to continue playing family-friendly games; others migrate toward more violent or otherwise non-family-friendly titles; while still others end up buying Nintendo titles for children of their own.

Hence, Nintendo faces a varied and ever-shifting set of segments; it must maintain a family-friendly image to appeal to gamers buying classic Nintendo-series games for themselves and their children, while branching out into diverse segments to maximize the chances of retaining gamers as they proceed through various life stages. Further complicating matters, Nintendo's software strategy involves lengthy development cycles—several years, in some cases—for their own games and complex, sometimes long-term publishing arrangements for other game developers to release titles for Nintendo consoles. This makes planning for changing customer tastes, rather than reacting on the fly, a necessity. As you plan a game release schedule for the next five years, you will need to consider which genres or styles of games your segments prefer now, as well as how those preferences will change over an extended period.

Critical thinking:

1. Name at least two events in an individual's life that could cause their preferences for Nintendo software to change. Explain why each shift in preferences would occur.
2. Describe three ways in which you would incorporate potential changes in customer preferences into your planned software lineup.

INTRODUCTION TO MARKETING PRINCIPLE #2

The opening example illustrates that even the most fundamental strategic planning decisions a business makes—which products to launch—cannot proceed without acknowledging that future outcomes depend on how customers and their needs change over time. This illustrates another First Principle of Marketing, namely, **Marketing Principle #2: all customers change**; customers' preferences and needs for goods and services tend to change over time.[1]

Marketing Principle #2: all customers change Customers' preferences and needs for goods and services tend to change over time

Managing Customer Dynamics

The Greek philosopher Heraclitus supposedly once said "The only constant in life is change." This proverb is equally true for marketers and for their customers; customers' own lives and needs change over time and in response to different situations, while marketers face an ever-evolving marketplace and competitive landscape. Thus, "*all customers change*" is a fundamental Marketing Principle because of the inevitable nature of change in life and business. The resulting challenge for marketers is **managing customer dynamics**, where dynamics refer to change, growth, decline, or transformation over time.[2]

managing customer dynamics Adapting to customers' and segments' needs as they change, grow, decline, or transform

The year 2020 saw a golden opportunity for entrepreneurs to respond to customer dynamics. Some small sellers, such as those on US-based handicrafts

Source: Ricarda Mölck/Pixabay

Handheld gaming has been a pillar of Nintendo's approach to managing customer dynamics. The Nintendo Switch can transition from a home console to a handheld as consumers' situations and needs change.

platform Etsy, specialized in custom textile products such as T-shirts and socks. When the coronavirus pandemic in 2020 created unprecedented demand for personal protective equipment such as masks, and large producers' factories could not rapidly scale up to demand, these small sellers stepped in and used their skills to fill the gap. During April 2020 alone, $133 million in face masks were sold on Etsy.[3] In responding to this opportunity, these Etsy entrepreneurs answered the **three questions for managing customer dynamics**:

three questions for managing customer dynamics (1) Where will customer preferences be in the future? (2) What capabilities do we have to match future customer preferences? (3) Which changing customer preferences should we prioritize?

1. ***Where will customer preferences be in the future?***

   In the case of Etsy sellers, those who were early to identify the upcoming demand for protective equipment were better positioned to meet the demand (e.g., by stocking up on materials and planning time to craft items). As the pandemic accelerated, astute sellers could note that, while customer needs for traditional purchases such as T-shirts would not disappear, these needs would likely be eclipsed by items such as masks as well as other protective gear for health professionals. In practice, estimating how customer preferences will change is the most challenging part of managing customer dynamics—predicting the future is no small feat! Chapter 9 addresses this challenge in more detail.

2. ***What capabilities do we have to match future customer preferences?***

   Etsy sellers specializing in sewn and knit items had capabilities clearly aligned with crafting masks and certain other protective gear (e.g., scrubs). On the other hand, the growing number of customers looking for items such as face shields and hand sanitizer were a poor fit for these sellers' capabilities.

3. ***Which changing customer preferences should we prioritize?***

   Just because a seller *can* meet a shifting customer need doesn't mean they *should*. Few health authorities, let alone individual entrepreneurs, were able to predict how long the pandemic would last. Had it been short-lived, sellers that were late to the mask market may not have profited from trying to adapt to this need. More generally, marketers need to assess the long-term business value of chasing customer preferences: do these changes represent fundamental shifts in the marketplace or mere fads?

Large firms face these same three questions. For example, the diffusion of digital technology in India led many consumers who previously used feature phones ("dumb" phones) or low-budget Android smartphones to develop growing preferences for more powerful and capable smartphones. Apple responded to this preference by launching the iPhone SE, adapting the premium iPhone's capabilities into a mid-budget phone. The iPhone SE has continued to be a success story in India, having a sustained positive impact on Apple's performance.

WHY ARE CUSTOMER DYNAMICS SO IMPORTANT?

Many events in a person's life, such as graduating college or having a child, change what products and services that person buys and when they buy them. Some marketers embrace this core marketing principle. US-based media company the Knot Worldwide operates multiple lifestyle magazines and websites under the brand names "The Knot" (for wedding planning), "The Nest" (for interior design), and "The Bump" (for pregnancy). These brands are designed to shepherd consumers through life stages and major events, remaining relevant at each step as the consumer's needs change from wedding dresses, to living room design ideas, to pregnancy health products. Hence, customer dynamics are at the core of the Knot Worldwide's business model.[4]

Although some firms may choose to ignore customer dynamics, this is unlikely to succeed except for brands with a strong "classic" appeal such as Coca-Cola. Even then, this strategy does not work forever or for all segments; Coca-Cola continuously adjusts its beverage portfolio to meet changing customer needs. Therefore, virtually all firms must face the challenge of customer dynamics if they hope to survive. If not properly managed, customer dynamics can be an existential threat. Laura Ashley is an apparel brand known for traditional women's clothing that recalled the Victorian and Edwardian eras. As women increasingly left the home and took on careers in the second half of the twentieth century, the core of the brand's appeal become a liability. Although the firm's sales of home furnishings blunted this decline, it eventually faced bankruptcy and the closure of dozens of stores.[5]

Thus, taken together with Marketing Principle #1 (all customers differ), Marketing Principle #2 implies a complex challenge for marketers. Customers are segmented based on needs and preferences at a single point in time to manage customer differences, as outlined in Chapter 4. In the process, marketers see a static snapshot. Unfortunately, reality is not a snapshot but a moving picture, as customer needs are dynamic and evolving. If a coffee shop assigns a consumer to a segment that primarily buys dessert-style premium beverages during leisure hours, that consumer need not stay in that segment; for example, after accepting a new job they may buy more utilitarian drinks during their morning commute.

five sources of customer dynamics Five types of factors that cause customer preferences to change

To solve the problem of customer dynamics and implement the strategies described later in the chapter, it is important to first understand the **five sources of customer dynamics.** Better understanding *why* customers change can help marketers see *how* to manage these changes.

MARKETING FAIL Pizza Hut Botches its Makeover

Source: M4rtine/Pixabay

Pizza Hut drew criticism for seeming to excessively pander to shifting millennial tastes with its overhauled topping selection.

Starting from humble roots in 1950s Kansas, United States, Pizza Hut has grown into the world's largest pizza chain with over 18,000 restaurants. Although originally a dine-in restaurant concept, the chain is now better known for its delivery and takeaway options featuring modestly priced pizza, pasta, salad, and desserts.[6] It hasn't always been smooth sailing, though. In 2014, after losing market share to competitors such as Domino's Pizza for two years in a row, Pizza Hut executives decided it was time for a total makeover of the brand. These executives recognized that the young adult segment—a crucial market for a value-focused pizza chain—had a growing desire to move beyond the standard margherita or pepperoni pizza and pursue more diverse and interesting flavors. As Pizza Hut Chief Marketing Officer Carrie Walsh explained, "We'll still have all the traditional pizzas, [but we'll now fulfill] a desire for more flavor and more adventure."[7]

USA

Introducing new pizzas was critical to meeting this evolving need. These new pizzas certainly brought the desired novelty. The expanded flavors grabbed headlines both for their wildly diverse ingredients and their apparent desire to appear as on-trend as possible. "The 56-year-old company appears to have just discovered Sriracha," quipped one journalist regarding the several new Sriracha-themed pizzas.[8] Ultimately, it seems that Pizza Hut miscalculated. As sales slumped throughout 2014 and 2015, Greg Creed, CEO of Pizza Hut's parent company, reflected: "Unfortunately, we haven't been as effective as we've liked with our marketing, and need to balance its appeal to millennials with mainstream pizza customers."[9] The chain rolled back many of the menu changes, which were increasing costs without providing much payoff, and refocused on families by providing better value and deals on its classic offerings.[10]

Diagnose the problem:

1. Explain exactly why Pizza Hut's overhaul failed. What customer dynamics were they trying to manage, and how did they miss the mark?
2. How could Pizza Hut have better met the evolving needs of younger consumers without alienating its core customers?

FIVE REASONS WHY CUSTOMERS CHANGE

Customer needs and preferences can change for many reasons. Broadly, these reasons fall into five categories (Table 7.1):

1. major life events;
2. personal life stages;
3. learning effects;
4. product-market evolution; and
5. influence from the environment.

Reason 1: Major Life Events

First, customer needs change following **major life events,** including graduation, starting a career, marriage, becoming a parent, or retiring. These events abruptly change how individuals make buying decisions. Someone starting a new job will shop for professional clothes, new parents buy a crib and stroller, and those approaching retirement may look to move to a warmer climate. After a divorce, a person might avoid brands that their ex-spouse favored, to avoid distressing reminders.[11] Recent college graduates change their store and brand preferences, as they transition from the role of being a student to becoming an employee.[12] Even comparatively smaller events—such as a change in television viewing habits or picking up a fitness routine—can lead to shifts in brand preferences.[13]

major life events Abrupt and significant occurrences in an individual's life that change buying behavior; one of the five sources of customer dynamics

Reason 2: Personal Life Stages

Second, as a customer ages and matures they will transition through multiple **personal life stages**. Compared to major life events, these are more gradual

personal life stages Gradual changes in an individual's values and priorities tied to age; one of the five sources of customer dynamics

Table 7.1 Five Sources of Customer Dynamics.

Individuals experience changes in preferences and buying behavior for many reasons, which can generally be grouped into five categories.

Source	Definition	Examples
Major life events	Abrupt and significant occurrences in an individual's life that change buying behavior	The birth of a child spurs a new parent to buy a crib and other baby products, while also eating out less and going on different vacations
Personal life stages	Gradual changes in an individual's values and priorities tied to age	With age, people's preferences become more fixed, the value they place on novelty and risk-taking decreases, and the value they place on comfort and stability increases
Learning effects	Preference changes that occur as customers develop knowledge and experience with a product or service	People using a voice assistant learn which commands are most useful and most easily recognized, increasing their perceived usefulness of this technology
Product-market evolution	Changes in customer preferences due to the shifts in product attributes and variety of brands as the category grows over time	As smartphones have become ubiquitous and many competitors exist at all price levels, individuals have become much pickier in selecting a phone that matches their needs
Influence from the environment	Changes in customer preferences due to external factors such as actions from marketers, regulators, and society at large	As gender-neutral or gender-bending clothing gains popularity in high fashion and acceptance in society at large, more individuals may experiment with these styles

changes in values and priorities tied to age. Marketers have identified several psychological and sociological changes that come with growing maturity. For example, younger consumers are often drawn to products that promise to make them appealing to potential partners (e.g., perfume, fitness centers, and high-end clothing). As these consumers age, they will tend to shift priorities toward financial security and stability. In the later years of life, individuals may become more rigid in their brand preferences and less willing to take risks or invest time in a relationship with a new seller.[14] Although it is problematic to assume that these stages hold for all consumers, such generalizations offer an accurate sense of typical changes. Most consumers shift in their willingness to take risks or try new things, and life stage frameworks in marketing effectively describe some of these general trends.

Reason 3: Learning Effects

learning effect Preference changes that occur as customers develop knowledge and experience with a product or service; one of the five sources of customer dynamics

Third, as customers develop knowledge and experience with a product or service, they experience a **learning effect** that influences their preferences. Through this learning effect, a customer becomes familiar with a type of product over time, and this familiarity causes the customer to change which features and attributes they find most important. For example, a consumer might buy a smart watch primarily for its ability to mirror phone notifications, but subsequently learn about and value the watch's extensive fitness tracking capabilities. These capabilities become an important factor when the customer buys his next smart watch.[15]

Experience with specific brands, rather than product attributes, also influences preferences and choices.[16] For example, a consumer who is accustomed to an Android phone has invested time in learning the features and interface of the Android operating system. This consumer might be reluctant to try an iPhone due to the need to learn a new operating system, regardless of the phone's other specifications and capabilities.

Because of such learning effects, some marketers focus more effort on consumers who are new to the brand. For example, to encourage these customers to learn more about the brand and continue using it, marketers can employ communication strategies to ensure some interaction with the customer within the first ninety days of their relationship with the brand.[17] It is worth noting, though, that a learning effect only benefits brands when the customer likes what they learn; if they instead find a useless and bloated set of features, they will be less likely to buy the brand in the future.

Reason 4: Product-Market Evolution

Product-market evolution Changes in customer preferences due to the shifts in product attributes and variety of brands as the category grows over time; one of the five sources of customer dynamics

Fourth, such experience and learning effects apply not only at the individual level but also at the level of the entire market as a product or service category becomes more mature. **Product-market evolution** changes customer preferences due to the shifts in product attributes and variety of brands as the category grows over time. Right after an innovative new product is introduced, for example, most of its sales are from first-time purchases, so marketers may offer free samples or discounts to encourage trial. As the product gains popularity, consumers are instead rebuying and influencing the product's trajectory through positive (or negative) word of mouth.

Therefore, firms may pull back discount or free sample offers, focus on more competitive pricing, and launch loyalty programs to better retain customers and encourage positive word of mouth. This notion is fundamental for many "free-to-play" video games and mobile apps such as the FarmVille series, which allow consumers to play for free with limited features or slower progression. Eventually, the mature game becomes so central to consumers' leisure time that they pay to attain special status, items, or features within the game.

Reason 5: Influence from the Environment

Fifth, customer preferences do not develop in a vacuum, but instead are constantly bombarded by **influence from the environment.** These are changes in customer preferences due to external factors such as actions from marketers, regulators, and society at large. For example, strict packaging regulations on tobacco products, such as required cancer warnings, affect how these products are perceived. Influences from slower-moving societal shifts are equally important and are often linked to broad generation labels (Gen Z, millennial, etc.). Boomers who experienced civil unrest in the 1960s in the United States, for example, were often shaped and transformed by this experience. Likewise, millennials' experience growing up with the rise of computers and internet technologies shifted their preferences toward products and services that maximize convenience. These sorts of generational differences, in part, inspired Pizza Hut's poorly conceived foray into unusual Pizza toppings in the 2010s (see Marketing Fail in this chapter).

influence from the environment Changes in customer preferences due to external factors such as actions from marketers, regulators, and society at large; one of the five sources of customer dynamics

The five sources of customer dynamics jointly determine how a customer's preferences and desires change with time. As Table 7.1 shows, these sources can have diverse and potentially unpredictable effects on customer needs. In addition, some sources can take months or years to take effect (e.g., personal net worth, norms on smoking, trends regarding home sizes) while others exert a more immediate influence (e.g., first child, well-publicized product failures).

corporate sociopolitical advocacy A firm publicly announcing a position on a contentious partisan issue

boycott Refusing to buy a firm's products/services for sociopolitical reasons

buycott Enthusiastically buying a firm's products/services for sociopolitical reasons

OPPOSING VIEWS Boycotts and Buycotts

Under pressure from customers, other stakeholders, and society at large, firms both large and small are increasingly choosing to take a stand on social and political issues. By engaging in **corporate sociopolitical advocacy**, firms publicly announce a position on a contentious partisan issue, such as a major election.[18] This can effectively divide the customer base; those against the firm's stance may organize a **boycott** (refuse to buy the firm's products/services), while those in favor may counter with a **buycott** (enthusiastically buy the firm's products/services).

UK USA

Whether the firm benefits or suffers as a result depends on the core values of its most important customers, among other factors.[19] For example, after Unilever-owned ice cream maker Ben & Jerry's announced its opposition to Israel's policy of settlements in the occupied Palestinian territories, it faced controversy.[20] Nevertheless, it saw continued sales growth, possibly indicating that many of the ice cream brand's loyal fans were not unsettled by this stance.[21] Likewise, JD Wetherspoon, a UK-based restaurant and pub chain, made waves when its CEO publicly supported Brexit, going so far in 2018 as to make 500,000 informational Brexit beermats to place in the chain's pubs.[22] Much like Ben & Jerry's, the firm continued to enjoy sales growth comparable to its industry.[23]

Yet even when sociopolitical advocacy helps (or at least doesn't hurt) the firm overall, there can be no doubt that it alters individual customer relationships. Some consumers grow their relationship with the brand, while others stop buying entirely. It can also increase pressure on competitors to take a stance on the same issue, prompting further change in customer preferences. It is an open question whether this type of politicized consumption, in which people's buying behavior diverges depending on their social and political views, should be encouraged.

On the one hand, firms' executives always held such stances privately; publicizing these stances only gives consumers more information to support enterprises that align with their values. On the other hand, the end result is a social landscape that seems to be even more divided along political, social, religious, racial, and class lines, in which individuals have fewer opportunities to share consumption experiences with those who have different views.[24] In either case, this trend will continue to make managing customer dynamics more challenging for marketers.

See the issue from two sides:

1. Craft an argument in favor of firms increasingly taking a public stand on social and political issues. Provide at least one example of a firm that you remember doing this, and why it might be beneficial.
2. Craft an argument against firms taking public stances on sociopolitical issues. Given the pressure that firms face to break their silence on such issues, brainstorm at least one way that the frequency of these public stands could be reduced.

TRADITIONAL APPROACHES FOR MANAGING CUSTOMER DYNAMICS

Marketing strategies for dealing with changing customers have evolved considerably since the postwar period. Beginning in the 1950s, theorists focused on **life cycle models** to generalize dynamics at the level of the customer, industry, and product market.[25] These models were inspired by biological concepts. As an organism grows, it experiences distinct stages with unique features—for example, a frogspawn becomes a tadpole, which grows into a froglet and eventually an adult frog. Traditional life cycle models include:

life cycle models Frameworks that generalize dynamics over distinct stages at the level of the customer, industry, and product market

customer life cycle Models that predicted consumer buying behavior based on stages in a typical consumer's life, or a portion thereof

- **Customer life cycle:** Marketers in the 1960s predicted consumer buying behavior based on stages in a typical customer life cycle.[26] These life cycle models could align with the generic personal life stages outlined earlier, or a more targeted set of stages. For example, a toy manufacturer might focus on distinct stages within a childhood life cycle (infant, toddler, primary school, secondary school), and devise marketing mix strategies—such as unique toys and advertising messages—for each stage. So popular were these models, that even leading economists incorporated personal life cycle assumptions into their models of consumer spending.[27]

In relation to the five sources of customer dynamics, customer life cycles mainly focus on personal life stages and the major life events that might

Source: Michelle Raponi/Pixabay

Graduating college is a critical moment in many consumers' life stages. How do you anticipate your buying behavior changing after graduation?

trigger movement to the next stage (e.g., graduating triggers movement toward adulthood). Learning effects are indirectly tied to these stages, as each new phase introduces a different set of products and services to learn about. For example, new parents begin learning about bottles and other baby products. On the other hand, customer life cycles are comparatively silent about influences from the environment and product-market evolution.

- **Product life cycle**: Product life cycle models predict that a new product or service will go through four stages over its lifespan:
  1. introduction, in which a small group of enthusiastic adopters try the product;
  2. growth, in which the product gains a mainstream following;
  3. maturity, in which the product's popularity reaches its apex and competition intensifies; and
  4. decline, in which the product's relevance and value give way to other innovations in the marketplace.

product life cycle Models that predict that a new product will go through four stages over its lifespan: introduction, growth, maturity, and decline

These stages can be observed for many products that have come and gone, such as the bulky cathode-ray tube (CRT) televisions and Video Home System (VHS) tapes that dominated the 1980s and 1990s. Hence, this model remains quite popular to this day, with marketing strategies being rolled out according to the

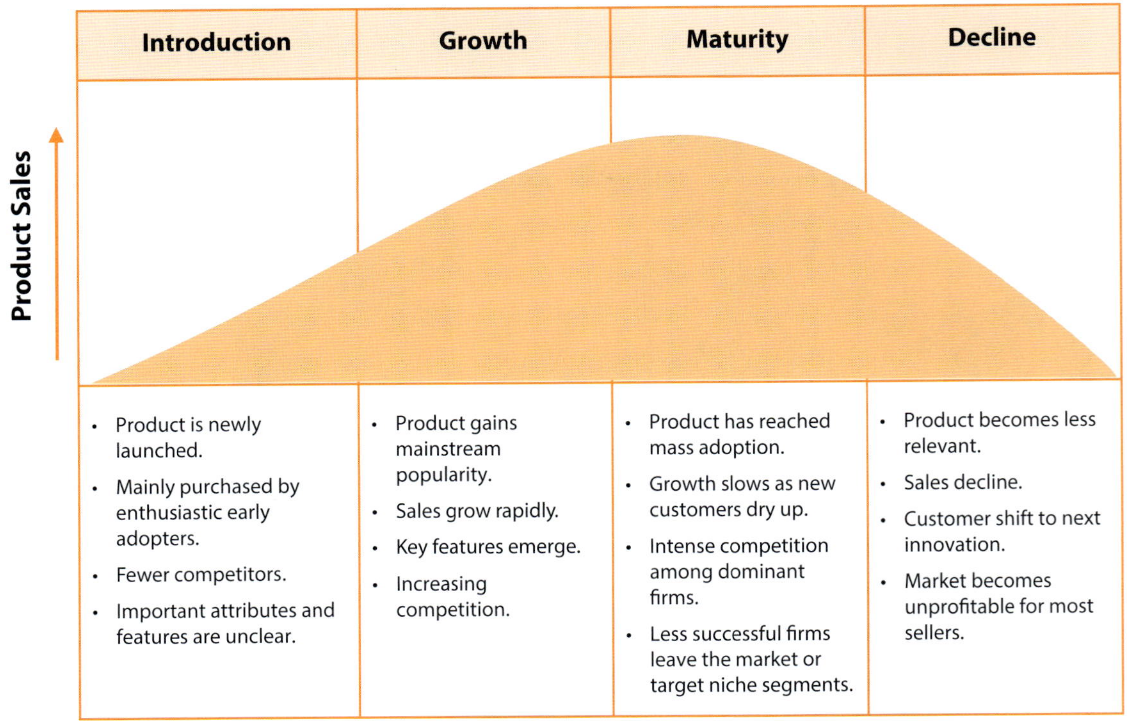

Figure 7.1 Generic Product Life Cycle.
Illustration of typical product life cycle stages, including competitive dynamics at each stage.

product's life cycle stage; for example, customer referral bonuses are a common tactic in the introduction and growth stages to spread word of mouth. Figure 7.1 depicts a generic product life cycle and its four stages.

Product life cycle models identify product-market evolution as the primary source of customer dynamics, without explicitly defining the role of personal life stages or major life events at the customer level. These models implicitly incorporate learning effects, as customers develop more expertise in using the product as the market matures, affecting preferences. For example, while early smart TVs shipped with remote controls comparable to traditional TVs (e.g., with a full panel of number button and input selectors), consumers over time realized that they were mainly using these remotes to launch smart TV apps. Hence, in the mature market for this product, manufacturers shipped smaller remotes with less cluttered faces.[28] Product life cycle models also account for environmental influences, to an extent. As the product-market matures, consumers have been exposed to more messages from competitors, effectively creating a "conversation" that grows and evolves with the market. For example, after the smartphone market reached maturity in developed nations in part due to the iPhone's success, Samsung took advantage of consumers' familiarity with Apple's hype-based messaging (e.g., major announcement events) to poke fun at this very hype with Samsung's "next big thing" campaign.[29]

industry life cycle Models that predict that an industry as a whole will go through five stages over its lifespan: establishment, innovation, shakeout, maturity, and decline

- **Industry life cycle:** Industry life cycles closely parallel product life cycles, but at the level of an entire market sector. A typical life cycle includes five stages:

1. establishment, in which the nature of the industry and its boundaries are defined;
2. innovation, in which competitors converge on dominant strategies and offerings;
3. shakeout, where larger firms consolidate their power and market share, as smaller firms with higher costs cannot keep up;
4. maturity, where the dominant firms battle for market share; and
5. decline, when the industry begins to lose relevance.[30]

The length of these stages varies tremendously across industries. For example, the COVID-19 vaccine market (see this chapter's AstraZeneca case) began in late 2020, exploded through rapid growth and maturity phases, and was in decline by 2024. In contrast, the horse-drawn carriage industry's early stages arguably lasted over a thousand years, before reaching maturity in the late 1800s and decline in the 1900s following the popularity of the automobile. Hence, while industry life cycles are useful for scholars and think tanks that want to understand the history of an industry, they are less useful for marketers. The most decision-relevant portions of the industry life cycle model are captured in product life cycles, as marketers typically set budgets and make decisions (advertising, pricing, etc.) at the product level. Industry life cycle stages can become more relevant when industries as a whole take action, such as through trade associations. For example, Cotton, Inc., a major cotton trade association, ran its famous "fabric of our lives" advertisements for over twenty-five years to stave off the decline of cotton products in the face of modern, synthetic fabrics.[31]

Industry life cycle models also mirror product life cycle models in terms of how they capture sources of customer dynamics. Industry life cycles highlight product-market effects, influences from the environment, and learning effects, while remaining ambivalent about individual customers' personal life stages and major life events. Environmental effects tend to be particularly important due to the long-lived nature of many industries. The apparel industry, for example, has seen consumer preferences affected by social movements, wars, and even the fall of nations. For example, the collapse of the Soviet Union in 1991 saw the Russian Federation and its former client states flooded with Western brands and 1990s fashion trends, such as bright colors and denim.[32]

blockchain An emerging technology that enables unchangeable, digital, public transaction ledgers; the basis for cryptocurrencies and NFTs

SHADES OF GRAY Big Brands Bounce on the Blockchain Bandwagon

Global

Bitcoin. Ethereum. Non-fungible tokens. Decentralized finance. In the last several years, a variety of mysterious-sounding tech jargon gained popularity in the public sphere. This is all thanks to **blockchain** technology. In a nutshell, a blockchain is an unchangeable, digital, public transaction ledger. A new set of transactions can only be added to the ledger if they are validated by a large network of people running powerful computers. For example, as people make transactions online using bitcoins,

Source: WhaleMaster420/Pixabay

NFT collections often feature generic artwork of an animal wearing different accessories. Nonetheless, the most coveted NFTs, such as some in the Bored Ape Yacht Club series (not pictured), can still sell for tens of thousands of US dollars.

these transactions enter a queue; when a block of transactions is validated (essentially, by solving extremely complex math problems), those who helped validate receive newly minted bitcoins.

To say that this technology went mainstream is an understatement. In 2024, the total value of all cryptocurrencies in circulation—primarily consisting of bitcoin and ether—exceeded $1.7 *trillion*.[33] This was roughly the value of Alphabet (Google's parent company) at the time.[34] The industry is well into its innovation phase and may be progressing through a shakeout stage. Major brands have sought ways to jump on this bandwagon, especially in the case of **non-fungible tokens (NFTs)**—a blockchain technology in which each ledger entry is linked with artwork, music, or some other intellectual property. For a time, Twitter (X) even allowed users to link NFT artwork to their profile picture,[35] while French video game developer Ubisoft continues to incorporate NFTs into games for buying and selling digital items (e.g., character outfits).[36] These efforts have accelerated both the growth of cryptocurrencies and NFTs, and public skepticism of them.

This increasing adoption obscures troubling facts about blockchain technology. Because of their fundamentally anonymous and decentralized nature, these technologies are notoriously difficult to regulate and police. As a result, cryptocurrency in particular has become a haven for money laundering and other criminal activity, while NFT buyers routinely fall victim to scams—for example, "rug pulls" in which a social media influencer conspires with the creator of a set of NFTs to build hype around them, then conducts a coordinated sell-off once an influx of buyers elevates the price. Blockchain technology is also extraordinarily complex and assets such as bitcoin can change price dramatically. Many novice adopters fail to understand or appreciate the risks they are taking on. And, last but not least, the computing power needed to operate blockchains is immense, potentially accelerating energy shortages and environmental impacts of energy production.[37] Whether it is advisable for trusted brands to nudge consumers into blockchain technologies, or whether they have a duty to educate consumers on the risks of these technologies, remains an open question.

Ethical dilemmas:

1. Who is potentially harmed when brands encourage their customers to buy cryptocurrency or NFTs? How are they harmed?
2. What can marketers who incorporate blockchain technology into their marketing efforts do to *reduce* risks for their consumers? In your opinion, do they have a responsibility to undertake such risk-reduction efforts?

non-fungible tokens (NFTs) A popular blockchain technology in which each ledger entry is linked with artwork, music, or some other intellectual property

The main advantage of life cycle models is their simplicity to understand and use. This advantage is the very reason that life cycles continue to be taught in business schools and seminars and continue to be a starting point for marketing mix decisions. Yet the elegant simplicity of life cycle models comes with major drawbacks. The overarching problem is a one-size-fits-all approach: each customer, product, or industry goes through the same series of stages. This makes actionable recommendations for a *specific* customer, product, or industry difficult to formulate. For example, personal life stages can progress differently for each individual. While one person may graduate college, get married, have children, and focus on family oriented products, his friend might focus exclusively on advancing her career and buying luxury products, and yet another friend might embark on some combination of these paths.

In essence, the weakness of life cycle models is their failure to incorporate Marketing Principle #1 (all customers differ). In their quest to understand customer dynamics, these models assume away customer differences by averaging across customers, products, and industries to develop generic developmental stages.

As Chapter 4 shows, though, firms assume away such differences at their peril. Customers and products behave in remarkably diverse ways. Even a firm focused on products for the millennial generation must contend with the fact that this generation has at least six distinct subgroups with vastly divergent lifestyles and buying behaviors.[38] The trouble with a life cycle model that simply averages across all groups is that the average may appeal to no one at all. For example, if some consumers are trying to reduce costs, save time, and buy with low-touch experiences while others want more expensive, feature-rich products bought in high-touch environments, then the "average" would inaccurately predict demand for a medium-priced product sold with medium touch. This would appeal to very few consumers in this setting.

MANAGING CUSTOMER DYNAMICS THROUGH THE ACQUISITION–EXPANSION–RETENTION (AER) MODEL

Life cycle models provide useful insights into customer dynamics and can serve as a starting point for marketing mix decisions, particularly for smaller firms focused on a single segment. But marketers making complex decisions across a varied product and service portfolio and numerous segments will be better served by models that incorporate both Marketing Principle #1 and Marketing Principle #2.

One such model that has gained wide acceptance is the **Acquisition–Expansion–Retention (AER) model**. Just as segmentation, targeting, and positioning (STP) was a solution to the problem of customer differences, so may AER be seen as a solution to customer dynamics. Indeed, another name for the AER approach is **dynamic segmentation.** Under this model, customer dynamics are captured in terms of the customer's relationship with the firm: acquisition, when this relationship begins; expansion, when this relationship grows; and retention, when this relationship is sustained over time. The model also incorporates a fourth possible relationship: none at all, which applies to both prospective customers and lost customers. Crucially, the AER model allows different customers to take different paths in their relationships with the firm, thereby accounting for Marketing Principle #1. Figure 7.2 shows the various relationship migration paths in an AER model.

Acquisition–Expansion–Retention (AER) model
A framework that captures customer dynamics in terms of the customer's relationship with the firm: acquisition, expansion, and retention

dynamic segmentation
A framework that captures changing customer preferences over time; commonly refers to the AER approach

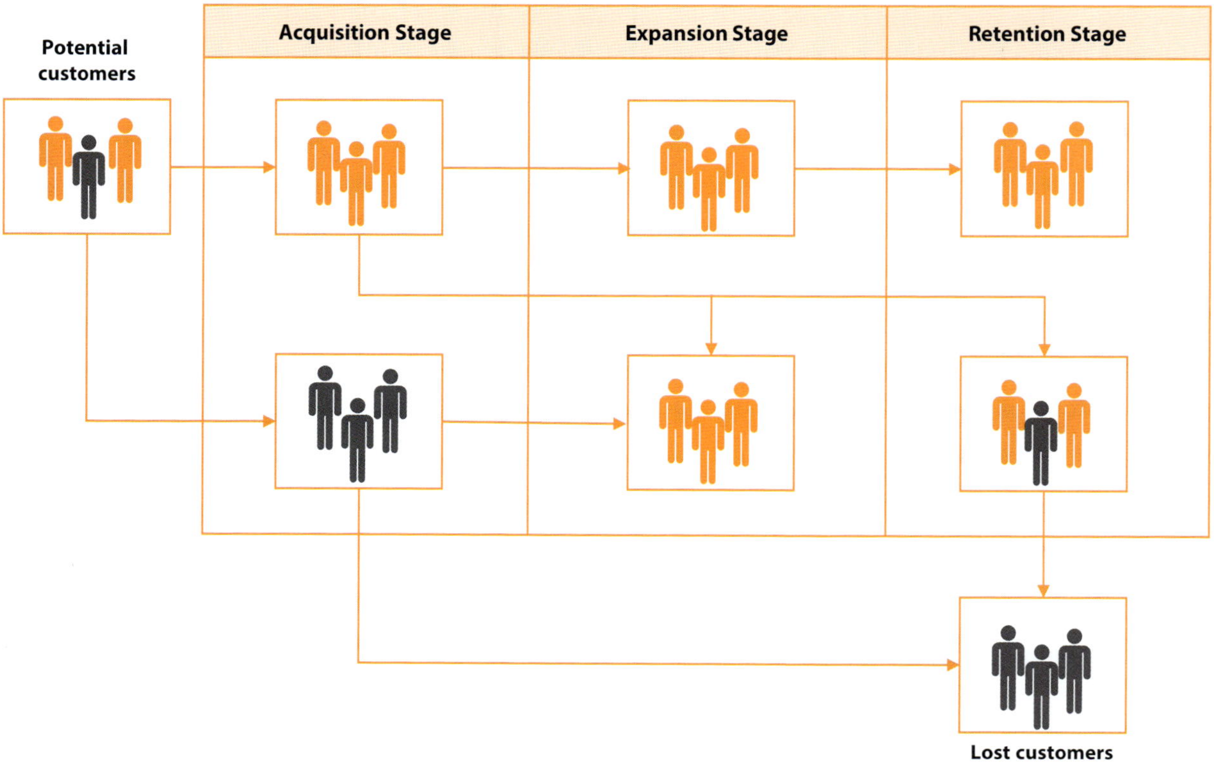

Figure 7.2 AER Model.

In the Acquisition–Expansion–Retention model, customers "migrate" across stages at different times and for different reasons, according to their unique segment profile. Firms try to maximize profitable movement along the stages. Gray customers represent those who will leave the firm, due to a poor fit, failed onboarding, or a stale relationship.

IN OTHER WORDS ...

The AER framework can be thought of as a leaky bathtub, where customers are the water. Marketers try to increase the flow of water into the bath (acquisition) and raise the water level (expansion) while proactively plugging whatever leaks they can (retention). Lost customer analysis is akin to following spilled water to find the leaks. In fact, the AER model has also been referred to as the bathtub model.

Acquisition Stage

acquisition stage The first stage of the AER model, characterized by onboarding efforts

customer onboarding The process by which new customers are introduced to a firm

Customers begin by evaluating several firms' offerings and contacting those that interest them—for example, by visiting a store or website. The **acquisition stage** begins with this first contact, often before a purchase even occurs, and continues through a customer's initial set of purchases when she forms impressions of the firm. Customers at this stage usually have more in common than typical customers in the broader market; they have each selected the same seller, implying they might have similar preferences. For example, two customers shopping at a BMW dealership share more similarities than two customers selected at random from all car dealerships.

The firm's main challenge in this stage is **customer onboarding,** or the process by which new customers are introduced to the firm. Onboarding may last up to six months, depending on the nature and complexity of the purchase and the type of customer relationship (e.g., B2C versus B2B). Successful onboarding can set a relationship up for success by lowering future costs, enhancing loyalty, and boosting cross-selling.[39] Onboarding tactics can be as simple as a "health check" phone call within the first month to ask if the customer's needs are being met. The reason onboarding is so critical is that customers are still evaluating and forming impressions of the firm and its offerings during the acquisition stage, so any effort to provide enhanced service can improve these impressions and elevate the relationship's trajectory.[40] Failed onboarding efforts, or a poor fit between the customer and the firm, can result in lost customers during this stage.

Expansion Stage

After the acquisition stage—up to six months after the first purchase, depending on the context—customers' needs will likely shift and diverge. Some may seek enhanced service and engagement with the brand, for example, while other customers simply buy more frequently over time. During this **expansion stage,** firms attempt to meet these diversifying customer needs by upselling (selling more expensive versions of the same products/services or selling them in greater quantities) and cross-selling (selling different products/services). However, when expansion tactics focus solely on growing sales in the present, they may fail to anticipate future needs. With more proactive efforts to avoid relationship pitfalls, firms can shield a growing customer relationship from competitors' advances. For example, banks know that a new customer acquired in college with an easy-qualification credit card usually needs more financial services and hands-on assistance when she starts her first job, such as car financing and setting up checking and savings accounts. If the bank doesn't offer these additional services after graduation, competitors will instead seize the opportunity. As in this example, lost customers in the expansion stage usually result from the firm's failure to adapt to growing and changing needs.

expansion stage The second stage of the AER model, characterized by attempts to upsell and cross-sell

Retention Stage

The last and potentially most crucial step is the **retention stage**, focused on preventing customers from switching to competitors. As a relationship matures, it faces a significant risk of growing stale. This is particularly true for consumer products where variety is important, such as clothes and restaurants. A consumer might have a favorite bar, but eventually they might grow tired of it and just want something new.

retention stage The third stage of the AER model, characterized by efforts to build strong loyalty to the brand

One way to enhance retention is by imposing switching costs on consumers. Annual phone plans with penalties for prematurely breaking the contract take this approach. Although these tactics appeal to marketers as a quick fix to lock in consumers, they can backfire. When consumers feel trapped with a seller and experience negative attitudes toward its brand, an opportunity opens for competitors to swoop in with a more consumer-friendly offering—in the phone plan example, the month-to-month plans that have grown popular. Rather than imposing penalties on consumers who switch, marketers are better served by strategies that generate strong, positive ties. This can take the form of deeply held brand loyalty, such as that generated and sustained by spontaneous "drops" of Supreme-branded apparel, or relational ties with employees of the firm, such as a salesperson in B2B settings. These relational ties are among the most potent ways for marketers to enhance long-term retention.[41]

lost customer analysis A postmortem examination of a terminated customer relationship, with the goal of diagnosing why customers fall out of the AER stages

customer lifetime value (CLV) A concept that assigns a value to each customer based on the future cash flows that customer will generate for the firm

Despite the firm's best efforts, 100 percent retention is impossible, and some customers will switch to competitors or leave the product category altogether. Hence, **lost customer analysis** is a critical tool to understand outcomes of the retention stage. This analysis, a postmortem examination of terminated customer relationships, can diagnose exactly what led a customer to leave the firm and suggest potential fixes for similar relationships in the future. Typically, firms execute lost customer analyses by employing marketing research methods described in Chapter 9 to solicit feedback from a sample of former customers at regular intervals. Some customers may have left due to a fundamentally poor fit; in other words, they never should have been acquired in the first place. Others, though, left despite fitting squarely in the firm's target market. These customers provide learning opportunities for marketers. For example, talking to former customers can reveal shortcomings in the onboarding process that hinder later retention; if a B2B seller never bothers to explain to a new customer how to place an order on its website, the customer may develop a sticky impression of the seller as uncaring or indifferent about the relationship.

THEORY SPOTLIGHT Customer Lifetime Value

The precise origins of the **customer lifetime value (CLV)** concept are unclear, but it has existed in some form since at least 1988.[42] Formally, CLV is "the present value of the future cash flows attributed to the customer during his/her entire relationship with the company."[43] It is often viewed primarily as a metric, a way of translating concepts from valuing stocks—treating them as a source of future cash flows, and "discounting" these cash flows to the present—to valuing customers. But conceptually, CLV is intriguing because *it can be negative.* That is, some customers bring in less profit than it takes to retain them, due to marketing and sales costs. This means that CLV has an interesting relationship with the AER model. Ordinarily, a marketer might employ an AER framework with the goal of maximizing migration from each stage to the next and minimizing lost customers. But if CLV is incorporated into the dynamic segmentation scheme, there may be some low value (or negative value) customers that are not worth acquiring in the first place. If they are acquired, marketers should *avoid* investing in such relationships to *minimize* migration to a more costly stage. For example, onboarding should be deprioritized for such customers under this view.

The AER model has two advantages for marketers. As noted earlier, it neatly encapsulates the first two Marketing Principles and can manage customer differences as well as customer dynamics. Second, the three stages in the model align well with how modern firms organize marketing efforts. For example, customer acquisition is often a distinct function with its own budget.[44] Despite these advantages, some of the life cycle approach's shortcomings apply here too. For example, no segmentation scheme is perfect, and marketers risk grouping customers with fundamentally different preferences at each stage in the model. In addition, the three AER stages create the illusion of hard cutoffs or clean transitions from one stage to the next, when in reality a customer's relationship with the firm evolves continuously and gradually.

CHAPTER CASE STUDY

A BUMPY ROAD FOR ASTRAZENECA

UK **Sweden**

British-Swedish conglomerate AstraZeneca is one of the world's largest producers of pharmaceuticals and biotechnology products. The firm seeks to differentiate itself from major competitors, such as GlaxoSmithKline and Pfizer, Inc., by aggressively pouring research and development funds into projects focused on rare diseases, cancer, respiratory illnesses, immune disorders, and a handful of other focal areas.[45] Given AstraZeneca's emphasis on respiratory products, it is unsurprising that it was one of the first firms to launch a vaccine for the SARS-CoV-2 coronavirus. In early 2020, the company reached an agreement to be the sole distributor for a vaccine being developed by researchers at Oxford University and an Oxford-affiliated firm called Vaccitech. Clinical trial results were promising, indicating effectiveness of 70–90 percent.[46] The resulting vaccine, codenamed AZD1222, was ready to launch by the end of autumn.

Launching the vaccine: The introduction phase. Given that vaccines, at that time, were to be distributed to individual consumers free of charge, the actual customers for AZD1222 were government entities such as health departments, which would allocate doses across their territories, and militaries, which would distribute doses to service members. Hence, AstraZeneca was facing a business-to-government (B2G) selling situation, with all the political hurdles that entailed. Further complicating matters were the heavily regulated nature of pharmaceuticals and the innovative technology employed by the vaccines, meaning that obtaining even an emergency approval from each government could be an uphill battle.

AZD1222 received a much-needed boost in late 2020 when it was approved in the United Kingdom, the product's home market, with the first dose administered in January 2021.[47] Approval in continental Europe and several Asian and South American countries shortly followed. Within a similar timeframe, competing vaccines from US-based Pfizer and Moderna also reached the market. In a worrying sign for AstraZeneca, these competing vaccines reported effectiveness of 95 percent.[48] Nonetheless, AZD1222 had acquired its first customers in the

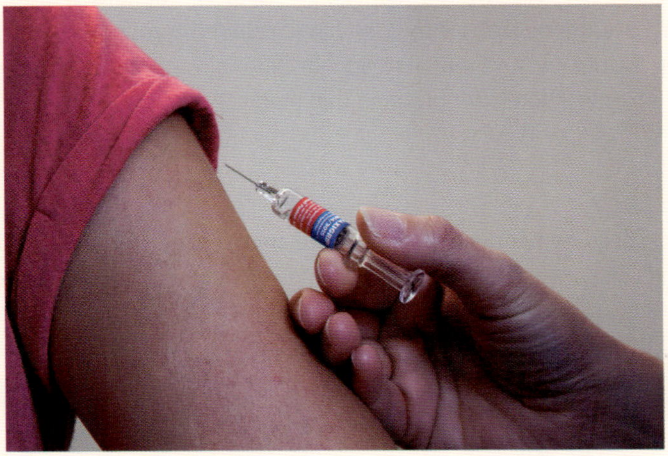

Source: Katja Fuhlert/Pixabay

While AstraZeneca's jab excelled in the early stages of the COVID-19 vaccine market, it stumbled relative to competitors as the market grew and matured.

form of major world governments. In fact, out of the gate, AstraZeneca's market share was leaps and bounds ahead of competitors. It could boast 2.4 billion doses ordered, compared to just 526 million for Pfizer's shot.[49] Now AstraZeneca just had to grow and maintain these relationships. Although the firm was initially selling the vaccine at cost, as a public service, these government relationships were critical to potential future profits.

Weathering the growth and maturity phases. The early months of 2021 brought challenges for AstraZeneca. Closer scrutiny of clinical trial data, as well as ongoing reports of adverse reactions to the jab, led to growing worries that AZD1222 had a small impact on the development of blood clots, and in particular a deadly condition called thrombocytopenia.[50] AstraZeneca sought to protect its fledgling market by pointing out that the benefits of the shot outweighed the risk for the vast majority of patients.[51] Worries over thrombocytopenia, combined with doubts about the vaccine's effectiveness against novel virus variants, led to government regulators temporarily or permanently halting distribution. South Africa, for example, cancelled all orders for AZD1222 and sold its existing inventory to other African countries.[52] Even Europe, which had been an early adopter, suspended the jab.[53] Although some of these interruptions were brief, they created doubt in the minds of consumers, affecting orders placed by governments. According to one survey conducted among Middle Eastern consumers in April 2021, 23 percent saw a risk of severe, life-threatening side effects from AstraZeneca's jab, versus just 6 percent for Pfizer.[54] A thorough review by European regulators, released around the same time, found the link to blood clots to be tenuous at best, but by this time it was difficult to reverse the damage to the product's reputation[55]

In the meantime, it was competitors such as Pfizer and Moderna, rather than AstraZeneca, that reaped the largest benefit throughout the growth stage of the COVID-19 vaccine market. In the same survey noted above, only 6 percent of consumers preferred AstraZeneca compared to 54 percent for Pfizer. As the major competitors lifted their at-cost pricing schemes and COVID-19 vaccines accelerated into the maturity phase, AstraZeneca was ill-positioned to take advantage. In the year following the blood clot scare, Pfizer began to dominate the market. By April 2022, it had accounted for over 60 percent of doses in virtually all EU countries, compared to under 20 percent in nearly all member states for AstraZeneca.[56]

While AstraZeneca reaped a respectable $4 billion from its vaccine in 2021,[57] Pfizer garnered a whopping *$37 billion*. This result surely comes as a disappointment for a product that initially seemed to dominate the market. As the pandemic receded throughout 2022, the COVID-19 vaccine market eventually entered a steady decline, closing the door on AstraZeneca's opportunity to become a dominant player in that market.

CASE QUESTIONS

1. What sources of customer dynamics did AstraZeneca's vaccine encounter during this case? Give at least one example of how it could have better managed one of these sources.
2. Apply the product life cycle model to the AstraZeneca case. Pick one stage of the model and explain what the firm could have done to achieve a better outcome from that stage.
3. Apply the Acquisition–Expansion–Retention (AER) model to the AstraZeneca case. Explain what steps the firm might have taken to improve the flow of customers through these stages.

CHAPTER SUMMARY

A second underlying challenge facing firms that make short- and long-term marketing decisions is the basic principle that all customers change, captured by Marketing Principle #2. Events in people's lives—graduation, marriage, new jobs, the birth of children—change their existing routines and buying habits. Not all customer change is event driven though; it also results, for example, from changes in customers' underlying needs and desires due to cultural change or other gradual shifts. This chapter therefore highlights five specific sources of changes in customers: (1) major life events, (2) personal life stages, (3) learning effects, (4) product-market evolution, and (5) influence from the environment. Marketers must account for both static variation in customers' needs, due to their inherent differences (MP#1), and the dynamic variation that arises as customer needs change over time (MP#2). The increased desire of certain segments to play a role in the co-creation of products and services illustrates this dynamism. However, efforts to closely track dynamism in individual preferences can raise moral and privacy concerns. Thus, Marketing Principle #2: all customers change, can represent either an opportunity or a threat, depending on how the firm understands and manages it. This chapter highlights several concepts that can be leveraged in managing customer dynamics within the marketing mix, including life cycle and Acquisition–Expansion–Retention (AER) approaches.

APPLICATION QUESTIONS

1. Can you think of any firm that appears to ignore Marketing Principle #2? Why does this firm seem to get away with it?
2. Think about a product you used to love, but now you are neutral or negative about. Why did your attitude change? How does this reason align with the five sources of customer dynamics?
3. Create a customer life cycle model for your life so far, divided into at least three stages. Describe how your preferences and buying behaviors shifted with each stage.
4. Think of one of your favorite products. Map out a product life cycle for this product, with rough years corresponding to each stage. Where do you think the product currently sits in its life cycle?
5. Think of an example of a company's sociopolitical advocacy that you saw in the news or heard about from a friend. Why do you think the company took this stance? Do you think that they benefited from the announcement?
6. Think about the first time you bought something from a specific company. Can you think of anything the company did that could be considered an onboarding effort? Do you think this effort was effective? Why or why not?
7. Consider your favorite clothing brand. Why have you stuck with this brand for as long as you have? What is the role, if any, of the brand's retention strategies?

Visit the companion website, **https://bloomsbury.pub/palmatier-marketing**, or **https://samsinstitute.com**, for additional learning and teaching tools, including professional videos outlining the Four Principles, PowerPoint tutorials with voice-over commentary, sample syllabi for marketing courses, testbank and more.

Chapter 8

THE CHANGING WORLD OF RETAIL AND OMNICHANNEL MARKETING

CHAPTER OVERVIEW

In this chapter, you will learn the essentials of retailing, a core marketing activity that has faced more change over the years than arguably any other aspect of marketing. The chapter will proceed by answering the following questions:

- Why is retailing so important today?
- How did retail stores and their various formats (department stores, etc.) evolve to become what they are today? What are the purposes of these different formats for consumers and businesses?
- How do manufacturers choose what retailers should carry their products?

You will also learn about some of the major challenges facing specific retailers today throughout the chapter's cases and features. For example, you will read about:

- IKEA's rough track record with online retailing (Marketing Fail).
- Zalando's efforts to integrate its e-commerce channel with brick-and-mortar stores (Chapter Case).
- Ethical dilemmas involving the Wish retail app (Shades of Gray) as well as telemedicine services in Bangladesh (Opposing Views).

LEARNING OBJECTIVES

- Identify key terms and concepts in modern retailing and omnichannel marketing.
- Recognize the key trends and challenges of the four major eras of retailing.
- Associate sources of customer dynamics with changes in retail and omnichannel marketing.
- Recognize connections between marketing dynamics and the success and failure of retailers in recent decades.
- Evaluate moral and ethical concerns for modern retailers.

IMAGINE Opening a Rush Hair Salon

Founded in 1994 in Croydon, United Kingdom, Rush Hair & Beauty has grown to nearly 100 locations across the country.[1] Rush operates a **franchising** business model. This means that entrepreneurs, known as franchisees, enter a contract with Rush; under this contract, franchisees run a business using Rush's branding, products, and expertise, while Rush receives a portion of the business' sales. This provides opportunities for entrepreneurs to start a business with the help of an established brand. For Rush, it allows an expanded retail presence with less risk than company-owned stores.

You are based in the United Kingdom and looking to start a business. Inspired by the success of existing Rush franchisees, you decide to take the leap and invest in a franchise of your own. You're putting most of your savings into this venture, so you are motivated to see it succeed. Thinking back to your marketing class, you recall that service-based businesses such as Rush have 7Ps to manage: product, price, place, promotion, people, processes, and physical evidence.[2] You wonder what each of these marketing mix decisions means when you are selling services—what is your product, for example? You also wonder what types of decisions you will be able to make, given your franchising arrangement with Rush; for example, the licensing agreement requires you to offer a standard menu of haircuts and prices. How will you be able to develop or enact a strategy that accounts for customer differences and dynamics?

Critical thinking:

1. For each element of the 7P marketing mix, consider what kind of choices this element entails for a hair salon, and explain how being a franchisee might narrow this range of choices.
2. What kind of challenges related to customer differences (MP#1) and customer dynamics (MP#2) does a hair salon face? What can you do to manage these challenges?

THE CENTRALITY OF RETAIL IN A CHANGING WORLD

Think about the things you do every day: buying groceries at Safeway, shopping for clothes on H&M's website, getting your hair done at Rush, checking your bank account on Barclays' app, visiting your dentist, or eating at KFC. These are all examples of **retailing**. Retailing, or the marketing activities that enable consumers to buy and receive value from goods and services, is central to consumers' understanding of what a business does and how consumers perceive major brands. Likewise, retailing helps marketers reach customers who want their products and services.

Retailing includes not only selling physical products but also providing services that customers need. **Consumer service providers** such as banks and restaurants exist for this reason. Telemedicine services (see Opposing Views in this chapter) fall under this category. Also, some firms sell to both consumers and businesses, and so include retailing and non-retailing operations. For example, US-based H&R Block is a retail business when it prepares tax returns for consumers, but a non-retail business when it does the same for a local coffee chain. Globally, total retail sales of goods and services are approaching $30 *trillion*.[3] For perspective, that is over ten times the entire gross domestic product of France. It should not be surprising, then, to learn that retailing is one of the most important areas of marketing.

franchising A business model common in retail, in which an entrepreneur, known as a franchisee, enters a contract with a retail brand (e.g., a restaurant); under this contract, the franchisee runs a business using the larger firm's branding, products, and expertise, in exchange for paying royalties on the business's sales

retailing The marketing activities that enable consumers to buy and receive value from goods and services

consumer service providers Businesses that provide labor on behalf of the consumer; a major type of retailer

THEORY SPOTLIGHT Service-Dominant Logic

Businesspeople and academics used to view goods—physical items sold in stores—as the norm in marketing. Services—the intangible benefits provided by a company's frontline workers—were the exception, a special case that did not merit as much attention.[4] One popular framework, championed by marketing scholars Stephen Vargo and Robert Lusch, argues that this distinction is irrelevant, and that both goods and services can be thought of using the *logic* of services. This concept, **service-dominant logic**, holds that the factors that traditionally helped service businesses such as law firms succeed—having valuable expertise, building relationships with customers, and being responsive to customers and market conditions—are crucial for *all* businesses.[5] For example, a grocery store, despite being a goods-focused retailer, will be more successful (and provide a better customer experience) when it knows which food items are most in demand and which items go together, when it knows its customers and their buying habits very well, and when it keeps an eye on new food trends.

The rise of service-dominant logic also explains the growing importance of retailers' loyalty programs and other customer relationship management (CRM; see Chapter 13) tools that aim to build deep customer knowledge. This deep knowledge can be used to build customer relationships, respond to changing customer needs, and provide better customer service.

service-dominant logic A theory that holds that the factors that lead service businesses to success—having valuable expertise, building relationships with customers, and being responsive to customers and market conditions—are crucial for all businesses

Source: Adam Winger/Unsplash

Service providers, such as local barber shops and hair salons, are just as much a part of the retail world as supermarkets and e-commerce shops.

retailer (or retail business) An enterprise that sells goods or services directly to consumers

The activity of retailing implies the existence of a **retailer**, a business that sells goods or services directly to consumers. A Lowe's home improvement store is a retailer, as is a BNP Paribas branch and a Sainsbury's grocery store. Retailers are important to learn about not only because they are a massive part of the economy but also because of retail's unique relationship with Marketing Principle #2 (all customers change). Types of retailers that will be defined and discussed in this chapter include:

- independent retailers
- department stores
- food retailers, including supermarkets
- megastores, including hypermarkets and category killers
- shopping malls
- specialty stores
- digital goods retailers
- consumer service providers, including online service providers

For many years, but especially since the 1990s, retailing has been a proving ground for surviving customer changes. Retailers that have adapted have become some of the most powerful firms in the world, such as Amazon, while those that fail to do so have collapsed in dramatic fashion. Such is the scale of disruption caused by changing customer preferences in the retail sector that the phrase "**retail apocalypse**" is routinely applied.[6] Age-old retail brands are closing stores, going bankrupt, being acquired by rivals, or outright shutting down.

retail apocalypse A popular term for the ongoing trend of major retail brands closing stores, going bankrupt, being acquired by rivals, or outright shutting down entirely

One of the major victims of this apocalypse is US department store chain Lord & Taylor, which closed in 2021. **Department stores**—large, diversified retail locations with goods divided into curated areas called departments—once dominated the retail world. Lord & Taylor was significant because it was the oldest such chain in the United States, having been founded by English immigrants Samuel Lord and George Washington Taylor in 1826.[7] Unfortunately, its leaders failed to invest in updating the store's image or product lineup as it came to be viewed as a stuffy, out-of-touch offering and its core segment—middle-class women—shrank in size. This spelled doom for Lord & Taylor.[8]

department stores Large, diversified retail locations with goods divided into distinct, curated areas called departments

Lord & Taylor's story stands in contrast to menswear store Brooks Brothers, which has survived since 1818. Although the brand has maintained its core identity as a classic menswear destination—after all, men's formalwear tends to change more slowly than the rest of the fashion world—Brooks Brothers has been continuously reinvigorated with new ideas that complement its classic styles. For example, its 2022 lineup featured a range of Instagram-ready looks with neo-prep and pastel flairs.[9]

As these examples show, retailers must evolve their products and services as customer preferences shift and diverge. When examining the retail sector as a whole, four broad eras of this evolution emerge.

CUSTOMER DYNAMICS AND RETAIL FORMATS ACROSS FOUR ERAS OF RETAILING

Retailing has transformed as new technologies emerge and consumers' priorities shift. This transformation can be divided into four eras: the **chain store era**

chain store era A period of time, roughly 1800 to 1960, in which large, multiple-location retail enterprises such as department stores, supermarkets, and convenience stores rose to prominence

Fewer retail formats and channels → Time → More retail formats and channels

	Chain store era ca. 1800–1960	Megastore era ca. 1960–1995	Dotcom era 1995–2005	Omnichannel era 2005–present
Definition	Multiple-location enterprises such as department stores, supermarkets, and convenience stores rise to prominence.	Large retailers with wide assortments and low prices, and related enterprises like malls, become commonplace.	The first introductions of successful ecommerce retailers, as well as norms around ecommerce, emerge.	Retailers learn to efficiently and effectively combine offline and online channels to meet customer needs.
Major trends in preferences	Industrialization, urbanization, and consumerism	Desire for efficiency, low prices, and one-stop shopping	Web-based technology alongside continued desire for efficiency and low prices	Increasingly differentiated preferences for product and service channels
Emerging formats	Department stores, supermarkets, convenience stores	Megastores, hypermarkets, category killer, specialty stores	Ecommerce stores, ecommerce platforms	Digital goods retailers, online service providers
Main retail channels	Brick-and-mortar, catalog	Brick-and-mortar, catalog, brick-and-mortar (within a shopping mall)	Brick-and-mortar, ecommerce, brick-and-mortar (within a shopping mall)	Brick-and-mortar, ecommerce, brick-and-mortar (within a shopping mall), online service channel

Figure 8.1 Evolution of Retail.

Customer preferences and technology have evolved dramatically over four eras. Across these eras, retailers have responded with innovative store formats and new sales channels.

megastore era A period of time, roughly 1960 to 1995, in which large retail locations with wide assortments and low prices, as well as related enterprises such as shopping malls, became commonplace

dotcom era A period of time, roughly 1995 to 2005, that saw the first introductions of successful e-commerce retailers, as well as the development of norms around e-commerce

omnichannel era A period of time, beginning roughly in 2005, in which retailers are learning to efficiently and effectively combine offline and online channels to meet customer needs

(*c.* 1800–1960), the **megastore era** (*c.* 1960–95), the **dotcom era** (*c.* 1995–2005), and the **omnichannel era** (*c.* 2005–present). Figure 8.1 provides an overview of the preference trends, store formats, and retail channels in each of these eras.

Period 1: Chain Store Era (1800–1960)

Although retailing activities have technically always been part of human societies—consider people buying vegetables and pottery in ancient Greek marketplaces—we begin in the industrial period, around 1800, when formal retailing strategies and large-scale retailers emerged. The defining trend of this era was the ever-expanding impact of industrialization. This impact took two primary forms.

First, new ways of making and moving things from the Industrial Revolution (e.g., the railroad) through the Second World War (e.g., the jet plane) helped businesses produce more standardized products and ship them to more places. Standardized products supported major brands, which needed consistent quality. Better transportation allowed retail chains to build complex distribution networks and also allowed even smaller stores to stock goods from far-away locales.[10]

Second, industrialization contributed to the explosive growth of the middle class, which increasingly had the money and time to demand this growing quantity and variety of goods. Consumers developed loyalty to specific stores and brands, leading retailers to develop advertising campaigns and service improvements to win loyal consumers away from competitors.[11] These factors helped create modern **consumerism**, which in this context refers to the market trend toward consumers buying more and more goods and services.[12]

consumerism The market trend toward consumers buying more and more goods and services

The dominant retail players of this era took two forms: independent retailers and department stores. Independent retailers were the local goods and services businesses that locals had long relied on. They were the "mom and pop," "main street," or "high street" establishments owned by local families, who would have personal relationships with their customers. Department stores were completely different. Many iconic department stores, such as Lord & Taylor in the United States or Selfridges in the United Kingdom, were founded during this period. These stores were important in laying down norms of chain retail, such as a predictable service experience and consistent branding at different locations, shopping as a fun outing, and an impersonal relationship with the shopkeeper. Due to their large scale, department stores were also influential in nineteenth- and twentieth-century style trends; a floral-patterned skirt displayed at every location of a department store chain, for example, could influence women's fashion across a nation.[13] Thus, influence from the environment (specifically, marketers) was a key source of customer dynamics in this period.

The later decades of this period saw the growth of two other innovative retail formats. One was the **supermarket**: a store combining all major categories of grocery products that would otherwise be found at a butcher, baker, produce seller, or creamery. This was a major evolution in the **food retailer** category (i.e., non-restaurant sellers of food products), replacing specialized stores with one all-purpose location. Fast-paced twentieth-century consumers wanted efficiency and one-stop shopping, and these stores gave it to them.[14] US chains such as Piggly Wiggly pioneered this type of store, but supermarkets soon spread to Europe during the reconstruction following the Second World War.[15] A second major retail format, the **convenience store**—selling a small selection of on-demand household goods and food, typically alongside fuel—also grew prominent in this era. This type of store became more common as automobiles (and hence gas/petrol stations) gained popularity, and also as urban centers with a strong demand for "corner stores" grew.[16]

supermarket A store combining all major categories of grocery products that would otherwise be found at specialty food retailers such as a butcher, baker, produce seller, or creamery

food retailer A retailer that sells good products (not to be confused with restaurants, which are service providers)

convenience store Small-format retail store with a modest selection of on-demand household goods and food, often alongside fuel

Period 2: Megastore Era (1960–95)

The department store and supermarket innovations of consistency and hyper-convenience would continue in the 1960s. Driven by these trends, **megastores** carried a large selection of goods, either in a single category (e.g., home improvement) or many categories (e.g., groceries and home goods) at very competitive prices. Diversified **hypermarkets** such as Carrefour and Super Target belong to this group, as do **"category killer" stores** focused on one type of product, such as Best Buy and MediaMarkt.[17] These emerging stores, as well as other store formats discussed in this chapter, are reviewed in Table 8.1.

megastores A retailer that carries a large selection of goods, either in a single category or many categories at very competitive prices

hypermarkets A megastore with a diversified product selection, including both groceries and non-food products

"category killer" stores A megastore focused on one product category, such as electronics or home improvement

The growth of megastores changed consumers' expectations and fed even greater consumer demand for convenience; retailers, in turn, had to respond

Table 8.1 Different Types of Retailers.

Many store formats have evolved to meet the changing needs of consumers throughout the four eras of retailing. This table describes most of the important major formats that continue to exist today.

Products	Format	Definition	Examples
Food	**Supermarkets**	Stores combining all major categories of grocery products that would otherwise be found at specialty food retailers such as a butcher, baker, produce seller, or creamery	Safeway, Morrisons, Hy-Vee, Spar, Sainsbury's, Kroger
	Hypermarkets	Megastores with a diversified product selection, including both groceries and non-food products	Super Target, Carrefour, Walmart Supercenter, Tesco Extra
	Convenience stores	Small-format retail stores with a modest selection of on-demand household goods and food, often alongside fuel	7-Eleven, Tesco Express, Couche-Tard, Casey's General Store
Non-food	**Department stores**	Large, diversified retail locations with goods divided into distinct, curated areas called departments	Macy's, Selfridges, Harrods, Nordstrom, Myer
	Category killers	Megastores focused on one product category, such as electronics or home improvement	MediaMarkt, Best Buy, Barnes & Noble, Staples, B&Q
	Specialty stores	Smaller-format retailers focused on one category	Journeys, Zales, The Gap, Pandora, Reiss, Scribbler
	E-commerce retailers	Firms that sell products exclusively through an online channel	ASOS, PrettyLittleThing, Newegg, Alibaba, American Apparel
	Digital goods retailers	Firms that sell intangible computer code, such as downloadable software or movies, to consumers	iTunes Store, Google Play Store, Steam, Epic Games Store, Amazon Video
Services	**Consumer service providers (traditional)**	Firms that perform labor on behalf of the consumer in the consumer's physical location (may also offer online service channel)	Pizza Hut, H&R Block, Barclays, Formula One Autocentres
	Online service providers	Firms that exclusively operate an online service channel	Priceline, Booking.com, Capella University, Talkspace

shopping mall Gigantic, typically enclosed structures that house multiple megastores as "anchors" to draw consumers in, as well as dozens of smaller specialty stores

specialty stores Smaller-format retailers focused on one category

to this demand with new types of stores. One format that gained traction in the 1960s was the **shopping mall**, which took one-stop shopping to the extreme. As with supermarkets, the concept took off in the United States before gaining popularity in Europe and the rest of the world.[18] These gigantic structures housed multiple megastores as "anchors" to draw consumers in, as well as dozens of smaller **specialty stores**, smaller-format chain retailers focused on one category. These stores varied widely in their focus (e.g., jewelry or maternity clothes) as well as their price point (e.g., low-price or luxury), such that any individual or family could get all their shopping done in one trip to the mall.

Malls also served as hubs for additional retailers, with other megastores as well as smaller retailers and service providers springing up outside of them. Many of the world's most popular chain restaurants, such as Burger King, experienced rapid growth during this period, including locations in and around malls.[19] The growth of malls, megastores, and chain specialty stores often came at the expense of independent retailers, further pushing consumers away from the close, personal exchanges that were common in earlier centuries.[20] Thus, the concept of a "trip to the mall" influenced how, when, and why people bought goods and services in rich and varied ways. Ironically, though, the very desire for convenience that led to the shopping mall's creation would be its undoing.

Source: Eduardo Soares/Unsplash

Beginning in the 1960s and 1970s, retail stores grew larger and larger. Many stores eschewed carefully curated aesthetics in favor of barebones, "warehouse"-style designs, such as this Brazilian hypermarket. How did this change reflect shifting consumer preferences?

Period 3: Dotcom Era (1995–2005)

The driving force that changed customer preferences in the dotcom (".com") era was technology. Although the technology underlying the World Wide Web had existed for years by 1990, it was the 1990s that made this technology accessible for the average consumer. Particularly notable was the 1994 launch of the Netscape Navigator web browser, which pioneered many of the user-friendly, point-and-click browser norms that we take for granted today.[21] Savvy entrepreneurs noticed the wide consumer potential of inventions such as Netscape. The result was a simple proposition: what if the **catalog channel**—a traditional retail channel featuring a physical booklet or magazine and call-in or mail-in ordering—could be translated into a website? Product entries could be updated on-the-fly, consumers could place orders without calling or filling out a form, and the retailer could save money on printing physical catalogs.

Many "dotcom" businesses tried this approach in 1995, such as Amazon.com and eBay.com. Major players such as these were immensely successful. Amazon, for example, fed on decades of growing consumer desire for convenience and low prices, thanks to its simple ordering process and its streamlined business model with no **brick-and-mortar channel** (i.e., physical locations). Instead, its *e-commerce channel* (see Chapter 3) could list an endless variety of goods for sale, with no need to worry about physically fitting these goods in a store. Countless other dotcom start-ups failed though. Perhaps most infamously, Pets.com spent millions of investors' dollars on advertising, including an advertisment during the Super Bowl, but never turned a profit; shipping bulky pet food turned out to be a money-losing proposition.[22]

catalog channel A traditional retail channel featuring a physical booklet or magazine and call-in or mail-in ordering

brick-and-mortar channel Selling through physical retail locations; a term popularized in the dotcom era to distinguish this channel from online retail

Despite success stories such as Amazon, in many ways Pets.com's story is more emblematic of the dotcom era. The hallmark of this period was uncertainty and experimentation. For investors, this meant pouring money into internet start-ups without really understanding which ones might take off. For consumers, this uncertainty meant widespread disagreement about the future of online retail and the Web in general. Engineer Robert Metcalfe's assertion that "I predict the Internet will soon go spectacularly supernova and in 1996 catastrophically collapse" captured the uncertain mood of the time.[23]

Retailers themselves likewise faced experimentation and ambiguity. Aging brick-and-mortar sellers, for example, had to decide whether to open an e-commerce channel. Would it bring new sales, or cannibalize (steal sales from) the brick-and-mortar channel? US electronics retailer Best Buy was aggressive in building an e-commerce presence starting in 2000, while others such as UK department store Selfridges held off until 2010 or later. And within the e-commerce channel, retailers experimented with various strategies. For example, shipping and return policies varied a lot across sellers: some had costlier shipping fees with larger orders, while others offered free shipping if the consumer reached a minimum purchase amount;[24] and some retailers offered free, no-hassle returns, while others had consumers pay the return shipping cost.[25] Other experiments fell by the wayside—for example, some online stores automatically played background music, much like the music a customer would hear in a brick-and-mortar shop. Unsurprisingly (at least in hindsight), blaring music into the consumer's home was not well received.[26]

The dotcom era is often seen as a transformative period driven by technological breakthroughs. In some ways, this characterization is accurate; online technologies were critical to the future of retailing. But in other ways, this brief period was more transitional than transformational. It was the adolescence to the coming era's adulthood, as the e-commerce channel found its place in the marketing landscape.

Period 4: Omnichannel Era (2005–present)

The fourth and current era of retail marketing came as the online strategies of the dotcom era matured. Retailers during the dotcom era questioned whether online retail was just a fad, or whether it might completely replace brick-and-mortar retail; it was a question of online *or* offline. In contrast, retailers in the new omnichannel era realized that the future was online *and* offline.

omnichannel retailing The practice of combining offline and online channels to maximize the value offered to each customer in each situation; also called multichannel retailing

channel integration Strategies to allow offline and online channels to work cohesively and support one another, instead of contradicting or undermining one another

"adding clicks to bricks" Integrating a new e-commerce channel with existing brick-and-mortar operations

e-commerce platform An online store that connects buyers and sellers for a fee, rather than selling goods itself

Omnichannel retailing (also called multichannel retailing) refers to the practice of combining offline and online channels to maximize the value offered to each customer.[27] Classic omnichannel tactics include allowing customers to order products online to pick up in store, and a doctor's office following up an in-office appointment with online blood test results. A key challenge of omnichannel retailing is **channel integration**, meaning that offline and online channels work together and support one another, instead of contradicting or undermining one another:

- For example, US apparel retailer Marshalls delayed opening an e-commerce store until 2019 for fear that it would hurt the brand's brick-and-mortar stores; in other words, Marshalls management struggled with channel integration.[28] For older retailers such as Marshalls, the challenge is "**adding clicks to bricks**," that is, how to integrate e-commerce with brick-and-mortar retail. This strategy can also help retailers compete against *showrooming*, where consumers look at items in the physical store only to buy on their phones from a convenient online competitor.

SHADES OF GRAY "When You Order Brand-Name Goods from Wish"

Source: Gohnarch/Wikimedia Commons

US-based retail platform Wish has developed a reputation for sellers listing goods of questionable quality. Some have even accused Wish of turning a blind eye to counterfeit or knockoff goods, similar to this imitation Adidas sneaker.

US-based e-commerce app Wish was created by Piotr Szulczewski with the goal of making everyday items more affordable for ordinary people. As Szulczewski put it, "Forty-one percent of U.S. households don't have $400 worth of liquidity," often have their credit cards declined, and struggle to buy basic necessities such as clothes and shoes.[29] Taking a hint from Wal-Mart's tagline ("Save money, live better"), Szulczewski developed a solution to connect consumers to cheaper products. The result was Wish, a price-focused **e-commerce platform**. A platform differs from an ordinary retailer in that it connects buyers and sellers, rather than selling goods itself. Wish separates itself from other platforms such as the Amazon Marketplace in that it focuses on the lowest-cost sellers, primarily from China, and offers no bells and whistles, for instance, fast or free shipping. A $2 sweater with a $2 fee for four-week shipping is a typical Wish purchase. The platform was a hit, becoming the most downloaded app in 2018.

USA

Despite this success, it soon became apparent that Wish had a dark side: counterfeit and knock-off goods. This problem was no secret, and even resulted in a popular meme format at the time that would poke fun at anything that looks like an inferior version of a well-known product (e.g., the poorly received 2019 remake of Disney's *Lion King* film might appear in a meme as "When you order Lion King from Wish"). Underneath this humor, though, is a serious legal and ethical issue. Small overseas sellers on Wish routinely sell goods that claim to be prestigious brands such as Gucci or Supreme, or that use logos meant to resemble these brands; the counterfeiters profit while the consumer receives a subpar imitation.[30] Luxury streetwear brand Off-White has even sued over 100 such sellers.[31]

It can be challenging to keep such sellers off the platform, though; even if Wish bans a seller, the same goods can just resurface under a "new" seller that might be linked to the same counterfeiters. It is an open question whether buyers are also responsible for this state of affairs. After all, if a consumer orders a $5 Gucci bag, she almost certainly knows that it is fake.

These issues contributed to Wish's decline in 2022 and 2023 and created opportunities for competing e-commerce apps, such as Temu, to gain prominence.

Ethical dilemmas:

1. Who is potentially harmed by the sale of counterfeit goods on e-commerce platforms such as Wish? How exactly are they harmed?
2. Can you think of any ways that platforms such as Wish could discourage or prevent transactions involving counterfeit goods on its platform? Do you think that platforms have a responsibility to do so?

- IKEA initially struggled in this arena as well, as you will see in this chapter's Marketing Fail. For born-digital online retailers such as Amazon—which has built or acquired physical retail space, for instance, Whole Foods stores—the challenge is instead "**adding bricks to clicks**," or integrating brick-and-mortar stores into an existing online channel. This chapter's case on fashion retailer Zalando also illustrates a bricks-to-clicks approach, featuring smaller "pop-up" stores that incur less cost and risk for the retailer.[32]

"adding bricks to clicks" Integrating a new brick-and-mortar channel with an existing e-commerce channel

German electronics retailer MediaMarkt has been a pioneer in successful omnichannel retailing and channel integration. The brand sums up its own omnichannel strategy as follows:

> By closely linking the online shops in all the countries in which it operates with the local bricks-and-mortar stores, customers can now decide between a number of different sales channels. … Customers can, for example, pick up purchases made online at a local MediaMarkt store the very same day, subject to availability, and take advantage of services offered at the store. Alternatively, they can obtain advice at a local store and then order online and have the products delivered to their home. … The individual combination of sales channels – i.e. omnichannel – is the name of the game at MediaMarkt. And this is first and foremost beneficial to the customers' shopping experience as they get the best of both worlds. Whatever customers need, whenever they need it, they will find it at MediaMarkt.[33]

In this description, MediaMarkt shows a keen awareness of the central benefit of omnichannel retailing: *adaptability*. Based on Marketing Principle #1 (all customers differ), we know that not all customers want to shop online, and not all customers want to visit a store. And based on Marketing Principle #2 (all customers change), we know that the same customer's preference for each channel might change over time and in different situations. An omnichannel approach embraces customer differences and dynamics by providing each customer the type of retail experience they want, when they want it.

The omnichannel era has also seen the growth of digital goods and services. These services fall into four categories.

digital goods retailers Firms that sell intangible computer code, such as downloadable software or movies, to consumers

1. With the rise of digital media such as music, movies, and video games, **digital goods retailers** are vital in today's economy. For example, Steam, the most popular online storefront for buying and downloading PC games, took in $4.3 billion in revenue in 2017.[34] Digital goods retailers such as Steam tend to work like typical e-commerce sites, including wish lists, product recommendations, and user reviews of products. The key difference is that the product itself is a bundle of computer code to be downloaded rather than a tangible good.
2. Physical goods providers increasingly offer digital services. Possibly the most successful example of this trend is grocery delivery service. For example, in 2017 UK supermarket chain Tesco launched a service allowing London consumers to order groceries from their local store using an app, and have them delivered within one hour by a worker driving a moped.[35]
3. Brick-and-mortar service providers are offering an **online service channel**, where customers can receive the same (or similar) service,

online service channel A means for customers to receive the same service (or a near analogue) as they would in a physical service provider location but through digital means such as web conferencing

MARKETING FAIL IKEA's Early Omnichannel Setbacks

Perhaps no company better illustrates the challenges of an omnichannel world than IKEA. The famed furniture and home goods retailer opened its first store in southern Sweden in 1958; fifty years later, it was the largest furniture retailer in the world and now boasts over 400 stores. So successful is the firm that its most popular item, the Billy bookcase, has sold over *110 million* units.[36] That is about one bookcase for every seventy-two humans on the planet.

Each massive store is a testament to IKEA's expertise in the brick-and-mortar retail experience. The stores feature furniture arranged in natural and pleasing room layouts along a defined path; the furniture itself can conveniently be picked up at the end of this path; and the stores feature restaurants and even children's play areas. Everything about the in-store experience, from the meatballs to the quirky product names such as Örfjäll, inspires loyalty among IKEA's core shoppers.[37]

IKEA's e-commerce operation did not initially achieve such acclaim. As this chapter highlights, trying to run an omnichannel retailer is like trying to ride a skateboard and a rollerblade at the same time; the two work completely differently but must somehow be made to move in the same direction. This takes a lot of expertise in both areas, and IKEA's brick-and-mortar knowledge did not initially translate to the online space. The firm also failed to invest seriously in this space for many years, as it became known for clunky online store layouts and inaccurate information.[38] These problems came to a head during the coronavirus pandemic in 2020 as consumer demand shifted to the online channel, and demand for furniture increased with the rising need for home-based offices. Although IKEA tried to improve its online store in 2020, it was too little, too late, resulting in negative customer experiences. For example, consumers would see an item in-stock on the website, place an order, wait over a month, and then, only if the consumer was proactive in contacting customer service, find out that some of the items ordered were never in stock to begin with.[39]

Sweden

For IKEA, this experience taught a valuable lesson, and it has since improved its online experience. Yet its failure to proactively invest in omnichannel capabilities led to a missed opportunity to fully take advantage of shifting customer needs at a time of increased demand.

Diagnose the problem:

1. Why do you think that IKEA had not invested as much into its e-commerce operation, compared to some other retailers, before 2020?
2. What could IKEA have done to invest more extensively in omnichannel operations? In what ways could the brick-and-mortar and online channels work together to meet customer needs?

but through digital means such as web conferencing. Online classes at universities and telemedicine appointments at doctor's offices (see Opposing Views in this chapter) are notable examples. Obviously, this trend accelerated during coronavirus lockdowns, but it shows no signs of disappearing.

4. Some firms exclusively operate an online service channel: **online service providers**. Such businesses take a service that would traditionally be provided by visiting a local business and offer it exclusively in a digital format. Wholly online colleges such as Capella University, digital travel agencies such as Booking.com, and online mental health counseling firms all fit into this category.

online service providers Firms that exclusively operate an online service channel

telemedicine An online service channel that provides healthcare services over long distances; also known as telehealth and e-health

As we can see, the omnichannel era has seen an explosion in retail formats that offer goods and/or services using various combinations of offline and online channels. As a result, retailers' abilities to meet diverse and changing customer needs are greater than ever before. This cycle will likely continue in the future: as customer needs change, retailers will develop new store formats and strategies to meet these needs, and older formats and strategies will become obsolete or diminished.

OPPOSING VIEWS Expanding Telemedicine in Bangladesh

Source: Tumisu/Pixabay

Telemedicine has responded to customer preferences for digital interactions and expanded access to healthcare services, but critics point to serious limitations and abuses that are unique to online health care.

Telemedicine, also known as telehealth and e-health, refers to providing healthcare services over long distances. Nowadays, this generally means an online channel for healthcare services, in which patients speak to a doctor or nurse using tools such as Zoom.[40] Telemedicine has been very important in Bangladesh, where most people live in rural areas and access to in-person healthcare services is often limited. With the expansion of broadband internet access in the last twenty years, these rural Bangladeshis increasingly rely on telemedicine appointments for regular checkups, diagnosing illnesses, and prescribing medication.[41] The increased demand for remote healthcare options during the coronavirus pandemic only accelerated this growth.

Although having an online channel for healthcare services is a lifeline for those with no access to a local clinic, the widespread use of telemedicine among urban and suburban residents has drawn criticism. Some healthcare providers have been accused of pushing this service to cut costs, since telehealth appointments are cheaper to provide than office visits.[42] This push is especially problematic as surveys show that many Bangladeshis are skeptical of diagnoses provided over telemedicine; without building trust in a doctor through in-person appointments, these patients are reluctant to accept any surprising or unusual diagnoses.[43] Critics also note that telemedicine is vulnerable to fraud and abuse. For example, US-based telehealth start-up Cerebral came under fire for its providers allegedly being too lax in prescribing Adderall, a medication for ADHD (attention deficit hyperactivity disorder).[44]

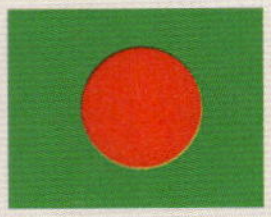

Bangladesh

Although telemedicine's critics acknowledge its advantages for rural areas, they also highlight the important limitations of translating an in-person service to an online channel.

See the issue from two sides:

1. Craft an argument in favor of widespread use of telemedicine in Bangladesh, including in urban areas. How can problems such as consumer trust and provider fraud be overcome?
2. Craft an argument against widespread use of telemedicine outside of Bangladesh's rural areas. As you develop arguments against this service, consider: are these arguments unique to health care, or do they apply to other online services?

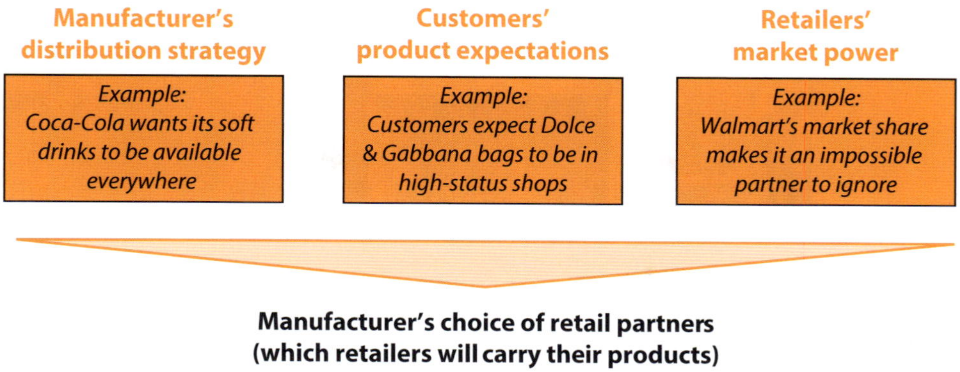

Figure 8.2 Retail Partner Selection.

Manufacturers usually pick which retailers will carry their products based on three factors: (1) the manufacturer's distribution strategy; (2) the customers' product expectations; and (3) the retailers' market power.

RETAILING FROM THE MANUFACTURER'S PERSPECTIVE: CHOOSING PARTNERS

So far, we have taken the perspective of retailers and consumers. But it is also worth considering a third set of players in the retail world: the manufacturers whose products line the store shelves of product retailers. For manufacturers, the key question in retailing is "Where should my products be?" This question is at the heart of the *place* dimension of the marketing mix for manufacturers. Producers of digital goods (e.g., music production companies) have a similar concern ("Which digital storefront should carry my music?"), but for simplicity's sake this section will focus on physical goods. Manufacturers have three factors to consider, as shown in Figure 8.2.

Manufacturers answer the "place" question based on three sets of factors. First, the *manufacturer's own distribution strategy* must be considered. There are three broad approaches:

- **Intensive distribution**, the manufacturer tries to get its product on the shelves in as many places as possible. Coca-Cola's Fanta soft drink, for example, can be found at supermarkets, convenience stores, hypermarkets, restaurants and bars, and virtually any retail location that sells or serves soft drinks. Intensive distribution is used when the product has wide appeal and the manufacturer wants to make it broadly available.

intensive distribution A strategy in which the manufacturer tries to get its product on the shelves in as many retailers as possible

- **Exclusive distribution** is the opposite of intensive distribution and designates only *one* retailer as a distribution partner. For example, when Australian apparel brand Woolmark entered the Indian market, it exclusively partnered with Tata Cliq, a luxury e-commerce platform.[45] This strategy is common when the manufacturer wants to maintain tighter control of the brand's image. The retailer's service quality and the aesthetic environment of its stores can affect how consumers view the products being sold there, so the manufacturer only associates with a partner that it can trust to deliver a suitable customer experience.[46]

exclusive distribution A strategy in which one retailer is designated as the manufacturer's sole distribution partner

Source: Pexels/Pixabay

Manufacturers of luxury goods, such as high-end handbags, often rely on exclusive or selective distribution strategies with a limited number of retail partners. These strategies also align with customer expectations that such products should be rare and special.

selective distribution A strategy in which several retailers are designated as the manufacturer's distribution partners

- **Selective distribution**, driven by a similar motivation, is a happy medium between intensive and exclusive distribution. The manufacturer makes its products more broadly available than it does in exclusive distribution by having multiple retail partners; but unlike with intensive distribution, the manufacturer carefully screens these partners to ensure that they will align with the brand's positioning and image.

Two other factors are important in selecting retail partners: *customers' product expectations* and *retailers' market power*:

- Customers' expectations are closely related to the issue highlighted above, namely, that consumers associate the image of the retailer with the image of the brands on its shelves. Different consumers shop at different stores depending on personal factors (e.g., income and social status) as well as situational factors (e.g., everyday purchases versus gift buying). Each of these factors affects the consumer's expectations when they enter a store. If a woman enters a store to buy groceries, she does not expect to see Dolce & Gabbana handbags for sale and will be puzzled by the manufacturer's actions. Likewise, if a wealthy woman enters a high-end department store, she might be perplexed by plastic bottles of Fanta offered for sale, as this product doesn't match her expectations for a premium retail experience.
- The relative power of retailers and the manufacturer also affects how products are placed in retail stores. It directly relates to issues such as how prices are

negotiated between the two companies and whether the manufacturer, for example, pressures the retailer to offer more of its products on store shelves. In the case of retail stores *owned* by the manufacturer, such as jewelry brand Tiffany & Co.'s own stores, this factor becomes irrelevant. That is because the retailer and manufacturer are the same entity, so the power dynamic between them is moot. But in most other cases, power dynamics become critically important. Retail shelf space is limited, so it can be difficult for a manufacturer to persuade a powerful retailer to carry its products at all. Yet a retailer can be so powerful that it is virtually impossible to gain broad market access without that retailer. US-based Walmart is a classic example. In dozens of major metropolitan areas, Walmart owns the *majority* of grocery market share, so food suppliers have no choice but to deal with Walmart.[47] In cases such as these, a supplier might earn 100 percent of its revenue from a single dominant retailer—not because of an exclusive distribution strategy, but because of the overwhelming power of the retailer.[48]

IN OTHER WORDS . . .

When a manufacturer develops a retail distribution plan for its product, it aims for a plan that aligns with its overall strategy and goals for the product. But this strategy must accommodate and adapt to the realities of the marketplace, including powerful retailers and influential customer expectations.

Thus, manufacturers have to consider three interrelated factors—their own strategy, their customers, and their potential retail partners—when devising a strategy for the "place" component of the marketing mix. They must do so while also considering the relative advantages of specific retail formats and offline and online channels discussed earlier in the chapter.

CHAPTER CASE STUDY

Germany

ZALANDO'S TWO-PRONGED APPROACH TO OMNICHANNEL STRATEGY

Zalando SE is a great success story of digital European retail. The German online apparel store started out in 2008 focused on shoes, before expanding into other apparel. By building alternate-language versions of its e-commerce store and growing its distribution network, it was able to expand its online sales presence out of Germany and into France, the Netherlands, Italy, and the United Kingdom.[49] Following expansion to additional countries and the acquisition of several smaller fashion brands, Zalando became the EU's largest e-commerce fashion store and held about 10 percent of the overall European apparel market.[50] In the late 2010s, around the same time that Amazon was establishing a brick-and-mortar presence by acquiring Whole Foods, Zalando wanted to expand its market with an omnichannel strategy.[51] It aimed to do so with two approaches: a direct entry into the brick-and-mortar channel with Zalando Beauty Station, and an indirect expansion into brick-and-mortar via the Zalando Connected Retail program. Each approach came with unique benefits and risks.

A direct approach: Zalando Beauty Station. In 2018, following Zalando's successful launch of beauty products such as makeup and shampoo, the firm's executives took a bold step. The online-native brand not only opened its first brick-and-mortar store but did so with a retail format focused entirely on this emerging beauty category. Dubbed "Zalando Beauty Station," the Berlin outlet stocked famous beauty brands, for instance Estée Lauder, and focused on hands-on experiences such as expert-guided makeup tutorials.[52] This was a textbook approach for an "adding bricks to clicks" strategy,[53] as the brick-and-mortar store: (1) focused on the unique benefits of a physical store, such as hands-on product experiences, and (2) heavily featured Zalando logos and branding, enhancing the physical presence of the brand and doubling as a powerful advertisement for the online store.

An indirect approach: Zalando Connected Retail. At first glance, Connected Retail seems to be an odd way for Zalando to expand its brick-and-mortar presence. Through Connected Retail, small, European brick-and-mortar fashion retailers can list their goods on Zalando's site as third-party sellers. The program differs from platforms such as the Amazon Marketplace in that it includes a curated set of retailers with local, physical stores, rather than thousands of anonymous overseas sellers.[54] Thus, with Connected Retail, Zalando is using an "adding clicks to bricks" strategy, adding an online channel for *other* retailers.

This may seem strange, but by tying its fortunes to local brick-and-mortar retailers that its customers see every day, Zalando gains two advantages: (1) it adds more products to its online catalog, and (2) it builds more tangible connections with customers, as participating stores can actively promote their ties to Zalando. As the firm states in its own promotional materials, part of the goal is for Zalando to become "more locally relevant."[55] It remains to be seen whether these omnichannel strategies will pay off for Zalando, but the brand continues to see modest growth.

CASE QUESTIONS

1. The case highlighted several potential benefits of Zalando Beauty Station. List and explain at least two significant risks of this strategy.
2. The case described some notable advantages of the Zalando Connected Retail program. List and explain at least two significant risks that come with this approach.
3. Given a limited budget to expand future omnichannel efforts, which of the two programs do you think Zalando should focus on growing in the future (e.g., adding more Connected Retail partners or building more brick-and-mortar stores)? Why?

CHAPTER SUMMARY

Retail and omnichannel marketing give rise to unique marketing challenges, while representing perhaps the most striking example of changing customer preferences. Retail and omnichannel marketing have changed tremendously over the years. Retail titans such as Sears, once a mainstay of consumer shopping habits, have disappeared from the landscape, with e-commerce giants and numerous smaller players vying to fill the void. This chapter examines the historical and ongoing sources of customer dynamics in this industry. Shifting preferences, the current state of the art, and relevant terminology are introduced in the areas of the evolution of retailing, retail store formats, retail partner selection, and omnichannel operations. For example, understanding the various categories of online and offline channels lays the groundwork for studying the evolution in preferences from traditional department stores to larger discount stores, to pure-play e-commerce stores, to online-native omnichannel retailers.

APPLICATION QUESTIONS

1. Try to think of your first memory of visiting a retail store. What do you remember about the experience? How would a visit to the same store, or a similar store, be different today?
2. Think of your favorite online retailer. If it has brick-and-mortar stores, explain why these stores are beneficial (or not beneficial) for the retailer. If it does not have physical locations, explain why added them would be useful (or not) to you.
3. Recall the "retail apocalypse" discussed in this chapter. Think of a retailer that has "died" in this apocalypse. In your opinion, what led to this store's demise?
4. Imagine starting an independent store selling musical instruments in the year 1900. Describe at least two types of marketing mix decisions you would have to make, and what factors would be important in these decisions.
5. Recent decades have seen the closure of many shopping malls. Do you think that shopping malls will disappear entirely? Why or why not?
6. Think of your favorite omnichannel retailer. Describe at least two ways that it employs channel integration strategies.
7. Think of (or find) an example of a retailer taking either an "adding clicks to bricks" or "adding bricks to clicks" strategy. What was the retailer's goal in adopting this strategy, and do you believe it was successful?

Visit the companion website, **https://bloomsbury.pub/palmatier-marketing**, or **https://samsinstitute.com**, for additional learning and teaching tools, including professional videos outlining the Four Principles, PowerPoint tutorials with voice-over commentary, sample syllabi for marketing courses, testbank and more.

Chapter 9

MARKETING RESEARCH AND ANALYTICS FOR MANAGING CUSTOMER DYNAMICS AND CUSTOMER DIFFERENCES

CHAPTER OVERVIEW

In this chapter, you will learn about marketing research and analytics. These are the processes that companies use to gather data and learn about customers and competitors. The chapter will answer the following questions:

- What is the value of marketing research and analytics?
- What five steps are involved in performing marketing research and analytics? What challenges arise in each step?
- What are the four fundamental ways that marketers can approach data analysis, and how do these differ?

You will also hear of cutting-edge practices as well as failures from some of today's major companies in this chapter's cases and features. For example, you will learn about:

- IBM's data-mining practices (Chapter Case).
- LG's poorly researched efforts to make 3D TV mainstream (Marketing Fail).
- Ethical challenges facing marketing researchers, such as data privacy (Opposing Views) and deception (Shades of Gray).

LEARNING OBJECTIVES

- Recognize the importance of marketing research and analytics for managing customer differences and dynamics.
- Identify key terms and concepts in the marketing research process.
- Associate various research methods with problems of customer differences and dynamics.
- Compare different categories of marketing analytics.
- Evaluate moral and ethical concerns in conducting and using marketing research.

IMAGINE Trying to Sell Lab-Grown Steak

A handful of biotechnology start-ups want to sell lab-grown meat: real animal muscle cells grown in a lab, with the same texture as natural meat. Some are even focusing on exotic meats, such as lion and tiger.[1] Imagine you are working in marketing for a start-up that has perfected the technology to grow a well-marbled sirloin steak from cow cells in the lab at a reasonable cost. As exciting as this breakthrough is, you have some difficult work ahead of you. You need to sort out who exactly will want to buy this meat. You are worried that some people might find meat grown in a lab a bit off-putting. You also wonder what vegetarians and vegans might think of it. After all, no animals are harmed in the steak's production. Could hardcore steak aficionados go for the product, or would their finely tuned palettes detect subtle differences between lab steak and natural steak? And what about restaurants? You will need to do some research to find out which segments will be interested, and what kinds of messages might encourage them to try lab-grown steak.

Critical thinking:

1. Pick a group of customers that might be interested in lab-grown steak. What kind of research could you do to assess the potential of this segment? How could you gauge what advertising messages might appeal to this segment?
2. Think of a potential objection or source of hesitancy that could stop someone from trying lab-grown meat. What kind of research could you do to determine how severe or common this objection is? How could you measure what types of advertising messages might overcome this objection?

THE IMPORTANCE OF INSIGHT

The combination of Marketing Principle #1, all customers differ, and Marketing Principle #2, all customers change, results in a complex landscape that shifts under marketers' feet. To see customers' preferences, where they are headed, and what threats competitors pose, marketers need to gather intelligence. This is the role of **marketing research**: planning, executing, and analyzing studies that help marketing decision-makers see more clearly. The critical output of marketing research is **insight**, meaning information that results in better decisions.

marketing research The functional role in the firm responsible for planning, executing, and analyzing studies that help marketing decision-makers see more clearly

insight The output of marketing research; information that results in better decisions

Insights About Customers

One key goal of marketing research is learning about customers. Decisions about managing customer differences and customer dynamics rely on marketing research:

- For example, marketers need to do a segmentation study to build a segmentation, targeting, and positioning (STP) strategy. This may involve gathering data about existing customers, surveying customers more broadly, or both.
- Likewise, Acquisition–Expansion–Retention (AER) models require marketers to track customers as they move between relationship stages. This tracking involves frequent collection and analysis of customer data, therefore it becomes the responsibility of marketing research and marketing analytics.

Source: Werner Moser/Pixabay

Modern marketers can derive insights about customers by mining sentiment (feelings and attitudes) from posts on social media.

With more advanced marketing research techniques, marketers can glean ever-deeper insights about attitudes and behaviors of customers. For example, analyzing thousands of posts scraped from individual users on social media, such as Facebook, allows analysts to measure real-time brand sentiments such as delight, disgust, anger, and surprise.[2]

Insights About Competitors

Marketing research and analytics are also crucial to understanding and predicting competitors. Because competitor reactions are at the heart of Part 4, this chapter focuses primarily on customer insights. But it should come as no surprise that a well-thought-out marketing plan could fizzle out when a competitor has an even better plan. Marketers can reduce this risk by using marketing research and analytics to learn about competitors' strategies. For example, interviewing customers of a competing restaurant allows a restaurateur to understand the competitor's service tactics.

FIVE STEPS FOR INSIGHTS: THE MARKETING RESEARCH PROCESS

Each business does marketing research differently, with some using a rigid series of steps and others approaching research more informally. Generally, though, a marketing research project goes through five steps to generate insights for decision makers, as shown in Figure 9.1 with additional detail in Table 9.1:

MARKETING FAIL LG's Shortsighted Foray into 3D TV

Source: NikolayF.com/Pixabay

LG gambled on 3D television being the future. This turned out to be a gamble based on faulty intelligence. Perhaps these glasses bear part of the blame.

South Korean technology firm LG Electronics, Inc. is known for televisions at the leading edge of technology. In 2010 the firm released the first LED TV to have 3D capabilities. Proclaimed by LG as "a radical departure from the past," this technology seemed to have a bright future.[3] Competitors such as Samsung agreed, as several brands of 3D TVs soon entered the market. Practical constraints, such as having to wear 3D glasses, seemed trivial next to the transformational entertainment experience on offer. After all, LG's research showed that consumers could put up with wearing glasses to access 3D content.

South Korea

Unfortunately, neither LG's 3D TVs nor any of its competitors earned the level of success that they had hoped for. By 2017, the feature was nearly gone from LG's product lineup.[4] Analysts placed the blame on the high prices for the TVs and comparatively low value, since 3D content was especially sparse on streaming services.[5] It seemed that studios and other content producers had a different view of 3D technology, and never quite took the plunge in the same way that LG did. Some observers noted that social media chatter in the early 2010s was seldom particularly positive, hinting at the uphill battle the technology faced.[6] Although 3D TVs retain a niche market presence, it is unlikely that they will ever reach the level of widespread adoption predicted by LG.

Diagnose the problem:

1. Explain why LG's 3D TVs did not achieve their anticipated success.
2. What was the role of marketing research in this failure? Could LG have used marketing research to better recognize the limitations of the 3D TV market?

---

1. Understand research objectives.
2. Design a research plan.
3. Gather data.
4. Analyze data.
5. Report findings.

Each of these steps is explained in detail in this section.

understanding research objectives The first step of the marketing research process; it involves identifying what problem the research is trying to solve and whose problem it is

research stakeholders The individuals in the firm who will rely on a marketing research project's insights

Step 1: Understand Research Objectives

The first step in designing marketing research, **understanding research objectives**, includes identifying what problem the research is trying to solve and also *whose problem it is*. Researchers must speak with the people in the company who will rely on the project's insights, known as **research stakeholders**. For example, a project to estimate market potential for a new line of sneakers should know what metrics the product manager is interested in and how the market potential should be broken down by segment.

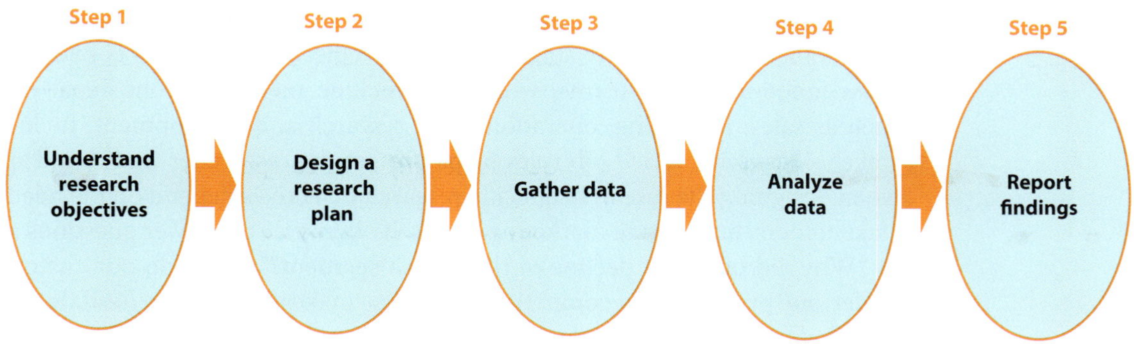

Figure 9.1 Marketing Research Process.

The five steps of a typical marketing research process: (1) understand research objectives; (2) design a research plan; (3) gather data; (4) analyze data; and (5) report findings. Not every business performs exactly these steps in exactly this order.

Table 9.1 Five Steps of the Marketing Research Process.

Although firms vary in how they execute marketing research, and how formalized their processes are, generating marketing research insights typically involves five steps.

Step	Definition	Examples
1. Understand research objectives	Identifying what problem the research is trying to solve and whose problem it is (i.e., who are the stakeholders)	PwC's consulting practice forms cross-functional teams with members from many departments to incorporate diverse perspectives into the research objectives
2. Design a research plan	Developing the overall research methodology in a way that flows from the objectives	An experiment had B2B buyers read a description of a supplier across conditions based on what combination of online, self-service channels and salesperson-based, high-touch channels were offered
3. Gather data	Collecting the input for planned analyses by executing the research plan	Researchers wanting to track customer sentiment on social media can scrape external secondary data from sites such as Twitter and Instagram
4. Analyze data	Trying to extract insights that address the research objectives from the data that was collected	A project seeking to map customers' movements across AER stages over time will involve repeated measurements of each customer's relationship and longitudinal analyses of these measurements
5. Report findings	Communicating insights from the data so that they can be used by decision-makers	CRM analytics functionality in Salesforce allows live estimates of conversion probability to be displayed to salespeople when choosing which prospects to pursue, and allows automated reporting of findings

In multinational consulting firm PwC, clients are urged to include diverse stakeholders from an early stage in projects. One way to do this is by forming cross-functional work teams, which can include members from departments such as sales, marketing, operations, and research and development. Including stakeholders with varied job roles helps protect the researcher from blind spots when designing the research. Specific research objectives depend on the needs of stakeholders, but routine marketing research often tries to answer questions such as "Why did our sales decline in the largest segment?" "Why do our customers prefer our product over competitors?" "What makes consumers hesitate to use our product?" "How much do we expect to sell next quarter?"

Step 2: Design a Research Plan

design a research plan The second step of the marketing research process; it involves developing the overall research methodology in a way that flows from the objectives

The researcher must next **design a research plan**, in which the overall research method is developed; this method should flow from the objectives, and can involve *qualitative* and *quantitative* studies. Building on the chapter's opening case, exploring potential objections to lab-grown meat might require more open-ended dialogues with consumers. In other words, this case calls for qualitative research, in which the researcher is not trying to predict a sales outcome or measure a relationship between variables but instead delve deeply into a subject—such as attitudes about lab-grown meat—and uncover patterns and themes in consumer responses.[7] Such research is best suited to open-ended questions, such as "Why do customers leave us?" and "How does our product mesh with our customers' day-to-day lives?" but ill-suited to questions with a quantifiable answer, such as "What is the optimal price for our product?" or "How much will the overall market grow next year?" Typical qualitative research plans will include some combination of methods such as:

interviews A primary data methodology, typically used for qualitative research, in which the researcher asks customers a series of probing questions

focus groups A primary data methodology, typically used for qualitative research, which involves the researcher jointly interviewing a group of consumers to get focused feedback on a product or other aspect of the marketing mix

qualitative observation A primary data methodology, typically used for *qualitative* research, which involves the researcher passively observing consumer behavior in a live marketing setting

quantitative research A research paradigm which involves data that can be tabulated as numbers in a spreadsheet and tested for relationships between variables

surveys A primary data methodology, typically used for quantitative research, which require each respondent to answer a battery of questions, often on a scale of 1 to 7 to gauge attitudes and intentions

- **Interviews**, in which the researcher asks customers a series of probing questions. For example, interviewers can ask consumers if they have heard of the brand, or what emotions the brand evokes.
- **Focus groups**, which involve the researcher interviewing a group of consumers to get focused feedback on a product or other aspect of the marketing mix. For example, the researcher can bring prototypes of a new virtual reality (VR) device to a focus group, and allow consumers to use the device and provide their impressions of it.
- **Qualitative observation**, which requires the researcher to observe consumer behavior in a live marketing setting. This could involve watching how consumers navigate placing an order in a coffee shop, for example.

The flipside of qualitative research is **quantitative research**, which involves data that can be tabulated as numbers in a spreadsheet and tested for relationships between variables (e.g., correlations). As lab-grown meat evolves out of the introduction phase of the product life cycle and faces more routine problems, such as how to set competitive prices for the product, quantitative research will be warranted. Classic quantitative research involves surveys and experiments.

Surveys require each respondent to answer a battery of questions, often on a 1–7 scale (e.g., from 1 = Strongly disagree to 7 = Strongly agree), to gauge attitudes about the product and purchase intentions. For example, one survey found that tradeshow attendees prefer booths with open, rather than closed, architectures.[8] **Experiments** randomly assign participants to different conditions to test the effects of the differences between those conditions. For example, an experiment in which B2B buyers read about a supplier said they were more likely to buy when the supplier was described as offering a combination of online, self-service channels and salesperson-based, high-touch channels.[9] More modern quantitative methods also use **observational studies** (not to be confused with qualitative observation), in which researchers look for patterns in preexisting data. For example, researchers can measure the performance of publicly traded companies that form alliances to understand the effectiveness of those alliances.[10]

Quantitative and qualitative methodologies are complements, not competitors. Open-ended probing with qualitative studies can set the stage for more specific, targeted questions to test in quantitative studies. In other cases, quantitative studies deliver puzzling findings, and **qualitative research** can help unravel the puzzle. After all, numbers don't lie, but they also don't tell the whole story. For example, quantitative analyses might reveal that a new phone targeted to younger consumers instead performed better with older consumers, leaving marketers scratching their heads. Follow-up qualitative research provides an opportunity to explain these gaps.

experiments A primary data methodology, typically used for quantitative research, in which participants are randomly assigned to different conditions to test the effects of the differences between those conditions

observational studies A secondary data methodology (not to be confused with qualitative observation), typically used for quantitative research, in which researchers look for patterns in preexisting data

qualitative research A research paradigm in which the researcher is not trying to predict an outcome or measure a relationship between variables, but instead delve deeply into an open-ended phenomenon and uncover patterns and themes in consumer responses

Step 3: Gather Data

Gathering data involves the researcher collecting the information to analyze, and is largely a matter of executing the research plan. The different kinds of data correspond to the type of research being done. Interviews collect interview responses, surveys collect survey responses, and so on. An important distinction exists, though, between *primary* and *secondary* data:

- Data collected specifically for the study is called **primary data**. Qualitative observation, interviews, surveys, focus groups, and experiments (all described in Step 2) generate primary data.
- Data that already existed prior to the study is known as **secondary data**. While observational studies typically rely on secondary data. Secondary data may be further broken down based on its source: **internal secondary data** includes transaction and customer relationship information from the company's digital database, while **external secondary data** can involve a combination of free, publicly available data (e.g., from the Census Bureau in the United States) and private, purchased data (e.g., from data brokers such as IRI and Nielsen). Data gathered from social media websites, such as Twitter posts, would be considered external secondary data.

Marketing researchers typically use a combination of primary and secondary data in their projects. For example, a segmentation study of the candy market might include primary survey data, asking about customer preferences (for specific flavors, textures, etc.), with purchased external secondary data (featuring demographic information such as age and income).

gathering data The third step of the marketing research process; it involves the researcher collecting the input for planned analyses by executing the research plan

primary data Data collected specifically for a marketing research study

secondary data Data that already existed prior to a marketing research study commencing

internal secondary data Secondary data that resides within the firm, such as transaction logs

external secondary data Secondary data that resides outside of the firm, such as government agency statistics

SHADES OF GRAY Deception in Marketing Research

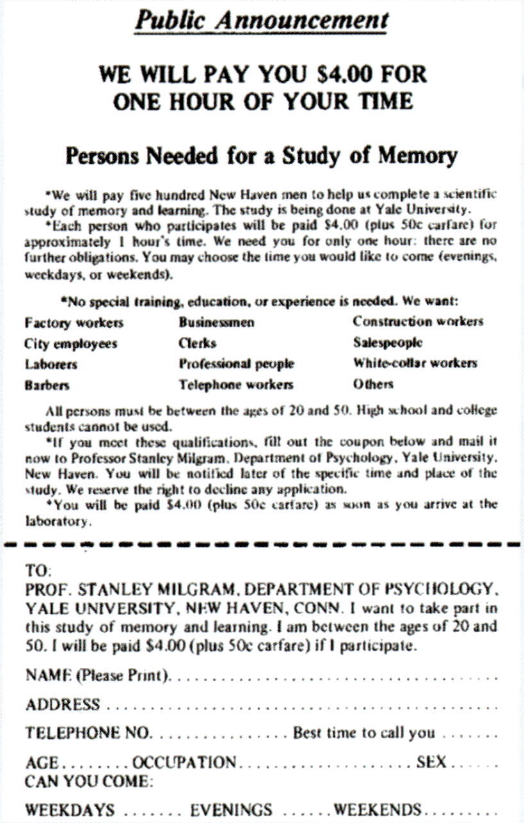
Public Announcement

WE WILL PAY YOU $4.00 FOR ONE HOUR OF YOUR TIME

Persons Needed for a Study of Memory

*We will pay five hundred New Haven men to help us complete a scientific study of memory and learning. The study is being done at Yale University.

*Each person who participates will be paid $4.00 (plus 50c carfare) for approximately 1 hour's time. We need you for only one hour: there are no further obligations. You may choose the time you would like to come (evenings, weekdays, or weekends).

***No special training, education, or experience is needed. We want:**

Factory workers	Businessmen	Construction workers
City employees	Clerks	Salespeople
Laborers	Professional people	White-collar workers
Barbers	Telephone workers	Others

All persons must be between the ages of 20 and 50. High school and college students cannot be used.

*If you meet these qualifications, fill out the coupon below and mail it now to Professor Stanley Milgram, Department of Psychology, Yale University, New Haven. You will be notified later of the specific time and place of the study. We reserve the right to decline any application.

*You will be paid $4.00 (plus 50c carfare) as soon as you arrive at the laboratory.

TO:
PROF. STANLEY MILGRAM, DEPARTMENT OF PSYCHOLOGY, YALE UNIVERSITY, NEW HAVEN, CONN. I want to take part in this study of memory and learning. I am between the ages of 20 and 50. I will be paid $4.00 (plus 50c carfare) if I participate.

NAME (Please Print)..

ADDRESS..

TELEPHONE NO. .... Best time to call you ....

AGE........ OCCUPATION.................... SEX......
CAN YOU COME:

WEEKDAYS .... EVENINGS ...... WEEKENDS.........

Source: © Photograph from the New Haven Register published in June 1961.

A flyer for Stanley Milgram's famous experiment on obedience to authority. The experiment was a classic example of deception in research, as it masqueraded as a study of memory.

Marketers are often stereotyped as tricksters and as slick, deceptive communicators in the popular imagination. Although this stereotype is usually not true, there is one area in which marketers have unapologetically lied: marketing research. This is because the objectives of a research study, such as a survey or experiment, sometimes cannot be achieved without deception. For example, a study that aims to measure racially biased attitudes will fail to collect useful data if it opens with "This is a study of racist attitudes"; people with such prejudices are likely to either drop out of the study or mask their biases when answering questions. This is due to **social desirability bias**, in which participants act inauthentically to meet the expectations of other people.[11] In this example, racial prejudices would have to be teased out with subtle questions—for example, after telling a story about a fictional crime and randomly varying the race of the perpetrator—and without mentioning the true purpose of the study.

Global

An iconic example of deception in research is psychologist Stanley Milgram's experiment on obedience to authority. Subjects were recruited to what they believed was a simple study of memory. They were assigned the role of teacher and an unseen partner in another room was assigned the role of student. They were told by a stern professor to administer electric shocks to the student if they incorrectly answered a question. As the experiment progressed, subjects were told to administer increasingly intense shocks. Most participants delivered a shock of 450 volts, believing another research subject was receiving that voltage.[12] Subjects later found out that the "student" was one of the researchers and was only pretending to receive electric shocks. The true purpose of the experiment was to learn whether ordinary people would harm an innocent person on the command of an authority figure. Obviously, this study could not have been conducted in this way without deception.

Although modern marketing research does not go to the extremes of Milgram's experiment, deception is alive and well in the field and remains in use when research questions cannot be achieved another way.

Ethical dilemmas:

1. Who is potentially harmed by deception in research, and how? Consider both the example of Milgram's experiment and the racial prejudice example.
2. For marketing research, where the direct or indirect goal is usually simply to enhance sales, is deception ever truly justified in your opinion? Why or why not?

Step 4: Analyze Data

social desirability bias The phenomenon in which research participants behave inauthentically to align with the expectations of other people

analyzing data The fourth step of the marketing research process; it involves trying to extract insights that address the research objectives from the data that was collected

The fourth step is **analyzing data**, in which marketers try to extract insights that address the research objectives from the data that was collected. Most of the discussion of this step will be reserved for the analytics section later in this chapter. At this point, it is important to mention three key points:

- The analysis should be planned at an early stage, before data are collected. Different analyses require different data. For example, advanced machine learning methods need thousands of data points. Similarly, getting fine-grained insights from the data—for example, understanding the factors that make some customer relationships more profitable than others—requires that data be collected at a sufficiently fine-grained level.
- When insights about customer dynamics are needed, **longitudinal data**—that is, repeated measurements of a customer's relationship over time—are needed. Such data can provide an early warning system about migration between AER states, such as by identifying growing or shrinking purchases.
- Finally, it is easy for analysts to arrive at incorrect conclusions, either by accident (see later discussion on correlation and causation) or on purpose (e.g., through deception; see the Chapter Case Study on challenges in data mining). To mitigate these problems, marketing research teams should seldom leave an analysis in the hands of one individual without oversight or a "second set of eyes" on the work.

longitudinal (customer) data Data that include repeated measurements of a customer relationship over time

Step 5: Report Findings

reporting findings The fifth step of the marketing research process; it involves communicating insights from the data so that they can be used by decision-makers

Reporting findings involves communicating analysis insights so that marketers can make better decisions. Traditionally, this involved a lengthy research report with four sections: the executive summary, featuring a quick overview of the most important insights; the body of the report, detailing the methods and findings; the conclusion, laying out the insights in detail; and lastly, charts and tables that supplement the report.

Increasingly, this formal report style is not agile enough for the pace of modern business. By the time an analyst prepares a fifty-page report, its insights are stale and no longer actionable. *Timeliness* is a critical feature of research insights. To rapidly get actionable recommendations to decision-makers, researchers and analysts look for ways to automate reporting. For example, using the CRM Analytics features within Salesforce, analytics can build a predictive model that estimates the probability that a specific prospect can be successfully converted into a sale. Taking it a step further, this prediction—in the form of a simple percentage probability—can be automatically generated as each prospect enters the database or is updated, and displayed on an informational card in the CRM page for that prospect.[13] In this way, salespeople have instant access to up-to-date analytical reporting so they know which prospects to spend time on. As sales and marketing technology advance, these agile reporting tools will become increasingly widespread.

THEORY SPOTLIGHT Marketing Research with Design Thinking

The principles of **design thinking** are applied in more and more fields, from product design to advertising, service innovation, crisis response, and even marketing research.[14] Design thinking is a solution-building philosophy and process with five steps:[15]

1. *Empathize*: The marketing researcher gains a deep empathetic understanding of the problem, in terms of what the problem is and *why* it is a problem. In marketing research, this often means dialogue with stakeholders of the research, such as product managers who will make decisions based on research insights.
2. *Define*: The researcher defines the problem based on the empathetic understanding developed in the first step.
3. *Ideate*: The researcher brainstorms as many research ideas that might solve the problem as possible, because a larger pool of potential solutions is more likely to include an optimal solution.
4. *Prototype*: The researcher selects an idea, mocks up a rough research plan, and probes the "prototype" plan for weaknesses.
5. *Test*: The research plan is implemented with live participants or data.

Design thinking requires multiple iterations; a prototype plan with a fatal flaw could lead to further ideation, while a thoroughly tested research plan will inform future studies. The design thinking process also maps onto most of the five-step process for marketing research discussed in this chapter. Empathizing and defining can be encapsulated in "Understanding research objectives"; ideating and prototyping fall under "Design a research plan"; while testing occurs in the "Gather data" and "Analyze data" steps. By breaking down the early steps of the process and highlighting the role of empathy, a design thinking approach challenges researchers to define their problems and plans more rigorously.

design thinking
A solution-building philosophy and process with five steps: empathize, define, ideate, prototype, and test

marketing analytics
The machine that takes data as fuel at one end and generates marketing insights at the other end

GETTING INSIGHTS FROM DATA WITH MARKETING ANALYTICS

The word "analytics" tends to bring scary thoughts to the surface: statistics, equations, Greek letters, and all manner of complicated concepts favored by self-described "quants" in the world. But **marketing analytics** is conceptually a simple machine: it takes data as fuel at one end and rolls out shiny new marketing insights at the other end. The inner workings of the machine—statistical models and coding and assumptions—are not a focus of this textbook. Increasingly, though, these details have less importance for analysts as well. Popular analysis software tools such as SAS, SPSS, Tableau, and Power BI are adopting powerful point-and-click interfaces, built-in metrics to evaluate the reliability of findings, and extensive plain-English help files. As a result, an analyst with only a basic statistical background can generate a wider range of insights than ever before. Extensive training never hurts, and remains necessary for certain tools, but it is no longer the barrier to entry that it once was.

This democratization of analytics is not without risks, though. The end-of-chapter case on data mining highlights several forms of analysis malpractice, and a novice researcher could be even more vulnerable to these. In addition, analysis software sometimes has no way of knowing that the data are bad. For example, the program has no way of knowing if a survey question is poorly worded (e.g., "Don't

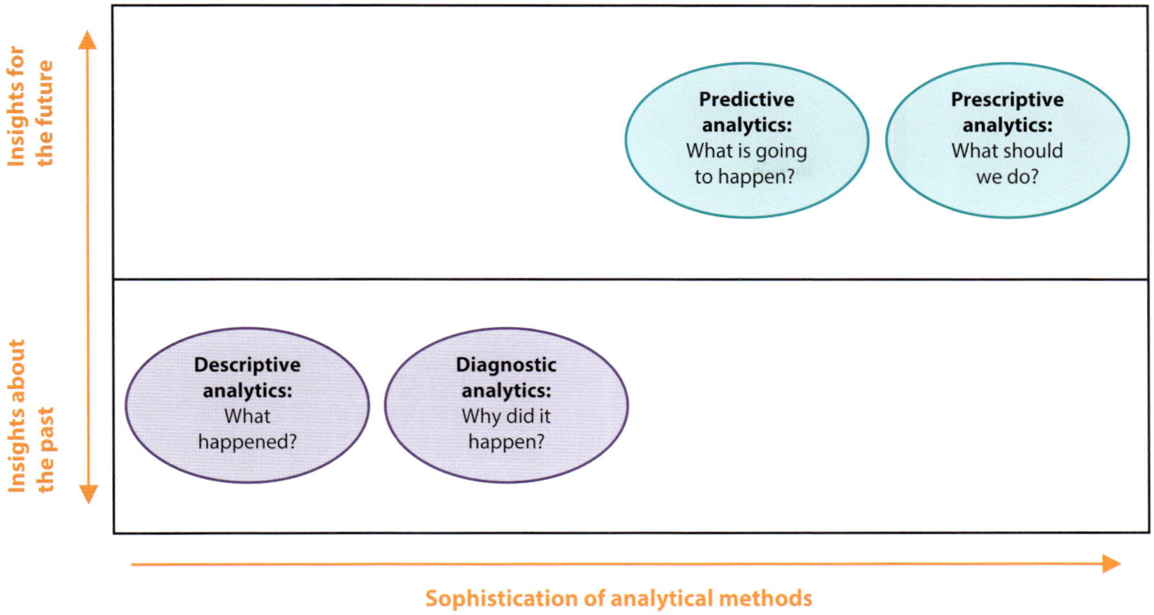

Figure 9.2 Types of Analytics.

A comparison of the four flavors of marketing analytics. Descriptive and diagnostic analytics examined the present and past and are comparatively less sophisticated. Predictive and prescriptive analytics focus on the future and require more advanced methods. All four types of analytics are needed for marketers to understand the past and plan for the future.

you agree that Honda is one of the most reliable automobile brands?") and would take the overly positive responses to this question at face value. This results in an ever-present problem: **garbage in, garbage out (GIGO)**. If the analytics machine is fed poor-quality fuel, it will not produce very useful insights—worse, they may be outright misleading. Hence, marketing researchers and analysts should work in tandem to ensure that only the best fuel goes into these analyses.

garbage in, garbage out (GIGO) The principle that feeding poor-quality data into marketing analytics will result in poor-quality or misleading insights

So far, this discussion has treated all analytics the same. In reality, distinct types of analytics have different objectives and levels of sophistication, as shown in Figure 9.2. These types can be grouped into categories focused on *the past and present* and focused on *the future*.

Analyzing the Past and the Present: Descriptive and Diagnostic Analytics

Descriptive Analytics

The simplest and most widespread flavor of analytics is **descriptive analytics**. These analyses answer the question: "*What happened*?"[16] They typically involve taking the average or sum of past sales or another outcome of interest, perhaps grouped by product categories or time period, and displaying them in a table or chart. One of the most common examples of descriptive analytics is the performance dashboard that a salesperson sees when she opens a CRM app, such as Salesforce. A **dashboard** displays multiple key performance metrics and charts in one place to be examined at a glance by a broad audience. This can show a salesperson, for example, a line chart that visualizes their progress toward meeting their sales quota.

descriptive analytics Analyses that involve averages or sums of past outcomes, sometimes by group, to answer the question: "What happened?"

dashboard A display of multiple key performance metrics and charts in one place to be examined at a glance by a broad audience

Source: Pexels/Pixabay

Performance dashboards, featuring multiple visualizations and tables arrayed on a single page, are a popular way to communicate descriptive analytics to managers.

data visualization The graphical display of quantitative information

Dashboards heavily rely on **data visualization**—the "graphic representation of quantitative information," usually in a chart—by using performance history line charts, sales quota attainment gauges, product category mix pie charts, and other graphical elements.[17] This visualization is powerful for communicating to a general audience of managers, salespeople, and other employees because of the way the human brain is wired for graphical information; it can process an image in as little as *13 milliseconds*.[18] Therefore, dashboards allow decision-makers to quickly process descriptive analytics on the go.

Diagnostic Analytics

diagnostic analytics Analyses that build on descriptive analytics by answering the question: "Why did it happen?"

At the next level of analytical sophistication, marketers can perform **diagnostic analytics**. Building on descriptive output, these analyses provide an answer to the question: "*Why did it happen*?" The most basic diagnostics involve breaking descriptive analytics into more specific groupings. For example, a medical equipment sales manager who sees that her division did not meet its sales goal can drill down to the individual sales representatives and notice that a pair of salespeople performed poorly this month, causing the entire division's performance to sag. At a more advanced level, the analyst can measure what variables are associated (i.e., correlated) with marketing outcomes; for example, if advertising expenses are positively correlated with sales, it could be that sales declined this quarter because the firm cut back on advertising to save money.

causation When a variable, such as advertising, is directly responsible for a change in an outcome, such as sales

Finally, the most complex diagnostic analytics involve statistical models that attempt to go beyond correlation and establish **causation**—for example, proving that advertising expenses truly cause increases in sales. This is important because correlations can often be spurious, meaning that both variables are driven by something else. If one looks hard enough, such correlations are everywhere. The divorce rate in the US state of Maine is highly correlated with US per capita margarine consumption. Similarly, the number of people who drown in US swimming pools in a year strongly correlates with the number of films in which actor Nicholas Cage appears in a year.[19] Or, to return to the advertising example, a retail firm likely both advertises more and sells more during the holiday season, and advertises less and sells less during other seasons, such that a correlation will exist regardless of whether causation does.

General Data Protection Regulation (GDPR) A set of data privacy regulations, centered around individual ownership of personal data, that marketers in the EU and UK must follow

OPPOSING VIEWS Data Privacy in the European Union versus the United States

Marketing researchers and analysts are limited by government regulations in terms of what types of customer data they can collect and use. Depending on where a firm is operating, those limitations can look quite different. The United States and European Union (EU) provide a stark illustration of this.

In the EU, customers' personal data is governed by the 2018 **General Data Protection Regulation (GDPR)** (the United Kingdom passed a nearly identical privacy law after it exited the EU). Under this regulation, people have clear, explicit rights to their own data, such as the right to consent or refuse any data collection, the right to access any data collected, the right to correct any inaccurate data, the right to erase data, and several other protections along these lines.[20] The guiding principle is that a person owns her personal data, and firms can only collect and use this data as long as that person grants her consent, which may be withdrawn at any time. While a boon to consumers, these regulations are costly for technology companies, and this may reduce their desire to further expand in the EU.

In the United States, consumers have much less certainty about their data. Although health records and financial information can be protected under laws known as HIPAA and GLBA, individual rights for other forms of personal data are limited to a patchwork of state laws and court rulings. Broadly speaking, large technology firms such as Google in the United States—the most prolific data harvesters—are left to self-regulate in accordance with free market principles.[21] Some evidence suggests that this approach is at least partially effective, as the most high-profile firms have an incentive to protect their reputations by treating data responsibly. For example, Apple grants iPhone users tight control over apps' access to personal data, while Google has vowed to stop using tracking cookies in web browsers. Unfortunately, smaller players with less valuable brand names may lack this reputation incentive. It remains to be seen whether the US market will converge toward a GDPR-style privacy scheme or not.

See the issue from two sides:

1. Craft an argument in favor of the EU's approach to data privacy. Why do the benefits outweigh the costs?
2. Craft an argument in favor of the US's approach to data privacy. Why do the benefits outweigh the costs?

Analyzing the Future: Predictive and Prescriptive Analytics

Perfectly predicting the future is impossible, especially for marketing outcomes that depend on the buying behavior of fickle humans. Even weather forecasts, which rely only on natural phenomena, are notoriously unreliable. It is tempting, then, for an analyst to throw up his hands and stay out of the prediction business. But if he does this, marketers are rudderless in planning for the future, and will fall back on naïve projections and optimistic assumptions. As psychologist and management professor Philip Tetlock explains, "Fuzzy thinking can never be proven wrong. And only when we are proven wrong so clearly that we can no longer deny it to ourselves will we adjust our mental models of the world—producing a clearer picture of reality. Forecast, measure, revise: it is the surest path to seeing better."[22] The point is that prediction challenges the analyst to "call her shots," instead of waiting for outcomes to occur and proclaiming "I knew that would happen!" Only then can she learn to generate more accurate forecasts.

Predictive Analytics

Predictive analytics Analyses that project future outcomes by answering the question: "What is going to happen?"

Predictive analytics, as the name implies, involve projecting future outcomes by answering the question: "*What is going to happen*?" The most common use of predictive analytics is forecasting near-to-medium-term sales to plan inventory levels and set quotas for salespeople. They can also be used for estimating market potential, second-guessing competitors' actions, and countless other applications. In practice, predictions require a model of how outcomes are determined. This model can be a simple rule of thumb (e.g., next month's sales will be this month's sales plus 1 percent) or a more sophisticated statistical construction. More advanced models can involve extraordinarily complex statistical or machine learning methods that incorporate thousands of factors—at the level of the customer, the product, marketing actions, and the external environment—which could affect marketing outcomes. Even so, in markets with fast-changing customer preferences, the model's predictive power can quickly suffer if it is not frequently updated. As this chapter's Marketing Fail illustrates, LG did a poor job predicting the size of the 3D TV market and spent resources to support this segment that could have been more productively spent elsewhere.

Prescriptive Analytics

prescriptive analytics Analyses that build on predictions by offering (i.e., prescribing) recommendations to improve outcomes. These analyses answer the question: "What should we do?"

what-if analysis A prescriptive tool in which an analyst plugs different values into a predictive model to see how outcomes will be affected

Closely related to predictive analytics, **prescriptive analytics** build on predictions by offering (i.e., prescribing) recommendations to improve outcomes.[23] These analyses answer the question: "*What should we do*?" As the most sophisticated flavor of analytics, prescriptive recommendations require an underlying statistical model of how different factors affect an outcome such as sales. If a marketer knows exactly how strongly the price level or amount of advertising affects sales for a segment, then it is possible to "plug in" different values for these variables and see when the segment's sales will be highest. Based on this **what-if analysis**, different recommended pricing and advertising levels can be recommended for each segment. For example, if Netflix is considering increasing its subscription prices, it can first construct a model of how prices influence the number of subscribers. Then, it can run the model under different scenarios (e.g., high versus low future economic growth) and assumptions (what-if analysis) and select the path forward that leads to the highest profitability (the "prescription").

IN OTHER WORDS ...

Predictive and prescriptive analytics are two sides of the same coin. A predictive model must explain what factors cause an outcome (e.g., sales) to occur. Prescriptive analytics play with the hypothetical levels of these factors to see what can be done to increase sales. Or, for a more whimsical metaphor, prescriptive analytics involve peering into the future and examining all possible outcomes—much like Dr. Strange in the Marvel films—and recommending the choices that will lead to the best possible outcome.

Although the continuum from descriptive to prescriptive analytics entails increasing levels of sophistication, none of these flavors are substitutes or replacements for one another. Just as predictive and prescriptive analytics go hand in hand (see the preceding section), so do descriptive and diagnostic analytics work. After all, it makes little sense to ask "Why did this happen?" without first knowing the answer to "What happened?" Likewise, the two forward-looking branches of analytics cannot replace backward-looking analytics. Understanding past performance, and why it occurred, is a key step in building a predictive model for future performance. Thus, the four types of analytics work together to generate a cohesive set of insights that allow marketers to both understand the past and plan for the future.

CHAPTER CASE STUDY

ANALYTICS WITH CRISP-DM

Global

data mining The practice of conducting large-scale searches for interesting relationships between variables

CRISP-DM Cross-industry standard process for data mining; a series of formalized steps for using business understanding to inform data mining efforts, which in turn build up greater business understanding

In the late 1990s, the rise of computing technology created a new problem: analysts had more data than they knew what to do with. Hundreds or even thousands of variables could be used to describe a single customer's relationship with the firm, such as recency and frequency of purchasing specific products, geographic spread of buying across retail locations, and growth in spending across categories. Traditional marketing research-based analytics, in which narrow analyses are conducted to test a well-defined research question, could never touch the vast majority of available data. Hence, a consortium of five firms (Integral Solution, Teradata, Daimler AG, NCR Corporation, and OHRA), with funding from the European Union, came together to develop a standardized system for **data mining**, the practice of conducting large-scale searches for interesting data insights.[24]

Birth of CRISP-DM. The consortium's efforts culminated in 1999 with the publication of the cross-industry standard process for data mining, or **CRISP-DM**. The model was developed as an open standard for other firms to follow, rather than a process owned by the consortium companies. In the years to come the process became most closely associated with IBM, the long-lived US technology firm, which incorporates the process into its SPSS analysis software.[25]

Understanding CRISP-DM. CRISP-DM is almost always depicted with the somewhat confusing Figure 9.3. As the figure shows, the process has six interconnected steps:[26]

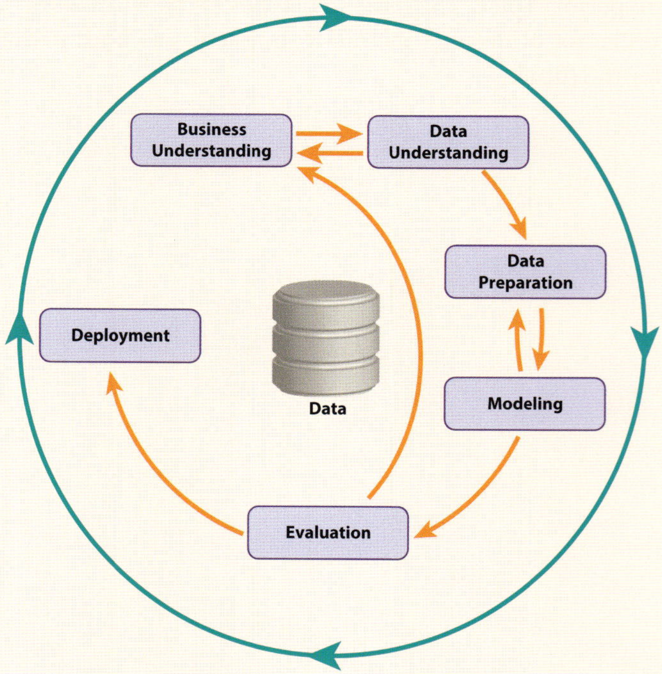

Figure 9.3 CRISP-DM Process.

The CRoss-Industry Process for Data Mining (CRISP-DM) has become a standard way to approach large-scale analytics. Critically, it begins with a deep understanding of underlying business problems.

Source: Kenneth Jensen/Wikimedia Commons

1. *Business understanding*: The analyst should develop a deep knowledge of the business problem that needs to be solved, in consultation with research stakeholders. This step is closely related to empathizing in the design thinking approach.
2. *Data understanding*: The analyst should know the available data inside and out, including its limitations and what questions cannot be asked of it.
3. *Data preparation*: The analyst processes the data, including eliminating poor-quality or out-of-date elements.
4. *Modeling*: The analyst develops a useful model that will deliver insights to solve the business problem from step 1.
5. *Evaluation*: The analyst judges whether the insights, in fact, solve the problem from step 1.
6. *Deployment*: The analyst rolls out the insights where stakeholders can use them, whether in a report or embedded as a prediction tool in CRM software.

As the figure shows, the process is iterative, with later steps providing feedback to inform future repetitions of the process. For example, insights from the analysis can develop new business understanding that aids future data-mining efforts.

Criticisms of data mining. Because CRISP-DM needs human input to define the business problem and the model, it is subject to human biases. In general, data mining encourages the analyst to go **data fishing**, meaning that they search for any notable relationships in the data regardless of whether such relationships could be explained based on any logic. Or, perhaps worse, the analyst might specifically seek out insights that she already believes exist in the data, for example, searching only for evidence that a new product launch was successful. With enough variables and freedom to define the model, the analyst can generate any insights she wants. This type of selective, self-serving analysis is also known as **p-hacking** (a reference to a statistical concept known as a p-value).[27]

data fishing Searching for any salient relationships in the data regardless of whether such relationships could be explained based on any logic

p-hacking Selective, self-serving analysis to generate a specific insight that the analyst wants to report

But despite these critiques, corporations with mountains of data have little choice but to engage in some form of data mining, or else they will ignore large swathes of valuable data. Going forward, they must continue to navigate the practical and ethical challenges of data mining.

CASE QUESTIONS

1. Explain how the six steps in CRISP-DM relate to the five steps of the marketing research process.
2. What measures can firms take to ensure that business analysts behave ethically and abstain from p-hacking and excessive data fishing?

CHAPTER SUMMARY

Marketers must understand, anticipate, and adapt to changing needs and preferences to retain existing customers and address new needs in the future. At any point in time, customers can be segmented into various groups, according to their needs and desires for a product or service—the common approach for dealing with customer heterogeneity, as outlined in Chapter 4. Even after customers get assigned to a segment, their needs and preferences continue to evolve, at different rates and in different directions, so at some point in the future, the customers in a once homogenous segment will develop very different preferences, as discussed in Chapters 7 and 8. It is therefore useful to understand and predict what causes customer preferences to change and evolve. To do so, techniques, methods, and processes for collecting and analyzing reliable data on customer preferences and behaviors over time are needed. This chapter provides an overview of the steps in a typical marketing research process as well as a high-level overview of the marketing research function, the data to be collected, the analyses to be performed, and how insights from these studies and data sources inform the evolution of customer preferences. Marketing research data also gives rise to privacy and other ethical concerns that markets must manage, particularly for firms such as tech companies that harvest extensive and intimate customer information.

APPLICATION QUESTIONS

1. Recall the lab-grown meat example at the beginning of the chapter. Provide an example of insights you would wish to know about competing start-ups in this space. How could you glean such insights?
2. Imagine you are embarking on a new customer segmentation study. In defining the study objectives, why would it be useful to include other departments, for example, sales, in the discussion?
3. How do you know when to use qualitative research, and when to use quantitative research? Give an example of a research objective that might call for each.
4. Compare and contrast interviews and focus groups. Can you give an example of when you might want to use one over the other?
5. Compare and contrast interviews and surveys. Can you give an example of when you might want to use one over the other?
6. Explain the difference between correlation and causality. Provide an example of two variables that might be correlated but do not cause one another.
7. Compare and contrast descriptive and diagnostic analytics. How do these two types complement one another?
8. Compare and contrast predictive and prescriptive analytics. How do these two flavors complement one another?

Visit the companion website, **https://bloomsbury.pub/palmatier-marketing**, or **https://samsinstitute.com**, for additional learning and teaching tools, including professional videos outlining the Four Principles, PowerPoint tutorials with voice-over commentary, sample syllabi for marketing courses, testbank and more.

Part 4

MARKETING PRINCIPLE #3: ALL COMPETITORS REACT

Part Overview

Welcome to Part 4. Against the backdrop of Marketing Principle #1 (all customers differ) and Marketing Principle #2 (all customers change), the three chapters of this unit add the actions of competing businesses to the mix. When making decisions, marketers must consider how their competitors will respond, much like a game of chess. The complexity of this challenge means that Part 4 is also the most content-packed section of this book. Chapter 10 introduces Marketing Principle #3 (all competitors react). This chapter also highlights that the solution is to build sustainable competitive advantage (SCA), meaning that the firm has an edge over its competitors that can't be copied or overcome very easily. There are three core strategies for building and maintaining SCA: *brands, offerings,* and *relationships.* Chapter 11 focuses on how valuable, iconic brands can create competitive advantage, especially when paired with effective advertising. Chapter 12 emphasizes the importance of unique and differentiated offerings (products/services), that must be crafted and nurtured through innovation. Finally, Chapter 13 discusses how irreplaceable customer relationships can drive competitive advantage, and how strategies such as customer relationship management and channel management build close customer connections.

Taken together, these chapters highlight the importance of thinking several moves ahead of competitors by creating value in unique, difficult to imitate, ways.

Chapter 10

MANAGING SUSTAINABLE COMPETITIVE ADVANTAGE

CHAPTER OVERVIEW

In this chapter, you will be introduced to the third Marketing Principle: all competitors react. You will learn why this principle is so critical to marketers and how to manage this challenge. The chapter will proceed by answering the following questions:

- What is Marketing Principle #3, and what problems does it involve?
- Why is MP#3 so central to the First Principles framework?
- What are the three routes that marketers can use to develop a sustainable competitive advantage?
- How can marketers use the Brands, Offerings, Relationships (BOR) Equity concept to manage sustainable competitive advantage?

You will also encounter many examples of companies' successes and failures in managing sustainable competitive advantage in this chapter's cases and features. For example, you will read about:

- Nokia's struggle to remain relevant in the world of smartphones (Marketing Fail).
- Uniqlo's expansion in the face of international competition (Chapter Case).
- Questionable ethical practices that emerge under stiff competition, such as aggressive mergers and acquisitions (Opposing Views) as well as fly-by-night online merchants (Shades of Gray).

LEARNING OBJECTIVES

- Define Marketing Principle #3 and its associated key marketing challenge.
- Recognize the consequences of failing to account for competitive reactions.
- Identify the three primary sources of sustainable competitive advantage.
- Evaluate moral and ethical concerns in marketers' pursuit of SCA.

IMAGINE Starting a Digital Marketing Agency

Imagine that you want to put your marketing skills to use by becoming an entrepreneur. You want to leverage your social media savvy and digital media know-how to provide marketing services to businesses. After conducting a segmentation, targeting, and positioning analysis, you decide that small and medium businesses in your hometown would be well served by your abilities. But after searching the web and social media, you realize that your hometown already has several digital marketing agencies, including one run by a recent graduate of your own university! Since that agency has the same knowledge and tools as you—along with more experience and a growing reputation—how can you compete? You consider simply offering rock-bottom prices, but you worry about developing a reputation as an "off-brand" agency. In any case, you wouldn't be able to stop rivals from matching your prices. You clearly have more planning to do before you launch this venture.

Critical thinking:

1. Name at least two ways that you could make your agency stand out, compared to your rivals. How would you get these advantages?
2. Suppose your agency is successful enough that a larger, regional agency sees you as a threat. What can you do to successfully compete against larger rivals?

INTRODUCTION TO MARKETING PRINCIPLE #3

The chapter's opening scenario demonstrates that even very small businesses cannot ignore the competition. The reactions of rival companies should enter the strategic planning process before a venture even begins. This notion is

Source: JESHOOTS.COM/Unsplash

Dealing with inevitable competitive reactions is akin to a chess match. The players (marketers) position their pieces (products, brands, and other assets) to create a strong defense against their rivals. To do this well, they must plan ahead and anticipate how opponents might counter their moves.

Marketing Principle #3: all competitors react The idea that other firms will persistently try to innovate, copy, and respond to marketing mix actions

encapsulated in **Marketing Principle #3: all competitors react**; other firms will persistently try to innovate, copy, and respond to marketing mix actions.[1] The core idea behind this principle is far older than modern marketing. As early as the fifth century BCE, Sun Tzu wrote that: "The art of war teaches us to rely not on the likelihood of the enemy not coming, but on our own readiness to receive him, not on the chance of his not attacking, but rather on the fact that we have made our position unassailable."[2] As in a chess match, it would be foolish for marketers to assume that a rival will not go on the offensive; instead, marketers should carefully arrange their pieces (brands, products, etc.) to defend against and counter their opponents' attacks. This chapter summarizes the techniques that marketers can use to protect against competitors' moves.

Competitive Reactions As Part of the Broader Marketing Environment

marketing environment Conditions surrounding marketing decisions, comprised of the 4Cs: customers, company, context, and competitors

Before analyzing how rivals react and how marketers can respond, it is important to understand the unique role that competitors play in the marketing environment. The **marketing environment** refers to the conditions surrounding marketing decisions and may be broken down into 4 Cs (see Figure 10.1):

1. customers
2. company
3. context
4. competitors

Customers

The first C represents the needs, desires, and preferences across *customers* in the firm's industry, geographic region, or product category. As discussed in Chapter 4, customers have different perceptions of firms and brands in the marketplace. These different perceptions can be grouped into segments and visualized in perceptual maps. Segmentation, targeting, and positioning (Chapter 4) are the key to understanding the customer dimension of the marketing environment. Because marketing is fundamentally a customer-centered discipline, this aspect of the environment is strongly represented within the four First Principles of Marketing, both in #1 (all customers differ) and #2 (all customers change).

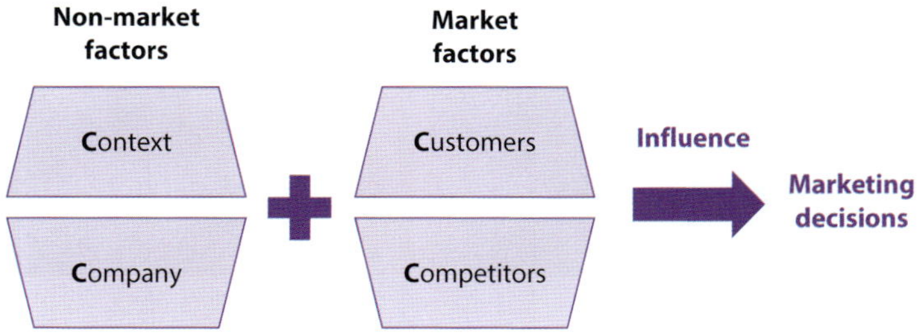

Figure 10.1 Four Cs of the Marketing Environment.

Marketing decisions must take into account the environment, which can be summarized based on 4 Cs: (1) customers, (2) company, (3) context, and (4) competitors.

Company

The second C is the *company* itself. Marketing decisions are influenced by the company's history, resources, personnel, structure, culture, and processes.[3] An understanding of that backdrop should guide marketing decisions. For example, Google's culture encourages experimentation and prototyping of new ideas and services, but also unceremonious abandonment of services such as its Google+ social media network. When considering a new consumer service, Google must assess whether this culture will cause consumers to believe that the company won't stand behind the new service. Likewise, limited company resources affect marketing decisions as we will see in Marketing Principle #4 (Chapters 14 and 15).

Context

The third C is the broader external *context*, such as technological and political trends, as well as the industry as a whole. Throughout 2020 and 2021, for example, marketing mix decisions in the restaurant industry had to weigh routine concerns about the level of in-person staffing and menu decisions against public health and supply chain factors. As another example, the trend of large-scale layoffs in the high-technology industry in 2023 had implications for marketing strategy (e.g., labor resources to develop new products). Context is arguably the most unpredictable of the 4 Cs, since it can change rapidly without any input from firms themselves.

Competitors

Finally, the fourth C is the set of *competitors* that vie for market share with a focal firm. Competitors, obviously, are the focus of this chapter, but what is special about this facet of the marketing environment? Why are competitors worthy of their own core marketing principle? The answer lies in the unique nature of competitors: they are the antagonists. While customers, the company, and context can sometimes make marketers' lives harder, they are ultimately the landscape underlying marketing decisions and do not actively work against marketers. *Competitors, on the other hand, are the players on the other side of the chess board and operate with an intent to undermine the firm's goals.* Therefore, understanding their role in marketing decisions requires special consideration.

Managing Competitive Reactions

Given that rival firms actively try to capture market share, *"all competitors react"* is a fundamental Marketing Principle. The resulting challenge for marketers is managing sustainable competitive advantage, such that competitors cannot easily counter or replicate the firm's success.[4] When devising a sustainable competitive advantage (SCA), marketers can evaluate a potential advantage by asking the three questions for **managing sustainable competitive advantage**:

managing sustainable competitive advantage (SCA) The key marketing mix challenge associated with MP#3

1. ***Can the firm do it better than competitors?***

   First, doing something (product quality, service, brand recognition, etc.) better than competitors is critical. There can be no sustainable competitive advantage without an advantage! This is especially true in mature segments. In rapidly growing segments (e.g., facemasks in 2020), when products are in high demand and scarce, even firms that offer weaker versions can seem to do well. But as the segment matures and demand stalls, firms often fight over customers, then those firms that are not the best in class cannot claim victory in head-to-head matchups. Their lack of relative advantage means that such firms are susceptible to competition. Strong past financial performance does not always imply an SCA.

2. ***Will customers care about the advantage?***

   Second, if a firm develops an advantage but customers don't want it, it has little value. Food delivery app Grubhub launched a successful innovation in the 2000s, matching drivers, customers, and restaurants in a smooth, app-based experience that expanded restaurant choice—a factor that customers cared about a great deal. On the other hand, Segway launched a revolutionary product innovation with its advanced motorized scooter. This innovation was supported by both patent protections and high brand awareness. But the end user market for these vehicles was minimal, so the patents, technology, and brand had little long-term value. Of course, because all customers change (MP#2), a firm's existing SCA can lose value when customers stop caring about it. At one point in time, Netflix nearly monopolized the streaming industry; it had SCA based in the brand and its one-of-a-kind offering, featuring an extensive library and reliable service. But soon other competitors, such as Max and Disney+, offered similarly extensive libraries and smooth user experiences, as well as iconic brand names. As a result, Netflix is now one streamer among many, differentiated only by the specific shows on offer.

3. ***Will the advantage be difficult to duplicate?***

   Third, being hard to duplicate is foundational to any SCA; it is what the "sustainable" part of the term means. A new offering might fit customers' needs better than existing offerings, but if a competitor can easily copy it, the innovator will struggle to profit. There are countless examples of pioneers that failed to build an SCA and were surpassed by later entrants. Nokia built the first mainstream smartphone but was soon virtually wiped out of the market by slick Apple and Android devices (see Marketing Fail in this chapter). The first major social network, Friendster, gained popularity through its first-of-its-kind features that enabled easy connections with friends and acquaintances. But when Myspace and later Facebook launched with the same features, as well as better technical performance, users jumped ship; there was nothing unique or difficult to duplicate about the concept of a digital social network.[5] Thus, being first to market with a new idea is not enough to stave off competitors. Deep-pocketed market leaders can recognize the threat of an innovative new entrant and

THEORY SPOTLIGHT Competitive Response Theory

It is important to have tools to understand who your competitors are and how they might respond. **Competitive response theory** provides one such tool, in the form of a framework for predicting rivals' reactions. The framework can be boiled down to three steps:[6]

1. The firm must define its set of competitors. Those who are selling to the *same customers* (e.g., car buyers) and have the *same resources* (e.g., economy car brands) are more likely to be direct competitors. These direct competitors will be motivated to respond. For example, for a potential new product launch (e.g., a VR headset), this can involve qualitative market research studies. Researchers ask consumers what needs the product fills and what alternative products or services might meet these needs.
2. To respond, the competitor must also be aware of the firm's action and have the capability (e.g., cash on hand) to respond. Awareness generally relates to the firm's *market-sensing* capabilities, or how well it can scan the industry environment, for example, based on social networks within the industry or based on predictive analytics.
3. The nature of the response will depend in part on the nature of the firm's action. Although predicting exact responses is difficult, a general rule—the principle of "**like-kind response**"—is that close competitors will respond with an action that closely mirrors the firm's action.[7] For example, a price cut will often be met with a matching price cut.

use their resources to copy and overwhelm the innovator. To make an SCA hard to imitate, firms often turn to the three routes described later in this chapter.

competitive response theory A theoretical process framework for predicting competitive responses

like-kind response The principle, from competitive response theory, that close competitors are more likely to respond to a firm's action with a similar type of action

WHY ARE COMPETITIVE REACTIONS SO IMPORTANT?

Consider Costa Coffee. It has a well-regarded brand name and a strong offering known for a consistently high level of quality, leading to advantages over competitors. Will it remain successful in the future? If history is any guide, no firm can count on any one advantage to withstand the test of time without adaptation and continued investment. Competitors displace firms by overcoming their SCA in many ways, including:

1. Launching disruptive products based on technical innovations.
2. Exploiting changes in customers' desires due to cultural, environmental, or other factors.
3. Creating copycats that improve the efficiency or effectiveness of an existing offering.

First, technical innovations are a powerful foundation for launching a new offering that will make existing products or services obsolete. Google's Maps app offers nearly all the navigation features anyone could ask for, and it can be installed on smartphones for free. Thus, following years of strong growth, standalone GPS device makers struggled; TomTom lost nearly 85 percent of their stock value and Garmin lost 70 percent within the months after the Google Maps app

Source: Omid Armin/Unsplash

Garmin was muscled out of the car navigation market by bigger rivals such as Google, but found its footing by excelling in a niche where it could better sustain an advantage: fitness wearables, such as watches.

was introduced. Garmin more successfully navigated this change, pivoting toward fitness watches and other wearable GPS technology.

Second, customers' desires change with cultural, environmental, or even seemingly random factors. A once-strong brand name might become less relevant or even detrimental to the firm's performance. For example, in the late 2010s, US National Football League (NFL) team the Washington Redskins came under heavy pressure as the team's name was increasingly seen as offensive toward Indigenous peoples. The team eventually adopted "The Washington Football Team" as a temporary moniker before settling on the Commanders. In the meantime, fans and viewers were spending their entertainment dollars elsewhere, such as to nearby NFL teams such as the Baltimore Ravens. In the 2021 season, Washington saw the lowest attendance in the league.[8]

Third, competitors also might copy a firm's offering and be better at executing its strategy. This "copycat" approach allows the competitor to tweak the mimicked offering to reduce cost, target an emerging growth segment, or pair the offering with complementary resources. For example, Apple's Siri delighted users with its natural dialogue skills when it launched, but the Google Assistant leveraged Google's AI expertise to quickly imitate and surpass Siri in its conversational ability.[9] Or, in a classic example from the 1970s, VHS videotapes learned from the mistakes of the pioneering Betamax videotapes and quickly became the dominant market player, demonstrating a sort of "second mover" advantage.

In summary, technology, customers, and business environments constantly change, and competitors continuously try to create new ways to satisfy customers' needs and desires, all of which has great potential to disrupt a firm's SCA and its market position. The more successful a firm is, the harder competitors will try to attack its position. As Apple co-founder Steve Jobs once said, "profits attract imitators and innovators." But because competitors are always reacting, firms need to build and adapt their SCA to withstand the competitive assault.

THREE ROUTES TO SUSTAINABLE COMPETITIVE ADVANTAGE

three routes to sustainable competitive advantage Three generic, non-mutually exclusive approaches for gaining and sustaining an edge over rivals (brands, offerings, and relationships)

We saw in the preceding section that building and maintaining an SCA that lasts is extremely difficult. This section introduces three approaches to overcoming this challenge. These are the **three routes to sustainable competitive advantage**: iconic brands, unique offerings, and valuable relationships (Table 10.1). It should be noted that these strategies are not mutually exclusive; many successful firms use all three.

MARKETING FAIL Nokia's Fall from Grace in the Smartphone Market

Finnish telecommunications provider Nokia was once a giant in the mobile phone industry. In 2007, it had cornered *half* of the global smartphone market.[10] The company built its fame in the pre-smartphone era on reliable, good-looking cellular phones, for instance, the popular Nokia 8810. It consistently edged out competitors such as Motorola by combining cutting-edge hardware with a trusted brand name. In 2001, it even launched one of the first commercially successful smartphones, the 7650, running on a mobile operating system (OS) called Symbian that could install basic Java applications. Nokia took Symbian's success and ran with it, making limited improvements to the OS but continuing to install it on a long series of well-built devices.[11]

Unfortunately for Nokia, other tech companies better recognized the potential of smartphone software. Most importantly, Apple launched the iPhone in 2007. This device came with the first iteration of iOS, a new smartphone platform with a centralized app store and a strong focus on supporting app developers. Other smartphone manufacturers, such as Motorola and Samsung, soon followed suit by adopting the similarly app-centric Android OS. Consumers appreciated the ability to customize their experience with iOS and Android devices through an extensive library of productivity, entertainment, and gaming apps. While Nokia clung to the Symbian platform and made only incremental improvements, the once-invincible brand saw its market share fall to just 3 percent within six years of the iPhone's launch.[12] Despite remaining a recognizable brand, continuing to provide strong hardware, and getting a helping hand in the form of an acquisition by Microsoft, Nokia never regained its dominant market position.

Finland

Diagnose the problem:

1. Explain exactly why Nokia's market share collapsed. What was Nokia's strategy for maintaining a competitive advantage, and how was it undone by competitive reactions?
2. What could Nokia have done differently to protect their market share, both proactively (before the iPhone's launch) and reactively (after the iPhone's launch)?

Table 10.1 Three Routes to Sustainable Competitive Advantage.

Firms can get an edge over competitors through three different, but not mutually exclusive, routes.

Source	Barriers to Imitation	Examples
Brands	Brand names and symbols create strong mental associations for consumers, and these are often subconscious; trademark protects the brand	Milka is a trusted snacking brand name; Lamborghini's brand evokes extremely high status and wealth
Offerings	Patents and copyrights can legally prevent duplication, for a time; performance and cost advantages of greater experience with production/service delivery	Pfizer's shifting portfolio of patented medicines can't be copied while under patent; Tesla tends to be ahead of the curve in mass-market electric car technology
Relationships	The interpersonal rapport, trust, and reciprocal bonds between two specific individuals cannot be replaced or replicated, although they might be substituted with time	State Farm insurance agents build personal rapport with clients in their communities; Airbus builds teams of personnel around meeting the needs of specific airlines

Brands As a Route to SCA

Brands can linger in customers' minds and are hard to copy or duplicate, such that they provide a valuable SCA. Using brands as an SCA is often most effective for businesses that serve large consumer markets (e.g., soft drinks, beer, fashion, automobiles). These companies spend a great deal on advertising, public relations (PR), and celebrity sponsorships to build brand awareness and strong brand images. These brands establish SCA through multiple means. Very strong awareness causes consumers to buy based simply on familiarity, which reduces their cognitive effort. For example, a consumer might automatically reach for Cheerios brand cereal at the grocery store, without spending even a moment looking at the store's own Tastee-O's brand. If brands also provide a clear meaning, consumers may buy based on a desire for status or because they identify with the brand's values. In line with the second question for managing SCA, a brand that aligns better with customers' needs than competitors' brands can provide a relative advantage.

Moreover, brands can be very hard to copy due to the unique value attached to the specific, trademarked brand name in the mind of consumers. The Louis Vuitton brand, for example, is worth an estimated $47 billion.[13] Brand consultants likewise offer evidence that it would take $64 billion for another company to replicate Coca-Cola's brand. Pepsi and other colas may win blind taste tests, but more people still habitually enjoy Coke than other soft drinks. Brands usually operate at subconscious levels, improving the experience on top of what is provided by objective elements, such as taste. So powerful is the typical consumer's subconscious association with the Coca-Cola brand, that given an image of a blank red can, they are likely to infer the iconic brand name. The role of branding in SCA is discussed in greater detail in Chapter 11.

Source: Marc Pascual/Pixabay

For many consumers, the brand power of Coca-Cola is so powerful that the combination of the top of a beverage can and the color red generate an immediate mental association with the brand.

Offerings As a Route to SCA

Using offerings (e.g., innovative products or services) as an SCA can be effective, because new and innovative products and services have the potential to disrupt the market. An innovative product can outperform competing offerings on the market and quickly capture market share.

Thus, firms spend vast budgets on research and development (R&D) so that they can introduce the newest or most feature-rich product, reduce costs, add supporting services, or change the customer experience. If the new offerings meet customers' needs better than existing options, and customers care about the new feature, a strong SCA emerges. For example, the home décor market has grown swiftly in India and China as the middle classes in these nations have expanded. In turn, start-ups such as https://Foyr.com and https://www.Furdo.com have combined technology and data science to provide online shoppers with 3D virtual tours of homes that they can decorate digitally.[14] Through this technology, consumers quickly and cheaply sort through hundreds of decorating possibilities. This innovative service produces a meaningful SCA compared with traditional rivals that provide 2D renderings.

In some cases, though, explaining the value of new features to customers is costly and difficult. New and innovative is not necessarily better, at least in customers' minds. As many as 75 percent of newly launched consumer packaged goods fail, and the top reason reported for product failures often is the lack of need for the new offering.[15] Windows Vista's launch in 2007, for example, was hampered by the quality and popularity of its predecessor, Windows XP, which reduced the need for an upgrade.

When a firm overcomes the odds and launches a new product that meets customers' needs better than alternatives, it still may succumb to a copycat. Competitors can see how the first customers react to the new product and then add slight refinements that better meet customer needs, whereas the first mover has already launched its product and committed to its manufacturing process. There have been many now-unfamiliar industry pioneers that were quickly overtaken by their early followers: Bow-mar Instruments (hand-held electronic calculators), Osborne (portable computer market), and Royal Crown Cola (diet and caffeine-free colas). In some cases, the copycat positioning is explicit; Xiaomi, for example, may benefit from being referred to as the "Apple of China," given Apple's reputation for premium products.

Whether an offering is hard to copy depends on the type of innovation. In some cases (e.g., pharmaceuticals such as COVID-19 medication Paxlovid), a firm can patent its innovation and prevent competitors from copying it, so it enjoys a legally enforceable SCA. But patents are not feasible in all industries. Even in the pharmaceutical sector, patents don't last forever, so companies that introduce a new drug gain an SCA with a fixed expiration date. Still, being the first in a market may provide benefits, in the form of an innovative brand image, strong customer relationships, or cost advantage. In some cases, a firm develops new offerings continuously, such that the SCA really reflects the firm's ability to maintain a strong research and development team and launch a sequence of successful innovations, rather than withstand competitors' assaults on any one innovative offering. Offerings as a source of SCA are examined in greater detail in Chapter 12.

Relationships As a Route to SCA

Relationships also meet the criteria for SCA. Many customers care about relational benefits such as enhanced trust, adaptability, and cooperation, as well as the intrinsic enjoyment that comes with interpersonal relationships. Relational sales organizations and customer service personnel often provide the best barriers to competitive entry. At Saks Fifth Avenue, a high-end US department store, the sales associates are a powerful SCA for the retailer, because the relationships between these sales associates and their customers often span years. This SCA

Source: Blake Wisz/Unsplash. Model Credit: Jasmine Wisz and Ashley Brown

Personal relationships are often recognized as a key advantage in business-to-business markets, but they can also be critical in B2C settings. Many consumers, for example, treat their hair stylist as a friend.

can create some confusion: the firm might assume customers are loyal to it, but in fact, they are bonded with the firm's salespeople.[16] One study of loyalty among more than 300 B2B firms showed that buyers would try to shift an average of 26 percent of their current purchases to follow a salesperson that left their company for a new supplier, due to their bonds with the individual salesperson.

Using relationships as an SCA is most critical in business-to-business, service, and complex offering settings. Strong relationships between customers and a firm's salespeople can establish powerful barriers to customer defection. For example, business-to-business transactions tend to be complex, require two-way communication, and span long periods of time, so strong personal relationships help buyers and sellers develop trust, cooperation, and flexibility. In addition, there are typically fewer customers in business markets, compared with consumer markets, so advertising is somewhat less cost effective. Relationships then produce SCA through higher levels of trust, commitment, and interpersonal bonds, which enable sellers to adapt to changing circumstances and give buyers confidence that they will be treated fairly.

Because relationships often take years to build, they are hard to duplicate, which makes for an enduring SCA. Continuing our example of B2B salespeople, when a sales rep leaves their job, replacement reps try to reinitiate and reinvigorate customer relationships that might have been placed at risk by the former salesperson's departure. But finding the right replacement is tricky, because this salesperson must find a way to meet or exceed the expectations established by the predecessor.[17] And even strong relational bonds are not immune to changing customer trends and preferences. In a recent B2B survey, one-third of respondents indicated that e-commerce was the most important purchasing method, as B2B customers increasingly know exactly what to buy without talking to a salesperson.[18] Coupled with the increasing use of the internet, it is not surprising to find some B2B competitors are trying to build relationships over easy-to-use e-commerce sites, rather than through personal contact. W.W. Grainger, for example, one of the largest industrial wholesalers in the world, offers over 1 million distinct items through its online store. We discuss the benefits and challenges of this approach and other facets of relationship-based SCA in Chapter 13.

MANAGING COMPETITIVE ADVANTAGE: THE BRANDS, OFFERINGS, RELATIONSHIPS (BOR) EQUITY CONCEPT

Starbucks has it all: an internationally recognized brand that customers are attached to; a unique offering of coffee-based drinks and appealing store environments; and relationships with local store employees who remember customers' names and drink orders. Customers have been known to walk past an identical store to visit another Starbucks and buy coffee from their favorite barista. These sources of SCA work together to increase customers' loyalty, and competitors find it hard to overcome these barriers. Rather than a franchising strategy, Starbucks maintains direct control over its coffee shops to ensure customers' experiences reflect its unique offering, reinforced by custom-made products that provide a unique customer relationship encounter. Furthermore, Starbucks continues to innovate its offerings (e.g., with Nitro cold brew-based drinks) and technology-based services (e.g., mobile payment) to maintain its SCA in this category.

Hence, these three sources of sustainable competitive advantage—brands, offerings, and relationships (BOR)—are not only additive but also often work synergistically to give a firm a strong relative position in the marketplace. Managing the overall SCA from these three interdependent sources is **BOR management**.

BOR management Managing the overall SCA from three interdependent sources: brands, offerings, and relationships

The BOR Equity Stack

Effective management of brands, offerings, and relationships should ideally account for all four Cs of the marketing environment: customers (and implicitly Marketing Principles #1 and #2), the company, the context, and competitors (Marketing Principle #3). The **BOR equity stack** (Figure 10.2) is a framework for visualizing and integrating these four factors when planning an SCA-based marketing strategy.

BOR equity stack A framework for visualizing and integrating competitive considerations and other marketing environment factors when planning a marketing strategy

To understand this concept (and Figure 10.2), it is helpful to work backwards. The outcome in the figure is **BOR equity**, or the monetary value of the firm's sustainable competitive advantages from brands, offerings, and relationships. It has three components:

BOR equity The total value of the firm's sustainable competitive advantages

1. *Brand equity* is evident in the multiple examples of valuable brands throughout this chapter. It equals the market value of that brand, that is,

OPPOSING VIEWS Buying the Competition in the Disney-Fox Acquisition

When faced with the threat of competitive reactions, large companies have a powerful tool at their disposal: buy the competition! For example, in the film and television industry, rival studios can produce competing films (possibly entering theaters head-to-head) and launch competing streaming services with similar genres of shows. This forces consumers to split their entertainment spending. Conversely, when a studio buys a major competitor, it can schedule major releases to avoid box office conflict and bring the competitor's entertainment catalog into its own streaming service. The Walt Disney Company recognized this threat (and opportunity) when it acquired 21st Century Fox for $71 billion in 2019.[19] Although this acquisition did not give Disney a monopoly—it still faces threats from Universal, Sony, and others—it bolstered the Disney+ streaming service with more content while consolidating Disney's position atop the box office. For example, in 2019, Disney and Fox films combined for almost 40 percent of US box office revenue.[20] Many consumers were pleased with this acquisition as it increased the value of a Disney+ subscription by adding hit shows such as *The Simpsons*.

And yet unrestricted purchasing of direct competitors is one path toward a monopoly. For example, acquisitions and other cutthroat business practices by US petroleum giant Standard Oil in the nineteenth century gave the company over 90 percent market share.[21] Such monopolistic business combinations or "trusts" were the motivation for modern antitrust law, which is designed to protect free competition. Throughout the world, laws exist to prevent abusive buyouts of competitors, such as the Clayton Antitrust act in the United States and the EC Merger Regulation in the European Union.[22]

USA

Despite such laws and scrutiny from regulators, this deal (like many others) successfully closed. Critics wonder whether these mergers hurt the industry as a whole; when firms don't have to worry as much about competitive reactions, they may not invest as much in beneficial brands, offerings, and relationships.[23] The trend of underperformance of Disney films in recent years only adds to this skepticism and leaves the future of the film and streaming industries uncertain.

See the issue from two sides:

1. Craft an argument in favor of firms freely acquiring direct competitors. In the case of Disney and Fox, what are the benefits that justify the potential loss of competition?
2. Craft an argument against firms acquiring direct competitors. Can you think of specific ways that the Disney-Fox acquisition might hurt the entertainment industry in the long run?

what one would have to pay to acquire all rights to it. Strong, iconic brands have higher equity.

2. *Offering equity* is likewise the market value of the firm's offering portfolio, divorced from the value of associated brands. In other words, how much is the uniqueness or novelty of the product/service itself worth? For firms with easily imitated products, this value is minimal. For firms with an extensive portfolio of patents, such as Pfizer, it is a large part of the company's value.
3. *Relationship equity* (i.e., customer equity) is the value of the firm's customer base. Under a relationship equity perspective, customers act as financial assets, such that they can be measured, managed, and maximized, similar to any other firm asset (e.g., land, buildings, equipment, intellectual

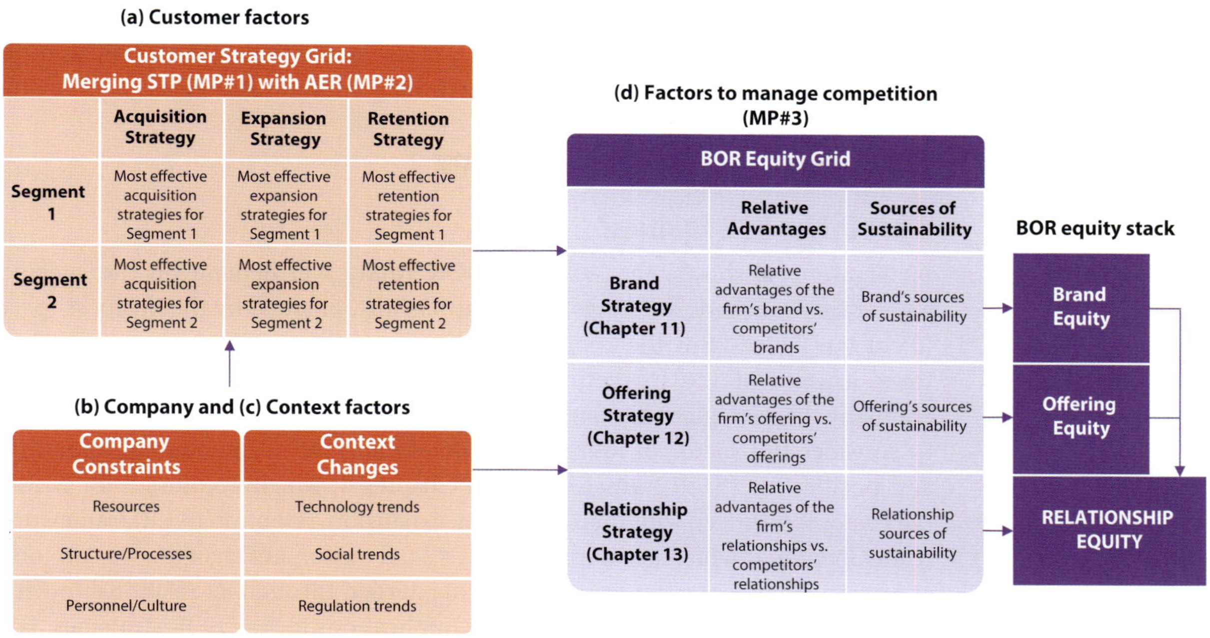

Figure 10.2 BOR Equity Stack.

The BOR equity stack visualizes and organizes the decisions to be made when planning a marketing strategy in the face of competition. The factors are organized according to the four dimensions of the marketing environment: customer, company, context, and competitors.

property). Relationship equity for a firm, then, is the value of all the future cash flows from its customers. When a business hires and trains salespeople who can improve relationships with clients, it should increase that firm's relationship equity.

Importantly, relationship equity can be viewed as directly incorporating brand equity and offering equity. That is, iconic brands and innovative offerings have market value *because* they affect customer cash flows in the form of more frequent purchases, higher prices paid, or greater loyalty. For example, the Milka chocolate brand is valuable not for some purely abstract reason, but because the brand name and its subconscious associations lead customers to buy more chocolate bars, increasing relationship equity. Likewise, the Uniqlo brand is valuable because its association with affordable, good-looking, functional clothes causes customers to keep coming back (see Chapter Case). In this way, brand equity and offering equity influence relationship equity, which in turn determines overall BOR equity.

Even though BOR equity is a useful managerial concept, it is not an accounting term. Yet BOR equities are similar to tangible assets reported on balance sheets: they generate a return on assets (ROA), can be built through investments, and depreciate over time if not maintained. For example, a report that compiled nearly 100 empirical studies published between the 1960s and the 2010s revealed that investments in personal selling produce positive, incremental financial benefits to firms.[24] Many firms have in-house metrics, or else use industry metrics, to assess their brand or offering equity. These measures provide helpful, intermediate ways of determining the performance of the brand and innovative offerings. Once a firm can measure relationship equity, it can use marketing analytics techniques (see Chapter 9) to learn which marketing investments and strategies generate the greatest equities.

What Drives BOR Equities?

As Figure 10.2 shows, the extent of BOR equity will depend on the specific advantages in brands, offerings, and relationships, pursued by the business (part (d) of the figure). But the choice of advantages ought to depend on the other three aspects of the marketing environment: customers ((a) in the figure), company (b), and context (c). In the case of customers, we already have the tools to consider this factor in more detail. Combining the segmentation, targeting, and positioning (STP) framework from Chapter 4, which accounted for MP#1 (all customers differ), with the acquisition, expansion, retention (AER) framework from Chapter 7, which accounted for MP#2 (all customers change), we can look at how each customer segment will be shepherded through its relationship with the firm. These STP/AER strategies have implications for the BOR strategies. For example, if retention for Segment 2 relies on brand loyalty, the firm should invest in advertising to build strong brand equity.

IN OTHER WORDS …

Based on the BOR equity stack framework, the firm should consider its company constraints and ongoing changes in the external environment. It should then perform an STP analysis to account for customer differences and apply the AER framework to each segment to account for customer dynamics. This results in a grid containing strategies for each segment at each stage of the relationship. The firm should then, with company and context factors still in mind, determine what BOR strategies can be applied to implement this customer strategy grid and obtain advantages over competitors.

Moreover, there is a natural order for making BOR strategic decisions in part (d) of Figure 10.1. First, a firm should make brand decisions, which are influenced by the firm's overall positioning objectives from MP#1 and MP#2 and largely determine how the firm will be positioned in the marketplace and in customers' minds. Second, the firm can focus on its offering decisions; product and service innovation as well as R&D efforts need to support both brand strategies and the firm's positioning objectives. Third and finally, relationship strategies are often determined last because they involve the delivery and experiential aspect of offerings (which must first be defined). This ordering is especially evident when the offering has a large service component because, in this case, salespeople and customer service personnel are critical to the customer experience and the firm's overall value proposition. The detailed discussion of brands, offerings, and relationships in the coming chapters thus follows this sequence.

SHADES OF GRAY Fly-by-Night Online Sellers

Global

Imagine a firm that lacks a strong brand, offering, or relationships. All who deal with this business regret doing so. Based on the principles of this chapter, you would be forgiven for assuming that this business would fail. And yet some sellers on e-commerce platforms defy this reasoning. These "fly-by-night" sellers win sales through outright fraud and deception. For example, a seller on Amazon's Marketplace might list a USB cable for a rock-bottom price under a generic (often nonsensical) brand name such as Utekit. The cable itself might also be of rock-bottom quality and less reliable than alternatives from other sellers. But the seller manipulates reviews—either through outright buying reviews from third-party services or giving buyers a rebate for leaving favorable reviews—to create the illusion of a great deal on a quality product, and to gain a higher listing rank in Amazon's search results. Eventually, Amazon might discover these practices and ban the seller, as they frequently do.[25] Yet some allege that these sellers have bribed Amazon employees to avoid these bans or repackaged their listings under new brand names and storefronts and repeated the scam.[26] They are the cockroaches of e-commerce: we all agree that they are unpleasant, but we cannot seem to put an end to them. E-commerce platforms must continue to contend with this problem if they want to retain consumers' trust.

Ethical dilemmas:

1. Who is harmed when e-commerce platforms such as the Amazon Marketplace allow fraudulent sellers to persist? How are they harmed?
2. What exactly can e-commerce platforms do to more effectively police fraudulent sellers? What can legitimate sellers do to compete with these sellers?

CHAPTER CASE STUDY

Japan

THE UNIQUE RISE OF UNIQLO

Uniqlo is now one of the world's largest clothing retailers with over 2,000 stores, but it arose from humble beginnings. It was founded in 1949 under the name Ogori Shōji as a small chain of menswear stores based in Yamaguchi, Japan. Growing alongside Japan's postwar economic boom, the company opened stores across Japan throughout the 1950s, 1960s, 1970s, 1980s, and 1990s, became a unisex brand, and began using its current brand name. In a twist of fate, the intended name of uni-clo (unique clothing) was misregistered with a government office as Uniqlo, and the company simply adopted this name rather than correcting the error.[27]

Building a unique offering. Uniqlo found success by exclusively selling its own Uniqlo-branded clothing. It worked with select manufacturers (mostly in China initially), produced a narrow mix of items in extremely large quantities, and sent technicians to manufacturing plants to keep an eye on the process and materials being used.[28,29] This strategy granted Uniqlo tight control over the cost and quality of its items, and the brand quickly gained a reputation in its home market as providing excellent value and extremely functional clothes. This enabled it to survive and even thrive during recessions, when many of its higher-priced competitors struggled.

Expanding the brand against international competition. Throughout the 2000s and 2010s, Uniqlo focused on expanding outside of its home market of Japan, which long accounted for the vast majority of its sales. Most notable was its growth into mainland China in 2002, where Uniqlo successfully applied the same formula it applied in Japan. The brand's affordability and

Source: Manh LE/Unsplash

Uniqlo's meteoric rise owes a lot to the company's ability to be more agile than competitors in responding to consumer tastes.

functionality have been hard to match for competitors in China, where it recently earned over $3 billion in revenue.[30] The brand has likewise made inroads in Southeast Asia and Europe, with several dozen stores in France, for example. It has outcompeted European fast fashion chains such as Zara and H&M by, counterintuitively, being *slower*. By not chasing short-term trends, Uniqlo tends to make its customers' wardrobes more affordable in the long run.[31]

Penetrating the US market, on the other hand, has been harder; it still only has about fifty US stores, almost all in large cities. First, the company lacks significant brand recognition in the western hemisphere. Second, it has faced stiff competition from discount retailers such as Target and Amazon.[32] For example, Target's function-focused private labels such as All in Motion and Goodfellow & Co offer styles and price points that closely rival Uniqlo, and that likewise avoid chasing short-term fashion trends.

Although Uniqlo has gained a foothold with young, urban consumers who are drawn to the brand's cosmopolitan image—and who often have less access to big-box retailers such as Walmart—it has struggled to build a broader following in the United States.[33] Going forward, Uniqlo will need to reckon with its seeming lack of uniqueness in the US market, and its brand alone may not be strong enough to compensate.

CASE QUESTIONS

1. Explain each source of competitive advantage for Uniqlo.
2. Which of these sources are most sustainable, and why? Be sure to reference the **three questions for managing sustainable competitive advantage**.
3. If you were managing Uniqlo, how would you go about overcoming competitors in the United States?

three questions for managing sustainable competitive advantage (1) Can the firm do it better than competitors? (2) Will customers care about the advantage? (3) Will the advantage be difficult to duplicate?

CHAPTER SUMMARY

The previous two First Principles focus on a firm's potential and existing customers, in an effort to understand and manage customer differences and dynamics. In turn, the firm can develop a positioning that matches its targeted customers' needs and track these needs over time as the firm continues to engage these customers. Each firm selects target markets and positioning strategies based on its own relative strengths compared with those of competitors, but the true effectiveness of these choices really depends on how competitors react to them. No matter how well a firm addresses MP#1 and MP#2—and perhaps especially if it addresses them effectively—competitors constantly seek to copy successful strategies or innovate their own business processes and offerings to match customers' existing and future needs and desires. These persistent efforts to copy and innovate, such that all competitors react, constitute a third challenge that marketers confront. To do so, they need to build and maintain barriers to competitive attacks, in the form of sustainable competitive advantage (SCA). Of the four First Principles, managing SCA may be the most difficult. This is due not only to the complexity of predicting and managing competitors' reactions, but also to the ethical and moral tensions that arise as marketers consider whether the ends justify the means in pursuing a competitive edge. The different sources of SCA in the marketing domain can be grouped into three main categories: brands, offerings, and relationships (BOR). This is the focus of MP#3, and the subject of this and the next three chapters.

APPLICATION QUESTIONS

1. Can you think of any firm, besides the examples in the chapter, that ignored or mismanaged Marketing Principle #3? What consequences did they suffer?
2. Think about a major new product launch by one of your favorite brands. In your opinion, how was the decision to launch this product affected by *context* factors?
3. Consider the three questions for managing sustainable competitive advantage. Think of a time when a brand seemed to have the wrong answer for the *first* question. What should they have done differently?
4. Once again consider the three questions for managing sustainable competitive advantage. Think of a time when a brand seemed to have the wrong answer for the *second* question. What should they have done differently?
5. Think of a recent positive change or product/service introduction made by a brand that you follow. If you were that brand's competitor, how would you enact a like-kind response? To what extent do you think that response would be effective?
6. Name a firm that you think has been successful in *all three* routes to SCA and explain why.
7. Revisit the opening scenario from this chapter about opening a digital marketing agency. After reading the concepts and examples throughout the chapter, can you think of any additional ways that your start-up could compete against a larger, more established agency?

Visit the companion website, **https://bloomsbury.pub/palmatier-marketing**, or **https://samsinstitute.com**, for additional learning and teaching tools, including professional videos outlining the Four Principles, PowerPoint tutorials with voice-over commentary, sample syllabi for marketing courses, testbank and more.

Chapter 11

BRAND-BASED ADVANTAGES AND ADVERTISING

CHAPTER OVERVIEW

This chapter focuses on one of the main routes to a sustainable competitive advantage: branding. You will learn what brands are, how they contribute to SCA, and how effective advertising builds and maintains brands. The chapter will proceed by answering the following questions:

- What are the key features of a brand?
- What is it about brands that creates sustainable competitive advantage?
- How is effective advertising planned and measured? How does it contribute to strong brands?

In this chapter's cases and features, you will also learn how companies have successfully and unsuccessfully maintained competitive advantages through branding and advertising. For example, you will read about:

- The decline and downfall of Oldsmobile's automotive brand (Marketing Fail).
- The World Health Organization's need for strong branding to fulfill its mission (Chapter Case).
- Dilemmas that branding and advertising managers face, such as the effectiveness of comparative advertising (Opposing Views) and Nestlé's struggles with offensive brand names (Shades of Gray).

LEARNING OBJECTIVES

- Identify key terms and concepts in brand management.
- Identify key terms and concepts in advertising.
- Associate advertising decisions with branding outcomes in various contexts.
- Compare various advertising and brand management strategies for achieving SCA.

IMAGINE Designing a Brand Advertising Campaign for ASOS

ASOS is a British online-only apparel retailer founded in 2000. Originally focused on selling imitations of outfits worn in films—ASOS was an acronym for "as seen on screen"—the company shed this limited positioning and became a globally recognized fashion brand.[1] The website markets the ASOS brand, several other house brands gained through acquisitions, as well as global name brands such as Adidas, with competitive prices and convenient shipping options offered for each quality tier. ASOS defines its own brand identity as: "We believe in a world where you have total freedom to be you, without judgement. To experiment. To express yourself. To be brave and grab life as the extraordinary adventure it is .... We exist to give you the confidence to be whoever you want to be." The website also announces support for several progressive causes, including body positivity and ecological consciousness.[2]

Imagine that you have been recently hired by ASOS to help design an advertising campaign in a new market. The objective of the campaign is to raise awareness of the ASOS brand and its unique features, and the centerpiece of the campaign will be a 30-second television and streaming advertisement.

Critical thinking:

1. What message would you try to convey in the advertisement? Explain your reasoning.
2. At a high level, how would you use the advertisement to convey that message? For example, what types of music and sounds would you include? What visual style and types of scenes might you depict?

WHAT MAKES A BRAND?

brand A unique name, word, symbol, or mark that a company uses to set its product or service apart from those offered by other companies

brand elements All the unique, outward components that mark the brand as separate from other brands

brand name A word or set of words (fictional or otherwise) that serves as the brand's official moniker

brand symbol A graphical shorthand for the brand name

As we saw in Chapter 10, brands are critically important to achieving and sustaining a competitive advantage for many companies. A **brand** is a unique name, word, symbol, or mark that a company uses to set its product or service apart from those offered by other companies.[3] The term originates from the "brands" that farmers would apply to livestock; in line with this origin, it is a way of *identifying* a product or service. In other words, it is all the unique, outward components that show that the brand is separate from other brands. These outward features are **brand elements** (Table 11.1). Some of the most important brand elements include:

- The **brand name** (e.g., Nike) defines the official moniker of the brand. Some firms, for instance, Target, use the firm's name as the brand; other firms give unique names to each product they offer, such as P&G's Vicks, Tide, and Pampers brands.
- The **brand symbol** (or logo) is a graphical shorthand for the brand name. While many well-known brands use a symbolic representation for their logo (e.g., Nike's swish), others such as Saks and Tesco simply use a stylized version of the brand name. Symbolic representations have the advantage of achieving more universal impact across languages and writing systems.

Table 11.1 Common Brand Elements.

A brand's identity is defined by its set of brand elements: recognizable, tangible features. The list of possible brand elements is endless, but several common categories and examples are provided here.

Format	Definition	Examples
Brand name	A word or set of words (fictional or otherwise) that serves as the brand's official moniker	Vicks, Tide, Lexus, Ferrero Rocher, Nokia, Adidas
Brand symbol (logo)	A graphical shorthand for the brand name	Target bullseye, Nike swish, Mercedes-Benz 3-pointed star, Zara black-and-white text logo, Banco Santander flame
Brand slogan	A short phrase that embodies the brand's spirit	Tesco "every little helps," Audi "Vorsprung durch Technik," De Beers "A diamond is forever"
Brand characters	Fictional personalities designed to promote the brand	Geico's gecko, Quaker Oats' Captain Crunch, McDonald's Ronald McDonald
Brand sounds	Sound effects or musical elements that belong to the brand	Netflix's TUDUM, Law & Order's dun-dun, Kit Kat's "Give me a break" jingle, Cornetto's "Just one Cornetto" jingle
Others	Other brand elements deployed to a greater or lesser extent across various industries	Celebrity spokespeople, URLs, alliances with other bands, fonts, colors, recurring advertising messages/themes

- A **brand slogan**, or short phrase that embodies the brand's spirit, is a core element of many brands. Nike's "Just Do It" or McDonald's "I'm Lovin' it" are well known examples.

brand slogan A short phrase that embodies the brand's spirit

- **Brand characters**—fictional personalities designed to promote the brand—are also commonly associated with brands. Children's brands heavily feature this element (e.g., Nesquik's Quiky bunny). For teens and adults, brand characters are perhaps most commonly associated with entertainment franchises, such as Star Wars (e.g., Darth Vader) and Game of Thrones (e.g., Jon Snow).

brand characters A fictional personality designed to promote the brand

- **Brand sounds** are sound effects or musical elements that belong to the brand. While not as widely used as other elements, they tend to be extremely memorable when deployed. Netflix's signature "TUDUM" sound on start-up and Kit Kat's "Give me a break" jingle are hard to forget (much as we might try).

brand sounds Sound effects or musical elements that belong to the brand

This is not an exhaustive list, as the only limit to what can be a brand element is the creativity of marketers. URLs (e.g., ebay.com), long-term celebrity spokespeople (e.g., Samuel L. Jackson for Capital One), alliances with other brands (e.g., Disney licensing Spider-Man from Sony Pictures in films), and personality conveyed on brand social media accounts can all define a brand. For example, US fast food chain Wendy's is well known for operating its Twitter handle with a snarky, flippant personality. In one instance, it replied to a mistakenly sent, garbled McDonald's tweet with "When the tweets are as broken as the ice cream machine."[4] Collectively, all of the brand elements determine the **brand identity**, or the set of marketer-defined tangible attributes that make the brand recognizable.[5]

brand identity The set of marketer-defined tangible attributes that make the brand recognizable

Source: Yixian Zhao/Unsplash

Brands can have deep connections to our senses and our memories. The sense of smell is no exception, as the name of a favorite fragrance can immediately trigger a pleasant memory and a desire to purchase.

Brand identity is vital for many firms. As discussed in Chapter 10, a firm's brand equity can be a large portion of its overall value. Forbes' list of the top global brands in 2020 valued Apple's brand at the top of the list at $241.2 billion, followed by Google ($207.5 billion) and Microsoft ($162.9 billion). Notable non-US brands in the top 15 include Samsung ($50.4 billion), Louis Vuitton ($47.2 billion), and Toyota ($41.5 billion).[6] To understand how brands drive sustainable competitive advantage (and the company's value), we must understand the psychology of brands—that is, how they function in the minds of customers.

HOW BRANDS BUILD SUSTAINABLE COMPETITIVE ADVANTAGE

How Do Brands Affect the Human Mind?

Understanding Brands and Memory

Brands affect humans by lingering in our memory; to understand brands, one must understand memory. The **associative network memory model** argues that the human mind is a network of nodes and connecting links. If you think of Coca-Cola (a node), related neurons will fire and connect (link) to other nodes, such as the red-and-white logo, the overall can or bottle design, and the taste, as well as summertime, fast food, and vending machines.

associative network memory model A theory that views the human mind as a network of nodes and connecting links between nodes

brand awareness How commonly individuals can identify a brand

brand image A customer's overall perception of the brand

The characteristics of a brand operate through nodes and links.[7] **Brand awareness** is a central attribute of a brand, indicating how often individuals can identify a brand. Marketing researchers measure awareness as the percentage of a sample of customers that could recall the brand's name, either when prompted with the name (aided recall) or from the top of their mind (unaided recall).[8] In the associative network memory model, an individual consumer's level of awareness is the size or strength of the node for that brand's memory, as shown in Figure 11.1.

Brand image is another core brand characteristic and reflects a customer's overall perception of the brand. While brand identity is the signal *sent* by marketers, brand image is the signal *received*. In the memory model, brand image describes the links that fire from the focal node. For example, unique links to a brand name might capture the brand's intended identity: its symbols, sounds, slogans, and favorable attributes. Yet the brand's image can also contain unintended links. For example, news reports of Uber drivers attacking passengers could make some consumers activate a link to "danger" when they think of Uber. In Figure 11.1, the thickness of a line between two nodes represents the strength of the association between two memories in a consumer's mind.

SHADES OF GRAY Nestle's Offensive Product Names

Swiss food conglomerate Nestlé is famous for its chocolate bars and candies, among countless other products. Famous treats such as its chocolate bars, Kit Kats, Crunch bars, and Nesquik sit alongside bottled water and Maggi noodles in a massive portfolio of recognizable sub-brands.[9] Yet with such a large stable of brand names, problems with some of them are inevitable, whether they stem from changing customer preferences, quality problems, or scandals.

This was the case in 2020 when, following global protests by Black Lives Matter and similarly aligned organizations, many companies faced scrutiny over outdated brand names. In Nestlé's case, two of its Australian brands, Red Skins and Chicos (brown candies in the shape of children), were criticized for being demeaning to minority communities.[10] Nestlé's Colombian candy called Beso de Negra ("kiss from a black woman") faced similar pushback.[11] In response to the backlash, Nestlé temporarily pulled the products from the market—a costly move—and rereleased two of them with new names: Red Ripperz and Cheekies. The Colombian candy awaits a new name. Yet some have criticized Nestlé for not going far enough; they note, for example, that the Cheekies candies still visually resemble small, brown-skinned children.[12]

Switzerland

In this situation, the strong and memorable associations consumers have with brands turned into liabilities as those associations became tinged with racial concerns. As a result of this and similar cases, as well as increasing globalization, firms are more careful nowadays when choosing brand names. For example, having a marketing team from diverse countries of origin—as well as doing diligent market research in different cultures—can give the company advance notice of naming problems.

Ethical dilemmas:

1. Who is harmed by the continued sale of products with names that demean specific ethnic groups? How exactly are they harmed?
2. How should firms manage brands that become tainted by racial connotations? What role should external backlash play in this decision-making process?

A key component of the brand's image is its perceived advantage, which is composed of **points of parity** and **points of difference**. Points of parity are the "boxes to tick": the aspects of the brand that are shared with competitors and that all customers expect as a baseline. Breakfast cereal having functional packaging that does not easily puncture or spill is a point of parity, for example. Points of difference are the key factors that differentiate the brand from its competition. "Gluten-free," "rich in protein," and "affordable" might be points of difference for a breakfast cereal. A firm has many ways to strengthen or build positive links from a brand node to points of parity and difference, to ensure that the brand identity matches the ideal positioning in a target market. For example, Figure 11.1 represents an associative network memory model for a potential customer of Vivo (a Chinese smartphone manufacturer) phones;

points of parity The aspects of the brand that are shared with competitors and that all customers expect as a baseline

points of difference The key factors that differentiate the brand from its competition

Source: Michal Jarmoluk/Pixabay

The human mind makes connections and finds memories much more quickly than thumbing through a photo book. Instead, memories are a web of interconnected nodes; recalling a memorable node, such as hearing the brand name Nestlé, can activate connections to a variety of linked nodes, such as images of packaging or the taste of chocolate.

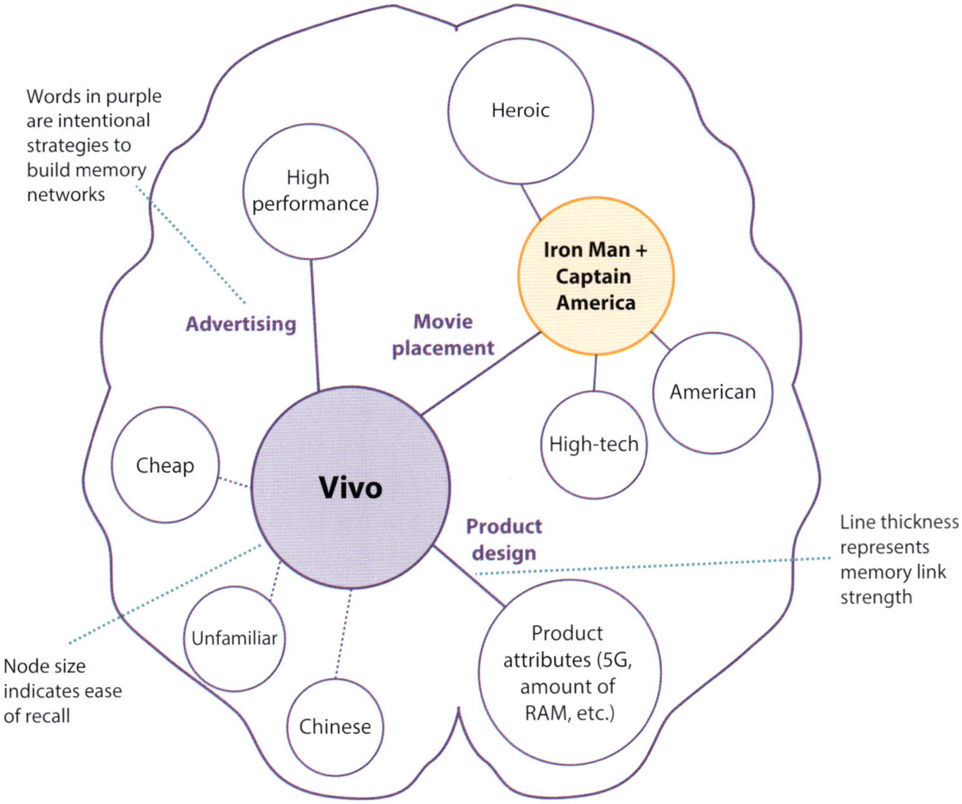

Figure 11.1 Memory Model of Brands.

The associative network memory model views the memory as composed of nodes and links. In this case, smartphone manufacturer Vivo used product placement in 2016's *Captain America: Civil War* to increase its awareness and appeal in Western markets.

the size of the Vivo node represents a particular customer's awareness of Vivo. The more often a customer is exposed to Vivo advertisements, tries a friend's Vivo phone, or just sees people using Vivo phones in public, the stronger Vivo's brand node becomes.

If Vivo's marketing department wants to build more links with this node—especially in Western markets—it could pay to have Captain America and Iron Man use Vivo phones in a Marvel movie, establishing a link between Vivo and the Marvel superheroes node, as well as those heroes' existing links (e.g., heroic, American, high-tech), as shown in Figure 11.1. This scenario isn't hypothetical; Vivo used exactly this strategy to promote their V3 and V3 max devices with over 60 seconds of screen time in 2016's *Captain America: Civil War*.[13] A movie placement can be very effective, because this single move can link a constellation of characteristics to the central brand node, which would be more difficult to achieve through traditional television or print advertisements. In addition, movie placements often make these links more subtly, so they can avoid the skepticism that customers often feel toward obvious paid advertising.[14] But as Figure 11.1 shows, other product design features and points of difference (e.g., favorable price-to-performance ratio) can be linked to the brand node using more traditional marketing strategies.

In the network memory model, brand strategy involves first building awareness to provide an anchor point, then building links to positive, unique memory nodes to establish an identity that matches target customers' needs.[15] When a customer sees (hears, touches) the brand name, it activates that brand node, leading to the cascading activation of other connected nodes—as long as strong links exist—which create the customer's brand experience. Research has shown that these links can activate a wide range of thoughts and feelings.[16] Sometimes these links can even be negative, creating new challenges for marketers (see this chapter's case study on the World Health Organization, as well as the Marketing Fail feature on Oldsmobile). Given the powerful impact that brands have on the human mind, marketers must put thought into developing the most effective brand strategy.

Brand Positioning

brand positioning How and where the firm hopes to appear in customers' minds

Brand positioning reflects how and where the firm hopes to appear in customers' minds. In a way, it reflects the firm's ideal associative network memory model, the one it hopes that customers hold in mind. It captures the aspirational level of awareness, key associations, and overall product or company image the firm seeks in the marketplace. The BOR (brands, offerings, relationships) equity stack from Chapter 10 provides a starting point for this discussion, because it describes the marketing objectives associated with the brand strategy, the relative advantage(s) that the brand can offer over relevant competitors, and the source of the sustainability of this advantage. That is, it captures many of the elements that brand managers need to develop their brand strategies. The firm's positioning statements (based on STP [segmentation, targeting, positioning]; see Chapter 4) are also important, though they can be more abstract or high level, rather than specific to the brand strategy. Furthermore, the AER (Acquisition–Expansion–Retention) strategies across segments (Chapter 7) are helpful, but they are unique to each segment and AER stage, whereas the brand usually needs to be consistent across all segments and stages. Generally, it is extremely hard to offer differentiated brand strategies at this level of specificity, since consumers widely share information about brands.

Thus, the BOR equity stack framework informs the objectives, sources of sustainability, image, identity, and level of awareness that comprise the brand's positioning strategy. If brand managers can describe all these components, they gain a clear picture of what they want the brand to do, know the key methods they are going to use to achieve their goals, and recognize many of the building blocks needed to develop a brand strategy. Two other strategic decisions also describe how these brand elements will apply to a firm's various offerings over time: brand extensions and brand architecture.

Managing Multiple Brands and Brands Across Multiple Products

Brand Extensions

Brand extensions pertain to the approach the firm uses to launch new offerings by leveraging an existing brand, whether through line or category extensions. In **brand line extensions** (often called line extensions), the new offering is in the same product category but targets a different segment of customers, usually with a slightly different set of attributes. Thus, Crest toothpaste has launched at least twelve different types of toothpaste, for kids, people with dentures, and those who want whiter teeth. In **brand category extensions**, the new offering instead moves to a completely different product category, such as when Smith & Wesson, known for manufacturing firearms, began producing bicycles.[17]

brand extensions Launching a new offering by leveraging an existing brand

brand line extensions A brand extension where the new offering is in the same product category but targets a different segment of customers

brand category extensions A brand extension where the new offering moves to a completely different product category

Source: Matt Bero/Unsplash

American Outdoor Brands, formerly Smith & Wesson, was long famous for selling firearms. In the 1990s, it extended its brand into a totally different category: mountain bikes, initially for police and later for the general public.

Most brand extensions are line extensions, which are less risky and enable the firm to address multiple customer segments with just slight variants to their focal product. Of the many benefits that brand extensions offer a firm, two are especially vital.[18] First, launching the new product with an established brand reduces customers' perceived risk in trying the product, as well as retailers' (or other channel partners') perceived risk in carrying the new product. Second, it enables the firm to serve new segments without the cost of building a new brand.

However, not all brand extensions achieve all these benefits, as evidenced by the many failed extensions over the years. Richard Branson extended the Virgin brand to the unfortunately named "Virgin Brides" wedding dress brand, soldiering on for a decade before shuttering the struggling boutiques. Zippo, known for high-quality butane cigarette lighters, tried their hand at launching a fragrance in a lighter-shaped bottle, with predictably poor results. These examples highlight the limits on a firm's ability to stretch its brand into new segments and categories.

Over time, researchers have developed some guidelines for improving the chances of success for brand extensions:

1. There must be perceived fit between the parent brand's image and the extension on an attribute that is relevant to the customer. Customers might evaluate the "fit" of the brand extension based on similarity in aesthetics, technology, or other factors that might not be easy to predict in advance.[19] The earlier Zippo example illustrates poor fit between a core brand attribute (the smell of butane) and the new category (fragrance).
2. Brand extensions can be stretched farther if done incrementally. For example, Amazon.com began as an online bookstore. Soon, it offered a variety of other household and electronic items online. Before long, it was selling grocery items and its own Amazon-branded private labels across dozens of product categories. And now, Amazon has applied its brand name, in whole or in part, to countless other services and ventures, from Amazon Video to Amazon Game Studios. Amazon increased its involvement in consumers' lives over time, until it became sufficiently ubiquitous and linked to every conceivable attribute that few extensions would be viewed as a stretch.
3. Higher-quality brands generally can be extended further. Disney (or one of the other brands it owns, for instance, Marvel) can adorn almost any merchandise under the sun with its own name—and they do, in their theme parks and online store. This works because Disney has legions of adoring fans that hold their films in the highest regard. In contrast, Illumination's serviceable *Minions* and *Sing* franchises must tread more carefully.

Brand Architecture

Brand architecture defines both the rationale and the structure among the firm, its products, and its brand extensions—in essence, how the brand is used at different levels in the organization. At one extreme is a **house of brands architecture**, such that the firm focuses on branding each major product with its own unique set of brand elements (e.g., P&G's Tide, Folgers, and Pampers).

brand architecture How the firm's portfolio of brands are used at different levels of the organization

house of brands architecture Brand architecture in which the firm focuses on branding each major product with its own unique set of brand elements

MARKETING FAIL Oldsmobile Fades Away

Oldsmobile was one of the first auto manufacturers in the world, dating back to its founding by Ransom E. Olds in 1897. It was Olds, not Henry Ford, who was the first to manufacture cars on an assembly line in 1902.[20] The company's growth accelerated after its 1908 acquisition by General Motors, peaking in the United States in the 1970s and 1980s with boxy classics such as the Cutlass Supreme. The brand had a reputation for comfort, quality, reliability, and a timeliness style.

Yet soon the party was over, as sales plunged by more than 50 percent in the decade following 1985.[21] The US auto market was facing new entries from Japan, such as Toyota, that were fast winning over consumers with innovative designs and reliable performance. Moreover, General Motors struggled to maintain distinct positionings for each of its brands, including Oldsmobile, Chevrolet, Buick, and Cadillac; Oldsmobile in particular developed a reputation as an outdated brand.[22] Without a new vehicle with attractive features to lure back consumers, or especially distinct brand attributes compared to its GM stablemates, Oldsmobile was left without a role in its parent company's brand portfolio.

USA

Its last new model was introduced in 2001, before the brand faded into obscurity. Unfortunately, when a brand no longer supports a sustainable competitive advantage, it tends to be discarded.

Diagnose the problem:

1. Explain why Oldsmobile's strong brand was not enough to preserve its competitive advantage.
2. What could Oldsmobile (and its parent company, GM) have done differently to save the brand? What would be the implications of your recommendation for GM's portfolio of other auto brands?

branded house architecture Brand architecture in which a firm uses a single set of brand elements for all of its products

At the other end is a **branded house architecture**, where a firm uses a single set of brand elements for all its products (e.g., Google's Google Books, Google Translate, Google Maps, and so on). Thus, P&G applies different brand elements to each of its major household products but devotes little effort or money to promoting the P&G parent brand. Google uses one set of brand elements for all its products, across such diverse categories as search, home routers, and video streaming. Why do firms select such different brand architectures when designing their brand strategies? Overall, firms should shift toward a house of brands approach if they need a separate brand for each entity (divisions, categories, products) to avoid a problematic association or confusion.

endorsed brand Brand architecture that links a brand to a parent brand with approval words such as "by" or "presents"

sub-branding Brand architecture in which a product/service has its own distinct brand identity, while retaining that of its parent brand

Despite this presentation of brand architecture as two extremes on a spectrum, in reality, firms often use intermediate or hybrid brand structures to gain the benefits of both approaches. Two types of hybrid brand architectures are endorsed brands and sub-branding. Marriott hotels use an **endorsed brand** strategy for the Courtyard by Marriott chain: it suggests the approval of the Marriott brand—known as a relatively upmarket brand of large resorts and business-focused hotels—but also makes it clear to customers that Courtyard hotels stand on their own and offer something different from, and more accessible than, typical Marriott hotels. Toyota (like most car manufacturers) instead uses a **sub-branding** strategy, where each model (Camry, Corolla, Prius, etc.) acquires its own brand identity and image. Branding a car as a Toyota Prius means that it enjoys spillover benefits from Toyota (awareness and links to attributes such as reliability) but also differentiates the Prius name so that it can establish links unique to the hybrid vehicle category (e.g., eco-friendly).

SUPPORTING BRAND EQUITY WITH EFFECTIVE ADVERTISING

advertising A form of communication that businesses use to influence customers to act or think in ways favorable to their firm

Advertising is a form of communication that businesses use to influence customers to act or think in ways favorable to their firm. Its implementation may involve print, audio, or visual media; these formats have evolved to fit customers' appetite for different channels of communication. Advertising offers an important means to improve customer awareness and perceptions of a brand, gain access to new customers, and improve the company's standing.[23] The benefits of a successful advertising campaign also can detract from the standing of rival firms, which improves the relative position of the brand, both within its targeted market and beyond.

Although brands can be critical in both business and consumer markets, advertising is especially effective at building brands with consumer segments. This is because one of the key strengths of advertising—reaching many individuals per dollar spent—is most advantageous when the target market is very large. This occurs, more often than not, in B2C contexts. Advertising is one of marketers' best tools for building and sustaining brand equity because of its potent ability to build links between the brand name, brand elements, and points of difference/parity. Examples of brand elements attached to the minds of consumers through aggressive advertising campaigns abound, including characters such as the Geico gecko, jingles such as McDonald's "I'm lovin' it," the logos for major film releases, for instance, *The Avengers*, and countless others. Using advertising to forge these and other links requires an understanding of the process for both planning, and measuring the effectiveness, of advertising campaigns.

Advertising Planning Process

Marketers generally make advertising decisions and build effective campaigns using a four-step process (Figure 11.2), detailed in the following section:

1. selecting a target audience and goal
2. selecting appropriate media and content
3. selecting an advertising schedule
4. measuring the reach and impact of advertising

Step 1: Selecting a Target Audience and Goal

audience The intended recipients of the advertising message

The first step in any advertising campaign is knowing the **audience**. These are the intended recipients of the message, whose associative memory networks the company hopes to influence in some way that benefits the brand. Having an ongoing marketing planning process, including conducting segmentation,

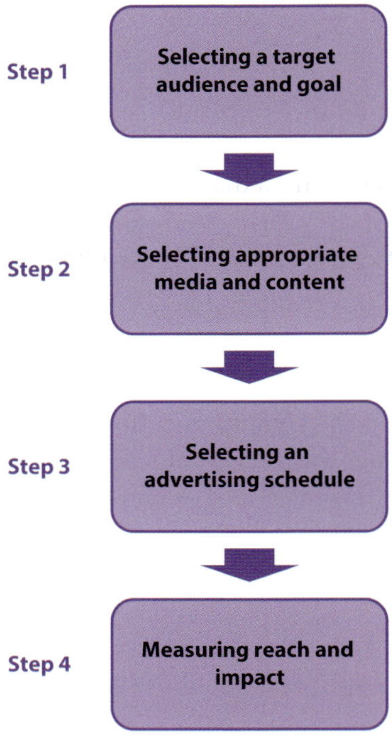

Figure 11.2 Advertising Planning Process.

Advertising processes vary across companies and industries but can generally be thought of as including four steps: (1) selecting a target audience and goal; (2) selecting appropriate media and content; (3) selecting an advertising schedule; and (4) measuring the reach and impact of advertising.

targeting, and positioning, greatly eases identifying the target audience, since the *target segments* that were most appropriate for the product or service are also, generally, the *target audience* who marketers would like to influence. At times, though, marketers may wish to run different campaigns for different segments of the same product (i.e., separate audiences). For example, Nike targets different advertising messages to consumers buying their products for an "athleisure" aesthetic, versus serious athletes who buy Nike products for improved performance. In other cases, marketers may wish to target only a portion of a focal segment (i.e., a smaller audience); for Nike, this could mean ads focusing specifically on women within the athleisure segment.

Once the audience is selected, marketers ought to set a measurable goal with respect to that audience. Typical objectives pertaining to the target audience might include: to raise awareness by 5 percent within six months; to increase web traffic by 20 percent year-over-year by quarter's end; generate $2,000,000 in sales this quarter; or increase subscriber count by 5,000 this month. In each case, the goal should feature a metric (e.g., awareness), a target level (e.g., 5 percent increase), and a time frame (e.g., within six months). This allows marketers to properly evaluate whether it is on track during the campaign, and whether it accomplished its goals after the campaign.

Step 2: Selecting Appropriate Media and Content

Once marketers have determined the campaign's audience and goal, these inputs should inform the medium or media in which the advertisements appear and the content of the adverts. Media and content are intertwined decisions. Some content works better on certain media; attempts to convey the striking silhouette of a laptop will likely fall short in a radio advert. Likewise, the choice of media will influence the direction of the content, as billboard adverts lend themselves to extremely simple, eye-catching visuals that can be processed in milliseconds. So strong and integral is this relationship that Marshall McLuhan, a Canadian expert in communication theory, famously asserted that "The medium is the message."[24]

In terms of media choice, **traditional media** consists of television, radio, print (direct mail, newspaper, magazine), and outdoor (billboard, bus stop, etc.). The category of "**new media**" is constantly evolving, but includes social media (e.g., TikTok adverts), streaming (e.g., Hulu adverts), sponsored search results, mobile, and display adverts (e.g., banner advert on a website). A rule of thumb for media selection is that it should follow the audience, that is, where their eyes linger, the advert should live. If Lululemon wants to target college-age women who enjoy athleisure clothing, and those women typically spend significant time on Snapchat, then digital advertisements on Snapchat are a natural medium to select.

traditional media Classic media, including television, radio, print, and outdoor

new media Media that has evolved within the digital age, including social media, streaming, sponsored search results, mobile, and display advertisements

The content of an advert is guided by two key factors, aside from the medium: (1) the aim of the advert with respect to influencing nodes and links in the associative memory model, and (2) the type of appeal that will be used to enact this influence. The three core types of influence that marketers hope to achieve through advertising are to *inform*, *persuade*, and *remind*.[25]

- **Informative advertising** looks to tell consumers about the brand and the product or service's features. In doing so, it can expand the focal brand node and forge links to other nodes, reflecting attributes of the brand or underlying offering. For example, the digital campaign for Google Fi in 2022 heavily leaned on informative elements, including substantial details of the phone plan's pricing and convenient features.

informative advertising Advertisements that look to tell consumers about the brand and the product's or service's features

- **Persuasive advertising** explicitly aims to change existing attitudes about the brand, as commonly seen in repositioning advertisements. Buick's repositioning campaign throughout the late 2010s tried to shift the prevailing perception of Buick as a boring brand by having actors express disbelief ("That's not a Buick!") when they saw sleek, high-tech Buick vehicles. So persuasive adverts may try to weaken *or* strengthen existing links to the focal brand node, create new connections, or even affect links to *other* brands' nodes (see Opposing Views in this chapter).

persuasive advertising Advertisements that aim to change existing attitudes about the brand

- Lastly, **reminder advertising** focuses on *maintaining* existing nodes and links by repeating information or brand elements that are already familiar to the audience. Certain government public service announcements, such as advertisements about the importance of wearing seatbelts, fall under this category.

reminder advertising Advertisements that repeat information or brand elements that are already familiar to the audience

informational appeals Advertisements that focus on facts, logic, and reason

emotional appeals Advertisements that try to influence the audience's feelings

The last major factor influencing advertising content is the type of appeal, which may be informational or emotional. **Informational appeals** focus on facts, logic, and reason. Despite the overlapping terminology, informative advertising is not the only type of advertising that uses informational appeals. Persuasive and reminder advertising can also change attitudes with rational arguments or remind consumers about important facts. The aforementioned Google Fi adverts use an informational appeal, while also being informative advertising. As the name implies, **emotional appeals** instead try to influence the audience's feelings. Such appeals are common, for example, in Dior fragrance advertisements; these are often music videos that have evocative imagery and songs but little to no information conveyed.

The choice of informational versus emotional appeals is complex and depends on many factors, including the nature of the audience and the objectives of the advert. For example, contrary to stereotypes, emotional appeals have been found to be more effective on *male* audiences. In general, emotional appeals fare better for influencing the preliminary stages of the buying process (e.g., awareness), while informational appeals are more effective at persuading buyers who were already considering a purchase.[26]

Step 3: Selecting an Advertising Schedule

advertising schedule The frequency and timing with which the advertisement is deployed across various media

continuous scheduling A steady deployment of an advertisment throughout its run

flighting scheduling Intermittent bursts of adverts, followed by long periods of zero activity

pulsing scheduling A schedule that combines continuous and flighting schedules. A baseline level of constant advertising frequency, with intermittent periods of heightened intensity

Once audience, goal, media, and content are defined, an **advertising schedule** must be produced. This is the frequency and timing with which the advert is deployed across various media. Although advertising schedules for major campaigns can be incredibly complex, they generally boil down to variations on three main strategies:

1. **Continuous scheduling** is, as the name implies, a steady deployment of the advertisement throughout its run. For example, a small business might purchase a Google display advert to run every day, from midday until midnight, for ninety days. This is typically the default scheduling option for goods and services with stable demand over time.
2. **Flighting scheduling** is quite different; it consists of intermittent bursts of adverts, followed by long periods of *zero* activity. A farm that sells fir trees, for example, could buy local newspaper adverts to run in every issue from November 15 to December 24. Flighting is typical for highly seasonal offerings and avoids wasting money on advertising when consumers are unlikely to buy.
3. **Pulsing scheduling** simply combines continuous and flighting schedules; it features a baseline level of constant advert frequency, with intermittent periods of heightened intensity. The motivation for pulsing is similar to flighting—minimizing wasteful adverts when demand is lower—except that the firm still expects reasonable demand outside of peak seasons, and therefore does not cut off adverts entirely.

OPPOSING VIEWS Comparative Advertising

Advertising professionals have historically held favorable views of a type of persuasive advertising called **comparative advertising**, in which the firm explicitly calls out a competing brand in the advertisement.[27] Samsung's advertising campaigns, for example, frequently target Apple; one advertisement mocks the devotion of Apple fans waiting outside a store for an iPhone launch. Such adverts provide consumers with a reference point for evaluating the brand and are believed to be potentially more involving and engaging for consumers.[28]

Yet more recent marketing research suggests that advertising should exercise caution when planning a comparison-focused advertisement. This style of advertising is less effective in certain national cultures. For example, in some cultures, nonverbal context plays a heavier role in communication, making verbal explicit comparisons appear out of touch; or in other cultures such as the United States, comparative advertising is excessively common and can lead to consumer annoyance.[29,30] Other research suggests that direct comparisons to the market leader (as in the Samsung/Apple adverts) could be viewed by consumers as manipulative and potentially backfire.[31]

Global

In answering the questions below, imagine you are designing an advert for your favorite smartphone manufacturer.

See the issue from two sides:

1. Craft an argument in favor of including comparisons to your chosen smartphone manufacturer's closest rival in the advertising content. What exact aspects would you compare?
2. Craft an argument against such a direct comparative approach. What content would you include in the advert instead?

Step 4: Measuring the Reach and Impact of Advertising

To know whether advertising succeeded, marketers must be able to accurately track and measure its impact. Generally, this can involve many of the marketing research and analytics principles discussed in Chapter 9:

- **Pretesting**, or estimating the impact of an advert before it goes live, can be performed with focus groups or surveys that include exposure to the advertisement or, if different versions of the ad are being tested, an experiment can be employed. Pretest studies can capture goal-relevant metrics such as purchase likelihood, willingness to pay, likelihood to recommend the product, or brand recall (in a follow-up study after some time).
- **Post-testing**, conversely, involves analyses of real-world outcomes after the advert goes live and after the completion of the campaign. This can require ongoing consumer surveys in the case of brand awareness, simple sales metrics for revenue-based goals, or more sophisticated advert tracking (e.g., using browser cookies) for metrics related to how often the advert was viewed. Viewing is typically measured with a combination of two factors: **reach**, or the percentage of the target audience that experienced the advert in a given period (e.g., a month), and **frequency**, or the typical number of times those people will see the advert. Multiplying these two factors together provides **gross rating points (GRP)**, an industry-standard metric of advertising exposure.

comparative advertising Advertising content in which the firm explicitly calls out a competing brand in the advertisement

pretesting Estimating the impact of an advertisement before it goes live

post-testing Analyses of real-world outcomes after the advertisement goes live and after the completion of the campaign

reach The percentage of the target audience that experienced the advertisement in a given period

frequency The typical number of times those people will see the advertisement in a given period

gross rating points (GRP) An industry-standard metric of advertising exposure that is the product of reach and frequency

THEORY SPOTLIGHT Elaboration Likelihood Model in Advertising

Many theories exist to explain how consumers are influenced by external messages such as advertisements. One that has stood the test of time is the **elaboration likelihood model**. In this framework, consumers have two distinct routes for processing information. The first is the *central route*, in which we consciously weigh the merits and arguments present in the advertisement. For example, we might consider whether we agree with the advert's claim that a product's current price is a good deal. We are generally very aware of this persuasion route, as people consider themselves to be rational. The second is the *peripheral route*, in which we are more influenced by non-informational cues, such as the tone or emotions conveyed in the advert.[32]

Hence, if marketers want to use an informational appeal, they hope that consumers will process information via the central route; if they want to use an emotional appeal, they hope for peripheral persuasion. The challenge is that the central processing route requires much more attention and effort on the part of the consumer, who often does not want to devote this effort to advertisements.[33] Marketers, then, are tasked with the challenge of crafting engaging adverts that pull the viewer, reader, or listener in before delivering vital information.

IN OTHER WORDS ...

It is helpful to think of gross rating points as "total impact." A reach of 1 percent with frequency of one time means that the advertiser impacts 1 percent of the possible audience in total (1 GRP). A reach of 1 percent with a frequency of three times means that the adviser reaches 1 percent of the possible audience, but with three times the impact on each consumer (3 GRP).

elaboration likelihood model A framework where consumers have two distinct routes for processing information: central and peripheral

By intelligently planning a campaign and measuring its impact on brand-relevant goals, marketers can wield advertising as an indispensable tool for building brand equity and sustainable competitive advantage.

Keys to Building Brand Equity with Effective Advertising

MP#3 focuses on the importance of barriers to competitive attacks, because competitors are continually reacting to any firm's success. Investments to build brand awareness and brand image can produce a strong competitive barrier. The positioning statements generated in relation to MP#1 and MP#2 provide key information that help the firm design its brand message to make target customers aware of the brand and how it continues to meet their needs over time.

Customers' behaviors in response to a brand generate the firm's brand equity, one of the three major components of the BOR equity stack, along with offering and relationship equities (Chapter 10). Thus, brand equity exists in the customer's mind, which means that it is difficult for competitors to copy it, adding to the sustainability of brand-based barriers.[34] But this status also makes it hard for firms to adapt or change their brand identity. Apple could not rapidly gain a reputation as a low-price provider of basic computers, for example, because the strength of its identity as a higher-priced, innovative brand is entrenched. If the power of brands as SCA depends on the minds of customers, then an important question emerges: how can the company influence customers' associative memory networks and ultimately build brand equity?

Building brand equity to increase a firm's SCA can be divided into three steps:

1. First, *build a high level of brand awareness* among the firm's targeted customers, which then provides an anchor point for linking the easily recalled brand name to the elements that define its meaning and image. Building awareness involves making the brand easy to recall across a wide range of potential purchase and usage situations. Awareness should be high for the complete constellation of brand name elements: its name, logo, jingle, package shape, and other elements that the firm uses to identify its offering.[35] This requires linking the brand node to these elements in consumers' memory with consistent and memorable advertising.
2. Then *link the brand name to the brand's points of parity and difference,* which helps define the brand's relative advantage. This step defines how the brand will be positioned against its competition. Some links might get transferred from the parent brand, depending on the firm's brand architecture. For example, when Johnson & Johnson launches a new product that includes its strong parent brand, the new product's sub-brands immediately take on some meaning from that parent. Because points of difference are a key relative advantage of a brand when it first launches, significant financial resources and promotional efforts are applied to make these differentiation points memorable and link them strongly to the brand name when designing advertisements.
3. Finally, *build a deep emotional connection or "relationship" between the brand and targeted customers.* Moving beyond functional differentiation implies a true, emotional connection—the essence of building a powerful, long-lasting brand image. A strong brand image often is what provides a long-term sustainable advantage because it connects with consumers at a deep level and is hard for competitors to replicate. It also can drive positive word of mouth, transforming customers into strong brand advocates.[36] This requires sustained and strategic advertising efforts over time, such that links form between the brand and the consumer's self-image or values.

All three steps are evident in Absolut Vodka's "bottle" campaign. Launched in 1980, the campaign featured clean, simplistic adverts that spotlighted the vodka's unique bottle design. Over the years, as the bottle design changed, the campaign remained the same, such that it effectively chronicled this unique feature of the product over time. Brand awareness skyrocketed, as did knowledge of the bottle's design (a point of difference), such that Absolut is now the second best-selling vodka in the world. Moreover, the campaign spurred many enthusiasts to collect Absolut bottles over the years, forging a strong relationship with the brand.[37]

Converting Brand Equity to Customer Equity

There are many benefits of building brand equity; together, these benefits ultimately can improve a firm's sales, reduce its costs, and make it more difficult for competitors to encroach on the firm's business.[38] Brands change how people think, though often at a level below their conscious awareness, which makes it very difficult for customers to ignore brand effects. For example, one classic experiment shows that the taste of beer differs when the customer knows the brand of the beer he or she is drinking.[39] Customers are not just repeating the brand messaging, that is, the beer actually tastes different when linked to a brand name. Because brand identification activates a brand node associated with that beer, it spreads across other strongly linked nodes in the drinker's memory network. Thus, the part of the brain that processes taste receives input from both the customer's taste buds and the brand's memory network. These two inputs then merge to establish the customer's taste perceptions. In other words, *brands can change customers' actual experiences*, whether in a restaurant, trying on clothes, or driving a car.[40]

Most benefits from strong brands are associated with three general areas:

1. *Sales growth.* Sales benefit from strong brands, because brands make it easier to acquire new customers, who perceive less risk, higher quality, and better performance of a brand with strong equity.[41] Similarly, it is easier for firms to launch new products, product extensions, and brand extensions, because their strong brand name provides protection, even before the firm spends any of its advertising budget on the product launch. When Nintendo launches a new game that was developed in-house, its brand identity (i.e., well-designed, high-quality, family-friendly) immediately attaches to the new offering.
2. *Profit enhancement.* The benefits that drive sales growth also can boost a firm's profitability by reducing costs (e.g., less advertising is needed to retain brand-loyal customers) or allowing the firm to charge higher prices for its products. Higher prices often are inherently tied to brand positioning in a market. Louis Vuitton, Coach, and Ferrari all charge significant premiums for their products, mostly due to customers' perception of their exclusive brand image. These products help confer high status onto customers who use them, and that status is a key part of their brand equity. In addition, firms with strong brand equity can gain easier access to various sales channels (retailers, distributors, specialty catalogs, web platforms) than can competitors with less brand equity.[42] In one study of customer perceptions, Kellogg's brand value was found to be more than 25 percent higher than that of General Mills.[43]
3. *Loyalty effects.* A strong brand makes customers more loyal, which can provide a large barrier against competitors. This source of SCA arises

Source: JeepersMedia/Openverse

Despite Aldi's extremely low prices, its faithful customers have come to trust the brand to provide an acceptable standard of quality. These customers visit week after week, with their loyalty to the brand providing strong and predictable revenue.

because strong brands generate more positive attitudes (**attitudinal loyalty**), which skew customers' subsequent behaviors. If Samsung suffers supply chain problems that lead to late product deliveries, many loyal customers would attribute the problems to the company's offshore suppliers. Samsung's strong brand protects it from the repercussions of such service failures, but if a similar problem were to plague Motorola or Alcatel, their customers likely would blame these weaker brands for the problems and perhaps even switch to a competitor. Strong brands also generate repeat purchase behaviors (**behavioral loyalty**), in the form of habitual purchase behavior, which can be reinforced by high brand awareness and the connection between the customer's self-identity and the brand identity of the firm or product.

attitudinal loyalty Loyalty as indicated by the customer's feelings, cognitions, or perceptions of the brand

behavioral loyalty Loyalty as indicated by a customer's repeat purchase behaviors

Overall, high brand equity enhances a firm's sales and profits, allowing it to continue to market its products, conduct research and development, and fight competitors in a multitude of ways. A strong cash reserve earned from superior sales and profits gives the firm the resources and time it needs to respond to innovative product entries or low-cost competitors; in some cases, it even might use these resources to acquire a firm that threatens its survival. Because strong brands increase customers' attitudinal and behavioral loyalty, switching behavior diminishes. Very loyal customers avoid even evaluating competitive offerings, to prevent themselves from feeling tempted or disrupting their sense of attachment to the brand.

CHAPTER CASE STUDY

BRANDING AT THE WORLD HEALTH ORGANIZATION

Global

Brands are not the exclusive domain of for-profit companies. Individuals (e.g., real estate agents), governments, nonprofit charities, for instance, United Way, nongovernmental organizations such as Amnesty International, and intergovernmental agencies such as the World Health Organization all have brands to manage. Although these brands differ somewhat in purpose from their for-profit counterparts—they do not exist to generate financial value for stakeholders, for instance—they nonetheless are important and valuable assets that protect the organization from threats.

In this case, we focus on the implications of branding for the World Health Organization (WHO), a United Nations agency with a mission to help the world's nations collaborate to improve global public health. Its roles include guiding the direction of medical research, coordinating and advising nations on policy, collating and reporting global health statistics, and providing a leading voice during global health crises.[44] Gathering governmental data to map outbreaks and pandemics, as in the accompanying image, is a frequent task for the WHO.

Role of the WHO's brand. All these efforts rely on the strength of the WHO's brand. To guide medical research, the WHO needs to be able to garner respect, especially given the presence of other authorities such as the US National Institutes of Health. To gather and report reliable data—which sometimes requires collecting sensitive information from

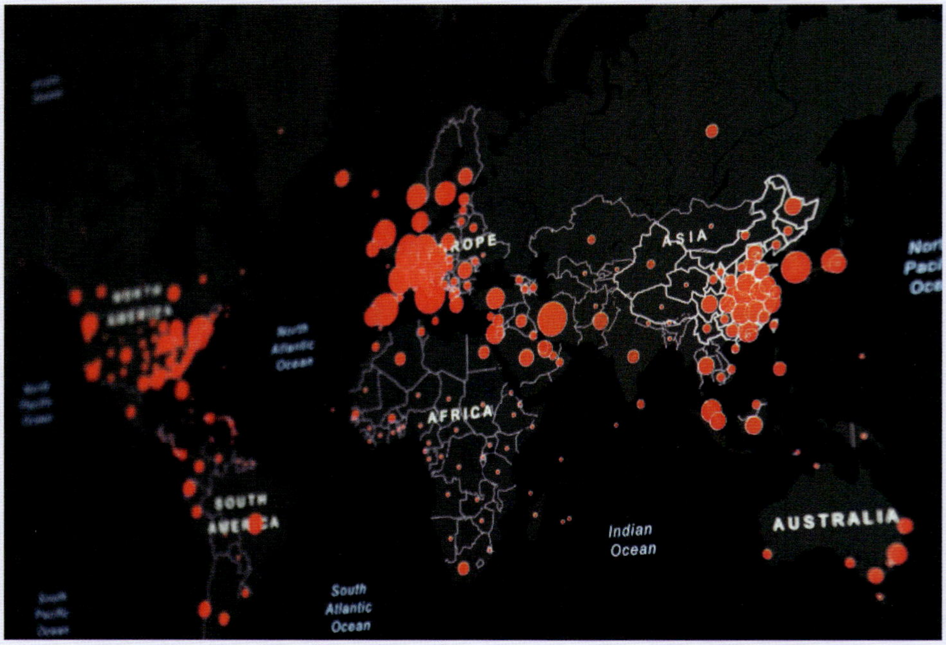

Source: Martin Sanchez/Unsplash

The World Health Organization has a role to play in coordinating different countries when a major disease outbreak spreads across national borders. The WHO relies on public trust in its brand, but it has drawn criticism both for its handling of the West African Ebola outbreak in 2013 and the COVID-19 pandemic in 2020.

member states—the WHO needs to be seen as unimpeachable. And to be taken seriously on policy advice and global leadership, its name must be associated with competence, foresight, and excellent judgment. Historically, the WHO has been successful in this regard. Its leadership, for example, was instrumental in the global campaign during the 1960s and 1970s to eliminate smallpox, which had killed *300 million* people in the twentieth century.[45] Against the backdrop of these past successes, the WHO developed a brand as an organization with a critical mission and the efficacy to carry out that mission.[46]

Threats to the WHO's brand power. In the past decade, external events have damaged the WHO's brand in such a way that it may have greater difficulty carrying out its mission in the future. First, the Ebola outbreak in West Africa, which began in 2013, "was catastrophic. Previously successful infection control mechanisms for haemorrhagic fevers were not enacted quickly enough, or to the extent required to bring the outbreak under control. The outbreak soon overwhelmed epidemic response mechanisms at national, regional and global levels" resulting in 11,000 deaths—exceeding all previous Ebola outbreaks combined.[47] Although some factors were beyond the WHO's control, such as a lack of national health infrastructure in the affected countries, the organization was widely criticized for its slow response and its difficulty in helping to coordinate efforts on the ground.[48]

The COVID-19 crisis further harmed favorable attributes of the WHO's brand. In the early days of the pandemic, the WHO was criticized for delaying in declaring a global pandemic—and hence underemphasizing the urgency of the situation—as well as its seeming lack of scrutiny of early outbreak data from China.[49] The WHO's later postmortem of the pandemic, its report on the origins of the virus, was likewise criticized for being inconclusive.[50]

Although the organization has called for greater resources and authority to confront future pandemics, the weakening of key attributes of its brand may complicate such efforts going forward.

CASE QUESTIONS

1. Summarize the brand positioning of the WHO, including its image and identity.
2. Which aspects of this positioning were hindered by the events noted above?
3. Explain how the WHO could go about using advertising and other mass communications efforts to strengthen its brand moving forward.

CHAPTER SUMMARY

This chapter emphasizes how marketers can establish and maintain a sustainable competitive advantage through valuable and iconic brands and effective advertising. Using brands as an SCA is often most effective in large consumer markets. These firms invest in advertising to support strong brands. When advertising is effective, it builds brand equity and brand images that match firms' positioning strategies. This chapter provides an overview of key advertising concepts such as message content and media planning, and links effective brand advertising to SCA through multiple mechanisms. For example, very strong awareness causes consumers to buy based on their recognition or habit, which reduces their cognitive effort. Or, if brands also provide a strong and unique meaning, consumers may act according to their desire for status, to enhance their self-identity, or because of their strong positive attachment to the brand. Thus, a brand that aligns better with customers' needs than competitors' brands can provide a relative advantage. This advantage, and the brand itself, can be very hard to copy, and this inimitability heightens the power of brands as a source of SCA. This chapter also highlights several tools and concepts to manage brand-based SCA, such as brand architecture and advertising metrics.

APPLICATION QUESTIONS

1. Think of your favorite brand, and name all the brand elements that you associate with it. Why do you think these elements came to mind?
2. Continue thinking about the same brand, but now also consider the brand's image as a whole—everything that you associate with it. In which ways do you think this image aligns with the company's intended brand identity, and in what ways does it differ?
3. Choose one brand element. What is the most successful example of this element that you have seen? What made it so memorable?
4. Remember that "where their eyes linger, the advert should live." What type of media do you consume the most? Describe your experience with adverts on this media—do you feel they have been appropriately targeted?
5. Recall (or find) an example of a persuasive advert. Were you persuaded? Why or why not?
6. Compare your experience with informational and emotional appeals. Which do you find more effective? Memorable? Enjoyable?
7. Imagine designing an ad to promote your favorite brand. What audience, media, and content would you select, and why?

Visit the companion website, **https://bloomsbury.pub/palmatier-marketing**, or **https://samsinstitute.com**, for additional learning and teaching tools, including professional videos outlining the Four Principles, PowerPoint tutorials with voice-over commentary, sample syllabi for marketing courses, testbank and more.

Chapter 12

OFFERING-BASED ADVANTAGES, INNOVATION, AND PRODUCT-SERVICE STRATEGY

CHAPTER OVERVIEW

While Chapter 11 focused on the symbolic power of brands, Chapter 12 emphasizes the substance of the company's products or services. What benefits does the firm offer that competitors do not? You will learn the fundamentals of marketing strategy related to products and services, the fundamentals of how firms innovate, and how an innovative portfolio of products and services leads to sustainable competitive advantage (SCA). The chapter will proceed by answering the following questions:

- How do firms manage a portfolio of products and services?
- What types of innovations do firms develop, and how do they develop them?
- What five key factors make innovations more successful?
- How do innovations lead to SCA and build offering equity for the firm?

In the chapter's cases and features, you will encounter high-profile examples of companies succeeding, or failing, to build better products and services in the face of tough competition. These include:

- A poorly conceived Adidas product launch (Marketing Fail).
- Barclays Bank's unconventional approach to innovation (Chapter Case).
- Practical and ethical dilemmas in product and service strategy, such as the merits of gacha offerings in popular video games (Shades of Gray) and "flights to nowhere" in the airline industry (Opposing Views).

LEARNING OBJECTIVES

- Recognize dimensions of the product-service portfolio, and related terms and concepts.
- Identify terms and common practices in the new product development process.
- Assess the effect of customer differences and dynamics on innovation and product/service strategy.
- Compare various innovation and product/service strategies for achieving SCA.

IMAGINE Launching the Steam Deck

In July 2021, Valve Corporation announced an innovative new product: a handheld personal computer running on a Linux operating system that would be optimized for playing video games—complete with built-in joysticks and Valve's integrated game storefront. This product would be available at a price ranging from $400 to $650, depending on features.[1] Although this device—the Steam Deck—was hotly anticipated by those wanting to play PC games on the go, others questioned the limitations of a Linux (rather than Windows) platform and raised practical concerns about performance and battery life. And still others wondered who was meant to adopt this product. Was it a competitor to traditional handheld consoles such as the Nintendo Switch, and aiming for mainstream audiences? Or was it a niche alternative to a gaming laptop?[2]

We now know that the Steam Deck successfully launched and satisfied users, selling at least 2 million units. But a lot of planning from Valve's side went into this effort. Imagine that you are part of Valve's marketing team in 2021, and you are tasked with helping assemble a plan to maximize the number of consumers who adopt the Steam Deck. You have several challenges to navigate in moving this product toward mass appeal.

Critical thinking:

1. What kinds of consumers would be your initial target when trying to encourage adoption of the Steam Deck? How would you reach them and what would be your message?
2. To maximize adoption, how would you close the gap between this initial segment and mainstream video game players?

BASICS OF PRODUCT-SERVICE STRATEGY

As noted in Chapter 1, *offering* is a broad term that captures both tangible products and intangible services. Brands and relationships enhance the customer's experience, but they must build on the platform of a core offering. Accordingly, firms spend most of their research and development (R&D) budgets to improve their offerings or create new ones that can have advantages over competitors' offerings. For example, Intel spends a great deal to build its brand and ensure that consumers want "Intel Inside" their computers. And yet, on top of this, Intel still spends $15 *billion* each year on R&D, dedicated to efforts to maintain its leading performance in the semiconductor industry.[3] It thus retains a market share lead over its rival AMD, despite significant offering improvements by the latter.[4]

Various factors (e.g., firm size, business diversity, industry competition) affect how much each firm spends on R&D, but as a general rule, most firms willingly tap both their cash reserves and outside financing (e.g., loans) to ensure they can spend enough to develop competitive new offerings.[5] But before delving into R&D and the innovation process, we must review some core concepts related to offerings themselves. These include:

- The difference between products and services.
- The difference between core and augmented products.
- The concept of the product-service mix.
- Breadth and depth in the product-service mix.

What Is a Product?

We defined *product* in Chapter 1 as a shorthand for the firm's offerings and a central element of the marketing mix. Yet in the context of managing offering-based SCA, product here refers to a physical, tangible good, in contrast with a service. In other words, it is the **core product**, such as a Lenovo laptop. When coupled with complementary services—in the Lenovo example, these might include bundled software subscriptions, a warranty, or the availability of live support—the core product becomes the **augmented product**. The augmented product is much more significant in terms of building offering equity because it represents the entire package that the firm is selling. Therefore, it is what determines the offering's value in the mind of the customer. Meal delivery services such as Uber Eats, for example, form an augmented product when combined with the meal itself.

core product A physical, tangible good, separated from any supplementary services

augmented product The core product along with any included complementary services

product mix The set of products offered by the firm

product lines Groupings within the product mix based on physical characteristics or use cases

services Intangible offerings that consist of value provided with no physical goods necessarily exchanged

The set of products offered by the firm are collectively the **product mix**, which is grouped into **product lines** based on the physical characteristics or use cases of the products. For example, Coca-Cola has a product mix comprising distinct product lines such as soft drinks (Coca-Cola, Diet Coke, Sprite, etc.), sports drinks (e.g., Powerade), and juices (e.g., Simply). The grouping of product lines is up to the firm and can align with brand architecture (e.g., sub-brands within a major brand product line) if it chooses.

What Is a Service?

Services are the intangible offering and consist of value provided with no physical goods necessarily exchanged. Restaurants, bars, banks, hair salons, healthcare facilities, education providers, athletic training facilities, and mechanics are all under the services umbrella. Some services exist not to be sold on their own but only as part of the augmented product—for example, certain automobile service plans from a car dealership. Other services stand alone, such as a haircut. Still others can be supplemented with products to meet the customer's needs. For example, a mechanic will sell a customer the pads to fix her brakes as well as install the pads. As with products, a firm can categorize its various services into service lines, which collectively comprise the service mix. Banco Santander, for example, groups their services into Personal, Small Business, Commercial, and Private Client, with numerous specific services (e.g., different types of deposit accounts and loans) within each line.

Source: Aleisha Kalina/Unsplash

When you order a food delivery service such as Uber Eats, you are getting a lot more than the core product (the food). You also receive service through the delivery app and the delivery person, as well as secondary products such as packaging and silverware.

Making Decisions About the Product-Service Mix

product-service mix The set of all products and services offered by the firm

breadth of the product-service mix The number of different product or service lines in the mix

depth of a product or service line The number of distinct products or services in a line

Together, the product mix and service mix form the **product-service mix**, which is the totality of what the firm can offer its targeted segments. Entire product or service lines can be added to or dropped from the mix; this is referred to as increasing (adding a line) or decreasing (removing a line) the **breadth of the product-service mix**. Entertainment conglomerate Paramount Global, for example, added a streaming service line when it launched Paramount+ in 2021. Meanwhile, individual lines can be extended or pruned, corresponding to the **depth of a product or service line**. Coca-Cola, for example, discontinued the Odwalla product from its juice line in 2020, reducing that line's depth.[6]

Figure 12.1 visualizes the product-service mix and decisions surrounding product-service lines. It should be noted that altering the breadth and depth of the product mix can sometimes overlap with brand management concepts discussed in Chapter 11. Specifically, if the firm organizes each product or service line under one brand name, then increasing the depth of a line corresponds to a brand line extension, while increasing the breadth would be a brand category extension. In Figure 12.1, extending the Simply brand from the juice category to the milk alternative category is indeed both a breadth expansion and a brand category extension.

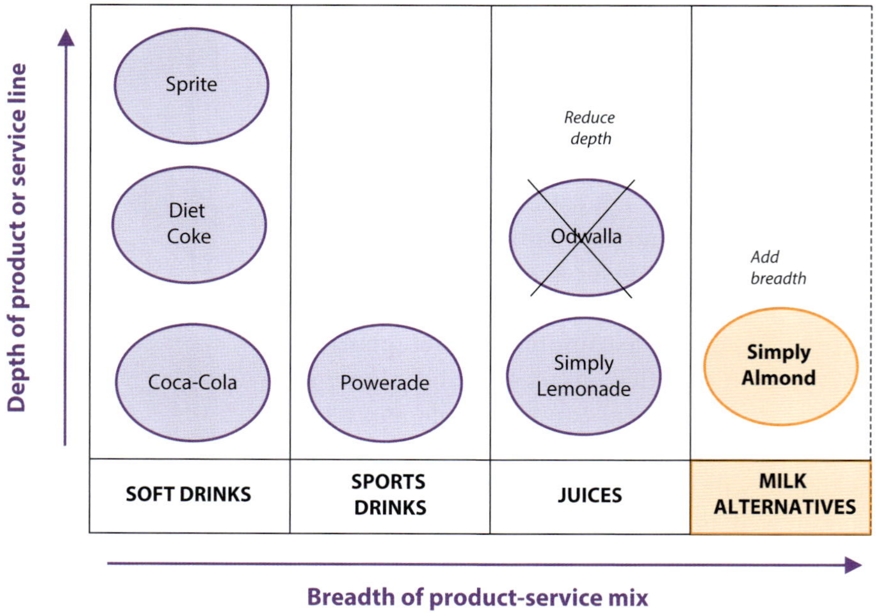

Figure 12.1 Product-Service Mix Decisions.

An example of managing the product-service mix, focusing on a small sample of Coca-Cola's core products. In the past several years, the company discontinued its Odwalla brand of juices (reducing the depth of the juice product line) but added almond milk under the Simply brand (adding a new product line, which increased the breadth of the product-service mix).

USING INNOVATION TO BUILD AND SUPPORT THE PRODUCT-SERVICE MIX

Innovation creates new value for customers by changing key facets of the firm or its product-service mix.[7] This process enables firms to develop valuable new offerings that ensure their sustainable competitive advantage (SCA). A recent survey of executives identifies innovation as a top strategic priority, with 59 percent expressing a desire to boost innovation *even if it involves collaborating with competitors*.[8] As the process for generating SCA through novel or improved offerings, innovation enables the firm to devise new, distinct solutions that separate it from its competitors. Using offerings as an SCA thus strongly reflects the underlying innovation process, in both theory and practice.

innovation Creating new value for the company and its customers by changing one or more key facets of the firm or its product-service mix

Types of Innovation

Innovation, its definition, and its process are expansive concepts, extending in scope beyond just product or technology innovation. Types of innovation can be grouped into four general categories:[9]

1. **Core offering-based innovation** is the type of innovation we typically imagine: engineers, chemists, physicists, and other science and technology professionals work on technological breakthroughs or novel applications, as in the case of self-driving cars; or creative professionals pouring their hearts and souls into the "next big thing," whether it is a new fashion line or blockbuster summer film release. General Electric, for example, once famously challenged its engineering teams to pursue 100 "imagination breakthrough" projects each year.[10]

core offering-based innovation Innovation to output new technology or creative work to improve core products or services

2. **Place-based innovation** involves creating value through novel approaches to *place* marketing mix decisions, such as seeking different retail locations or channel partners. For example, Enterprise Rent-A-Car was the first to locate its rental facilities in neighborhoods and commuter-heavy suburbs, rather than airports. Because a specific plot of land cannot be perfectly imitated, and moving facilities is costly and time-consuming, Enterprise held an advantage in these locations for several years.

place-based innovation Innovation that creates value through novel approaches to place marketing mix decisions

3. **Targeting-based innovation** requires finding segments to target that were previously neglected by competitors. Nintendo's 2006 launch of its Wii system, for example, explicitly took this route; as one executive at the time stated, "[Gaming is] no longer confined to just the few. It's about everyone." The console's signature motion control gimmick successfully appealed to segments, such as care home residents who had never played video games before, leading to over 100 million units sold.[11]

targeting-based innovation Innovation that finds segments to target that no competitor had significantly pursued previously

4. Lastly, **process-based innovation** changes how the firm transacts with customers. Geico's pioneering focus on an exclusively online business model, for example, made consumers realize that buying and managing insurance policies could involve less stress and paperwork. Similarly, Dell's notion of building-to-order "semi-custom" computer products and selling them directly to consumers online was radical when it first appeared. Providing new ways to pay for experiences, or parts of experiences, are also increasingly common process-based innovations (see Shades of Gray in this chapter).

process-based innovation Innovation that changes how the firm transacts with customers

SHADES OF GRAY Innovating Monetization with Gacha Games

Source: C M/Unsplash

Ubiquitous in Japan, gachapon are simple coin-operated dispensers of capsule toys. They have been the inspiration and namesake for an innovative type of chance-based video game monetization tactic. Gacha games are widely viewed as predatory.

Gachapon are simple coin-operated dispensers of capsule toys, common in Japan for decades and named for the distinctive sound they make when operated. Although they might be viewed as a gamble—a child doesn't know what toy they will get—they are harmless enough; they require visiting the machine with cash in hand, so parents can control spending.[12]

Their namesake in the world of mobile gaming, on the other hand, has stirred controversy. Rather than requiring an upfront purchase to play, so-called gacha games use an innovative strategy to monetize (i.e., extract money from) users' continuous engagement with the game. Much as with gachapon of old, players receive opportunities to "pull" for in-game items or characters of unpredictable value or gameplay benefit (often rated from one to five stars). Players receive a handful of free pulls, after which they must spend real-world money each time. This system is analogous to loot boxes, another popular monetization innovation.[13]

Two trends have caused this innovation to draw the ire of parents, the public, and even lawmakers:

1. Gacha systems have grown increasingly common in the past decade and feature heavily in some of the most popular mobile games globally, such as Genshin Impact.
2. They often appear in intellectual property-based mobile games focused on characters that appeal to kids and teens: Pokémon Masters EX, Star Wars: Galaxy of Heroes, Yu-Gi-Oh! Duel Links, Marvel Strike Force, and countless others.

These strategies have been shown to elicit repetitive spending behavior with a "just one more pull for a five-star" allure, to which children are especially susceptible.[14] So while game publishers insist that sufficient parental controls already exist on mobile devices, parents and lawmakers worry that more should be done to limit potential overspending and addiction. For example, Japan outlawed "multilevel" gacha in which a rare pull from one "tier" (e.g., a special token) would have to be spent to attempt a pull for even rarer second "tier" items. Going forward, game publishers may have to reckon with increasing scrutiny and regulation of these monetization strategies.

Ethical dilemmas:

1. Who is harmed by gacha practices in mobile games? Who is responsible for this harm, and why?
2. If you oversaw all gaming regulations, what (if anything) would you do to restrict this type of aggressive innovation in monetization?

A company need not focus on just one type of innovation. For example, Starbucks' successful innovation was not based only on technology; it revolved around designing a unique customer experience or "third place," other than home and work, where customers could relax and spend time. Starbucks also pursues product innovations, such as cold brew drinks, and technological innovations, such as its mobile ordering app. In blind taste tests, Starbucks often finds itself in the middle of the pack alongside McDonald's McCafe brand, yet millions of loyal Starbucks customers still visit daily and pay more per cup than they would at McDonald's.[15] In addition to its initial offering-based SCA, Starbucks takes an innovative strategic approach, focused on building a strong, authentic brand and avoiding a franchising model to expand. Therefore, it employs relatively well-compensated, motivated employees who are willing to build strong customer relationships.

Innovative new offerings help firms build and maintain SCA and barriers to the competitive attacks that arise because competitors continually react to a firm's success (MP#3). However, most offerings must be augmented by and linked to brands and relationships to ensure the firm's SCA because generally it is relatively easy for competitors to copy offerings, given enough time and money (unless the offering is protected by patents or trade secrets). Still, new innovations establish the foundation for the value that can be added by brands and relationships. Hence, it is useful for companies to have a formal process for conducting innovation.

The Innovation Process

Most firms rely on a **stage-gate development process** to increase the speed of their offering development and enhance their likelihood of success, while also reducing development costs.[16] As Figure 12.2 shows, a stage-gate process divides development into a series of steps or stages. The figure shows a typical four-stage process:

stage-gate development process An innovation process model in which a project gets evaluated from multiple perspectives on multiple dimensions at each stage of a funnel

1. **Concept and definition**, where the firm determines what the innovation *is* and *is not*. Returning to the Steam Deck example from the chapter opening, Valve had to decide early on whether it was building a portable device.
2. **Design and development**, where the concept becomes a tangible rendering and prototype (for a physical good) or detailed process plan (for a service). In the Steam Deck example, Valve would need to iterate on a prototype multiple times, for example, to test the ergonomics of the device.
3. **Validation and production**, when manufacturing ramp-up and other major launch preparations occur. In Valve's case, this would involve securing commitments from component suppliers, ensuring manufacturing capacity, and taking preorders from customers.
4. **Final audit**, in which details and estimates from previous stages are verified before launch.

concept and definition The first step of the stage-gate process, where the firm determines what the innovation is and is not

design and development The second step of the stage-gate process, where the concept becomes a tangible rendering and prototype (for a physical good) or detailed process plan (for a service)

validation and production The third step of the stage-gate process, when manufacturing ramp-up and other major launch preparations occur

final audit The fourth step of the stage-gate process, in which details and estimates from previous stages are verified before launch

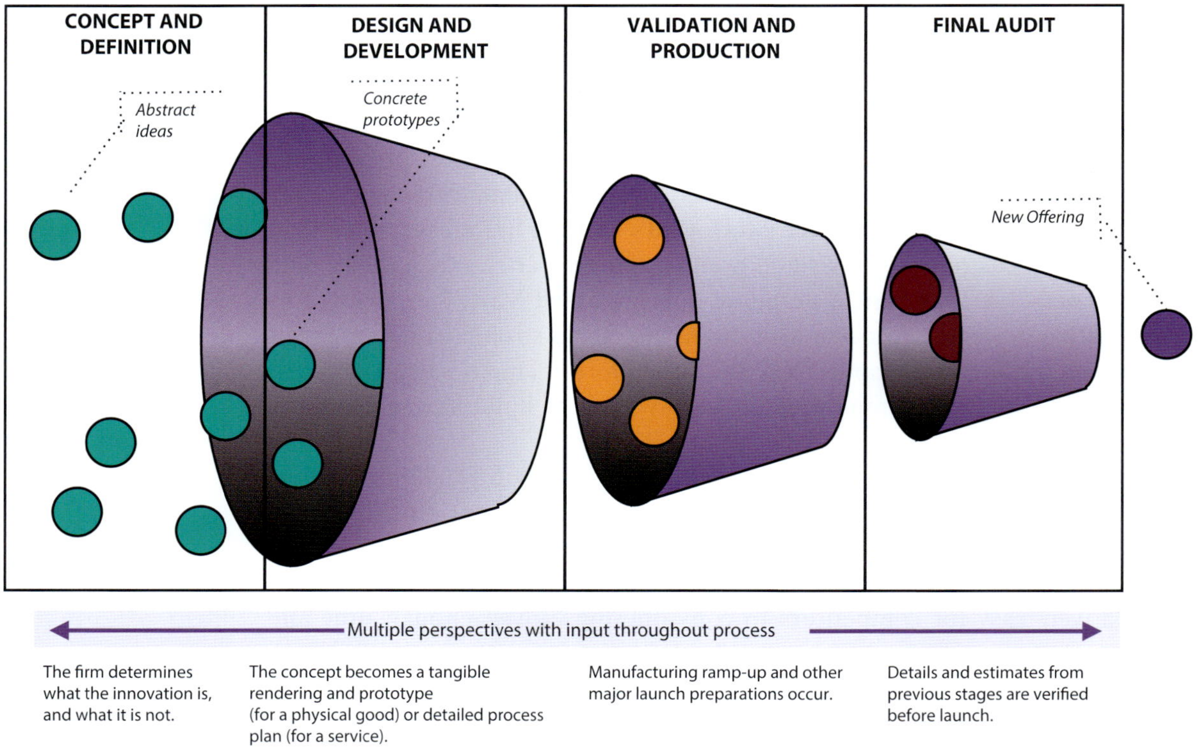

Figure 12.2 Stage-Gate Process.

The stage-gate process model lays out four approximate stages that ideas must pass before they can be launched as products. Innovation in real firms can be more complex and involve many more process steps. Yet the key feature of this process is not the breakdown of specific stages, but the fact that the project is evaluated on multiple dimensions from multiple perspectives, including those outside the core project team, at each stage.

In each of these four stages, a project gets evaluated from multiple perspectives on multiple dimensions. This method helps ensure effective development in three ways:

1. In each stage, the feasibility of the new project gets evaluated from multiple perspectives: customer, technology, financial, and operations, for example. If, say, a customer-responsible individual (e.g., a marketing research manager) is one of the evaluators from the early stages, acceptance and marketability can be given more attention before major funds are invested in development (for a negative example of this, see Marketing Fail in this chapter).
2. In each review stage, the evaluators who determine if the project will receive continued support must be external to the core project team. This requirement provides some degree of independence to the process. Members of a project team almost invariably become biased in favor of their own creation. Some studies even suggest that innovators or managers involved in a project provide ratings of the innovative features of the new offering that are up to nine times better than the ratings provided by general consumers.[17]

3. The stage-gate method gives firms plenty of opportunities to cancel projects at early stages. With timely cancellation, the resources (human, time, financial) that had been devoted to the new offering can be redeployed to other projects. Thus, poor projects cannot jam up the development pipeline, and good projects are less likely to be slowed down or starved of resources, simply because too many projects are in that pipeline (i.e., see Chapter 14; managing resource trade-offs, MP#4).

The stage-gate development process continues to see refinements, such as overlapping stages to shorten development time or increasing the customer input component at each stage to account better for customer dynamics during the development process (MP#2). Yet it also has one notable downside. Incremental, minor innovations often pass each stage-gate review more easily because they involve less risk and are easier to evaluate relative to past launches. Radical and potentially valuable innovations instead might struggle to pass through the stages, especially if their novelty is difficult to understand. Innovations related to the Metaverse draw skepticism, for example, because few people understand what exactly the Metaverse is.

In response, some firms establish alternative approaches for highly innovative projects (for one such approach, see Chapter Case). Many Indian firms employ a *jugaad* practice, in conjunction with traditional stage-gate processes. *Jugaad* is a Hindi word referring to an innovative fix or simple work-around, so these innovation practices seek creative, quick, unconventional, and frugal solutions to problems.[18] The basic intuition is that agile innovation practices can vary with each problem stage and product, rather than requiring the same stage-gate process for all innovative ideas. Without a set process, the main goals for this form of innovation are to reach unattainable outcomes and to push innovators beyond their existing mental boundaries. Thus, Tata Motors innovated the Nano, the cheapest car in the world, launched in 2009 at a sale price of just $2,000. Most car manufacturers use a sedan chassis to begin building new models; Tata challenged the conventional wisdom and started with a blueprint featuring a scooter's backbone. The ultimate product cost less to build and thus was affordable in the Indian market, but perhaps even more important, it turned out to be better suited to busy Indian traffic patterns, which require quick and frequent maneuvering.

WHAT MAKES INNOVATIONS SUCCESSFUL?

Passing the stage-gate process should greatly increase the likelihood of market success, but there are no guarantees. It is tempting to believe, for example, that **first movers**—the first player in a product category—will automatically gain the upper hand, but this tends to only hold in the short run. Returning to the earlier example of Enterprise being the first car rental agency to pursue suburban locations, competitors such as Hertz quickly caught on and, within a handful of years, Enterprise's advantage due to those locations had vanished. One historical study, spanning sixty-five years of first mover market entries, reveals a 47 percent outright failure rate among these pioneers; within a decade of their innovation,

first movers The first firm to market in a product category

MARKETING FAIL Adidas Unchained

Source: Sebastian Pociecha/Unsplash

Adidas' Unchained sneaker was meant to celebrate Black History Month in 2019. The all-white design was not well received.

German athletic apparel manufacturer Adidas generally manages its product lines effectively but even the world's second-largest sportswear company stumbles at the finish line occasionally. By way of background, it is important to know that Adidas views itself as more than just a seller of shoes and clothes. Per their corporate purpose statement: "Through sport, we have the power to change lives .... We will always strive to expand the limits of human possibilities, to include and unite people in sport, and to create a more sustainable world."[19] In other words, Adidas views inclusivity and social impact as inseparable from its broader success. It comes as no surprise, then, that Adidas went out of its way to celebrate Black History Month 2019 with a special edition version of its Ultra Boost sneaker. Adidas put considerable thought into innovating the design of the shoe, basing the textures, patterns, and colors on the historical jazz ballrooms of the Harlem Renaissance in turn-of-the-century New York City.

Germany

What did come as a surprise to many, though, was the result of this behind-the-scenes creative process. The special edition Ultra Boost, released for Black History Month, bore an all-white design and was positioned in a range named "Uncaged."[20] Consumer backlash was swift, and any attempt at rationalizing the legitimate historical inspiration for the shoes came too late. It seemed that somewhere along the line, Adidas' typically successful innovation process had veered off course, and it was forced to pull this sneaker from sale.

Diagnose the problem:

1. Speculate: what do you think it was about Adidas' innovation process that left this blind spot regarding the inevitable consumer reaction?
2. In light of question 1, what could Adidas have done differently to better achieve its goal of honoring Black History Month?

only 11 percent of them remained leaders in their categories.[21] According to a different study of 264 B2B products, first movers generally enjoy higher survival rates than later entrants—they don't go out of business—but they enjoy minimal market share advantage, especially when the product in question is radically new.[22]

The lesson? "Best Beats First."[23] Firms cannot rest on their laurels but instead must build additional SCA (e.g., brands, relationships) around new offerings if they hope to maintain a leadership position. Thus, moving first, whether in B2C or B2B markets, is not a guarantee of success. More generally, innovation failure rates are high. An estimated 40 percent of new offerings launched on the market fail to meet business objectives.[24] These failures might result from *poor designs*, such as when a new product fails to offer any relative advantage over existing solutions that is worth a price premium, or from *poor launches*, such that the new offering spreads too slowly throughout the potential customer base because it is inappropriately targeted, positioned, or not competitive.

Because the success of a new offering launch is determined by how fast and extensively it spread throughout a target population, we focus on the factors that drive new product's adoption. A long series of studies demonstrate that the following five factors are key to driving product/service adoption and a successful launch, as summarized in Table 12.1:[25]

1. Relative *advantage* over competitor's offerings.
2. *Compatibility* with customers' use cases and experiences.
3. *Complexity* of the offering.
4. Whether customers can easily *trial* the offering.
5. Whether the offering and its benefits are visible and *observable.*

Success Factor #1: Relative Advantage

If a customer perceives a higher relative advantage of a product, such that it appears better than an existing offering, it speeds up that product's diffusion. This relative advantage factor captures multiple dimensions, including technical performance, cost savings, and status, as discussed in Chapter 11 (points of parity/points of difference). Although this relative advantage is a necessary condition for product adoption, it is not a sufficient one. That is, if the other four factors fail to support product diffusion, even a significant relative advantage can lead to slow adoption rates. For example, a new keyboard layout for English language typists is significantly more efficient for professional typists than the traditional QWERTY keyboard, but it has attracted few users because of its lack of compatibility with what customers are used to.

Success Factor #2: Compatibility

Customers gauge new products according to how consistent they are with their existing values, uses, and experiences. Greater compatibility with existing product usages speeds product adoption. If a new offering instead requires consumers to break a habit or violate their traditional beliefs, adoption slows down considerably. Launching a new smartphone operating system is greatly hampered by this factor, as too many factors make consumers stuck in the Android or iOS ecosystem.

Success Factor #3: Complexity

A more complex product, which is more difficult to understand or use, generally suffers from slow adoption; education instead can speed up acceptance. Adoption of cryptocurrency and other blockchain technologies have suffered due to this factor, as few individuals understand their inner workings. In contrast, Google's very simple search screen helped expand its spread, in contrast with options that

Table 12.1 Innovation Success Factors.

Success is never guaranteed for new products and services. Yet generally, studies point to five factors that make an innovation more likely to catch on.

Step	Definition	Effect	Examples
1. Relative advantage	The new product or service provides meaningful benefits, compared to other options, in terms of technical performance, cost, status, or other value-relevant factors	Higher advantage enhances adoption	High advantage: Lenovo ThinkPad laptops are more durable than most options on the market, providing an advantage for many professionals working in rugged environments (e.g., construction management)
2. Compatibility	The new product or service is easy to fit into existing habits and/or aligns with customers' existing experience and knowledge	Higher compatibility enhances adoption	Low compatibility: subscription meal shipment services such as HelloFresh require advance planning of numerous meals at a time, which may not align with some customers' habits
3. Complexity	The benefits of the new product or service are difficult (or easy) to grasp and the product/service itself is difficult (or easy) to use	Higher complexity *hinders* adoption	High complexity: ChatGPT's inner workings are a black box, such that many experts are unsure why it produces a specific answer, which leads to confusion among users
4. Trialability	It is easy for customers to try out the product or service before committing to a purchase	Higher trialability enhances adoption	Most apparel retailers, such as Harrods, offer customers changing rooms to try on clothes before buying
5. Observability	The benefits of the product or service are plainly visible to others, including those who have not yet purchased	Higher observability enhances adoption	When Apple releases a sleek new iteration of the iPhone, onlookers can easily see the new design as early adopters use the new phone in public

demanded users enter multiple search criteria or other information. The nearly blank page and straightforward search options lowered the complexity of its use, even though the offering itself was highly sophisticated, which helped Google capture vast market share.

Success Factor #4: Trialability

More opportunities to try an offering speed up its adoption. Providing customers with free samples and demo versions or encouraging test drives are tactics that marketers use to enhance trialability. This factor is especially critical for costly offerings (e.g., cars), products that take time to learn (e.g., a streaming service's catalog), or offerings that are risky in some other way, to help consumers overcome these barriers to adoption.

Success Factor #5: Observability

Finally, when an offering's benefits are highly visible to others, it speeds up new product adoption because those others readily see the benefits, without the firm

Source: Arturs Budkevics/Pixabay

Even natural products such as tomatoes can be the focus of innovation, such as selective cross-breeding, genetic modification, additives, and improved storage and transportation. However, the complexity of the science involved, as well as the "genetically modified" label, sometimes frightens consumers.

needing to expend marketing resources to communicate about them. This factor is especially salient for status or prestige products, and especially fashion items such as Lacoste polo shirts. However, observability can have a negative effect if there is some social stigma involved with usage, which is why sellers promote some sensitive or embarrassing personal products by promising to ship them in unidentifiable packaging, with no distinguishing labels visible.

Marketers launching new offerings need to evaluate their innovations on these five factors, then develop plans for leveraging these factors to encourage adoption. For example, if a product is particularly complex, the firm likely needs to expend extra effort to increase its trialability and observability to help ensure its spread and enhance acceptance.

HOW INNOVATION GENERATES OFFERING EQUITY

Creating Offering Equity

Building offering equity involves three main steps:

1. Developing an offering with a significant advantage.
2. Segmenting, targeting, and positioning the offering to drive adoption.
3. Manage customer migrations into deeper relationships with the company.

THEORY SPOTLIGHT Adoption Life Cycle

Organization theorist Geoffrey Moore proposed that not only product and launch factors but also the characteristics of the population of potential customers (segment sizes, preferences, demographics, etc.) would influence adoption. He proposed the **adoption life cycle**, in which five groups of potential users adopt the product in sequence. *Innovators* are a small group of enthusiasts who will adopt the product with minimal persuasion. *Early adopters* also favor new technology, but wait for some positive signs (e.g., word of mouth from innovators) before trying the product. The *early majority* are pragmatic consumers, who are not opposed to newer technology but will evaluate it purely on its merits; the new technology must be confirmed to be just as reliable as that which preceded it. The last two groups, the *late majority* and the *laggards*, share a general distrust of new and disruptive ideas, and take the greatest amount of persuasion—in some cases, a near-consensus among other groups—before adopting.

Moore's framework has several important implications for innovation strategy. First, marketing efforts should be tailored to the five groups as the innovation moves along the adoption life cycle. Targeted product giveaways to social media influencers are likely to have a large impact on innovators and early adopters, spurring the initial phases of adoption. But once the innovation becomes mainstream, the ROI of such approaches is greatly diminished, and more traditional advertising strategies from Chapter 11 win out. Another key concept inherent in the framework is **crossing the chasm**, that is, moving from the early adopters to the early majority. This step of going mainstream is the most common failure point for new offerings; the novelty wins over innovators and early adopters but relevant advantages are insufficient (or inadequately communicated) for the majority of consumers to adopt the product on its own merits.[26]

adoption life cycle A theory in which five groups of potential users adopt the product in sequence

crossing the chasm Moving from the early adopters to the early majority in the adoption life cycle

Developing an Advantageous Offering

First, the firm must *develop an offering that provides customers with a significant relative advantage*. The lack of a meaningful relative advantage, from a customer's perspective, is perhaps the greatest cause of new product failure, whereas a significant advantage speeds diffusion and raises higher barriers to competition. Because so many firms use stage-gate development processes to speed their development and reduce costs, leading to incremental innovations, a competitive option can be to maintain a parallel strategy (e.g., *jugaad* innovation) to develop truly disruptive, radical innovations. Just like a balanced portfolio can help protect investors, firms might seek to mix their radical and incremental innovation efforts, instead of devoting all their energy to either big blockbuster innovations or continuous streams of minor product extensions. This recommendation reflects the importance of considering the entire offering portfolio that a firm develops; for example, pharmaceutical firms generally feature drugs in various stages of development (e.g., discover, testing, launch), some of which seek to address conventional health problems better, while others seek to cure cancer or find other ways to radically improve people's lives. Tracking the entire offering portfolio reveals a firm's existing advantages but also its potential for future revenue and success.[27]

Engage in STP to Drive Adoption

Second, in line with MP#1, offering equity requires a firm to *segment, target, and position* (STP; see Chapter 4) that new offering in a way that accounts for the favors that drive adoption. The segmentation and targeting strategies should focus on those segments with the greatest relative advantage and in which the new offering is most compatible with existing technologies. If they are introducing disruptive innovations, managers might want to focus proactively on the low-end of the market or new market segments, to avoid head-to-head competition with established offerings that perform better on certain factors. Marketing campaigns also should offer various ways for targeted users to experiment with the new offering, then make these early adopters highly visible to non-users (see Theory Spotlight in this chapter). Free samples, warranties, and trial periods are effective methods to reduce perceived risk; the free samples that pharmaceutical manufacturers provide to physicians have clear benefits in terms of finding the right patients for the latest drug options.[28] Similarly, positioning strategies should focus on the relative advantage, compatibility, and simplicity of the new offering. Because failed launches are expensive and damaging, many firms engage in test marketing to determine the most effective targeting, positioning, and marketing mix strategies for new consumer offerings.[29]

Craft AER Strategies to Manage Customer Migrations

Third, and associated with MP#2, firms need to *manage the customer migrations to deeper relationship stages with the firm, via acquisition, expansion, retention (AER) efforts* (see Chapter 7). To accelerate product acceptance across groups and ensure greater launch success, firms can devote most of their marketing resources to a few segments and persuade their gatekeepers, forming strong bonds with these individuals, who then provide the references and testimonials needed to persuade more pragmatic customers in subsequent stages. This method also helps ensure sufficient sales achieved through the initial target markets. Once the product has been accepted widely in these segments, the launch can be expanded to other segments, using testimonials and the lessons from the early successes.

IN OTHER WORDS ...

The three factors just noted emphasize the importance of innovators and early adopters in a product's success, even though they are a relatively small part of the market. Marketers should (1) have an advantage that these individuals will recognize, (2) build adoption likelihood (and the notion of adoption life cycle) into STP models, and (3) target and develop deep relationships with these earlier adopters. In turn, they will drive further adoption through positive buzz and word of mouth.

OPPOSING VIEWS Flights to Nowhere

Major disruptions can lead to opportunities for unconventional innovation. Starting in 2020, the COVID-19 pandemic produced unique challenges for airlines. With leisure and business travel both dramatically curtailed through most of 2020, airlines were largely reliant on loans and grants from governments to survive. Even consumers willing to risk spending an extended period on a crowded airplane had nowhere to go; tourist destinations and restaurants were often shuttered, while conventions and conferences were held remotely. In these conditions, some airlines chose to creatively find new ways to eke out revenue and give consumers something resembling an air travel experience.

One such airline was Singapore Airlines, which in September 2020 proposed offering "flights to nowhere," in which the aircraft would take off from Singapore's Changi Airport, fly in circles over a scenic route, and then return to the same airport.[30] The idea was to find some offering that could satisfy air travel aficionados during the pandemic and gain a relative advantage over competitors. The airline, however, faced an immediate and predictable backlash from environmental groups, since the flights would consume massive amounts of fuel to travel precisely nowhere, and also from those worried about COVID-19 spreading on crowded planes.[31] After scrapping that concept, Singapore Airlines instead launched on-the-ground airplane experiences, such as using a grounded jumbo passenger jet as a restaurant; naturally, this eased the former concern but not the latter.

Singapore

This experience during the pandemic informed airlines going forward about potential unconventional flight opportunities. For example, several airlines offered "eclipse" flights for the sole purpose of giving passengers an optimal view of the total solar eclipse in April 2024.[32]

See the issue from two sides:

1. Craft an argument in favor of Singapore Airlines conducting flights to nowhere during the pandemic. To which segment would this innovation appeal?
2. Craft an argument against pushing this innovation forward. Aside from the jet-as-restaurant alternative, can you think of any other ways that Singapore Airlines could have pursued a relative advantage during the pandemic?

Benefits of Offering Equity

By building offering equity, an innovative firm can make it more difficult for competitors to encroach on its business. As described in Chapter 10, *offering equity* refers to the core value that the performance of the product or service offers the customer, absent any brand or relationship equity effects. When a firm produces a product or service that is no different from competitors' offerings (i.e., copycat offerings), it generates little offering equity or SCA. Most firms attempt to develop innovative offerings, differentiated from competitors' products, to generate at least some relative advantage. As we know, competitors will quickly copy successful offerings, so each firm must constantly try to develop new and innovative offerings to stay ahead of its competitors. For example, Disney started out promoting Disney+ as a standalone film and television streaming service. But to outcompete Netflix and Max, and gain parity with Hulu, it increasingly focuses on advertising the Disney Bundle, including ESPN+ and access to live sports. In any cases, as in complex microprocessors, the manufacturing process may be so specialized, lengthy, and costly that copycat strategies are not viable, boosting the relative advantage from offering innovations.

At the firm level, offering equity translates to the market value of the firm's various offerings. Research conducted with thousands of firms shows that simply announcing a new product can increase a firm's stock price by 0.5 percent on that same day.[33] Thus, investors really believe in offering equity. But why?

In many cases, a new offering provides more value to customers, in the form of enhanced performance. New offerings often motivate customers to switch from competitors to gain access to the new product. Such switching behavior might signal that the customer really believes the new offering performs better than existing alternatives, or it might arise because the customer just wants to have the newest offering (these are the innovators or early adopters from the life cycle framework; see Theory Spotlight in this chapter). In any market, there are some early adopters who always want the newest offering, whether or not the new features or attributes add any material value for them (e.g., newest cell phone, dinner at the latest restaurant).[34]

New offerings also can help the firm acquire new customers or enter new markets when they offer similar performance but at a lower price. Customers often rebuy the same brand, out of habit or because it is convenient, with little thought. But if a firm offers a new innovation that can lower the prices they pay, it often provides a clear path to customer acquisition and sales expansion.

Source: Andreas Lischka/Pixabay

Developing, prototyping, and manufacturing modern computer processors requires incredibly complex and sensitive equipment as well as skilled personnel. This upfront investment in offerings makes things difficult for any would-be challengers to Intel, AMD, or Arm.

Whether the innovation is radically new or represents incrementally new offering, its arrival in the market sparks benefits for other departments in the firm too. For example, salespeople have a good reason to make sales calls to both new and existing customers, with a new sales pitch about an exciting new opportunity rather than just repeating the same sales line about older products that customers already know about. Similarly, advertising effectiveness increases when the firm has new products to offer.[35] The effect can carry over to human resources departments too, such that firms with innovative offerings are better able to recruit and keep the best talent, which in turn can create barriers to competitive attacks.[36] Thus, customer, employee, and market expansion all emerge as key potential benefits of offering innovative products.

Furthermore, offering new and innovative products tends to enhance the firm's brand, even if customers don't buy the new offering. Google, Apple, Mercedes-Benz, and OpenAI base their strong reputations largely on their innovativeness and strong offering performance. Such benefits influence customers' purchase decisions, even if they only buy an entry-level product that includes few of the truly innovative features that made the firm's reputation. These brands often seek to introduce new offerings with some minimal frequency to maintain a leading image.

Yet we must constantly remember that SCA based solely on new products tends to be short lived. Before competitors can react (as they always do; MP#3) and copy or even leapfrog an innovation, the firm should build other, more lasting SCA. Always having the newest and best offering is virtually impossible, so firms try to add brand-based or relational SCA to their offering, to enhance its equity, before direct competitors emerge. Tesla, for example, offered one of the first mass-market, commercially viable electric cars in North America. But it also offers drivers a highly personalized experience thanks to the advanced smart technology inside its vehicles, building sticky customer relationships. In addition, the brand's figurehead, Elon Musk, goes out of his way to keep his face in the international spotlight, directly or indirectly promoting Tesla's brand identity. The combination of these factors has created a strong SCA that has admirably kept extremely powerful electric car competitors, such as General Motors and Nissan, at bay.

Overall, greater offering equity, generated from the firm's new and innovative products and services, provides more value to customers, which leads to SCA and superior sales and profits. Innovative new offerings help firms expand their customer bases and increase the effectiveness of their advertising, direct selling, and employee recruitment and retention efforts. Even though the barriers to competitive copycat options typically are short in their duration (with the exception of patent-protected products), they still provide a powerful platform for firms to build synergistic, longer-lasting SCA using brands and relationships (see Chapters 11 and 13).

CHAPTER CASE STUDY

BARCLAYS RISE INITIATIVE

UK

Barclays Bank PLC is a British banking conglomerate with origins dating back centuries. One might expect such a venerable institution to have a staid, conservative approach to strategy and innovation, but recent years have proven otherwise. The new CEO of Barclays, C.S. Venkatakrishnan, immediately brought superficial change to the organization by being its first leader of Indian origin. But he also brought deeper shifts, in part by investing more deeply in the firm's existing Rise innovation initiative.[37]

Barclays Rise initiative. Rise was created by Barclays in 2015 as an incubator for **fintech** (financial technology) firms. It has offices in London and New York, over 100 start-ups, numerous mentors from Barclays and other industry leaders, and raised over $1 billion.[38] The stated goal of the incubator has been to focus on expanding access to newer finance technologies. For example, making digital payments and financing offers built-in features on delivery apps and social media would be in line with this goal.

fintech Financial technology industry, a present focus of innovation in the finance world

Painless, smooth user experiences have been an emphasis throughout projects in the initiative. One start-up involved with Rise, TapTrip, provides user-friendly integrated payment, booking, and expense reporting services for corporations looking to schedule travel for their employees. Another participant, Equipment Connect, is designed to provide small businesses easier access to finance, lease, and dispose of heavy equipment.[39] Venkatakrishnan sought to further accelerate this incubator program by forging a partnership with Rainmaking, which designs and implements start-up training programs and seminars for new media start-ups.[40]

Future challenges. Barclays is clearly coordinating resources toward innovation projects that stand to add value across various settings, but curiously, the direct advantage for Barclays is less clear. By embedding payment and banking systems into more aspects of everyday life for businesses and consumers, Barclays naturally could gain some benefit, but this benefit would also accrue to all of Barclays competitors in the banking industry. In many cases, fintech start-ups *undermine* the role of traditional banks in the finance system, for example, by facilitating peer-to-peer transactions. Moreover, while Barclays has secured external funds to cover most of the expenses for the New York and London offices, the firm itself has devoted a lot of resources to the initiative over the years, in terms of funding public relations campaigns, communications about Rise across various media, and the time of the CEO, CIO, and other executives to engage with and direct the initiative at a strategic level.

It remains to be seen whether the types of innovation being indirectly generated from these investments best serves Barclays interests.

CASE QUESTIONS

1. In terms of the different types of innovation we discussed in this chapter, how would you characterize Rise? Explain your answer.
2. In what way(s) could Barclays gain an offering-based sustainable competitive advantage through the Rise program?
3. Explain, with a fictional example, how the stage-gate process could hypothetically be used to manage start-ups within the Rise initiative.

CHAPTER SUMMARY

This chapter highlights how strong offerings—that is, innovative products or services—are frequently a sustainable source of competitive advantage. Using offerings as an SCA can be effective because new and innovative products and services have the potential to disrupt virtually any market segment. Firms allocate vast budgets to research and development so that they can introduce the newest or most innovative product, reduce costs, add supplementary services, or fundamentally alter the customer experience. Firms further invest large sums in their marketing mix to support and manage their existing product and service portfolios. If the resulting offerings meet customers' needs better than competing offerings, and customers care about the offerings' advantageous features, a strong SCA emerges. In some cases, though, the firm first must invest time and money to explain the offering and perhaps even convince customers that they "need" it. This is particularly challenging when attempting to craft offerings that meet emerging and evolving needs. New and innovative is not necessarily better though, at least in customers' minds, creating unique challenges in delivering offering-based SCA. These challenges can be addressed with a better understanding of concepts such as innovation processes and portfolio-based management of products and services.

APPLICATION QUESTIONS

1. Recall a time that you remember a company changing the breadth or depth of the product-service mix. What exactly did they do, and in your opinion, what was the reason for this change?
2. Think about an especially satisfying experience you had with a product or service recently. Identify which parts of that experience corresponded to a core product, a service, or an augmented product.
3. Think of your favorite retailer or restaurant. In which of the four types of innovation from this chapter do you think that business excels? Explain your reasoning.
4. Consider actually implementing the stage-gate process as part of the production team for a new film in your favorite entertainment franchise. How would you move from the concept to the design phase—that is, how would you filter out bad ideas?
5. Recall a time when a new product launched that, in your view, had no relative advantage. What should have been done differently in the design or function of the product?
6. Consider a recent time when you tried a new brand or a new product or service for the first time. Of the five innovation success factors discussed in this chapter, which one was the most important to your decision, and why?
7. Viral posts and videos on social media undergo a similar adoption life cycle to products. Think of one of your favorite examples of such media. What about the content do you think helped it "cross the chasm," namely, go viral and gain mainstream appeal?

Visit the companion website, **https://bloomsbury.pub/palmatier-marketing**, or **https://samsinstitute.com**, for additional learning and teaching tools, including professional videos outlining the Four Principles, PowerPoint tutorials with voice-over commentary, sample syllabi for marketing courses, testbank and more.

Chapter 13

RELATIONSHIP-BASED ADVANTAGES, CRM, AND CHANNEL MANAGEMENT

CHAPTER OVERVIEW

Chapters 11 and 12 detailed sources of competitive advantage that are built within the company and conveyed to customers: iconic brands and innovative offerings. Chapter 13, on the other hand, focuses on a source of advantage that must be co-developed with, and continuously adapted to, the customer, that is, relationship-based sustainable competitive advantage. You will learn why these advantages are unique and important, how modern technology accelerates relationship-based advantages, and how these advantages unfold in the context of marketing channel relationships. The chapter will address the following questions:

- What can firms do to build a relationship-based advantage?
- How does customer relationship management technology contribute to relationship-based advantage?
- What are the implications of marketing channel relationships for building relationship equity?

In the chapter's cases and features, you will witness companies' efforts—some admirable, some less so—to build competitive advantage through relationship marketing tools. Examples include:

- An ill-fated overhaul to NCBA bank's mobile app (Marketing Fail).
- Tesco's legendary loyalty program (Chapter Case).
- Ethical and moral dilemmas in product and service strategy, such as the perils of powerful partners such as Inditex (Shades of Gray) and Nike's cutthroat approach to independent retailers (Opposing Views).

LEARNING OBJECTIVES

- Recognize the factors driving the importance of relationship management.
- Associate CRM technology with the steps in the relationship marketing value chain.
- Identify key terms and concepts in marketing channel management.
- Recognize strategies to adapt relationship marketing to the channel environment.

IMAGINE Deciding Where to Get a Haircut

Imagine you have gotten your hair cut at the same location, by the same stylist (or barber), for the last ten years. Let's call them Alex. Obviously, you must like your haircut to have stuck with them for so long! But more than that, you enjoy talking to Alex during your haircut each time that you visit. You speak with each other about careers, relationships, current events, and so on—you even know their kids' names. You occasionally have friends recommend that you try out another salon (or barber), but you've never given that much thought.

One day, without warning, Alex tells you that their college friend is opening a new shop, and they intend to quit and cut hair for their friend's shop across town. You aren't sure what to do. You would have to travel a bit farther to go there, and you don't know if the salon (or barber) itself is as nice as the one you are used to. You could try out some of your other local options, but then you wouldn't get to talk to Alex during your haircut. Sure, this isn't a life-or-death decision, but it's frustrating that you have to choose!

Critical thinking:

1. What would you do? Explain what factors led to your decision, and how you weighed them.
2. Thinking about your own experiences buying products and services, when have you cared about personal relationships with frontline workers such as Alex? When has this been irrelevant? Why do you think you care about this in some settings and not others?

HOW STRONG RELATIONSHIPS BUILD SUSTAINABLE COMPETITIVE ADVANTAGE

relationship equity
The value of the firm's customer base, in terms of expected future cash flows from customers

Marketing Principle #3 focuses on building and maintaining barriers, or sustainable competitive advantages (SCA), to competitive attacks, based on the premise that competitors always react to a firm's success. As noted in Chapter 10, **relationship equity** is the value of the firm's customer base, in terms of expected future cash flows from customers. But this value is only secure if customers do not constantly shift their loyalty to competing firms. For example, streamers such as Max (formerly HBO Max) may find it difficult to estimate relationship equity when customers hop from one streaming service to another, canceling less-favored services when a trendy show hits another platform. So, how does the firm build barriers against competitors copying—or more accurately, stealing—valuable customer relationships? In other words, how does the firm build a relationship-based advantage?

What Is a Relationship-based Advantage and Why Is It Important?

Efforts to build relationship equity often come after generating brand and value equities, because relational interactions are part of the product and service delivery, which occurs after the product is launched and brands have been promoted to customers. For example, a car buyer only starts speaking to salespeople after she is already familiar with major car brands and the available cars have already entered the market.

Yet relationships powerfully affect behavior. Throughout recorded history, interpersonal relationships have been critical to trade and business.[1] Moreover, nearly one-third of human brain activity focuses on interpersonal relationships, because they support cooperation and evolutionary advances.[2] Firms pursue relationship-based SCA by leveraging this aspect of human nature, enacting tactics to build trust, loyalty, interpersonal rapport, and other intangible relational "glue" that keeps competitors at bay.

Although often associated with business-to-business transactions—where personal relationships with salespeople can be vital—relationship-based strategies are equally common in business-to-consumer settings. For example, US bakery chain Panera's customer rewards program offers a customized selection of rewards, based on the customer's preferences and purchase history. This feature creates a sense that Panera knows the customer and makes the rewards feel more personal, inspiring gratitude.[3] In a sense, Panera—a multibillion dollar corporation—is trying to mimic some of the benefits of a service that is tied to a personal relationship (e.g., a consumer's relationship with a hairdresser, as in the chapter's "Imagine" feature). The psychological processes and emotions associated with relational interactions (e.g., gift–gratitude, anger–punishment, guilt–reciprocation) help explain customers' responses to marketers' actions and thus the effectiveness of relationship-building efforts.[4]

Such effects have prompted researchers and managers to focus on relationship-based advantages. Research on mergers and acquisitions suggests that customer relationships often make up a larger percentage of firm value than brands do.[5] The value of relationships is especially prominent in light of the ongoing transition toward service-based economies.[6] Services now represent over 75 percent of the US economy.[7] Compared with products, they are more intangible, less consistent,

Source: istock.com/santypan

Relationships tend to be more valuable for some offerings than others. This is especially the case for services that require hands-on attention from another person. For example, many restaurant and bar patrons value a close relationship with a bartender.

more perishable, and harder to evaluate, so customers and frontline workers participate more closely in the production and consumption of services. The close resulting interactions and intangibility of the service also make relationships and trust more critical.[8]

How Does Relationship Marketing Contribute to Relationship-based SCA?

relationship marketing (RM) Efforts aimed at identifying, growing, and maintaining customer relationships to ultimately produce relationship equity

To achieve relationship-based advantage, firms invest in **relationship marketing (RM)**. These are efforts aimed at identifying, growing, and maintaining customer relationships to ultimately produce relationship equity. Relationship marketing is common in both B2B and B2C companies. For example, since 2007, Apple has relied on Corning, a specialty materials manufacturer, to make all iPhone touchscreens. To gain and sustain relationship equity, Corning must innovate and remain Apple's top supplier as new manufacturers release advanced touchscreens. Apple also informs Corning about the desired touchscreen properties for its R&D effort (e.g., size, toughness, texture).[9] In another example, Chinese e-commerce retailer Temu devotes resources to allowing extensive personalization and customization options for items sold on its site. In doing so, it creates a sense of a higher-touch, more engaged experience than similar low-cost e-commerce sites, enhancing customer loyalty.[10]

Relationship marketing investments generally fall into three categories:[11]

social RM A type of relationship marketing that uses social interactions to convey the customer's favored status

1. **Social RM** uses social interactions to convey the customer's favored status. Training coffee shop baristas to learn customers' names and ask about their days is a typical social RM strategy. Deep, personal bonds with customers are also critical for business-to-business salespeople. As a longtime IBM consultant explains, "Trust increases with investment and interaction. If there is a business opportunity, your partner will remember you and that trust which you have invested in will result in more business."[12] Personal rapport creates hard-to-replicate bonds that lead to repeat sales, recommendations, or ignoring competitive offers. Compared to other RM investments, social RM investments are massively profitable, generating up to 180 percent return on investment.[13] But social programs may also lead buyers to form ties with the salesperson rather than the selling firm, so they may defect if the salesperson goes.[14]

structural RM A type of relationship marketing that involves creating systems for customers, such as specialized packaging or inventory tracking systems, that customers might not make on their own

2. **Structural RM** involves creating systems for customers, such as specialized packaging or inventory tracking systems, that customers might not make on their own. These systems improve customer efficiency and even profitability, creating an advantage that is difficult to go without. These programs bind buyers and sellers, then, by creating switching costs. For this reason, structural RM investments have a powerful profit impact, with up to 120 percent return on investment.[15] Many firms set up mutually beneficial structural RM by partnering to serve shared customers. For example, Delta Airlines and Marriott International's

loyalty program partnership allows customers to exchange Delta SkyMiles for Marriott Bonvoy points.[16]

3. **Financial RM** takes the form of direct economic benefits. These may be rebates, discounts, sweepstakes and contests, free shipping promotions, or other efforts to woo customers with monetary gains. The weakness of financial RM is that, unlike a structural partnership or social bonds, competitors can easily duplicate these efforts. Moreover, the types of customers most attracted to short-term financial incentives also tend to be disloyal in the long run, as they flock to competing sellers' offers in the future.[17] It should be noted that not all injections of cash in a partner are simple financial RM. For example, Pfizer and BioNTech signed a deal in 2022 that provided hundreds of millions of dollars to BioNTech for research and development of new mRNA vaccines. But this investment came with much more lasting ties, including Pfizer buying a large stake in its partner, making this alliance an example of structural RM instead.[18]

financial RM A type of relationship marketing that takes the form of direct economic benefits, such as rebates, discounts, and free shipping promotions

A CUSTOMER RELATIONSHIP MANAGEMENT (CRM) PROCESS FOR BUILDING RELATIONSHIP EQUITY

These and other RM efforts lead to stronger customer relationships, but how do these relationships form barriers against competition? In other words, how exactly does relationship-based SCA and relationship equity form?

In this section, we outline a three-step process for building relationship equity. We explain this process against the backdrop of **customer relationship management (CRM)**. Despite the similar name, CRM and RM are distinct concepts. CRM is the fusion of RM with information technology tools to use customer data to improve relationship outcomes.[19] Firms spend billions of dollars on CRM each year in the hope of strengthening customer relationships.[20] For example, the UK division of Banco Santander partnered with Salesforce—the world's largest CRM technology provider—to build a subscription-based platform for small business clients. This platform allowed Santander to not only more easily monitor its relationships with these clients, but also offer customized recommendations and strategies for clients to grow their businesses (and, indirectly, grow their relationships with Santander).[21]

customer relationship management (CRM) The fusion of RM with information technology tools to use customer data to improve relationship outcomes

It is not just multinational giants investing in CRM, either; *among companies with at least ten employees, 91 percent use some form of CRM system.*[22] Therefore, an up-to-date understanding of how relationship management strategies lead to relationship equity requires grasping how CRM fits into this process. The three steps for building relationship equity, or **relationship marketing value chain**, are as follows (see also Figure 13.1):

relationship marketing value chain The three steps by which RM efforts lead to enhanced relationship equity

1. Designing and targeting relationship marketing strategies.
2. Measuring relationship improvement.
3. Observing outcomes of relationship improvement.

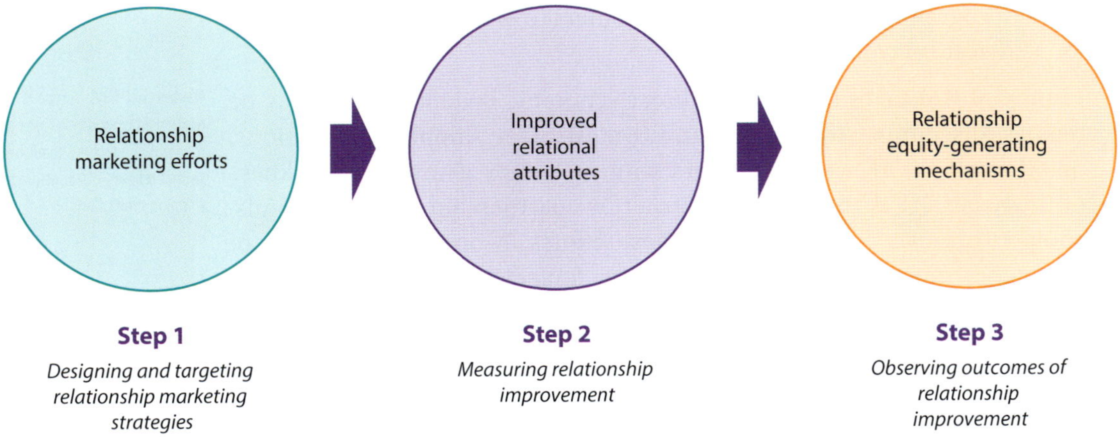

Figure 13.1 Relationship Marketing Value Chain.

The three steps of the relationship marketing value chain: (1) designing and targeting relationship marketing strategies; (2) measuring relationship improvement; and (3) observing outcomes of relationship improvement. Understanding the process allows marketers to monitor the steps with CRM systems and correct any problems.

These three steps cover the most common route to gaining equity from customer relationships. Exceptions exist, though, for example when extreme power imbalances exist (for an example of this, see Shades of Gray in this chapter).

SHADES OF GRAY Power Corrupts Inditex's Relationships

Spanish conglomerate Inditex is the largest purveyor of fast fashion brands in the world and the parent company of such brands as Pull and Bear, Zara, and Stradivarius.[23] For the network of suppliers—based in countries such as Brazil and Bangladesh—that manufacture clothes for Inditex's brands, the relationship is irreplaceable. If Inditex decided to stop working with one of its manufacturers, that company would struggle to find an alternative partner with enough demand for manufacturing capacity. This dynamic creates a massive power imbalance in Inditex's favor.[24] As a result, there is little need for Inditex to invest in improving relationships along the traditional vectors outlined in this chapter.

Instead, this power imbalance allows a buyer such as Inditex to simply extract relationship benefits, for instance, lower prices, from suppliers.[25] This ability has led to tragic consequences. The pressure to cheaply and quickly supply Inditex has occasionally led suppliers to subcontract work to less-than-reputable workshops, including sweatshops with documented human rights abuses. This pattern has played out in both Myanmar and Brazil.[26] Inditex espouses a commitment to human rights and denies prior knowledge of, and responsibility for, these abuses. Yet human rights campaigners note that "Inditex's demand for low prices and tight delivery deadlines inevitably led to an 'obscure supply chain' in which human rights abuses could occur."[27]

Spain

Ethical dilemmas:

1. Ultimately, workers in Inditex's supply chain are abused. Who is responsible for this harm, and why?
2. What can be done to minimize labor abuses in fashion supply chains? What, if anything, needs to change in the fast fashion industry to reduce this problem?

RM Value Chain Step #1: Designing and Targeting Relationship Management Strategies

Above, you read about three different types of RM strategies: social, structural, and financial. Although we can make some generalizations about these strategies—financial RM tends to have shorter-lived effects, as noted earlier—there is no one-size-fits-all approach to deploying relationship marketing efforts across customers.

The reasons should be obvious to astute readers: Marketing Principle #1 (all customers differ) and Marketing Principle #2 (all customers change)! Based on Chapters 4 and 7, marketers must use segmentation, targeting, and positioning (STP) frameworks to understand how the needs of customer segments vary, and acquisition–expansion–retention (AER) frameworks to see how these needs evolve over the course of a relationship. For example, while some customers want to be "wooed" with constant attention and contact, others might feel "stalked" by the same attention. US newspaper the *Dallas Morning News* learned this lesson the hard way when its telemarketing initiative—intended to win customers with personal contact—instead annoyed and pushed customers away.[28] And thinking back to the chapter's opening "Imagine" activity, the same customer might desire close personal contact for some products and services, but not others.

The upshot is that customers' *appetites for social, structural, and financial RM* should be key dimensions that are analyzed in the firm's STP and AER efforts, and used in targeting RM efforts. This is where CRM technology comes in. For example, Arizona State University uses CRM to keep detailed student records from the moment they are admitted, including application data, and tracks student activities as their academic careers proceed. These data are used to customize RM strategies. Data on students' backgrounds and past financial needs can influence scholarship opportunities (financial RM); data on students' classes and majors are used to automatically assign students to relevant Slack chat communities (social RM); and data on common sources of confusion and headaches for first-year students inform the design of convenient self-service processes (structural RM).[29] Typical data collected by retailers' loyalty programs, such as Tesco's Clubcard (see the Chapter Case) can be used in a similar way to target RM efforts.

RM Value Chain Step #2: Measuring Relationship Improvement

Although carefully designed and targeted relationship marketing should improve relationships, what does an "improved relationship" mean, exactly? And how do marketers know if they've succeeded? Once again, CRM is key. There are three main indicators of relationship improvement, and each can be inferred from CRM data: (1) relationship depth, (2) relationship breadth, and (3) relationship composition.[30]

Relationship Depth

Relationship depth refers to the quality and closeness of bonds between the buyer and seller. Depth has four drivers: commitment, trust, gratitude, and reciprocity.[31]

relationship depth
The quality and closeness of bonds between the buyer and seller

commitment A desire to continue an exchange relationship

trust Confidence in the other party's words and integrity in an exchange relationship

- The first two drivers, **commitment** (desire to continue the relationship) and **trust** (confidence in the other party's words and integrity), are detailed in this chapter's Theory Spotlight. Commitment and trust can be monitored and measured by carefully tracking the seller's conversations with the buyer. This requires that salespeople take careful notes and log them in the CRM system. If these notes indicate the customer is warming to the seller and showing less overt signals of suspicion (e.g., asking fewer questions about product quality), this may indicate improving commitment and trust.

gratitude A sense of thankfulness for the other party's extraordinary efforts in an exchange relationship

reciprocity A perceived need to repay extraordinary efforts in an exchange relationship

- The other two factors, **gratitude** (sense of thankfulness for the other party's extraordinary efforts) and **reciprocity** (perceived need to repay extraordinary efforts) go hand in hand. For example, a retailer that waives their usual return policy and allows a customer to refund a jacket after sixty days might make the customer feel grateful. In return, the customer may be more likely to shop at that retailer in the future. In other words, gratitude prompts reciprocity. Moreover, failing to reciprocate can even lead to feelings of guilt. Psychologists argue that gratitude and reciprocity are hardwired tendencies in humans, making them powerful sources of relationship depth.[32] Gratitude and reciprocity can be captured in CRM systems by identifying back-and-forth patterns in the data; do past efforts to go above and beyond (e.g., offering free expedited shipping or proactively addressing a problem with an order) seem to be followed by increased purchasing? If so, gratitude and reciprocity are evident.

In summary, commitment, trust, gratitude, and reciprocity are the drivers of relationship depth. Each of these can be tracked in modern CRM systems to evaluate whether customer relationships are improving.

THEORY SPOTLIGHT Commitment-Trust Theory

A wealth of knowledge is available to comprehend the effects of relationship marketing thanks to extensive research into the effects of relationships on human behavior. For instance, social exchange theory has demonstrated that commitment and trust are essential components of strong business relationships. As noted in this chapter, commitment is defined as an ongoing desire to uphold a valued relationship, and trust is defined as confidence in a relationship partner's dependability and integrity.

According to the commitment-trust theory of relationship marketing—one of the most well-known theories in all of marketing research—*trust is a prerequisite for commitment*. For a customer to want to continue doing business with a seller, they need to trust that the seller's word will be upheld.[33] Therefore, marketers should first look for ways to build trust with buyers—for example, by taking extra care to fulfill any promises they make, especially earlier in the relationship—to develop a committed relationship. In turn, committed partners put out extra effort and endeavor to uphold and strengthen relational ties, which improves collaboration, financial performance, and other favorable consequences.

Relationship Breadth

Relationship breadth, the number of distinct interpersonal ties between a buyer and seller, is beneficial in multiple ways. When many people in the selling firm (salespeople, product experts, executives, etc.) interact with many people in a buying firm (executives, purchasing personnel, etc.), the interconnected network between the two companies forms a strong relational "glue" that makes ending the relationship more difficult.[34] In addition, these multiple ties protect against the loss of any individual interpersonal connection (e.g., when a salesperson quits).[35] Relationship breadth is easily tracked and measured in CRM systems. Seller personnel, such as salespeople, record every individual contact person that they meet in the buyer-firm. A growing number of unique interpersonal connections with the customer indicates improving relationship breadth (and an improving relationship overall).

relationship breadth The number of distinct interpersonal ties between a buyer and seller

Relationship Composition

While relationship breadth refers to the quantity of unique contacts with the customer, **relationship composition** is the diversity and usefulness of the contacts. A diversified contact portfolio helps a seller confirm information from multiple angles and reach key decision-makers. Consider a potential new sale that involves the customer's engineering, production, quality, and purchasing departments. A good relationship with a quality control manager doesn't affect purchasing's cost-based calculations. That is, even high-quality connections with various contacts (breadth) are ineffective without key decision-makers in relevant roles. As with relationship breadth, relationship composition is easily measured in modern CRM systems by recording contacts and their roles within buying organizations. Achieving impactful connections with diverse decision-makers marks a significant improvement in the relationship.

relationship composition The diversity and usefulness of the contacts between a buyer and seller

Thus, firms enacting RM efforts should use CRM systems to track the effectiveness of these efforts in driving relationship depth, breadth, and composition. Seemingly well-targeted strategies that do not yield relational improvements should be revisited and revamped.

RM Value Chain Step #3: Observing Outcomes of Relationship Improvement

The chain of effect from relationship marketing to relationship equity concludes with four equity-generating mechanisms:

1. cooperation
2. loyalty
3. empathy
4. positive word of mouth

Each of these mechanisms has the power to directly influence financial outcomes, thus contributing to relationship equity and firm value. Further, each can be monitored with prudent use of CRM systems.

MARKETING FAIL NCBA Bank Fails to Keep Customers in the Loop

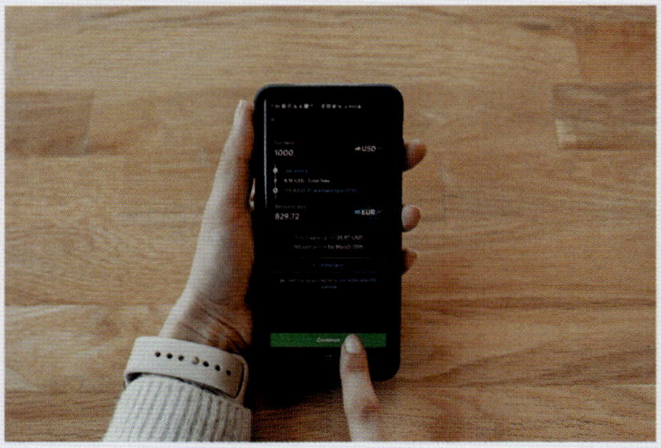

Source: Tech Daily/Unsplash

Loop started out as a simple and convenient online banking and money transfer app for young, unbanked Kenyans. Its overhaul into an "everything" app did not receive the universal praise that NCBA hoped for.

Kenya

Mobile phone-based banking services are a critical piece of financial infrastructure for individuals in many African countries, including Kenya. In 2006, only 14 percent of Kenyans had bank accounts. By 2019, this figure had risen to 83 percent, largely due to easily accessible, phone-based banking apps.[36] NCBA bank is a mid-sized banking services provider headquartered in Nairobi, Kenya. The firm joined the digital banking trend in 2017 by launching the NCBA Loop banking app in 2017. The main appeals of the app—especially for young, digital-native consumers—were being able to open a bank account in minutes with no paperwork, and easily depositing and sending funds to merchants and friends.[37]

But in January of 2023, NCBA launched a radically redesigned version of the app simply called Loop. Loop was now an "everything" app, including not only online banking features but also shopping and food delivery, rewards program features, and numerous other new sections of the app.[38] Ostensibly, this was an effort to expand customer relationships by touching more aspects of their financial lives. But the redesign sparked a swift backlash. Customers who valued the simplicity of the old app—it did a small number of jobs but did them well—resented the new app's attempts to intrude into other areas of their lives, such as shopping. Worse, the new app completely replaced the old one, removing customers' choice to have a more limited relationship with Loop.[39]

The backlash created an opportunity for competitors to fill the niche that NCBA Loop previously filled. For example, Ecobank Kenya launched its new Fingo Africa digital banking app later the same year.[40] It is unclear how many NCBA customers have abandoned the bank for competitors such as Ecobank Kenya as such figures have not been publicly reported. Yet the entry of competitors into this space is a sure sign that these customers were vulnerable to "poaching" by a more appealing alternative.

Diagnose the problem:

1. Would you classify the Loop app update as an attempt at social, structural, or financial relationship marketing? Why?
2. How could NCBA have adjusted its Loop strategy to keep the potential to grow customer relationships, without alienating longtime customers who did not want deeper relationships?

Cooperation

cooperation Coordinated, complementary actions between exchange partners to achieve a goal

Cooperation—coordinated, complementary actions between partners to achieve a goal—is the first mechanism. Cooperation increases customers' flexibility and adaptability to sellers' requests for changes, information, or reciprocation. Cooperation can be observed through diligent logging and tracking in CRM systems; for example, call logs indicating the customer's willingness to work together to achieve joint goals. In a committed and trusting partnership, cooperation can occur even if one party temporarily comes out ahead—for example, when a supplier takes a small loss on a sale to keep a longtime customer in business.[41] However, in relationships without trust or commitment, parties cooperate only when their benefits are equal and simultaneous. Starbucks customers can share their ideas for new products, better service, or the elimination of existing ideas on My Starbucks Idea, a crowdsourcing platform. The forum draws thousands of dedicated visitors daily, even though consumers know Starbucks is unlikely to implement their ideas. In this case, the consumer controls the extent of the relationship; each person can contribute as much as they want without having to commit fully. Cooperation enhances relationship equity, and firm value, through the value of such collaborative efforts with customers.

Loyalty

Second, **loyalty** is the likelihood that the customer repeatedly benefits the seller in the exchange due to their relational ties. Loyalty is easily observed with CRM data by capturing customers' repeat purchases, including frequency and amounts, over time. Loyal customers may buy again and again without looking for alternatives—although a major disruption to the product or service can change that (see Marketing Fail in this chapter).

loyalty The likelihood that the customer repeatedly benefits the seller in the exchange due to their relational ties

Relationships increase loyalty because customers feel safer dealing with trusted partners and save time and money in decision-making by buying from familiar sellers.[42] In competitive markets, loyalty is crucial to firm success. Chinese e-commerce is fiercely competitive and growing, with trillions of US dollars' worth of annual consumer spending and hundreds of notable players, but 80 percent of consumers are loyal to just four firms: Taobao, Tmall, JD, and Pinduoduo.[43] Smaller players and new entrants struggle to overcome loyalty to these major players, creating relationship equity for the e-commerce giants.

Empathy

Empathy, or a greater likelihood to be influenced by seller perceptions, is the third mechanism. Customers in a strong relationship may attribute service failures (e.g., defective product) to external causes the seller cannot control. Due to their empathy for the seller's difficult situation (e.g., offshore competition, reduced sales and profits), they may not withdraw from the relationship or demand price reductions in response to service failures or other missteps by the seller. Empathy contributes to relationship equity by stabilizing and safeguarding financial outcomes against relational missteps. Detecting the presence of empathy with CRM technology requires processes for monitoring service failures and identifying specific customers' patterns of responding—which may be more difficult than observing the other equity-generating mechanisms.

empathy A greater likelihood for a buyer to be influenced by seller perceptions

Positive Word of Mouth

positive word of mouth (WOM) The likelihood that a customer recommends a seller

The fourth and final mechanism is **positive word of mouth (WOM)**, or the likelihood that a customer recommends a seller. Deep, positive relationships motivate and encourage referrals.[44] Only customers with strong, trusting relationships are likely to risk their reputations by recommending a seller to another potential customer.[45] Unlike the other three equity-generating mechanisms; positive word of mouth builds relationship equity by generating new customers. Strong WOM can be very valuable among these new customers, especially since evidence shows that consumers are willing to pay more for a product with an "excellent" rating (a form of WOM by other consumers) than a "good" rating, promising premiums from 20 percent for real estate agents to 99 percent for legal services.[46] Word-of-mouth data can be collected and integrated into CRM systems using routine marketing research methods, such as post-purchase surveys, and asking new customers how they heard about the firm.

Thus, deep, broad, and diversely composed relationships build relationship equity through the equity-generating mechanisms of cooperation, loyalty, empathy, and positive word of mouth. By tracking each of these relationship indicators and outcomes, marketers can identify disconnects and take corrective action. If a deep relationship is not engendering cooperation, what is missing? Perhaps broader relationships across the two firms are also required for cooperation with a particular customer. For example, a sporting goods manufacturer cooperating with a major sporting goods retailer-customer on new product development, such as a new line of treadmills, would require deep, broad, and diverse interconnections among many departments across the two companies. Table 13.1 summarizes these various RM value chain concepts.

IN OTHER WORDS ...

The relationship marketing value chain can be thought of a bit like a manufacturing process. Imagine a candy factory with various steps: measuring and mixing ingredients, heating, cooling, packaging, etc. If the end product comes out wrong, how does the factory know what happened? In manufacturing operations, this problem is handled by proactively and diligently monitoring defects at each stage of the process. The failure rates of the mixing, heating, packaging, and other processes are each known and updated over time. This allows problems to be diagnosed and corrected. Just so with the relationship marketing value chain: CRM technology allows each step in the chain to be monitored, so marketers know where there is a breakdown.

USING RELATIONSHIP MARKETING STRATEGIES IN MARKETING CHANNELS

marketing channels The series of relationships that get a product from its manufacturer to its end user

As the discussion in this chapter emphasizes, relationship marketing strategies are vital in both B2B and B2C marketing. In the case of business-to-business marketing, relationships generally happen within the context of **marketing channels**, or the series of relationships that get a product from its manufacturer to its end user. For example, Samsung manufactures televisions. Some of these

Table 13.1 RM Value Chain Concepts.

The relationship marketing value chain outlines the links between many closely related concepts.

Step	Definition	Effect
Relationship marketing (RM)	Efforts aimed at identifying, growing, and maintaining customer relationships to ultimately produce relationship equity. Divided into types that …	*Relationship marketing efforts can improve the relationship in terms of depth, breadth, and composition*
Social RM	… use social interactions to convey the customer's favored status	
Structural RM	… involve creating systems for customers, such as specialized packaging or inventory tracking systems, which customers might not make on their own	
Financial RM	… take the form of direct economic benefits, such as rebates, discounts, and free-shipping promotions	
Relationship improvement factors	Dimensions along with RM efforts can enrich customer relationships, including:	*An improved relationship can generate relationship equity in the form of cooperation, loyalty, empathy, and positive word of mouth*
Relationship depth	The quality and closeness of bonds between the buyer and seller	
Commitment	A desire to continue an exchange relationship	
Trust	Confidence in the other party's words and integrity in an exchange relationship	
Gratitude	A sense of thankfulness for the other party's extraordinary efforts in an exchange relationship	
Reciprocity	A perceived need to repay extraordinary efforts in an exchange relationship	
Relationship breadth	The number of distinct interpersonal ties between a buyer and seller	
Relationship composition	The diversity and usefulness of the contacts between a buyer and seller	
Equity-generating mechanisms	The means by which an improved customer relationship can translate to financial value, including:	*The four equity-generating mechanisms result in improved financial outcomes and, ultimately, greater firm value*
Cooperation	Coordinated, complementary actions between exchange partners to achieve a goal	
Loyalty	The likelihood that the customer repeatedly benefits the seller in the exchange due to their relational ties	
Empathy	A greater likelihood for a buyer to be influenced by seller perceptions	
Positive word of mouth	The likelihood that a customer recommends a seller	

might be sold directly to electronics and big-box retailers, then to consumers (i.e., end users). Others might be sold to a generalist wholesaler, which sells to a hospital supply company that sells televisions for patient use in hospitals (i.e., end users). Because each B2B relationship typically exists within a *series* of relationships such as these, RM strategies should account for the overall channel structure and context.

Structure of Marketing Channels

Before considering how to adapt RM strategies, it is necessary to summarize some of the basic configurations of marketing channels (see also Figure 13.2). Channels can be described based on the number of *levels*, or intermediate steps, between the manufacturer and the end user.

zero-level channel A channel in which the end user buys directly from the manufacturer

one-level channel A channel with a single intermediary between the manufacturer and end user

two-level channel A channel with two intermediaries between the manufacturer and end user

- When the end user buys directly from the manufacturer, this is a **zero-level channel**. This would be the case when a consumer orders a car from Tesla online.
- When there is one party, such as a single wholesaler or retailer, between the manufacturer and retailer, a **one-level channel** exists, as in the example above of Samsung selling to retailers selling to consumers.
- And when two intermediaries exist, as in the hospital televisions example, this is a **two-level channel**.

Three- and four-level channels are also possible, and any level of channel may exist whether the end user is a consumer or a business. Generally, channel intermediaries such as retailers, distributors, and wholesalers exist to create useful assortments from multiple suppliers, to efficiently distribute physical goods, and to help suppliers access different markets—for example, if smartphone manufacturer OnePlus wants to enter a new country market, it might benefit from working with a local distributor or retailer that has expertise in the market.

As the case of Samsung above illustrates, the same manufacturer can *serve different end users through different channels*. It is also possible to *serve different end users through the same channel*. For example, Dewalt sells power tools to HD Supply, which sells them to Home Depot, which then sells them to both contractors (business end users) and consumers. Finally, manufacturers can even serve the same end user through multiple channels. For example, Nike sells shoes to consumers both directly through Nike stores (zero-level channel) and through

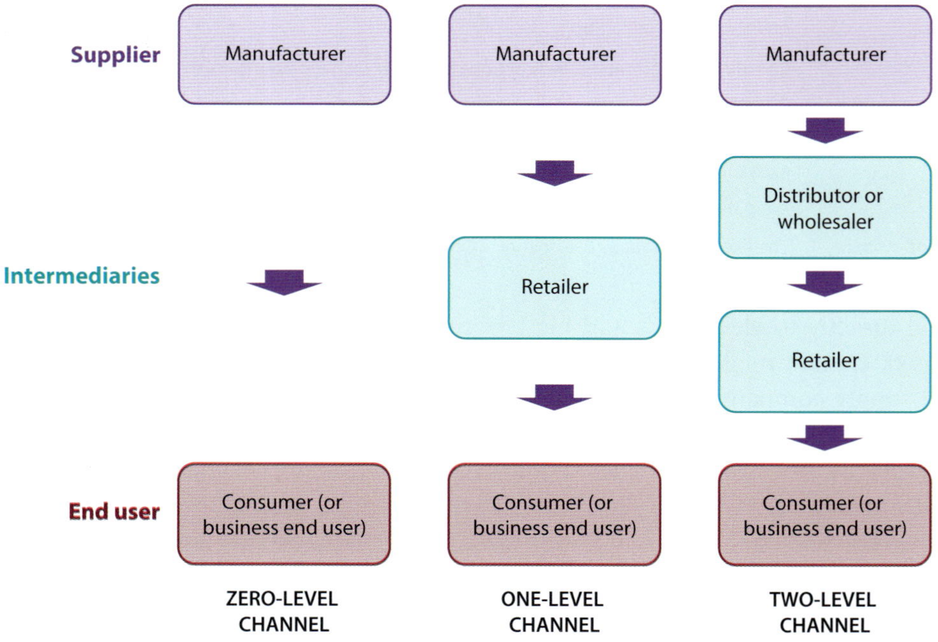

Figure 13.2 Marketing Channel Configurations.

Marketing channels vary in their number of intermediaries. For example, buying a car directly from Tesla's website is a zero-level channel (zero intermediaries or "middlemen"). The structure of the channel, as well as the prestige and power of channel members, affects how relationship marketing strategies must be adapted.

retailers such as JD Sports (one-level channel). This chapter's Opposing Views feature covers more information about Nike's marketing channels. As that feature further illustrates, the uniqueness and prestige of the manufacturer's brand affects the deployment of RM strategies as well.

OPPOSING VIEWS Nike Breaks Up with Retailers

Source: Tim Mossholder/Unsplash

Nike cut off thousands of independent retailers to focus its relationship marketing efforts on major partners such as JD Sports. This strategy boosted Nike's profits but devastated some small, local retail businesses by cutting off access to the most popular footwear brand.

American footwear and apparel giant Nike is ubiquitous. As of 2017, it was the largest athletic apparel brand at $9.6 billion in sales, and the largest footwear brand with $21 billion in sales in that year. It was also the leader in footwear in virtually every single market where it operated.[47] Yet it wanted to deliver ever-greater returns for its investors, leading to its "Triple Double Strategy," promising to double its speed of product innovation, double its speed in bringing products to market, and double its ability to directly connect with consumers.[48] As part of this strategy, it sought to streamline its network of 30,000, mostly independent, retailers and focus on its own direct-to-consumer Nike store as well as forty large, chain retailers.[49]

USA

Practically speaking, what this "streamlining" meant was cutting off independent retailers—typically small, owner-operated shops—from accessing the #1 footwear brand at wholesale prices. In other words, Nike was firing most of its B2B customers. The impact on those retailers was devastating. Moe Stein, the owner of New York City's century-old Frank's Sports Shop, reported receiving a letter from Nike stating that his shop "No longer aligns with our distribution policy." A frustrated Moe Stein told reports, "This is plain chutzpah. Let me tell you about Nike. We knew them when they had nothing. How do you like that? [We're] not an elite place to them."[50]

To strengthen relationships with select partners, Nike was putting livelihoods at risk. Yet the strategy paid off. By 2023, total Nike brand sales topped $48 billion, "driven by double-digit growth across NIKE Direct."[51]

See the issue from two sides:

1. Craft an argument in favor of Nike. Why is it just for Nike to "fire" its retail partners in this way?
2. Craft an argument against Nike. How could Nike have achieved its growth and profitability objectives without cutting off independent retailers?

Adapting RM Strategies in Marketing Channels

Marketing researchers have expended a lot of effort to try to determine how to adapt relationship marketing strategies to different channel environments, sometimes coming to conflicting conclusions. But generally, adaptation approaches can be categorized into three core ways of doing business:

1. arms-length transacting
2. cooperative relationships
3. integrative partnerships[52]

As we review each of these, keep in mind that these approaches are only general archetypes that must be fine-tuned to the specific relational context.

Arms-Length Transacting

Certain channel structures entail limited trust and limited opportunities to build trust with most buyers. For example, some channels have large, market-making middlemen whose primary function is to simply facilitate the flow of goods through the supply chain. For example, industrial wholesalers, such as W.W. Grainger, sell relatively undifferentiated products to tens of thousands of small retail buyers and small end users via an e-commerce website and operate on the understanding that most customers will receive little to no personal attention. Social, structural, and financial RM in these contexts is shallower and less personal, akin to what mass-market retailers such as Amazon offer: discounts, loyalty programs, customized promotions, and so on.[53]

arms-length transacting Exchanges where buyers and sellers conduct business at market prices without an automatic expectation of repeat purchases

In such environments, where the potential for relationship equity is more limited, **arms-length transacting** is a natural response. That is, buyers and sellers conduct business at market prices without an automatic expectation of

Source: Hannes Egler/Unsplash

Arms-length exchanges are common in contexts focused on efficiently distributing large amounts of relatively undifferentiated goods. Many wholesalers emphasize this approach. Extensive loading docks, like those pictured, reflect wholesalers' specialization in physical distribution of products.

repeat purchases. This way of doing business is also known as "market-based governance" since market norms around price and quality of goods, rather than features of the relationship, determine which deals are made.[54]

Cooperative Relationships

Other channel structures require more mutual involvement from channel members than simply moving goods through a supply chain. Consider, for example, franchising systems. McDonald's, the franchisor, acts like a "manufacturer" of the McDonald's branding, menu, and restaurant design. Franchisees, often medium-sized businesses that specialize in operating restaurant locations, act as the "buyer" that pays a percentage of sales (via a contract with McDonald's) in exchange for the ability to sell the McDonald's menu in retail locations. Naturally, in this arrangement, arms-length transacting would be a disaster; McDonald's cannot simply let anyone provide food service under their brand with no strings attached. Instead, the franchisor (McDonald's): performs careful due diligence on potential franchisees; uses a written contract to ensure that franchisees adhere to brand standards regarding ingredients, signage, and other details; and closely works with franchisees to support their stores' success and help them comply with brand standards.

Franchising is but one example of this type of context. For example, settings that require customized products also fit into this category. When CED, a major US commercial lighting distributor, sells electrical and lighting equipment to contractors and construction service providers, it often needs to visit the construction site and work closely with the buyer to determine their exact needs and deliver the right solution (see also *solution selling* in Chapter 15). These channel structures call for **cooperative relationships**: buyer–seller exchanges that require communication and collaboration to meet mutual needs. In these exchanges, buyers place a great deal of weight on the supplier performing exceptionally, compared to more limited expectations (i.e., providing goods on time) in arms-length transacting.[55] Thus, cooperative relationships place greater emphasis on social and structural RM efforts that are tailored to the individual buyer's needs.

cooperative relationships Exchanges that require communication and collaboration to meet mutual needs

Since these relationships place a greater emphasis on both parties accommodating each other, despite having their own goals, they are also known as *bilateral governance*.[56] This balancing act also creates the greatest potential, out of any arrangement, for **channel conflict**. Channel conflicts are disagreements between channel members about which party's goals will be met, and typically relate to how the financial rewards of the channel will be distributed.[57] They often relate to pricing (e.g., a buyer wants a discount), which products to carry (e.g., a supplier wants buyers to carry *all* of its products), or special attention (e.g., a buyer is upset that a supplier will not share details about an upcoming new product).

channel conflict Disagreements between channel members about which party's goals will be met, and typically relate to how the financial rewards of the channel will be distributed

Integrative Partnerships

Finally, some channel structures require a continuous, intense, and formalized level of collaboration. The most obvious example of this is vertical integration,

Source: ThisisEngineering RAEng/Unsplash

Volvo and Uber embarked on an equity joint venture—a jointly owned subsidiary—to design and engineer autonomous, self-driving cars. This reflected an integrative partnership between the eventual manufacturer of these cars, Volvo, and the buyer, Uber.

when a supplier in the channel owns a buyer (or vice versa). For example, IKEA owns the suppliers that manufacture its furniture and even owns many of the raw material suppliers that serve those manufacturers—including a logging operation in Romania.[58] In settings like these, IKEA has the ability and incentive to have eyes *inside* of the manufacturer's operation, and control every aspect of that operation to maximize IKEA's success. Similarly intense levels of collaboration can arise in equity joint ventures—a type of business alliance where two companies jointly own a shared subsidiary. For example, in 2016 Uber and Volvo each invested $150 million into a joint venture to develop autonomous cars; the designs from this subsidiary would eventually result in cars sold by the manufacturer (Volvo) to Uber.[59]

integrative partnerships Exchanges in which buyers' and suppliers' interests are fully synchronized, whether through vertical integration, equity joint ventures, or another mechanism

Marketing channel alliances such as these, in which buyers' and suppliers' interests are fully synchronized, whether through vertical integration, equity joint ventures, or another mechanism, are **integrative partnerships**.[60] In these relationships, there are typically no alternative partners due to formal mechanisms locking the partners together, such as exclusive distribution agreements or one company owning the other company. Therefore, the parties must maximize social RM efforts to create smooth interpersonal working relationships and structural RM to build seamless workflows that cross company boundaries.

Overall, as this section illustrates, the targeting of RM strategies in the relationship marketing value chain must consider not only STP and AER strategies, as noted earlier, but also the structure of relationships—and power dynamics—in the marketing channel.

CHAPTER CASE STUDY

TESCO CLUBCARD EVOLVES WITH THE TIMES

UK

Tesco PLC is the leading grocery retailer in the United Kingdom and one of the largest retailers in the world, with £54.8 billion ($69.0 billion) revenue in 2022. The chain launched the first supermarket loyalty card in the United Kingdom, the Clubcard, in 1995. The explicit goal was to gather data on customers' shopping habits, encourage customer loyalty in the form of repeat purchasing, and spur customers to buy all of their groceries at Tesco to maximize rewards.[61] The Clubcard's basic features included a 1 percent reward rate on purchases (higher when redeeming points with partner retailers) and customized offers, based on customers' purchase histories, in the form of loyalty letters sent in the mail. These features led those with Clubcards to increase spending at Tesco by 28 percent in the year following the card's launch.[62] Clubcard enabled mining and analyzing customer relationship data at a scale that was revolutionary for its time.

Evolving the Clubcard. Over the next twenty-five years, the Clubcard saw mostly minor changes, keeping its core 1 percent reward benefit and "every little helps" tagline, as well as the ability to multiply rewards by redeeming points at partner chains such as PizzaExpress. Even throughout Tesco's missteps in the mid-2010s, the company continued to stay at the cutting edge of customer data mining and analytics.[63] Incremental Clubcard changes included the ability to spend points on fuel and the shift toward a digital (i.e., mobile app-based) card to maximize convenience and provide a digital home for the old "loyalty letter" customized offers.

Yet beginning in 2020, Tesco started to make more drastic changes to the program. The value of fuel and partner point redemptions decreased; for example, where redeeming points with partner retailers could previously allow an effective reward rate of 4 percent, this was reduced to 2 percent across the board.[64] At the same time, Clubcard added two benefits. The first was an expansion of an existing benefit, as Tesco greatly expanded the use of personalized coupons offered to Clubcard members through the digital app.[65] The second, even more consequential change, was the introduction of Clubcard Prices. This program resulted in many products in the store having two prices: a lower price for Clubcard members and a higher price for non-members.[66] As a whole, the changes to the program reflect a greater focus on expending relationship marketing costs to keep customers in Tesco stores.

Uncertain future. Despite these intentions, reactions to the revised Clubcard program have been mixed. Although some customers appreciate the automatic member savings with Clubcard Prices, others have argued that the "special" member price is sometimes the ordinary price charged at other grocers, while the "normal" non-member price is exorbitant.[67] Moreover, the program lost some of its unique advantage over competitors when UK grocery rival Sainsbury's launched its near-identical Nectar Prices program.[68] It remains to be seen whether the Clubcard will be a source of advantage for Tesco in the future.

CASE QUESTIONS

1. Considering the different types of relationship marketing discussed in this chapter, how would you characterize Clubcard? Is your answer different before and after the card's evolution?
2. In what ways does Clubcard, in its current form, contribute to relationship equity?
3. In your opinion, does Clubcard contribute to relationship-based sustainable competitive advantage? What could be done to enable or enhance this advantage from the program?

CHAPTER SUMMARY

Enduring relationships with customers, channel partners, and other strategically vital individuals and institutions are a potentially sticky form of competitive advantage. This advantage is not easily replicated because it is grounded in the idiosyncratic histories of personal and channel relationships. The relationship management (RM) concept, supported by technological tools such as CRM as well as organizational processes, embodies this approach to competitive advantage. Strong relationships between customers or channel partners and a firm's salespeople or other boundary-spanning employees can establish powerful barriers to customer defection. Social, structural, and financial RM efforts promote higher levels of trust, commitment, and interpersonal reciprocal bonds, which enable customer relationships and channel partnerships to adapt to changing circumstances and give buyers confidence in the fairness of future outcomes. Improved relationships prompt customer loyalty and other relationship benefits that lead to relationship equity and superior financial performance. Channel relationships, in particular, produce complexity for this relationship marketing process. RM efforts must be adapted not only to the needs of specific buyers but also to the structure of the channel.

APPLICATION QUESTIONS

1. Think about a time that a retailer or another company directly contacted you via phone or email. What was the contact about? What type of relationship marketing effort was it?
2. Do you care a lot about your relationship with anyone working at a retailer or a service provider? Why or why not?
3. In the chapter, you read that almost all (except the very smallest) companies use some form of CRM system. Why do you think they do this? Why do the smallest companies often fail to adopt CRM?
4. Reflect on the idea that different customers want different levels of social, structural, and financial RM at different times. Which type of RM is most appealing to you currently? Do you think this will ever change—why or why not?
5. Consider the four drivers of relationship depth. Taking into account both your relationships with companies as well as interpersonal relationships (they operate on similar principles!), which of the four drivers is the most important to you, and why?
6. Think of a time when you spread positive word of mouth about a brand, product, or service. What inspired you to do this? Were you able to persuade someone to try out the brand? Why or why not?
7. As noted in the chapter, some marketing channels have two, three, or more levels. Why might a marketing channel have more than one intermediary—for example, manufacturer to *wholesaler* to retailer to consumer, instead of just manufacturer to retailer to consumer? How does the manufacturer benefit from organizing channel relationships in this way?

Visit the companion website, **https://bloomsbury.pub/palmatier-marketing**, or **https://samsinstitute.com**, for additional learning and teaching tools, including professional videos outlining the Four Principles, PowerPoint tutorials with voice-over commentary, sample syllabi for marketing courses, testbank and more.

Part 5

MARKETING PRINCIPLE #4: ALL RESOURCES ARE LIMITED

Part Overview

Welcome to Part 5. The two chapters in this unit explain how the three Marketing Principles we have discussed so far create complex challenges in terms of managing limited resources across segments, relationship phases, and sources of competitive advantage. Chapter 14 introduces Marketing Principle #4 (all resources are limited). This chapter also covers a central marketing decision lever that relates to both inflows of resources and outflows of resources: pricing. Chapter 15 focuses on several remaining key resource "buckets" that entail trade-off decisions. Specifically, marketers must allocate resources across integrated marketing communications (IMC) channels including the sales force.

These two chapters conclude the First Principles framework by explaining how resources are applied to activate strategies discussed in the prior units.

Chapter 14

MANAGING RESOURCE TRADE-OFFS AND PRICING STRATEGY

CHAPTER OVERVIEW

Chapter 14 introduces Marketing Principle #4: all resources are limited. It explains the various factors that lead to the pressing challenge of limited resources and the accompanying problem of managing resource trade-offs. It then describes two broad strategies for managing resource trade-offs with varying degrees of complexity. The second half of the chapter applies the notion of managing resource trade-offs to a key, resource-focused marketing mix decision: pricing. The chapter will proceed by answering the following questions:

- What is Marketing Principle #4 and its accompanying managerial challenge?
- What factors make managing resource trade-offs more challenging?
- What are the main strategies for managing resource trade-offs?
- How do typical approaches to pricing decisions embody resource trade-offs?

In the chapter's cases and features, you will run into companies that have struggled, and sometimes excelled, at managing resource trade-offs while sustaining profitability. These include:

- A high-profile, overbudgeted Disney film flop (Marketing Fail).
- Twitch's resource trade-off tango with livestreamers (Chapter Case).
- Ethical and moral dilemmas in resource trade-offs, such as the wild world of kids using real money in Roblox (Shades of Gray) and Netflix's embrace of "streamflation" (Opposing Views).

LEARNING OBJECTIVES

- Define the key marketing challenge associated with Marketing Principle #4.
- Recognize the five primary drivers of challenging resource trade-offs.
- Identify the main strategies for managing resource trade-offs.
- Apply Marketing Principle #4 to the problem of managing prices.

IMAGINE Managing Resources at Ben's Cookies

Source: Girl with red hat/Unsplash

Even more difficult than choosing from among an assortment of cookies, running a retail store requires making choices about how to invest limited resources into advertising, staffing, training, and more.

Ben's Cookies was founded as a single location in Oxford, United Kingdom, in 1984, and has since grown to encompass dozens of locations worldwide, including recently launched locations in the United States.[1] Ben's specializes in a modest assortment of chocolate chunk cookies in clean, cozy, counter-service shops. Although Ben's stores are all company-owned, imagine that you have control over a brand-new franchised location in your neighborhood. You have a limited start-up budget to place some advertisements for your new business. You also need to recruit and train employees to provide a friendly service. After that, you'll need revenue from customers coming in to continue promoting your business.

Given your limited start-up funds, you aren't certain where you can get the biggest bang for your buck. Should you focus on a low-cost social media campaign, leveraging your family, friends, and contacts to spread the word, and conserve resources for hiring the best staff? Should you blitz the internet and local radio and television with adverts to create buzz? Or perhaps go in some other direction?

Critical thinking:

1. How would you begin using your start-up resources in this scenario? Where would you focus?
2. This chapter is about resource trade-offs. Can you explain what about this scenario (and your choice above) reflects "trade-offs"?

INTRODUCTION TO MARKETING PRINCIPLE #4

Marketers Have Limited Resources

The last problem that managers face when making strategic marketing decisions is that there are only so many resources available, in terms of money, time, customer goodwill, and other resource pools. When a company makes marketing decisions, it has to choose between different goals. Because resources are limited, different needs have to be met based on decisions that are closely related. Every month, the marketing manager of a single retail store has to decide how to spend limited advertising dollars, sales staff hours, shelf space, and merchandise inventories for hundreds of categories. Imagine how hard it would be to make these kinds of decisions for an entire chain of stores. All these decisions about how to divide up the marketing mix are called resource trade-offs.[2]

If marketers make a mistake on any of these trade-off decisions, it can affect every other result that comes after that decision. For example, if the company spends most of its money on advertising instead of making sure it has enough inventory, customers might find stores that are out of stock. In the same way, wasting retail shelf space on products for customers who don't come into the store very often would lead to huge losses because the products would become obsolete, and the store would have to pay more for inventory than it needed to.

Firms' limited resources, along with the fact that the environment is always changing, mean that companies must always make choices about how to use their resources to make their marketing strategy successful. That is, the fact that all resources are limited is a basic problem that all businesses must solve to develop an effective marketing plan. The fourth and final first principle is **Marketing Principle #4**: all resources are limited. Based on this principle, the resulting challenge for marketers is that they must design strategies for intelligently **managing resource trade-offs**.[3]

Marketing Principle #4 A fundamental principle affecting all marketing decisions: all resources are limited

managing resource trade-offs The managerial challenge associated with Marketing Principle #4: scarce resources must be allocated strategically

Three Questions for Managing Resource Trade-offs

Managing resources is unavoidable because marketing resources are the main action levers that companies can use to put into practice what they've learned from the first three Marketing Principles. For example, a YouTube influencer with 1 million followers will earn well over $100,000 from the platform.[4] Yet, to continue growing the audience, much of this must be invested back into the channel, as high-quality videos are expensive and time-consuming. The influencer has to choose what new content to create to please a diverse audience, account for changing tastes, and remain unique among competing channels. Trading off resources based on the first three principles leads to the **three questions for managing resource trade-offs**:

three questions for managing resource trade-offs (1) How should resources be divided among customer segments? (2) How should resources be divided across customer relationship states? (3) How should resources be divided across sources of competitive advantage?

1. ***How should resources be divided among customer segments?***

   First, to effectively manage customer differences (Marketing Principle #1), managers conduct segmentation, targeting, and positioning (STP). Yet they also need to divide their fixed resources across these target segments effectively. In the YouTube example, some of the channel's audience might prefer reviews of video games, while other audience members enjoy reaction commentary about games industry news or about other video game influencers.

2. ***How should resources be divided across customer relationship states?***

   Second, to effectively manage customer dynamics (Marketing Principle #2), marketers develop acquisition–expansion–retention (AER) strategies that they use to serve customers as they move across life cycle stages. But to put these carefully thought-out strategies into action, managers need enough marketing funds to cover all three stages, and these costs can quickly get out of hand. For example, a YouTube channel might try to focus on new viewers by chasing trends, such as hosting livestreams of the latest popular video games—just as many influencers did following the shocking success of the Pokémon-inspired *Palworld* game in 2024.[5] But this choice would pull production funds and time away from creating the content that long-time fans have come to expect.

3. ***How should resources be divided across sources of competitive advantage?***

   Finally, to build sustainable competitive advantages (Marketing Principle #3), managers can never stop developing innovative products, building iconic brands, and investing in relationship marketing (BOR strategies). In our YouTube example, the influencer could choose to build interpersonal relationships with interactive livestreams, but this could reduce the time and resources available to develop more complex new offerings, such as long-form video essays about the state of the video game industry. Deciding which sources of competitive advantage to pursue entails trade-offs with complex implications for performance. If firms fail to develop reasonable methods to manage these complex trade-offs, they risk losing segments of customers or product market share to competitors, as well as suffering lower returns on their marketing investments.

These three questions are unavoidable for both small and large firms. For example, Procter & Gamble oversees dozens of brands that earn billions of dollars annually, but still must continuously introduce new products to keep its edge, and it must decide which customer segments and relationship stages to target with these products—while missing out on pursuing equally costly alternatives.[6] This chapter's Marketing Fail, about Disney's 2023 *Indiana Jones* flop, speaks to a large corporation's failure to properly manage these trade-off questions, leading to a costly waste of resources.

IN OTHER WORDS …

The first three Marketing Principles directly lead to the challenge of limited resources, since it is not possible to devote maximum resources to every segment, relationship stage, and source of advantage. The three questions for managing resource trade-offs capture the essence of the fourth Marketing Principle. That is, the firm must look at the challenges implied by the first three principles and decide what to prioritize. For example:

- Which segment should be the focus of advertising dollars (MP#1)?
- Which aspect of changing technology should the firm's new products adopt (MP#2)?
- Which customer relationships are the most important to invest in (MP#3)?

WHY ARE RESOURCE TRADE-OFFS SO CHALLENGING?

If every firm worked in a stable industry with infinite resources, selling to clients with the same needs that never changed over time, and competitors did not modify their strategy, then resource allocation decisions and trade-offs would be simple. Firms might learn what worked best, then maintain their resource allocation judgments over time and for all their customers. Of course, as we know from the three Marketing Principles, this depiction is far from accurate. Instead, enterprises must regularly make resource trade-off decisions for five major reasons, which we summarize in Table 14.1: (1) limited resource slack, (2) shifting customer needs, (3) shifting produce life cycle, (4) shifting market landscape, and (5) shifting marketing effectiveness.

Source #1: Limited Resource Slack

The awareness that the firm does not have spare funds available for any given project at any given time is the first and probably most fundamental factor that makes resource trade-offs so challenging and pervasive. The term for

Table 14.1 Resource Trade-off Drivers.

Resource trade-offs are a universal problem, but they are made even more challenging by five factors.

Driver	Explanation
1. Limited resource slack	Firms have some given level of resource slack, or potentially usable resources that can be diverted or redeployed to achieve organizational goals. However, this slack must be shared and allocated across many different marketing needs. Resource allocation processes therefore need to find ways to optimize the return on marketing investments.
2. Shifting customer needs	Market segmentation provides a description of the industry segments. A firm then moves from the overall market landscape to the specific segment(s) of interest to the firm. Yet over time, the size and attractiveness of each of the industry segments changes, which means that the number of targeted segments may change, and a firm's commitment among segments will change.
3. Shifting product life cycle	Firms try to balance their product portfolios to have products in all life cycle stages, to help offset resource needs. Introductory stage products require resource allocations to their launch, testing, and advertising to create awareness. They require different allocations as they enter the growth, maturity, and decline stages. Changes in technology and the success or failure of new products also alter any firm's product portfolio constantly.
4. Shifting market landscape	When the firm moves into a reasonably advantageous market position, competitors quickly make a countermove. Such counterattacks have the potential to negate the impact of the incumbent's advantage and often create jostling for secondary demand, that is, firms stealing market share from one another rather than creating primary demand. Firms have to constantly change their resource trade-off decisions during competitive counterattacks. In some cases, resource trade-offs have to be made simply in anticipation of new entrants.
5. Shifting marketing effectiveness	Even if a firm is operating during a stable economic window, with fixed consumer segments, homogenous preferences for products across different life cycle stages, and no major competitive entry, the effectiveness of marketing activities change over time, such that the aggregated market becomes less or more responsive to marketing efforts. For example, sales cycles have lengthened due to more relationship selling, product complexity, and informed and demanding customers.

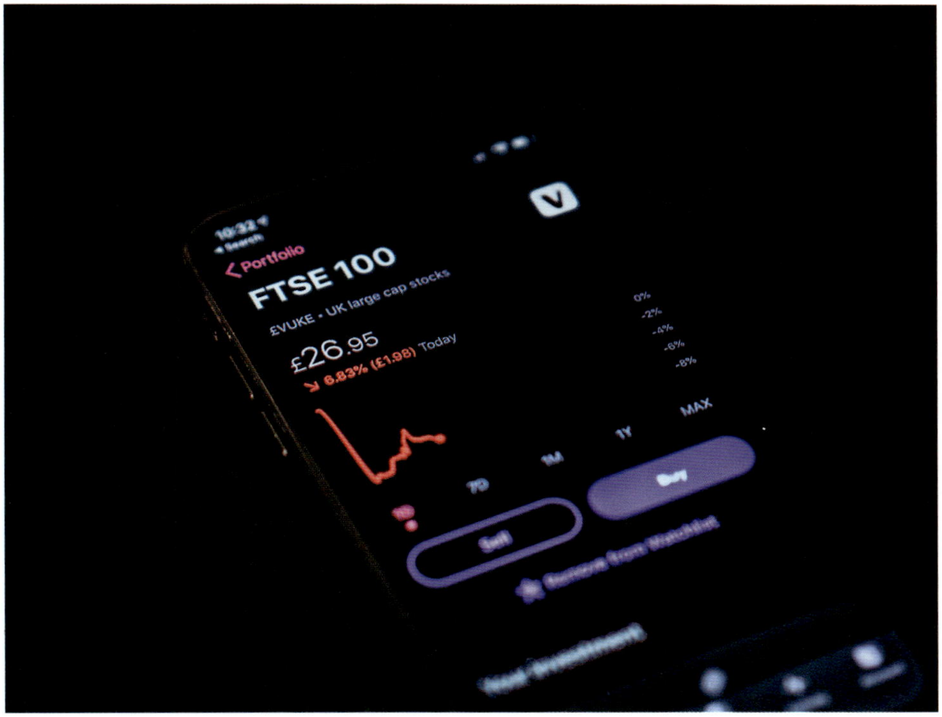

Source: Jamie Street/Unsplash

Resource slack is one of the main drivers of resource trade-offs. The availability of spare slack resources depends heavily on economic conditions. When markets drop, as in a recession, resources become further constrained.

the firm's surplus funds is **resource slack**, formally defined as "potentially utilizable resources a firm possesses that it could divert or redeploy to achieve organizational goals."[7] Resource slack supplies a company with actual or potential resources, allowing it to modify its marketing plan.

resource slack Potentially utilizable resources a firm possesses that it could divert or redeploy to achieve organizational goals

Firms vary greatly in how much emphasis they place on marketing, but their overall amount of resource slack is highly influenced by the economy. Major events in the global economy, such as recessions, have far-reaching consequences. These downturns dramatically reduce demand for goods and services, lowering most organizations' sales and earnings and leaving them with much less resource slack. Many companies choose to minimize marketing-related, brand-building investments if they believe they need to conserve those limited slack resources, which means marketers are compelled to operate with smaller budgets.[8] Following the 2008 financial crisis, nearly all firms reported some extent of budget cuts.[9] Similarly, chief marketing officers surveyed in 2022 reported cutting their budgets by as much as 15 percent as a result of the COVID-19-induced recession.[10]

Source #2: Shifting Customer Needs

A second reason that resource trade-offs are so challenging is that customer needs are diverse and always changing. Segmentation, targeting, and positioning techniques can provide descriptions of industry segments, including salient buying preferences, demographic factors, and segment potential for each identified segment. These precise definitions of target segments are vital and necessary, but the size and attractiveness of each industry sector, as well as the number of targeted segments, can change over time, as can the appropriate amount of a firm's commitment to the various segments.

For example, there are four classic sectors in the hospitality industry: backpackers, couples, families, and business travelers.[11] Backpackers prefer to explore the city rather than stay in a hotel, and thus demand more affordable lodging options. Couples instead prize room furnishings and hotel conditions. Families look for kid-friendly and affordable restaurants, on-site play spaces, entertainment, and savings on additional rooms for their children to stay in. Business travelers are willing to pay a premium. As a result, depending on which categories they target, hotels are likely to make quite diverse pricing, marketing, amenity, and loyalty program selections. They must make allocation decisions; the upscale JW Marriott hotel brand caters to business travelers more than backpackers. However, the size, demands, and financial payoffs of these divisions are not stable and fluctuate frequently. Following a STP analysis, a company's altered marketing strategy will almost certainly necessitate adjustments to its resource allocations, especially if the company decides to leave existing segments or join new segments.

Source #3: Shifting Product Life Cycle

The third cause for difficult resource trade-offs arises from changes in a company's product's life cycle stage. Firms attempt to balance their product portfolio to have items at all phases of the life cycle and so counterbalance resource needs. Products at the introduction stage, for example, need a lot of capital to introduce the offering, wait for sales to accumulate, conduct consumer studies to refine the product, and raise awareness through advertising. When such items reach the growth stage, the company's sales increase, but it must also alter its resource allocations and invest in production and distribution to satisfy rising demand. Later, the company will need to develop appropriate differentiation tactics for items in the maturity and decline stages, because these markets have grown saturated, consumers' wants are mainly met, and the company will most likely seek to minimize marketing expenses to retain profitability. Beyond this natural progression, as technology evolves or new goods enter the market, the firm's product portfolio moves as well, often in unanticipated ways, requiring the marketing manager to reallocate spending across the whole product life cycle.

For example, Smith's Snackfood Company, a British-Australian company known for packaged food items (e.g., corn chips), tracks all inputs and outputs throughout the life cycle of a product, from pre-farm preparations to on-farm operations to post-farm transportation. According to their statistics, one of the key trade-offs throughout the packaging and manufacturing step for corn chips is between resource utilization and greenhouse gas emissions. This type of monitoring enables Smith's to make more informed resource allocation decisions throughout the product life cycle stages.[12]

Source #4: Shifting Market Landscape

A fourth reason why marketers constantly struggle to adapt their resource trade-offs derives from changes in the market landscape caused by competitor entry and exit. Remember that once a company acquires a beneficial market position, competitors swiftly respond with their own efforts, based on Marketing Principle #3. Such counterattacks can result in battles for market share; in mature markets, this can mean more players fighting to split a pie that is not growing. For example, when patents expire on name-brand drugs, the entry of generic pharmaceuticals often leaves the name-brand competitors with limited room for growth. This can pressure their manufacturers to invest resources in innovating new and slightly improved versions of the drug to obtain renewed patent protection. For example, popular arthritis drug Humira had its patent extended multiple times in this manner, known as "evergreening."[13]

Source #5: Shifting Marketing Effectiveness

Changes in the effectiveness of marketing activities are the final issue that necessitates challenging resource trade-offs. Even in periods of economic stability, with relatively constant consumer preferences and no big competitor entry, marketing initiatives can lose or gain effectiveness over time, depending on customer responsiveness to specific marketing tools.

HSBC, a multinational banking and financial services firm based in the United Kingdom, revitalized its marketing activities to reconnect with its consumers following a number of significant organizational changes and poor financial performance. In its commercials, HSBC addressed challenging themes such as energy efficiency, an aging workforce, and growing markets, and it enhanced its use of social media channels to engage customers.[14] These advertisements resonated with consumers, and HSBC continued this approach for years, for example, with a 2023 advert featuring tennis star Emma Raducanu reading "fairy tales" that were meant to empower women. Yet the increasingly polarized political climate has potentially reduced the effectiveness of these adverts for some consumers, with media personalities such as Piers Morgan referring to the messages as "woke."[15]

Other marketing activities have seen their effectiveness shift due to long-term trends. Some sales cycles have stretched in B2B settings as more companies engage in personal selling and create more sophisticated products to deal with better-informed, more demanding clients. As a result, personal selling effectiveness has steadily declined over four decades in both the United States and Europe.[16] Similarly, the efficiency of mass media advertising has declined during the last two decades, particularly in the United States, Europe, and Asia.[17] Trading off resources can be difficult when the effectiveness of multiple marketing channels changes at the same time. Companies must constantly adjust their allocations and future marketing plans, accounting for these changes.

These five drivers of resource trade-offs highlight the ongoing nature and challenge of this type of marketing decision. Most marketing initiatives need substantial investments, so knowing how to efficiently spend available resources is critical to success.

MARKETING FAIL Indiana Jones and the Box Office Flop

Source: Karen Zhao/Unsplash

Indiana Jones and the Dial of Destiny failed to impress audiences or fill theaters, despite massive resources poured into its production and marketing budgets.

It has never been easy for film studios to turn a profit at the box office, but the sheer financial scale of box office failures has ballooned out of control in recent years. One of the most notable large-scale flops was 2023's *Indiana Jones and the Dial of Destiny*. The film grossed nearly $400 million worldwide, which sounds impressive.[18] That is, until one considers the film's $295 million production budget, including extensive special effects, such as those used to digitally de-age star Harrison Ford. And this figure does not account for the film's advertising blitz or theater distribution costs; the movie needed to earn close to $600 million to break even.[19]

USA

The devastating financial loss for Disney, which produced the film, along with lukewarm critic and audience reviews, led many to wonder why Disney invested such a lavish budget into a film franchise that no longer resonates with moviegoers.[20] Even worse for Disney, the film released during a string of misfires and middling reviews. Titles such as the third *Ant-Man* film and *The Little Mermaid* remake earned modest gains, therefore using up resources that could have been devoted to more profitable films; *The Haunted Mansion*, like Indiana Jones, lost money.[21]

Given Disney's wealth of classic stories and intellectual properties to lean on, Disney's string of missed opportunities to connect with audiences leave fans wondering why these films have been given oversized budgets, and if they will be able to make smarter decisions moving forward.

Diagnose the problem:

1. What mistakes has Disney made in allocating resources for its film division? What source of resource trade-offs is it overlooking?
2. Going forward, how can Disney use its knowledge of the first three Marketing Principles to better allocate film resources?

TYPICAL APPROACHES TO WEIGHING RESOURCE TRADE-OFFS

Firms have created many techniques and analytical tools to decide where to invest resources. For simplicity's sake, we divide these into two categories: (1) heuristics-based approaches and (2) attribution-based approaches.

Heuristics-based Approaches

heuristics Simple resource allocation decision rules with no ambiguity

Firms continually allocate resources between customer segments, relationship phases, services, regions, and marketing communication forms. Without hard data, managers use intuition and judgment to allocate resources. These solutions are called **heuristics**. Heuristics are simple decision rules with no ambiguity. They are straightforward to understand and utilize, making them appealing to managers facing complex resource allocations and tight deadlines. A heuristic might call for investing 4 percent of sales revenue into advertising, regardless of any other factors.

Even when improved information technology made performance data and complete marketing investment analyses more available, many managers still used rule-of-thumb heuristics and simply applied them based on more accurate data. Based on previous year's sales, they may distribute a portion of the funds to each marketing resource. A 2014 poll of 1,000 advertising and promotion managers indicated that 72 percent utilize heuristics to allocate resources among products, regions, and marketing technologies.[22] Heuristics remain appealing because firms tend to be risk averse and prefer transparent resource trade-offs, so they adopt simple, even if suboptimal, approaches to managing their resources.

Several common approaches to heuristics-based decisions exist:[23]

- In the **percentage of sales** method, marketing resources are expended as a predetermined proportion of sales revenue. Because the firm can only assign a set amount of sales revenue, this system is easy and prevents overspending. If competitors invest resources similarly, industry standards for marketing spending arise.

percentage of sales Resource allocation heuristic; marketing resources are expended as a predetermined proportion of sales revenue

- The **proportion of profits** technique allocates marketing resources based on product earnings instead of sales. This strategy is sometimes favored over the percentage of sales method because it prevents marketing expenditures from reversing a positive profit margin.

proportion of profits Resource allocation heuristic; allocates marketing resources based on product earnings instead of sales

- Managers who use the **historical method** make current resource allocations close to last year's spending. This heuristic assumes the market is stable and growing slowly, and that resource allocation levels do not require sudden changes. Thus, it is most beneficial in businesses with stable political, social, demographic, and economic environments.

historical method Resource allocation heuristic; makes current resource allocations close to last year's spending

- Finally, the **competitive parity** strategy requires managers to match resource allocation levels with rivals. This strategy is most common in competitive marketplaces, where extensive marketing budgets are table stakes for competing—think Coca-Cola versus Pepsi. Individual firms may not know the right resource allocations, but collective industry expertise can often result in reasonable decisions. Since it relies exclusively on competitive benchmarking, this strategy cannot accurately tell marketers what spending *should* be, though.

competitive parity Resource allocation heuristic; requires managers to match resource allocation levels with rivals

Heuristics are appealing because of their simplicity. Their problem lies in their failure to take the first three Marketing Principles into account. The proportion of sales method goes against Marketing Principle #1 because it assumes that all customers are the same and that advertising will pay off equally. Setting advertising expenditures at historical levels contradicts Marketing Principle #2 because it assumes that advertising will pay in the same way now as it did in the past, ignoring the fact that all customers change. Nonetheless, these approaches are not without their benefits. A five-year simulation study found that a percentage-of-sales rule (allocating funding proportionately to previous year's sales) beat an equal allocation (equal distribution across all products and activities).[24]

Attribution-based Approaches

attribution methods Resource allocation techniques that use data along with complex statistical and economic models to understand the effect of each marketing resource investment on outcomes

Although heuristics-based approaches remain widely used, the most sophisticated data-driven companies have moved on to **attribution methods** for managing resource trade-offs. Attribution methods use data along with complex statistical and economic models to understand the *effect* of each marketing resource investment on outcomes. For example, the firm can use an attribution model to precisely estimate how much sales it would gain from investing an additional $1 million in digital advertising versus television advertising. The main advantage of attribution techniques is that they explicitly consider how resource allocations *lead to* financial outcomes. This is in direct contrast to heuristics approaches such as percentage of sales, which take a backward approach by assigning marketing resources as a *result* of sales. By quantifying relationships between resource allocations and financial outcomes, the firm can more accurately predict which trade-offs will optimize sales and profit.

response modeling Resource allocation techniques that entail collecting detailed data about a response (usually sales) and one or more predictors (for example, advertising expenditures across different media)

There are two main drawbacks to the attribution approach. First, the models typically require significant knowledge of statistics to execute (see Theory Spotlight in this chapter on response models). Second, attribution approaches require collecting specific data. This can be historical data on the relationship between resource allocations and outcomes, as in the aforementioned response models, or data collected from pre-planned experiments. For example, the firm can test a digital-heavy resource allocation in one region and a television-heavy resource allocation in another, and compare the outcomes.

THEORY SPOTLIGHT Response Modeling

One data-forward way to implement an attribution-based approach to managing resource trade-offs is **response modeling**. Response modeling entails collecting detailed data about a response (usually sales) and one or more predictors (for example, advertising expenditures across different media). The model uses a statistical framework to estimate the shape of the mathematical relationship between the response and the predictors.[25] Although the approach requires a lot of data and at least a rudimentary knowledge of applied statistics, the result is a relatively straightforward equation. Marketers can simply set up the equation in any software program with calculation capabilities (even Excel), plug planned advertising expenditures into the equation, and the equation will spit out estimated sales. With this approach, marketers can plan out different resource trade-off scenarios and anticipate outcomes.

MANAGING RESOURCE TRADE-OFFS IN PRICING DECISIONS

Pricing decisions are not only a critical part of the marketing mix (see Chapter 1) but also central to resource trade-offs. Price is a direct component of revenue, and therefore influences the number of resources (and potentially slack resources) available to deploy. But in other ways, price acts similarly to marketing promotions. *Reducing* the price, for example, can be a strategic resource deployment—a form of financial relationship marketing (see Chapter 13)—that must be weighed against other resource deployments. This duality makes pricing decisions uniquely complex.

In addition, pricing decisions must be made frequently and by many different marketing-related personnel. Product line managers, pricing directors, salespeople, sales managers, and business analysts might all have a say in pricing decisions, depending on the firm and industry. Price changes can happen at regular intervals (e.g., monthly), at specific, irregular times (e.g., when a competitor launches a new product), or automatically at high frequency (e.g., by-the-minute price changes driven by artificial intelligence algorithms).

Firms handle the complexity of pricing decisions in numerous ways that vary in levels of complexity, sophistication, and effectiveness. Countless books and articles have been written on the subject. Some firms seem to change pricing structures arbitrarily (see this chapter's case on Twitch). Yet, many of these strategies can be characterized in one of three ways (Figure 14.1):

1. cost-plus pricing
2. competitive price matching
3. value-based pricing

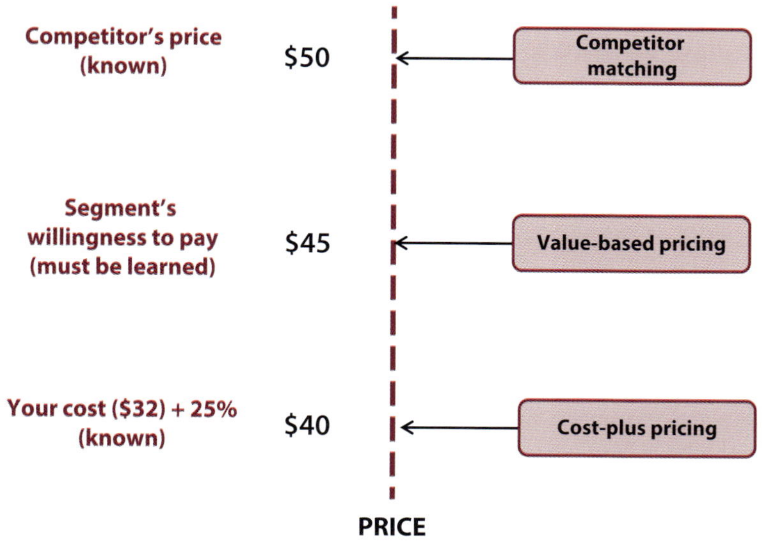

Figure 14.1 Pricing Strategies.

An example of cost-plus pricing, value-based pricing, and competitor matching in a specific scenario. In this case, the competitor's offering is overpriced, giving you an opening if you learn via market research that the segment isn't really willing to pay that much. Likewise, cost-plus pricing in this case results in underpricing, leaving profit on the table. Note that this is just one scenario; in other cases, cost-plus pricing could result in excessively high prices, for example.

Cost-Plus Pricing

cost-plus pricing A pricing strategy in which the seller takes the cost and adds some amount to it to earn a profit

markup The amount (expressed as a number or percentage) by which the price is increased, relative to cost

breakeven The number of units a firm needs to sell to begin to earn a profit

This approach is just what it sounds like. Under **cost-plus pricing**, the seller takes the cost and adds some amount to it to earn a profit. For example, if you run an eyewear shop and mark up all of your glasses by 50 percent, a pair that cost you $100 would sell for $150. **Markup** is the amount (expressed as a number or percentage) by which you increased the price, relative to cost; it also equals the amount of profit you will gain from the transaction. Cost-plus pricing remains the most widely used way of setting prices, due to its simplicity.[26] It relies on only two pieces of information: the cost (which you know) and your desired amount of profit (which you decide). It also makes calculations of **breakeven**, or the number of units you need to sell to begin to earn a profit, easy: breakeven equals any fixed costs that must be covered (e.g., rent and salaries) divided by the dollar markup on each unit.

Cost-plus pricing falls short, though, in its one-size-fits-all approach. It does not account for Marketing Principle #1, as different segments will be willing to pay different prices for glasses; it ignores Marketing Principle #2 by assuming that your profit margin should remain the same as customers' preferences and budgets for eyewear might change; and it sets aside Marketing Principle #3 by ignoring the possibility that competitors might undercut your price. Yet in an age

OPPOSING VIEWS Netflix Experiences "Streamflation"

Netflix, the world's most popular streaming service, saw its subscriber base grow from 34 million customers in 2013 up to 238 million in 2023.[27] Yet Netflix's growth has slowed in recent years. This is a problem as the streamer strategically took on massive amounts of debt to produce prestige films and shows, resulting in annual interest payments over $700 million.[28] As growth slows, Netflix has turned away from debt and expensive shows in a bid to reduce costs and protect profit margins.

At the same time, Netflix bolstered profits by jumping on an industry-wide trend: "streamflation."[29] Streamers from Disney+ to Max to Amazon Prime have increased prices against the backdrop of broader inflation in the economy, providing rationale for customers to accept once-in-a-generation large price increases. For its part, Netflix enthusiastically embraced this opportunity. Between 2019 and 2023, the price of Netflix's "Standard" ad-free plan increased from $10.99/month all the way up to $15.49/month (a 41 percent increase). At the same time, it dropped its cheaper, "Basic" plan entirely, eliminating a lower-cost option.[30]

USA

Customers have lamented the "streamflation" phenomenon, as they find themselves paying more for a basket of streaming services than the cost of traditional cable service. As consumers weigh how to balance their own resources across two, three, or even four or more streaming services, streamers, in turn, must continue to invest resources in quality content to attract and retain consumers.

See the issue from two sides:

1. Craft an argument in favor of Netflix's price hike. Is the hike justified on cost-plus, competitive matching, or value-based grounds?
2. Craft an argument against the price hike. What makes this price hike less justified or more opportunistic than other price increases in an inflationary economy?

of confusing pricing approaches driven by algorithms (e.g., constantly changing airfare prices), the simplicity and transparency of a cost-plus approach continues to appeal to many firms and consumers.

Competitive Price Matching

Under a **competitive price matching** strategy, the seller tries to maintain parity with rivals by setting prices based on competitors' prices. Like cost-plus pricing, competitive price matching has the advantage of relying on readily available (or easy to learn) information. Many airlines, for example, price-match their unsold seats behind the scenes by monitoring the prices of competitors' remaining seat inventory on equivalent routes. Further, competitive price matching explicitly incorporates Marketing Principle #3 by considering the actions of competitors—albeit in a simplistic way.

competitive price matching A pricing strategy in which the seller tries to maintain parity with rivals by setting prices based on competitors' prices

Mimicking competitors in this way can be advantageous especially if competitors have a firm understanding of value-based pricing (see below); in this way, marketers can piggyback off competitors' market research and demand

Source: Skyler Smith/Unsplash

In 1992, airlines in the United States got into a major price war, undercutting each other until they were losing money on flights. American Airlines and others experienced record losses due to poorly executed pricing strategies.

analyses. It can also make consumer's decision journeys easier, as price matching can mean one less factor for consumers to compare between options (i.e., the prices are the same). However, a reckless approach to price matching can lead instead to a price *war*. If competitors match and slightly *undercut* each other's prices repeatedly, a profit-destroying downward spiral ensues. The US airline industry famously fell into this trap in 1992, with American Airlines alone losing $1 billion as a result.[31]

Value-based Pricing

value-based pricing A pricing strategy in which the seller attempts to set prices based on the value that the target segment perceives in the product or service

willingness to pay The maximum amount of money that a customer will be satisfied with trading for the good or service

The most sophisticated approach, **value-based pricing**, attempts to set prices based on the value that the target segment perceives in the product or service. The core idea of this strategy is to charge each customer, to the extent feasible, based on their **willingness to pay**—that is, the maximum amount of money that they will be satisfied with trading for the good or service. This approach is more advanced because it accounts for all the first three Marketing Principles: it acknowledges that different segments may have different perceptions of value; it allows for these perceptions to shift over time; and it accounts for how competitors' offerings might alter value perceptions.

SHADES OF GRAY Roblox Pricing for Kids

Roblox is one of the most successful online virtual spaces in existence, but it is seldom discussed among adults. That's because most of its 52 million daily active users are under thirteen years old. In this virtual world, kids can make games, share them, play them, chat, and even buy and sell games and digital items.[32] Roblox makes money by selling "Robux" that can be used in-game. When a kid creates their own game, they receive about 28 percent of the real-world currency value of any Robux spent by other kids on items and abilities in their game. This has led to some extraordinary stories, such as one teenager paying for his college degree with Roblox sales.

Clearly, Roblox has mastered value-based pricing. It has managed to charge kids exactly what they are willing to pay, even if that means a ten-year-old girl spending over $3,000 of their parents' money.[33] Or in the case of creators, willingly letting Roblox keep 72 percent of their earnings (while grown-up creators on platforms such as Twitch keep 70 percent themselves; see Chapter Case). And of course, the unique blend of casino-level spending and a wide range of teens and preteens results in money changing hands in unconventional ways. Most notably, the platform has struggled to prevent teenage hackers from scamming children out of their parents' money.[34]

USA

Although Roblox remains immensely popular, its struggles with pricing and extracting resources from children have continued to create bad press and headaches for the now publicly traded company.

Ethical dilemmas:

1. In your opinion, is it moral to allow peer-to-peer financial transactions in a game for children? Why or why not?
2. What steps would you have Roblox take to balance its value-based pricing strategy with protecting the well-being (and finances) of children?

The real drawback in value-based pricing is in its difficulty of implementation. Whereas the prior two methods rely on easily known or knowable quantities (costs, desired profit, competitors' prices), value-based pricing relies on knowing a number that exists in the mind of each customer.[35] There are two ways to use data to infer this information:

- A special kind of market research study called a **conjoint analysis**, designed to measure customer preferences, can be used to estimate individual customers' willingness to pay. These studies can be expensive to conduct, though, and they gather data on only a small number of customers, so the results must be extrapolated to the entire customer base. This sample-and-extrapolate approach, of course, requires special care be taken to select a representative sample of customers.
- The use of historical sales data from different price levels. For example, if a price of $150 yields 1,000 units of sales, while a price of $200 results in 500 units of sales, what has happened? As the price increased from $150 to $200, 500 customers were no longer willing to pay, while 500 were willing to pay at least that much. Now, let's say that the price increases to $250 and only 200 units are sold. A further 300 customers were willing to pay at least $200 but *not* as high as $250, while only 200 customers were willing to pay at least $250. Although this technique does not reveal *individual* willingness to pay, with enough data points, it can provide extremely valuable insights about the *contours* of willingness to pay—that is, how many people are willing to buy at different price points.

conjoint analysis A market research technique designed to measure customer preferences, that can be used to estimate individual customers' willingness to pay

If one plots many data points like this, the resulting relationship between price and quantity sold is a classic, downward-sloping **demand curve**, familiar from the world of economics. If the demand curve is very steep—a lot of customers drop off and are unwilling to pay more as the price increases—we say that demand is **elastic**. If the curve is shallow—customers continue to buy even as the price increases a lot—we say that demand is **inelastic** (see Figure 14.2). Inelastic demand gives marketers more room to work with when changing prices; streamers such as Netflix, for example, must suppose that streaming demand is inelastic, based on their push for increased prices (see Opposing Views in this chapter). Elastic demand, on the other hand, gives marketers a narrower band of acceptable prices to work with, so price reductions, discounts, and other price-based marketing tools must be used cautiously.

demand curve A generally downward-sloping relationship between price and quantity sold

elastic A steep demand curve, where the quantity demanded drops off rapidly with price increases

inelastic A shallow demand curve, where the quantity demanded only drops off slowly with price increases

By understanding the demand curve and customers' willingness to pay, marketers can price products according to segments' willingness to pay. By doing so, they are more likely to maximize revenue and profit earned from each segment as well.

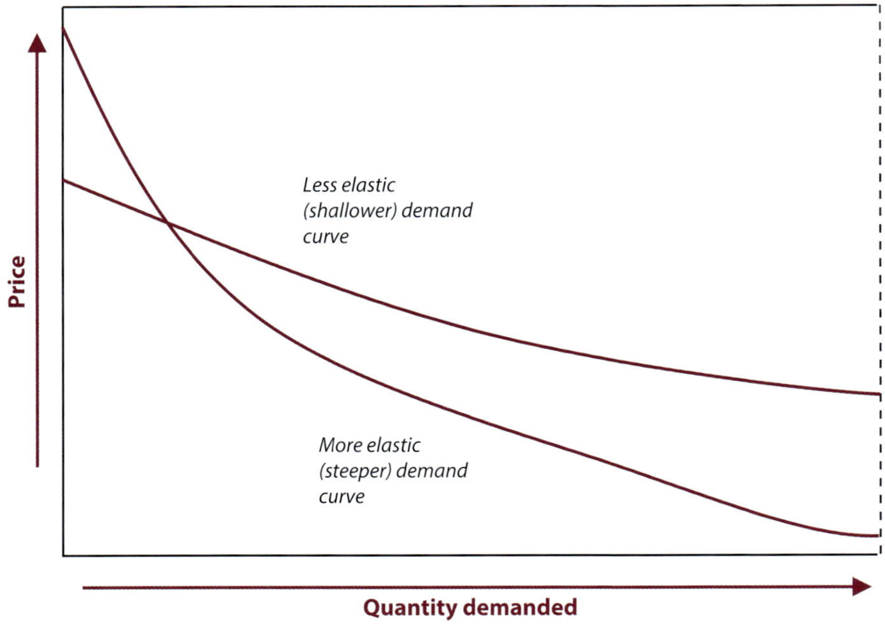

Figure 14.2 Demand Curves.

An example of two basic demand curves. As the price goes up, fewer and fewer people are willing to pay, and the quantity demanded goes down. As the price goes down, more people are willing to pay, and the quantity demanded goes up. When people's reactions are more extreme, demand is more elastic, and the curve is steeper.

CHAPTER CASE STUDY

TWITCH TRIES TO CLAW BACK RESOURCES

USA

As of 2022, an estimated 3.08 billion individuals worldwide tuned into livestreaming content, generating revenue approximated at $154 billion.[36] Streaming has emerged as a full-time profession for thousands of content creators and gamers across various platforms, with top earners commanding seven-figure incomes from subscriptions, advertisements, and brand partnerships.[37]

Among the livestreaming platforms, Twitch, established in 2011 to cater specifically to gaming content, is the market leader.[38] Twitch has set itself apart from its competitors, boasting 140 million monthly active users and 7.03 million streamers as of 2022.[39] Recognizing Twitch's business potential early, Amazon acquired the platform in 2014, integrating it with its Amazon Prime service. Twitch's business model is built around advertising and subscriptions, where viewers can choose to subscribe to their preferred streamers for a fixed monthly fee; Twitch takes a portion of this fee. Twitch likewise collects a percentage of advertising revenue earned by top streamers.[40]

Twitch claws back its revenue share. Historically, Twitch had allowed thousands of top streamers to keep 70 percent of subscription fees from viewers. This share may be viewed as a "price" of using the platform, from influencers' perspectives. This attracted numerous popular influencers to the platform, where they grew their following and contributed to Twitch's

Source: istock.com/Antonio_Diaz

Thousands of streamers make a living broadcasting video games and other activities on the Amazon-owned platform Twitch. Twitch's recent back-and-forth decisions on its revenue-sharing policies with streamers have left content creators shellshocked without improving the platform's resource constraints.

overall growth. After the platform grew in scale, Twitch sought more resources to support its server infrastructure and earn a profit. Therefore, it announced that these partners would have their share of subscription revenue reduced to 50 percent for any revenue over $100,000, with Twitch keeping the other 50 percent.[41] This policy shift would directly affect over ten thousand channels that rely on subscriptions as their primary income source and a broader segment of streamers who could be affected in the future as their revenues increase.

Backlash and stepping back from the precipice. The revised revenue split would substantially reduce the earnings of Twitch partners, leading to unrest within the streaming community. Consequently, some leading streamers expressed public disapproval, with some contemplating transitioning to competitor platforms. Others announced plans to run more adverts on their channels to make up for lost income, upsetting loyal viewers.[42] In the face of this backlash, Twitch offered improved access and revenue sharing for its advertising platform, but creators continued to threaten to leave for competitors such as YouTube and Kick.

After months of backlash, and only weeks after the new policy took effect, Twitch reversed course. It announced a new version of its 70/30 subscription revenue split, appeasing top creators as well as viewers and smaller creators.[43] Yet Twitch remains in a problematic position. It earns over $2 billion in revenue for its parent Amazon each year but *loses* money overall due to overwhelming costs.[44] Eventually, Twitch will need to find a balance between offering creators a fair price for their contributions and running a profitable business unit.

CASE QUESTIONS

1. Twitch is unique from many service providers in that it is a platform serving both viewers (who enjoy watching and subscribe to streamers) and streamers (who livestream for a career or hobby). How does this unique dimension affect Twitch's resource trade-off decisions?
2. Twitch's "cut" of streamers' subscription revenue may be thought of as the price Twitch collects for providing the streamers a platform. When Twitch increased its own "cut," was this a cost-, competition-, or value-based approach to pricing, and why? What about when it reversed course and decreased its own cut again?
3. Explain at least two ways that Twitch could reallocate resources and/or change its pricing strategy to improve its profitability.

CHAPTER SUMMARY

The final, perennial issue facing managers as they make marketing decisions is Marketing Principle #4: all resources are limited. A firm's marketing decisions require trade-offs across multiple objectives such as the competing priorities of marketing initiatives, so scarce resources get allocated to meet different needs, according to decisions that are closely interdependent. As a simple example, the marketing manager of just a single retail store must trade off scarce resources and efforts every month, across advertising dollars, sales staff hours, retail shelf space, and merchandise inventories for hundreds of categories—never mind the complexity involved in making such decisions for an entire chain of stores. All these marketing mix allocation decisions may be combined under the single descriptive term of resource trade-offs. This chapter highlights five key factors that accelerate the challenge of resource trade-offs: (1) Limited resource slack, (2) shifts in customers' needs, (3) shifts in the product life cycle, (4) shifts in the competitive environment, and (5) shifts in the effectiveness of marketing activities. These resource trade-off challenges are particularly critical in the context of pricing decisions. Cost-based, competitive matching, and value-based pricing strategies can affect both outflow and inflow of resources and are central to trade-off decisions.

APPLICATION QUESTIONS

1. We all face resource constraints in our daily life, too, in terms of money, time, and energy. Think of a trade-off you made in the past week. How did you arrive at your decision?
2. Consider the three questions for managing resource trade-offs. Think of a brand that you admire. Can you answer at least one of the three questions for that brand—for example, how does it allocate resources across customer relationship states?
3. Imagine you are running a small coffee shop in your hometown. Considering the five drivers of resource trade-offs, which of these would be the most difficult or unpredictable in influencing resource trade-off decisions?
4. Recall the Marketing Fail feature on movie flops as well as the Theory Spotlight on response models. Do you think it is possible to generate a response model that estimates box office revenue based on a movie's budget? What problems might a model such as that have?
5. Consider the four heuristic-based approaches to managing resource trade-offs. If you were in charge of advertising planning for a major brand, which of these four techniques would be most appealing to you? Why?
6. Consider the three pricing strategies discussed in this chapter. From the customer perspective, which feels the most fair to you, and which feels the least fair? Why?
7. Draw an imaginary demand curve for one of your favorite products. Now redraw the curve but make it more elastic. What would have to happen in the real world to make the shape of the curve change like this?

Visit the companion website, **https://bloomsbury.pub/palmatier-marketing**, or **https://samsinstitute.com**, for additional learning and teaching tools, including professional videos outlining the Four Principles, PowerPoint tutorials with voice-over commentary, sample syllabi for marketing courses, testbank and more.

Chapter 15

MANAGING RESOURCE TRADE-OFFS IN INTEGRATED MARKETING COMMUNICATIONS AND PERSONAL SELLING

CHAPTER OVERVIEW

In Chapter 14, you learned about Marketing Principle #4: all resources are limited. Nowhere is this more apparent than in integrated marketing communications (IMC). These efforts to unify the brand's communications—across advertising, salesperson effort, public relations, etc.—produce special resource trade-off challenges. The chapter will proceed by answering the following questions:

- What are integrated marketing communications, and how do they relate to previously discussed topics such as advertising?
- How can marketers successfully plan IMC campaigns?
- What is the role of the salesperson and personal selling in IMC?

In the various cases and features throughout the chapter, you will encounter brands that have taken diverse approaches to managing resource trade-offs within their IMC strategies. These include:

- A controversial marketing stunt by Paddy Power (Marketing Fail).
- Primark's efforts to rehabilitate its sustainability image (Chapter Case).
- Moral and practical issues related to IMC, such as the implications of successful IMC for Absolut (Shades of Gray) and how the field salesperson fits into an evolving digital landscape (Opposing Views).

LEARNING OBJECTIVES

- Recognize the interrelated components of integrated marketing communications.
- Understand the resource trade-off decisions in the IMC planning process.
- Identify key challenges in personal selling and sales management.
- Compare approaches to managing resource trade-offs in IMC and personal selling.

IMAGINE Selling Artificial Intelligence Tools

Source: Charanjeet Dhiman/Unsplash

Telesales representatives have difficult jobs. They must call individuals on a long list of leads, hoping that at least a small percentage will be interested in making a follow-up appointment with another representative. What would make this sort of work more appealing to you?

Imagine that you have just started a job working in telesales for a company that sells artificial intelligence-based tools to small- and medium-sized businesses. For example, your company provides custom generative AI tools (similar to ChatGPT) to help digital marketing agencies generate personalized content for social media advertisements. Your company purchased from a data broker a list of several thousand businesses that could potentially use your services. As a telesales representative your chief responsibilities include:

1. Calling and emailing businesses on this list to inform them about your services.
2. Persuading businesses to schedule an in-person product demonstration with one of your company's traveling field salespeople.
3. Keeping detailed records of your contact with these businesses, including repeated contact attempts.

Your first several weeks on the job have been challenging. Most of the businesses seem to have no interest in unsolicited phone calls and emails. When they do respond, they often seem annoyed that you have interrupted their day. Several of them explain that they have no interest in buying a hyped-up AI tool from a company they know nothing about. Even in the rare cases—less than 5 percent of the time—when a call goes well, the job is unfulfilling; after all your effort, you simply hand off the potential customer to a different salesperson and move on to the next name on the list. You wonder why these businesses are so uninterested in speaking with you and what the point is in setting up an appointment with the field salesperson.

Critical thinking:

1. In this scenario, what weaknesses do you see in the company's approach to communicating with potential customers? How might they improve this approach?
2. Here, two different salespeople (a telesales rep and a field salesperson) communicate with the customer. In your opinion, what are the potential advantages and disadvantages of this approach?

WHAT ARE INTEGRATED MARKETING COMMUNICATIONS?

Integrated Marketing Communications Explained

The modern marketing communications landscape is complex. For example, for the launch of the PlayStation 5 video game console, Japanese tech giant Sony designed a many-pronged multimedia campaign. They worked with marketing agency Amplify to coordinate a diverse set of costly communications to maximize hype for the launch, which consisted of:

1. standard television, search engine, and social media advertisements;
2. posts on YouTube, Facebook, and other social media; and
3. elaborate outdoor promotional stunts, including a ten-minute projection light show in London's Piccadilly Circus.[1]

integrated marketing communications (IMC) Allocating resources across multiple media and messaging channels that complement one another to influence customers and build brand equity

How did Sony and Amplify choose which elements to include in the campaign and what messaging to use? How did they decide which types of advertising would pay off or whether stunts such as the outdoor light shows were worthwhile? These sorts of resource trade-off questions are fundamental to **integrated marketing communications (IMC)**. IMC involves allocating resources across multiple media and messaging channels that complement one another to influence customers and build brand equity.[2] Throughout this chapter, we discuss how IMC incorporates what we learned in Chapter 11 about advertising—one of the most important messaging tools—with Marketing Principle #4 (all resources are limited) to see how advertising works together with other communications vehicles. Table 15.1 describes several high-profile examples of IMC campaigns.

Integrated marketing communications are best understood as part of a strategy or campaign (such as Sony's above) consisting of different communications elements. These elements can include:

1. advertising on television, radio, billboard, print (magazines, etc.) and other traditional channels
2. paper mail, such as flyers and catalogs, sent directly to customers' mailboxes (typically called *direct mail*)
3. embedded website adverts (banners, videos, etc.)
4. paid search adverts and paid social media adverts
5. messages posted on the brand's social media accounts, such as Twitter (X) and TikTok
6. public relations efforts, including public statements on the website and to the media, remarks made in interviews, and communications to investors (such as annual reports)
7. promotional email messages
8. mobile marketing, such as promotional notifications from apps

Table 15.1 Examples of Successful IMC Campaigns.

Advertising and public relations agencies help many companies design and launch successful IMC campaigns. Some of these examples are proactive strategies while others are reacting to a threat or problem.

Brand	Agency	Campaign	IMC channels	Explanation	Result
Hulu	*Max Pollak*	*HAHA Awards*	*YouTube; Twitter; website*	In 2020, streaming service Hulu noticed a gap in the awards show landscape: there was no awards show focused specifically on animated television. Hulu launched the Hilarious Animated Hulu awards (HAHA) to remedy this. The streamer used adverts on the Hulu platform itself as well as YouTube, and encouraged voting for awards on Twitter.	A successful launch of the HAHA awards with nearly half a million votes cast on Twitter
Aldi	*McCann Manchester*	*#FreeCuthbert*	*Twitter; public relations (e.g., talk show appearances)*	In 2021, Aldi's UK rival Marks & Spencer sued Aldi over Aldi's Cuthbert the Caterpillar cake, which allegedly was too similar to M&S's Colin the Caterpillar cake. Rather than face the legal questions head-on, Aldi embarked on a social media and public relations blitz, including appearances by Cuthbert himself on talk shows, to make Marks & Spencer's lawsuit look ridiculous.	Marks and Spencer settled the issue with Aldi and dropped the lawsuit, letting Cuthbert go
Old Spice	*Wieden + Kennedy*	*Smell like a man*	*Television adverts; YouTube; Twitter; Reddit; other social media*	By 2010, Old Spice had learned that a man's body wash purchases are often influenced by his partner. This inspired a Super Bowl advertisement focusing on "The Man Your Man Could Smell Like," which became a viral hit. Old Spice leveraged the viral success by interacting directly with consumers on social media and posting response videos on YouTube.	Sales doubled in a matter of months
Sony	*Amplify*	*PlayStation 5 launch*	*Television; outdoor; YouTube; Facebook*	In 2020, Sony was launching its hotly anticipated new video game console, the PlayStation 5. Sony wanted to maximize consumer hype and excitement for the launch. In addition to traditional advertising, Sony employed unique projection light shows and other outdoor installations in twenty-five major cities. For example, in London, Sony put on a ten-minute light show at Piccadilly Circus and changed Underground signs at Oxford Circus to reflect the four main button shapes of the PlayStation Controller.	PS5 preorders sold out, with subsequent restocks of the system also quickly selling out
The New York Times	*Droga5*	*The truth is hard*	*Short films; Facebook; Twitter; Instagram*	In 2018, US newspaper *The New York Times* was facing falling subscriber numbers as fewer people wanted to pay for news from media outlets that they trusted less and less. To improve their public image and boost subscriptions, *The New York Times* created a series of impactful short films about the value of journalism, first shown at the 2018 Oscars and later posted across various social media.	Over 5 billion social media ad impressions and a 100 percent increase in signups

9. sales promotions, such as contests, sweepstakes, and mail-in rebates
10. communications from various frontline employees and salespeople; these can be in-person, over the phone, via Zoom and other videoconferencing tools, and through email

Over time, elements are introduced or altered. For example, generative AI tools such as ChatGPT are being used to mass-customize advertising content on the web.[3] And changing customer preferences (Marketing Principle #2) mean that some communications elements become less important or are even phased out. The closure of many local newspapers has virtually eliminated print newspaper advertising in many markets.[4]

Why Are IMC Trade-offs Challenging?

As we can see, companies have a dizzying array of choices! Each of these are costly, even those that may initially appear costless. For example, in 2021, international supermarket chain Aldi faced a legal challenge from its UK competitor Marks & Spencer. M&S claimed that Aldi's Cuthbert the Caterpillar birthday cake illegally copied Marks & Spencer's famous Colin the Caterpillar cake. Aldi took on this challenge in the court of public opinion. It used a combination of cheeky #FreeCuthbert social media posts and appearances by a Cuthbert mascot on television talk shows to make its rival look foolish for blowing up such a trivial issue; Marks & Spencer eventually withdrew the lawsuit.[5]

Aldi was technically able to post messages on its social media accounts for free, but in practice it incurred many expenses, such as paying a professional social media manager to oversee the content and paying a designer to craft images used in the posts. Likewise, while appearing on a television program might not seem expensive, in reality Aldi needed to pay multiple actors to play the Cuthbert mascot, design and produce costumes, plan a script for the appearances, and coordinate travel for actors and support staff. All the while, Aldi was also paying its marketing agency McCann Manchester to plan and coordinate this IMC strategy. Although this strategy was not free, it was likely a wise resource investment that saved Aldi on the costs of legal representation and potential legal penalties.

Managing IMC is getting more difficult for multiple reasons:

1. Traditional advertising such as television commercials are getting less effective over time, even in industries such as film where they remain important.[6]
2. As the number of options increases (e.g., with the advent of mobile marketing), the menu of possible pairings and combinations of media multiplies. This is important because communications media work can complement one another. For example, some car insurance salespeople

pay for billboard adverts; these might have little effect on their own, but they can increase brand awareness, which might make the salesperson's job easier.[7]

3. And in business-to-business settings, deciding how to allocate resources to salespeople is growing more complex, as customers have higher expectations of salespeople and newer ways of communicating (e.g., Zoom and videoconferencing) become more important.

Therefore, modern IMC strategies involve complicated resource trade-off decisions among an evolving and interrelated set of options for communicating with existing and potential customers. Deciding which choices will maximize brand equity and sustainable competitive advantages is not straightforward, and the wrong decisions can lead to wasted time and money.

IN OTHER WORDS ...

Chapter 11 focused on advertising, or messages (typically paid) that the firm places in channels such as social media and television to influence customers' attitudes and behaviors. Under an integrated marketing communications (IMC) strategy, advertising works together with other communications to achieve a common goal. Sales promotions, public relations, salesperson communication, and other statements made by the company should work together in a cohesive strategy. For example, web advertising can generate brand awareness among customers, making them easier for salespeople to persuade. IMC is complex because it involves resource trade-offs between many interrelated ways of communicating with customers.

Source: Grzegorz Kaliciak/Unsplash

On their own, billboards such as those visible in this photograph from Japan's famous Shibuya Crossing, might have little effect on consumers. But when combined with complementary prongs of an IMC campaign, such as more detailed social media advertising, they can serve as important tools to reinforce the brand and remind consumers to buy.

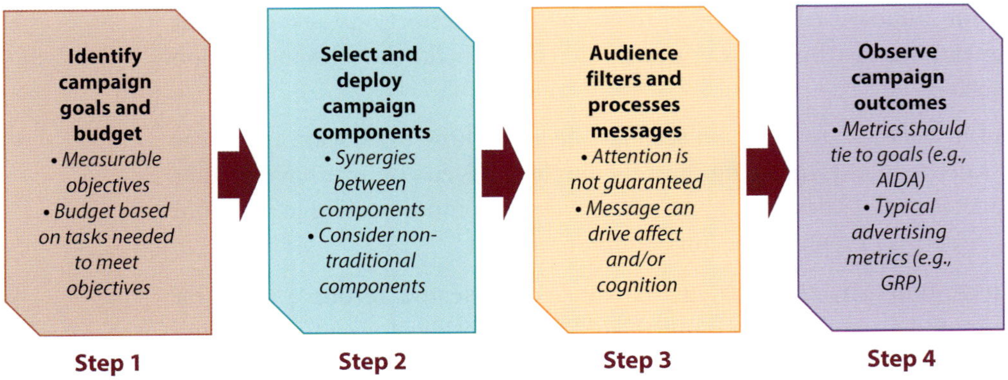

Figure 15.1 IMC Planning Process.

These four steps encapsulate the typical process for planning an integrated marketing communications campaign: (1) identify campaign goals and budget; (2) select and deploy campaign components; (3) audience filters and processes messages; and (4) observe campaign outcomes.

A PROCESS FOR IMC PLANNING

Given the difficulty of managing resource trade-offs in an IMC strategy, how can marketers ensure success? Unfortunately, there is no one-size-fits-all approach. In this section, we describe a four-step process that applies to most IMC strategies. Each of the four steps in this section (and in Figure 15.1) draws attention to the factors marketers must consider and the decisions that they must make:

1. The marketers identify the campaign goals and budget.
2. The marketers select and deploy the campaign components.
3. The audience filters and processes the messages.
4. The marketers observe the campaign outcomes.[8]

Step 1: Identify Campaign Goals and Budget

The process of setting goals for an IMC campaign involves selecting a target audience (e.g., young, suburban professionals) and a measurable objective (e.g., raise brand awareness by 10 percent) with respect to that audience. Objectives should relate directly to moving customers along the decision journey described in Chapter 5 (need recognition, initial consideration, active evaluation, and buying). An objective to raise brand awareness, for example, would help the brand enter the customers' mind in the initial consideration stage.

Decisions about audiences and objectives were already described with respect to advertising campaigns in Chapter 11, so we will not rehash that discussion. By way of example, though, in 2018, US newspaper *The New York Times* was struggling with declining print and digital subscriptions as well as plummeting advertising revenue. The paper's goal was to move from negative growth into positive growth among the segment of young adult-to-middle-age consumers who had grown distrustful of traditional news outlets. In collaboration with marketing agency Droga5, *The New York Times* launched a campaign across television (in particular, the Oscars awards show), Facebook, Twitter, and Instagram. This campaign featured short films with impactful messages about the value of journalism. The campaign achieved its goal, leading to a 100 percent increase in subscription signups.[9]

Once the goals are set, the campaign requires a workable budget. Deciding on the right resources to devote to the campaign is challenging, especially as marketing budgets are coming under more scrutiny within companies.[10] One common method of managing limited resources in the IMC budget is the **objective and task technique**. In this approach, marketers undergo a series of steps to set the budget:[11]

objective and task technique A multistep IMC budgeting technique in which the budget is determined by the tasks needed to meet the campaign objectives

1. Based on the selected audience and *objective*, determine what types of communications can feasibly reach them. For example, the younger-leaning primary audience of *The New York Times* campaign above would likely be difficult to reach with radio advertisements.
2. Gathering information about the audience and studying how receptive they will be to the different feasible communications methods such as advertising, salespeople, and public relations. This knowledge includes the ability to predict the level of advertising response (see the feature on response models in Chapter 14) and how different media complement one another. For example, salespeople are known to be more effective when the company invests enough in advertising.[12] Making these predictions also requires a smartly designed program of ongoing market research (see Chapter 9).
3. Based on these predictions and knowledge about the audience, determine what *tasks* are needed to meet the objective. These tasks include the adverts to be placed, in specific channels, at specific intervals (see Chapter 11 on the advertising planning process), as well as other communications (such as those from salespeople) that are needed to meet the objective.
4. Once the specific IMC tasks are known, a budget can be set by getting estimates from those who generate the communications (the company's own executives, advertising agencies, etc.).

The advantage of the objective and task technique is that *the budget is determined entirely by the need to meet the specific IMC campaign objectives.* More basic methods, such as setting the communications budget as a percentage of past sales, do not have this benefit.

Step 2: Select and Deploy Campaign Components

If the company closely follows the objective and task technique above, the decision about which components to use might already be made. Nonetheless, it is extremely challenging to sort out how well the various options will work, individually or in concert (see "What Are Integrated Marketing Communications?," above). IMC components broadly fall into two categories: interactive and noninteractive.[13] Each category includes *both* "traditional" and "new" media (see Chapter 11). As emphasized earlier, marketers must account for the interrelated nature of these different tools and their synergies with one another when deciding which ones to deploy and how to divide limited resources.

interactive communications Communications that not only allow messages from the company to customers but also from customers to the company

social media communications Messages the brand posts on social media to promote products or respond to an ongoing issue or controversy

Interactive Communications

Interactive communications are those that not only allow messages from the company to customers but also from customers to the company. They include:

1. **Social media communications**, or messages the brand posts on social media to promote products or respond to an ongoing issue or controversy. As long as social media posts do not completely disable comments from consumers, they are interactive. Social media is important not only for its own effectiveness but because it has been shown to increase consumer responsiveness to traditional communications such as television adverts and in-store coupons.[14] For example, in 2010, the men's body wash brand Old Spice launched its famous "The man your man could smell like" campaign. Although it started with a Super Bowl advert, it took an aggressively interactive approach on social media. The brand's Twitter and Reddit accounts responded directly to customers, and its YouTube channel posted video responses to customer questions. The campaign, masterminded by marketing agency Wieden + Kennedy, revitalized what had been a stagnant brand.[15]

mobile marketing Promotional actions targeted to customers' mobile devices, typically through an app

2. **Mobile marketing,** defined as promotional actions targeted to customers' mobile devices, typically through an app. These actions usually give customers some opportunity to interact through the app. For example, US restaurant chain Chick Fil A delivers app notifications about surveys customers can take to earn rewards.

sales promotions Unique communications designed to act as an immediate incentive to buy

3. **Sales promotions** are unique communications designed to act as an immediate incentive to buy. Some promotions are interactive in that they require customer participation, especially contests (skill-based competitions) and sweepstakes (luck-based competitions). Snack brand Oreo's #MYOreo Creation Contest, for example, invites customers to design and submit new flavors, which are judged on taste and creativity. The winner receives $500,000 and gets to see their flavor sold in stores.[16]
4. Messages from salespeople and other frontline employees. Salespeople are a long-standing and critical part of IMC strategy (discussed in more detail in "How Salespeople Make IMC Personal," below).

noninteractive communications One-way messages to which the customer cannot easily respond

Noninteractive Communications

Noninteractive communications, then, are one-way messages to which the customer cannot easily respond. Examples of these are:

direct mail Physical print material that the company sends to customers' mailboxes

email marketing Email messages targeted to specific customers' digital inboxes

1. Communications using traditional advertising media such as print, billboard, television, and radio. These are described in detail in Chapter 11.
2. **Direct mail** includes physical print material that the company sends to customers' mailboxes. These can be simple print adverts, product catalogs, or promotions such as coupons. **Email marketing**, defined as email messages targeted to specific customers' digital inboxes, serve a similar purpose.

3. **Web advertising** includes paid messages that the customer encounters while browsing the internet. Examples of web advertising include display adverts (banners, videos, etc.) embedded in news articles and sponsored links at the top of search engine results. These sponsored links, specifically, are known as **search engine marketing** and have historically been critical ways for customers to learn about brands.[17] The increasing use of generative AI tools such as ChatGPT to get information (bypassing search engines entirely) has created uncertainty about the future of search engine marketing.[18]

web advertising Paid messages that the customer encounters while browsing the internet

search engine marketing Sponsored links at the top of search engine results

4. Aside from contests and sweepstakes, many types of sales promotions are not interactive. Mail-in rebates, free trial or free sample offers, and cardboard displays in the store do not encourage customers to communicate with the brand in any meaningful way.
5. **Public relations (PR)** are also a key part of the IMC toolkit. PR is defined as direct statements, by the company or its leaders, to the media, investors, or society at large. PR can be applied proactively, for example, by Primark in the chapter's case to improve its sustainability image. Marketers can also use PR reactively; in the earlier Aldi and Cuthbert the Caterpillar example, the PR strategy focused on responding to Marks & Spencer's accusations.

public relations (PR) Direct statements, by the company or its leaders, to the media, investors, or society at large

Step 3: Audience Filters and Processes Messages

Unlike the other steps, this one occurs in the minds of customers. Once the company's messages are out in the wild, they must be received. But this does not always happen the way the company hopes it will. Individuals have limited attention—as emphasized in Chapter 14, all resources are limited! We are surrounded by information, messages, and stimuli throughout the day: conversations, phone notifications, background noise and music, distractions from peers, children, or coworkers, and communications from brands. We must decide how to divide limited attention between these different demands.

Consumers do this through **information filtering**, meaning that they ignore or de-emphasize incoming information and stimuli that seem to be less urgent, believable, or important. Advertising can fall into this category; since consumers know the brand has an ulterior motive to sell products, they often distrust and filter out marketing communications.[19] One way to think about whether customers will pay attention to IMC efforts is the **motivation-ability-opportunity** test: (1) do they gain something from paying attention (motivation), (2) are they capable of processing the information (ability), and (3) do they have time to listen (opportunity)?[20] For example, a commuter on a subway train might have the opportunity to read adverts posted on the train but see no advantage in doing this instead of looking at their phone. This limited attention raises the stakes for marketers to avoid wasting resources on IMC elements that will be ignored.

information filtering Consumers ignoring or de-emphasizing incoming information and stimuli that seem to be less urgent, believable, or important

motivation-ability-opportunity A perspective on the three conditions necessary for an individual to spend effort on something (like paying attention)

MARKETING FAIL Paddy Power Courts Controversy

Earlier in the chapter, Aldi playfully used a legal controversy to its advantage in its IMC campaign. This is not an uncommon approach; after all, as the old adage goes, there is no such thing as bad publicity. But is that really true? Paddy Power, a major Irish gambling company (owned by Flutter, whose other subsidiaries include Betfair and FanDuel), put it to the test in 2015.

Paddy Power had long been running a campaign that used both social media and outdoor advertising (such as billboards) to push messages with an edgy, irreverent, attention-grabbing brand of humor. For example, in 2010 it ran an advert on television and digital media showing a blind athlete kicking a cat into a tree, sparking complaints. In 2014, when it was controversially allowing bets on the outcome of the murder trial of paralympic star and double amputee sprinter Oscar Pistorius, it offered to pay "money back if he walks." The distasteful pun, like the previous campaign, led to complaints and the adverts eventually being discontinued following an order from the United Kingdom's Advertising Standards Authority.[21]

When Paddy Power continued this strategy in 2015, it ran into problems. This time, it emblazoned the side of a truck with "Immigrants, jump in the back! (But only if you're good at sport)" along with a picture of notable immigrant athletes, in addition to Scottish tennis star Andy Murray. According to Paddy Power, it was primarily a joke about how "Andy Murray is Scottish when he loses and British when he wins."[22] Yet whatever the intent may have been, the fact that the advert appeared on the side of a cargo truck, and the fact that the truck traveled from Dover to Calais, made the situation more complicated. The advert was run in the middle of a major migrant crisis, in which Dover and Calais were primary immigration centers and migrants were regularly smuggled on cargo vehicles, sometimes leading to their deaths.[23] The advert resulted in a fierce backlash, a record number of complaints, and a censure from the Advertising Standards Authority. Although it may have succeeded in grabbing attention, the campaign likely hurt Paddy Power's image worse than it had planned.

Ireland

Diagnose the problem:

1. Paddy Power's approach to using controversy to grab attention in its communications was consistent. How was the 2015 incident similar to the 2014 incident, and how was it different?
2. In your view, was there any way that Paddy Power could have softened the messaging in its 2015 campaign while retaining its irreverent brand image?

Assuming consumers pay attention to the messages, they can process them in several ways (some of these ways have been noted in Chapter 5 [how marketing mix elements influence the decision journey] and Chapter 11 [how different advertising appeals work]):

cognition Rational thoughts about an object, such as an advertisement or brand

affect Feelings and emotions about an object, such as an advertisement or brand

- Consumers might think rationally about the claims that the brand is making. In this case, they are activating **cognition**, that is, thinking. Information appeals typically aim to engage cognition.
- Consumers might process the message in terms of their emotions and feelings, known as **affect**. Emotional appeals tend to target this pathway.

Source: takahiro taguchi/Unsplash

Marketing messages don't always reach their audience. Distractions are one reason for this. For example, the various messages on this subway train get very little attention from commuters that are distracted by their phones and the noise of the train.

- As marketers consider how messages will be processed in terms of cognition and affect, they must also keep in mind that the consumers' **experiences**—past events that are relevant to the message, including experience with other messages from the brand—can influence whether the message is viewed as credible or not.[24]

experiences Past events in the consumer's life that are relevant to the message, including experience with other messages from the brand

Ultimately, based on how the audience filters and processes information, they might move forward in their buying decision journeys in ways that are favorable to the brand (such as buying) or not.

Step 4: Observe Campaign Outcomes

Finally, after the audience has been exposed to the campaign, filtered and processed the messages, and taken action (or not) on their decision journeys, marketers get to see the fruits of their labors. Did the campaign rocket the brand to success, or fail to launch?

The most important consideration here is to judge the success of the campaign *strictly by the measurable goals set out at the* beginning, whether these are specific levels of brand awareness, sales, gross rating points, or some other metric (see Step 1 and also Chapter 11). It is easy for marketers to decide, after a campaign, that the original goal was unrealistically high and pat themselves on the back for a successful effort. It is similar to a student who, after setting out

THEORY SPOTLIGHT Information Integration

When consumers process messages from different sources, such as the same brand's adverts on Instagram and TikTok, how do they make sense of it? Information integration theory provides a useful way for marketers to think about this problem in designing IMC strategy.

In the **information integration theory**, consumers make a decision by "adding" information from different sources, almost like a math equation, but they give different "weights" to each source of information. If a source is more believable—for example, if a trusted friend speaks highly of the brand—it gets a higher weight, and it may retroactively increase the weights applied to consistent information that was received before (e.g., an advertising message). And if the information is not consistent, such as when a television ad contradicts what the trusted friend said, a consumer will give it less weight. Also, if a consumer hears from one source of information before others, it might give later adverts and sources of information less weight, since the advert is no longer providing the first impression of a product.[25] Consumers giving less weight to a piece of information is called **information discounting**.

Thinking about IMC from an information integration perspective has several advantages for marketers:

1. It changes the focus of decision-making away from "How much should I spend on each type of advertising and other communications?" toward "What conversation am I having with each individual consumer?"
2. By thinking about these individual "conversations," the company can think critically about how, when, and in what environment its messages reach its audience. For example, are messages reaching consumers when they are distracted and not paying much attention, resulting in information discounting?
3. The company can also carefully evaluate how to maximize the weight given to its messages, for example, by using trusted influencers or celebrity endorsers to increase credibility.

information integration theory A perspective holding that consumers make a decision by "adding" information from different sources, almost like a math equation, but they give different "weights" to each source of information

information discounting Consumers giving less weight to a piece of information

hindsight bias People believing, after the fact, that they knew more than they truly did

personal selling Direct, one-on-one communication with a current or potential customer to inspire purchases

for college with the goal of getting no grade lower than a B, gets a C in organic chemistry and declares that he was actually aiming for at least a B *on average*.

This phenomenon is known as **hindsight bias**: people believe, after the fact, that they knew more than they truly did.[26] While the student example is harmless, hindsight bias is a major threat to IMC strategies. If marketers cannot be honest about whether they have met their goals, they will not recognize their failures; and if they do not see their failures, they won't improve their strategies.

HOW SALESPEOPLE MAKE IMC PERSONAL

Salespeople (often called sales representatives or simply "reps") are one of the oldest components of integrated marketing communications strategies. Salespeople's fundamental task is **personal selling**, defined as direct, one-on-one communication with a current or potential customer to inspire purchases.[27]

Although most salespeople would not call themselves marketers, they are indeed a key piece of the IMC puzzle. They are also, perhaps surprisingly, the primary marketing-related job role in terms of total employment. In the United States, over 50 percent of university graduates find their first job in a

? SHADES OF GRAY The Problem of Absolut's Success

Absolut is a well-known Swedish vodka brand owned by the massive French spirits conglomerate Pernod Ricard. Absolut's IMC strategy has been remarkably consistent and successful. Beginning in the 1980s, when Absolut started working with New York-based advertising agency TBWA, Absolut began an iconic campaign across print and television media that simply featured the Absolut bottle with the tagline "Absolute Perfection." These adverts were paired with special edition bottlings that attracted collectors, putting the bottle at the center of the brand's messaging. This trend continued into the social media era.[28] After the COVID-19 pandemic subsided, Absolut modernized this approach with the digital-focused "Born to mix" campaign, emphasizing popular vodka-based mixed drinks and including messages about inclusivity.[29]

This chapter focuses on how marketers can maximize the effectiveness of IMC strategies, and Absolut has done a good job of that. But what happens when effective IMC is not in the best interests of society or individual consumers? This is arguably the case for **vice goods**, meaning products or services "that consumers are likely to overconsume … although they would later regret doing so."[30] This is a broad and subjective category, and includes extreme examples such as illicit drugs as well as common goods, for instance, ice cream and even some video games.

Sweden

Vodka is generally seen as a vice good. Spirits are heavily intoxicating and often abused. Alcohol abuse does immense harm to society, contributing to mental illness, unemployment, unstable households, and violence.[31] Because of this, governments and regulators face a dilemma when it comes to companies that market and sell spirits. On the one hand, they have a duty to protect free competition in the marketplace by allowing companies to advertise how they see fit. On the other hand, they have a duty to serve the common good and reduce harm in society. Different countries' regulators have landed at different decisions on this. For example, Norway has banned all marketing messages about alcohol since 1975, and this has reduced alcohol consumption by almost 10 percent.[32] Meanwhile, other European countries have taken a less extreme approach focused on public service messages to young adults (e.g., "Responsible party") and restricted advertising to children.[33]

Ethical dilemmas:

1. Who is potentially harmed by effective hard liquor (spirits) IMC campaigns such as those done by Absolut? How are they harmed?
2. Consider the dilemma that regulators have, as described above. In your opinion, how should they handle this issue? Is Norway's approach justified? Why or why not?

selling role![34] Universities have responded to this demand, offering certificate and degree programs in professional selling—you may have one at your own university—with more than 90 percent of students from these programs quickly finding jobs in sales.[35]

vice goods Products or services that consumers tend to overconsume, and regret doing so

Personal Selling's Importance and Synergies with Other IMC Components

Why does personal selling get its own section in this chapter? Salespeople are a vital tool for building relationship equity, especially in B2B selling situations, as noted in Chapter 13. But beyond this, persona selling has a special role in the IMC mix for three reasons:

1. It is *powerful*. It is the only element of IMC strategy that allows the company to have a direct, one-on-one conversation with a customer. This minimizes filtering and allows more influence over how the customer processes information.
2. It is *expensive*, by far the most expensive element of the communications mix on a per-customer basis. A single sales call often costs upwards of $200, due to the expense of paying the salesperson for their time.[36] It can take many salespeople to adequately meet the needs of all customers—creating countless attractive sales jobs for young university graduates!
3. It is *in conflict* with other elements of the communications mix, at least in many companies. This is a marketing textbook, and given that marketing is the customer discipline, we view personal selling as a part of marketing. Yet this is not the case within most companies. Marketing has its own department, typically led by a Vice President of Marketing, while sales has a separate division, often spearheaded by a Vice President of Sales. Marketers and salespeople often have different backgrounds, personalities, and skillsets due to the different demands of their jobs; marketers tend to specialize in analytical or creative skills, while salespeople love to make personal connections with buyers. The culture of sales and marketing departments differs, too, with salespeople receiving heavy **commission**—special pay calculated as a percentage of sales—and other incentive pay, leading to intensely competitive cultures, while marketers often lack these incentives. As a result, salespeople and marketers can end up "feud[ing] like Capulets and Montagues."[37] It is hard to manage resource trade-offs between two departments that are at war!

commission Salesperson incentive pay calculated as a percentage of sales

On top of its importance, the potential synergy between salespeople and other elements of IMC is noteworthy. Direct mail adverts have been shown to generate a greater response when the customer is also in contact with an experienced salesperson.[38] Direct mail and other mass-market advertising methods can lead a small percentage of potential customers to call the firm, creating opportunities for salespeople to close deals.[39] Salespeople are also a key part of B2B brands' presence at events such as trade shows and conventions, where they can speak face to face with current and potential business partners; moreover, manufacturers that build awareness with a major presence at these events find that their salespeople have an easier time selling afterward.[40]

As we can see, salespeople can be some of the most important pieces in an IMC strategy and can be complementary with other elements.

OPPOSING VIEWS What Is the Role of Field Salespeople?

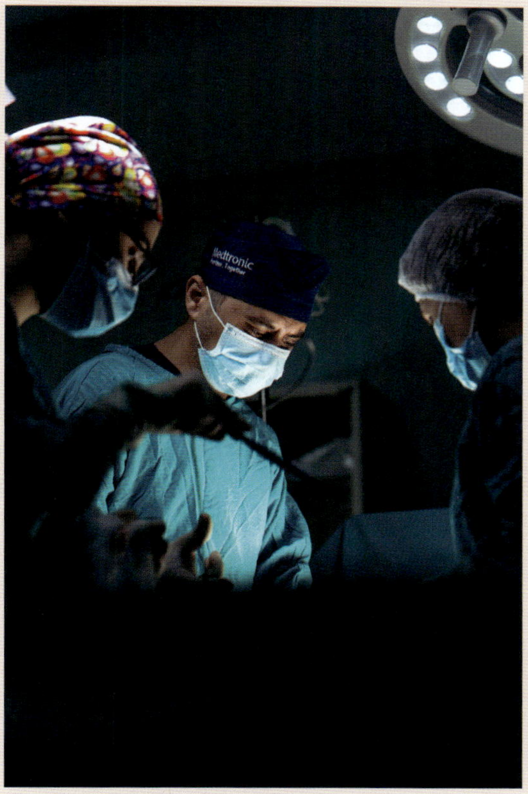

Source: Akram Huseyn/Unsplash

Many sales tasks can only be performed with an on-site visit. For example, sales representatives from medical device manufacturers such as Stryker and Medtronic help physicians as they learn device-enhanced techniques, such as laparoscopic surgery.

The traditional sales job is field sales. Field salespeople (also called outside salespeople) travel to the customer in-person to discuss customer needs, make presentations, negotiate deals, and close sales. Before widespread access to telecommunications, this was the only way to reach customers. Automobile salespeople, for example, would travel door-to-door to visit potential customers.

The growth of communications technology, including the telephone and later the internet, created different kinds of sales jobs, such as the "telesales" role described in this chapter's introductory "Imagine . . . " feature. **Telesales reps** can make outbound calls to lists of potential customers and receive inbound calls when customers place orders or ask questions. Another kind of sales job is "inside sales." Similar to telesales reps, inside salespeople do not visit customers in person. **Inside salespeople** manage an assigned territory or set of customer relationships over time, and therefore act much like field salespeople (but without the field visits). Inside salespeople are a growing part of the sales force, making up a majority of reps within many companies.[41]

Germany

At the same time, many business-to-business customers now prefer ordering online instead of buying from a salesperson at all. This leaves the proper role of the field salesperson in the IMC mix uncertain.[42] Companies now take drastically different approaches. German construction supply company Hilti, for example, still maintains an extensive field sales force. It augments these field sales reps with digital tools, such as automated predictions of when a customer's equipment will need replacing. Insurance company Allianz, also based in Germany, has gone in a different direction, as it replaced most of its field salespeople with digital self-service tools such as online insurance quotes.[43] Other companies combine field salespeople with inside salespeople, for example, by having outside salespeople find new customers and inside salespeople service existing customers.[44] Going forward, companies will approach a new equilibrium in terms of their mixes of inside and field salespeople.

See the issue from two sides:

1. Craft an argument in favor of abandoning the field sales model. Why should companies stop having salespeople visit customers in person?
2. Craft an argument against abandoning the field sales model. What unique value does visiting customers in person provide? If field salespeople are kept in place, what is the best way to use other salespeople, such as telesales reps and inside salespeople?

inside salespeople Salespeople who manage an assigned territory or set of customer relationships over time, and act much like field salespeople (but without the field visits)

telesales reps Salespeople who make outbound calls to lists of potential customers and receive inbound calls when customers place orders or ask questions

Trade-offs among Six Steps of Selling

Much of the expense and difficulty in selling comes from the need to complete multiple steps just to close a single sale. In some industries—consider closing a major deal for a fleet of passenger jets—one sale can take months as these steps unfold. Depending on how the firm (and the salesperson) divide resources across these six steps, they may have a smooth pipeline of deals being closed and sales being made, or an unreliable and rocky flow of revenue. For example, spending too much time trying to find potential customers (step 1 below) can overwhelm the salesperson with leads, without leading to any actual sales. In this section, we outline these steps.

six steps of selling The six phases that must be executed for a salesperson to acquire and serve a new customer

Although the activities needed to close a sale can be broken down or combined into a different number of steps, here we view them as **six steps of selling**—the six phases that must be executed for a salesperson to acquire and serve a new customer. Sometimes, different salespeople handle different parts of the process (see this chapter's introductory feature), and the sales process can involve other steps when trying to sell to current customers (e.g., steps 1 and 2 below might be skipped).[45] It is also worth mentioning that this process might be abbreviated in B2C settings, for example, at a jewelry store, a salesperson might complete most of the process in a single conversation. But in general, the six steps (see Figure 15.2) include:

1. prospecting
2. qualification
3. pre-approach
4. value proposition
5. closing the sale
6. follow-up

Figure 15.2 Six Steps of Selling.

An example of a typical series of steps that a salesperson might take with a new customer. This process is not rigid and might work differently depending on the sales job and situation. For example, with current customers, "prospecting" is more about finding opportunities to deepen the existing relationship rather than casting a wide net for potential new customers. Also, the same salesperson might not handle the entire process.

Step 1: Prospecting—Where Do I Find Customers?

Prospecting is the search for information about potential customers. Potential customers are also known as **leads**. Prospecting can take many forms. Some common ways include:

prospecting The search for information about potential customers

leads Potential customers

1. the salesperson cold-calling (i.e., calling or emailing strangers)
2. taking leads that telesales has already cold-called (these may already be qualified, see step 2)
3. buying or otherwise obtaining lists of leads

Prospecting has long been considered one of the least desirable tasks for salespeople, since it can involve a lot of impersonal conversations that do not lead to sales, as well as a lot of rejection.[46] No one likes to be told "no" all day! Yet failure to devote resources to prospecting can cause a salesperson's pipeline to dry up, as they run out of deals to work on and find themselves missing out on bonus pay.

Step 2: Qualification—Are My Leads Worth My Selling Time?

Qualification involves making sure that (1) the firm's products have a reasonable chance of meeting the potential customer's needs, and (2) the potential customer has the ability to buy.[47] For example, if a salesperson's company exclusively sells electric trucks for use in commercial fleets, then potential customers that are only interested in non-electric trucks, or consumers who can't buy a fleet, are not very good leads. Leads who meet the company's qualification criteria are often called **prospects**. As noted above, if telesales reps pass leads to other salespeople after a first phone conversation, these leads might already be qualified prospects.

qualification Making sure that (1) the firm's products have a reasonable chance of meeting the potential customer's needs, and (2) the potential customer has the ability to buy

prospects Leads who meet the company's qualification criteria

Together, prospecting and qualification are the front-end or early phase of the sales process. Spending resources on qualification is vital because, otherwise, salespeople can waste time in the later phases on individuals or companies that had no real chance of buying.

Step 3: Pre-approach—What Selling Strategy Should I Use with the Prospect?

Next begins the middle phase of the sales process. At this point, the salesperson has zeroed in on a specific customer where there is a reasonable chance of success. In **pre-approach**, the salesperson does their homework and researches the prospect. In the case of B2B sales, this involves detailed analysis of public information about the company and looking through any existing internal records (e.g., from attempted sales in the past).

pre-approach The salesperson doing research about the prospect

The goal is to identify who the decision-makers in the company are, understand the decision-making process, and plan out what products might best meet their needs. Essentially, the salesperson needs to understand the organizational buying decision journey (see Chapter 5). For example, a medical imaging equipment manufacturer selling to a large hospital might find out that several doctors and managers will influence which machine the hospital buys, and each have slightly different preferences about the machine's features.

If salespeople don't invest resources in the pre-approach stage, they might walk into sales meetings with people who have no influence over the buying decision or make the wrong sales pitch entirely.

Step 4: Value Proposition—How Do I Meet the Prospect's Needs?

value proposition A statement of how the seller's goods and services will benefit the customer

This step involves using the knowledge from step 3 to design and present a **value proposition**, or a statement of how the seller's goods and services will benefit the customer. Value propositions are best constructed by taking the customer's perspective and being able to explain, in concrete terms, how they will have easier lives, save money, perform better, or gain some other advantage from buying the seller's products. In the medical imaging example above, this could involve selling a machine that will reduce expenses by requiring maintenance 50 percent less often. Given the need to focus on the customer perspective, getting marketers involved at this stage can boost the salesperson's success. This can be difficult given the historic sales–marketing conflict noted earlier, but some companies have managed it. For example, *sales and marketing selling centers*—formal teams of salespeople and marketers that may be temporary or permanent—aid in developing more effective value propositions.

Naturally, a lack of effort and resources put into crafting a value proposition will lead to underwhelming sales presentations and a reduced success rate.

Step 5: Closing the Sale—How Can I Reach an Agreement with the Prospect?

closing the sale Getting the customer to definitively commit to buying

The final step before a prospect becomes a customer is **closing the sale**, or getting the customer to definitively commit to buying. This can be a handshake, a written signature, or a filled-out web form, but in each case it signals that the deal is complete. There are two main challenges in this stage. The first is getting the customer to commit; buyers often like to keep their options open as long as possible, so salespeople must show persistence and assertiveness to succeed.[48] The second is negotiating the terms of a deal, with price often being a sticking point. Salespeople tend to have better luck negotiating when the buyer believes that the salesperson has their best interests at heart.[49]

If salespeople do not put enough resources into closing sales, they will end up with poorly negotiated, underpriced deals or, worse, no deals at all.

Step 6: Follow-Up—How Do I Keep the Customer Coming Back?

follow-up The salesperson continuing to activate the relationship after closing the sale

If closing the sale was the final step in making a deal, what remains? As Chapter 13 emphasized, relationship equity only comes with loyalty and repeat purchasing. **Follow-up** means that the salesperson continues to activate the relationship after closing the sale. This can be as simple as checking in on the customer via email or phone on a regular basis, making sure they are satisfied with their purchase, and proactively looking to meet more of their needs in the future. Continuing the medical imaging example above, after the hospital buys an expensive imaging machine, the salesperson would benefit from keeping a close eye on the machine's performance and ensuring that the medical staff have no issues with it.

Failure to bother devoting resources to follow-up can result in a transactional approach to sales, closing deals but failing to win loyal customers as competitors get easy openings to develop relationship equity with these customers. Given that follow-up involves reactive, *service*-oriented tasks, while gaining new customers involves proactive, *selling*-oriented tasks, many salespeople struggle to balance these dual roles. In some firms, they are instead divided: *hunter* salespeople complete steps 1 through 5, while *farmer* salespeople handle step 6.

In summary, the six steps of the sales process each require resource investments. Trade-offs and synergies *among* these six steps, as well as *between* salespeople and other components of IMC, makes personal selling a complex and pivotal piece of IMC strategies.

CHAPTER CASE STUDY

Ireland

THE PRIMARK CARES CAMPAIGN

Primark Stores Limited is a major, multinational apparel retailer headquartered in Dublin, Ireland. After opening its first store in 1969, Primark (known as Penneys in its home country), expanded over several decades to cover over a dozen European countries plus the United States. Primark has a focus on *fast fashion*, or affordable and trendy clothes, for men, women, and children.[50] In recent years, one of the major challenges for Primark and other fast fashion retailers has been public perception, with some consumers even viewing the entire category as essentially a vice good. This is because the benefits of fast fashion—it is cheap to make and based on the latest runway styles—can be a nightmare for ethics and sustainability:

1. Low-cost production can mean underpaid employees or unsafe working conditions in suppliers' facilities in the Global South. The 2013 collapse of the Rana Plaza garment factory in Bangladesh, which killed over 1,000 workers, was especially damning for Primark and other brands that sourced clothing from Rana Plaza.
2. A focus on frequently changing runway styles, combined with cheap materials, can mean clothes that end up in the garbage, and later in landfills.[51]

Primark's problematic reputation as a fast fashion retailer, as well as incidents such as the Rana Plaza collapse, led it to take action.

Source: Hermes Rivera/Unsplash

Fast fashion retailers such as Primark developed a reputation for producing "disposable" clothes that end up in landfills such as this one in Nicaragua. The Primark Cares multimedia campaign aimed to improve this image by highlighting the company's sustainability efforts.

Introducing Primark Cares. In 2021, Primark officially launched its Primark Cares campaign. On the surface, this was an initiative aiming to source all its clothing materials from sustainable sources by 2030. This involved meaningful, tangible changes in how Primark managed its supply chain and designed its clothing—for example, by training farmers how to generate less waste in cotton production.[52] But beyond that, it was a multipronged, integrated marketing communications campaign with a clear objective to rehabilitate Primark's image among young, sustainability-conscious consumers. Elements included:

- in-store promotions in the form of "How change looks" displays, which had detailed panels showing how recycled materials could lead to fashionable clothes
- sustainability-focused advertisements on Spotify and other platforms
- a public relations blitz involving the company website, enthusiastic statements from executives, and many interviews with the media
- creative events focused on sustainability practices such as repairing clothing—for example, Primark stores hosted workshops that would teach consumers how to sew and have "Textile Takeback" boxes for recycling clothes into usable fabric.[53]

Uncertain results. In terms of sustainability, Primark Cares undoubtedly achieved results, leading to measurable reductions in waste and energy consumption and better lives for many of the workers in Primark's supply chain. In terms of the campaign's objective to repair the company's image, the jury is still out. Sustainability advocacy groups have expressed skepticism over some of the changes—for example, noting that many items in the store still contain minimal recycled material. And in more practical terms, there is little evidence that loyalty to the brand is increasing.[54] The brand seemingly received a much bigger boost from its recent push into e-commerce, suggesting that the sustainability focus in the Primark Cares campaign, while admirable, might not be as important to Primark consumers as convenience and low prices.[55] Going forward, Primark will need to re-evaluate how it allocates resources in deploying IMC messages to its customers.

CASE QUESTIONS

1. Following up on this chapter's "Shades of Gray" feature, do you think that fast fashion is a vice good? Why or why not, and to what degree should regulators play a role in the market?
2. Consider the elements included in Primark's IMC campaign. If you were already skeptical of Primark's motives and track record with sustainability, which of these elements might be the *most* convincing? Why?
3. Once again, consider these campaign elements and the perspective of a skeptical consumer. Which elements would probably be the *least* convincing? Why wouldn't you believe them?

CHAPTER SUMMARY

One important arena for managing trade-offs, grounded in the first three principles, is the allocation of integrated marketing communications and personal selling effort—the core of the promotion element of the 7Ps—across priorities. This chapter introduces the IMC concept and its components and illustrates approaches to deploying the IMC portfolio based on the First Principles. Main themes include the importance of having systematic processes for planning and deploying IMC while considering how different elements of IMC can impact one another. We lay out a four-step process for planning IMC efforts in general and describe the various types of communications that can typically comprise an IMC strategy. The chapter further provides a high-level overview of personal selling and establishes the concept of sales effort as a scarce resource to allocate. We explain why personal selling is an especially critical, and difficult to manage, component of IMC strategy and how salesperson resources need to be divided among six steps of selling.

APPLICATION QUESTIONS

1. Revisit the five integrated marketing communications campaigns described in Table 15.1. Choose one of these and look up a news article or two about it. What do you think made this campaign successful?
2. Try to think of times when you have received messages from the same brand in multiple different ways, for example, on two different social media platforms. Why do you think the brand chose this set of communications elements?
3. Consider the list of IMC elements mentioned in "A Process for IMC Planning." Given your experience with being targeted by marketing communications, in your opinion, which of these elements are the *most* effective, which are the *least* effective, and why?
4. Imagine you are running a small coffee shop in your hometown. Considering the five drivers of resource trade-offs, which of these would be the most difficult or unpredictable in influencing resource trade-off decisions?
5. Recall the Marketing Fail feature about Paddy Power, as well as the Aldi example. What is your opinion on campaigns such as these that are based primarily on controversy? Are they sustainable in the long run? Why or why not?
6. Consider the motivation-opportunity-ability test from the chapter. Thinking of a time that you decided *not* to spend effort on a task, use this test to explain why.
7. Review the six steps of selling. Which *two* steps seem the most difficult to you, and why?
8. "Sales representative" is one of the most common first job titles for new business school graduates. Based on how you perceive sales jobs, does this option appeal to you? Do you feel any differently about selling in B2B relationships?

Visit the companion website, **https://bloomsbury.pub/palmatier-marketing**, or **https://samsinstitute.com**, for additional learning and teaching tools, including professional videos outlining the Four Principles, PowerPoint tutorials with voice-over commentary, sample syllabi for marketing courses, testbank and more.

REFERENCES

CHAPTER 1: THE MODERN MARKETING CONCEPT

1 Palmatier, R. and Sridhar, S. (2017) *Marketing Strategy: Based on First Principles and Data Analytics*. London: Palgrave Macmillan.

2 *Oxford English Dictionary* (2021) sv. "Marketing." Available at: https://www.oed.com/view/Entry/114186?rskey=-2f8ayk&result=2#eid (accessed March 23, 2021).

3 *Merriam-Webster*. (2019) sv. "Marketing." Available at: https://www.merriam-webster.com/dictionary/marketing (accessed February 16, 2021).

4 American Marketing Association. (2017) "What is Marketing?—The Definition of Marketing." Available at: https://www.ama.org/the-definition-of-marketing-what-is-marketing/ (accessed February 16, 2021).

5 Singh, M. (2021) "Flipkart Doubles Down on Rewards Program, Partners with 5,000 Retail Outlets in India." *TechCrunch*, January 17. Available at: https://techcrunch.com/2021/01/17/flipkart-supercoin-pay-loyalty-rewards-program-india-amazon/ (accessed February 18, 2021).

6 FinSMEs. (2020) "Carrefour Acquires Bio c' Bon, for €60M," November 4. Available at: https://www.finsmes.com/2020/11/carrefour-acquires-bio-c-bon-for-e60m.html (accessed February 20, 2021).

7 Shah, D., Rust, R.T., Parasuraman, A., Staelin, R. and Day, G.S. (2006) "The Path to Customer Centricity." *Journal of Service Research*, 9(2), pp. 113–24. https://doi.org/10.1177/1094670506294666.

8 Light Reading. (2020) "Nokia and Polkomtel Turn on 5G Services in Poland," December 18. Available at: https://www.lightreading.com/5g/nokia-and-polkomtel-turn-on-5g-services-in-poland/d/d-id/766233 (accessed February 25, 2021).

9 Grodt, J. (2020) "Epic Games Store Holiday Sale Will Make a New Game Free Every Day." *ScreenRant*, December 11. Available at: https://screenrant.com/epic-games-store-holiday-sale-new-game-free/ (accessed February 25, 2021).

10 Friedman, M. (2007) "The Social Responsibility of Business is to Increase its Profits." In *Corporate Governance*. Heidelberg: Springer, pp. 173–78.

11 United States Environmental Protection Agency. (2019) "Deepwater Horizon—BP Gulf of Mexico Oil Spill," last updated August 14, 2023. Available at: https://www.epa.gov/enforcement/deepwater-horizon-bp-gulf-mexico-oil-spill (accessed March 1, 2021).

12 Post, J.E., Preston, L.E. and Sachs, S. (2002) "Managing the Extended Enterprise: The New Stakeholder View." *California Management Review*, 45(1), pp. 6–28.

13 Moshinsky, B. (2015) "Here's What Volkswagen Did and How It Got Caught." *Business Insider*, September 23. Available at: https://www.businessinsider.com/heres-what-volkswagen-did-and-how-they-got-caught-2015-9?r=UK#in-2013-the-international-council-on-clean-transportation-teams-up-with-west-virginia-university-for-a-study-on-the-volkswagen-diesel-cars-2 (accessed March 3, 2021).

14 Pennsylvania Office of Attorney General. (2018) "Attorney General Shapiro Announces $575 Million 50-State Settlement with Wells Fargo Bank for Opening Unauthorized Accounts and Charging Consumers for Unnecessary Auto Insurance, Mortgage Fees," December 28. Available at: https://www.attorneygeneral.gov/taking-action/press-releases/attorney-general-shapiro-announces-575-million-50-state-settlement-with-wells-fargo-bank-for-opening-unauthorized-accounts-and-charging-consumers-for-unnecessary-auto-insurance-mortgage-fees/ (accessed December 1, 2022).

15 Lipton, M., Cain, K. and Iannone, K. (2019) "Stakeholder Governance and the Fiduciary Duties of Directors." *Harvard.edu*, August 24. Available at: https://corpgov.law.harvard.edu/2019/08/24/stakeholder-governance-and-the-fiduciary-duties-of-directors/ (accessed March 5, 2021).

16 Friedman, M. (2007) "The Social Responsibility of Business is to Increase its Profits." In *Corporate Governance*. Heidelberg: Springer, pp. 173–78.

17 Burton, C. (2020) "What is Disney Plus? From the Content to the Price and Release Date, How to Subscribe to the New On-demand Streaming Service." *Daily Mail*, March 19. Available at: https://www.dailymail.co.uk/femail/article-8126585/What-Disney-Plus-Content-price-release-date.html (accessed March 7, 2021).

18 Daws, R. (2020) "Baidu's Robotaxi Service Apollo Go Hits the Streets of Beijing." *Internet of Things News*, September 11. Available at: https://iottechnews.com/news/2020/sep/11/baidu-robotaxi-service-apollo-go-beijing/ (accessed March 7, 2021).

19 Vodafone Public Sector Services. (2021) "Visit the Vodafone Public Sector Portal." Available at: https://publicsector.vodafone.co.uk/ (accessed March 7, 2021).

20 Palmatier and Sridhar, *Marketing Strategy*.

21 Sainsbury's. (2019) "Our Business Strategy." Available at: https://www.about.sainsburys.co.uk/about-us/our-business-strategy (accessed March 8, 2021).

22 Teece, D.J., Pisano, G. and Shuen, A. (1997) "Dynamic Capabilities and Strategic Management." *Strategic Management Journal*, 18(7), pp. 509–33.

23 McCarthy, E.J. (1960) *Basic Marketing: A Managerial Approach*. Homewood, IL: R.D. Irwin.

24 Lee, W. (2018) "Quibi Aims to Launch 5,000 'Quick Bite' Videos When It Debuts." *Los Angeles Times*, December 5. Available at: https://www.latimes.com/business/hollywood/la-fi-ct-quibi-20181205-story.html (accessed March 10, 2021).

25 Spangler, T. (2021) "Roku Acquires Global Rights to 75-Plus Quibi Shows, Will Stream Them for Free." *Variety*, January 8.

Available at: https://variety.com/2021/digital/news/roku-acquires-quibi-shows-free-streaming-1234881238/ (accessed March 12, 2021).

26 Lee, "Quibi Aims to Launch 5,000 'Quick Bite' Videos."

27 Alexander, J. (2020) "11 Reasons Why Quibi Crashed and Burned in Less than a Year." *The Verge*, October 22. Available at: https://www.theverge.com/2020/10/22/21528404/quibi-shut-down-cost-subscribers-content-tv-movies-katzenberg-whitman-tiktok-netflix (accessed March 12, 2021).

28 Meyersohn, N. (2019) "How a Cheap, Brutally Efficient Grocery Chain Is Upending America's Supermarkets." *CNN*, May 17. Available at: https://www.cnn.com/interactive/2019/05/business/aldi-walmart-low-food-prices/index.html (accessed March 14, 2021).

29 Asarch, S. (2020) "What Is the Rarest 'Fortnite' Skin? These Cosmetics Are the Most Valuable." *Newsweek*, May 28. Available at: https://www.newsweek.com/what-rarest-fortnite-skin-these-cosmetics-are-most-valuable-1507113 (accessed March 14, 2021).

30 LG USA. (2021) "LG: Mobile Devices, Home Entertainment & Appliances." Available at: https://www.lg.com/us/authorizeddealers/lg_online_authorized_retailers (accessed March 18, 2021).

31 Lawrence, F. (2013) "Horsemeat Scandal: Where Did the 29% Horse in Your Tesco Burger Come From?." *The Guardian*, October 22. Available at: https://www.theguardian.com/uk-news/2013/oct/22/horsemeat-scandal-guardian-investigation-public-secrecy (accessed March 18, 2021).

32 Alexander, G., ed. (2016) "The World's Largest Sales Forces." *Sales Benchmark Index Magazine*. Available at: https://salesbenchmarkindex.com/wp-content/uploads/2016/07/201602-SBIMag_e2e_Online_LR.pdf (accessed March 20, 2021).

33 Booms, B. and Bitner, M.J. (1981) "Marketing Strategies and Organizational Structures for Service Firms." In J.H. Donnelly and W.R. George, eds., *Marketing of Services*. Chicago: American Marketing Association, pp. 47–51.

34 Athey, S. and Luca, M. (2019) "Why Tech Companies Hire So Many Economists." *Harvard Business Review*, February 12. Available at: https://hbr.org/2019/02/why-tech-companies-hire-so-many-economists (accessed March 20, 2021).

35 Anderson, D.A. (2020) "A Profile of the Retail Workforce: Retail Jobs Among the Most Common Occupations." United States Census Bureau, September 8. Available at: https://www.census.gov/library/stories/2020/09/profile-of-the-retail-workforce.html (accessed March 21, 2021).

36 Nestlé Global. (2009) "WellNes Centre inaugurated in Vevey," January 15. Available at: https://www.nestle.com/media/pressreleases/allpressreleases/wellnescentre (accessed March 21, 2021).

37 Von Hippel, E. (1986) "Lead Users: A Source of Novel Product Concepts." *Management Science*, 32(7), pp. 791–805.

38 Anheuser-Busch (2013) "The 'King of Beers' Unveils Budweiser Black Crown on Jan. 21; First TV Spot Will Be Featured During Super Bowl XLVII." *PR Newswire*, January 8. Available at: https://www.prnewswire.com/news-releases/the-king-of-beers-unveils-budweiser-black-crown-on-jan-21-first-tv-spot-will-be-featured-during-super-bowl-xlvii-186002982.html (accessed March 22, 2021).

39 Gundry, K. (2015) "DEWALT Wins Vision Critical's North American Insight Community of the Year Award for DEWALT Insights." *Business Wire*, October 29. Available at: https://www.businesswire.com/news/home/20151029005087/en/DEWALT-Wins-Vision-Critical%E2%80%99s-North-American-Insight-Community-of-the-Year-Award-for-DEWALT-Insights (accessed March 22, 2021).

40 Lego Ideas. (2021) "LEGO IDEAS—Submit a Project." Available at: https://ideas.lego.com/projects/create (accessed March 23, 2021).

CHAPTER 2: THE FIRST PRINCIPLES OF MARKETING

1 Palmatier, R.W. and Crecelius, A.T. (2019) "The 'First Principles' of Marketing Strategy." *AMS Review*, 9(1), pp. 5–26.

2 Portions of this chapter were adapted from Palmatier, R.W. and Sridhar, S. (2017) *Marketing Strategy: Based on First Principles and Data Analytics*. London: Palgrave Macmillan.

3 Lee, C. (2021) "Netflix Just Paid Nearly Half a Billion for *Knives Out 2* and *3*." *New York Vulture*, March 31. Available at: https://www.vulture.com/2021/03/netflix-paid-nearly-half-a-billion-for-knives-out-2-and-3.html (accessed May 8, 2024).

4 Hempel, J. (2009) "Motorola Gets in the Game." *CNN Money*, September 29. Available at: https://money.cnn.com/2009/09/28/technology/motorola_google_android.fortune/index.htm (accessed May 8, 2024).

5 Motorola. (n.d.) "Motorola's Milestones." Available at: https://www.motorola.com/us/about/motorola-history-milestones (accessed May 8, 2024).

6 Statista. (2023) "Manufacturers' Market Share of Smartphone Sales in the United States from 1st Quarter 2016 to 2nd Quarter 2023," August. Available at: https://www.statista.com/statistics/620805/smartphone-sales-market-share-in-the-us-by-vendor/ (accessed May 8, 2024).

7 Whitwam, R. (2019) "Moto Mods: How a Modular Hardware Platform Locked Motorola into a Cycle of Failure." *Android Police*, February 21. Available at: https://www.androidpolice.com/2019/02/21/moto-mods-how-a-modular-hardware-platform-locked-motorola-into-a-cycle-of-failure/ (accessed May 8, 2024).

8 Oyedele, A. (2018) "GE Is Getting Booted from the Dow Jones Industrial Average: Here Are the Members of the Original 1896 Index." *Business Insider*, June 20. Available at: https://www.businessinsider.com/dow-original-companies-2016-12 (accessed May 8, 2024).

9 Hinckley Past & Present. (n.d.) "Hansom Cab." Available at: http://www.hinckleypastpresent.org/hansomcab.html (accessed May 8, 2024).

10 Howell, T. (2020) "Antitrust Spotlight: Does Amazon Abuse Its Third-Party Sellers?." Morning Brew, July 21. Available at: https://www.morningbrew.com/daily/stories/2020/07/21/antitrust-spotlight-amazon-improperly-abuse-thirdparty-sellers (accessed May 8, 2024).

11 Amazon (n.d.) "Standard Selling Fees." Available at: https://sell.amazon.com/pricing.html (accessed May 8, 2024).

12 Palmer, A. and Novet, J. (2020) "Amazon Bullies Partners and Vendors, Says Antitrust Subcommittee." CNBC, October 6. Available at: https://www.cnbc.com/2020/10/06/amazon-bullies-partners-and-vendors-says-antitrust-subcommittee.html (accessed May 8, 2024).

13 Germann, F., Lilien, G.L. and Rangaswamy, A. (2013) "Performance Implications of Deploying Marketing Analytics." *International Journal of Research in Marketing*, 30(2), pp. 114–28.
14 Davenport, T.H. (2013) "Big Data and the Role of Intuition." *Harvard Business Review*, December 24. Available at: https://hbr.org/2013/12/big-data-and-the-role-of-intuition (accessed May 8, 2024).
15 Kozlenkova, I.V., Samaha, S.A. and Palmatier, R.W. (2014) "Resource-Based Theory in Marketing." *Journal of the Academy of Marketing Science*, 42(1), pp. 1–21; Barney, J.B., Ketchen Jr, D.J. and Wright, M. (2011) "The Future of Resource-Based Theory: Revitalization or Decline?." *Journal of Management*, 37(5), pp. 1299–315.
16 Capritto, A. "Impossible Burger vs. Beyond Meat Burger: Taste, Ingredients and Availability, Compared." *CNET*, October 25. Available at: https://www.cnet.com/health/nutrition/beyond-meat-vs-impossible-burger-whats-the-difference/ (accessed May 8, 2024).
17 Goldfine, J. (2020) "A Brief History of Impossible Foods: How 'Bleeding' Plant-Based Burgers Started a Food Industry Trend." *The Business of Business*, May 11. Available at: https://www.businessofbusiness.com/articles/impossible-foods-plant-based-burgers-milk-food-industry-trend-data/ (accessed May 8, 2024).
18 Morning Consult. (n.d.) "Tracking Impossible Foods's Recent Growth in the U.S." Available at: https://morningconsult.com/form/impossible-foods-growth/ (accessed May 8, 2024).
19 Shanker, D. (2021) "Impossible and Beyond Slash Prices As Fake-Meat Market Heats Up." *Bloomberg UK*, April 16. Available at: https://www.bloomberg.com/news/articles/2021-04-16/beyond-meat-bynd-impossible-foods-battle-over-future-of-fake-meat-industry (accessed May 8, 2024).
20 Kapadia, S. (2020) "Beyond Meat Incurs $6M in Repacking Expense to Handle Pandemic Demand Shift." *Supply Chain Dive*, August 5. Available at: https://www.supplychaindive.com/news/coronavirus-beyond-meat-expenses-repack-inventory-transportation/582948/ (accessed May 8, 2024).

CHAPTER 3: FIRST PRINCIPLES IN ACTION—NAVIGATING THE WORLD OF DIGITAL MARKETING

1 Salesforce. (n.d.) "What Is Digital Transformation?." Available at: https://www.salesforce.com/products/platform/what-is-digital-transformation/ (accessed May 9, 2024).
2 Lamberton, C. and Stephen, A.T. (2016) "A Thematic Exploration of Digital, Social Media, and Mobile Marketing: Research Evolution from 2000 to 2015 and an Agenda for Future Inquiry." *Journal of Marketing*, 80(6), pp. 146–72.
3 Zhang, J. and Hon, H.W. (2020) "Towards Responsible Digital Transformation." *California Management Review*, 62(3), pp. 1–10.
4 Kannan, P.K. (2017) "Digital Marketing: A Framework, Review and Research Agenda." *International Journal of Research in Marketing*, 34(1), pp. 22–45.
5 Rosen, D.E. and Purinton, E. (2004) "Website Design: Viewing the Web as a Cognitive Landscape." *Journal of Business Research*, 57(7), pp. 787–94.
6 Lawrence, J.M., Crecelius, A.T., Scheer, L.K. and Patil, A. (2019) "Multichannel Strategies for Managing the Profitability of Business-to-Business Customers." *Journal of Marketing Research*, 56(3), pp. 479–97.
7 Nagpal, M. and Petersen, J.A. (2020) "Keyword Selection Strategies in Search Engine Optimization: How Relevant is Relevance?." *Journal of Retailing*, 97(4), pp. 746–63.
8 Newtek. (2014) "Five Important Digital Marketing Elements to Consider." *Forbes*, October 13. Available at: https://www.forbes.com/sites/thesba/2014/10/13/five-important-digital-marketing-elements-to-consider/?sh=5901502b3a3e (accessed May 9, 2024).
9 Volterra, A. (2019) "How Rolex Is Revamping Its Digital Channels: 3 Marketing Innovations Not to Miss." *LuxurySociety*, April 2. Available at: https://www.luxurysociety.com/en/articles/2019/04/how-rolex-revamping-its-digital-channels-3-marketing-innovations-not-miss (accessed May 9, 2024).
10 Xiao, B., Huang, M. and Barnes, A.J. (2015) "Network Closure among Sellers and Buyers in Social Commerce Community." *Electronic Commerce Research and Applications*, 14(6), pp. 641–53.
11 History.com Editors. (2019) "'Gangnam Style' Becomes the First YouTube Video to Reach One Billion Views." *History*, August 8. Available at: https://www.history.com/this-day-in-history/gangnam-style-first-youtube-video-to-hit-one-billion-views (accessed May 9, 2024).
12 Smith, A. (2017) "Pepsi Pulls Controversial Kendall Jenner Ad After Outcry." *NBC News*, April 5. Available at: https://www.nbcnews.com/news/nbcblk/pepsi-ad-kendall-jenner-echoes-black-lives-matter-sparks-anger-n742811 (accessed May 9, 2024).
13 Roggeveen, A.L. and Grewal, D. (2016) "Editorial." *Journal of Consumer Marketing*, 33(2). https://doi.org/10.1108/JCM-12-2015-1649.
14 Sehl, K. and Mikolajczyk, K. (2024) "Engagement Rate Calculator + Tips for 2024." *Hootsuite*, March 20. Available at: https://blog.hootsuite.com/calculate-engagement-rate/ (accessed May 9, 2024).
15 *Statista*. (2024) "Influencer Marketing Market Size Worldwide from 2016 to 2024." Available at: https://www.statista.com/statistics/1092819/global-influencer-market-size/ (accessed August 28, 2024).
16 Wong, J.C. (2019) "The Cambridge Analytica Scandal Changed the World – But It Didn't Change Facebook." *The Guardian*, March 18. Available at: https://www.theguardian.com/technology/2019/mar/17/the-cambridge-analytica-scandal-changed-the-world-but-it-didnt-change-facebook (accessed May 9, 2024).
17 Federal Trade Commission. (2019) "FTC Issues Opinion and Order Against Cambridge Analytica for Deceiving Consumers About the Collection of Facebook Data, Compliance with EU-U.S. Privacy Shield." Press Release, December 6. Available at: https://www.ftc.gov/news-events/press-releases/2019/12/ftc-issues-opinion-order-against-cambridge-analytica-deceiving (accessed May 9, 2024).
18 Davies, H. (2015) "Ted Cruz Using Firm that Harvested Data on Millions of Unwitting Facebook Users." *The Guardian*, December 11. Available at: https://www.theguardian.com/us-news/2015/dec/11/senator-ted-cruz-president-campaign-facebook-user-data (accessed May 9, 2024).
19 Wong, J.C. (2019) "Zuckerberg Says Facebook Is Pivoting to Privacy after Year of Controversies." *The Guardian*, March 6. Available at: https://www.theguardian.com/technology/2019/

mar/06/mark-zuckerberg-facebook-privacy-vision (accessed May 9, 2024).
20 Newberry, C. and Macready, H. (2022) "What Is Social Listening, Why It Matters + 14 Tools to Help." *Hootsuite*, December 1. Available at: https://blog.hootsuite.com/social-listening-business/#:~:text=Social%20listening%20is%20the%20process,crucial%20component%20of%20audience%20research (accessed May 9, 2024).
21 Stewart, A. (2019) "Social Listening Made L'Oreal the Leader of the Cosmetics Market." *Medium*, August 26. Available at: https://medium.com/latent/social-listening-made-loreal-the-leader-of-the-cosmetics-market-d794208ed877 (accessed May 9, 2024).
22 Baker, K. (2024) "What Will Influencer Marketing Look Like in 2024?." *Hubspot*, April 2. Available at: https://blog.hubspot.com/marketing/how-to-work-with-influencers#:~:text=80%25%20of%20marketers%20say%20influencer,is%20better%20than%20other%20sources (accessed May 9, 2024).
23 Williams, R. (2019) "Instagram Influencer Engagement Hovers Near All-Time Lows, Study Says." *Marketing Dive*, July 9. Available at: https://www.marketingdive.com/news/instagram-influencer-engagement-hovers-near-all-time-lows-study-says/558331/ (accessed May 9, 2024).
24 Pringle, R. (2019) "Double or Nothing? Social Media Influencers' Value Is Open to Debate." *CBC*, July 11. Available at: https://www.cbc.ca/news/science/pringle-influencers-social-media-1.5207258 (accessed May 9, 2024).
25 Baker, "What Will Influencer Marketing Look Like in 2024?."
26 Statista. (n.d.) "Global Smartphone Penetration Rate as Share of Population from 2016 to 2023." Available at: https://www.statista.com/statistics/203734/global-smartphone-penetration-per-capita-since-2005/ (accessed May 9, 2024).
27 Hanbury, M. (2019) "Peloton Cut the Price of One of Its Memberships But Ignored Another, Infuriating Some of Its Most Loyal Customers." *Business Insider*, December 11. Available at: https://www.businessinsider.com/peloton-cuts-cost-digital-membership-annoying-customers-2019-12 (accessed May 9, 2024).
28 *Harvard Business Review*. (2013) "How People Really Use Mobile," January–February. Available at: https://hbr.org/2013/01/how-people-really-use-mobile (accessed May 9, 2024).
29 Fong, N.M., Fang, Z. and Luo, X. (2015) "Geo-Conquesting: Competitive Locational Targeting of Mobile Promotions." *Journal of Marketing Research*, 52(5), pp. 726–35.
30 *Marketing Dive* (n.d.) "Starbucks Breaks First Location-based Mobile Campaign with Major Carrier." Available at: https://www.marketingdive.com/ex/mobilemarketer/cms/news/database-crm/7754.html (accessed May 9, 2024).
31 Seibert, M. (2017) "A Take on 3 Confusing Terms: Content Marketing, Content Strategy, Content Marketing Strategy." *Content Marketing Institute*, November 24. Available at: https://contentmarketinginstitute.com/2017/11/confusing-content-marketing-terms/ (accessed May 9, 2024).
32 Ng, K. (2016) "Vegetarians and Vegans Boycott Gourmet Burger Kitchen Over 'Antagonising' Ad Campaign." *Independent*, January 18. Available at: https://www.independent.co.uk/news/uk/home-news/vegetarians-and-vegans-boycott-gourmet-burger-kitchen-over-antagonising-ad-campaign-a6819751.html (accessed May 9, 2024).
33 Maguire, L. (2020) "Gen Z Is Reinventing Social Media Marketing." *Vogue Business*, January 8. Available at: https://www.voguebusiness.com/consumers/gen-z-reinventing-social-media-marketing-tiktok-youtube-instagram-louis-vuitton (accessed May 9, 2024).
34 Asghar, R. (2018) "Why the IHOP Name Change? Because Hotcakes Aren't Selling Like Hotcakes." *Forbes*, June 10. Available at: https://www.forbes.com/sites/robasghar/2018/06/10/why-the-ihop-name-change-because-hotcakes-arent-selling-like-hotcakes/?sh=12f05c44203d (accessed May 9, 2024).
35 Limbachia, D. (n.d.) "IHOP Grilled by Burger King, Wendy's on Twitter Over IHOb Name Change." *USA Today Money*. Available at: https://www.usatoday.com/story/money/food/2018/06/11/ihop-becomes-ihob-burgers/691380002/ (accessed May 9, 2024).
36 Hoffman, D.L. and Fodor, M. (2010) "Can You Measure the ROI of Your Social Media Marketing?." *MIT Sloan Management Review*, 52(1), p. 41.
37 Packaging Gateway. (2023) "Walkers' Crisps Production Facility, Leicester, UK," July 6. Available at: https://www.packaging-gateway.com/projects/walkerscrisps/ (accessed May 9, 2024).
38 McKirdy, E. (2017) "'Nice Selfie?' Trolls Hijack Walkers' Social Media Campaign." *CNN*, May 26. Available at: https://www.cnn.com/2017/05/26/europe/walkers-wave-twitter-campaign-disaster-trnd/index.html (accessed May 9, 2024).
39 BBC News. (2017) "Walkers Crisps Gary Lineker Campaign Suffers Twitter Sabotage," May 25. Available at: https://www.bbc.com/news/uk-40047816 (accessed May 9, 2024).
40 Hoffman and Fodor, "Can You Measure the ROI of Your Social Media Marketing?," p. 41.
41 Edelman, D.C. (2010) "Four Ways to Get More Value from Digital Marketing." *McKinsey Quarterly*, March 1. Available at: https://www.mckinsey.com/business-functions/marketing-and-sales/our-insights/four-ways-to-get-more-value-from-digital-marketing (accessed May 9, 2024).
42 Hoffman and Fodor, "Can You Measure the ROI of Your Social Media Marketing?," p. 41.
43 Amaro. (n.d.) "OI, SOMOS A AMARO." Available at: https://amaro.com/br/pt/sobre-nos (accessed May 9, 2024).
44 Orland, K. (2021) "Why Animal Crossing: New Horizons' 31 Million Sales Are So Incredible." *ars TECHNICA*, February 1. Available at: https://arstechnica.com/gaming/2021/02/putting-31-million-animal-crossing-new-horizons-sales-in-context/#:~:text=35.12%20million%3A%20Total%20combined%20sales,previous%20Animal%20Crossing%20console%20games (accessed May 9, 2024).
45 Deighton, K. (2020) "Animal Crossing Is Emerging as a Media Channel for Brands in Lockdown." *The Drum*, April 21. Available at: https://www.thedrum.com/news/2020/04/21/animal-crossing-emerging-media-channel-brands-lockdown (accessed May 9, 2024).
46 Gianatasio, D. (2020) "This Fashion Brand Is Developing a Collection Inside Animal Crossing." *MUSE*, June 23. Available at: https://musebycl.io/gaming/fashion-brand-developing-collection-inside-animal-crossing (accessed May 9, 2024).

CHAPTER 4: MANAGING CUSTOMER DIFFERENCES

1 Palmatier, R.W. and Crecelius, A.T. (2019) "The 'First Principles' of Marketing Strategy." *AMS Review*, 9(1–2), pp. 5–26. https://doi.org/10.1007/s13162-019-00134-y.
2 Palmatier, R. and Sridhar, S. (2017) *Marketing Strategy: Based on First Principles and Data Analytics*. London: Palgrave Macmillan.

3 Bhasin, K. (2011) "15 Facts About Coca-Cola That Will Blow Your Mind." *Business Insider*. Available at: https://www.businessinsider.com/facts-about-coca-cola-2011-6 (accessed September 3, 2020).

4 Wittendorfer, F. (2020) "Shining Bright." Siemens. Available at: https://new.siemens.com/global/en/company/about/history/news/siemens-and-osram.html (accessed September 3, 2020).

5 Ford Corporate. (2000) "Ford Motor Company Timeline." Available at: https://corporate.ford.com/history.html (accessed September 3, 2020).

6 Winer, R. and Neslin, S. (2014) *The History of Marketing Science*. Singapore: World Scientific Publishing Company.

7 The Coca-Cola Company. (2011) "A Short History of the Coca-Cola Company." Available at: https://www.coca-colacompany.com/content/dam/journey/us/en/our-company/history/coca-cola-a-short-hisotry-125-years-booklet.pdf (accessed September 3, 2020).

8 Peppers, D. and Rogers, M. (1992) *The One to One Future: Building Relationships One Customer at a Time*. New York: Doubleday.

9 Arora, N., Dreze, X., Ghose, A., Hess, J.D., Iyengar, R., Jing, B., Joshi, Y. and Kumar, V. (2008) "Putting One-to-One Marketing to Work: Personalization, Customization, and Choice." *Marketing Letters*, 19(3–4), pp. 305–21.

10 BBC Newsbeat. (2017) "Netflix Introduces New Thumbs-up, Thumbs-down Rating System," April 5. Available at: http://www.bbc.co.uk/newsbeat/article/39502995/netflix-introduces-new-thumbs-up-thumbs-down-rating-system (accessed September 3, 2020).

11 Alphabet Investor Relations. (2019) "Alphabet Investor Relations." Available at: https://abc.xyz/investor/ (accessed September 3, 2020).

12 Morris, C. (2019) "Hands on with Google's Stadia Game-Streaming Service." *Fortune*, June 14. Available at: https://fortune.com/2019/06/14/hands-on-google-stadia-game-streaming-service/ (accessed September 3, 2020).

13 Park, G. (2019) "Google Stadia, the Cloud-Fueled Game Console You Play on Your Browser, Ships Nov. 19." *Washington Post*, October 15. Available at: https://www.washingtonpost.com/video-games/2019/10/15/google-stadia-cloud-fueled-game-console-you-play-your-browser-ships-nov/ (accessed September 4, 2020).

14 Murnane, K. (2019) "Stadia Is Walking a Thin Line Between Revolutionary Success and Epic Failure." *Forbes*, November 19. Available at: https://www.forbes.com/sites/kevinmurnane/2019/11/19/stadia-is-walking-a-thin-line-between-revolutionary-success-and-epic-failure/#13dd8ac11b4b (accessed September 4, 2020).

15 Tassi, P. (2020) "Google Stadia Needs Its Free Tier Immediately as Its Numbers Continue to Fall." *Forbes*, January 17. Available at: https://www.forbes.com/sites/paultassi/2020/01/17/google-stadia-needs-its-free-tier-immediately-as-its-numbers-continue-to-fall/#423e54b37da1 (accessed September 4, 2020).

16 Wilde, D. (2019) "Google Stadia Review: Gaming's Future Is Here Far too Early." 9to5Google, December 3. Available at: https://9to5google.com/2019/12/03/google-stadia-review/ (accessed September 4, 2020).

17 Saxe, R. and Weitz, B.A. (1982) "The SOCO Scale: A Measure of the Customer Orientation of Salespeople." *Journal of Marketing Research*, 19(3), 343–51. https://doi.org/10.1177/00222437820190030.

18 Sylt, C. (2018) "The Marvellous Marketing Vehicle for the New Lexus." *Forbes*, February 26. Available at: https://www.forbes.com/sites/csylt/2018/02/26/the-marvellous-marketing-vehicle-for-the-new-lexus/#5679e9c27176 (accessed September 4, 2020).

19 Strand, O. (2017) "How Cold Brew Changed the Coffee Business." *The New York Times*, June 5. Available at: https://www.nytimes.com/2017/06/05/dining/cold-brew-coffee.html (accessed September 4, 2020).

20 John, O.P. and Srivastava, S. (1999) "The Big Five Trait Taxonomy: History, Measurement, and Theoretical Perspectives." *Handbook of Personality: Theory and Research*, 2, pp. 102–38.

21 Gecas, V. (1982) "The Self-Concept." *Annual Review of Sociology*, 8(1), pp. 1–33.

22 Salesforce.com. (2020) "Why You Need to Use Behavioral Segmentation." Available at: https://www.salesforce.com/products/marketing-cloud/best-practices/behavioral-segmentation/ (accessed September 4, 2020).

23 Sahni, N.S., Narayanan, S. and Kalyanam, K. (2019) "An Experimental Investigation of the Effects of Retargeted Advertising: The Role of Frequency and Timing." *Journal of Marketing Research*, 56(3), pp. 401–18.

24 Electronic Frontier Foundation. (2009) Legislative Primer September 2009. Available at: https://www.eff.org/files/onlineprivacylegprimersept09.pdf (accessed September 4, 2020).

25 Magid, L. (2019) "Magid: YouTube Settlement Has Unintended Consequence." *The Mercury News*, September 6. Available at: https://www.mercurynews.com/2019/09/06/magid-youtubes-ftc-childrens-privacy-settlement-makes-sense-but-has-unintended-consequence/ (accessed September 4, 2020).

26 Meyer, S. (2018) "Online Behavioral Tracking: Who's Spying on Your Every Move?." *CPO Magazine*, March 19. Available at: https://www.cpomagazine.com/data-privacy/online-behavioral-tracking-whos-spying-on-your-every-move/ [accessed September 4, 2020].

27 Clauser, G. (2019) "Amazon's Alexa Never Stops Listening to You. Should You Worry?." *Wirecutter: Reviews for the Real World*, August 8. Available at: https://www.nytimes.com/wirecutter/blog/amazons-alexa-never-stops-listening-to-you/ (accessed September 5, 2020).

28 Cerullo, M. (2019) "Influencer Marketing Fraud Costs Companies $1.3 Billion." *CBS News*, July 25. Available at: https://www.cbsnews.com/news/influencer-marketing-fraud-costs-companies-1-3-billion/ (accessed September 5, 2020).

29 Conklin, A. (2020) "How Much Money Do Social Media Influencers Make?." *FOXBusiness*, March 11. Available at: https://www.foxbusiness.com/lifestyle/social-media-influencer-pay (accessed September 5, 2020).

30 Constine, J. (2020) "FTC Votes to Review Influencer Marketing Rules & Penalties." *TechCrunch*, February 12. Available at: https://techcrunch.com/2020/02/12/ftc-influencer-marketing-law/ (accessed September 5, 2020).

31 Zucker, M. (2019) "Influencer Marketing Fraud—Heroes Among Us." *Forbes*, September 25. Available at: https://www.forbes.com/sites/matzucker/2019/09/25/influencer-marketing-solutions-but-no-hero/#75bc23663e8a (accessed September 5, 2020).

32 Webb, K. (2020) HBO Max is WarnerMedia's Ambitious Attempt to Take on Netflix, and It's Now Available to Stream—Here's How to Sign Up." *Business Insider*, May 23. Available at: https://www.businessinsider.com/hbo-max-streaming-service (accessed September 5, 2020).

33 Buss, D. (2018) "Buick Refreshes Its Branding to Appear More Refined and Modern." *brandchannel*, March 13. Available at: https://www.brandchannel.com/2018/03/13/buick-new-logo-031318/ (accessed September 5, 2020).

34 Jaguar Land Rover North America. (2020) "About Jaguar—Overview | Jaguar USA." Available at: https://www.jaguarusa.com/about-jaguar/index.html (accessed September 8, 2020).

35 Jaguar Land Rover North America. (2014) "Our History—Jaguar Heritage | Jaguar USA." Available at: https://www.jaguarusa.com/about-jaguar/heritage/index.html (accessed September 8, 2020).

36 Tata Motors Limited. (2020) Tata Motors Limited—Profile & Capabilities Brief History and Range of Current Business. Available at: https://www.tatamotors.com/wp-content/uploads/2016/11/18070456/TML-Capabilities.pdf (accessed September 8, 2020).

37 Tata Motors Limited. (2020) Annual Reports, Financial Statements, Balance Sheet of Tata Motors. Available at: https://www.tatamotors.com/investors/annual-reports/?annual_report_search=annual_report_search&areport_year=2008 (accessed September 8, 2020).

38 Schuster, T. and Holtbrügge, D. (2011) "Tata Nano: The Car for the Bottom-of-the-Pyramid." *Fallstudien zum Internationalen Management*, pp. 83–102. https://doi.org/10.1007/978-3-8349-6793-0_7.

39 Statista. (2020) "Luxury Cars—Global Market Size 2010–2019." Available at: https://www.statista.com/statistics/281574/size-of-the-luxury-car-market/ (accessed September 12, 2020).

40 Carty, S.S. (2008) "Tata Motors to Buy Jaguar, Land Rover for $2.3B." *ABC News*, March 26. Available at: https://abcnews.go.com/Business/story?id=4528213&page=1 (accessed September 12, 2020).

41 *Forbes*. (2008) "A Case of Reverse Imperialism," June 6. Available at: https://www.forbes.com/2008/06/06/tata-uk-imperialism-oped-cx_bw_0606india.html#4002fb7e341f (accessed September 12, 2020).

42 Arnott, S. (2010) "Booming Sales at Jaguar Land Rover Boost Tata Motors Profits." *The Independent*, August 11. Available at: https://www.independent.co.uk/news/business/news/booming-sales-at-jaguar-land-rover-boost-tata-motors-profits-2049056.html (accessed September 12, 2020).

43 Tata Motors Limited. (2019) "Investors | Financials & Filings | Annual Reports." Available at: https://www.tatamotors.com/investors/annual-reports/?annual_report_search=annual_report_search&areport_year=2019 (accessed September 12, 2020).

CHAPTER 5: UNDERSTANDING CONSUMER AND ORGANIZATIONAL BUYER BEHAVIOR

1 Edelman, D.C. and Singer, M. (2015) "Competing on Customer Journeys." *Harvard Business Review*, 93(11), pp. 88–100.

2 Chevalier, S. (2024) "Retail E-commerce Sales Worldwide from 2014 to 2027." *Statista*, February 6. Available at: https://www.statista.com/statistics/379046/worldwide-retail-e-commerce-sales/ (accessed May 11, 2024).

3 Steward, M.D., Narus, J.A., Roehm, M.L. and Ritz, W. (2019) "From Transactions to Journeys and Beyond: The Evolution of B2B Buying Process Modeling." *Industrial Marketing Management*, 83, pp. 288–300.

4 Sheth, J.N., Newman, B.I. and Gross, B.L. (1991) *Consumption Values and Market Choices: Theory and Applications.* Cincinnati, OH: South-Western Publishing, pp. 16–74.

5 Paulssen, M. and Bagozzi, R.P. (2005) "A Self-Regulatory Model of Consideration Set Formation." *Psychology & Marketing*, 22(10), pp. 785–812.

6 Kahn, B.E. and Baron, J. (1995) "An Exploratory Study of Choice Rules Favored for High-Stakes Decisions." *Journal of Consumer Psychology*, 4(4), pp. 305–28.

7 Caplin, A., Dean, M. and Martin, D. (2011) "Search and Satisficing." *American Economic Review*, 101(7), pp. 2899–922.

8 Steward et al., "From Transactions to Journeys and Beyond."

9 Oliver, R.L., Rust, R.T. and Varki, S. (1997) "Customer Delight: Foundations, Findings, and Managerial Insight." *Journal of Retailing*, 73(3), p. 311.

10 Aslam, S. (2024) "YouTube by the Numbers: Stats, Demographics & Fun Facts." *Omnicore*, January 10. Available at: https://www.omnicoreagency.com/youtube-statistics/ (accessed May 11, 2024).

11 Deahl, D. (2018) "Parents Can Now Limit YouTube Kids to Only Show Human-Approved Videos." *The Verge*, April 25. Available at: https://www.theverge.com/2018/4/25/17281654/youtube-kids-parental-controls-approved-content (accessed May 11, 2024).

12 Federal Trade Commission. (2019) "Google and YouTube Will Pay Record $170 Million for Alleged Violations of Children's Privacy Law." Press Release, September 4. Available at: https://www.ftc.gov/news-events/press-releases/2019/09/google-youtube-will-pay-record-170-million-alleged-violations (accessed May 11, 2024).

13 Jennings, R. (2019) "The Golden Age of Kids' YouTube Is Over. Good." *Vox*, December 20. Available at: https://www.vox.com/the-goods/2019/12/20/21025139/youtube-kids-coppa-law-ftc-2020 (accessed May 11, 2024).

14 Court, D., Elzinga, D., Mulder, S. and Jørgen Vetvik, J. (2009) "The Consumer Decision Journey." *McKinsey Quarterly*, June 1. Available at: https://www.mckinsey.com/business-functions/marketing-and-sales/our-insights/the-consumer-decision-journey (accessed May 11, 2024).

15 Yahoo Style Contributors. (2016) "A Lot of People Think Vera Bradley's New Ads Are a Sexist Fail." *Yahoo!Life*, September 21. Available at: https://www.yahoo.com/lifestyle/a-lot-of-people-think-very-bradleys-new-ads-are-a-sexist-fail-170937198.html (accessed May 11, 2024).

16 Liffreing, I. (2016) "Vera Bradley Changes Course After Ads Are Labeled a 'Sexist Fail.'" *Campaign US*, October 6. Available at: https://www.campaignlive.com/article/vera-bradley-changes-course-ads-labeled-sexist-fail/1411269 (accessed May 11, 2024).

17 Coppola, D. (2024) "B2B E-commerce Volume in the United States from 2018 to 2021." *Statista*, March 6. Available at: https://www.statista.com/statistics/239366/us-b2b-e-commerce-volume-since-2006/#:~:text=In%202018%2C%20

combined%20manufacturing%20and,in%20B2B%20e%2D-commerce%20volume (accessed May 11, 2024).

18 Konkel, F. (2019) "Government's Contract Spending Approaches $600B, Highest Since 2010." *Nextgov/FCW*, August 1. Available at: https://www.nextgov.com/cio-briefing/2019/08/governments-contract-spending-approaches-600b-highest-2010/158880/ (accessed May 11, 2024).

19 *Business Wire*. (2016) "How Many Products Does Amazon Actually Carry? And in What Categories?," June 14. Available at: https://www.businesswire.com/news/home/20160614006063/en/Products-Amazon-Carry-Categories (accessed May 11, 2024).

20 Schwartz, B. (2004) *The Paradox of Choice: Why More Is Less*. New York: Ecco.

21 DeCarlo, T.E. (2016) *Distribution Management*, 5th edn. Createspace Independent Publishing Platform.

22 Ronchetto Jr., J.R., Hutt, M.D. and Reingen, P.H. (1989) "Embedded Influence Patterns in Organizational Buying Systems." *Journal of Marketing*, 53(4), pp. 51–62.

23 Block Imaging. (2024) "1.5T MRI Machine Price Guide," April 3. Available at: https://info.blockimaging.com/1.5t-mri-machine-price-cost-guide (accessed May 11, 2024).

24 Mehra, S.K. (2015) "Antitrust and the Robo-seller: Competition in the Time of Algorithms." *Minnesota Law Review*, 100, p. 1323.

25 Gustafson, B.M., Pomirleanu, N., Mariadoss, B.J. and Johnson, J.L. (2019) "The Social Buyer: A Framework for the Dynamic Role of Social Media in Organizational Buying." *Journal of Business Research*, 125, pp. 806–14.

26 Chase, K.S. and Murtha, B. (2019) "Selling to Barricaded Buyers." *Journal of Marketing*, 83(6), pp. 2–20.

27 Barnes, D.C. and Krallman, A. (2019) "Customer Delight: A Review and Agenda for Research." *Journal of Marketing Theory and Practice*, 27(2), pp. 174–95.

28 Lawrence, J.M., Crecelius, A.T., Scheer, L.K. and Lam, S.K. (2019) "When It Pays to Have a Friend on the Inside: Contingent Effects of Buyer Advocacy on B2B Suppliers." *Journal of the Academy of Marketing Science*, 47(5), pp. 837–57.

29 Čater, T. and Čater, B. (2010) "Product and Relationship Quality Influence on Customer Commitment and Loyalty in B2B Manufacturing Relationships." *Industrial Marketing Management*, 39(8), pp. 1321–333.

30 Scheer, L.K., Miao, C.F. and Garrett, J. (2010) "The Effects of Supplier Capabilities on Industrial Customers' Loyalty: The Role of Dependence." *Journal of the Academy of Marketing Science*, 38(1), 90–104.

31 Madden, M. (2008) "Networked Workers." Pew Research Center, September 24. Available at: https://www.pewresearch.org/internet/2008/09/24/networked-workers/ (accessed May 11, 2024).

32 Candi, M. and Kahn, K.B. (2016) "Functional, Emotional, and Social Benefits of New B2B Services." *Industrial Marketing Management*, 57, pp. 177–84.

33 Casidy, R., Nyadzayo, M.W., Mohan, M. and Brown, B. (2018) "The Relative Influence of Functional versus Imagery Beliefs on Brand Sensitivity in B2B Professional Services." *Industrial Marketing Management*, 72, pp. 26–36.

34 Diba, H., Vella, J.M. and Abratt, R. (2019) "Social Media Influence on the B2B Buying Process." *Journal of Business & Industrial Marketing*, 34(7), pp. 1482–496.

35 Miller, R. (2017) "Zoom Video Conferencing Service Raises $100 Million from Sequoia on Billion-Dollar Valuation." *TechCrunch*, January 17. Available at: https://techcrunch.com/2017/01/17/sequoia-invests-100-million-in-zoom-video-conferencing-service/ (accessed May 11, 2024).

36 Cohan, P. (2017) "Zoom Scoops Customers from Cisco in $16 Billion Video Conferencing Market." *Forbes*, October 3. Available at: https://www.forbes.com/sites/petercohan/2017/10/03/zoom-scoops-customers-from-cisco-in-16-billion-videoconferencing-market/#38db91d7979b (accessed May 11, 2024).

37 Owl Labs (2018) "45% of Companies Choose Either Zoom or Skype for Business for Video Conferencing." *PR Newswire*, May 17. Available at: https://www.prnewswire.com/news-releases/45-of-companies-choose-either-zoom-or-skype-for-business-for-video-conferencing-300650065.html (accessed May 11, 2024).

38 European Centre for Disease Prevention and Control. (n.d.) "Timeline of ECDC's Response to COVID-19." Last updated April 14, 2021. Available at: https://www.ecdc.europa.eu/en/covid-19/timeline-ecdc-response (accessed May 11, 2024); BBC News. (2020) "Coronavirus: UK Worst Hit Among Major Economies," August 26. Available at: https://www.bbc.com/news/business-53918568 (accessed May 11, 2024).

39 McRae, E.R. and Aykens, P. (2022) "9 Future of Work Trends for 2023." Gartner, December 22. Available at: https://www.gartner.com/smarterwithgartner/9-future-of-work-trends-post-covid-19/ (accessed May 11, 2024).

40 Widdicombe, L. (2020) "The Great Zoom-School Experiment." *The New Yorker*, April 2. Available at: https://www.newyorker.com/news/our-local-correspondents/the-great-zoom-school-experiment (accessed May 11, 2024).

41 Kirby, J. (2020) "How to Run the World Remotely." *Vox*, May 8. Available at: https://www.vox.com/2020/5/8/21244105/coronavirus-remote-voting-zoom-parliament-congress (accessed May 11, 2024).

42 Roy, J. (2020) "How to Have Zoom Parties That Are Actually Fun." *Los Angeles Times*, April 20. Available at: https://www.latimes.com/lifestyle/story/2020-04-20/zoom-party-tips-etiquette-virtual-hangout-ideas-fun-game-night (accessed May 11, 2024).

43 Sloan, M. (2020) "The 3 Secrets Behind Zoom's Triple-Digit Growth." DRIFT, April 10. Available at: https://www.drift.com/blog/how-zoom-grew/ (accessed May 11, 2024).

44 Haselton, T. (2020) "Zoom Falls 11% After CEO Apologizes for Security Lapses, Says Daily Users Spiked to 200 Million in March." *CNBC*, April 2. Available at: https://www.cnbc.com/2020/04/02/zoom-ceo-apologizes-for-security-issues-users-spike-to-200-million.html (accessed May 11, 2024).

45 O'Flaherty, K. (2020) "Zoom Security: 100 New Features Later, Can You Trust Zoom?." *Forbes*, July 2. Available at: https://www.forbes.com/sites/kateoflahertyuk/2020/07/02/zoom-security-100-new-features-later-can-you-trust-zoom-yet/#4140d346336e (accessed May 11, 2024).

46 Lamont, T. (2020) "'After Boris Johnson's Zoom Call, All Hell Broke Loose': Inside the World's Favourite Video App." *The Guardian*, August 1. Available at: https://www.theguardian.com/technology/2020/aug/01/boris-johnson-zoom-call-world-favourite-video-app (accessed May 11, 2024).

47 Kaur, H. (2020) "Why Rural Americans Are Having a Hard Time Working from Home." *CNN US*, April 29. Available at: https://www.cnn.com/2020/04/29/us/rural-broadband-access-coronavirus-trnd/index.html (accessed May 11, 2024).

48 Abril, D. (2023) "Zoom Made Employees Return to the Office to Feel Your Hybrid Pain." *The Washington Post*, October 5. Available at: https://www.washingtonpost.com/technology/2023/10/05/zoom-return-to-office-hybrid-remote-work/ (accessed May 11, 2024).

CHAPTER 6: MARKETING FOR GLOBAL AND CROSS-CULTURAL DIFFERENCES

1 Oxford Reference. (n.d.) s.v. "Globalization." Available at: https://www.oxfordreference.com/view/10.1093/oi/authority.20110803095855259 (accessed May 11, 2024).

2 Nestlé. (2019) Annual Review 2019. Available at: https://www.nestle.com/sites/default/files/2020-03/2019-annual-review-en.pdf (accessed May 11, 2024).

3 Nestlé. (2014) Annual Report 2014. Available at: https://www.nestle.com/sites/default/files/asset-library/documents/library/documents/annual_reports/2014-annual-report-en.pdf (accessed May 11, 2024).

4 Spencer, N. (2020) "Nestlé Focuses on Meeting 'Nutritional Needs of Mexicans in All Stages of Life.'" *NutraIngredient*, March 2. Available at: https://www.nutraingredients-latam.com/Article/2020/03/02/Nestle-focuses-on-meeting-nutritional-needs-of-Mexicans-in-all-stages-of-life (accessed May 11, 2024).

5 Glusker, A. (2018) "Lessons for Success from the Founder of Sleepwear Disruptor Lunya." *Forbes*, November 12. Available at: https://www.forbes.com/sites/anneglusker/2018/11/12/lessons-for-success-from-the-founder-of-sleepwear-disruptor-lunya/#2b8dca384fb8 (accessed May 11, 2024).

6 Schomer, S. (2018) "How the Entrepreneur Behind a Luxury Sleepwear Startup Looks to Her Founder Husband for Mentorship." *Entrepreneur*, May 24. Available at: https://www.entrepreneur.com/article/311729 (accessed May 11, 2024).

7 London Business School. (2008) "Born Global," December 1. Available at: https://www.london.edu/think/born-global (accessed May 11, 2024).

8 Vanham, P. (2019) "A Brief History of Globalization." World Economic Forum, January 17. Available at: https://www.weforum.org/agenda/2019/01/how-globalization-4-0-fits-in-to-the-history-of-globalization/ (accessed May 11, 2024).

9 IMF Staff. (2008) "Globalization: A Brief Overview." International Monetary Fund, May. Available at: https://www.imf.org/external/np/exr/ib/2008/053008.htm (accessed May 11, 2024).

10 Wood, F. (2002) *The Silk Road: Two Thousand Years in the Heart of Asia*. Berkeley: University of California Press.

11 Editors of Encyclopaedia Britannica. (2024) "Silk Road." Britannica, last updated April 15, 2024. Available at: https://www.britannica.com/topic/Silk-Road-trade-route (accessed May 11, 2024).

12 Deputy Directors-General. (2018) "DDG Wolff: Trade and Foreign Policy Have Always Been Intertwined." World Trade Organization, February 5. Available at: https://www.wto.org/english/news_e/news18_e/ddgra_09feb18_e.htm (accessed May 11, 2024).

13 Brush, S.G., Spencer, J.B. and Osler, M.J. (2019) "Scientific Revolution." Britannica, November 26. Available at: https://www.britannica.com/science/Scientific-Revolution (accessed May 11, 2024).

14 Vanham, "A Brief History of Globalization."

15 Vanham, "A Brief History of Globalization."

16 Atterbury, P. (2011) "History: Victorian Technology." BBC, last updated February 17, 2011. Available at: http://www.bbc.co.uk/history/british/victorians/victorian_technology_01.shtml (accessed May 11, 2024).

17 Scott, W., Garden, F. and Mozley, J.B. (1827) "Monthly Register: Society for the Propagation of the Gospel: Liverpool District Committee." *The Christian Remembrancer, or the Churchman's Biblical, Ecclesiastical & Literary Miscellany*, 9, p. 589.

18 Bairoch, P. (1982) "International Industrialization Levels from 1750 to 1980." *Journal of European Economic History*, 11(2), p. 269.

19 Parnell, S. and Robinson, J. (2012) "(Re)theorizing Cities from the Global South: Looking Beyond Neoliberalism." *Urban Geography*, 33(4), pp. 593–617.

20 Deputy Directors-General, "DDG Wolff."

21 Dumke, R.H. (1978) "The Political Economy of German Economic Unification: Tariffs, Trade and Politics of the Zollverein Era." *Journal of Economic History*, 38(1), pp. 277–78.

22 Santana, R. (n.d.) "Clash of the GATT Negotiators." World Trade Organization. Available at: https://www.wto.org/english/tratop_e/gatt_e/clash_gatt_negotiators_e.htm (accessed May 11, 2024).

23 World Trade Organization. (n.d.) "The GATT Years: From Havana to Marrakesh." Available at: https://www.wto.org/english/thewto_e/whatis_e/tif_e/fact4_e.htm (accessed May 11, 2024).

24 World Trade Organization. (n.d.) "Fiftieth Anniversary of the Multilateral Trading System." Press Brief. Available at: https://www.wto.org/english/thewto_e/minist_e/min96_e/chrono.htm#:~:text=GATT%20entered%20into%20force.%20The%2023%20founding%20members,United%20States.%20The%20first%20Session%20of%20the%20Contracting (accessed May 11, 2024).

25 World Trade Organization, "The GATT Years."

26 Clingingsmith, D. and Williamson, J.G. (2004) "India's De-industrialization under British Rule: New Ideas, New Evidence." *National Bureau of Economic Research*, no. w10586.

27 Irwin, D.A. (1995) "The GATT in Historical Perspective." *American Economic Review*, 85(2), pp. 323–28.

28 World Trade Organization. (n.d.) "History of the Multilateral Trading System." Available at: https://www.wto.org/english/thewto_e/history_e/history_e.htm (accessed May 11, 2024).

29 Ritchie, H., Mathieu, E., Roser, M. and Ortiz-Ospina, E. (2023) "Internet." Our World in Data. Available at: https://ourworldindata.org/internet (accessed May 11, 2024).

30 Starbucks. (n.d.) "Our Company." Available at: https://www.starbucks.com/about-us/company-information/starbucks-company-timeline (accessed May 11, 2024).

31 Rajesh, M. (2013) "India's Unfair Obsession with Lighter Skin." *The Guardian*, August 14. Available at: https://www.theguardian.com/world/shortcuts/2013/aug/14/indias-dark-obsession-fair-skin (accessed May 11, 2024).

32 Shevde, N. (2008) "All's Fair in Love and Cream: A Cultural Case Study of Fair & Lovely in India." *Advertising & Society Review*, 9(2). https://doi.org/10.1353/asr.0.0003.

33 Literally Darling. (2015) "Growing Up with India's Light-Skinned Beauty Standards." *Huff Post* [blog], October 19. Available at: https://www.huffpost.com/entry/growing-up-with-indias-light-skinned-beauty-standards_b_8294810 (accessed May 11, 2024).

34 Shankar, P.R., Giri, B.R. and Palaian, S. (2006) "Fairness Creams in South Asia–A Case of Disease Mongering?." *PLoS Medicine*, 3(7), e315.

35 Goon, P. and Craven, A. (2003) "Whose Debt: Globalisation and Whitefacing in Asia." *Intersections: Gender, History and Culture in the Asian Context*, 9.

36 Oppenheim, M. (2016) "Emma Watson Responds to Criticism over 'skin Whitening' Advert." *Independent*, March 30. Available at: https://www.independent.co.uk/news/people/emma-watson-skin-whitening-twitter-galdem-a6959701.html (accessed May 11, 2024).

37 Gibson, K. (2020) "Unilever to Rename Skin-lightening Cream in India After Outcry." CBS News, June 25. Available at: https://www.cbsnews.com/news/unilever-skin-lightening-business-india-questioned/ (accessed May 11, 2024).

38 Ramirez, R. (2020) "Beauty Companies Are Changing Skin-whitening Products. But the Damage of Colorism Runs Deeper." *Vox*, July 1. Available at: https://www.vox.com/first-person/2020/6/30/21308257/skin-lightening-colorism-whitening-bleaching (accessed May 11, 2024).

39 Office of Foreign Assets Control. (n.d.) "Sanctions Programs and Country Information." Available at: https://home.treasury.gov/policy-issues/financial-sanctions/sanctions-programs-and-country-information/north-korea-sanctions (accessed May 11, 2024).

40 Edmondson, D. (2019) "Analysis: Fortune 500 Companies Global Footprint." Urbanist.co, May 29. Available at: https://urbanist.co/analysis-fortune-500-companies-global-footprint/ (accessed May 11, 2024).

41 Cavusgil, S.T., Kiyak, T. and Yeniyurt, S. (2004) "Complementary Approaches to Preliminary Foreign Market Opportunity Assessment: Country Clustering and Country Ranking." *Industrial Marketing Management*, 33(7), pp. 607–17.

42 Cavusgil, Kiyak, and Yeniyurt, "Complementary Approaches to Preliminary Foreign Market Opportunity Assessment."

43 Kim, A.B. (2024) "2024 Index of Economic Freedom." Heritage Foundation, 30th edn. Available at: https://www.heritage.org/index/ (accessed May 11, 2024).

44 McNamara, G. and Vaaler, P.M. (2000) "The Influence of Competitive Positioning and Rivalry on Emerging Market Risk Assessment." *Journal of International Business Studies*, 31(2), pp. 337–47.

45 Porter, M.E. (1985) *Competitive Advantage: Creating and Sustaining Competitive Advantage*. New York: Free Press.

46 Buckley, P.J. and Casson, M.C. (1998) "Analyzing Foreign Market Entry Strategies: Extending the Internalization Approach." *Journal of International Business Studies*, 29(3), pp. 539–61.

47 Buckley and Casson, "Analyzing Foreign Market Entry Strategies."

48 BusinessNews Staff. (2011) "KFC to Invest N1.5bn on 19 New Outlets." *BusinessNews*, April 15. Available at: http://businessnews.com.ng/2011/04/15/kfc-to-invest-n1-5bn-on-19-new-outlets/ (accessed May 11, 2024).

49 BMW Brilliance Automotive Ltd. (n.d.) "Company Introduction." Available at: http://www.bmw-brilliance.cn/cn/en/pr/bba.html (accessed May 11, 2024).

50 Buckley and Casson, "Analyzing Foreign Market Entry Strategies."

51 Ortiz-de-Mandojana, N. and Bansal, P. (2016) "The Long-Term Benefits of Organizational Resilience through Sustainable Business Practices." *Strategic Management Journal*, 37(8), pp. 1615–631.

52 Pagell, M., Wu, Z. and Wasserman, M.E. (2010) "Thinking Differently About Purchasing Portfolios: An Assessment of Sustainable Sourcing." *Journal of Supply Chain Management*, 46(1), pp. 57–73.

53 Segran, E. (2019) "H&M, Zara, and Other Fashion Brands Are Tricking Shoppers with Vague Sustainability Claims." *Fast Company*, August 7. Available at: https://www.fastcompany.com/90385370/hm-zara-and-other-fashion-brands-are-tricking-consumers-with-vague-sustainability-claims (accessed May 11, 2024).

54 Slater, S. (2019) "The 'Greenwashing' Hiding the Truth of Your Favourite Fashion Brands." *Vice*, May 1. Available at: https://www.vice.com/en/article/kzmw5a/the-greenwashing-hiding-the-truth-of-your-favourite-fashion-brands (accessed May 11, 2024).

55 Kale, S.H. and Sudharshan, D. (1987) "A Strategic Approach to International Segmentation." *International Marketing Review*, 4(2), pp. 60–70.

56 Schwartz, S.H. (1994) "Beyond Individualism/Collectivism: New Cultural Dimensions of Values." In Kim, U., Triandis, H.C., Kagitcibasi, C., Choi, S.-C. and Yoon, G. (eds.), *Individualism and Collectivism: Theory, Method, and Applications*. Thousand Oaks, CA: Sage, pp. 85–119.

57 Ng, S.I., Lee, J.A. and Soutar, G.N. (2007) "Are Hofstede's and Schwartz's Value Frameworks Congruent?." *International Marketing Review*, 24(2), pp. 164–80.

58 Torelli, C. and Cheng, S. (2011) "Cultural Meanings of Brands and Consumption: A Window into the Cultural Psychology of Globalization." *Social and Personality Psychology Compass*, 5(5), pp. 251–62.

59 Schwartz, "Beyond Individualism/Collectivism."

60 Schwartz, S.H. (2008) "The 7 Schwartz Cultural Value Orientation Scores for 80 Countries." Research Gate Publication. Available at: https://www.researchgate.net/publication/304715744_The_7_Schwartz_cultural_value_orientation_scores_for_80_countries (accessed May 11, 2024).

61 Schwartz, "The 7 Schwartz Cultural Value Orientation Scores for 80 Countries."

62 Hofstede, G. and Bond, M.H. (1984) "Hofstede's Culture Dimensions: An Independent Validation Using Rokeach's Value Survey." *Journal of Cross-Cultural Psychology*, 15(4), pp. 417–33.

63 Ng, Lee, and Soutar, "Are Hofstede's and Schwartz's Value Frameworks Congruent?"; Berry, H., Guillén, M.F. and Zhou, N. (2010) "An Institutional Approach to Cross-National Distance." *Journal of International Business Studies*, 41(9), pp. 1460–480.

64 Schwartz, "The 7 Schwartz Cultural Value Orientation Scores for 80 Countries."

65 Hopper, P. (2007) *Understanding Cultural Globalization*. Cambridge, UK: Polity Press.

66 Crane, D. (2014) "Cultural Globalization and the Dominance of the American Film Industry: Cultural Policies, National Film Industries, and Transnational Film." *International Journal of Cultural Policy*, 20(4), pp. 365–82.

67 Theodore, L. (1983) "The Globalization of Markets." *Harvard Business Review*, 61(3), pp. 92–102.

68 Business Insider. (2017) "The Rags-to-Riches Life Story of Alibaba Founder Jack Ma." Inc., March 2. Available at: https://www.inc.com/business-insider/alibaba-jack-ma-life-story.html (accessed May 11, 2024).

69 Baker, L.B., Toonkel, J. and Vlastelica, R. (2014) "Alibaba Surges 38 percent on Massive Demand in Market Debut." Reuters, September 19. Available at: https://www.reuters.com/article/us-alibaba-ipo/alibaba-surges-38-percent-on-massive-demand-in-market-debut-idUSKBN0HD2CO20140919 (accessed May 11, 2024).

70 Reuters. (2019) "Alibaba Opens to Sellers in the U.S." VentureBeat, July 23. Available at: https://venturebeat.com/2019/07/23/alibaba-opens-to-sellers-in-the-u-s/ (accessed May 11, 2024).

71 Arcieri, K. (2019) "Alibaba, Amazon Battle over US B2B Market with Rival Platforms." S&P Global, December 12. Available at: https://www.spglobal.com/marketintelligence/en/news-insights/latest-news-headlines/alibaba-amazon-battle-over-us-b2b-market-with-rival-platforms-55774891 (accessed May 11, 2024).

72 Hu, K. (2019) "Alibaba Takes on Amazon in a $1.8 Trillion US Market." Yahoo!Finance, July 23. Available at: https://finance.yahoo.com/news/alibaba-launches-us-b2b-business-compete-with-amazon-123932927.html?guccounter=1&guce_referrer=aHR0cHM6Ly93d3cuZ29vZ2xlLmNvbS8&guce_referrer_sig=AQAAABsQRI1-gTv0VrEjf3bhsXfZTsl95Yc2GGm-3986QpYIFoKVlEzasCm5ouyLH7CnMQZvEmUyMpYTItBVyX3A_XI6771HFnfkr6gfHSzA8_xNNTAoUhgiVhHTlioIwDi1-_cWAgE7CZ2OAzdYCrJy5KL-4hi6hkwQZzLF-jjugtZa (accessed May 11, 2024).

73 Arcieri, "Alibaba, Amazon Battle over US B2B Market with Rival Platforms."

74 FreightWaves. (2020) "Alibaba.com Taxis toward the B2B E-commerce Runway." BENZINGA, September 4. Available at: https://www.benzinga.com/tech/20/09/17391029/alibaba-com-taxis-toward-the-b2b-e-commerce-runway (accessed May 11, 2024).

75 Bary, E. (2020) "Alibaba Sees Growth of Its Business-to-Business Platform Accelerate Amid COVID-19." MarketWatch, May 20. Available at: https://www.marketwatch.com/story/alibaba-sees-growth-of-its-business-to-business-platform-accelerate-amid-covid-19-2020-05-20 (accessed May 11, 2024).

76 Yu, E. (2020) "Alibaba Unveils B2B Initiative for US SMBs, As More Look for Online Trade." ZDNET, January 15. Available at: https://www.zdnet.com/article/alibaba-unveils-b2b-initiative-for-us-smbs-as-more-look-for-online-trade/ (accessed May 11, 2024).

CHAPTER 7: MANAGING CUSTOMER DYNAMICS

1 Palmatier, R.W. and Crecelius, A.T. (2019) "The 'First Principles' of Marketing Strategy." *AMS Review*, 9(1–2), pp. 5–26. https://doi.org/10.1007/s13162-019-00134-y.

2 Palmatier, R. and Sridhar, S. (2017) *Marketing Strategy: Based on First Principles and Data Analytics*. London: Palgrave Macmillan.

3 Clifford, T. (2020) "'It Was Suddenly Cyber Monday' — Etsy CEO Says Sales Spiked 79% in April." CNBC, May 7. Available at: https://www.cnbc.com/2020/05/07/etsy-ceo-says-sales-jumped-79percent-in-april-likens-it-to-cyber-monday.html (accessed May 11, 2024).

4 Sherwood, I-H. (2020) "The Knot Worldwide's Chief Marketing Officer on How the Pandemic Is Reshaping Weddings." AdAge, May 25. Available at: https://adage.com/article/qaa/knot-worldwides-chief-marketing-officer-how-pandemic-reshaping-weddings/2258861 (accessed May 11, 2024).

5 Smithers, R. (2020) "Laura Ashley Returns to UK High Street After Deal with Next." *The Guardian*, October 31. Available at: https://www.theguardian.com/business/2020/oct/31/laura-ashley-returns-to-uk-high-street-after-deal-with-next (accessed May 11, 2024).

6 Yum. (n.d.) "Pizza Hut." Available at: https://www.yum.com/wps/portal/yumbrands/Yumbrands/company/our-brands/pizza-hut (accessed May 11, 2024).

7 Elliott, S. (2014) "In Overhaul, Pizza Hut Tries Adventurous Menu Offerings and a Dash of Irreverence." *The New York Times*, November 18. Available at: https://www.nytimes.com/2014/11/19/business/media/in-overhaul-pizza-hut-tries-adventurous-menu-offerings-and-a-dash-of-irreverence.html (accessed May 11, 2024).

8 Shah, K. (2014) "Pizza Hut Hopes Putting Sriracha on Everything Will Make It Cool Again." Eater, November 10. Available at: https://www.eater.com/2014/11/10/7186125/pizza-hut-hopes-putting-sriracha-on-everything-will-make-it-cool-again (accessed May 11, 2024).

9 Ruggless, R. (2015) "Pizza Hut Works to Readjust Brand Overhaul." Nation's Restaurant News, May 29. Available at: https://www.nrn.com/pizza-hut/pizza-hut-works-readjust-brand-overhaul (accessed May 11, 2024).

10 Ruggless, "Pizza Hut Works to Readjust Brand Overhaul."

11 Lee, E., Mathur, A. and Moschis, G. (2003) "Life Events and Brand Preference Changes." *Journal of Consumer Behavior* 3(2), pp. 129–41.

12 Yang, H. (2011) "College Student's Apparel Shopping Orientation Changes in Relation to Life Events." MS thesis, Louisiana State University.

13 Lee, Mathur, and Moschis, "Life Events and Brand Preference Changes."

14 Palmatier, R.W. (2006) *Relationship Marketing*. Cambridge, MA: Marketing Science Institute.

15 Leonhard, D. and Schüßler, E. (2013) "Theorizing Path Dependence: A Review of Positive Feedback Mechanisms in Technology Markets, Regional Clusters, and Organizations," *Industrial & Corporate Change*, 22(3), pp. 617–47.

16 Carpenter, G.S. and Nakamoto, K. (1988) "Market Pioneering, Learning, and Preference." *Advances in Consumer Research*, 15, pp. 275–79.

17 Troake, J. and McAdam, P. (2008) "Customer relationship White Paper: Growing Customer Relationships: 90 Days that Make It or Break It." *Xerox Global Services and BAI Research.*

18 Hydock, C., Paharia, N., and Weber, T.J. (2019) "The Consumer Response to Corporate Political Advocacy: A Review and Future Directions." *Customer Needs and Solutions*, 6(3), pp. 76–83.

19 Bhagwat, Y., Warren, N.L., Beck, J.T. and Watson IV, G.F. (2020) "Corporate Sociopolitical Activism and Firm Value." *Journal of Marketing*, 84(5), pp. 1–21.

20 TOI Staff. (2021) "Ben & Jerry's Founders: It's a Boycott of Settlements, Not of Israel." *Times of Israel*, October 11. Available at: https://www.timesofisrael.com/ben-jerrys-founders-its-a-boycott-of-settlements-not-of-israel/ (accessed May 11, 2024).

21 Naidu, R. and Kerber, R. (2022) "Unilever Expects New Ben & Jerry's 'Arrangement' for Israel by Year-End." Reuters, February 10. Available at: https://www.reuters.com/markets/

europe/unilever-expects-new-ben-jerrys-arrangement-israel-by-year-end-2022-02-10/ (accessed May 11, 2024).

22 Events. (2018) "Wetherspoon Launches 500,000 New Brexit Beer Mats in Its Pubs." Wetherpoon, August 25. Available at: https://www.jdwetherspoon.com/news/2018/08/wetherspoon-launches-500000-new-brexit-beer-mats-in-its-pubs (accessed May 11, 2024).

23 Statista Research Department. (2023) "Annual Sales of JD Wetherspoon in the United Kingdom (UK) and Ireland from 2007 to 2022." Statista, September 7. Available at: https://www.statista.com/statistics/641568/wetherspoon-revenue-united-kingdom-ireland/ (accessed May 11, 2024).

24 Machado, R.P. and Scalco, L.M. (2022) "The Right to Shine: Poverty, Consumption and (De)politicization in Neoliberal Brazil." *Journal of Consumer Culture*, 23(2), pp. 312–30.

25 Bauer, B. and Auer-Srnka, K.J. (2012) "The Life Cycle Concept in Marketing Research." *Journal of Historical Research in Marketing*, 4(1), pp. 68–96; Wells, W. and Gubar, G. (1966) "Life Cycle Concept in Marketing Research." *Journal of Marketing Research*, 3(4), pp. 355–63.; Rich, S. and Jain, S. (1968) "Social Class and Life Cycle as Predictors of Shopping Behavior." *Journal of Marketing Research*, 5(1), pp. 41–9.; Ghez, G. and Becker, G. (1975) *The Allocation of Time and Goods over the Life Cycle.* New York: National Bureau of Economic Research; Stampfl, R. (1978) "The Consumer Life Cycle." *Journal of Consumer Affairs*, 12(2), pp. 209–19.; Arndt, J. (1979) "Family Life Cycle as a Determinant of Size and Composition of Household Expenditures." *Advances in Consumer Researchi*, 6, pp. 128–32.; Wagner, J. and Hanna, S. (1983) "The Effectiveness of Family Life Cycle Variables in Consumer Expenditure Research." *Journal of Consumer Research*, 10(3), pp. 281–91.

26 Wells and Gubar, "Life Cycle Concept in Marketing Research"; Rich and Jain, "Social Class and Life Cycle as Predictors of Shopping Behavior."

27 Arndt, J. (1979) "Toward a Concept of Domesticated Markets." *Journal of Marketing*, 43(4), pp. 69–75; Wagner and Hanna, "The Effectiveness of Family Life Cycle Variables in Consumer Expenditure Research"; Rouse, M. (2007) "Customer Life Cycle Definition." *SearchSalesforce.* Available at: http://searchcrm.techtarget.com/definition/customer-life-cycle (accessed January 27, 2016).

28 Samsubg Newsroom. (2014) "[Infograhic] Evolution of Samsung TV Remote Controls," January 1. Available at: https://news.samsung.com/global/evolution-of-samsung-tv-remote-controls (accessed May 11, 2024).

29 Kim, E. (2014) "Here's How Samsung Spent Billions of Dollars to Destroy Apple with Attack Ads." Business Insider, September 24. Available at: https://www.businessinsider.com/samsung-apple-parody-ads-2014-9 (accessed May 11, 2024).

30 Inc. (n.d.) "Industry Life Cycle," January 5. Available at: http://www.inc.com/encyclopedia/industry-life-cycle.html (accessed January 27, 2016); The Investopedia Team. (2006) "Understanding the Industry Life Cycle: Phases and Examples." Investopedia, December 13. Available at: http://www.investopedia.com/terms/i/industrylifecycle.asp (accessed May 11, 2024).

31 Salfino, C. (2014) "Cotton Still the 'Fabric of Our Lives' After 25 Years." *Sourcing Journal*, December 1. Available at: https://sourcingjournal.com/topics/lifestyle-monitor/cotton-still-fabric-lives-25-years-21163/ (accessed May 11, 2024).

32 Fedorova, I. (2014) "The Heady Style of the Heady 1990s." Russia Beyond, April 8. Available at: https://www.rbth.com/arts/2014/04/08/getting_it_right_and_getting_it_wrong_the_heady_style_of_the_heady_1990s_35759.html (accessed May 11, 2024).

33 CoinMarketCap. (n.d.) "Today's Cryptocurrency Prices by Market Cap." Available at: https://coinmarketcap.com/ (accessed May 11, 2024).

34 Dyvik, E.H. (2023) "The 100 Largest Companies in the World by Market Capitalization in 2023." *Statista*, August 30. Available at: https://www.statista.com/statistics/263264/top-companies-in-the-world-by-market-capitalization/ (accessed May 11, 2024).

35 Wong, Q. (2022) "Twitter Rolls Out a Way to Showcase Your NFTs." CNET, January 20. Available at: https://www.cnet.com/personal-finance/crypto/twitter-rolls-out-a-way-to-showcase-nfts/ (accessed May 11, 2024).

36 Tan, E. (2021) "Crypto Fans Rejoice, Gamers Revolt as Ubisoft Announces NFT Plans." CoinDesk, December 7. Available at: https://www.coindesk.com/business/2021/12/07/crypto-fans-rejoice-gamers-revolt-as-ubisoft-announces-nft-plans/ (accessed May 11, 2024).

37 Carmona, T. (2022) "Mayors: Cryptocurrency Won't Solve Your Cities' Problems." Brookings, March 22. Available at: https://www.brookings.edu/blog/the-avenue/2022/03/22/mayors-cryptocurrency-wont-solve-your-cities-problems/ (accessed May 11, 2024).

38 FutureCast. (2012) "At Last, a Millennial Segmentation." *Millennial Marketing*, April. Available at: http://www.millennial-marketing.com/2012/04/at-last-a-millennial-segmentation/ (accessed January 29, 2016).

39 Accenture. (2011) *Smarter Onboarding: The Key to Higher Client Retention and Cross-Sell.* Available at: https://www.accenture.com/us-en/~/media/Accenture/Conversion-Assets/DotCom/Documents/Global/PDF/Industries_5/Accenture-Client-Onboarding2011.pdf (accessed May 11, 2024).

40 Che, H., Erdem, T. and Öncü, T.S. (2008) "Consumer Learning and Evolution of Consumer Brand Preferences," *Quant itative Marketing and Economics*, 13(3), pp. 173–202; Troake, J. and McAdam, P. (2008) "Customer Relationship White Paper: Growing Customer Relationships: 90 Days that Make It or Break It." *Xerox Global Services and BAI Research.*

41 Palmatier, R.W. (2008) *Relationship Marketing.* Cambridge: Marketing Science Institute; Palmatier, R.W. and Steinhoff, L. (2014) "Understanding Loyalty Program Effectiveness: Managing Target and Bystander Effects," *Journal of the Academy of Marketing Science*, 44(1), pp. 88–107; Yohn, D.L. (2014) "Great Brands Aim for Customers' Hearts, Not Their Wallets," *Forbes*, January 8.

42 Shaw, R. and Stone, M. (1988) *Database Marketing.* London: Gower.

43 Farris, P., Bendle, N., Pfeifer, P.E. and Reibstein, D. (2015) *Marketing Metrics: The Manager's Guide to Measuring Marketing Performance.* London: Pearson FT Press.

44 Weinstein, A. (2002) "Customer Retention: A Usage Segmentation and Customer Value Approach." *Journal of Targeting, Measurement and Analysis for Marketing*, 10(3), pp. 259–69.

45 AstraZeneca. (n.d.) "Our Company." Available at: https://www.astrazeneca.com/our-company/our-strategy.html (accessed May 11, 2024).

46 Oxford Science Enterprises. (2020) "The Backstory: Vaccitech and Its Role in Co-inventing the Oxford COVID-19 Vaccine," November 23. Available at: https://enterprise-labs.oxfordscienceenterprises.com/news/the-backstory-vaccitech-and-its-role-in-co-inventing-the-oxford-covid-19-vaccine/ (accessed May 11, 2024).

47 BBC News. (2021) "Covid: Brian Pinker, 82, First to Get Oxford-AstraZeneca Vaccine," January 4. Available at: https://www.bbc.com/news/uk-55525542 (accessed May 11, 2024).

48 Katella, K. (2024) "Comparing the COVID-19 Vaccines: How Are They Different?." Yale Medicine, April 24. Available at: https://www.yalemedicine.org/news/covid-19-vaccine-comparison (accessed May 11, 2024).

49 The Economist. (2020) "An Effective Covid-19 Vaccine Is a Turning Point in the Pandemic," November 14. Available at: https://www.economist.com/briefing/2020/11/14/an-effective-covid-19-vaccine-is-a-turning-point-in-the-pandemic (accessed May 11, 2024).

50 Kupferschmidt, K. and Vogel, G. (2021) "Hard Choices Emerge As Link between AstraZeneca Vaccine and Rare Clotting Disorder Becomes Clearer." Science, April 11. Available at: https://www.science.org/content/article/hard-choices-emerge-link-between-astrazeneca-vaccine-and-rare-clotting-disorder-becomes (accessed May 11, 2024).

51 World Health Organization. (2022) "The Oxford/AstraZeneca (ChAdOx1-S [Recombinant] Vaccine) COVID-19 Vaccine: What You Need to Know," June 13. Available at: https://www.who.int/news-room/feature-stories/detail/the-oxford-astra-zeneca-covid-19-vaccine-what-you-need-to-know (accessed May 11, 2024).

52 Reuters. (2021) "South Africa Sells AstraZeneca COVID-19 Vaccines to Other African Countries," March 21. Available at: https://www.reuters.com/article/us-health-coronavirus-safrica-vaccine-idUSKBN2BD0K4 (accessed May 11, 2024).

53 Henley, J. (2021) "Spain, Belgium and Italy Restrict Astra-Zeneca Covid Vaccine to Older People." *The Guardian*, April 8. Available at: https://www.theguardian.com/society/2021/apr/08/spain-belgium-and-italy-restrict-astrazeneca-covid-vaccine-to-older-people (accessed May 11, 2024).

54 Hatmal, M.M.M., Al-Hatamleh, M.A., Olaimat, A.N., Hatmal, M., Alhaj-Qasem, D.M., Olaimat, T.M. and Mohamud, R. (2021) "Side Effects and Perceptions Following COVID-19 Vaccination in Jordan: A Randomized, Cross-sectional Study Implementing Machine Learning for Predicting Severity of Side Effects." *Vaccines*, 9(6), p. 556.

55 Mahase, E. (2021) "Covid-19: AstraZeneca Vaccine Is Not Linked to Increased Risk of Blood Clots, Finds European Medicine Agency." *thebmj*, 372:n774.

56 Stewart, C. (2022) "Distribution of COVID-19 Vaccine Doses Distributed to the European Economic Area (EEA) as of July 21, 2022, by Manufacturer." *Statista*, July 26. Available at: https://www.statista.com/statistics/1219343/covid19-vaccine-doses-distributed-in-europe-by-manufacturer/ (accessed May 11, 2024).

57 Dunleavy, K. (2022) "AstraZeneca's COVID Vaccine Sales Reached $4B Last Year, But Don't Expect that Much in 2022." FIERCE Pharma, February 10. Available at: https://www.fiercepharma.com/pharma/astrazeneca-vaccine-sales-reached-4-billion-last-year-but-don-t-expect-2022-company-says (accessed May 11, 2024).

CHAPTER 8: THE CHANGING WORLD OF RETAIL AND OMNICHANNEL MARKETING

1 Crunchbase. (n.d.) "Rush Hair." Available at: https://www.crunchbase.com/organization/rush-hair (accessed May 12, 2024).

2 Booms, B. and Bitner, M.J. (1981) "Marketing Strategies and Organizational Structures for Service Firms." In Donnelly, J.H. and George, W.R. (eds.), *Marketing of Services*. Chicago: American Marketing Association, pp. 47–51.

3 Sabanoglu, T. (2024) "Retail Market Worldwide—Statistics & Facts." *Statista*, April 19. Available at: https://www.statista.com/topics/5922/retail-market-worldwide/#dossierContents__outerWrapper (accessed May 13, 2024).

4 Rathmell, J.M. (1966) "What Is Meant by Services?." *Journal of Marketing*, 30(4), pp. 32–6.

5 Vargo, S.L. and Lusch, R.F. (2004) "Evolving to a New Dominant Logic for Marketing." *Journal of Marketing*, 68(1), pp. 1–17.

6 Mende, M. (2019) "Retail Apocalypse or Golden Opportunity for Retail Frontline Management?." *Journal of Retailing*, 95(2), p. 84.

7 Hudson;s Bay Company. (n.d.) "Lord & Taylor." Available at: https://www.hbcheritage.ca/history/acquisitions/lord-taylor (accessed May 13, 2024).

8 Howland, D. (2020) "What Happened to Lord & Taylor." Retail Dive, August 4. Available at: https://www.retaildive.com/news/what-happened-to-lord-taylor/582847/ (accessed May 13, 2024).

9 Tashjian, R. (2022) "Does Brooks Brothers Really Need to Be Reinvented?." *GQ*, February 3. Available at: https://www.gq.com/story/brooks-brothers-michael-bastian-quality (accessed May 13, 2024).

10 Alexander, N. and Akehurst, G. (1998) "Introduction: The Emergence of Modern Retailing, 1750–1950." *Business History*, 40(4), pp. 1–15.

11 Stearns, P.N. (1997) "Stages of Consumerism: Recent Work on the Issues of Periodization." *Journal of Modern History*, 69(1), pp. 102–17.

12 Higgs, K. (2021) "How the World Embraced Consumerism." BBC Future, January 20. Available at: https://www.bbc.com/future/article/20210120-how-the-world-became-consumerist (accessed May 13, 2024).

13 Crossick, G. and Jaumain, S. (eds.). (2019) *Cathedrals of Consumption: European Department Stores, 1850–1939*. New York: Routledge.

14 Ross, A. (2016) "The Surprising Way a Supermarket Changed the World." *Time*, September 9. Available at: https://time.com/4480303/supermarkets-history/ (accessed May 13, 2024).

15 Shaw, G., Curth, L. and Alexander, A. (2004) "Selling Self-Service and the Supermarket: The Americanisation of Food Retailing in Britain, 1945–60." *Business History*, 46(4), pp. 568–82.

16 Anzilotti, E. (2016) "A Brief History of the 24-Hour Convenience Store." Bloomberg, February 1. Available at: https://www.bloomberg.com/news/articles/2016-02-01/a-brief-history-of-the-24-hour-convenience-store (accessed May 13, 2024).

17 NPR Staff. (2012) "The Past and Future of America's Biggest Retailers." NPR, November 19. Available at: https://www.npr.org/2012/11/19/165295840/the-past-and-future-of-americas-biggest-retailers (accessed May 13, 2024).

18 Feinberg, R.A. and Meoli, J. (1991) "A Brief History of the Mall." *ACR North American Advances*, 18, pp. 426–27.

19 Diamond, A. (2019) "A Crispy, Salty, American History of Fast Food." *Smithsonian Magazine*, June 24. Available at: https://www.smithsonianmag.com/history/crispy-salty-american-history-fast-food-180972459/ (accessed May 13, 2024).

20 Brennan, D.P. and Lundsten, L. (2000) "Impacts of Large Discount Stores on Small US Towns: Reasons for Shopping and Retailer Strategies." *International Journal of Retail & Distribution Management*, 28(45), pp. 155–61.

21 Blitz, M. (2019) "Later, Navigator: How Netscape Won and Then Lost the World Wide Web." *Popular Mechanics*, April 4. Available at: https://www.popularmechanics.com/culture/web/a27033147/netscape-navigator-history/ (accessed May 13, 2024).

22 Goldman, D. (2010) "10 Big Dot.com Flops." CNN Money, March 10. Available at: https://money.cnn.com/galleries/2010/technology/1003/gallery.dot_com_busts/ (accessed May 13, 2024).

23 Russell, K. (2013) "11 Hilariously Wrong Predictions About the Internet." *Business Insider*, November 4. Available at: https://www.businessinsider.com/11-hilariously-wrong-internet-predictions-2013-11#robert-metcalfe-the-inventor-of-ethernet-wrote-an-article-for-infoworld-in-december-1995-in-which-he-predicted-i-predict-the-internet-will-soon-go-spectacularly-supernova-and-in-1996-catastrophically-collapse-2 (accessed May 13, 2024).

24 Koukova, N.T., Srivastava, J. and Steul-Fischer, M. (2012) "The Effect of Shipping Fee Structure on Consumers' Online Evaluations and Choice." *Journal of the Academy of Marketing Science*, 40(6), pp. 759–70.

25 Bower, A.B. and Maxham III, J.G. (2012) "Return Shipping Policies of Online Retailers: Normative Assumptions and the Long-Term Consequences of Fee and Free Returns." *Journal of Marketing*, 76(5), pp. 110–24.

26 Wang, L., Baker, J., Wakefield, K. and Wakefield, R. (2017) "Is Background Music Effective on Retail Websites?." *Journal of Promotion Management*, 23(1), pp. 1–23.

27 Bell, D.R., Gallino, S. and Moreno, A. (2014) "How to Win in an Omnichannel World." *MIT Sloan Management Review*, 56(1), p. 45.

28 Wassel, B. (2019) "Marshalls to Launch E-commerce Site for the First Time in 2019." *Retail Touchpoints*, February 27. Available at: https://www.retailtouchpoints.com/features/news-briefs/marshalls-to-launch-e-commerce-site-for-the-first-time-in-2019 (accessed May 13, 2024).

29 Olson, P. (2019) "Meet the Billionaire Who Defied Amazon and Built Wish, the World's Most-Downloaded e-Commerce App." *Forbes*, March 13. Available at: https://www.forbes.com/sites/parmyolson/2019/03/13/meet-the-billionaire-who-defied-amazon-and-built-wish-the-worlds-most-downloaded-e-commerce-app/?sh=2aa39ab770f5 (accessed May 13, 2024).

30 Bloomberg News. (2018) "Wish Faces Criticism Over Suspected Counterfeits." *Digital Commerce 360*, July 17. Available at: https://www.digitalcommerce360.com/2018/07/17/wish-faces-criticism-over-suspected-counterfeits/ (accessed May 13, 2024).

31 Hays, K. (2018) "Off-White Going After Fakes Being Sold on Wish.com with Lawsuit." *WWD*, April 4. Available at: https://wwd.com/business-news/legal/off-white-going-after-fakes-being-sold-on-wish-com-with-lawsuit-1202643968/ (accessed May 13, 2024).

32 Herhausen, D., Binder, J., Schoegel, M. and Herrmann, A. (2015) "Integrating Bricks with Clicks: Retailer-Level and Channel-Level Outcomes of Online–Offline Channel Integration." *Journal of Retailing*, 91(2), pp. 309–25.

33 MediaMarkt. (n.d.). Available at: http://www.mediamarkt.com/ (accessed May 13, 2024).

34 Statt, N. (2018) "Valve's New Steam Revenue Agreement Gives More Money to Game Developers." The Verge, November 30. Available at: https://www.theverge.com/2018/11/30/18120577/valve-steam-game-marketplace-revenue-split-new-rules-competition (accessed May 13, 2024).

35 Lomas, N. (2017) "Tesco Launches One-Hour Grocery Deliveries in London, Powered by Quiqup." TechCrunch, June 26. Available at: https://techcrunch.com/2017/06/26/tesco-launches-one-hour-grocery-deliveries-in-london-powered-by-quiqup/ (accessed May 13, 2024).

36 Brzezinski, V. (2019) "IKEA Billy Bookcase Remains King of Shelves." *The Times*, April 19. Available at: https://www.thetimes.co.uk/article/ikeas-billy-bookcase-remains-king-of-shelves-pf2qnptl7 (accessed May 15, 2024).

37 Clifford, C. (2019) "Meatballs and DIY Bookcases: The Psychology Behind Ikea's Iconic Success." CNBC, October 5. Available at: https://www.cnbc.com/2019/10/05/psychology-behind-ikeas-huge-success.html (accessed May 13, 2024).

38 Santos, M.R. (2018) "I Love You IKEA, But Why Is Your Website so...?." Medium, August 15. Available at: https://uxdesign.cc/i-love-you-ikea-but-why-is-your-website-so-abae4ce8658 (accessed May 13, 2024).

39 Co.Design. (2020) "Ikea's E-commerce Was Already Pretty Bad. During COVID-19, It Absolutely Fell Apart." Fast Company, September 8. Available at: https://www.fastcompany.com/90547486/ikeas-e-commerce-was-already-pretty-bad-during-covid-19-it-absolutely-fell-apart (accessed May 13, 2024).

40 Wootton, R. (2001) "Recent Advances: Telemedicine." *BMJ*, 323(7312), pp. 557–60. https://doi.org/10.1136/bmj.323.7312.557.

41 Hill, A. (2020) "Telemedicine in Bangladesh: The Way Forward." Borgan Project, February 19. Available at: https://borgenproject.org/telemedicine-in-bangladesh/ (accessed May 13, 2024).

42 Gajarawala, S.N. and Pelkowski, J.N. (2021) "Telehealth Benefits and Barriers." *Journal for Nurse Practitioners*, 17(2), pp. 218–21. https://doi.org/10.1016/j.nurpra.2020.09.013.

43 Uddin Quadery, S.E., Hasan, M. and Khan, M.M. (2021) "Consumer Side Economic Perception of Telemedicine During COVID-19 Era: A Survey on Bangladesh's Perspective." Informatics in Medicine Unlocked, 27, 100797. https://doi.org/10.1016/j.imu.2021.100797.

44 Winkler, R. (2022) "Cerebral's Preferred Pharmacy Truepill Halts Adderall Prescriptions for All Customers." *The Wall Street Journal*, May 2. Available at: https://www.wsj.com/articles/cerebrals-preferred-pharmacy-truepill-halts-adderall-prescriptions-for-all-customers-11651504078?mod=article_inline (accessed May 15, 2024).

45 Martins, M. (2018) "Tata Cliq Luxury Named Exclusive Retail Partner for Woolmark in India." Fashion Network, January 9.

Available at: https://in.fashionnetwork.com/news/tata-cliq-luxury-named-exclusive-retail-partner-for-woolmark-in-india,933954.html (accessed May 15, 2024).

46 Simonin, B.L. and Ruth, J.A. (1998) "Is a Company Known by the Company It Keeps? Assessing the Spillover Effects of Brand Alliances on Consumer Brand Attitudes." *Journal of Marketing Research*, 35(1), pp. 30–42.

47 Mitchell, S. (2019) "Walmart's Monopolization of Local Grocery Markets." Institute for Local Self-Reliance. Available at: https://ilsr.org/wp-content/uploads/2019/06/Walmart_Grocery_Monopoly_Report-_final_for_site.pdf (accessed May 15, 2024).

48 Wilmers, N. (2018) "Wage Stagnation and Buyer Power: How Buyer-Supplier Relations Affect US workers' Wages, 1978 to 2014." *American Sociological Review*, 83(2), pp. 213–42.

49 Scott, M. (2016) "In Shadow of Amazon, European Challenger Looks to China for Inspiration." *The New York Times*, December 16. Available at: https://www.nytimes.com/2016/12/16/technology/amazon-zalando-eu-online-shopping.html (accessed May 15, 2024).

50 Reuters. (2021) "Zalando Aims for More Than 10% of Europe Fashion Market," March 16. Available at: https://www.reuters.com/article/us-zalando-results-idUSKBN2B80PU (accessed May 15, 2024).

51 Van Looveren, Y. (2018) "Zalando Expands Collaboration with German Retailers." Retail Detail, February 16. Available at: https://www.retaildetail.eu/news/fashion/zalando-expands-collaboration-german-retailers/ (accessed May 15, 2024).

52 Brown, H. (2018) "First Look: Zalando to Open Berlin Beauty Store." *Drapers*, July 27. Available at: https://www.drapersonline.com/news/first-look-zalando-to-open-berlin-beauty-store (accessed May 13, 2024).

53 Avery, J., Steenburgh, T.J., Deighton, J. and Caravella, M. (2012) "Adding Bricks to Clicks: Predicting the Patterns of Cross-Channel Elasticities Over Time." *Journal of Marketing*, 76(3), pp. 96–111.

54 Van Looveren, "Zalando Expands Collaboration with German Retailers."

55 Zalando. (n.d.) "Connected Retail." Available at: https://corporate.zalando.com/en/brands-retailers/partnership-models/connected-retail (accessed May 22, 2024).

CHAPTER 9: MARKETING RESEARCH AND ANALYTICS FOR MANAGING CUSTOMER DYNAMICS AND CUSTOMER DIFFERENCES

1 Tonkin, S. (2022) "Lab-grown Lion Burgers, Tiger Steaks and Zebra Sushi Rolls Could Soon Be on the Menu in Britain After Start-up Reveals Plans for 'Cultivated' Exotic Meat Products." *Mail Online*, April 12. Available at: https://www.dailymail.co.uk/sciencetech/article-10710861/Lab-grown-exotic-meat-tiger-steaks-lion-burgers-soon-British-dinner-tables.html (accessed May 13, 2024).

2 Ma, L., Sun, B. and Kekre, S. (2015) "The Squeaky Wheel Gets the Grease—An Empirical Analysis of Customer Voice and Firm Intervention on Twitter." *Marketing Science*, 34(5), pp. 627–45.

3 LG. (2011) "LG Cinema 3D TV Is the Most Startling Innovation I Have Seen – Soyinka." Press Release, June 24. Available at: https://www.lg.com/africa/about-lg/press-and-media/lg-cinema-3d-tv-is-the-most-startling-innovation-i-have-seen-soyinka (accessed May 13, 2024).

4 Leswing, K. (2017) "3D TV Is Dead." *Business Insider*, January 24. Available at: https://www.businessinsider.com/3d-tv-is-dead-2017-1 (accessed May 13, 2024).

5 Charlton, A. (2016) "3D Television Is Dead: Samsung and LG Cut Back on 3D TV Production." *International Business Times*, February 8. Available at: https://www.ibtimes.co.uk/3d-television-dead-samsung-lg-cut-back-3d-tv-production-1542580 (accessed May 13, 2024).

6 Munford, M. (2014) "How Social Media Predicted the Failure of 4K and 3D TVs." *Forbes*, November 4. Available at: https://www.forbes.com/sites/montymunford/2014/11/04/how-social-media-predicted-the-failure-of-4k-and-3d-tvs/?sh=23bf92fe596d (accessed May 13, 2024).

7 Calder, B.J. (1977) "Focus Groups and the Nature of Qualitative Marketing Research." *Journal of Marketing Research*, 14(3), pp. 353–64.

8 Bloch, P.H., Gopalakrishna, S., Crecelius, A.T. and Scatolin Murarolli, M. (2017) "Exploring Booth Design as a Determinant of Trade Show Success." *Journal of Business-to-Business Marketing*, 24(4), pp. 237–56.

9 Lawrence, J.M., Crecelius, A.T., Scheer, L.K. and Patil, A. (2019) "Multichannel Strategies for Managing the Profitability of Business-to-Business Customers." *Journal of Marketing Research*, 56(3), pp. 479–97.

10 Crecelius, A.T., Lawrence, J.M., Lee, J.Y., Lam, S.K. and Scheer, L.K. (2019) "Effects of Channel Members' Customer-centric Structures on Supplier Performance." *Journal of the Academy of Marketing Science*, 47(1), pp. 56–75.

11 Grimm, P. (2010) "Social Desirability Bias." *Wiley International Encyclopedia of Marketing.* https://doi.org/10.1002/9781444316568.wiem02057.

12 Milgram, S. (1963) "Behavioral Study of Obedience." *Journal of Abnormal and Social Psychology*, 67(4), p. 371.

13 Donneau-Golencer, T. (2020) "Einstein Prediction Builder: How to Turn Your Idea Into a Prediction." Salesforce Admins, November 24. Available at: https://admin.salesforce.com/blog/2020/einstein-prediction-builder-how-to-turn-your-idea-into-a-prediction (accessed May 13, 2024).

14 Magistretti, S., Pham, C.T.A. and Dell'Era, C. (2021) "Enlightening the Dynamic Capabilities of Design Thinking in Fostering Digital Transformation." *Industrial Marketing Management*, 97, pp. 59–70.

15 Liedtka, J. (2018) "Why Design Thinking Works." *Harvard Business Review*, 96(5), pp. 72–9.

16 Mosavi, N.S. and Santos, M.F. (2020) "How Prescriptive Analytics Influences Decision Making in Precision Medicine." *Procedia Computer Science*, 177, pp. 528–33.

17 Friendly, M. (2008) "A Brief History of Data Visualization." In Chen C.-h., Härdle, W. and Unwin, A. (eds.), *Handbook of Data Visualization*. Berlin: Springer, pp. 15–56.

18 Potter, M.C., Wyble, B., Hagmann, C.E. and McCourt, E.S. (2014) "Detecting Meaning in RSVP at 13 ms per Picture." *Attention, Perception, & Psychophysics*, 76(2), pp. 270–79.

19 Tyler Vigen. (n.d.) "Spurious Correlations." Available at: http://www.tylervigen.com/spurious-correlations (accessed May 13, 2024).

20 Congressional Research Services. (2020) EU Data Protection Rules and U.S. Implications. Report, updated July 17. Available at: https://sgp.fas.org/crs/row/IF10896.pdf (accessed May 13, 2024).
21 Arkansas State University. (2020) "Differences Between EU and US Data Protection," October 8. Available at: https://degree.astate.edu/articles/media-management/eu-and-us-data-protection.aspx (accessed May 13, 2024).
22 Tetlock, P.E. and Gardner, D. (2016) *Superforecasting: The Art and Science of Prediction*. New York: Random House.
23 Mosavi and Santos, "How Prescriptive Analytics Influences Decision Making in Precision Medicine."
24 Chapman, P., Clinton, J., Kerber, R., Khabaza, T., Reinartz, T., Shearer, C. and Wirth, R. (1999) "The CRISP-DM User Guide." In *4th CRISP-DM SIG Workshop in Brussels*, March 1999.
25 IBM. (2021) "CRISP-DM Help Overview," August 17. Available at: https://www.ibm.com/docs/en/spss-modeler/SaaS?topic=dm-crisp-help-overview (accessed May 13, 2024).
26 Schröer, C., Kruse, F. and Gómez, J.M. (2021) "A Systematic Literature Review on Applying CRISP-DM Process Model." *Procedia Computer Science*, 181, pp. 526–34.
27 Baron, A.S., Zaltman, G. and Olson, J. (2017) "Barriers to Advancing the Science and Practice of Marketing." *Journal of Marketing Management*, 33(11–12), pp. 893–908.

CHAPTER 10: MANAGING SUSTAINABLE COMPETITIVE ADVANTAGE

1 Palmatier, R.W. and Crecelius, A.T. (2019) "The 'First Principles' of Marketing Strategy." *AMS Review*, 9(1–2), pp. 5–26. https://doi.orghttps/10.1007/s13162-019-00134-y.
2 Tzu, S. ([fifth century BCE] 1963) *The Art of War*, translated by Griffith, S.B. Oxford: Clarendon Press.
3 Shah, D., Rust, R.T., Parasuraman, A., Staelin, R. and Day, G.S. (2006) "The Path to Customer Centricity." *Journal of Service Research*, 9(2), 113–24.
4 Palmatier, R. and Sridhar, S. (2017) *Marketing Strategy: Based on First Principles and Data Analytics*. London: Palgrave Macmillan.
5 Saint, N. (2009) "10 First-to-Market Products That Lost." *Business Insider*, December 1. Available at: https://www.businessinsider.com/10-first-to-market-companies-that-lost-out-to-latecomers-2009-11#friendster-1 (accessed May 13, 2024).
6 Chen, M.J. (1996) "Competitor Analysis and Interfirm Rivalry: Toward a Theoretical Integration." *Academy of Management Review*, 21(1), pp. 100–134.
7 Leeflang, P.S. and Wittink, D.R. (2001) "Explaining Competitive Reaction Effects." *International Journal of Research in Marketing*, 18(1–2), pp. 119–37.
8 Caldwell, D. (2021) "Empty Seats and Scandals: It Appears No One Wants to Be a Washington Fan." *The Guardian*, November 17. Available at: https://www.theguardian.com/sport/2021/nov/17/empty-seats-and-scandals-it-appears-no-one-wants-to-be-a-washington-fan (accessed May 13, 2024).
9 Satell, G. (2016) "Why You Shouldn't Copycat Strategy." *Forbes*, November 12. Available at: https://www.forbes.com/sites/gregsatell/2016/11/12/why-you-shouldnt-copycat-strategy/?sh=7dee1cd73311 (accessed May 13, 2024).
10 Statista Research Department. (2011) "Global Smartphone Market Share of Nokia Symbian and Microsoft from 2008 to 2015." *Statista*, December 31. Available at: https://www.statista.com/statistics/219966/global-smartphone-market-shareforecast-of-symbian-and-microsoft/ (accessed May 13, 2024).
11 Doz, Y.L. (2017) "The Strategic Decisions That Caused Nokia's Failure." *Knowledge*, November 23. Available at: https://knowledge.insead.edu/strategy/strategic-decisions-caused-nokias-failure (accessed May 13, 2024).
12 BBC News. (2013) "Nokia: The Rise and Fall of a Mobile Giant," September 3. Available at: https://www.bbc.com/news/technology-23947212 (accessed May 13, 2024).
13 Swart, M. (2019) "The World's Most Valuable Brands." *Forbes*. Available at: https://www.forbes.com/the-worlds-most-valuable-brands/#48246ea7119c (accessed May 13, 2024).
14 Kashyaap, S. (2015) "Three Entrepreneurs Join Hands to Help You Visualise Your Home Décor in 3D." *YOURSTORY*, August 12, Available at: https://yourstory.com/2015/08/furdo/amp (accessed May 13, 2024).
15 Schneider, J. and Hall, J. (2011) "Why Most Product Launches Fail." *Harvard Business Review*, April. Available at: https://hbr.org/2011/04/why-most-product-launches-fail#:~:text=Most%20won%27t.,million%20during%20their%20first%20year (accessed May 13, 2024).
16 Palmatier, R.W., Scheer, L.K. and Steenkamp, J.B.E. (2007) "Customer Loyalty to Whom? Managing the Benefits and Risks of Salesperson-Owned Loyalty." *Journal of Marketing Research*, 44(2), pp. 185–99.
17 Shi, H., Sridhar, S., Grewal, R. and Lilien, G. (2017) "Sales Representative Departures and Customer Reassignment Strategies in Business-to-Business Markets." *Journal of Marketing*, 81(2), 25–44.
18 Oracle. (2022) *Pivotal Trends in B2B Ecommerce*, March. Available at: https://www.oracle.com/a/ocom/docs/dc360-pivotal-trends-b2b-ecommerce.pdf (accessed May 15, 2024).
19 BBC News. (2020) "Disney Ends the Historic 20th Century Fox Brand," August 12. Available at: https://www.bbc.com/news/business-53747270 (accessed May 15, 2024).
20 Whitten, S. (2019) "Disney Accounted for Nearly 40% of the 2019 US Box Office." CNBC, December 29. Available at: https://www.cnbc.com/2019/12/29/disney-accounted-for-nearly-40percent-of-the-2019-us-box-office-data-shows.html (accessed May 15, 2024).
21 The Editors of Encyclopaedia Britannica. (2021) "Standard Oil." *Britannica Money*, last updated March 28. Available at: https://www.britannica.com/topic/Standard-Oil (accessed May 15, 2024).
22 Baumgardner, L. (2005) "Antitrust Law in the European Union: The Law Is Changing – But to What Effect?" *Graziadio Business School Report*, 8(3). Available at: https://gbr.pepperdine.edu/2010/08/antitrust-law-in-the-european-union/ (accessed March 1, 2023).
23 Schwartz, M. (2019) "Disney Officially Owns 21st Century Fox." NPR, March 20. Available at: https://www.npr.org/2019/03/20/705009029/disney-officially-owns-21st-century-fox (accessed May 15, 2024).
24 Albers, S., Mantrala, M.K. and Sridhar, S. (2010) "Personal Selling Elasticities: A Meta-Analysis." *Journal of Marketing Research*, 47(5), pp. 840–53.
25 Dzieza, J. (2018) "Dirty Dealing in the $175 Billion Amazon Marketplace." The Verge, December 19. Available at: https://www.theverge.com/2018/12/19/18140799/amazon-market-

place-scams-seller-court-appeal-reinstatement (accessed May 15, 2024).

26 Dzieza, "Dirty Dealing in the $175 Billion Amazon Marketplace."

27 Marino, T. (n.d.) "Iniqlo Logo." Available at: https://tonimarino.co.uk/uniqlo-logo/ (accessed March 1, 2023).

28 Usui, T., Kotabe, M. and Murray, J.Y. (2017) "A Dynamic Process of Building Global Supply Chain Competence by New Ventures: The Case of Uniqlo." *Journal of International Marketing*, 25(3), pp. 1–20.

29 Marino, "Iniqlo Logo."

30 Bain, M. (2021) "How Uniqlo Became the World's Most Valuable Clothing Company." Quartz, February 22. Available at: https://qz.com/1975658/how-uniqlo-became-the-worlds-most-valuable-clothing-company/ (accessed May 15, 2024).

31 White, G.B. (2019) "Why Urban Millennials Love Uniqlo." *The Atlantic*, April. Available at: https://www.theatlantic.com/magazine/archive/2019/04/uniqlo-millennials-gap/583219/ (accessed May 15, 2024).

32 Chitrakorn, K. (2021) "How Can Uniqlo Succeed in America?." *Vogue Business*, September 13. Available at: https://www.voguebusiness.com/consumers/uniqlo-fast-retailing-retail-and-marketing-strategy-to-succeed-in-america (accessed May 15, 2024).

33 White, "Why Urban Millennials Love Uniqlo."

CHAPTER 11: BRAND-BASED ADVANTAGES AND ADVERTISING

1 Kollewe, J. (2014) "Asos Timeline: From Tiny Startup to Dressing Michelle Obama." *The Guardian*, June 5. Available at: https://www.theguardian.com/business/2014/jun/05/asos-timeline-startup-michelle-obama (accessed May 14, 2024).

2 ASOS. (n.d.) "Who We Are." Available at: https://www.asos.com/about/who-we-are/?ctaref=aboutus|whoweare (accessed May 14, 2024).

3 American Marketing Association. (n.d.) *Dictionary: B*. Available at: https://www.ama.org/resources/Pages/Dictionary.aspx?dLetter=B (accessed September 8, 2015).

4 Atchinson, J. (2020) "4 Strategies for Increasing Brand Awareness." *Business 2 Community*, last updated December 2. Available at: https://www.business2community.com/strategy/4-strategies-for-increasing-brand-awareness-02367227 (accessed May 14, 2024).

5 Aaker, J.L. (1997) "Dimensions of Brand Personality." *Journal of Marketing Research*, 34(3), pp. 347–56; Escalas, J.E. and Bettman, J.R. (2005) "Self construal, Reference Groups, and Brand Meaning." *Journal of Consumer Research* 32(3), pp. 378–89.

6 Swant, M. (2019) "The World's Most Valuable Brands." *Forbes*. Available at: https://www.forbes.com/the-worlds-most-valuable-brands/#5291af20119c (accessed May 14, 2024).

7 Anderson, J.R. (1983) *The Architecture of Cognition*. Cambridge, MA: Harvard University Press; John, D.R., Loken, B., Kim, K. and Alokparna, B.M. (2006) "Brand Concept Maps: A Methodology for Identifying Brand Association Networks." *Journal of Marketing Research*, 43(4), pp. 549–63; Keller, K.L. (1993) "Conceptualizing, Measuring, and Managing Customer-based Brand Equity." *Journal of Marketing Research*, 57(1), pp. 1–22.

8 Schöntag, K. and Teichert, T.A. (2010) "Exploring Consumer Knowledge Structures Using Associative Network Analysis." *Psychology & Marketing*, 27(4), pp. 369–98; Pitta, D.A. and Prevel Katsanis, L. (1995) "Understanding Brand Equity for Successful Brand Extension." *Journal of Consumer Marketing*, 12(4), pp. 51–64.

9 Nestlé. (2023) Annual Report. Available at: https://www.nestle.com/investors/annual-report (accessed May 14, 2024).

10 Guy, J. (2020) "Nestlé Renames 'Out of Step' Australian Candy Products." CNN Business, November 16. Available at: https://www.cnn.com/2020/11/16/intl_business/nestle-renames-sweets-scli-intl/index.html (accessed May 14, 2024).

11 Barrie, L. (2020) "Nestle to Re-Brand Racially-Insensitive Beso de Negra in Colombia." *Just Food*, June 24. Available at: https://www.just-food.com/news/nestle-to-re-brand-racially-insensitive-beso-de-negra-in-colombia/ (accessed May 14, 2024).

12 ABC News. (2020) "Nestle Renames Allen's Lollies Brands Red Skins and Chicos to Red Ripper and Cheekies to Avoid Marginalising People," November 15. Available at: https://www.abc.net.au/news/2020-11-16/red-ripper-and-cheekies-the-new-name-of-allens-red-skin-chicos/12887278 (accessed May 22, 2024).

13 Donnelly, M. (2016) "'Captain America: Civil War' Product Placement, From Smartphones to Designer Suits." *Y!entertainment*, May 5. Available at: https://www.yahoo.com/entertainment/captain-america-civil-war-product-placement-smartphones-designer-020455319.html?guccounter=1&guce_referrer=aHR0cHM6Ly93d3cuZ29vZ2xlLmNvbS8&guce_referrer_sig=AQAAADiMe9f5Lyu0Y-8DgRRlKbzhCTjorKTgAx8NFqf7R8XETa9pQXpLSdoS6dvnsQDHYRKSp6OL-vVD_LN3I2rSyFD6uF2w-ZS6BFDDDUdPxDz7krUXckB9nDCvI19koUELlMciOVuTiMbNkFOdbIZvmTMxdcOEPrt3APU9PgqmxRFX (accessed May 14, 2024).

14 Balasubramanian, S.K. (1994) "Beyond Advertising and Publicity: Hybrid Messages and Public Policy Issues." *Journal of Advertising*, 23(4), pp. 29–46.

15 Baker, W.E. (2003) "Does Brand Name Imprinting in Memory Increase Brand Information Retention?." *Psychology & Marketing*, 20(12), pp. 1119–135.

16 Dimofte, C.V. and Yalch, R.F. (2011) "The Mere Association Effect and Brand Evaluations." *Journal of Consumer Psychology*, 21(1), pp. 24–37.

17 Weinmann, K. (20110 "11 Bizarre Crossover Products." *Business Insider*, November 4. Available at: https://www.businessinsider.com/13-bizarre-products-from-brands-you-know-and-love-2011-11#smith-and-wesson-mountain-bikes-4 (accessed May 14, 2024).

18 Keller, K.L. (2012) *Strategic Brand Management*, 4th edn. Upper Saddle River, NJ: Pearson/Prentice Hall.

19 Keller, *Strategic Brand Management*.

20 Wojdyla, B. (2009) "Henry Ford Did Not Invent the Assembly Line." *Jalopnik*, December 9. Available at: https://jalopnik.com/henry-ford-did-not-invent-the-assembly-line-5412420 (accessed May 14, 2024).

21 Yates, B. (2000) "How GM Wrecked Oldsmobile." *The Wall Street Journal*, December 18. Available at: https://www.wsj.com/articles/SB977092974412937757 (accessed May 14, 2024).

22 Yates, "How GM Wrecked Oldsmobile."

23 Edell, J.A. and Burke, M.C. (1987) "The Power of Feelings in Understanding Advertising Effects." *Journal of Consumer Research*, 14(3), pp. 421–33; Zhao, H. (2000) "Raising Awareness and Signaling Quality to Uninformed Consumers: A Price-Advertising Model." *Marketing Science* 19(4), pp. 390–96.

24 McLuhan, M. (1994) *Understanding Media: The Extensions of Man*. Cambridge, MA: MIT Press.
25 Curti, M. (1967) "The Changing Concept of 'Human Nature' in the Literature of American Advertising." *Business History Review*, 41(4), pp. 335–57.
26 Teichert, T., Hardeck, D., Liu, Y. and Trivedi, R. (2018) "How to Implement Informational and Emotional Appeals in Print Advertisements: A Framework for Choosing Ad Appeals Based on Advertisers' Objectives and Targeted Demographics." *Journal of Advertising Research*, 58(3), pp. 363–79.
27 Rogers, J.C. and Williams, T.G. (1989) "Comparative Advertising Effectiveness: Practitioners' Perceptions versus Academic Research Findings." *Journal of Advertising Research*, 29(5), pp. 22–37.
28 Gotlieb, J.B. and Sarel, D. (1991) "Comparative Advertising Effectiveness: The Role of Involvement and Source Credibility." *Journal of Advertising*, 20(1), pp. 38–45.
29 Jeon, J.O. and Beatty, S.E. (2002) "Comparative advertising effectiveness in different national cultures." *Journal of Business Research*, 55(11), pp. 907–13.
30 Shao, A.T., Bao, Y. and Gray, E. (2004) "Comparative Advertising Effectiveness: A Cross-Cultural Study." *Journal of Current Issues & Research in Advertising*, 26(2), pp. 67–80.
31 Kalro, A.D., Sivakumaran, B. and Marathe, R.R. (2017) "The Ad Format-Strategy Effect on Comparative Advertising Effectiveness." *European Journal of Marketing*, 51(1), pp. 99–122.
32 Petty, R.E. and Cacioppo, J.T. (1986) "Message Elaboration versus Peripheral Cues." In *Communication and Persuasion*. New York: Springer, pp. 141–72.
33 Rucker, D.D. and Petty, R.E. (2006) "Increasing the Effectiveness of Communications to Consumers: Recommendations Based on Elaboration Likelihood and Attitude Certainty Perspectives." *Journal of Public Policy & Marketing*, 25(1), pp. 39–52.
34 Keller, K.L. (2000) "The Brand Report Card." *Harvard Business Review*, 78(1), pp.147–58.
35 Keller, K.L. (1987) "Memory Factors in Advertising: The Effect of Advertising Retrieval Cues on Brand Evaluations." *Journal of Consumer Research*, 14(3), pp. 316–33.
36 Kim, S.S., Morris, J.G. and Ray, S. (2014) "The Central Role of Engagement in Online Communities." *Information Systems Research*, 25(3), pp. 528–46.
37 Goldfarb, A. (2021) "Absolut Obsessive: 30 Years After the Campaign Launched, Passion for Collecting Remains." *VinePair*, November 19. Available at: https://vinepair.com/articles/absolut-vodka-ad-collectors/ (accessed May 14, 2024).
38 *The Hartford*. (2015) "Advantages of Strong Brand Equity." *Business Owner's Playbook*. Available at: https://www.thehartford.com/business-playbook/in-depth/advantages-strong-brand-equity (accessed August 31, 2015); Keller, *Strategic Brand Management*; Mizik, N. (2014) "Assessing the Total Financial Performance Impact of Brand Equity with Limited Time-Series Data." *Journal of Marketing Research*, 51(6), pp. 691–706.
39 Allison, R.I. and Uhl, K.P. (1964) "Influence of Beer Brand Identification on Taste Perception." *Journal of Marketing Research*, 1(3), pp. 36–9.
40 Lowrey, T.M. and Shrum, L.J. (2007) "Phonetic Symbolism and Brand Name Preference." *Journal of Consumer Research*, 34(3), pp. 406–14; Rao, A.R. and Monroe, K.B. (1989) "The Effect of Price, Brand Name, and Store Name on Buyers' Perceptions of Product Quality: An Integrative Review." *Journal of Marketing Research* 26(3), pp. 351–57; Yorkston, E. and Menon, G. (2004) "A Sound Idea: Phonetic Effects of Brand Names on Consumer Judgments." *Journal of Consumer Research*, 31(1), pp. 43–51; Wänke, M., Herrmann, A. and Schaffner, D. (2007) "Brand Name Influence on Brand Perception." *Psychology & Marketing*, 24(1), pp. 1–24.
41 Stahl, F., Heitmann, M., Lehmann, D.R. and Neslin, S.A. (2012) "The Impact of Brand Equity on Customer Acquisition, Retention, and Profit Margin." *Journal of Marketing*, 76(4), pp. 44–63.
42 Palmatier, R., Stern, L. and El-Ansary, A. (2014) *Marketing Channel Strategy*, 8th edn. Upper Saddle River, NJ: Prentice Hall.
43 Goldfarb, A., Lu, Q. and Moorthy, S. (2009) "Measuring Brand Value in an Equilibrium Framework." *Marketing Science*, 28(1), pp. 69–86.
44 KFF. (2023) "The U.S. Government and the World Health Organization," May 22. Available at: https://www.kff.org/global-health-policy/fact-sheet/the-u-s-government-and-the-world-health-organization/ (accessed May 14, 2024).
45 Flight, C. (2011) "Smallpox: Eradicating the Scourge." BBC, last updated February 17. Available at: https://www.bbc.co.uk/history/british/empire_seapower/smallpox_01.shtml (accessed May 14, 2024).
46 KFF, "The U.S. Government and the World Health Organization."
47 Wenham C. (2017) "What We Have Learnt About the World Health Organization from the Ebola Outbreak." *Philosophical Transactions of the Royal Society of London. Series B, Biological Sciences*, 372(1721), 20160307.
48 Kamradt-Scott, A., Harman, S., Wenham, C. and Smith III, F. (2015) Saving Lives: The Civil-Military Response to the 2014 Ebola Outbreak in West Africa. Sydney: The University of Sydney.
49 BBC News. (2021) "Covid: Serious Failures in WHO and Global Response, Report Finds," May 12. Available at: https://www.bbc.com/news/world-57085505 (accessed May 14, 2024).
50 U.S. Department of State. (2021) "Joint Statement on the WHO-Convened COVID-19 Origins Study." Media Note, March 30. Available at: https://www.state.gov/joint-statement-on-the-who-convened-covid-19-origins-study/ (accessed May 14, 2024).

CHAPTER 12: OFFERING-BASED ADVANTAGES, INNOVATION, AND PRODUCT-SERVICE STRATEGY

1 Webb, K. (2022) "Valve's Steam Deck Is Like a Switch for PC Games — It Launches February 25 for $399." *Business Insider*, January 26. Available at: https://www.businessinsider.com/guides/tech/steam-deck-price-release-date-preorder (accessed May 14, 2024).
2 Allan, D. (2022) "Linux Gaming Surges in Popularity – Is This the Steam Deck Effect?." Techradar, May 3. Available at: https://www.techradar.com/news/linux-gaming-surges-in-popularity-is-this-the-steam-deck-effect (accessed May 14, 2024).
3 Manners, D. (2022) "Intel's $15bn 2021 R&D Spend." Electronics Weekly.com, May 6. Available at: https://www.electronicsweekly.com/news/business/intel-leads-rd-spend-

2022-05/#:~:text=Industry%20R%26D%20spending%20will%20rise,to%20the%20McLean%20Report%202022.&text=The%20top%2010%20raised%20spending,more%20on%20R%26D%20in%202021 (accessed May 14, 2024).

4 Alsop, T. (2024) "Distribution of Intel and AMD x86 Computer Central Processing Units (CPUs) Worldwide from 2012 to 2024, by Quarter." *Statista*, April 23. Available at: https://www.statista.com/statistics/735904/worldwide-x86-intel-amd-market-share/ (accessed May 14, 2024).

5 Erickson, G. and Jacobson, R. (1992) "Gaining Comparative Advantage through Discretionary Expenditures: The Returns to R&D and Advertising." *Management Science*, 38(3), pp. 1264–279.

6 Wiener-Bronner, D. (2020) "Coca-Cola Is Shutting Down Odwalla Juice." CNN, last updated July 2. Available at: https://www.cnn.com/2020/07/01/business/odwalla-juice-coca-cola/index.html (accessed May 14, 2024).

7 Sawhney, M., Wolcott, R.C. and Arroniz, I. (2006) "The 12 Different Ways for Companies to Innovate." *MIT Sloan Management Review*, 47(3), p. 75.

8 Bain & Company. (n.d.) "Management Tools & Trends." Available at: https://www.bain.com/insights/topics/management-tools-and-trends/ (accessed May 14, 2024).

9 Sawhney, Wolcott, and Arroniz, "The 12 Different Ways for Companies to Innovate," p. 75.

10 Bartlett, C.A., Hall, B.J. and Bennett, N. (2007) "GE's Imagination Breakthroughs: The Evo Project." *HBS Case Collection*, June. Available at: https://www.hbs.edu/faculty/Pages/item.aspx?num=34629 (accessed May 14, 2024).

11 Kirk, C. (2012) "Wii Revolution." Slate, October 22. Available at: https://slate.com/business/2012/10/nintendo-wii-the-console-that-beat-the-xbox-and-playstation-and-saved-nintendo.html (accessed May 14, 2024).

12 Rich, N. (2021) "All About Gachapon." All About Japan, March 4. Available at: https://allabout-japan.com/en/article/2169/ (accessed May 14, 2024).

13 McKenzie, B. (2018) "Loot Boxes in Japan: Legal Analysis and Kompu Gacha Explained." Lexology, August 2. Available at: https://www.lexology.com/library/detail.aspx?g=9207df10-a8a2-4f67-81c3-6a148a6100e2 (accessed May 14, 2024).

14 Shibuya, A., Teramoto, M., Shoun, A. and Akiyama, K. (2019) "Long-Term Effects of In-Game Purchases and Event Game Mechanics on Young Mobile Social Game Players in Japan." *Simulation & Gaming*, 50(1), pp. 76–92.

15 Taylor, K. (2015) "Iced Coffee Challenge: How Do Fast-Food Restaurants Measure Up to Coffee Chains?." Entrepreneur, August 28. Available at: https://www.entrepreneur.com/slideshow/250002 (accessed May 14, 2024).

16 Cooper, R.G. (2008) "Perspective: The Stage-Gate® Idea-to-Launch Process—Update, What's New, and NexGen System." *Journal of Product Innovation Management*, 25(3), pp. 213–32; Cooper, R.G. (1990) "Stage-Gate Systems: A New Tool for Managing New Products." *Business Horizons*, 33(3), pp. 44–54.

17 Gourville, J.T. (2006) "Eager Sellers and Stony Buyers: Understanding the Psychology of New-Product Adoption." *Harvard Business Review*, 84(6), pp. 98–106.

18 Radjou, N., Prabhu, J. and Ahuja, S. (2010) *Jugaad Innovation: Think Frugal, be Flexible, Generate Breakthrough Growth*. San Francisco, CA: John Wiley & Sons.

19 Adidas. (n.d.) "About: Profile." Available at: https://www.adidas-group.com/en/about/profile/ (accessed May 14, 2024).

20 Wade, R. (2019) "Adidas Faces Backlash for Mostly White Black History Month Sneaker." Yahoo!Finance, last upated February 6. Available at: https://finance.yahoo.com/news/adidas-faces-backlash-for-mostly-white-black-history-month-sneaker-210640912.html?guccounter=1 (accessed May 14, 2024).

21 Golder, P. and Tellis, G. (1993) "Pioneer Advantage: Marketing Logic or Marketing Legend?." *Journal of Marketing Research*, 30(2), pp. 158–70.

22 Robinson, W.T. and Min, S. (2002) "Is the First to Market the First to Fail? Empirical Evidence for Industrial Goods Businesses." *Journal of Marketing Research*, 39(1), pp. 120–28.

23 Collins, J. (2000) "Best Beats First." *Inc.*, 22(11), pp. 48–50.

24 Castellion, G. and Markham, S.K. (2012) "Perspective: New Product Failure Rates: Influence of Argumentum ad Populum and Self-Interest." *Journal of Product Innovation Management*, 30(5), pp. 976–79.

25 Rogers, E.M. (1995) *Diffusion of Innovations*, 4th edn. New York: Free Press.

26 Moore, G.A. (2006) *Crossing the Chasm: Marketing and Selling Disruptive Products to Mainstream Customers*, 1st rev. edn. New York: Collins Business Essentials.

27 Grewal, R., Chakravarty, A., Ding, M. and Liechty, J. (2008) "Counting Chickens Before the Eggs Hatch: On the Valuation of New Product Development Portfolios in the Pharmaceutical Sector." *International Journal of Research in Marketing*, 25(4), pp. 261–72.

28 Joseph, K. and Mantrala, M. (2009) "A Model of the Role of Free Drug Samples in Physicians' Prescription Decisions." *Marketing Letters*, 20(1), pp. 15–29.

29 Ladik, F., Kent, L. and Nahl, P.C. (1960) "Test Marketing of New Consumer Products." *Journal of Marketing*, 24(4), pp. 29–34.

30 Sully, E. (2020) "Singapore Airlines Reportedly Plans to Offer Sightseeing 'Flights to Nowhere' that Take Off and Land at the Same Airport." *Business Insider*, September 15. Available at: https://www.businessinsider.com/singapore-airlines-flights-nowhere-take-off-land-same-airport-report-2020-9 (accessed May 14, 2024).

31 Hosie, R. (2020) "Singapore Airlines Has Cancelled Its Proposed 'Flights to Nowhere' After Criticism from Environmental Campaigners." *Business Insider*, October 1. Available at: https://www.businessinsider.com/singapore-airlines-drops-flights-to-nowhere-after-environmental-concerns-2020-10 (accessed May 14, 2024).

32 Chow, D. (2024) "Delta Adds Another Eclipse Flight As Companies Look to Capitalize on Solar Event." NBC News, February 26. Available at: https://www.nbcnews.com/science/science-news/delta-adds-another-eclipse-flight-companies-look-capitalize-solar-even-rcna140588 (accessed May 14, 2024).

33 Chaney, K.W., Devinney, T.M. and Winer, R.S. (1991) "The Impact of New Product Introductions on the Market Values of Firms." *Journal of Business*, 64(4), pp. 573–610; Lee, H., Smith, K.G., Grimm, C.M. and Schomburg, A. (2000) "Timing, Order, and Durability of New Product Advantages with Imitation." *Strategic Management Journal*, 21(1), pp. 23–30; Sood, A. and Tellis, G.J. (2009) "Demystifying Disruption: A New Model for Understanding and Predicting Disruptive Technologies." *Marketing Science*, 30(2), pp. 339–54.

34 Meyer, R.J., Zhao, S. and Han, J.K. (2008) "Biases in Valuation vs. Usage of Innovative Product Features." *Marketing Science*, 27(6), pp. 1038–096.

35 Bruce, N.I., Foutz, N.Z. and Kolsarici, C. (2012) "Dynamic Effectiveness of Advertising and Word of Mouth in Sequential Distribution of New Products." *Journal of Marketing Research*, 49(4), pp. 469–86; Bruce, N.I. (2008) "Pooling and Dynamic Forgetting Effects in Multitheme Advertising: Tracking the Advertising Sales Relationship with Particle Filters." *Marketing Science*, 27(4), pp. 659–78.

36 Pitta, D.A., Wood, V.R. and Franzak, F.J. (2008) "Nurturing an Effective Creative Culture within a Marketing Organization." *Journal of Consumer Marketing*, 25(3), pp. 137–48; Mast, K. (2011) "How to Create a Culture of Innovation that Attracts & Retains Top Talent." *InnovationManagement.se*, February 17.

37 Spezzati, S. (2021) "Staley to Step Down As Barclays CEO Amid Epstein Probe." *BNN Bloomberg*, November 1. Available at: https://www.bnnbloomberg.ca/staley-to-step-down-as-barclays-ceo-amid-epstein-probe-1.1675015 (accessed May 14, 2024).

38 Girling, W. (2021) "Rise by Barclays: Embedded Finance and the Future of Fintech." *FinTech Magazine*, July 8. Available at: https://fintechmagazine.com/sustainability/rise-barclays-embedded-finance-and-future-fintech (accessed May 14, 2024).

39 Barclays. (n.d.) "Companies." Available at: https://home.barclays/who-we-are/innovation/barclays-accelerator/companies/ (accessed May 14, 2024).

40 Barclays. (2022) "Barclays Announces Strategic Partnership with Global Corporate Venture Builder Rainmaking to Drive FinTech Innovation." Available at: https://home.barclays/news/press-releases/2022/02/Barclays-announces-strategic-partnership-with-global-corporate-venture-builder-Rainmaking/ (accessed May 14, 2024).

CHAPTER 13: RELATIONSHIP-BASED ADVANTAGES, CRM, AND CHANNEL MANAGEMENT

1 Sheth, J.N. and Parvatiyar, A. (1995) "The Evolution of Relationship Marketing." *International Business Review*, 4(4), pp. 397–418.

2 Becker, H.S. (1986) *Doing Things Together: Selected Papers*. Evanston, IL: Northwestern University Press; Trivers, R.L. (1971) "The Evolution of Reciprocal Altruism." *Quarterly Review of Biology*, 46(1), pp. 35–57; Trivers, R.L. (1985) *Social Evolution*. Menlo Park, CA: Benjamin/Cummings.

3 Canham-Clyne, A. (2022) "Panera Will Allow Loyalty Customers to Choose Rewards." Restaurant Dive, September 20. Available at: https://www.restaurantdive.com/news/Panera-myPanera-loyalty-choose-rewards/632222/ (accessed May 15, 2024).

4 Cialdini, R.B. and Rhoads, K.V. (2001) "Human Behavior and the Marketplace." *Marketing Research*, 13(3), pp. 8–13; Dahl, D.W., Honea, H. and Manchanda, R.V. (2003) "The Nature of Self-Reported Guilt in Consumption Contexts." *Marketing Letters*, 14(3), pp. 159–71; Dahl, D.W., Honea, H. and Manchanda, R.V. (2005) "Three Rs of Interpersonal Consumer Guilt: Relationship, Reciprocity, Reparation." *Journal of Consumer Psychology*, 15(4), pp. 307–15; Palmatier, R.W., Jarvis C., Bechkoff, J. and Kardes F.R. (2009) "The Role of Customer Gratitude in Relationship Marketing." *Journal of Marketing*, 73(5), pp. 1–18; Palmatier, R.W., Scheer, L.K., Houston, M.B., Evans, K.R. and Gopalakrishna, S. (2007) "Use of Relationship Marketing Programs in Building Customer–Salesperson and Customer–Firm Relationships: Differential Influences on Financial Outcomes." *International Journal of Research in Marketing*, 24(3), pp. 210–23.

5 Brinder, C. and Hanssens, D.M. (2015) "Why Strong Customer Relationships Trump Powerful Brands." *Harvard Business Review*, April 14.

6 Palmatier, R.W., Stern, L.W. and El-Ansary, A.I. (2014) *Marketing Channel Strategy*, 8th edn. Upper Saddle River, NJ: Pearson Prentice Hall.

7 Statista Research Department. (2023) "Value Added to Gross Domestic Product Across Economic Sectors in the United States from 2000 to 2021." *Statista*, November 3. Available at: https://www.statista.com/statistics/270001/distribution-of-gross-domestic-product-gdp-across-economic-sectors-in-the-us/ (accessed May 15, 2024).

8 Palmatier, R.W., Dant, R.P., Grewal, D. and Evans, K.R. (2006) "Factors Influencing the Effectiveness of Relationship Marketing: A Meta-Analysis." *Journal of Marketing*, 70(4), pp. 136–53.

9 Dormehl, L. (2014) "How Corning Won Apple Back and Built the Strongest Gorilla Glass Yet." *CultofMac.com*, November 26. Available at: http://www.cultofmac.com/304120/corning-gorilla-glass-4/ (accessed August 25, 2016).

10 Salon Privé. (2023) "Custom Creations: The Growing Trend of Personalized Fashion in Online Shopping." *Salon Privé Magazine*, August 9. Available at: https://www.salonprivemag.com/personalized-fashion-in-online-shopping/ (accessed May 15, 2024).

11 Berry, L.L. (1995) "Relationship Marketing of Services–Growing Interest, Emerging Perspectives." *Journal of the Academy of Marketing Science*, 23(4), pp. 236–45; Bolton, R.N., Smith, A.K. and Wagner, J. (2003) "Striking the Right Balance Designing Service to Enhance Business-to-Business Relationships." *Journal of Service Research*, 5(4), pp. 271–91; Cannon, J.P., Achrol, R.S. and Gundlach, G.T. (2000) "Contracts, Norms, and Plural Form Governance." *Journal of the Academy of Marketing Science*, 28(2), pp. 180–94; Palmatier, R.W., Gopalakrishna, S. and Houston, M.B. (2006) "Returns on Business-to-Business Relationship Marketing Investments: Strategies for Leveraging Profits." *Marketing Science*, 25(5), pp. 477–93.

12 Aurora, R. (2021) "Is Relationship Is Equivalent To Business." IBM, October 27. Available at: https://www.ibm.com/blogs/digital-transformation/in-en/blog/is-relationship-is-equivalent- to-business/ (accessed May 15, 2024).

13 Palmatier, Gopalakrishna, and Houston, "Returns on Business-to-Business Relationship Marketing Investments."

14 Palmatier, R.W., Scheer, L.K. and Steenkamp, J.B.E. (2007) "Customer Loyalty to Whom? Managing the Benefits and Risks of Salesperson-Owned Loyalty." *Journal of Marketing Research*, 44(2), 185–99.

15 Palmatier, Gopalakrishna, and Houston, "Returns on Business-to-Business Relationship Marketing Investments."

16 Arghandewal, A. (2023) "Everything You Need to Know About the Delta SkyMiles Loyalty Program." CNN, October 27. Available at: https://www.cnn.com/cnn-underscored/travel/delta-skymiles-loyalty-program (accessed May 15, 2024).

17 Cao, Y. and Gruca, T.S. (2005) "Reducing Adverse Selection through Customer Relationship Management." *Journal of Marketing*, 69(4), pp. 219–29; Bolton, R.N., Kannan, P.K. and Bramlett, M.D. (2000) "Implications of Loyalty Program Membership and Service Experiences for Customer Retention and Value." *Journal of the Academy of Marketing Science*, 28(1), pp. 95–108.

18 Pfizer. (2022) "Pfizer and BioNTech Sign New Global Collaboration Agreement to Develop First mRNA-based Shingles Vaccine." Press Release, January 5. Available at: https://www.pfizer.com/news/press-release/press-release-detail/pfizer-and-biontech-sign-new-global-collaboration-agreement (accessed May 15, 2024).

19 Frow, P. and Payne, A. (2005) "A Strategic Framework for Customer Relationship Management." *Journal of Marketing*, 69(4), pp. 167–76.

20 Columbus, L. (2013) "Gartner Predicts CRM Will Be a $36B Market by 2017." *Forbes.com*, June 18. Available at: http://www.forbes.com/sites/louiscolumbus/2013/06/18/gartner-predicts-crm-will-be-a-36b-market-by-2017/#617f75b0c1ec (accessed October 8, 2015).

21 Salesforce. (n.d.) "Santander UK Sets Up Businesses for Global Success with Salesforce." Available at: https://www.salesforce.com/resources/customer-stories/santander-personalization-customer- conversations/ (accessed May 15, 2024).

22 Scheiner, M. (2024) "17 CRM Statistics: Growth, Revenue & Adoption Trends in 2024." CRM.ORG, February 5. Available at: https://crm.org/crmland/crm-statistics (accessed May 15, 2024).

23 Inditex. (2022) Inditex Annual Report 2021. Available at: https://www.inditex.com/itxcomweb/api/media/9f9bb2e5-99da-4127-8337-4f829b874628/inditex_annual_report_2021.pdf (accessed May 15, 2024).

24 Ali, T. (2023) "Rana Plaza 10 Years on: UK High Street Brands Continue to Abuse Cheap Labour in Bangladesh, Say Workers." *i*, April 21. Available at: https://inews.co.uk/news/world/rana-plaza-10-years-uk-high-street-brands-abuse-cheap-labour-bangladesh-2283118 (accessed May 15, 2024).

25 Butler, S. (2015) "Zara Owner Inditex Faces Fines in Brazil over Poor Working Conditions Claim." *The Guardian*, May 12. Available at: https://www.theguardian.com/fashion/2015/may/12/zara-owner-inditex-fines-brazil-working-conditions-claim (accessed May 15, 2024).

26 Reid, H. (2023) "H&M Probes Alleged Myanmar Factory Abuses As Pressure Intensifies." Reuters, August 16. Available at: https://www.reuters.com/business/retail-consumer/hm-probes-myanmar-factory-abuses-pressure-intensifies-2023-08-16/ (accessed May 15, 2024).

27 Butler, "Zara Owner Inditex Faces Fines in Brazil over Poor Working Conditions Claim."

28 Reichheld, F.F., Schefter, P. and Rigby, D. (2002) "Avoid the Four Perils of CRM." *Harvard Business Review*, February. Available at: https://hbr.org/2002/02/avoid-the-four-perils-of-crm (accessed May 15, 2024).

29 Salesforce. (n.d.) "How Do You Provide Premier Education at Scale? ASU Goes Cutting Edge." Available at: https://www.salesforce.com/resources/customer-stories/asu-personalization-boosts-recruitment/ (accessed May 15, 2024).

30 Palmatier, R.W. (2008) "Interfirm Relational Drivers of Customer Value." *Journal of Marketing*, 72(4), pp. 76–89; Palmatier, R.W. (2008) *Relationship Marketing*. Cambridge, MA: Marketing Science Institute.

31 Crosby, L.A., Evans, K.R. and Cowles, D. (1990) "Relationship Quality in Services Selling: An Interpersonal Influence Perspective." *Journal of Marketing*, 48(1), pp. 68–81; Kumar, N., Scheer, L.K. and Steenkamp, J.B.E.M. (1995) "Interdependence, Punitive Capability, and the Reciprocation of Punitive Actions in Channel Relationships." *Journal of Marketing Research*, 35(2), pp. 225–36.

32 Emmons, R.A. and McCullough M.E. (2004) *The Psychology of Gratitude*. Oxford: Oxford University Press; Gouldner, A.W. (1960) "The Norm of Reciprocity: A Preliminary Statement." *American Sociological Review*, 25(2) pp. 161–78; Ostrom, E. and Walker, J. (2003) "Trust and Reciprocity: Interdisciplinary Lessons for Experimental Research." *Contemporary Sociology*, 33(4), pp. 493–94.

33 Morgan, R.M. and Hunt, S.D. (1994) "The Commitment-Trust Theory of Relationship Marketing." *Journal of Marketing*, 58(3), pp. 20–38; Moorman, C., Zaltman, G. and Deshpande, R. (1992) "Relationships between Providers and Users of Market Research: The Dynamics of Trust." *Journal of Marketing Research*, 29(3), pp. 314–28.

34 Borgatti, S.P. and Foster, P.C. (2003) "The Network Paradigm in Organizational Research: A Review and Typology." *Journal of Supply Chain Management*, 45(2), pp. 5–22; Van den Bulte, C. and Wuyts, S.H.K. (2007) *Social Networks in Marketing*. MSI Relevant Knowledge Series. Cambridge, MA: MSI Science Institute.

35 Bendapudi, N. and Leone, R.P. (2002) "Managing Business-to-Business Customer Relationships Following Key Contact Employee Turnover in a Vendor Firm." *Journal of Marketing*, 66(2), pp. 83–101; Shi, H., Sridhar, S., Grewal, R. and Lilien, G. (2017) "Sales Representative Departures and Customer Reassignment Strategies in Business-to-Business Markets." *Journal of Marketing*, 81(2), 25–44.

36 Reuters. (2019) "M-Pesa Helps Drive Up Kenyans' Access to Financial Services—Study," April 3. Available at: https://www.reuters.com/article/kenya-banking/m-pesa-helps-drive-up-kenyans-access-to-financial-services-study-idUSL8N21L2HK (accessed May 15, 2024).

37 NCBA. (n.d.) "Loop." Available at: https://ke.ncbagroup.com/loop/ (accessed May 15, 2024).

38 LOOP. (n.d.) "Evolution of LOOP – From Banking to Platform." Available at: https://loop.co.ke/stories/evolution-of-loop-from-banking-to-platform/ (accessed May 15, 2024).

39 Otieno, D. (2023) "NCBA LOOP Update; A Masterclass on How to Annoy Customers." Tech-ish, January 25. Available at: https://tech-ish.com/2023/01/25/ncba-loop-update-masterclass/ (accessed May 15, 2024); Abuya, K. (2023) "Top 5 Issues with the New NCBA LOOP App." Techweez, January 23. Available at: https://techweez.com/2023/01/23/top-5-issues-with-the-new-ncba-loop-app/ (accessed May 22, 2024).

40 Kanali, N. (2023) "Ecobank Kenya Takes on NCBA LOOP with New Fingo Africa App." TechTrends KE, May 4. Available at: https://techtrendske.co.ke/2023/05/04/ecobank-kenya-takes-on-ncba-loop-with-new-fingo-africa-app/ (accessed May 15, 2024).

41 Anderson, J.C. and Narus, J.A. (1990) "A Model of Distributor Firm and Manufacturer Firm Working Partnerships." *Journal of Marketing*, 54(1), pp. 42–58; Palmatier et al., "Factors Influencing the Effectiveness of Relationship Marketing."

42 Doney, P.M. and Cannon, J.P. (1997) "An Examination of the Nature of Trust in Buyer-Seller Relationships." *Journal of*

Marketing, 61(2), pp. 35–51; Garbarino, E. and Johnson, M.S. (1999) "The Different Roles of Satisfaction, Trust, and Commitment in Customer Relationships." *Journal of Marketing*, 63(2), pp. 70–87; Hewett, K., Money, R.B. and Sharma, S. (2002) "An Exploration of the Moderating Role of Buyer Corporate Culture in Industrial Buyer-Seller Relationships." *Journal of the Academy of Marketing Science*, 30(3), pp. 229–39; Macintosh, G. and Lockshin, L.S. (1997) "Retail Relationships and Store Loyalty: A Multi-Level Perspective." *International Journal of Research in Marketing*, 14(5), pp. 487–97.

43 International Trade Administration. (2023) "eCommerce." Last updated April 7. Available at: https://www.trade.gov/country-commercial-guides/china-ecommerce (accessed May 15, 2024).

44 Barksdale, H.C., Johnson, J.T. and Suh, M. (1997) "A Relationship Maintenance Model: A Comparison between Managed Health Care and Traditional Fee-for-Service." *Journal of Business Research*, 40(3), pp. 237–47; Hennig-Thurau, T., Gwinner, K.P. and Gremler, D.D. (2002) "Understanding Relationship Marketing Outcomes: An Integration of Relational Benefits and Relationship Quality." *Journal of Service Research*, 4(3), pp. 230–47.

45 Verhoef, P.C., Franses, P.H. and Hoekstra, J.C. (2002) "The Effect of Relational Constructs on Customer Referrals And Number Of Services Purchased from a Multiservice Provider: Does Age of Relationship Matter?." *Journal of the Academy of Marketing Science*, 30(3), pp. 202–16.

46 comScore (2007) "Online Consumer-Generated Reviews Have Significant Impact on Offline Purchase Behavior." Press Release, November 29. Available at: http://www.comscore.com/Press_Events/Press_Releases/2007/11/Online_Consumer_Reviews_Impact_Offline_Purchasing_Behavior (accessed February 18, 2016).

47 Nike. (2017) "2017 Nike, Inc. Investor Day," October 25. Available at: https://investors.nike.com/investors/news-events-and-reports/events-and-presentations/event-details/2017/2017-NIKE-INC-INVESTOR-DAY/ (accessed May 15, 2024).

48 Danziger, P.N. (2018) "Nike's New Consumer Experience Distribution Strategy Hits the Ground Running." *Forbes*, December 1. Available at: https://www.forbes.com/sites/pamdanziger/2018/12/01/nikes-new-consumer-experience-distribution-strategy-hits-the-ground-running/?sh=25fb53bf1d06 (accessed May 15, 2024).

49 Deng, V. (2019) "Nike Will Reportedly Stop Supplying Some Independent Stores by 2021." COMPLEX, October 14. Available at: https://www.complex.com/sneakers/a/cmplxvictor-deng/nike-end-supplying-products-independent-stores-2021 (accessed May 15, 2024).

50 Deng, V. (2020) "Nike Cuts Ties with Independent Retailer after 50 Years of Business." COMPLEX, October 12. Available at: https://www.complex.com/sneakers/a/cmplxvictor-deng/nike-ends-partnership-with-franks-sport-shop (accessed May 15, 2024).

51 Nike. (2023) "NIKE, Inc. Reports Fiscal 2023 Fourth Quarter and Full Year Results," June 29. Available at: https://investors.nike.com/investors/news-events-and-reports/investor-news/investor-news-details/2023/NIKE-Inc.-Reports-Fiscal-2023-Fourth-Quarter-and-Full-Year-Results/default.aspx (accessed May 15, 2024).

52 Golicic, S.L., Foggin, J.H. and Mentzer, J.T. (2003) "Relationship Magnitude and Its Role in Interorganizational Relationship Structure." *Journal of Business Logistics*, 24(1), pp. 57–75.

53 Cannon, J.P. and Perreault Jr., W.D. (1999) "Buyer–Seller Relationships in Business Markets." *Journal of Marketing Research*, 36(4), pp. 439–60.

54 Heide, J.B. (1994) "Interorganizational Governance in Marketing Channels." *Journal of Marketing*, 58(1), pp. 71–85.

55 Cannon and Perreault, "Buyer–Seller Relationships in Business Markets."

56 Heide, "Interorganizational Governance in Marketing Channels."

57 Eliashberg, J. and Michie, D.A. (1984) "Multiple Business Goals Sets As Determinants of Marketing Channel Conflict: An Empirical Study." *Journal of Marketing Research*, 21(1), pp. 75–88.

58 Pringle, K.G. (2022) "Supply-Chain Problems? Not for Tesla, Apple, and IKEA." Barron's, last updated March 10. Available at: https://www.barrons.com/articles/tesla-apple-ikea-supply-chain-51646778444 (accessed May 15, 2024).

59 Volve. (2016) "Volvo Cars and Uber Join Forces to Develop Autonomous Driving Cars." Press Release, August 18. Available at: https://www.media.volvocars.com/global/en-gb/media/pressreleases/194795/volvo-cars-and-uber-join-forces-to-develop-autonomous-driving-cars (accessed May 15, 2024).

60 Golicic, Foggin, and Mentzer, "Relationship Magnitude and Its Role in Interorganizational Relationship Structure."

61 Fleming, M. (2019) "'We Had to Make Sure It Didn't Fall on Its Arse': How Tesco Revolutionised Loyalty with Clubcard." *Marketing Week*, March 13. Available at: https://www.marketingweek.com/tesco-clubcard-loyalty/ (accessed May 15, 2024).

62 *The Guardian* (2003) "The Card Up Their Sleeve," July 19. Available at: https://www.theguardian.com/lifeandstyle/2003/jul/19/shopping.features (accessed May 15, 2024).

63 Schrage, M. (2014) "Tesco's Downfall Is a Warning to Data-Driven Retailers." *Harvard Business Review*, October 28. Available at: https://hbr.org/2014/10/tescos-downfall-is-a-warning-to-data-driven-retailers (accessed May 15, 2024).

64 BBC News. (2023) "Tesco to Cut the Value of Clubcard Rewards Scheme," March 21. Available at: https://www.bbc.com/news/business-65024091 (accessed May 15, 2024).

65 PYMNTS. (2023) "Tesco Offers 90 Million Personalized Coupons to Maintain Customer Loyalty," April 13. Available at: https://www.pymnts.com/earnings/2023/tesco-offers-90-million-personalized-coupons-to-maintain-customer-loyalty/ (accessed May 15, 2024).

66 Carroll, N. (2023) "Tesco's CMO on Making Clubcard Stand Out in a Sea of Loyalty Schemes." *Marketing Week*, July 6. Available at: https://www.marketingweek.com/tesco-clubcard-stand-out/ (accessed May 15, 2024).

67 Sandercock, H. (2022) "Tesco Clubcard Prices: What Are Price Differences for Card Holders—and Why Has Supermarket Been Criticised?." NationalWorld, April 29. Available at: https://www.nationalworld.com/lifestyle/money/tesco-clubcard-prices-what-price-differences-card-holders-supermarket-criticised-3675716 (accessed May 15, 2024).

68 Faithfull, M. (2023) "Sainsbury's Ramps Up Loyalty Battle As Tesco Reduces Clubcard Value." *Forbes*, April 11. Available at: https://www.forbes.com/sites/markfaithfull/2023/04/11/sainsburys-ramps-up-loyalty-battle-as-tesco-reduces-clubcard-value/?sh=2a8b30ec4d73 (accessed May 15, 2024).

CHAPTER 14: MANAGING RESOURCE TRADE-OFFS AND PRICING STRATEGY

1 Ben's Cookies. (n.d.) "Our Story." Available at: https://www.benscookies.us/our-story/ (accessed May 15, 2024).

2 Mantrala, M.K. (2002) "Allocating Marketing Resources." In Weitz, B. and Wensley, R. (eds.), *Handbook of Marketing*. London: Sage, pp. 409–35.

3 Palmatier, R.W. and Crecelius, A.T. (2019) "The 'First Principles' of Marketing Strategy." *AMS Review*, 9, pp. 5–26.

4 McAlone, N. and Perelli, A. (2023) "How Much YouTubers Make for 1 Million Subscribers." *Business Insider*, July 3. Available at: https://www.businessinsider.com/how-much-youtube-pays-for-one-million-subscribers (accessed May 15, 2024).

5 Denzer, TJ. (2024) "Palworld's Success Lifted It onto Twitch's Top 10 Most Viewed Games in January." *ShackNews*, February 13. Available at: https://www.shacknews.com/article/138707/streamelements-state-of-the-stream-january-2024-palworld (accessed May 15, 2024).

6 Procter & Gamble (n.d.) *P&G's Billion Dollar Brands: Trusted, Valued, Recognized*. Available at: http://www.pg.com/en_US/downloads/media/Fact_Sheets_BDB.pdf (accessed July 27, 2015).

7 George, G. (2005) "Slack Resources and the Performance of Privately Held Firms." *Academy of Management Journal*, 48(4), pp. 661–76.

8 Ryan, B. (1991) *Advertising in a Recession*. New York: American Association of Advertising Agencies.

9 Scanlon, J. (2010) "Is Recession the Time to Boost Ad Spending?." *Business Week*, May 4.

10 Blum, K. (2021) "Marketing Budgets Drop to Lowest Levels in Recent History." *Gartner*, July 20. Available at: https://www.gartner.com/en/marketing/insights/articles/marketing-budgets-drop-to-lowest-levels-in-recent-history (accessed May 15, 2024).

11 Capozzi, C. (n.d.) "Consumer Segments in the Hotel Industry." *Houston Chronicle*. Available at: http://smallbusiness.chron.com/consumer-segments-hotel-industry-13764.html (accessed March 7, 2016).

12 Grant, T. and Beer T. (2008) "Life Cycle Assessment of Greenhouse Gas Emissions from Irrigated Maize and Their Significance in the Value Chain." *Australian Journal of Experimental Agriculture*, 48, pp. 375–81.

13 Lovelace Jr., B. (2022) "'Gaming' of U.S. Patent System Is Keeping Drug Prices Sky High, Report Says." *NBC News*, September 15. Available at: https://www.nbcnews.com/health/health-news/gaming-us-patent-system-keeping-drug-prices-sky-high-report-says-rcna47507 (accessed May 15, 2024).

14 Brownswell, A. (2012) "HSBC's Chris Clark on a New Era for the Bank's Marketing." *Campaign*, May 31. Available at: http://www.campaignlive.co.uk/article/1134018/hsbcs-chris-clark-new-era-banks-marketing (accessed August 5, 2016).

15 Tennis365. (2023) "Piers Morgan Rips into Emma Raducanu for Taking Part in 'Woke And Absurd' Advert," September 26. Available at: https://www.tennis365.com/tennis-news/piers-morgan-emma-raducanu-woke-advert (accessed May 15, 2024).

16 Albers, S., Mantrala, M.K. and Sridhar, S. (2010) "Personal Selling Elasticities: A Meta-Analysis." *Journal of Marketing Research*, 47(5), pp. 840–53.

17 Sethuraman, R., Tellis, G.J. and Briesch, R.A. (2011) "How Well Does Advertising Work? Generalizations from Meta-Analysis of Brand Advertising Elasticities," *Journal of Marketing Research*, 48(3), pp. 457–71.

18 Rubin, R., Lang, B. and Donnelly, M. (2023) "Big Budgets, Big Headaches: Why 'Indiana Jones 5' and 'Mission: Impossible 7' Are Struggling to Make a Profit." *Variety*, August 15. Available at: https://variety.com/2023/film/news/indiana-jones-5-mission-impossible-7-box-office-flops-explained-1235690262/ (accessed May 15, 2024).

19 Kelley, A. (2023) "'Indiana Jones and the Dial of Destiny' Budget Breakdown: Has Indy's Swan Song Officially Flopped?." *Collider*, updated July 31. Available at: https://collider.com/indiana-jones-and-the-dial-of-destiny-box-office-budget/ (accessed May 15, 2024).

20 Caoile, P. (2023) "Indiana Jones and the Dial of Destiny's Reliance on Nostalgia Led to Its (Temple of) Doom." *Collider*, September 1. Available at: https://collider.com/indiana-jones-dial-of-destiny-nostalgia/ (accessed May 15, 2024).

21 Reid, C. (2023) "The 4 Flops of 2023 that Cost Disney $1 Billion." *Forbes*, August 4. Available at: https://www.forbes.com/sites/carolinereid/2023/08/04/the-four-flops-of-2023-that-cost-disney-1-billion/?sh=357b14243bed (accessed May 15, 2024).

22 Farris, P.W. (2015) "How Advertising Budgets Are Like Fly Balls." *Darden Ideas to Action*, April 10. Available at: https://ideas.darden.virginia.edu/how-advertising-budgets-are-like-fly-balls (accessed May 13, 2024).

23 Chand, S. (n.d.) "15 Methods for Setting up of Advertisement Budget under Top down Budgeting Method." Your Article Library. Available at: http://www.yourarticlelibrary.com/advertising/15-methods-for-setting-up-of-advertisement-budget-under-top-down-budgeting-method/22291/ (accessed February 22, 2016).

24 Fischer, M., Albers, S., Wagner, N. and Frie, M. (2011) "Practice Prize Winner-Dynamic Marketing Budget Allocation Across Countries, Products, And Marketing Activities." *Marketing Science*, 30(4), pp. 568–85.

25 Manchanda, P., Rossi, P.E. and Chintagunta, P.K. (2004) "Response Modeling with Nonrandom Marketing-Mix Variables." *Journal of Marketing Research*, 41(4), 467–78.

26 Dholakia, U.M. (2018) "When Cost-Plus Pricing Is a Good Idea." *Harvard Business Review*, July 12. Available at: https://hbr.org/2018/07/when-cost-plus-pricing-is-a-good-idea (accessed May 15, 2024).

27 Stoll, J. (2024) "Number of Netflix Paid Subscribers Worldwide from 1st Quarter 2013 to 1st Quarter 2024." *Statista*, April 22. Available at: https://www.statista.com/statistics/250934/quarterly-number-of-netflix-streaming-subscribers-worldwide/#:~:text=How%20many%20paid%20subscribers%20does,the%20second%20quarter%20of%202023 (accessed May 15, 2024).

28 Green, T. (2022) "Netflix's Mountain of Debt Isn't a Problem...Yet." *The Motley Fool*, April 21. Available at: https://www.fool.com/investing/2022/04/21/netflixs-mountain-of-debt-isnt-a-problemyet/ (accessed May 15, 2024).

29 Whelan, R., Flint, J. and Rattner, N. (2023) "Streamflation Is Here and Media Companies Are Betting You'll Pay Up." *The Wall Street Journal*, August 15. Available at: https://www.wsj.com/articles/disney-max-hulu-netflix-streaming-price-2c3bac2a (accessed May 15, 2024).

30 Munkachy, A. (2023) "The Complete History of Netflix Price Hikes—From 2007 to Now." Flixed, updated December 15. Available at: https://flixed.io/us/en/netflix-price-hikes (accessed May 15, 2024).
31 Sanchez, J. (1993) "American Loses Record $1 Billion in '92: Airlines: Last Year Stands to Rank As One of the Worst in History for the Beleaguered Industry." *Los Angeles Times*, January 21. Available at: https://www.latimes.com/archives/la-xpm-1993-01-21-fi-2074-story.html (accessed May 15, 2024).
32 Kutuchief, B. (2022) "What Is Roblox? Everything You Need to Know About the Social Gaming Platform." *Hootsuite*, August 24. Available at: https://blog.hootsuite.com/what-is-roblox/ (accessed May 15, 2024).
33 Currie, R. (2023) "Parent Discovers the Cost of Ignoring Roblox: £2,500 and Heart Palpitations." *The Register*, May 22. Available at: https://www.theregister.com/2023/05/22/roblox_shopping_spree/ (accessed May 15, 2024).
34 Winkie, L. (2022) "Inside Roblox's Criminal Underworld, Where Kids Are Scamming Kids." *IGN*, December 28. Available at: https://www.ign.com/articles/inside-robloxs-criminal-underworld-where-kids-are-scamming-kids (accessed May 15, 2024).
35 Dean, J. (1976) "Pricing Policies for New Products." *Harvard Business Review*, November. Available at: https://hbr.org/1976/11/pricing-policies-for-new-products (accessed May 15, 2024).
36 Stoll, J. (2023) "Video Streaming Worldwide—Statistics & Facts." *Statista*, December 18. Available at: https://www.statista.com/topics/7527/video-streaming-worldwide/#topicOverview (accessed May 15, 2024).
37 Houssard, A., Pilati, F., Tartari, M., Sacco, P.L. and Gallotti, R. (2023) "Monetization in Online Streaming Platforms: An Exploration of Inequalities in Twitch. TV." *Scientific Reports*, 13(1), p. 1103.
38 Clement, J. (2023) "Most Popular Platform to Watch Live Streams According to Gamers in the United States as of February 2021." *Statista*, August 29. Available at: https://www.statista.com/statistics/1221858/most-popular-livestream-platform-watch-us/ (accessed May 15, 2024).
39 Turner, A. (2024) "Twitch Statistics: How Many Users Are on Twitch (2024)." Bankmycell.com, April 8. Available at: https://www.bankmycell.com/blog/number-of-twitch-streamers/ (accessed May 15, 2024).
40 Twitch (n.d.) "Frequently Asked Questions." Available at: https://www.twitch.tv/p/de-de/partners/faq/ (accessed May 15, 2024).
41 Twitch. (2022) "A Letter from Twitch President Dan Clancy on Subscription Revenue Shares." [Blog] September 21. Available at: https://blog.twitch.tv/en/2022/09/21/a-letter-from-twitch-president-dan-clancy-on-subscription-revenue-shares/ (accessed May 15, 2024).
42 Tassi, P. (2022) "Twitch Announces Pay Cuts for Top Streamers, And Everyone's Mad." *Forbes*, September 21. Available at: https://www.forbes.com/sites/paultassi/2022/09/21/twitch-announces-pay-cuts-for-streamers-and-everyones-mad/ (accessed May 15, 2024); Parrish, A. (2022) "How Twitch Lost the Battle for Its Soul." *The Verge*, September 26. Available at: https://www.theverge.com/2022/9/26/23369070/twitch-revenue-split-70-30-streamers-reaction-amazon (accessed May 15, 2024).
43 Twitch. (2023) "Introducing the Partner Plus Program." [Blog] June 15. Available at: https://blog.twitch.tv/en/2023/06/15/introducing-the-partner-plus-program/ (accessed May 15, 2024).
44 Tassi, P. (2023) "Twitch Is Starting to Feel Like a Failed State." *Forbes*, June 16. Available at: https://www.forbes.com/sites/paultassi/2023/06/16/twitch-is-starting-to-feel-like-a-failed-state/?sh=305d8e951ff1 (accessed May 15, 2024).

CHAPTER 15: MANAGING RESOURCE TRADE-OFFS IN INTEGRATED MARKETING COMMUNICATIONS AND PERSONAL SELLING

1 Amplify. (2020) "Global PlayStation 5 Launch," November 20. Available at: https://www.weareamplify.com/news/global-playstation-5-launch (accessed May 16, 2024); Douglas, F. (2020) "Sony PlayStation 5 Takeover of London Landmarks Culminates with Piccadilly Lights." *Campaign UK*, November 20. Available at: https://www.campaignlive.co.uk/article/sony-playstation-5-takeover-london-landmarks-culminates-piccadilly-lights/1700662 (accessed May 16, 2024).
2 Naik, P.A. and Raman, K. (2003) "Understanding the Impact of Synergy in Multimedia Communications." *Journal of Marketing Research*, 40(4), pp. 375–88.
3 Reisenbichler, M., Reutterer, T., Schweidel, D. and Dan, D. (2022) "Frontiers: Supporting Content Marketing with Natural Language Generation." *Marketing Science*, 41(3), pp. 441–52. https://doi.org/10.1287/mksc.2022.1354.
4 Twenge, J.M., Martin, G.N. and Spitzberg, B.H. (2019) "Trends in US Adolescents' Media Use, 1976–2016: The Rise of Digital Media, the Decline of TV, and the (near) Demise of Print." *Psychology of Popular Media Culture*, 8(4), p. 329.
5 Lim, E. (2021) "Aldi's #FreeCuthbert Campaign Takes Grand Prix at The Drum Awards for Social Media." *The Drum*, November 12. Available at: https://www.thedrum.com/news/2021/11/12/aldis-freecuthbert-campaign-takes-grand-prix-the-drum-awards-social-media (accessed May 16, 2024).
6 Schöndeling, A., Burmester, A.B., Edeling, A., Marchand, A. and Clement, M. (2023) "Marvelous Advertising Returns? A Meta-Analysis of Advertising Elasticities in the Entertainment Industry." *Journal of the Academy of Marketing Science*, 51, pp. 1019–1045.
7 Gopalakrishna, S., Crecelius, A.T. and Patil, A. (2022) "Hunting for New Customers: Assessing the Drivers of Effective Salesperson Prospecting and Conversion." *Journal of Business Research*, 149, pp. 916–26.
8 Vakratsas, D. and Ambler, T. (1999) "How Advertising Works: What Do We Really Know?." *Journal of Marketing*, 63(1), pp. 26–43.
9 Droga (n.d.) "New Yok Times." Available at: https://droga5.com/work/new-york-times/ (accessed May 16, 2024).
10 Blum, K. (2021) "Marketing Budgets Drop to Lowest Levels in Recent History." *Gartner*, July 20. Available at: https://www.gartner.com/en/marketing/insights/articles/marketing-budgets-drop-to-lowest-levels-in-recent-history (accessed May 16, 2024).
11 Barnes, J.D., Moscove, B.J. and Rassouli, J. (1982) "An Objective and Task Media Selection Decision Model and Advertising Cost Formula to Determine International Advertising Budgets." *Journal of Advertising*, 11(4), pp. 68–75.

12 Smith, T.M., Gopalakrishna, S. and Chatterjee, R. (2006) "A Three-Stage Model of Integrated Marketing Communications at the Marketing-Sales Interface." *Journal of Marketing Research*, 43(4), pp. 564–79.

13 Majid, K.A. (2020) "Effect of Interactive Marketing Channels on Service Customer Acquisition." *Journal of Services Marketing*, 35(3), pp. 299–311.

14 Kumar, V., Choi, J.B. and Greene, M. (2017) "Synergistic Effects of Social Media and Traditional Marketing on Brand Sales: Capturing the Time-Varying Effects." *Journal of the Academy of Marketing Science*, 45, pp. 268–88.

15 Wieden + Kennedy. (2010) "Old Spice: Smell Like a Man, Man," February. Available at: https://www.wk.com/work/old-spice-smell-like-a-man-man/ (accessed May 16, 2024).

16 Odell, P. (2017) "OREO Launches $500,000 #MYOreo Creation Contest." Chief Marketer, May 10. Available at: https://www.chiefmarketer.com/oreo-launches-500000-myoreo-creation-contest/ (accessed May 16, 2024).

17 Sun, H., Fan, M. and Tan, Y. (2020) "An Empirical Analysis of Seller Advertising Strategies in an Online Marketplace." *Information Systems Research*, 31(1), pp. 37–56.

18 MTS Staff Writer (2023) "SEO and ChatGPT: How ChatGPT Will Impact the SEO Journey." MartechSerii, June 7. Available at: https://martechseries.com/mts-insights/staff-writers/seo-and-chatgpt-how-chatgpt-will-impact-the-seo-journey/ (accessed May 16, 2024).

19 Rumbo, J.D. (2002) "Consumer Resistance in a World of Advertising Clutter: The Case of Adbusters." *Psychology & Marketing*, 19(2), pp. 127–48.

20 Maclnnis, D.J., Moorman, C. and Jaworski, B.J. (1991) "Enhancing and Measuring Consumers' Motivation, Opportunity, and Ability to Process Brand Information from Ads." *Journal of Marketing*, 55(4), pp. 32–53.

21 Baird, D. (2015) "Paddy Power's Oscar Pistorius Ad Named Most Complained-About of 2014." *The Guardian*, February 20. Available at: https://www.theguardian.com/media/2015/feb/20/paddy-power-oscar-pistorius-ad-complaints-2014-asa (accessed May 16, 2024).

22 McCarthy, J. (2015) "Paddy Power Has 'No Regrets' for 'Good at Sport' Immigrant Stowaway Ad." *The Drum*, July 3. Available at: https://www.thedrum.com/news/2015/07/03/paddy-power-has-no-regrets-good-sport-immigrant-stowaway-ad (accessed May 22, 2024).

23 Tran, M. (2015) "Migrant Dies on UK-Bound Freight Train near Calais." *The Guardian*, July 7. Available at: https://www.theguardian.com/world/2015/jul/07/migrant-dies-uk-bound-freight-shuttle-near-calais-france (accessed May 16, 2024).

24 Vakratsas and Ambler, "How Advertising Works."

25 Anderson, N.H. (1971) "Integration Theory and Attitude Change." *Psychological Review*, 78(3), p. 171.

26 Christensen-Szalanski, J.J. and Willham, C.F. (1991) "The Hindsight Bias: A Meta-Analysis." *Organizational Behavior and Human Decision Processes*, 48(1), pp. 147–68.

27 Wotruba, T.R. (1991) "The Evolution of Personal Selling." *Journal of Personal Selling & Sales Management*, 11(3), pp. 1–12.

28 Goldfarb, A. (2021) "Absolut Obsessive: 30 Years after the Campaign Launched, Passion for Collecting Remains." *VinePair*, November 19. Available at: https://vinepair.com/articles/absolut-vodka-ad-collectors/ (accessed May 16, 2024).

29 Kemp, A. (2022) "Absolut's Largest Global Campaign in a decade Says We're All 'Born to Mix'." *The Drum*, June 6. Available at: https://www.thedrum.com/news/2022/06/06/absolut-s-largest-global-campaign-decade-says-we-re-all-born-mix (accessed May 16, 2024).

30 Jain, S. (2012) "Marketing of Vice Goods: A Strategic Analysis of the Package Size Decision." *Marketing Science*, 31(1), pp. 36–51.

31 Moss, H.B. (2013) "The Impact of Alcohol on Society: A Brief Overview." *Social Work in Public Health*, 28(3–4), pp. 175–77.

32 Rossow, I. (2021) "The Alcohol Advertising Ban in Norway: Effects on Recorded Alcohol Sales." *Drug and Alcohol Review*, 40(7), pp. 1392–395.

33 World Health Organization. (2020) *Alcohol Marketing in the WHO European Region*, June 6. Available at: https://www.who.int/publications/i/item/2020-1266-41016-55678 (accessed May 16, 2024); Michalopoulos, S. (2017) "'Responsible Party' Has Some Impact on Students' Drinking Habits, Report Finds." Euractiv, December 3. Available at: https://www.euractiv.com/section/alcohol/news/responsible-party-has-impact-on-students-drinking-habits-report-finds/ (accessed May 16, 2024).

34 Sales Education Foundation. (2023) "Key Statistics on Professional Sales Education." Available at: https://salesfoundation.org/resources/2023/2023-key-stats-sales-education.pdf (accessed May 16, 2024).

35 Sales Education Foundation. (n.d.) "A Professional Sales Education Is the First Step." Available at: https://salesfoundation.org/who-we-serve/students/index.php (accessed May 16, 2024).

36 Inc. Staff. (1991) "The Cost of a Sales Call." *Inc.*, May 1. Available at: https://www.inc.com/magazine/19910501/4595.html (accessed May 16, 2024).

37 Kotler, P., Rackham, N. and Krishnaswamy, S. (2006) "Ending the War between Sales and Marketing." *Harvard Business Review*, 84(7/8), p. 68.

38 Gopalakrishna, S., Crecelius, A.T. and Patil, A. (2022) "Hunting for New Customers: Assessing the Drivers of Effective Salesperson Prospecting and Conversion." *Journal of Business Research*, 149, pp. 916–26.

39 Smith, Gopalakrishna, and Chatterjee, "A Three-Stage Model of Integrated Marketing Communications at the Marketing-Sales Interface."

40 Smith, T.M., Gopalakrishna, S. and Smith, P.M. (2004) "The Complementary Effect of Trade Shows on Personal Selling." *International Journal of Research in Marketing*, 21(1), pp. 61–76.

41 Zoltners, A.A., Sinha, P.K. and Lorimer, S.E. (2013) "The Growing Power of Inside Sales." *Harvard Business Review*, July 29. Available at: https://hbr.org/2013/07/the-growing-power-of-inside-sa (accessed May 16, 2024).

42 Josephson, B., Lee, J.Y. and Sridhar, S. (2021) "The Death of the Salesmen? Effect of B2B Online Channel Introduction on Offline Sales Performance." *SSRN*, March 11; Roff-Marsh, J. (2015) *The Machine: A Radical Approach to the Design of the Sales Function*. Austin, TX: Greenleaf Book Group Press.

43 Guenzi, P. and Habel, J. (2020) "Mastering the Digital Transformation of Sales." *California Management Review*, 62(4), pp. 57–85.

44 Lawrence, J.M., Crecelius, A.T. and Palmatier, R.W. (2023) "Understanding Effects of Customer Assignment to Outside or Inside Salespeople." *MSI Working Paper Series*, 23(129), pp. 1–46.

45 Lawrence, Crecelius, and Palmatier, "Understanding Effects of Customer Assignment to Outside or Inside Salespeople."

46 Jolson, M.A. and Wotruba, T.R. (1992) "Selling and Sales Management in Action: Prospecting: A New Look at This Old Challenge." *Journal of Personal Selling & Sales Management*, 12(4), pp. 59–66.

47 Söhnchen, F. and Albers, S. (2010) "Pipeline Management for the Acquisition of Industrial Projects." *Industrial Marketing Management*, 39(8), pp. 1356–364.

48 Chaker, N.N., Zablah, A.R. and Noble, C.H. (2018) "More Than One Way to Persist: Unpacking the Nature of Salesperson Persistence to Understand Its Effects on Performance." *Industrial Marketing Management*, 71, pp. 171–88.

49 Lawrence, J.M., Scheer, L.K., Crecelius, A.T. and Lam, S.K. (2021) "Salesperson Dual Agency in Price Negotiations." *Journal of Marketing*, 85(2), pp. 89–109.

50 Primark. (n.d.) "About Us." Available at: https://www.primark.com/en-gb/about-us (accessed May 16, 2024).

51 Hendriksz, V. (2017) "Case Study on Primark Sustainability, Ethics, Supply Chain." *Fashion United*, April 20. Available at: https://fashionunited.uk/primark-sustainability (accessed May 16, 2024).

52 Weston, S. (2022) "Primark Cares' Director on the Retailer's First Sustainability Report." *Drapers*, November 30. Available at: https://www.drapersonline.com/news/primark-cares-director-on-the-retailers-first-sustainability-report (accessed May 16, 2024).

53 Quagga Design. (n.d.) "Primark Cares: Birmingham." Available at: https://www.quaggadesign.co.uk/projects/primark-cares; Spotify Advertising Team. (2021) "Audio Ads Help Primark Drive In-Store Traffic." Spotify Advertising, October. Available at: https://ads.spotify.com/en-US/inspiration/primark-ad-studio-case-study/; Weston, "Primark Cares' Director on the Retailer's First Sustainability Report" (accessed May 13, 2024).

54 Pomp. (n.d.) "Sustainable Fashion Roundup—November." Available at: https://pomp.store/blogs/journal/sustainable-fashion-roundup-november (accessed May 16, 2024); Wightman-Stone, D. (2019) "Two in Five Consumers Feel No Loyalty to Fashion Retailers." *Fashion United*, April 2. Available at: https://fashionunited.uk/news/retail/two-in-five-consumers-feel-no-loyalty-to-fashion-retailers/2019040242500 (accessed May 16, 2024); Bottomley, T. (2021) "Primark's New Sustainability Drive May Not Increase Customer Loyalty." *The Industry.Fashion*, September 16. Available at: https://www.theindustry.fashion/primarks-new-sustainability-drive-may-not-increase-customer-loyalty/ (accessed May 16, 2024).

55 Rigby, C. (2022) "Primark Meets Overwhelming Levels of Interest As It Sells Online—for In-Store Collection—for the First Time." *Internet Retailing*, November 14. Available at: https://internetretailing.net/primark-meets-overwhelming-levels-of-interest-as-it-sells-online-for-in-store-collection-for-the-first-time/ (accessed May 16, 2024).

INDEX

Bold page numbers indicate tables, *italic* numbers indicate figures.

C

S

T

U

V

W

Y

Z